Caring for Your Baby and Young Child

This invaluable volume was prepared under the editorial direction of distinguished pediatricians Steven P. Shelov, M.D., M.S., and Robert E. Hannemann, M.D., and draws on the contributions and practical wisdom of more than 100 pediatric subspecialists and an editorial review board. Written in a warm, accessible style and illustrated with more than 350 helpful drawings and diagrams, this book gives you the information you need to safeguard your child's most precious asset: his or her health.

In *Caring for Your Baby and Young Child* you'll find:

- A month-by-month guide to your baby's first year that lets you know what to expect in terms of growth, behavior, and development

- A yearly guide to ages one through five with practical advice for dealing with sleeping, toilet training, and temper tantrums

- "Health Watch" features that alert you to potential medical problems at each stage

- "Safety Check" reminders for home, outdoors, and car travel

- A discussion of family issues—from grandparents and siblings to working mothers and single parenting

Plus reliable information on:

- All common infectious diseases, from chickenpox and measles to flu and ear infections

- Developmental disabilities, such as congenital abnormalities, cerebral palsy, hearing loss, autism, and mental retardation

- Skin problems, from birthmarks to head lice and sunburn

- Emergencies, including bites, poisoning, choking, and CPR

- Feeding and nutrition

- Car safety seats

Parenting Books from
the American Academy of Pediatrics

Caring for Your Baby and Young Child
Birth to Age 5

El Cuidado De Su Hijo Pequeño
Desde Que Nace Hasta Los Cinco Años

Caring for Your School-Age Child
Ages 5 to 12

Caring for Your Teenager

Your Baby's First Year

El Primér Año De Su Bebé

Guide to Your Child's Symptoms
Birth through Adolescence

Guide to Your Child's Sleep
Birth through Adolescence

Guide to Your Child's Allergies and Asthma
Breathing Easy and Bringing Up Healthy, Active Children

Guide to Your Child's Nutrition
Making Peace at the Table and Building Healthy Eating Habits for Life

New Mother's Guide to Breastfeeding

Nueva Guía De Lactancia Materna

Guide to Toilet Training

Guía Para Enseñar Al Niño A Usar El Inodoro

ADHD: A Complete and Authoritative Guide

CARING FOR YOUR BABY AND YOUNG CHILD

Birth to Age Five

Steven P. Shelov, MD, MS, FAAP
Editor-in-Chief
Chairman, Department of Pediatrics
Maimonides Medical Center and
    Lutheran Medical Center
Vice President, Infants and Children's
    Hospital of Brooklyn
Professor of Pediatrics, Mount Sinai
    School of Medicine

Robert E. Hannemann, MD, FAAP
Associate Medical Editor
Visiting Professor, Child Psychology and
    Biomedical Engineering
Purdue University

Richard Trubo
Writer

Editorial Board:
Phyllis F. Agran, MD, MPH, FAAP
Professor, Department of Pediatrics
Director, Child Injury and Traffic Safety
    Research Group
Health Policy and Research
University of California Irvine

Tanya Remer Altmann, MD, FAAP
Community Pediatrics Medical Group,
    Westlake Village, CA
Clinical Instructor, Mattel Children's
    Hospital at UCLA

Susan S. Baker, MD, PhD, FAAP
Professor of Pediatrics
Co-Director, Digestive Diseases and
    Nutrition Center
State University of New York at Buffalo
Children's Hospital of Buffalo

William L. Coleman, MD, FAAP
Professor of Pediatrics
Department of Pediatrics
Center for Development and Learning
University of North Carolina School of
    Medicine

Paul H. Dworkin, MD, FAAP
Professor and Chairman of Pediatrics
University of Connecticut School of
    Medicine
Physician-in-Chief
Connecticut Children's Medical Center

H. Cody Meissner, MD, FAAP
Chief, Pediatric Infectious Disease
Tufts–New England Medical Center
Associate Professor of Pediatrics
Tufts University School of Medicine

Henry L. Shapiro, MD, FAAP
Assistant Professor of Pediatrics
University of South Florida
Medical Director of Developmental-
    Behavioral Pediatrics
All Children's Hospital

BANTAM BOOKS

CARING FOR YOUR BABY AND YOUNG CHILD: BIRTH TO AGE FIVE
A Bantam Book

PUBLISHING HISTORY
Bantam hardcover edition published May 1991
Revised edition / May 1993
Revised edition / June 1998
Revised trade paperback edition / May 1993
Revised trade paperback edition / June 1998
Fourth trade paperback edition / June 2004
Updated in May 2005

A note about revisions:
Every effort is made to keep CARING FOR YOUR BABY AND
YOUNG CHILD consistent with the most recent advice and
information available from the American Academy of Pediatrics. In addition to major revisions identified as "Revised
Editions" and "Fourth Edition," the text has been updated as
necessary for each additional reprinting listed above.

Drawings on page 453
by Nancy Beaumont.
Used by permission.

Bantam Books and the rooster colophon are registered
trademarks of Random House, Inc.

Library of Congress Cataloging in Publication Data
is on file with the publisher.

ISBN: 0-553-38290-X

Manufactured in the United States of America
Published simultaneously in Canada

RRH   10

Reviewers and Contributors

Acknowledgments

Writer:
Richard Trubo

Writer, first edition:
Aimee Liu

Illustrators:
Wendy Wray/Morgan Gaynin Inc.
Alex Grey

Designer:
Richard Oriolo

Secretarial Support:
Debbie Carney
Patti Coffin
Donita Kennedy
Delores Menting
Giselle Reynolds
Gale Ringeisen

Marilyn Rosenfeld
Nancy Wagner
Mary Ellen Watson

Additional Assistance:
Susan A. Casey
Betty L. Crase, IBCLC
Michelle Esquivel
Becky Levin-Goodman, MPH
Sarah Hale
Eleanor Hannemann
Brent Heathcott
Christine Kang
Marlene Lawson, RN
Nancy Macagno
Lisa Miller
Veronica Laude Noland
Marsha L. Shelov, PhD
Mary Claire Walsh
Kathy Whitaker, RN

This book is dedicated to
all the people who recognize that children are our greatest inspiration
in the present and our greatest hope for the future.

We also appreciate the contributions of the late
Leonard P. Rome, MD, to the original publication of this book.

PLEASE NOTE

The information contained in this book is intended to complement, not substitute for, the advice of your child's pediatrician. Before starting any medical treatment or medical program, you should consult with your child's pediatrician, who can discuss your child's individual needs and counsel you about symptoms and treatment. If you have questions regarding how the information in this book applies to your child, speak to your child's pediatrician.

The information and advice in this book apply equally to children of both sexes (except where noted). To indicate this, we have chosen to alternate between masculine and feminine pronouns throughout the book.

The American Academy of Pediatrics constantly monitors new scientific evidence and makes appropriate adjustments in its recommendations. For example, future research and the development of new childhood vaccines may alter the regimen for the administration of existing vaccines. Therefore, the schedule for immunizations outlined in this book is subject to change. These and other potential situations serve to emphasize the importance of always checking with your child's pediatrician for the latest information concerning the health of your child.

Contents

RESOURCES FROM THE AMERICAN ACADEMY OF PEDIATRICS

The American Academy of Pediatrics (AAP) develops and produces a wide variety of public education materials that teach parents and children the importance of preventive and therapeutic medical care. These materials include books, brochures, videos, and other educational resources. Examples of these materials include:

- Brochures and fact sheets on relevant topics such as asthma and allergies, early childhood growth and development, childhood sickness and symptoms, divorce and single parenting, immunizations, learning disabilities, media, nutrition and fitness, sleep problems, teen issues, and more!

- Videos on ADHD, African American families, and other helpful topics.

- First-aid and growth charts, as well as child health records in English and Spanish.

- Award winning and best selling books for parents and children:
  - Caring for Your Baby: Birth to Age 5*
  - Caring for Your School-Age Child Ages 5 to 12
  - Caring for Your Teenager
  - Your Baby's First Year*
  - ADHD: A Complete and Authoritative Guide
  - New Mother's Guide to Breastfeeding*
  - Guide to Toilet Training*
  - Guide to Your Child's Nutrition
  - Guide to Your Child's Symptoms
  - Guide to Your Child's Allergies and Asthma
  - Guide to Your Child's Sleep

For more information on these products and many others, visit the AAP online bookstore at: www.aap.org/bookstore or call toll free: 888/227-1770. Or, get a printed brochure with information on all the AAP parenting books in our Parent Resource Guide by sending a self-addressed, stamped #10 envelope to:

American Academy of Pediatrics
Attention: Marketing Department—PRG request
141 Northwest Point Blvd.
Elk Grove Village, IL 60007

* Denotes this book is also available in Spanish.

Foreword

This fourth edition of *Caring for Your Baby and Young Child: Birth to Age 5* is the first in a three-volume series of child care books developed by the American Academy of Pediatrics (AAP). The other books in this series include *Caring for Your School-Age Child: Ages 5 to 12* and *Caring for Your Teenager*. The Academy has also published books for parents on topics ranging from breastfeeding, nutrition, and toilet training to sleep, allergies and asthma, and attention-deficit/hyperactivity disorder.

The AAP is an organization of 60,000 primary-care pediatricians, pediatric medical subspecialists, and pediatric surgical specialists dedicated to the health, safety, and well-being of all infants, children, adolescents, and young adults. This book is part of the ongoing educational efforts of the Academy to provide parents and caregivers with high-quality information on a broad spectrum of children's health issues.

What distinguishes this book from the many others in bookstores and on library shelves is that it has been developed and extensively reviewed by members of the American Academy of Pediatrics. A six-member editorial board developed the initial material with the assistance of more than 100 contributors and reviewers. Because medical information is constantly changing, every effort has been made to ensure that this book contains the most up-to-date findings. Readers can visit the AAP website at www.aap.org to keep current on the latest information.

It is the Academy's hope that this book will become an invaluable resource and reference guide for parents and caregivers. We believe it is the best comprehensive source of information on matters of children's health and well-being. We are confident that parents and caregivers will find the book extremely valuable. We encourage its use along with the advice and counsel of our readers' own pediatricians, who will provide individual guidance and assistance related to the health of children.

Errol R. Alden, MD, FAAP
Executive Director
American Academy of Pediatrics

INTRODUCTION:

THE GIFTS OF PARENTHOOD

*Y*our child is the greatest gift you will ever receive. From the moment you first hold this miracle of life in your arms, your world will be broader and richer. You will experience a flood of feelings, some of wonder and joy and others of confusion and of being overwhelmed and wondering whether you can ever measure up to the needs of your new baby. These are feelings you could barely imagine before— feelings that no one can truly experience without having a child.

Even describing them can be difficult because the bond between parent and child is so intensely personal. Why do tears come to your eyes the first time your baby smiles or reaches for you? Why are you so proud of her first words? Why does your heart suddenly start to pound the first time you watch her stumble and fall? The answer lies in the unique two-way giving relationship between you and your child.

Your Child's Gifts to You

Although simple, your child's gifts to you are powerful enough to change your life positively.

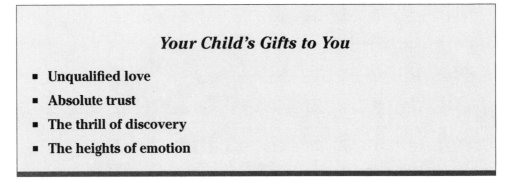

Your Child's Gifts to You

- **Unqualified love**
- **Absolute trust**
- **The thrill of discovery**
- **The heights of emotion**

Unqualified Love. From birth, you are the center of your child's universe. He gives you his love without question and without demand. As he gets older, he will show this love in countless ways, from showering you with his first smiles to giving you his handmade Valentines. His love is filled with admiration, affection, loyalty, and an intense desire to please you.

Absolute Trust. Your child believes in you. In her eyes, you are strong, capable, powerful, and wise. Over time, she will demonstrate this trust by relaxing when you are near, coming to you with problems, and proudly pointing you out to others. Sometimes she also will lean on you for protection from things that frighten her, including her own sensitivities. For example, in your presence she may try out new skills that she would never dare to try alone or with a stranger. She trusts you to keep her safe.

The Thrill of Discovery. Having a child gives you a unique chance to rediscover the pleasure and excitement of childhood. Although you cannot relive your life through your child, you can share in his delight as he explores the world. In the process, you probably will discover abilities and talents you never dreamed you possessed. Feelings of empathy mixed with growing self-awareness will help shape your ability to play and interact with your growing child. Discovering things together, whether they are new skills or words or ways to overcome obstacles, will add to your experience and confidence as a parent and will better prepare you for new challenges that you never even envisioned.

The Heights of Emotion. Through your child, you will experience new heights of joy, love, pride, and excitement. You probably also will experience anxiety, anger, and frustration. For all those delicious moments when you hold your baby close and feel her loving arms around your neck, there are bound to be times when you feel you cannot communicate. The extremes sometimes become sharper as your child gets older and seeks to establish her independence. The same child who at three gaily dances across the room with you may at four have a rebellious and active period that surprises you. The extremes are not contradictions, but simply a reality of growing up. For you as a parent, the challenge is to accept and appreciate all the feelings your child expresses himself and arouses in you, and to use them in giving him steady guidance.

The Gifts You Give Your Child

As his parent, you have many vital gifts to offer your child in return. Some are subtle, but all are very powerful. Giving them will make you a good parent. Receiving them will help your child become a healthy, happy, capable individual.

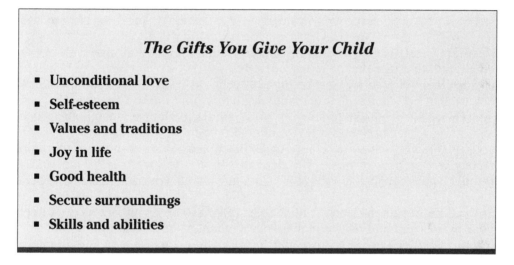

The Gifts You Give Your Child

- **Unconditional love**
- **Self-esteem**
- **Values and traditions**
- **Joy in life**
- **Good health**
- **Secure surroundings**
- **Skills and abilities**

Unconditional Love. Love lies at the core of your relationship with your child. It needs to flow freely in both directions. Just as she loves you without question, you must give her your love and acceptance absolutely. Your love shouldn't depend on the way she looks or behaves. It shouldn't be used as a reward or withheld as a threat. Your love for your child is constant and indisputable, and it's up to you to convey that, especially when she misbehaves and needs to have limits set or behavior corrected. Love must be held separate and above any fleeting feelings of anger or frustration over her conduct. Never confuse the actions with the child, and never let her think that you do. The more secure she feels in your love, the more self-assurance she will have as she grows up.

Self-Esteem. One of your most important gifts as a parent is to help your child develop self-esteem. It's not an easy or quick process. Self-respect, confidence, and belief in oneself, which are the building blocks of self-esteem, take years to become firmly established. Your child needs your steady support and encouragement to discover his strengths. He needs you to believe in him as he learns to believe in himself. Loving him, spending time with him, listening to him, and praising his accomplishments are all part of this process. If he is confident of your love, admiration, and respect, it will be easier for him to develop the solid self-esteem he needs to grow up happy and emotionally healthy.

Values and Traditions. Regardless of whether you actively try to pass on your values and beliefs to your child, she is bound to absorb some of them just by living with you. She'll notice how disciplined you are in your work, how deeply you hold your beliefs, and whether you practice what you preach. She'll participate in family rituals and traditions and think about their significance. You can't expect or demand that your child subscribe to all your opinions, but you can present your beliefs honestly, clearly, and thoughtfully, in keeping with the child's age and maturity level. Give her guidance and encouragement, not only commands. Encourage questions and discussions, when age and language permit, instead of trying to force your values on your child. If your beliefs are well reasoned and if you are true to them, she probably will adopt many of them. If there are inconsistencies in your actions—something we all live with—often your child will make that clear to you, either subtly by his behavior or, when he is older, more directly by disagreeing with you. The road to developing values is not straight and unerring. It demands flexibility built on firm foundations. Self-awareness, a willingness to listen to your child and change when appropriate, and, above all, a demonstration of your commitment to traditions will best serve your relationship with your child. While the choice of values and principles ultimately will be hers to make, she depends on you to give her the foundation through your thoughts, shared ideas, and, most of all, your actions and deeds.

Joy in Life. Your baby doesn't need to be taught to be joyful, but he does need your permission and occasional encouragement to let his natural enthusiasm fly free. The more joyful you are, particularly when you are with him, the more delightful life will seem to him and the more eagerly he will embrace it. When he hears music, he'll dance. When the sun shines, he'll turn his face skyward. When he feels happy, he'll laugh. This exuberance often is expressed through his being attentive and curious, willing to explore new places and things, and eager to take in the world around him and incorporate the new images, objects, and people into his own growing experience. Remember, different babies have different temperaments—some are more apparently exuberant than others, some are more noisily rambunctious, some are more playful, some are more reserved. But all babies demonstrate their joy in life in their own ways, and you as the parent will discover what those ways are and will nurture your child's joy.

Good Health. Your child's health depends significantly on the care and guidance you offer her during these early years. You begin during pregnancy by taking good care of yourself and by arranging for obstetric and pediatric care. By taking your child to the doctor regularly for consultations, keeping her safe from injuries, providing a nutritious diet, and encouraging exercise throughout childhood, you help protect and strengthen her body. You'll also need to maintain good health habits yourself, while avoiding unhealthy ones, such as smoking, excessive drinking, drug use, and lack of adequate physical activity. In this way, you'll give your child a healthy example to follow as she grows up.

Secure Surroundings. You naturally want to give your child a safe, comfortable home. This means more than a warm place to sleep and a collection of toys. As important as it is to provide shelter that is physically safe and secure, it is even more important to create a home that is emotionally secure with a minimum of stress and a maximum of consistency and love. Your child can sense problems between other family members and may be very troubled by them, so it's important that all family problems, even minor conflicts, be dealt with directly and resolved as quickly as possible through cooperation. This may entail seeking advice, but remember, your family's well-being helps maintain an environment that promotes your child's development and will allow him to achieve his potential. The family's dealing effectively with conflicts or differences ultimately will help him feel secure in his ability to manage conflicts and disagreements and will provide him a positive example for resolving his own challenges.

Skills and Abilities. As your child grows up, she'll spend most of her time developing and polishing a variety of skills and abilities in all areas of her life. You should help her as much as possible by encouraging her and providing the equipment and instruction she needs. Books, magazines, play groups, and nursery schools will fast take on a central role as your toddler becomes a preschooler. But it's important not to forget some of the most important learning tools: Your child will learn best when she feels secure, confident, and loved; she will learn best when information is presented in a way that she will respond to positively. Some information is best presented through play—the language of children. Young children learn a tremendous amount through play, especially when with parents or playmates. Other information is best learned or incorporated through actual experience. This may mean learning through exposure to diverse places, people, activities, and experiences. Other things are learned through stories, picture books, magazines, and activity books. Still other things are learned by watching—sometimes just watching you, sometimes watching other children or adults. Preschool experiences also promote socialization.

If you enjoy learning and making discovery fun for your child, she soon will recognize that achievement can be a source of personal satisfaction as well as a way to please you. The secret is to give her the opportunities and let her learn as best fits her style and at her own rate.

How to Make Giving a
Part of Your Daily Family Life

Giving your child the guidance and support he needs to grow up healthy involves all the skills of parenthood: nurturing, guiding, protecting, sharing, and serving as an example or model. Like other skills, these must be learned and perfected through practice. Some will be easier for you than others. Some will seem easier on certain days than on others. These variations are a normal part of raising a child, but they do make the job challenging. The following suggestions will help you make the most of your natural parenting skills so you can give your child the best possible start.

Enjoy Your Child as an Individual. Recognize that your child is unique—different from everyone else—and appreciate her special qualities. Discover her special needs and strengths, her moods and vulnerabilities, and especially her sense of humor, which starts to show itself early in infancy. Let her show you the joy of play. The more you enjoy your child and appreciate her individuality, the more successful you'll be in helping her develop a sense of trust, security, and self-esteem. You'll also have a lot more fun being a parent!

Educate Yourself. You probably know much more than you think you do about being a parent. You spent years observing your own parents and other families. Perhaps you've taken care of other people's children. And you have many instinctive responses that will help make you a giving parent. In other times, this probably would have been all the preparation you needed to raise a child. However, our society is extremely complex and is constantly changing. In order to guide their children in this new world, parents often benefit from some extra education. Talk to your pediatrician and other parents, and ask questions. Read about issues and problems that affect your family. Contact your local religious organizations, school systems and PTAs, child care centers, parent education classes, and other groups that specialize in child-related concerns. Often these groups serve as networks for concerned and interested parents. These networks will help you feel more comfortable and secure when issues seem puzzling or frustrating, a not uncommon state today.

As you gather advice, sift through it for information that is right for you and your child. Much of what you receive will be very valuable, but not all of it. Because child rearing is such a personal process, there is bound to be disagreement. You are not obligated to believe everything you hear or read. In fact, one of the purposes of educating yourself is to protect your child from advice that does not fit your family. The more you know, the better equipped you'll be to decide what works best for your family.

Be a Good Example. One of the ways your child shows her love for you is by imitating you. This is also one of the ways she learns how to behave, develop new skills, and take care of herself. From her earliest moments, she watches you closely and patterns her own behavior and beliefs after yours. Your examples become permanent images, which will shape her attitudes and actions for the rest of her life. Setting a good example for your child means being responsible, loving, and consistent not only with her but with all members of the family. The way you conduct your marriage and/or relationship, whether it is within legally recognized marriage or long-term partnership, for example, influences your child. Show your affection and nurture your relationships. If your child sees her parents communicating openly, cooperating, and sharing household responsibilities, she'll bring these skills to her own future relationships.

Setting good examples also means taking care of yourself. As an eager, well-meaning parent, it's easy to concentrate so hard on your family that you lose sight of your own needs. That's a big mistake. Your child depends on you to be physically and emotionally healthy, and she looks to you to show her how to keep herself healthy. By taking care of yourself, you demonstrate your self-esteem, which is important for both you and your child. Getting a sitter and resting when you're overtired or ill teaches your child that you respect yourself and your needs. Setting aside time and energy for your own work or hobbies teaches your child that you value certain skills and interests and are willing to pursue them. Ultimately she will pattern some of her own habits after yours, so the healthier and happier you keep yourself, the better it will be for both of you.

You can set an example in still another important area, too, and that's in demonstrating tolerance and acceptance in an increasingly multicultural society. As the United States has become a melting pot of nationalities and cultures, it is more important than ever to teach tolerance to your child when relating to people of other racial, ethnic, and religious groups and alternate lifestyles. Make an effort to help your child understand and even celebrate diversity. No boy or girl is born a racist, but prejudice can be learned at a very young age. By four years old, children are aware of differences among people. The way you relate to people in your life will provide a foundation for how your child will treat her peers and others throughout her childhood and adulthood. Let your child know that there are many similarities among people and make an effort to dispel stereotypes that she is exposed to, replacing them with the belief that all people deserve to be respected and valued.

Show Your Love. Giving love means more than just saying "I love you." Your child can't understand what the words mean unless you also treat him with love. Be spontaneous, relaxed, and affectionate with him. Give him plenty of physical contact through hugging, kissing, rocking, and playing. Take the time to talk, sing, and read with him every day. Listen and watch as he responds to you. By paying attention and freely showing your affection, you make him feel special and secure and lay a firm foundation for his self-esteem.

Communicate Honestly and Openly. One of the most important skills you teach your child is communication. The lessons begin when she is a tiny baby gazing into your eyes and listening to your soothing voice. They continue as she watches and listens to you talking with other members of the family and, later, as you help her sort out her concerns, problems, and confusions. She needs you to be understanding, patient, honest, and clear with her. Good communication within a family is not always easy. It can be especially difficult when both parents are working, overextended, or under a great deal of stress, or when one person is depressed, ill, or angry. Preventing a communications breakdown requires commitment, cooperation among family members, and a willingness to recognize problems as they arise. Express your own feelings, and encourage your child to be equally open with you. Look for changes in her behavior—such as frequent or constant crying, irritability, sleep problems, or appetite loss— that may signal sadness, fear, frustration, or worry, and show her that you're aware of and understand these emotions. Ask questions, listen to the responses, and offer constructive suggestions.

Listen to yourself, as well, and consider what you say to your child before the words leave your mouth. It's sometimes easy to make harsh, even cruel, statements in anger or frustration that you don't really mean but that your child may never forget. Thoughtless comments or jokes that seem incidental to you may be hurtful to your child. Phrases like "You stupid idiot," "That's a dumb question," or "Don't bother me" make your child feel worthless and unwanted and may seriously damage her self-esteem. If you constantly criticize or put her off, she also may back away from you. Instead of looking to you for guidance, she may hesitate to ask questions and may mistrust your advice. Like everyone else, children need encouragement to ask questions and speak their minds. The more sensitive, attentive, and honest you are, the more comfortable she'll feel being honest with you.

Spend Time Together. You cannot give your child all that he needs if you only spend a few minutes a day with him. In order to know you and feel confident of your love, he has to spend a great deal of time with you, both physically and emotionally. Spending this time together is possible even if you have outside commitments. You can work full time and still spend some intimate time with your child every day. The important thing is that it be time devoted just to him, meeting his needs and your needs together. Is there any fixed amount? No one can really say. One hour of quality time is worth more than a day of being in the same house but in different rooms. You can be at home full time and never give him the undivided attention he requires. It's up to you to shape your schedule and direct your attention so that you meet his needs.

It may help to set aside a specific block of time for your child each day and devote it to activities he enjoys. Also make an effort to include him in all family activities—meal preparation, mealtimes, and so forth. Use these times to talk about each other's problems (Do be attentive, however, to overburdening your child with adult problems; kids don't need to shoulder your anxieties), personal concerns, and the day's events.

Nurture Growth and Change. When your child is a newborn, it may be difficult for you to imagine her ever growing up, and yet your main purpose as a parent is to encourage, guide, and support her growth. She depends on you to provide the food, protection, and health care her body needs to grow properly, as well as the guidance her mind and spirit need to make her a healthy, mature individual. Instead of resisting change in your child, your job is to welcome and nurture it.

Guiding your child's growth involves a significant amount of discipline, both for you and for your child. As she becomes increasingly independent, she needs rules and guidelines to help her find what she can do and grow from there. You need to provide this framework for her, establishing rules that are appropriate for each stage of development and adjusting them as your child changes so they encourage growth instead of stifling it.

Confusion and conflict do not help your child to mature. Consistency does. Make sure that everyone who cares for her understands and agrees on the way she is being raised and the rules she's expected to follow. Establish policies for all her caregivers to observe when she misbehaves, and adjust these policies along with the rules as she becomes more responsible.

Another way you nurture your child's growth is by teaching her to adapt to changes around her. You can help her with this lesson by coping smoothly with change yourself and by preparing her for major changes within the family. A new baby, the death or illness of a family member, a new job for a parent, marital problems, separation, divorce, remarriage, unemployment, and chronic illness all deeply affect your child as well as you. If the family faces these challenges as a mutually supportive unit, your child will feel secure in accepting change and adjusting to it. By being open and honest with her, you can help her meet these challenges and grow through them.

You also should create an environment that encourages the healthy brain development of your youngster. His world—including where he lives and plays and who he interacts with—will affect how his brain grows. Your child's environment and experiences need to be nurtured constantly, with warm and loving caregivers who give him the freedom to explore and learn safely. (Throughout this book, you'll find guidelines on ensuring the optimal development of your child's brain.)

Minimize Frustrations and Maximize Success. One of the ways your child develops self-esteem is by succeeding. The process starts in the crib with his very first attempts to communicate and use his body. If he achieves his goals and receives approval, he soon begins to feel good about himself and eager to take on greater challenges. If, instead, he's prevented from succeeding and his efforts are ignored, eventually he may become so discouraged that he quits trying and either withdraws or becomes angry and even more frustrated.

As a parent, you must try to expose your child to challenges that will help him discover his abilities and achieve successes while simultaneously preventing him from encountering obstacles or tasks likely to lead to too great a series of frustrations and defeats. This does not mean doing his work for him or keeping him from tasks you know will challenge him. Success is meaningless unless it involves a certain amount of struggle. However, too much frustration in the face of challenges that really are beyond your child's current abilities can be self-defeating and perpetuate a negative self-image. The key is to moderate the challenges so they're within your child's reach while asking him to stretch a bit. For example, try to have toys that are appropriate for his age level, neither too young for him nor too difficult for him to handle. See if you can find a variety of playmates, some older and some younger. Invite your child to help you around the house and have him do chores as he gets older, but don't expect more of him than he realistically can manage.

As you raise your child, it's easy to get carried away by your hopes and dreams for him. You naturally want him to have the best education, all possible opportunities, and eventually a successful career and lifestyle. But be careful not to confuse your own wishes with his choices. In our highly competitive society, a great deal of pressure is placed on children to perform. Some nursery schools have entrance requirements. In some professions and sports, youngsters are considered out of the running if they haven't begun training by age ten. In this atmosphere, the popularity of programs that promise to turn "ordinary babies" into "super babies" is understandable. Many well-meaning parents want desperately to give their children a head start on lifetime success. Unfortunately, this is rarely in the children's best interests.

Children who are pressured to perform early in life do not learn better or achieve higher skills over the long run than do other children. On the contrary, the psychological and emotional pressures may be so negative that the child develops learning or behavioral problems. If a child is truly gifted, he might be able to handle the early learning barrage and develop normally, but most gifted children require less pressure, not more. If their parents push them, they may feel overloaded and become anxious. If they don't live up to their parents' expectations, they may feel like failures and worry that they'll lose their parents' love.

Your child needs understanding, security, and opportunity geared to his own special gifts, needs, and developmental timetable. These things cannot be packaged in a program and they don't guarantee the future, but they will make him a success on his own terms.

Offer Coping Strategies. Some disappointment and failure are inevitable, so your child needs to learn constructive ways to handle anger, conflict, and frustration. Much of what she sees in movies and on television teaches her that violence is the way to solve disputes. Her personal inclination may be either to erupt or to withdraw when she's upset. She may not be able to distinguish the important issues from the insignificant ones. She needs your help to sort out these confusing messages and find healthy, constructive ways to express her negative feelings.

Begin by handling your own anger and unhappiness in a mature fashion so that she learns from your example. Encourage her to come to you with problems she can't solve herself, and help her work through them and understand them. Set clear limits for her so that she understands that violence is not permissible, but at the same time let her know it's normal and okay to feel sad, angry, hurt, or frustrated.

Recognize Problems and Get Help When Necessary. Although it is an enormous challenge, parenthood can be more rewarding and enjoyable than any other part of your life. Sometimes, though, problems are bound to arise, and occasionally you may not be able to handle them alone. There is no reason to feel guilty or embarrassed about this. Healthy families accept the fact and confront difficulties directly. They also respect the danger signals and get help promptly when it's needed.

Sometimes all you need is a friend. If you're fortunate enough to have parents and relatives living nearby, your family may provide a source of support. If not, you could feel isolated unless you create your own network of neighbors, friends, and other parents. One way to build such a network is by joining organized parent-child groups at your local YM/YWCA or community center. The other parents in these groups can be a valuable source of advice and support. Allow yourself to use this support when you need it.

Occasionally you may need expert help in dealing with a specific crisis or ongoing problem. Your personal physician and pediatrician are sources of support and referral to other health professionals, including family and marriage counselors. Don't hesitate to discuss family problems with your pediatrician. If not resolved, eventually many of these problems can adversely affect the family's health. Your pediatrician should know about them and is interested in helping you resolve them.

If your child has special needs, you and your family may face particularly difficult challenges. Families whose children have chronic illnesses or disabilities often deal with and conquer everyday obstacles in order to ensure that their youngsters have access to optimal care to support their well-being and proper development. In such situations, one of your immediate goals is to find a pediatrician who is accessible and knowledgeable, can coordinate your child's treatment with other health care providers, and can help you navigate through the conflicting advice that you may encounter. The term "medical home" often is used to describe care that is accessible, family-centered, continuous, comprehensive, coordinated, compassionate, and culturally effective. This is the optimal system of medical care for all children, particularly those with special health-care needs. Creating a medical home is a partnership between pediatric health-care professionals, parents, and child care providers, and is a goal you should strive for in helping your child lead a fulfilling life that is as normal and healthy as possible.

Your journey with your child is about to begin. It will be a wondrous time filled with many ups and downs, times of unbridled joy and times of sadness or frustration. The chapters that follow provide a measure of knowledge intended to make fulfilling the responsibilities of parenthood a little easier and, it is hoped, a lot more fun.

PART I

1

PREPARING FOR A
NEW BABY

*P*regnancy is a time of anticipation, excitement, preparation, and, for many new parents, uncertainty. You dream of a baby who will be strong, healthy, and bright—and you make plans to provide her with everything she needs to grow and thrive. You probably also have fears and questions, especially if this is your first child, or if there have been problems with this or a previous pregnancy. What if something goes wrong during the course of your pregnancy, or what if labor and delivery are difficult? What if being a parent isn't everything you've always dreamed it would be? These are perfectly normal feelings and fears to have. Fortunately, most of these worries are needless. The nine months of pregnancy will give you time to have your questions answered, calm your fears, and prepare yourself for the realities of parenthood.

Some of these preparations should begin when you first learn you're pregnant. The best way to help your baby develop is to take good care of yourself, since medical attention and good nutrition will directly benefit your baby's health. Getting plenty of rest and exercising moderately will help you feel better and ease the physical stresses of pregnancy. Talk to your physician about prenatal vitamins, and avoid smoking and alcohol.

As pregnancy progresses, you're confronted with a long list of related decisions, from planning for the delivery to decorating the nursery. You probably have made many of these decisions already. Perhaps you've postponed some others because your baby doesn't yet seem "real" to you. However, the more actively you prepare for your baby's arrival, the more real that child will seem, and the faster your pregnancy will appear to pass.

Eventually it may seem as if your entire life revolves around this baby-to-be. This increasing preoccupation is perfectly normal and healthy and actually may help prepare you emotionally for the challenge of parenthood. After all, you'll be making decisions about your child for the next two decades—at least! Now is a perfect time to start.

Here are some guidelines to help you with the most important of these preparations.

GIVING YOUR BABY A HEALTHY START

Virtually everything you consume or inhale while pregnant will be passed through to the fetus. This process begins as soon as you conceive. In fact, the embryo is most vulnerable during the first two months, when the major body parts (arms, legs, hands, feet, liver, heart, genitalia, eyes, and brain) are just starting to form. Chemical substances such as those in cigarettes, alcohol, illegal drugs, and certain medications can interfere with the developmental process and with later development, and some can even cause congenital abnormalities.

Take smoking, for instance. If you smoke cigarettes during pregnancy, your baby's birth weight may be significantly decreased. Even inhaling smoke from the cigarettes of others (passive smoking) can affect your baby. Stay away from smoking areas and ask smokers not to light up around you. If you smoked before you got pregnant and still do, this is the time to stop—not just until you give birth, but forever. Children who grow up in a home where a parent smokes have more ear infections and more respiratory problems during infancy and early childhood. They get more sore throats, they cough and wheeze more and have a harder time getting over colds, and they are more prone to hoarseness. They also have been shown to be more likely to smoke themselves when they grow up.

There's just as much concern about alcohol consumption. Alcohol intake during pregnancy increases the risk for a condition called fetal alcohol syndrome (FAS), which is responsible for birth defects and below-average intelligence. A baby with fetal alcohol syndrome may have heart defects, malformed limbs (e.g., club foot), a curved spine, a small head, abnormal facial characteristics, small body size, and low birth weight. Fetal alcohol syn-

WHERE WE STAND

Drinking alcohol during pregnancy is one of the leading preventable causes of birth defects, mental retardation, and other developmental disorders in newborns. There is no known safe amount of alcohol consumption during pregnancy. For that reason, the American Academy of Pediatrics recommends that women who are pregnant, or who are planning to become pregnant, abstain from drinking alcoholic beverages of any kind.

---

drome is also the leading cause of mental retardation in newborns. Alcohol consumption during pregnancy increases the likelihood of a miscarriage or preterm delivery, as well.

Although no one has determined exactly how much alcohol is too much for a pregnant woman, there is evidence that the more you drink, the greater the risk to the fetus. It is safest not to drink *any* alcoholic beverages during pregnancy.

You also should avoid all medications and supplements except those your physician has specifically recommended for use during pregnancy. This includes not only prescription drugs that you may have already been taking, but also nonprescription or over-the-counter products such as aspirin, cold medications, and antihistamines. Even vitamins can be dangerous if taken in high doses. (For example, excessive amounts of vitamin A have been known to cause congenital [existing from birth] abnormalities.) Consult with your physician before taking drugs or supplements of any kind during pregnancy, even those labeled "natural."

Your caffeine intake also should be limited while you are pregnant. While no adverse effects from minimal caffeine intake (one cup of caffeinated coffee per day) have yet been proven, recent studies suggest that consuming large amounts of caffeine during pregnancy might affect fetal growth. Caffeine is also found in many soft drinks and foods such as chocolate. It also tends to keep adults awake and make them irritable, which can only make things less comfortable and restful for you.

Another cause of congenital abnormalities is illness during pregnancy. You should take precautions against these dangerous diseases:

German measles (rubella) can cause mental retardation, heart abnormalities, cataracts, and deafness. Fortunately, this illness now can be prevented by immunization, although *you must not get immunized against rubella during pregnancy.*

The majority of adult women are immune to German measles because they had the disease during childhood or already have been immunized against it. If you're not sure whether you're immune, ask your obstetrician to order a blood test for you. In the unlikely event that the test shows you're not immune, you

WHERE WE STAND

The Academy message is clear—don't smoke when pregnant. Many studies now show that if a woman smokes during pregnancy, her child's birth weight and growth during the first year of life may be reduced. The range of indisputable effects runs from depressed breathing movements during fetal life to cancer, respiratory disorders, and heart disease in later years.

If you smoke, quit. If you can't quit, don't smoke around children (especially indoors or in the car). Children of parents who smoke have more respiratory infections, bronchitis, pneumonia, and reduced pulmonary function than children of nonsmokers. The Academy supports legislation that would prohibit smoking in public places frequented by children. The Academy also supports a ban on tobacco advertising, harsher warning labels on cigarette packages, and an increase in the cigarette excise tax. For more information, visit www.aap.org.

must do your best to avoid sick children, especially during the first three months of your pregnancy. It is then recommended that you receive this immunization after giving birth to prevent this same concern in the future.

Chickenpox is particularly dangerous if contracted shortly before delivery. If you have not already had chickenpox, avoid anyone with the disease or anyone recently exposed to the disease. You also should receive the preventive vaccine when you are not pregnant.

Toxoplasmosis is primarily a danger for cat owners. This illness is caused by a parasitic infection common in cats, but it also is found in uncooked meat and fish. The infected animal excretes a form of the parasite in its stools, and people who come in contact with infected stools could become infected themselves.

If you own a cat, have it checked for toxoplasmosis before you become pregnant or as early as possible in your pregnancy. You can reduce the chances that your cat will contract toxoplasmosis by feeding it only commercially prepared cat food, which is processed in a way that destroys the parasites. Also, to decrease your own chances of being infected, have someone who is not pregnant clean the litter box daily. (The toxoplasmosis parasites cannot infect humans until forty-eight hours after the cat excretes them.) If you do clean the litter box or handle cat litter, make sure to wash your hands thoroughly afterward. As previously mentioned, toxoplasmosis also is found in uncooked meat and fish, so avoid eating uncooked or partially cooked meat or fish such as sushi, and practice good hand-washing techniques after handling uncooked meat products.

GETTING THE BEST PRENATAL CARE

Throughout your pregnancy, you should work closely with your obstetrician to make sure that you stay as healthy as possible. Regular doctor's visits up until the birth of your baby can significantly improve your likelihood of having a healthy newborn. During each doctor's visit, you will be weighed, your blood pressure will be checked, and the size of your uterus will be estimated to evaluate the size of your growing fetus.

Here are some areas that deserve attention during your pregnancy.

Nutrition

Follow your obstetrician's advice regarding your use of prenatal vitamins. As mentioned, you should only take vitamins in the doses recommended by your doctor. Perhaps more than any other single vitamin, make sure you have an adequate intake (generally, 400 micrograms a day) of folic acid, a B vitamin that can reduce the risk of certain birth defects, such as spina bifida. Your obstetrician may recommend a daily prenatal vitamin pill, which includes not only folic acid and other vitamins, but also iron, calcium, and other minerals. Make sure your doctor knows about any other supplements you may be taking, including herbal remedies.

Eating for Two

When it comes to your diet, do some planning to ensure that you're consuming balanced meals. Make sure that they contain protein, carbohydrates, fats, vitamins, and minerals. This is no time for fad or low-calorie dieting. In fact, as a general rule, you need to consume about 300 more calories per day than you did before you became pregnant. You need these extra calories and nutrients so your baby can grow normally.

Exercise

Physical activity is just as important when you're pregnant as at any other time of life. Discuss a fitness program (including any video fitness tapes you may be interested in) with your doctor. Particularly if you haven't been exercising regularly, she may suggest a moderate walking or swimming regimen. Don't overdo it. Take it particularly slowly during the first few workouts—even just five to ten minutes a day is beneficial and a good place to start. Drink plenty of water while working out, and avoid activity with jumping or jarring movements.

Tests During Pregnancy

Even when your pregnancy is progressing normally, your obstetrician may recommend some of the following tests.

- An *ultrasound* exam is one of the most common tests given to pregnant women. It monitors your fetus's growth and the well-being of his internal organs by taking sonograms (images made from sound waves) of him.

- A *nonstress test* monitors the fetus's heart rate. In this test, a belt is positioned around your abdomen to measure the fetus's heart rate.

- A *contraction stress test* is another means of checking the fetus's heart rate, but this time it is measured and recorded in response to mild contractions of the uterus that are induced during the test.

Other tests may be recommended, depending on your own physical health and personal and family history. For example, particularly for women with a family history of genetic problems or for those who are age thirty-five or older, your obstetrician may advise tests that can detect genetic disorders. The most common genetic tests are *amniocentesis* and *chorionic villus sampling*.

CHOOSING A PEDIATRICIAN

Every pediatrician is committed to helping parents raise healthy children with the greatest possible ease, comfort, pleasure, and success. However, different pediatricians have different approaches, so you may want to interview several before selecting the one who best suits your family's particular preferences and needs. Conduct these visits before the baby arrives, so the pediatrician you choose can give your newborn her very first exam.

Here are some considerations to help you make your choice.

Training of Pediatricians

Pediatricians are graduates of four-year medical schools with three additional years of residency training solely in pediatrics. Under supervised conditions, the pediatrician-in-training acquires the knowledge and skills necessary to treat a broad range of conditions, from the mildest childhood illnesses to the most serious diseases.

With the completion of residency training, the pediatrician is eligible to take a written examination given by the American Board of Pediatrics. Once she passes this examination, a certificate is issued, which you probably will see hanging on the pediatrician's office wall. If you see the initials "FAAP" after a pediatrician's name, it means he has passed his board exam and is now a Full Fellow of the American Academy of Pediatrics. Only board-certified pediatricians can add the designation "FAAP" after their name, which means they have reached the highest status of membership in this professional organization.

Following their residency, some pediatricians elect an additional one to three years of training in a subspecialty, such as neonatology (the care of sick and premature newborns) or pediatric cardiology (the diagnosis and treatment of heart problems in children). These pediatric subspecialists generally are called on to consult with general pediatricians when a patient develops uncommon or special problems. If a subspecialist is ever needed to treat your child, your regular pediatrician will help you find the right one for your child's problem.

How to Find a Pediatrician

The best place to start looking for a pediatrician is by asking other parents you know and trust. They are likely to know you, your style, and your needs. You also should consider asking your obstetrician for advice. She will know local pediatricians who are competent and respected within the medical community. If you're new to the community, you may decide to contact a nearby hospital, medical school, or county medical society for a list of local pediatricians. If you are a member of a managed care plan, you probably will be required to choose a pediatrician from among their approved network of doctors. (For more information about managed care, see "Managed Care Plans: Getting Good Care for Your Child" on pages 12–13).

Once you have the names of several pediatricians you wish to consider, start by contacting and arranging a personal interview with each of them during the final months of your pregnancy. Many pediatricians are happy to fit such preliminary interviews into their busy schedules. Before meeting with the pediatrician, his office staff should be able to answer some of your more basic questions:

- Is the pediatrician accepting new patients with my insurance or managed care plan?

- What are the office hours?

- What is the best time to call with routine questions?

- How does the office handle billing and insurance claims? Is payment due at the time of the visit?

Both parents should attend the interviews with pediatricians, if possible, to be sure you both agree with the pediatrician's policies and philosophy about child rearing. Don't be afraid or embarrassed to ask any questions. Here are a few suggestions to get you started.

- *How soon after birth will the pediatrician see your baby?*
Most hospitals ask for the name of your pediatrician when you're admitted to deliver your baby. The delivery nurse then will phone that pediatrician or her associate on call as soon as your baby is born. If you had any complications

during either pregnancy or the delivery, your baby should be examined at birth. Otherwise, the examination can take place anytime during the first twenty-four hours of life. Ask the pediatrician if you can be present during that initial examination. This will give you an opportunity to learn more about your baby and get answers to any questions you may have.

- *When will your baby's next exams take place?*

Pediatricians routinely examine newborns and talk with parents before the babies are discharged from the hospital. This lets the doctor identify any problems that may have arisen and also gives you a chance to ask questions that have occurred to you during your hospital stay, before you take the baby home. Your pediatrician also will let you know when to schedule the first office visit for your baby and how she may be reached if a medical problem develops before then.

- *When is the doctor available by phone? E-mail?*

Some pediatricians have a specific call-in period each day when you can phone with questions. If members of the office staff routinely answer these calls, consider asking what their training is. Also ask your pediatrician for guidelines to help you determine which questions can be resolved with a phone call and which require an office visit. Some pediatricians prefer using e-mail to communicate. There are security concerns here, but overall it can help foster your relationship with the doctor.

- *What hospital does the doctor prefer to use?*

Ask the pediatrician where to go if your child becomes seriously ill or is injured. If the hospital is a teaching hospital with interns and residents, find out who would actually care for your child if he were admitted.

- *What happens if there is an emergency?*

Find out if the pediatrician takes her own emergency calls at night. If not, how are such calls handled? Also, ask if the pediatrician sees patients in the office after regular hours, or if you must take your child to an emergency room or urgent care center. When possible, it's easier and more efficient to see the doctor in her office, because hospitals often require lengthy paperwork and extended waits before your child receives attention. However, serious medical problems usually are better handled at the hospital, where staff and medical equipment are always available.

- *Who "covers" the practice when your pediatrician is unavailable?*

If your physician is in a group practice, it's wise to meet the other doctors, since they may treat your child in your pediatrician's absence. If your pediatrician practices alone, he probably will have an arrangement for coverage with other doctors in the community. Usually your pediatrician's answering service will refer you to the doctor on call automatically, but it's still a good idea to ask for the names and phone numbers of all the doctors who take these calls—just in case you have trouble getting through to your own physician.

If your child is seen by another doctor at night or on the weekend, you should check in by phone with your own pediatrician the next morning (or first thing Monday, after the weekend). Your doctor probably will already know what has taken place, but this phone call will give you a chance to bring him up to date and reassure yourself that everything is being handled as he would recommend.

- *How often will the pediatrician see your baby for checkups and immunizations?*

Your baby should undergo a physical exam within her first twenty-four hours of life (plus a follow-up checkup before you and she are discharged from the hospital). The American Academy of Pediatrics recommends another checkup by one month and at two, four, six, nine, twelve, fifteen, eighteen, and twenty-four months, and annually after that. If the doctor routinely schedules examinations more or less frequently than this, discuss the difference with her. The American Academy of Pediatrics immunization schedule is on page 73.

- *What are the costs of care?*

Your pediatrician should have a standard fee structure for hospital and office visits as well as after-hours visits and home visits (if he makes them). Find out if the charges for routine visits include immunizations. Be sure to familiarize yourself with the scope of your insurance coverage before you actually need services.

After these interviews, ask yourself if you are comfortable with the pediatrician's philosophy, policies, and practice. You must feel that you can trust him and that your questions will be answered and your concerns handled compassionately. You also should feel comfortable with the staff and the general atmosphere of the office.

Once your baby arrives, the most important test of the pediatrician you have selected is how he cares for your child and responds to your concerns. If you are unhappy with any aspect of the treatment you and your child are receiving, you should talk to the pediatrician directly about the problem. If the response does not address your concerns, or if the problem simply cannot be resolved, seek out another physician.

ISSUES TO DISCUSS WITH YOUR PEDIATRICIAN

Once you have found a pediatrician with whom you feel comfortable, let her help you plan for your child's basic care and feeding. Certain decisions and preparations should be made before the baby arrives. Your pediatrician can advise you on such issues as the following.

Managed Care Plans: Getting Good Care for Your Child

Many Americans now receive their health care in managed care plans. These plans, typically offered by employers and state Medicaid programs, provide services through health maintenance organizations (HMOs) or preferred provider organizations (PPOs). The plans have their own network of pediatricians and other physicians, and if you or your employer changes from one managed care plan to another, you may find that the pediatrician you've been using and whom you like is not part of the new network. Once you have a pediatrician whom you like, ask what plans she is in, and see if you can join one of them if there's a need to switch from one HMO or PPO to another.

Managed care plans attempt to reduce their costs by having doctors control patient access to certain health care services. Your pediatrician may act as a "gatekeeper," needing to give approval before your child can be seen by a pediatric medical subspecialist or surgical specialist. Without this approval, you'll have to pay for part or all of these services out of pocket.

To help you maneuver effectively through your managed care plan, here are some points to keep in mind:

- To determine what care is provided in your managed care plan, carefully read the materials provided by the plan (often called a certificate of coverage). If you have questions, talk to a plan representative or your employer's benefits manager. All plans limit some services (e.g., mental health care, home health care), so find out what's covered and what's not.

- When you're part of a managed care plan, primary and preventive care visits usually will be covered, including well-child checkups, treatment for illnesses or injuries, and immunizations. In many plans, you'll have to pay a portion of the primary care services that your family receives—usually between $5 and $20—called a copayment, for each doctor's visit.

When Should the Baby Leave the Hospital?

Each mother and baby should be evaluated individually to determine the best time of discharge. The timing of the discharge should be the decision of the physician caring for the infant, not the insurance company.

- Once you've chosen a pediatrician, it's best to stay with her. But if you feel the need to switch, all plans allow you to select another doctor from among those who are part of their network. The plan administrator can give you information on how to make this change; some plans allow you to switch only during certain time periods called open enrollment.

- If you feel that your child needs to see a pediatric subspecialist, work with your pediatrician to find one who is part of your plan, and obtain approval to schedule an appointment with him. Check your plan contract for details about whether your insurer will pay at least a portion of these costs. Also, if hospital care is needed, use your pediatrician's guidance in selecting a hospital in your plan that specializes in the care of children. (Most hospital procedures and surgeries require prior approval.)

- Know in advance what emergency services are covered since you won't always have time to contact your pediatrician. Most managed care plans will pay for emergency room care in a true emergency, so in a life-threatening situation, go immediately to the nearest hospital. In general, follow-up care (e.g., removing stitches) should be done in your pediatrician's office.

- To file a complaint—for example, if coverage of certain procedures is denied—start by expressing your concern to your pediatrician. If she is unable to resolve the problem, contact your plan's member service representative or employee benefits manager about filing a complaint. If a claim has been denied, you typically have fifteen to thirty days to file an appeal, and you should receive a decision about the appeal within thirty to ninety days of the request. If you still are dissatisfied, you may decide to seek help from the office of your state insurance commissioner, or you can take legal action.

Should the Baby Be Circumcised?

If you have a boy, you'll need to decide whether to have him circumcised or not. Unless you are sure you're having a girl, it's a good idea to make a decision about circumcision ahead of time, so you don't have to struggle with it amid the fatigue and excitement following delivery.

Circumcision

At birth, most boys have skin that completely covers, or almost covers, the end of the penis. Circumcision removes some of this foreskin so that the tip of the penis (glans) and the opening of the urethra, through which the baby urinates, are exposed to air. Routine circumcisions are performed in the hospital within a few days of birth. When done by an experienced physician, circumcision takes only a few minutes and is rarely complicated. (The complications, when they occur, are minor, such as soreness or bruising.) After consultation with you, your doctor will provide local anesthesia to reduce the pain the baby experiences during the procedure. The doctor should inform you in advance about the type of anesthesia he recommends.

Circumcision has been practiced as a religious rite for thousands of years. In the United States, most boys are circumcised, but usually for social rather than religious reasons. It is done because "all the other men in the family were circumcised" or because parents don't want their sons to feel "different."

At present, there is controversy over whether circumcision is advisable from a medical standpoint. New information suggests there are potential medical benefits to circumcision. Recent studies have concluded that male infants who are circumcised may be less likely to develop urinary tract infections than those who aren't; they also have a reduced chance of developing penile cancer. Further studies are needed to confirm these observations.

Cancer of the penis, a very rare condition, has long been known to occur al-

WHERE WE STAND

The American Academy of Pediatrics believes that circumcision has potential medical benefits and advantages, as well as inherent disadvantages and risks. The existing scientific evidence is not sufficient to recommend routine circumcision. Therefore, because the procedure is not essential to a child's current well-being, we recommend that the decision to circumcise is one best made by parents in consultation with their pediatrician, taking into account what is in the best interest of the child, including medical, religious, cultural, and ethnic traditions. Your pediatrician should discuss the benefits and risks of circumcision with you and the forms of analgesia that are available.

most exclusively in uncircumcised men. New reports find that cervical cancer may be more common among females whose partners are uncircumcised. Thus far, these reports are inconclusive. Also inconclusive is new evidence regarding the relationship of circumcision to sexually transmitted diseases.

Circumcision does, however, pose certain risks, such as infection and bleeding. Although the evidence also is clear that infants experience pain, there are several safe and effective methods to reduce the pain, such as EMLA cream, dorsal penile nerve blocks, and subcutaneous ring blocks. If the baby is born prematurely, has an illness at birth, or has congenital abnormalities or blood problems, he should not be circumcised immediately. The procedure should be performed only on stable, healthy infants.

Should I Breastfeed or Bottle-Feed?

Before your baby arrives, you'll want to decide whether you're going to breast-feed or use formula. The American Academy of Pediatrics advocates breast-feeding as the optimal form of infant feeding. While not identical to breastmilk, formulas do provide appropriate nutrition. Both approaches are safe and healthy for your baby, and each has its advantages.

The most obvious benefits of breastfeeding are convenience and cost, but there are some real medical benefits, too. Breastmilk provides your baby with natural antibodies that help her resist some infections that involve the ears, lungs, or bowel. Breastfed babies also are less likely to suffer from allergies that occasionally occur in babies fed cow's milk formulas.

Mothers who nurse their babies feel there are many emotional rewards. Once the milk supply is established and the baby is nursing well, both mother and

The American Academy of Pediatrics advocates breastfeeding as the optimal form of infant feeding.

If you cannot breastfeed or you choose not to do so, you still can achieve similar feelings of closeness during bottle-feedings.

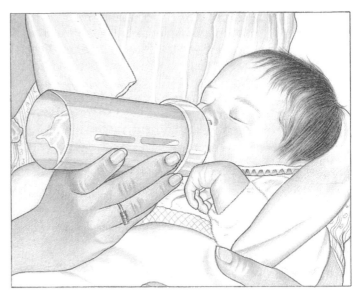

child experience a tremendous sense of closeness and comfort, a bond that continues throughout infancy. The first week or two can be challenging for some, but most pediatricians can offer guidance or refer you to a certified lactation consultant for assistance if needed.

If there is a medical reason you cannot breastfeed or you choose not to do so, you still can achieve similar feelings of closeness during bottle-feedings. Rocking, cuddling, stroking, and gazing into your baby's eyes will enhance the experience for both of you, regardless of the milk source.

Before making your decision on this issue, read Chapter 4 (pages 79–120), so that you thoroughly understand the advantages and disadvantages of breastfeeding and bottle-feeding, and you are aware of all the options available to you.

Should I Store My Newborn's Cord Blood?

Recently umbilical cord blood has been used successfully to treat a number of genetic, blood, and cancer disorders in children. Some parents are choosing to store their baby's cord blood for possible future use. However, there are no accurate estimates on the likelihood of children someday needing their own stored cells, with estimates ranging from 1 in 1,000 to 1 in 200,000. As a result, the American Academy of Pediatrics believes that private storage of cord blood as "biological insurance" is not currently recommended. Nevertheless, banking should be considered if there is a family member with a current or potential need to undergo a stem cell transplantation (because of diseases such as leukemia or a severe blood disorder called hemoglobinopathy). This is certainly an issue that you should discuss with your obstetrician and/or pediatrician *before* your baby is born, not during the emotionally stressful time of delivery.

PREPARING YOUR HOME AND FAMILY FOR THE BABY'S ARRIVAL

Choosing a Layette

As your due date nears, you'll need to acquire a layette, the basic collection of baby clothes and accessories that will get your newborn through his first few weeks. A suggested starting list includes:

3 or 4 pajama sets (with feet)
6 to 8 T-shirts
3 newborn sacques
2 sweaters
2 bonnets/hats
4 pairs of socks or booties
4 to 6 receiving blankets
1 set of baby washcloths and towels (look for towels with hoods)
3 to 4 dozen newborn-size diapers
3 to 4 onesies/T-shirts with snaps

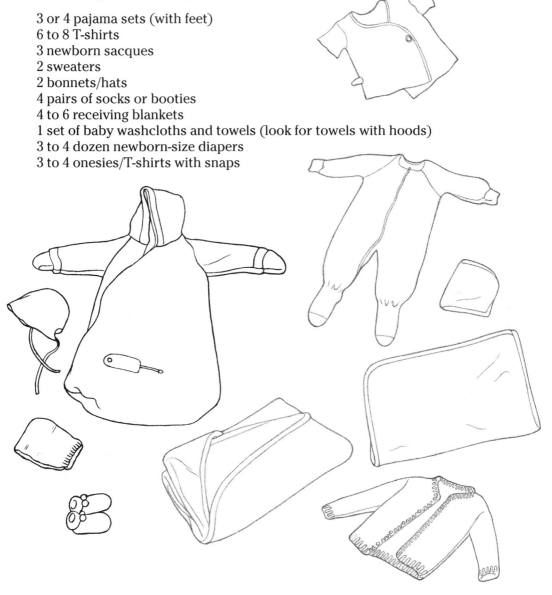

Safety Alert: Bassinets and Cradles

Many parents prefer to use a bassinet or cradle for the first few weeks, because it's portable and allows the newborn to sleep in the parents' room. But remember that infants grow very fast, so a cradle that is sturdy enough one month may be outgrown the next. To get the longest and safest possible use from your baby's first bed, check the following before buying:

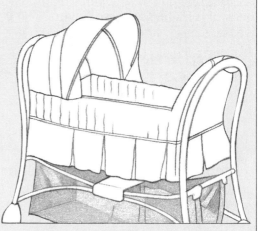

1. The bottom of the cradle or bassinet should be well supported so it cannot possibly collapse.

2. The bassinet or cradle should have a wide base so it can't tip over even if someone bumps against it. If the bassinet or cradle has folding legs, they should be locked straight whenever the bed is in use. Your baby should graduate to a crib around the end of the first month or by the time he weighs 10 pounds (4.5 kg).

If you have other children, most of this layette probably will consist of hand-me-downs. If this is your first child, you may receive many of the items from friends and relatives. Here are some guidelines to help you make your selections for the rest of the items you need.

- Buy big. Unless your baby is born prematurely or is very small, he probably will outgrow "newborn" sizes in a matter of days—if he ever fits into them at all! Even three-month sizes may be outgrown within the first month. You'll want a couple of garments that your child can wear in the very beginning, but concentrate on larger sizes for the rest of the wardrobe. Your baby won't mind if his clothes are slightly large for a while.

- To avoid injury from a garment that accidentally catches fire, all children should wear flame-retardant sleepwear and clothing. Make sure the label indicates this. These garments should be washed in laundry detergents, not soap, because soap will wash out the flame retardant. Check garment labels and product information to determine which detergents to use.

- Make sure the crotch opens easily for diaper changes.

- Avoid any clothing that pulls tightly around the neck, arms, or legs or has ties or cords. These clothes are not only safety hazards, but are also uncomfortable.

- Check washing instructions. Clothing for children of all ages should be washable and require little or no ironing.

- Do *not* put shoes on a newborn's feet. Shoes are not necessary until after he starts to walk. Worn earlier, they can interfere with the growth of his feet. The same is true of socks and footed pajamas if they're too small and worn for a prolonged period of time.

Buying Furniture and Baby Equipment

Walk into any baby store and you probably will be overwhelmed by the selection of equipment available. A few items are essential, but most things, while enticing, are not necessary. In fact, some are not even useful. To help you sort through the options, here is a list of the basic necessities you should have on hand when your baby arrives.

- A crib that meets all safety specifications (see *Safety Alert: Cribs,* page 20). New cribs sold today must meet these standards, but if you're looking at used cribs, check them carefully to make sure they meet the same standards and have not been recalled. Unless you have money to spare, don't bother with a bassinet. Your baby will outgrow it in just a few weeks.

- A crib mattress that is firm and covered with material that can be cleaned easily. If this covering is made of plastic or other nonabsorbent material, place a thick fabric pad on top of it so your baby won't lie in moisture caused by perspiration, drooling, or spit-up. The mattress must fit snugly so your baby can't get trapped between the mattress and the crib.

- Crib bumpers to keep your baby from hitting her head on the crib bars. Make sure these bumpers are tied to the crib railings, using all the strings. The bumpers should be removed when your child starts to stand; otherwise she may climb up on them and out of her crib. It is unnecessary and potentially dangerous to use pillows in a newborn's crib.

- Bedding for the crib, including a flannel-backed, waterproof mattress cover (which is cooler and more comfortable for your baby than plain plastic or rubber covers), and two fitted sheets. Never use infant cushions that have soft fabric coverings and are loosely filled with plastic foam beads or pellets. These cushions have been banned by the U.S. Consumer Product Safety Commission because they have been involved in thirty-six infant suffocations. Remove all pillows, quilts, comforters, sheepskins, and other pillowlike soft products. Remember that the safest position for baby to sleep is on her back (see *Positioning for Sleep,* page 45).

Safety Alert: Cribs

Your baby usually will be unattended when in his crib, so this should be a totally safe environment. Falls are the most common injury associated with cribs, even though they are the easiest to prevent. Children are most likely to fall out of the crib when the mattress is raised too high for their height or when the side rail is left down.

If you use a new crib or one manufactured since 1985, it will meet current safety standards. If you plan to use an older crib, inspect it carefully for the following features:

- Slats should be no more than 2⅜ inches (6 cm) apart so a child's head cannot become trapped between them.

- There should be no cutouts in the headboard or footboard, as your child's head could become trapped in them.

- If the crib has corner posts (sometimes called finials), unscrew them or cut them off. Loose clothing can become snagged on these and choke your baby.

Many older cribs were painted with lead-based paint, which can poison children if they gnaw on the crib rails. (It does happen.) As a precaution, strip the old paint and then repaint the crib using high-quality, new enamel. Let it dry thoroughly in a well-ventilated room. Then place plastic strips (available at most children's furniture stores) over the top of the side rails.

You can prevent other crib hazards by observing the following guidelines:

1. If you purchase a new mattress, remove and destroy all plastic wrapping material that comes with it, because it can suffocate a child. If you cover the mattress with heavy plastic, be sure the cover fits tightly; zippered covers are best.

2. As soon as your baby can sit, lower the crib mattress to the level where he cannot fall out either by leaning against the side or by pulling himself over it. Set the mattress at its lowest position by the time your child learns to stand. The most common falls occur when a baby tries to climb out, so move your child to another bed when he is 35 inches (88.9 cm) tall, or the height of the side rail is at or below his nipple line while standing.

3. When fully lowered, the top of the crib's side rail should be at least 4 inches (10.16 cm) above the mattress, even when the mattress is set at its highest position. Be sure the locking latch that holds the side up is sturdy and can't be released by your child accidentally. Always leave the side up when your child is in the crib.

4. The mattress should fit snugly so your child cannot slip into the crack between it and the crib side. If you can insert more than two fingers between the mattress and the sides or ends of the crib, replace the mattress with one that fits snugly.

5. Periodically check the crib to be sure there are no rough edges or sharp points on the metal parts and no splinters or cracks in the wood. If you notice tooth marks on the railing, cover the wood with a plastic strip (available at most children's furniture stores).

6. Use a crib bumper when your child is an infant. Be sure the pad goes all the way around the crib and is secured with at least six straps or ties, to keep the bumper from falling away from the sides. To prevent strangulation, the ties should be no more than 6 inches (15.24 cm) long.

7. As soon as your child can pull to a standing position, remove the crib bumpers, which could be used as a step for climbing out.

8. If you hang a mobile over your child's crib, be sure it is securely attached to the side rails. Hang it high enough so your baby cannot reach it to pull it down, and remove it when he starts to sit or when he reaches five months, whichever comes first.

9. Remove crib gyms as soon as your child can get up on all fours. Even though these gyms are designed to withstand a child's grabbing and tugging, he could fall forward onto the gym and become entangled.

10. To prevent the most serious of falls, don't place a crib—or any other child's bed—beside a window. Do not hang pictures or shelves above the child's bed; they can pose hazards in the event of an earthquake.

- A changing table that meets all safety specifications (see *Changing Tables,* page 433). It should be placed on a carpet or padded mat and against a wall, not a window, so there is no danger of your child falling. Put shelves or tables to hold diapers, pins, and other changing equipment within immediate reach (but away from the baby's reach), so you will not have to step away from the table—even for a second—to get anything.

- A diaper pail with deodorizer. Keep the diaper pail securely closed. If you are going to wash your own diapers, you'll need a second pail so you can separate wet diapers from "soiled" ones. If you use a diaper service, it usually will provide the pail. Diaper services usually offer a full line of supplies that make using cloth diapers as convenient as using disposable diapers. Look into the services in your area before your baby arrives.

- A large plastic washtub for bathing the baby. As an alternative to the washtub, you can use the kitchen sink to bathe your newborn, provided the faucet swings out of the way and the dishwasher is off. (The water from the dishwasher could dump into the sink, resulting in scalding.) After the first month, it's safer to switch to a separate tub, because the baby will be able to reach and turn on the faucet from the sink. Always make sure the bathing area is very clean prior to bathing your baby. It is advisable to set the thermostat on your water heater to its coolest setting. This will be hot enough for your household needs (120 degrees Fahrenheit [48.9 degrees Celsius]) but cool enough to reduce accidental scald injuries.

Everything in the nursery should be kept clean and dust-free. (See Chapter 14 for safety specifications.) All surfaces, including window and floor coverings, should be washable. So should all toys that are left out. Although stuffed animals look cute around newborns (they seem to be a favorite shower gift), they tend to collect dust and may contribute to stuffy noses. Since your baby won't actively play with them for many months, you might consider storing them until she's ready for them.

If the air in the nursery is extremely dry, your pediatrician may recommend using a cool mist humidifier. This also may help clear your child's stuffy nose when she has a cold. If you do use a humidifier, clean it frequently as directed in the package instructions and empty it when not in use. Otherwise, bacteria and molds may grow in the still water. Steam vaporizers are not recommended because of the danger of scalding.

One object that your baby is sure to enjoy is a mobile. Look for one with bright colors (the first color she'll see is red) and varied shapes. Some also play pleasant music. When shopping for a mobile, look at it from below so that you'll know how it appears from your baby's point of view. Avoid the models that look good only from the side or above—they were designed more for your enjoyment than for the infant's. Make sure you remove the mobile at five months of age or as soon as your baby can sit up, because that's when she'll be able to pull it down and risk injury.

A rocking chair, music box, and record or tape player are also wise additions to the nursery. The rocking motion of the chair will increase the soothing effect your baby feels when you hold her. Playing soft music for your baby will comfort her when you're not nearby and will help her fall asleep.

You will want to keep the lights in the nursery soft once your newborn has arrived and leave a night-light on after dark. The night-light will allow you to check on the baby more easily, and as she gets older, it will reassure her when she awakens at night. Make sure all lights and cords are kept safely out of the baby's reach.

Preparing Your Other Children
for the Baby's Arrival

If you have other children, you'll need to plan carefully how and when to tell them about the new baby. A child who is four or older should be told as soon as you start telling friends and relatives. He also should be apprised of the basic facts about conception and pregnancy so he understands how he is related to his new brother or sister. Fables about storks and such may seem cute, but they won't help your youngster understand and accept the situation. Using one of the picture books published on the subject may help you to explain "where babies come from." Too much detail can be scary for him. It's usually enough to say: "Like you, this baby was made from a little bit of Mommy and a little bit of Daddy."

If your child is younger than four when you become pregnant, you can wait awhile before telling him. When he's this young, he's still very self-centered and may have difficulty understanding an abstract concept like an unborn baby. But once you start furnishing the nursery, bringing his old crib back into the house, and making or buying baby clothes, he should be told what's going on. Also take advantage of any questions he may ask about Mom's growing "stomach" to explain what's happening. Picture books can be helpful with very young children, too. Sharing ultrasound pictures with him can be helpful, as well. Even if he doesn't ask any questions, start talking to your older child about the baby by the last few months of pregnancy. If your hospital offers a sibling preparation class, take him so that he can see where the baby will be born and where he can visit you. Point out other newborns and their older siblings, and tell him how he's going to be a big brother soon.

Don't promise that things will be the same after the baby comes, because they won't be, no matter how hard you try. But reassure your child that you will love him just as much, and help him understand the positive side of having a baby sibling.

Breaking the news is most difficult if your child is between two and three. At this age, he's still extremely attached to you and doesn't yet understand the concept of sharing time, possessions, or your affection with anyone else. He's also very sensitive to changes going on around him and may feel threatened by the idea of a new family member. The best way to minimize his jealousy is to include him as much as possible in the preparations for the new baby. Let him shop with you for the layette and the nursery equipment. Show him pictures of

Take advantage of any questions your child may ask about Mom's growing "stomach" to explain what's happening.

Picture books can be helpful with very young children.

himself as a newborn, and if you're recycling some of his old baby equipment, let him play with it a bit before you get it in order for the newcomer.

Any major changes in your preschooler's routine, such as toilet training, switching from a crib to a bed, changing bedrooms, or starting nursery school, should be completed before the baby arrives. If that's not possible, put them off until after the baby is settled in at home. Otherwise, your youngster may feel overwhelmed when the upheaval caused by the baby's arrival is added to the stress of his own adjustments.

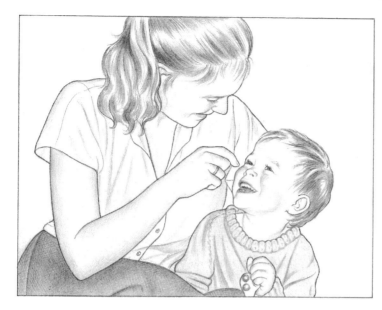

Make sure you reserve some special time each day just for you and your older child.

Don't be alarmed if news that a baby is coming—or, later, the baby's arrival—prompts your older child's behavior to regress a little. He may demand a bottle, ask to wear diapers again, or refuse to leave your side. This is his way of demanding your love and attention and reassuring himself that he still has it. Instead of protesting or telling him to act his age, simply grant his requests, and don't get upset about it. A three-year-old toilet-trained child who demands a diaper for a few days, or the five-year-old who wants his outgrown (you thought long-forgotten) security blanket for a week, will soon return to his normal routine when he realizes that he now has just as important a place in the family as his new sibling. Similarly, an older sibling who wants to try nursing again will quickly lose interest.

However busy or preoccupied you may be with your new arrival, make sure you reserve some special time each day just for you and your older child. Read, play games, listen to music, or simply talk together. Show him that you're interested in what he's doing, thinking, and feeling—not only in relation to the baby, but about everything else in his life. You don't have to spend more than five or ten minutes per day of protected time—time when the baby is asleep or being cared for by another adult—to make your older child feel special.

Preparing Yourself for Delivery

Toward the end of pregnancy, you may start feeling a little frantic. You'll be eager for the baby to arrive, but at the same time worried that your baby will be born before you have everything in perfect order. As your due date approaches (and, in some cases, passes), you'll have to fend off countless callers who are almost as excited as you are and also concerned about your welfare. This social pressure, added to the physical discomfort of late pregnancy, can make the ninth month seem endless. But the story does have a nice ending, so try to enjoy your leisure time as much as you can.

If you use this time wisely, you can get some chores out of the way that otherwise would have to be done after delivery. For example:

- Make a list of people who will receive birth announcements, select the announcement style, and address the envelopes in advance.

- Cook a number of meals and freeze them. You may not feel up to cooking for a while after the baby arrives.

- Look for child care and/or housekeeping help if you can afford it, and interview candidates in advance. (See *Finding Temporary Child Care Help,* page 163.) Even if you don't think you'll need extra help, you should have a list of names to call in case the situation changes.

Before entering your ninth month, make your last-minute preparations for delivery. Your checklist should include the following:

- Name, address, and phone number of the hospital

- Name, address, and phone number of the doctor or nurse-midwife who will deliver your baby and of the person who covers the practice when your doctor is not available

- The quickest and easiest route to the hospital or birthing center

- The location of the hospital entrance you should use when labor begins

- The phone number of an ambulance service, in case you need such assistance in an emergency

- The phone number of the person who will take you to the hospital (if that individual does not live with you)

- A bag packed with essentials for labor and for the rest of your hospital stay, including toiletries, clothing, addresses and phone numbers of friends and relatives, reading material, and a receiving blanket and suit of clothes for the baby to wear home

- A car safety seat for the vehicle so you can take your baby home safely. Make sure the seat meets all federal safety standards. (It should state this on the label.) Install it in the backseat, facing the rear. *(Never* place a rear-facing car safety seat in front of an air bag.) It should stay in this position until your baby reaches one year of age *and* weighs at least 20 pounds (9 kg). Then position it facing forward. (See *Car Safety Seats,* page 447, for complete details.)

- If you have other children, arrangements for their care during the time you will be at the hospital.

Preparing the Father for Delivery

If you're the father-to-be, remember that having a baby is a family event. You can help your spouse in the tasks and preparations for the baby's arrival described above. At the same time, you'll be making your own adjustments, which are just as challenging as those of your spouse. Of course, your role during the nine-month pregnancy has been quite different from hers, but you still have had adjustments to make. At times you've felt excited and elated; other times, fearful, exhausted, and perhaps just tired of waiting for the baby to arrive. There probably have been times when you've been an emotional anchor for your wife or partner during some of the more difficult moments of pregnancy, from periods of extreme fatigue to morning sickness.

When you accompany your wife on prenatal visits to the obstetrician, discuss what role you'll play in the delivery room. Be sure to get all your questions answered about what will take place and how you can be most supportive of your wife (as well as of the doctor and support staff). If you can do any advance planning in order to take off a few days or weeks from work once the baby arrives, make those arrangements now. And, of course, be ready to play a very active role in your child's life, not only in the first few days after her birth, but for the rest of your lives together. (For a further discussion about the unique role of fathers—and grandparents—upon the birth of their baby, see Chapter 6, pages 167–169.)

For both parents, once your baby finally arrives, all the waiting and discomforts of pregnancy will seem like minor inconveniences. Suddenly you'll get to meet this new person who's been so close and yet so mysterious all these months. The rest of this book is about the child she will become and the job that awaits you as a parent.

There's only so much preparation you can do before you start any journey. We have discussed a lot of the supplies you will need as well as many of the dos and don'ts. Ultimately, the way you assume your role as a parent will be determined more by the way you prepare yourself spiritually and emotionally than by what color you choose for the nursery wallpaper or the style of crib you buy. Only you know how you respond to stress and change. Try to prepare yourself for parenthood in a way that feels most comfortable to you. Some parents find support groups helpful; others prefer to meditate, sketch, or write.

Preparing yourself might be more difficult for some soon-to-be parents than others, especially if you are the kind of person who likes spontaneity more than figuring everything out in advance, but preparation is important, since it gives rise to greater confidence. It takes a stunning amount of confidence for a child to begin to walk. Similarly, you will need that type of confidence to take your own first steps into parenting.

2

BIRTH AND THE FIRST
MOMENTS AFTER

Giving birth is one of the most extraordinary experiences of a woman's life. Yet after all the months of careful preparation and anticipation, the moment of birth is almost never what you had expected. Labor may be easier or more physically demanding than you had imagined. You may end up in a delivery room instead of the birthing room you'd wanted, or you could have a cesarean section instead of a vaginal delivery. Your health, the condition of the fetus, and the policies of the hospital will all help determine what actually happens. But fortunately, despite what you may have thought when you were pregnant, these are not the issues that will make your child's birth a "success." What counts is the baby, here at last and healthy.

ROUTINE VAGINAL DELIVERY

In the days and weeks leading up to the birth of your baby, you'll probably feel a bit of apprehension along with your excitement, wondering when this much-anticipated event finally will happen. Then, usually between the thirty-seventh and forty-second week of your pregnancy, you'll go into labor. Although no one knows for certain what triggers this process, shifts in hormone levels appear to play a role. Your amniotic sac may seem to begin the process by rupturing, commonly referred to as breaking your water. As you proceed through labor, your uterus will contract, or squeeze, which will move your baby down the birth canal. At the same time, these contractions will fully open, or dilate, your cervix to an opening of about 10 centimeters (4 in.) so the baby can make his appearance through the opening of the vagina.

In a routine vaginal delivery, your first view of your child may be the top, or crown, of his head seen with the help of a mirror. After the head is delivered, the obstetrician will suction the nose and mouth, and your baby will take his first breath. He doesn't need to be slapped or spanked to begin breathing, nor will he necessarily cry; many newborns take their first breath quietly.

With the most difficult part of the birth now over, there is usually one last pause before the push that sends the rest of your child's body, which is smaller than his head, gliding smoothly into the doctor's waiting arms. After another, more thorough suctioning of his nose and mouth, your child may be handed to you to hold—and behold.

Even if you've seen pictures of newborns, you're bound to be amazed by the first sight of your own infant. When she opens her eyes, they will meet yours with curiosity. All the activity of birth may make her very alert and responsive to your touch, voice, and warmth. Take advantage of this attentiveness, which may last for the first few hours. Stroke her, talk to her, and look closely at this child you've created.

Fresh from birth, your child may be covered with a white cheesy substance called vernix. This protective coating is produced toward the end of pregnancy by the sebaceous (oil-producing) glands in his skin. He'll also be wet with amniotic fluid from the uterus. If there was an episiotomy (surgical cutting) or tearing of tissue in the vaginal area, he may have some of your own blood on him. His skin, especially on the face, may be quite wrinkled from the wetness and pressure of birth.

Your baby's shape and size also may surprise you, especially if this is your first child. On one hand, it's hard to believe that a human being can be so tiny; on the other, it's incredible that this "enormous" creature could possibly have fit inside your body. The size of his head in particular may alarm you. How could the head possibly have made it through the birth canal? The answer lies in its slightly elongated shape. The head was able to adapt to the contours of the passageway as it was pushed through, squeezing to fit. Now free, it may take up to several days to revert to its normal oval shape.

Your baby's skin color may be a little blue at first, but gradually will turn pinker as his breathing becomes regular. His hands and feet will be cold, and may remain so, on and off, for several weeks until his body is better able to adjust to the temperature around him.

You also may notice that your newborn's breathing is irregular and very rapid. While you normally take twelve to fourteen breaths per minute, your newborn may take as many as forty to sixty breaths per minute. An occasional deep breath may alternate with bursts of short, shallow breaths followed by pauses. Don't let this make you anxious. It's normal for the initial days after birth.

DELIVERY BY CESAREAN SECTION

More than twenty out of every hundred babies born in the United States are delivered by cesarean section (also called C-section or, simply, section). In a C-section, surgery is performed, with an incision made in the mother's abdomen and uterus, so the baby can be taken directly from the uterus instead of traveling through the birth canal.

Cesarean sections are done most often when the mother has had a previous baby by cesarean delivery or when the obstetrician feels that the baby's health might suffer if born vaginally. Usually, if the fetus's heartbeat slows abnormally or becomes irregular, the obstetrician will perform an emergency C-section instead of taking the chance of allowing labor to progress.

If your baby has assumed a breech position, your obstetrician will recommend a cesarean section as the best means of delivery. The reason is because breech babies are more difficult to deliver vaginally, and complications are more likely to occur with a vaginally delivered breech baby. While most babies are in a head-down position in the mother's uterus, about three of a hundred newborns have their buttocks, feet, or both in a place to come out first during birth (a breech presentation). A doctor can determine the baby's position by feeling the mother's lower abdomen at particular points; the physician may decide to confirm the breech position by ordering an ultrasound or other tests.

The birth experience with a C-section is very different from that of a vaginal delivery. For one thing, the whole operation ordinarily takes no more than an hour, and—depending on the circumstances—you may not experience any labor at all. An important difference is the need to use medication that affects both mother and baby. If given a choice of anesthetic, most women prefer to have a regional anesthesia—an injection in the back that blocks pain by numbing the spinal nerves—such as an epidural or a spinal. Administration of a regional anesthesia numbs the body from the waist down, has relatively few side effects, and allows you to witness the delivery. But sometimes, especially for an emergency C-section, a general anesthetic must be used, in which case you are not conscious at all. Your obstetrician and the anesthesiologist in attendance will advise you which approach they think is best, based on the medical circumstances at the time.

Even if you've seen pictures of newborns, you're bound to be amazed by the first sight of your own infant.

Because of the effects of the anesthesia, babies born by C-section sometimes have difficulty breathing in the beginning and need extra help. A pediatrician or other person skilled in newborn problems usually is present during a cesarean section to examine and assist the baby, if necessary, immediately after birth.

If you were awake during the operation, you may be able to see your baby as soon as she's been examined and proclaimed healthy. She then will be taken to the nursery to spend several hours in a temperature-controlled crib. This allows the hospital staff to observe her while the anesthesia wears off and she adjusts to her new surroundings.

If a general anesthesia was used during the delivery, you may not wake up for a few hours. When you do, you may feel groggy and confused. You'll probably also experience some pain where the incision was made. But you'll soon be able to hold your baby, and you'll quickly make up for the lost time.

Your C-section baby may look "prettier" than newborns delivered vaginally, because she didn't have to squeeze through the birth canal. As a result, instead of being elongated, her head retains its roundish shape.

Don't be surprised if your baby is still being affected by the anesthesia for six to twelve hours after delivery and appears a little sleepy. If you're going to breastfeed, try to nurse her as soon as you feel well enough. Even if she's drowsy, her first feeding will provide a reason for her to wake up and meet her new world—and you.

As mentioned, many obstetricians believe that once a woman has a C-section, her subsequent babies should be delivered the same way. If you're the father-to-be, discuss your role and presence in the delivery room and ways you can best support your partner during the birth.

DELIVERY ROOM PROCEDURES FOLLOWING A NORMAL VAGINAL BIRTH

As your baby lies with you following a routine delivery, his umbilical cord still will be attached to the placenta. The cord may continue to pulsate for several minutes, supplying the baby with oxygen while he establishes his own breathing. Once the pulsing stops, the cord will be clamped and cut. (Because there are no nerves in the cord, the baby feels no pain during this procedure.) The clamp will remain in place for twenty-four to forty-eight hours, or until the cord

Bonding

If you have a delivery without complications, you'll be able to spend the first hour or so after birth holding, stroking, and looking at your baby. Because babies are usually alert and very responsive during this time, researchers have labeled this the sensitive period.

The first exchanges of eye contact, sounds, and touches between the two of you are all part of a process called bonding, which helps lay the foundation for your relationship as parent and child. Although it will take months to learn your child's basic temperament and personality, many of the core emotions you feel for him may begin to develop during this brief period immediately after birth. As you gaze at him and he looks back, following your movements and perhaps even mirroring some of your expressions, you may feel a surge of protectiveness and awe. This is part of the attachment process.

It's also quite normal if you do *not* immediately have tremendously warm feelings for your baby. Labor is a demanding experience, and your first reaction to the birth may well be a sense of relief that at last it's over. If you're exhausted and emotionally drained, you may simply want to rest. That's perfectly normal. Give yourself a half hour or so until the strain of labor fades and then request your baby. Bonding has no time limit.

Also, if your baby must be taken to the nursery right away for medical attention, or if you are sedated during the delivery, don't despair. You needn't worry that your relationship will be harmed because you didn't "bond" during this first hour. You can and will love your baby just as much, even if you weren't able to watch his birth or hold him immediately afterward. Your baby also will be fine, just as loving of you, and connected to you.

is dry and no longer bleeds. The stump that remains after the clamp is removed will fall off sometime between ten days and three weeks after birth.

Once you've had a few moments to get acquainted with your baby, she will be dried to keep her from getting too cold, and a doctor or nurse will examine her briefly to make sure there are no obvious problems or abnormalities. One minute after birth, and again at five minutes, she will be given Apgar scores (see pages 36–37), which measure her overall responsiveness. Then she will be wrapped in a blanket and given back to you.

Depending on the hospital's routine, your baby also may be weighed, measured, and receive medication before leaving the delivery room. All newborns are slightly low in vitamin K, which is necessary for normal blood clotting, so they are given an injection of this vitamin to prevent excessive bleeding.

Because bacteria in the birth canal can infect a baby's eyes, your baby will be given antibiotic eyedrops or erythromycin ointment or other hospital-approved medication, either immediately after delivery or later, in the nursery, to prevent any infection.

At least one other important procedure must be done before either you or your newborn leaves the delivery room: Both of you will receive matching labels bearing your name and other identifying details. After you verify the accuracy of these labels, one will be attached to your wrist and the other to your baby's. Each time the child is taken from or returned to you while in the hospital, the nurse will check the bracelets to make sure they match. Many hospitals also footprint newborns as an added precaution.

PROCEDURES FOLLOWING PREMATURE BIRTH

About five or six out of every one hundred births in this country are premature. Because these babies are born before they are physically ready to leave the womb, they often have problems. For this reason, premature babies are given extra medical attention and assistance immediately after delivery. Depending on how early the baby is, your pediatrician may call in another pediatrician (called a neonatologist), who specializes in premature intensive care (also known as neonatal intensive care), to help determine what, if any, special treatment the infant needs.

If your baby is born prematurely, she may neither look nor behave like a full-term infant. While the average full-term baby weighs about 7 pounds (3.17 kg) at birth, a premature newborn might weigh 5 pounds (2.26 kg) or even considerably less. But thanks to medical advances, children born after twenty-eight weeks of pregnancy, and weighing more than 2 pounds 3 ounces (1 kg), have almost a full chance of survival; eight out of ten of those born after the thirtieth week have no long-term health or developmental problems.

The earlier your baby arrives, the smaller she will be, the larger her head will seem in relation to the rest of her body, and the less fat she will have. With so little fat, her skin will seem thinner and more transparent, allowing you actually to see the blood vessels beneath it. She also may have fine hair, called lanugo, on

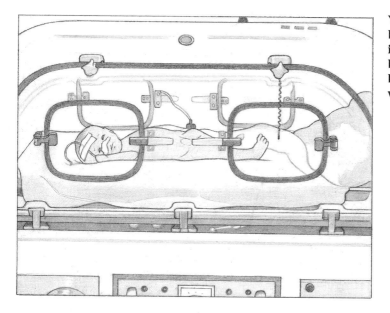

Your premature baby will be placed immediately after birth in an enclosed bed to keep her warm.

Nursing After Delivery

Do you plan to breastfeed your baby? If so, ask ahead of time about the hospital's policies on nursing in the delivery area. Today most hospitals encourage immediate breastfeeding following routine delivery unless the baby's Apgar scores are low or he's breathing very rapidly, in which case nursing would be delayed temporarily.

Breastfeeding right away benefits the mother by causing the uterus to contract, thus reducing the amount of uterine bleeding. (The same hormone that stimulates the milk ejection reflex, or letdown response, triggers the uterine contractions.)

The first hour or so after birth is a good time to begin breastfeeding, because your baby is very alert and eager. When put to the breast he may first lick it. Then, with a little help, he'll grasp the nipple and suck vigorously for several minutes. If you wait until later, he may be sleepier and have more difficulty holding the nipple effectively.

For the first two to five days after delivery, your body produces colostrum, a thin, yellowish fluid that contains protein and antibodies to protect him from infection. Colostrum provides all the nutrients and fluids your baby needs in the first few days of life. (For a complete discussion of breastfeeding, see Chapter 4.)

Apgar Scores

As soon as your baby is born, a delivery nurse will set one timer for one minute and another for five minutes. When each of these time periods is up, a nurse or physician will give your baby her first "tests," called Apgars.

This scoring system (named after its creator, Virginia Apgar) helps the physician estimate your baby's general condition at birth. The test measures your baby's heart rate, breathing, muscle tone, reflex response, and color. It cannot predict how healthy she will be as she grows up or how she will develop; nor does it indicate how bright she is or what her personality is like. But it does alert the hospital staff if she is sleepier or slower to respond than normal and may need assistance as she adapts to her new world outside the womb.

Each characteristic is given an individual score; then all scores are totaled. For example, let's say your baby has a heart rate of more than 100, cries lustily, moves actively, grimaces and coughs in response to the syringe, but is blue; her one-minute Apgar score would be 8. About nine out of ten newborns in this country score in the 8 to 10 range. Because their hands and feet remain blue until they are quite warm, few score a perfect 10.

If your baby's Apgar scores are between 5 and 7 at one minute, she may have experienced some problems during birth that lowered the oxygen in her blood. In this case, the staff probably will dry her vigorously with a towel while oxygen is held under her nose. This should start her breathing deeply and improve her oxygen supply so that her five-minute Apgar scores total between 8 and 10.

A small percentage of newborns have Apgar scores of less than 5. For example, babies born prematurely or delivered by emergency C-section are more likely to have low scores than infants with normal births. These scores may reflect difficulties the baby experienced during labor or problems with her heart or respiratory system.

If your baby's Apgar scores are very low, a mask may be placed over her face to pump oxygen directly into her lungs. If she's not breathing on her own within a few minutes, a tube can be placed into

her back and shoulders. Her features will appear sharper and less rounded than they would at term, and she probably won't have any of the white, cheesy vernix protecting her at birth, because it isn't produced until late in pregnancy. Don't worry, however; in time she'll begin to look like a typical newborn.

Because she has no protective fat, your premature baby will get cold in normal room temperatures. For that reason, she'll be placed immediately after

her windpipe, and fluids and medications may be administered through one of the blood vessels in her umbilical cord to strengthen her heartbeat. If her Apgar scores are still low after these treatments, she will be taken to the special-care nursery for more intensive medical attention.

Apgar Scoring System

Score	0	1	2
Heart Rate	Absent	Less than 100 beats per minute	More than 100 beats per minute
Respiration	Absent	Slow, irregular; weak cry	Good; strong cry
Muscle Tone	Limp	Some flexing of arms and legs	Active motion
Reflex*	Absent	Grimace	Grimace and cough or sneeze
Color	Blue or pale	Body pink; hands and feet blue	Completely pink

* Reflex judged by placing a catheter or bulb syringe in the infant's nose and watching her response.

birth in an incubator (an enclosed bed) in which the temperature can be adjusted to keep her warm. After a quick examination in the delivery room, she'll probably be moved to a special-care nursery (often called a neonatal intensive care unit [NICU]).

You also may notice that your premature baby will cry only softly, if at all, and may have trouble breathing. This is because her respiratory system is still im-

Health Issues of Premature Babies

When babies are born prematurely, they are more susceptible to a number of health problems. Here are some of the most common conditions:

- *Respiratory distress syndrome* is a breathing disorder related to the baby's immature lungs. It occurs because the lungs of preterm babies often lack surfactant, a liquid substance that gives lungs the elasticity that makes breathing easier. Artificial surfactants can be used to treat these babies, along with a ventilator to help them breathe.

- *Bronchopulmonary dysplasia,* or chronic lung disease, is a term used to describe babies who require oxygen for several weeks or months. They tend to outgrow this uncommon condition, which varies in severity, as their lungs grow and mature.

- *Apnea* is a temporary pause (more than fifteen seconds) in breathing that is common in preterm infants. It often is associated with a decline in the heart rate, called bradycardia. Your pediatrician can prescribe medication that helps regulate the breathing of babies with apnea, and most infants outgrow the condition by the time they leave the hospital for home.

- *Retinopathy of prematurity (ROP)* is an eye disease in which the retina is not fully developed. Most cases resolve without treatment, although serious cases may need treatment, including surgery in the most severe instances.

- *Jaundice* develops in babies whose liver is not mature enough to completely filter a normal blood breakdown product called bilirubin. As a result, the skin may develop a yellowish hue. The treatment for jaundice involves placing the baby under special lights (while her eyes are covered to protect them). For additional information about jaundice, see pages 139–140.

- Other conditions sometimes seen in preterm babies include *anemia of prematurity* (a low red blood cell count) and *heart murmurs.* For additional information on heart murmurs, see pages 667–668.

mature. If she's more than two months early, her breathing difficulties can cause serious health problems, because the other organs in her body may not get enough oxygen. To make sure this doesn't happen, doctors will keep her under close observation, watching her breathing and heart rate with equipment called a cardiorespiratory monitor. If she needs help breathing, she may be given extra oxygen, or special equipment such as a ventilator; or another breathing assistance technique called CPAP (continued positive airway pressure) may be used temporarily to do some of her breathing for her.

As important as this care is for your baby's survival, her move to the special-care nursery probably will be wrenching for you. On top of all the worry about her health, you may miss the experience of holding, breastfeeding, and bonding with her right after delivery. You won't be able to hold or touch her whenever you want, and you can't have her with you in your room.

What's your and her father's best defense against the stress of an experience like this? Ask to see your baby as soon as possible after delivery, and become as active as you can in caring for her. Spend as much time with her in the special-care nursery as your condition—and hers—permit. Even if you can't hold her, touch her through the portholes of the enclosed bed. Feed her as soon as advised by her doctor. The nurses will instruct on either breast and bottle feeding techniques, whichever is appropriate for the baby's needs and your desires. Because premature babies have a great need for food in order to become stronger and increase their resistance to disease, they may require fluids given intravenously or through a feeding tube. But breastmilk is the best possible nutrition, and once you start breastfeeding, your baby should nurse frequently to increase your milk supply.

You may be ready to return home before your newborn is, which can be very difficult, but remember that your baby is in good hands, and you can visit her as often as you'd like. You can use your time away from the hospital to get some needed rest and prepare your home and family for your baby's homecoming.

The more you participate in her process of recovery and the more contact you have with her during this time, the better you'll feel about the situation and the easier it will be for you to care for her when she leaves the special-care nursery. As soon as your doctor says it's OK, gently touch, hold, and cradle your newborn. If you have questions, be sure to ask them of the doctors and nurses. Also, don't forget that your own pediatrician will be participating in, or at least will be informed about, your infant's immediate care. Because of this, he will be able to answer most of your questions. Your baby will be ready to come home once she's breathing on her own, able to maintain her body temperature, able to be fed by breast or bottle, and is gaining weight steadily.

LEAVING THE DELIVERY AREA

If you've given birth in a birthing room or alternative birth center, you probably won't be moved right away. But if you've delivered in a conventional delivery room, you'll be taken to a recovery area where you can be watched for problems such as excessive bleeding. Your baby may be taken to the nursery at that time, or he may receive his first physical examination by your side.

This exam will measure his vital signs: temperature, respiration, and pulse rate. The pediatrician or nurse will check his color, activity level, and breathing pattern. If he didn't receive his vitamin K and eyedrops earlier, they will be administered now. And once he's warm, he'll be given his first bath, and the stump of his cord may be painted with a blue antibacterial dye or other medication to prevent infection. Then he'll be wrapped in a blanket and, if you wish, returned to you.

NEWBORN SCREENING TESTS

Shortly after birth, and before you and your baby are discharged from the hospital to return home, he'll be given a number of screening tests to detect a variety of congenital conditions. These tests are designed to detect problems early in order to treat them promptly, prevent disabilities, and save lives. However, while some tests are mandated by law, the tests required in one state are often different from those required in another (and they change periodically). For instance, three-fourths of states have legislation governing newborn hearing screening. Only a few mandate screening for cystic fibrosis, HIV, or toxoplasmosis. However, all fifty states and the District of Columbia test for PKU (phenylketonuria), a rare condition in which the body lacks the ability to break down a particular amino acid that, at high levels, can cause brain damage. All states also mandate screening for congenital hypothyroidism, a developmental defect of the thyroid gland that causes mental and physical disabilities and for galactosemia (a metabolic disorder). Forty-nine states screen for sickle cell diseases; fewer require testing for conditions such as maple syrup urine disease (branched-chain ketoaciduria), biotinidase deficiency, homocystinuria, tyrosinemia, and congenital adrenal hyperplasia. Talk to your pediatrician about which screening tests your baby will undergo. (The American Academy of Pediatrics has urged the adoption of nationwide standards to ensure that all newborns are screened uniformly for important genetic or metabolic disorders.)

REFLECTING ON YOUR BABY'S ARRIVAL

After all this activity during his first few hours of life, your baby probably will fall into a deep sleep, giving you time to rest and think back over the exciting things that have happened since labor began. If you have your baby with you, you may stare at him in wonder that you could possibly have produced such a miracle. Such emotions may wipe away your physical exhaustion temporarily, but don't fool yourself. You need to relax, sleep, and gather your strength. You have a very big job ahead of you—you're a parent now!

BASIC INFANT CARE

When your baby first arrives, you may feel a bit overwhelmed by the job of caring for her. Even such routine tasks as diapering and dressing her can fill you with anxiety—especially if you've never spent much time around babies before. But it doesn't take long to develop the confidence and calm of an experienced parent, and you'll have help. While you are in the hospital, the nursery staff and your pediatrician will give you instructions and support your needs. Later, family and friends can be helpful; don't be bashful about asking for their assistance. But your baby will give you the most important information—how she likes to be treated, talked to, held, and comforted. She'll bring out parental instincts that will guide you automatically to many of the right responses, almost as soon as she's born.

The following sections address the most common questions and concerns that arise during the first months of life.

DAY TO DAY

Responding to Your Baby's Cries

Crying serves several useful purposes for your baby. It gives him a way to call for help when he's hungry or uncomfortable. It helps him shut out sights, sounds, and other sensations that are too intense to suit him. And it helps him release tension.

You may notice that your baby has fussy periods throughout the day, even though he's not hungry, uncomfortable, or tired. Nothing you do at these times will console him, but right after these spells, he may seem more alert than before, and shortly thereafter he may sleep more deeply than usual. This kind of fussy crying seems to help babies get rid of excess energy so they can return to a more contented state.

Pay close attention to your baby's different cries. You'll soon be able to tell when he needs to be picked up, consoled, or tended to, and when he is better off left alone. You may even be able to identify his specific needs by the way he cries. For instance, a hungry cry is usually short and low-pitched, and it rises and falls. An angry cry tends to be more turbulent. A cry of pain or distress generally comes on suddenly and loudly with a long, high-pitched shriek followed by a long pause and then a flat wail. The "leave-me-alone" cry is usually similar to a hunger cry. It won't take long before you have a pretty good idea of what your baby's cries are trying to tell you.

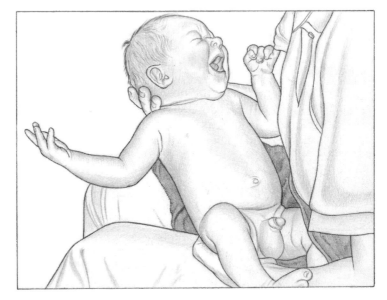

It won't take long before you have a pretty good idea of what your baby's cries are trying to tell you.

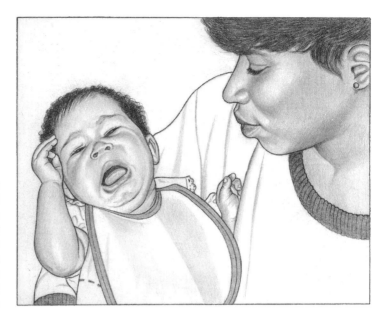

Respond promptly to your infant whenever he cries during his first few months. You cannot spoil a young baby by giving him attention.

Sometimes different types of cries overlap. For example, newborns generally wake up hungry and crying for food. If you're not quick to respond, your baby's hunger cry may give way to a wail of rage. You'll hear the difference. As your baby matures, his cries will become stronger, louder, more insistent. They'll also begin to vary more, as if to convey different needs and desires.

The best way to handle crying is to respond promptly to your infant whenever he cries during his first few months. You cannot spoil a young baby by giving him attention, and if you answer his calls for help, he'll cry less overall.

When responding to your child's cries, try to meet his most pressing need first. If he's cold and hungry and his diaper is wet, warm him up, change his diaper, and then feed him. If there's a shrieking or panicked quality to the cry, consider the possibility that a diaper pin is open or a strand of hair is caught around a finger or toe. If he's warm, dry, and well fed but nothing is working to stop the crying, try the following consoling techniques to find the ones that work best for your baby:

- Rocking, either in a rocking chair or in your arms as you sway from side to side

- Gently stroking his head or patting his back or chest

- Swaddling (wrapping him snugly in a receiving blanket)

- Singing or talking

- Playing soft music

- Walking him in your arms, a stroller, or a carriage

- Riding in the car (Be sure to properly secure him in his car safety seat.)

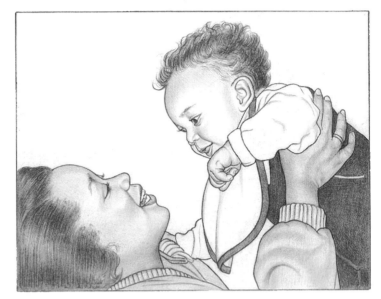

Enjoy all those wondrous moments with your child.

- Rhythmic noise and vibration

- Burping him to relieve any trapped gas bubbles

- Warm baths (*Most* babies like this, but not all.)

Sometimes, if all else fails, the best approach is simply to leave the baby alone. Many babies cannot fall asleep without crying, and will go to sleep more quickly if left to cry for a while. The crying shouldn't last long if the child is truly tired.

If your baby is inconsolable no matter what you do, he may be sick. Check his temperature (see *Taking a Rectal Temperature,* page 66). If it is over 100.4 degrees Fahrenheit (38 degrees Celsius)(taken rectally), he could have an infection. Contact your pediatrician.

The more relaxed you remain, the easier it will be to console your child. Even very young babies are sensitive to tension around them and react to it by crying. Listening to a wailing newborn can be agonizing, but letting your frustration turn to anger or panic will only intensify your infant's screams. If you start to feel that you can't handle the situation, get help from another family member or a friend. Not only will this give you needed relief, but a new face sometimes can calm your baby when all your own tricks are spent. No matter how impatient or angry you feel, *do not* shake the baby. Shaking an infant hard can cause blindness, brain damage, or even death.

Above all, don't take your newborn's crying personally. He's not crying because you're a bad parent or because he doesn't like you. All babies cry, often without any apparent cause. Newborns routinely cry a total of one to four hours a day. It's part of adjusting to this strange new life outside the womb.

No mother can console her child *every* time he cries, so don't expect to be a miracle worker with your baby. Instead, take a realistic approach to the situation, line up some help, get plenty of rest, and enjoy all those wondrous moments with your child.

Helping Your Baby Sleep

Initially your infant doesn't know the difference between day and night. Her stomach holds only enough to satisfy her for three or four hours, regardless of the time, so there's no escaping round-the-clock waking and feeding for the first few weeks. But even at this age, you can begin to teach her that nighttime is for sleeping and daytime is for play. Do this by keeping nighttime feedings as subdued as possible. Don't turn up the lights or prolong late-night diaper changes. Instead of playing, put her right back down after feeding and changing her. If she's napping longer than three or four hours, particularly in the late afternoon, wake her up and play with her. This will train her to save her extra sleeping for nighttime.

Positioning for Sleep

Historically, it was recommended that infants, particularly those between birth and four months of age, be placed on their stomachs for sleep. This was thought to be the best way to avoid aspiration (sucking food into the trachea [windpipe]) in case of vomiting or spitting up. We know now that *the back is a safer position, particularly as it relates to the sudden infant death syndrome (SIDS), which is responsible for more infant deaths in the United States than any other cause during the first year of life. Therefore, the American Academy of Pediatrics recommends that healthy infants be placed on their backs for sleep.* The exact reason for this finding is not certain, but it may be related to the infant sleeping on her stomach getting less oxygen or eliminating less carbon dioxide because she is "rebreathing" air from a small pocket of bedding pulled up around the nose. Although sleep position is probably not the only reason for SIDS, it seems so strongly related that the Academy feels obligated to make this recommendation. Please note that there are a few exceptions to this recommendation, including babies with certain medical conditions, which your pediatrician can discuss with you.

This recommendation of putting the baby down on her back applies to infants throughout the first year of life. However, it is particularly important during the first six months, when the incidence of SIDS is the highest. At times, even though sleeping on the back is best, you also can place your baby on her side to sleep—and alternate from one side to the other. Both back and side sleeping positions have a lower risk of SIDS than sleeping on the stomach.

Even when you are sure your baby is lying on her back, it is also important to avoid placing her on soft, porous surfaces such as pillows, quilts, comforters, sheepskins, or bean bags—even soft materials used for stuffed toys—which may block her airway if she burrows her face in them. Also avoid having her sleep on waterbeds, sofas, or soft mattresses. A firm crib mattress covered by a sheet is the safest bedding. Keep all soft toys and stuffed animals out of your child's crib. Keep the temperature in your baby's room comfortable and do not place your baby near air-conditioning or heating vents, open windows, or other sources of drafts. Use sleep clothing (such as a one-piece sleeper) with no other covering, as an alternative to blankets. If you use a thin blanket, tuck it in around the crib mattress, reaching only as far as your baby's chest, to reduce the risk of getting her face covered by the blanket.

As she gets older and her stomach grows, your baby will be able to go longer

How Your Baby Sleeps

Even before birth your baby's days were divided between periods of sleep and wakefulness. By the eighth month of pregnancy or earlier, her sleep periods consisted of the same two distinct phases that we all experience:

1. **Rapid eye movement (or REM) sleep,** the times during which she does her active dreaming. During these periods, her eyes will move beneath her closed lids, almost as if she were watching a dream take place. She also may seem to startle, twitch her face, and make jerking motions with her hands and feet. All are normal signs of REM sleep.

2. **Non-REM sleep,** which consists of four phases: drowsiness, light sleep, deep sleep, and very deep sleep. During the progression from drowsiness to deepest sleep, your baby becomes less and less active, and her breathing slows and becomes very quiet, so that in deepest sleep she is virtually motionless. Very little, if any, dreaming occurs during non-REM sleep.

At first your newborn probably will sleep about sixteen hours a day, divided into three- or four-hour naps evenly spaced between feedings.

Each of these sleep periods will include relatively equal amounts of REM and non-REM sleep, organized in this order: drowsiness, REM sleep, light sleep, deep sleep, and very deep sleep.

After about two to three months the order will change, so that as she grows older, she will cycle through all the non-REM phases before entering REM sleep. This pattern will last into and through adulthood. As she grows older, the amount of REM sleep decreases, and her sleep generally will become calmer. By the age of three, children spend one-third or less of total sleep time in REM sleep.

between feedings. In fact, you'll be encouraged to know that more than 90 percent of babies sleep through the night (six to eight hours without waking) by three months. Most infants are able to last this long between feedings when they reach 12 or 13 pounds (5.44–5.89 kg), so if yours is a very large baby, she may begin sleeping through the night even earlier than three months. As encouraging as this sounds, don't expect the sleep struggle to end all at once. Most children swing back and forth, sleeping beautifully for a few weeks, or even months, then returning abruptly to a late-night wake-up schedule. This may have to do with growth spurts increasing the need for food, or, later, it may be related to teething or developmental changes.

Where We Stand

Based on an evaluation of current sudden infant death syndrome (SIDS) data, the American Academy of Pediatrics recommends that healthy infants, when being put down to sleep, be placed on their backs. Despite common beliefs, there is no evidence that choking is more frequent among infants lying on their backs (the supine position) when compared to other positions, nor is there evidence that sleeping on the back is harmful to healthy babies. In some circumstances, there are still good reasons for placing certain infants on their stomachs for sleep. Discuss your individual circumstances with your pediatrician.

Since 1992, when the American Academy of Pediatrics began recommending that babies be put to sleep on their backs, the annual SIDS rate has declined more than 50 percent.

From time to time, you will need to help your baby fall asleep or go back to sleep. Especially as a newborn, she probably will doze off most easily if given gentle continuous stimulation. Some infants are helped by rocking, walking, patting on the back, or by a pacifier in the mouth. For others, music from a radio or a CD or tape player can be very soothing if played at moderate volume. Even the sound of the television, played quietly, can provide comforting background noise. Certain stimulation, however, is irritating to any baby—for example, ringing telephones, barking dogs, and roaring vacuum cleaners.

There is no reason to restrict your baby's sleeping to her crib. If, for any reason, you want her closer to you while she sleeps, use her infant seat or bassinet as a temporary crib and move it around the house with you. (She'll be perfectly happy in a padded basket if you don't have an "official" bassinet.)

How to Diaper Your Baby

Before you start to change your baby, make sure you have all the necessary supplies within easy reach. Never leave your baby alone on the changing table—not even for a second. It won't be long before he will be able to turn over, and if he does it when your eyes or attention is diverted, a serious injury could result.

When changing a newborn, you will need:

- a clean diaper (plus fasteners if a cloth diaper is used)
- cotton balls and a small basin with lukewarm water and a washcloth (commercial diaper wipes also can be used, although some babies are sensitive to them; if any irritation occurs, discontinue use)
- ointment or petroleum jelly (for use only if the baby has a rash)

This is how you proceed:

1. Remove the dirty diaper and use the lukewarm water and cotton to gently wipe your baby clean. (Remember to wipe front to back on female infants.)

2. Use the damp washcloth to wipe the diaper area.

3. Use the diaper rash preparation recommended by your pediatrician if needed.

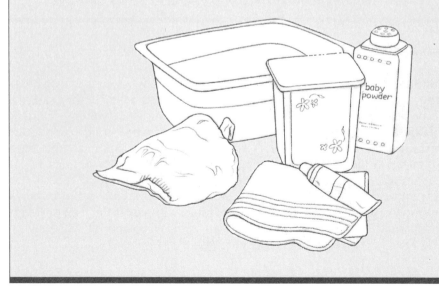

4. Put on the new diaper as shown on the following pages. Cloth diapers are available either prefolded (14 × 20 inches, or 35.6 × 50.8 cm) or in a 27-inch (68.6 cm) square, which you can fold to fit your child precisely. Initially you will need to fold about a third of the diaper down from the end so it's not too long. This also increases the absorbency. If the diapers have extra padding and your baby is a boy, place the padding in front. For girls, the padding goes in back.

Rectangular-fold diaper

The tab fasteners on disposables make the job of diapering very easy, but there are ways to fasten cloth diapers that many parents find just as convenient. Most use diaper pins (oversize safety pins with plastic heads). To prevent pricking the baby when using pins, you must keep your hand between the pin and his skin. If this procedure makes you nervous, try using diaper tape, which comes in a dispenser like household tape and adheres to the cloth. A third alternative is the diaper wrap, which requires neither pins nor tape. Available from diaper services and most stores that carry baby supplies, diaper wraps literally wrap around the baby's body, fastening with Velcro around the waist to hold the diaper in place. You also can use these wraps when you're away from home to cover wet diapers until you can dispose of them properly.

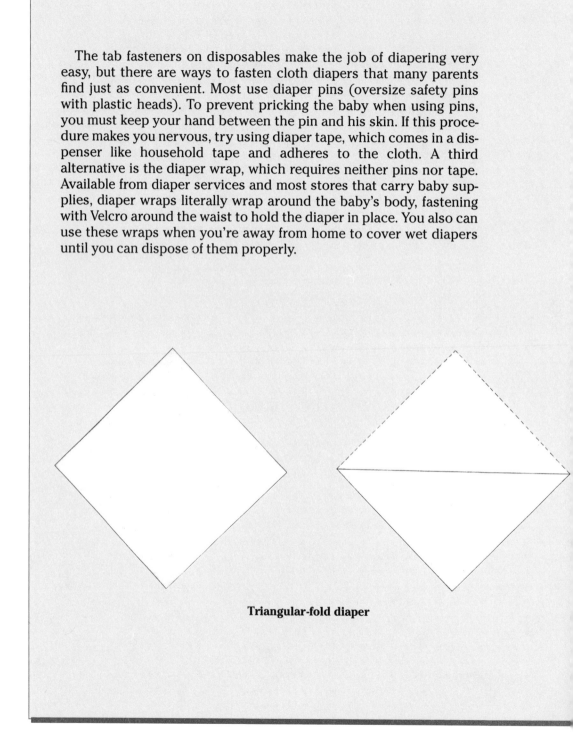

Triangular-fold diaper

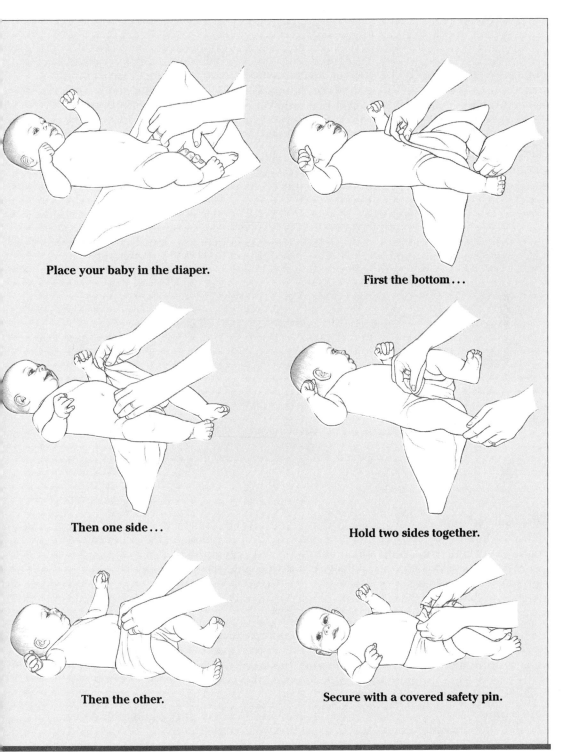

Place your baby in the diaper.

First the bottom...

Then one side...

Hold two sides together.

Then the other.

Secure with a covered safety pin.

Diapers

Until disposable diapers were introduced about thirty-five years ago, the only choice was to use cloth diapers, and either launder them at home or use a commercial diaper service. Today modern disposable diapers meet the needs and expectations of most parents and make up 80 percent or more of all diaper changes in virtually all developed countries. However, diaper choice is a decision that every new parent faces. Ideally, you should choose between cloth and disposable diapers before the baby arrives, so you can stock up or make delivery arrangements ahead of time. In order to plan ahead, you should know that most newborns go through about ten diapers a day.

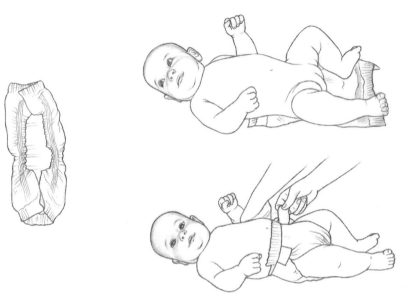

Disposable Diapers. Most disposable diapers today consist of an inner liner next to the baby to help keep wetness away from the skin, an absorbent core made of purified wood pulp and superabsorbent polymers, and an outer waterproof covering. They may have elastics at the waist and legs to provide better fit and help prevent leaks, and have various kinds of fastening tabs to make application and removal easier. Over the years, disposable diapers have become thinner and lighter, while continuing to meet the needs for containment, comfort, ease of use, and skin care. They also come in different sizes.

To fit a disposable diaper, place the baby on the open diaper so the fastening tabs are in back of the baby, and bring the front of the diaper between the baby's legs. Then bring the back edges of the diaper over the front and press the tabs into place to fasten. When changing a soiled diaper, dump loose stool into a toilet. Do not flush the diaper, because it can block your plumbing. Wrap the diaper in its outer cover, and discard in a waste receptacle.

Cloth Diapers. Like disposable diapers, reusable cloth diapers have improved over the years, and are available in a variety of absorbencies and textures. The original single-layer cotton diaper that is folded down to size has been largely replaced with the double-layered rectangular cotton diaper that has a multi-ply or fiber-filled center strip. Most parents fasten them with diaper pins. To prevent pricking the baby when using pins, you need to keep your hand between the pin and your baby's skin. You also can use diaper tape, which comes in a dispenser like household tape, and adheres to the cloth. The correct way to apply cloth diapers is shown in the diagrams. To prevent wet clothes and bedding, cloth diapers can be covered with a waterproof pant or overwrap. Also available are cloth diapers that combine the diaper and overwrap into a single unit.

If you want to use a diaper service, shop around before you make a choice. Ideally, a diaper service should pick up dirty diapers and drop off clean ones twice a week. Some services ask you to rinse the diapers yourself, while others prefer that you leave them intact, waste and all, in the diaper pail. If a diaper service is not available, or if you choose to wash diapers yourself, keep them separate from other clothes. After you dump stool into the toilet, rinse the diapers in cold water, then soak them in a mild detergent solution with bleach for thirty minutes. Wring them out, then wash in hot water with a mild detergent.

Diaper Choice. Diaper choice has been complicated in recent years by the debate on the environmental effects of diapers, mostly centered on the effects of disposable diapers on landfill space. Actually, a number of scientific studies have found that both cloth and disposable diapers have environmental effects, including raw material and energy usage, air and water pollution, and waste disposal. Disposable diapers add 1 to 2 percent to municipal solid waste, while cloth diapers use more energy and water in laundering and contribute to air and water pollution. It is difficult to judge whether solid waste issues are more important than energy, air, and water pollution issues. In the end, it is up to individuals to make their own decisions about diaper type based on their own concerns and needs.

The cost of disposable diapers from a supermarket or discount club and cloth diapers from a diaper service is roughly equivalent. Laundering your diapers at home can save money, but you must decide whether this is a good way to spend your time and energy.

There are also some health aspects to consider. Excessively wet skin and contact with urine and stool can cause diaper rash. Because cloth diapers can't keep wetness away from your baby's skin as effectively as disposables, it's especially important to change cloth diapers quickly after they become wet or soiled. If you use cloth diapers, you might consider using disposables overnight and during trips and outings, when changing diapers frequently may be less convenient.

Another health-related issue results from the ability of diapers to prevent leakage of urine and stool. This is particularly important in group child care settings such as child care centers, where intestinal diseases can be transmitted easily among the children. Disposable diapers generally are able to prevent leaks better than cloth ones because their superabsorbent polymers lock wet-

Diaper Rash

Diaper rash is the term used to describe a rash or irritation in the area covered by the diaper. The first sign of diaper rash is usually redness or small bumps on the lower abdomen, buttocks, genitals, and thigh folds—surfaces that have been in direct contact with the wet or soiled diaper. This type of diaper rash is rarely serious and usually clears in three or four days with appropriate care. The most common causes of diaper rash include:

1. Leaving a wet diaper on too long. The moisture makes the skin more susceptible to chafing. Over time, the urine in the diaper decomposes, forming chemicals that can further irritate the skin.

2. Leaving a stool-soiled diaper on too long. Digestive agents in the stool then attack the skin, making it more susceptible to a rash.

Regardless of how the rash begins, once the surface of the skin is damaged, it becomes even more vulnerable to further irritation by contact with urine and stool.

Another cause of rash in this area is yeast infection. This rash is common on the thighs, genitals, and lower abdomen but almost never appears on the buttocks.

Although most babies develop diaper rash at some point during infancy, it happens less often in babies who are breastfed (for reasons we still do not know). Diaper rash occurs more often at particular ages and under certain conditions:

- Among babies eight to ten months old
- If babies are not kept clean and dry

ness inside. Because of the increased risk for leaks and diaper handling issues, many child care centers require the use of disposable diapers.

Urination

Your baby may urinate as often as every one to three hours or as infrequently as four to six times a day. If she's ill or feverish, or when the weather is extremely hot, her usual output of urine may drop by half and still be normal. Urination should never be painful. If you notice any signs of distress while your infant is urinating, notify your pediatrician, as this could be a sign of infection or some other problem in the urinary tract.

- When babies have frequent stools (especially when the stools are left in their diapers overnight)

- When a baby starts to eat solid food (probably due to the introduction of more acidic foods and changes in the digestive process caused by the new variety of foods)

- When a baby is taking antibiotics (because these drugs encourage the growth of yeast organisms that can infect the skin)

To reduce your baby's risk of diaper rash, make these steps part of your diapering routine:

1. Change the diaper as soon as possible after a bowel movement. Cleanse the diaper area with a soft cloth and water after each bowel movement.

2. Change wet diapers frequently to reduce skin exposure to moisture.

3. Expose the baby's bottom to air whenever feasible. When using plastic pants or disposable diapers with tight gathers around the abdomen and legs, make sure air can circulate inside the diaper.

If a diaper rash develops in spite of your efforts and the skin is dried out, you may need to use a lotion or ointment; if it is a moist rash, use a drying lotion. The rash should improve noticeably within forty-eight to seventy-two hours. If it doesn't, consult your pediatrician.

In a healthy child, urine is light to dark yellow in color. (The darker the color, the more concentrated the urine; the urine will be more concentrated when your child is not drinking a lot of liquid.) Sometimes you'll see a pink stain on the diaper that you may mistake for blood. In fact, this stain is usually a sign of highly concentrated urine, which has a pinkish color. As long as the baby is wetting at least four diapers a day, there probably is no cause for concern, but if the pinkish staining persists, consult your pediatrician.

The presence of actual blood in the urine or a bloody spot on the diaper is never normal, and your pediatrician should be notified. It may be due to nothing more serious than a small sore caused by diaper rash, but it also could be a sign of a more serious problem. If this bleeding is accompanied by other symptoms, such as abdominal pain or bleeding in other areas, seek medical attention for your baby immediately.

Bowel Movements

In the first few days of life your baby will have his first bowel movement, which is often referred to as meconium. This thick, dark-green or black substance filled his intestines before birth, and it must be eliminated before normal digestion can take place. Once the meconium is passed, the stools will turn yellow-green.

If your baby is breastfed, his stools soon should resemble light mustard with seedlike particles. Until he starts to eat solid foods, the consistency of the stools should be soft, even slightly runny. If he's formula-fed, his stools usually will be tan or yellow in color. They will be firmer than in a baby who is breastfed, but no firmer than peanut butter.

Whether your baby is breastfed or bottle-fed, hard or very dry stools may be a sign that he is not getting enough fluid or that he is losing too much fluid due to illness, fever, or heat. Once he has started solids, hard stools might indicate that he's eating too many constipating foods, such as cereal or cow's milk, before his system can handle them. (Whole cow's milk is not recommended for babies under twelve months.)

Keep in mind that occasional variations in color and consistency of the stools are normal. For example, if the digestive process slows down because the baby has had a particularly large amount of cereal that day or foods requiring more effort to digest, the stools may become green; or if the baby is given supplemental iron, the stools may turn dark brown. If there is a minor irritation of the anus, streaks of blood may appear on the outside of the stools. However, if there are large amounts of blood, mucus, or water in the stool, call your pediatrician immediately. These symptoms may indicate severe diarrhea or an intestinal abnormality.

Because an infant's stools are normally soft and a little runny, it's not always easy to tell when a young baby has mild diarrhea. The telltale signs are a sudden increase in frequency (to more than one bowel movement per feeding) and unusually high liquid content in the stool. Diarrhea may be a sign of intestinal infection, or it may be caused by a change in the baby's diet. If the baby is breastfeeding, he can even develop diarrhea because of a change in the mother's diet.

The main concern with diarrhea is the possibility that dehydration can develop. If fever is also present and your infant is less than two months old, call your pediatrician immediately. If your baby is over two months and the fever lasts more than a day, check his urine output and rectal temperature; then report your findings to your doctor so she can determine what needs to be done.

The frequency of bowel movements varies widely from one baby to another. Many pass a stool soon after each feeding. This is a result of the gastrocolic reflex, which causes the digestive system to become active whenever the stomach is filled with food.

By three to six weeks of age, some breastfed babies have only one bowel movement a week and still are normal. This happens because breastmilk leaves very little solid waste to be eliminated from the child's digestive system. Thus, infrequent stools are not a sign of constipation and should not be considered a problem as long as the stools are soft (no firmer than peanut butter), and your infant is otherwise normal, gaining weight steadily, and nursing regularly.

If your baby is formula-fed, he should have at least one bowel movement a day. If he has fewer than this and appears to be straining because of hard stools, he may be constipated. Check with your pediatrician for advice on how to handle this problem. (See *Constipation,* page 503.)

Bathing

Your infant doesn't need much bathing if you wash the diaper area thoroughly during diaper changes. Two or three times a week during her first year is plenty. Bathing her more frequently may dry out her skin.

During her first week or two, until the stump of the umbilical cord falls off, your newborn should have only sponge baths. In a warm room, lay the baby anywhere that's flat and comfortable for both of you—a changing table, bed, floor, or counter next to the sink will do. Pad hard surfaces with a blanket or fluffy towel. If the baby is on a surface above the floor, use a safety strap or keep one hand on her *at all times* to make sure she doesn't fall.

Have a basin of water, a damp, double-rinsed washcloth (so there is no soap residue in it), and a supply of mild baby soap within reach before you begin. Keep your baby wrapped in a towel, and expose only the parts of her body you are actively washing. Use the dampened cloth first without soap to wash her

Baby towels with built-in hoods are the most effective way to keep your baby's head warm when she's wet.

Bathing Your Baby

Fill the basin with 2 inches of water that feels warm—not hot—to the inside of your wrist or elbow. Once you've undressed your baby, place her in the water immediately so she doesn't get chilled. Use one of your hands to support her head and the other to guide her in, feet first. Speak to her encouragingly, and gently lower the rest of her body until she's in the tub. Most of her body and face should be well above the water level for safety, so you'll need to pour warm water over her body frequently to keep her warm.

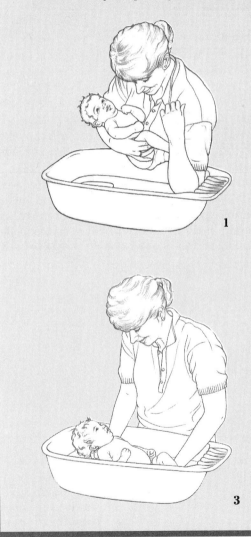

1

2

3

4

Use a soft cloth to wash her face and hair, shampooing once or twice a week. Massage her entire scalp gently, including the area over her fontanelles (soft spots). When you rinse the soap or shampoo from her head, cup your hand across her forehead so the suds run toward the sides, not into her eyes. Should you get some soap in her eyes, and she cries out in protest, simply take the wet washcloth and liberally wipe her eyes with plain, lukewarm water until any remains of the soap are gone, and she will open her eyes again. Wash the rest of her body from the top down.

5

6

7

face, so you don't get soap into her eyes or mouth. Then dip it in the basin of soapy water before washing the remainder of her body and, finally, the diaper area. Pay special attention to creases under the arms, behind the ears, around the neck, and, especially with a girl, in the genital area.

Once the umbilical area is healed, you can try placing your baby directly in the water. Her first baths should be as gentle and brief as possible. She probably will protest a little; if she seems miserable, go back to sponge baths for a week or two, then try the bath again. She will make it clear when she's ready.

Most parents find it easiest to bathe a newborn in a bathinette, sink, or plastic tub lined with a clean towel. Fill the basin with 2 inches (5.08 cm) of water that feels warm—not hot—to the inside of your wrist or elbow. If you're filling the basin from the tap, turn the cold water on first (and off last) to avoid scalding yourself or your child. In addition, make sure your hot water heater is set no higher than 120 degrees Fahrenheit (48.9 degrees Celsius).

Make sure that supplies are at hand and the room is warm before undressing the baby. You'll need the same supplies that you used for sponge bathing, but also a cup for rinsing with clear water. When your child has hair, you'll need baby shampoo, too.

If you've forgotten something or need to answer the phone or door during the bath, *you must take the baby with you,* so keep a dry towel within reach. *Never leave a baby alone in the bath, even for an instant.*

If your baby enjoys her bath, give her some extra time to splash and explore the water. The more fun your child has in the bath, the less she'll be afraid of the water. As she gets older, the length of the bath will extend until most of it is taken up with play. Bathing should be a very relaxing and soothing experience, so don't rush unless she's unhappy.

Bath toys are not really needed for very young babies, as the stimulation of the water and washing is exciting enough. Once a baby is old enough for the bathtub, however, toys become invaluable. Containers, floating toys, even waterproof books make wonderful distractions as you cleanse your baby.

When your infant comes out of the bath, baby towels with built-in hoods are the most effective way to keep her head warm when she's wet. Bathing a baby of any age is wet work, so you may want to wear a terry-cloth apron or hang a towel over your shoulder to keep you dry.

In the early months, you may find it easiest to bathe your infant in the morning, when she's alert and the house is quiet and warm. By the time she graduates to the bathtub (usually when she's sitting up or outgrows the basin), you may want to shift to an evening schedule on the days she's bathed. The bath is a relaxing way to prepare her for sleep.

Skin and Nail Care

Your newborn's skin may be susceptible to irritation from chemicals in new clothing and from soap or detergent residue on clothes that have been washed. To avoid problems, double-rinse all baby clothes, bedding, blankets, and other

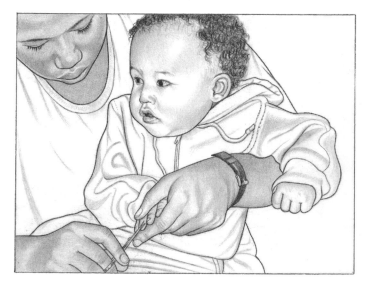

In the early weeks, your baby's fingers are so small and his nails grow so quickly you may have to trim them twice a week.

washable items before exposing the child to them. (Wash his new layette, too, before he uses it.) For the first few months, do your infant's wash separately from the rest of the family's.

Contrary to what you may read in ads for baby products, your infant does not ordinarily need any lotions, oils, or powders. If his skin is very dry, you can apply a small amount of nonperfumed baby lotion sparingly to the dry areas. Never use any skin-care products that are not specifically made for babies, because they generally contain perfumes and other chemicals that can irritate an infant's skin. Also avoid baby oil, which does not penetrate or lubricate as well as baby lotion. If the dryness persists, you may be bathing your child too often. Give him a bath just once a week for a while and see if the dryness stops. If not, consult your pediatrician.

The only care your child's nails require is trimming. You can use a soft emery board, baby nail clippers, or blunt-nosed toenail scissors. A good time to trim nails is after a bath if your baby will lie quietly, but you may find it easiest to do when he's asleep. Keep his fingernails as short and smoothly trimmed as possible so he can't scratch himself (or you). In the early weeks, his fingers are so small and his nails grow so quickly you may have to trim them twice a week.

By contrast, his toenails grow much more slowly and are usually very soft and pliable. They needn't be kept as short as the fingernails, so you may have to trim them only once or twice a month. Because they are so soft, they sometimes look as if they're ingrown, but there's no cause for concern unless the skin alongside the nail gets red, inflamed, or hard. As your baby gets older, his toenails will become harder and better defined.

Dressing Your Baby

Supporting your baby on your lap, stretch the garment neckline and pull it over your baby's head, using your fingers to keep it from catching on her face or ears.

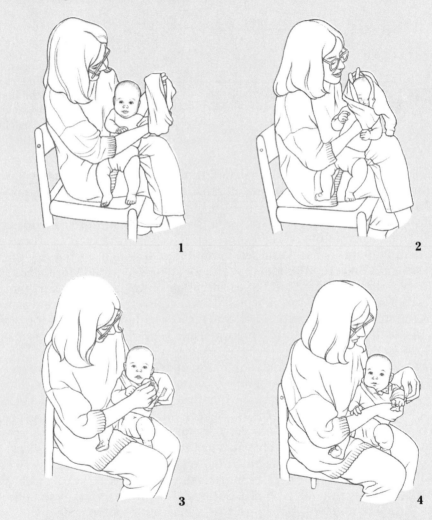

Don't try to push your baby's arm through the sleeve. Instead, put your hand into the sleeve from the outside, grasp your baby's hand, and pull it through.

Undressing Your Baby

Take off the sleeves one at a time while you support your baby's back and head.

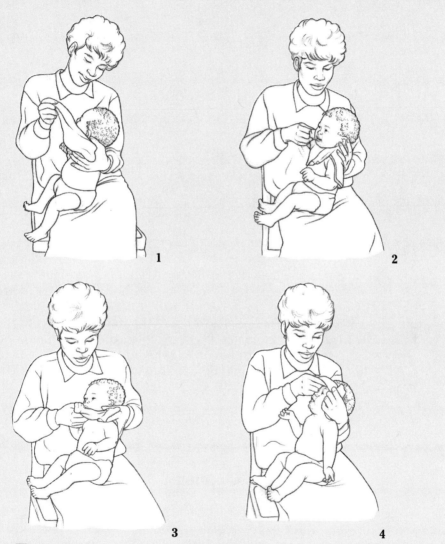

Then stretch the neckline, lifting it free of your baby's chin and face as you gently slip it off.

A Snug Bundle

During the first few weeks, your baby will spend most of his time wrapped in a receiving blanket. Not only does this keep him warm, but the slight pressure around the body seems to give most newborns a sense of security. To make a snug bundle, spread the blanket out flat, with one corner folded over. Lay the baby face-up on the blanket, with his head at the folded corner. Wrap the left corner over his body and tuck it beneath him. Bring the bottom corner up over his feet, and then wrap the right corner around him, leaving only his head and neck exposed.

Clothing

Unless the temperature is hot (over 75 degrees Fahrenheit [23.88 degrees Celsius]), your newborn will need several layers of clothing to keep her warm. It's generally best to dress her in an undershirt and diapers, covered by pajamas or a dressing gown, and then wrap her in a receiving blanket. If your baby is premature, she may need still another layer of clothing until her weight reaches that of a full-term baby and her body is better able to adjust to changes in temperature. In hot weather you can reduce her clothing to a single layer, but be sure to cover her when in air-conditioned surroundings or near drafts. A good

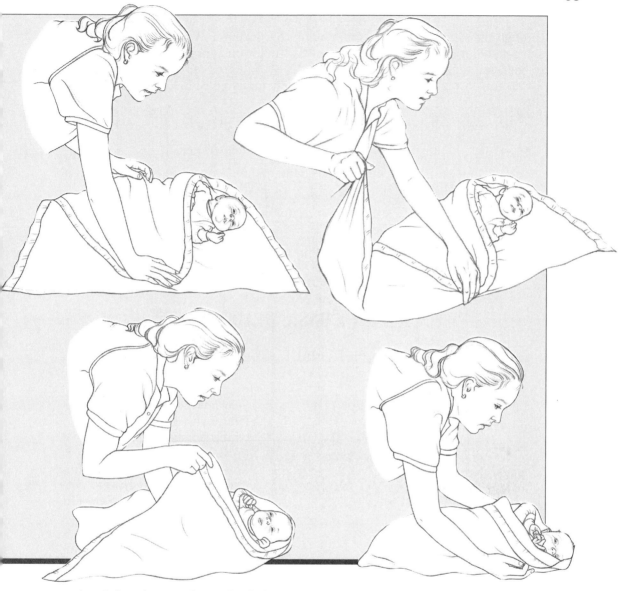

rule of thumb is to dress the baby in one more layer of clothing than you are wearing to be comfortable in the same environment.

If you've never taken care of a newborn baby before, the first few times you change her clothes can be quite frustrating. Not only is it a struggle to get that tiny little arm through the sleeve, but your infant may shriek in protest through the whole process. She doesn't like the rush of air against her skin, nor does she enjoy being pushed and pulled through garments. It may make things easier for both of you if you hold her on your lap while changing the upper half of her body, then lay her on a bed or changing table while doing the lower half. When you're dressing her in one-piece pajamas, pull them over her legs before putting on the sleeves. Pull T-shirts over her head first, then put one arm at a time through the sleeves. Use this opportunity to ask "Where's the baby's hand?" As she gets older this will turn into a game, with her pushing her arm through just to hear you say, "*There's* the baby's hand!"

Certain clothing features can make dressing much easier. Look for garments that

- Snap or zip all the way down the front, instead of the back

- Snap or zip down both legs to make diaper changes easier

- Have loose-fitting sleeves so your hand fits underneath to push the baby's arm through

- Have no ribbons or strings to knot up, unravel, or wrap around the neck (which could cause choking)

- Are made of stretchy fabric (Avoid tight bindings around arms, legs, or neck.)

YOUR BABY'S BASIC HEALTH CARE

Taking a Rectal Temperature

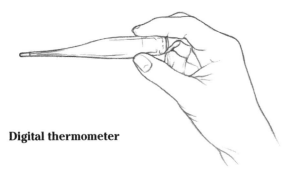

Digital thermometer

Very few babies get through infancy without having a fever, which is usually a sign of infection somewhere in the body. A fever indicates that the immune system is actively fighting viruses or bacteria, so—in this respect—it is a positive sign that the body is protecting itself. But if the body temperature gets too high too rapidly (over 104 degrees Fahrenheit [40 degrees Celsius], rising more than several degrees an hour), it is possible that a convulsion may occur.

An infant or toddler cannot hold a thermometer steady in his mouth for you to take an oral temperature, and "fever strips" that are placed on the child's forehead are not accurate. The best way to measure fever in a young child is by taking a rectal temperature. Once you know how to take a rectal temperature, it is really quite simple; but it's best to learn the procedures in advance so you're not nervous about them the first time your child is actually sick.

The American Academy of Pediatrics does not recommend the use of mercury thermometers, which can break easily. In fact, we advise parents to re-

Taking a rectal temperature

move any mercury thermometers from the home to prevent accidental exposure to mercury, which is a toxin. Instead, among your basic baby equipment, you should have a rectal digital thermometer and, if you wish, an ear (or tympanic) thermometer. For children under three years of age, a rectal digital thermometer provides the most accurate reading.

The procedure for taking a rectal temperature with a digital thermometer is as follows:

1. Clean the end of the thermometer with rubbing alcohol or soap and water. Rinse with cool *(not hot)* water.

2. Apply disposable plastic sleeve.

3. Place a small amount of lubricant such as petroleum jelly on the end.

4. Place your child belly-down across your lap or on a firm surface. Hold him steady by placing your palm against his lower back, just above his bottom.

5. With the other hand, turn on the thermometer's switch, and then insert the thermometer one-half to one inch into the anal opening. *(Do not insert it any farther.)* Hold the thermometer loosely in place using two fingers, while keeping your hand cupped around your child's bottom.

6. Hold the thermometer in place for about one minute, until you hear it beep.

7. Remove the thermometer and check the reading. Most digital thermometers come with disposable sleeves to cover the thermometer; once you've taken your baby's temperature, dispose of this plastic sleeve. Use a clean one next time you use the device.

A rectal reading over 100.4 degrees Fahrenheit (38 degrees Celsius) may indicate a fever. Retake the temperature in thirty minutes if you think the tempera-

RECOMMENDATIONS FOR PREVENTIVE PEDIATRIC HEALTH CARE

Committee on Practice and Ambulatory Medicine

Each child and family is unique; therefore, these **Recommendations for Preventive Pediatric Health Care** are designed for the care of children who are receiving competent parenting, have no manifestations of any important health problems, and are growing and developing in satisfactory fashion. **Additional visits may become necessary** if circumstances suggest variations from normal.

AGE[5]	PRENATAL[1]	NEWBORN[2]	INFANCY[4] 2-4d[3]	By 1mo	2mo	4mo	6mo	9mo	12mo	EARLY CHILDHOOD[4] 15mo	18mo	24mo	3y	4y
HISTORY Initial/Interval	●	●	●	●	●	●	●	●	●	●	●	●	●	●
MEASUREMENTS Height and Weight		●	●	●	●	●	●	●	●	●	●	●	●	●
Head Circumference		●	●	●	●	●	●	●	●	●	●	●		
Blood Pressure													●	●
SENSORY SCREENING Vision		S	S	S	S	S	S	S	S	S	S	S	O[6]	O
Hearing		O[7]	S	S	S	S	S	S	S	S	S	S	S	O
DEVELOPMENTAL/ BEHAVIORAL ASSESSMENT[8]		●	●	●	●	●	●	●	●	●	●	●	●	●
PHYSICAL EXAMINATION[9]		●	●	●	●	●	●	●	●	●	●	●	●	●
PROCEDURES-GENERAL[10] Hereditary/Metabolic Screening[11]			◄ ● ►											
Immunization[12]		●		●	●	●	●	●	●	●	●	●	●	●
Hematocrit or Hemoglobin[13]								●	►	★				
Urinalysis														
PROCEDURES-PATIENTS AT RISK Lead Screening[16]								★	►			★		
Tuberculin Test[17]									★	★	★	★	★	★
Cholesterol Screening[18]												★	★	★
STD Screening[19]														
Pelvic Exam[20]														
ANTICIPATORY GUIDANCE[21]	●	●	●	●	●	●	●	●	●	●	●	●	●	●
Injury Prevention[22]	●	●	●	●	●	●	●	●	●	●	●	●	●	●
Violence Prevention[23]	●	●	●	●	●	●	●	●	●	●	●	●	●	●
Sleep Positioning Counseling[24]	●	●	●	●	●	●	●							
Nutrition Counseling[25]	●	●	●	●	●	●	●	●	●	●	●	●	●	●
DENTAL REFERRAL[26]									◄				●	

1. A prenatal visit is recommended for parents who are at high risk, for first-time parents, and for those who request a conference. The prenatal visit should include anticipatory guidance, pertinent medical history, and a discussion of benefits of breastfeeding and planned method of feeding per AAP statement "The Prenatal Visit" (1996).
2. Every infant should have a newborn evaluation after birth. Breastfeeding should be encouraged and instruction and support offered. Every breastfeeding infant should have an evaluation 48-72 hours after discharge from the hospital to include weight, formal breastfeeding evaluation, encouragement, and instruction as recommended in the AAP statement "Breastfeeding and the Use of Human Milk" (1997).
3. For newborns discharged in less than 48 hours after delivery per AAP statement "Hospital Stay for Healthy Term Newborns" (1995).
4. Developmental, psychosocial, and chronic disease issues for children and adolescents may require frequent counseling and treatment visits separate from preventive care visits.
5. If a child comes under care for the first time at any point on the schedule, or if any items are not accomplished at the suggested age, the schedule should be brought up to date at the earliest possible time.
6. If the patient is uncooperative, rescreen within 6 months.
7. All newborns should be screened per the AAP Task Force on Newborn and Infant Hearing statement, "Newborn and Infant Hearing Loss: Detection and Intervention" (1999).
8. By history and appropriate physical examination: if suspicious, by specific objective developmental testing. Parenting skills should be fostered at every visit.
9. At each visit, a complete physical examination is essential, with infant totally unclothed, older child undressed and suitably draped.
10. These may be modified, depending upon entry point into schedule and individual need.
11. Metabolic screening (eg, thyroid, hemoglobinopathies, PKU, galactosemia) should be done according to state law.
12. Schedule(s) per the Committee on Infectious Diseases, published annually in the January edition of Pediatrics. Every visit should be an opportunity to update and complete a child's immunizations.
13. See AAP Pediatric Nutrition Handbook (1998) for a discussion of universal and selective screening options. Consider earlier screening for high-risk infants (eg, premature infants and low birth weight infants). See also "Recommendations to Prevent and Control Iron Deficiency in the United States." MMWR. 1998;47 (RR-3):1-29.
14. All menstruating adolescents should be screened annually.
15. Conduct dipstick urinalysis for leukocytes annually for sexually active male and female adolescents.
16. For children at risk of lead exposure consult the AAP statement "Screening for Elevated Blood Levels" (1998). Additionally, screening should be done in accordance with state law where applicable.
17. TB testing per recommendations of the Committee on Infectious Diseases, published in the current edition of Red Book: Report of the Committee on Infectious Diseases. Testing should be done upon recognition of high-risk factors.

Key: ● = to be performed   ★ = to be performed for patients at risk
S = subjective, by history   O = objective, by a standard testing method
◄ ● ► = the range during which a service may be provided, with the dot indicating the preferred age.

These guidelines represent a consensus by the Committee on Practice and Ambulatory Medicine in consultation with national committees and sections of the American Academy of Pediatrics. The Committee emphasizes the great importance of **continuity of care** in comprehensive health supervision and the need to avoid **fragmentation of care.**

MIDDLE CHILDHOOD[4]				ADOLESCENCE[4]										
5y	6y	8y	10y	11y	12y	13y	14y	15y	16y	17y	18y	19y	20y	21y
•	•	•	•	•	•	•	•	•	•	•	•	•	•	•
•	•	•	•	•	•	•	•	•	•	•	•	•	•	•
•	•	•	•	•	•	•	•	•	•	•	•	•	•	•
O	O	O	O	S	O	S	S	O	S	S	O	S	S	S
O	O	O	O	S	O	S	S	O	S	S	O	S	S	S
•	•	•	•	•	•	•	•	•	•	•	•	•	•	•
•	•	•	•	•	•	•	•	•	•	•	•	•	•	•
•	•	•	•	•	•	•[14]	•	•	•	•	•	•	•	•
◄				◄										►
•				◄					•[15]					►
★	★	★	★	★	★	★	★	★	★	★	★	★	★	★
★	★	★	★	★	★	★	★	★	★	★	★	★	★	★
				★	★	★	★	★	★	★	★	★	★	★
				★	★	★	★	★	★	★	★◄	★[20]	★	►★
•	•	•	•	•	•	•	•	•	•	•	•	•	•	•
•	•	•	•	•	•	•	•	•	•	•	•	•	•	•
•	•	•	•	•	•	•	•	•	•	•	•	•	•	•
•	•	•	•	•	•	•	•	•	•	•	•	•	•	•

18. Cholesterol screening for high-risk patients per AAP statement "Cholesterol in Childhood" (1998). If family history cannot be ascertained and other risk factors are present, screening should be at the discretion of the physician.
19. All sexually active patients should be screened for sexually transmitted diseases (STDs).
20. All sexually active females should have a pelvic examination. A pelvic examination and routine pap smear should be offered as part of preventive health maintenance between the ages of 18 and 21 years.
21. Age-appropriate discussion and counseling should be an integral part of each visit for care per the AAP *Guidelines for Health Supervision III* (1998).
22. From birth to age 12, refer to the AAP injury prevention program (TIPP*) as described in *A Guide to Safety Counseling in Office Practice* (1994).
23. Violence prevention and management for all patients per AAP statement "The Role of the Pediatrician in Youth Violence Prevention in Clinical Practice and at the Community Level" (1999).
24. Parents and caregivers should be advised to place healthy infants on their backs when putting them to sleep. Side positioning is a reasonable alternative but carries a slightly higher risk of SIDS. Consult the AAP statement "Changing Concepts of Sudden Infant Death Syndrome: Implications for Infant Sleeping Environment and Sleep Position" (2000).
25. Age-appropriate nutrition counseling should be an integral part of each visit per the AAP *Handbook of Nutrition* (1998).
26. Earlier initial dental examinations may be appropriate for some children. Subsequent examinations as prescribed by dentist.

American Academy of Pediatrics
DEDICATED TO THE HEALTH OF ALL CHILDREN™

ture may be unusually high because your child has been physically active or too warmly clothed. If your baby is younger than two months of age, contact your pediatrician right away if his temperature is 100.4 degrees Fahrenheit (38 degrees Celsius) or higher.

Tympanic thermometers are another option for older babies and children. They measure the temperature inside the ear, but for accuracy, they must be placed correctly in the youngster's ear. Excess earwax can cause inaccurate readings, too. Here is how to use this device:

1. Cover the end of the thermometer with the plastic shield.

2. Gently put in the ear canal.

3. Press the start button.

4. Within seconds, you can check the digital reading of your child's temperature.

Rectal or tympanic temperatures can be taken with children of all ages, but by age four or five years your child probably will be cooperative enough to let you take his temperature orally, using an oral digital thermometer. For an accurate oral temperature, wait at least fifteen minutes after your child has had a hot or cold drink to take her temperature. Then follow these steps:

1. Clean the oral digital thermometer with soapy water or rubbing alcohol, and then rinse with cool water.

2. Apply disposable plastic sleeve.

3. Turn on the thermometer's switch and place the sensor under the tongue, toward the back of the mouth. Hold it in place for about one minute, until you hear it beep.

4. Remove the thermometer and check the digital reading.

Using an oral or a rectal digital thermometer under the arm is another way to take a child's temperature, but it is not as accurate a measurement as the rectal, oral, or ear techniques. However, it can be used in children older than three months of age.

1. Place the sensor end of the thermometer in your child's armpit.

2. Hold his arm tightly against the side of his chest for about one minute, until the thermometer beeps.

3. Check the digital reading.

For more information about taking a child's temperature, see Chapter 23 (pages 634 and 637).

Visiting the Pediatrician

You probably will see more of your pediatrician in your baby's first year than at any other time. The baby's first examination will take place immediately after birth. The schedule on pages 68 to 69 lists the minimum routine checkups from infancy through adolescence. Your pediatrician may want to see your baby more often.

Ideally, both parents should attend these early visits to the doctor. These appointments give you and your pediatrician a chance to get to know each other and exchange questions and answers. Don't restrict yourself to medical questions; your pediatrician is also an expert on general child care issues and a valuable resource if you're looking for child care help, parent support groups, or other outside assistance. Many pediatricians hand out information sheets that cover the most common concerns, but it's a good idea to make a list of questions before each visit so you don't forget any important ones.

If only one parent can attend, try to get a friend or a relative to join the parent who does. It's much easier to concentrate on your discussions with the doctor if you have a little help dressing and undressing the baby and gathering all of her things. While you're getting used to outings with your newborn, an extra adult also can help carry the diaper bag and hold doors. Grandparents can fulfill this role quite well if they live nearby. (For additional information about the role of grandparents in your baby's life, see pages 168, 224, and 426 in Chapters 6, 8, and 14.)

The purpose of these early checkups is to make sure your child is growing and developing properly and has no serious abnormalities. Specifically, the doctor will check the following areas.

Growth. You will be asked to undress your baby, and then he'll be weighed on an infant scale. His length may be measured lying on a flat table with his legs stretched straight. A special tape is used to measure the size of his head. All of these measurements should be plotted on a graph in order to determine his growth curve from one visit to the next. (You can plot your baby's growth curve in the same way using the charts on pages 128–131.) This is the most reliable way to judge whether he's growing normally, and will show you his position on the growth curve in relation to other children his age.

Head. The soft spots (fontanelles) should be open (normal skin covered openings in the skull) and flat for the first few months. By two to three months of age, the spot at the back should be closed. The front soft spot should close before your child's second birthday (around eighteen months of age).

Ears. The doctor will look inside both ears with an otoscope, an instrument that provides a view of the ear canal and eardrum. This tells her whether there is any evidence of fluid or infection in the ear. You'll also be asked if the child responds normally to sounds. Formal hearing tests are done in the newborn nursery and later if there is suspicion that a problem exists.

Eyes. The doctor will use a bright object or flashlight to catch your baby's attention and track his eye movements. She also may look inside the baby's eyes with a lighted instrument called an ophthalmoscope—repeating the internal eye examination that was first done in the hospital nursery. This is particularly helpful in detecting cataracts (clouding of the lens of the eye). (See *Cataracts,* page 606.)

Mouth. The mouth is checked for signs of infection and, later, for teething progress.

Heart and Lungs. The pediatrician will use a stethoscope on the front and back of the chest to listen to your child's heart and lungs. This examination determines whether there are any abnormal heart rhythms, sounds, or breathing difficulties.

Abdomen. By placing her hand on the child's abdomen and gently pressing, the doctor makes sure that none of the organs is enlarged and there are no unusual masses or tenderness.

Genitalia. The genitalia are examined at each visit for any unusual lumps, tenderness, or signs of infection. In the first exam or two, the doctor pays special attention to a circumcised boy's penis to make sure it's healing properly. She checks all baby boys to make certain both testes are down in the scrotum.

Hips and Legs. The pediatrician will move your baby's legs to check for dislocations or other problems with the hip joints. Later, after the baby starts to walk, the doctor will watch her take a few steps to make sure the legs and feet are properly aligned and move normally.

Developmental Milestones. The pediatrician also will ask about the baby's general development. Among other things, she'll observe and discuss when the baby starts to smile, roll over, sit up, and walk, and how he uses his hands and arms. During the exam, she will test reflexes and general muscle tone. (See Chapters 5 through 12 for details of normal development.)

Immunizations

Your child should receive most of his childhood immunizations before his second birthday. These will protect him against eleven major diseases: polio, measles, mumps, rubella (German measles), chickenpox, pertussis (whooping cough), diphtheria, tetanus, *Haemophilus* (Hib) infections, hepatitis B, and pneumococcal infections. See page 73 for the schedule of immunizations recommended by the American Academy of Pediatrics.

Recommended Childhood and Adolescent Immunization Schedule   UNITED STATES · 2006

Vaccine ▼ \ Age ▶	Birth	1 month	2 months	4 months	6 months	12 months	15 months	18 months	24 months	4–6 years	11–12 years	13–14 years	15 years	16–18 years
Hepatitis B[1]	HepB	HepB		HepB[1]		HepB					HepB Series			
Diphtheria, Tetanus, Pertussis[2]			DTaP	DTaP	DTaP		DTaP			DTaP	Tdap	Tdap		
Haemophilus influenzae type b[3]			Hib	Hib	Hib[3]	Hib								
Inactivated Poliovirus			IPV	IPV	IPV					IPV				
Measles, Mumps, Rubella[4]						MMR				MMR	MMR			
Varicella[5]						Varicella			Varicella					
Meningococcal[6]											MCV4	MCV4 / MPSV4		MCV4
Pneumococcal[7]			PCV	PCV	PCV	PCV			PCV	PPV				
Influenza[8]						Influenza (Yearly)				Influenza (Yearly)				
Hepatitis A[9]									HepA Series					

Vaccines within broken line are for selected populations

Legend: Range of recommended ages | Catch-up immunization | 11–12 year old assessment

This schedule indicates the recommended ages for routine administration of currently licensed childhood vaccines, as of December 1, 2005, for children through age 18 years. Any dose not administered at the recommended age should be administered at any subsequent visit when indicated and feasible. ▇ Indicates age groups that warrant special effort to administer those vaccines not previously administered. Additional vaccines may be licensed and recommended during the year. Licensed combination vaccines may be used whenever any components of the combination are indicated and other components of the vaccine are not contraindicated and if approved by the Food and Drug Administration for that dose of the series. Providers should consult the respective ACIP statement for detailed recommendations. Clinically significant adverse events that follow immunization should be reported to the Vaccine Adverse Event Reporting System (VAERS). Guidance about how to obtain and complete a VAERS form is available at **www.vaers.hhs.gov** or by telephone, **800-822-7967.**

1. **Hepatitis B vaccine (HepB).** *AT BIRTH:* **All newborns** should receive monovalent HepB soon after birth and before hospital discharge. **Infants born to mothers who are HBsAg-positive** should receive HepB and 0.5 mL of hepatitis B immune globulin (HBIG) within 12 hours of birth. **Infants born to mothers whose HBsAg status is unknown** should receive HepB within 12 hours of birth. The mother should have blood drawn as soon as possible to determine her HBsAg status; if HBsAg-positive, the infant should receive HBIG as soon as possible (no later than age 1 week). **For infants born to HBsAg-negative mothers,** the birth dose can be delayed in rare circumstances but only if a physician's order to withhold the vaccine and a copy of the mother's original HBsAg-negative laboratory report are documented in the infant's medical record. *FOLLOWING THE BIRTHDOSE:* The HepB series should be completed with either monovalent HepB or a combination vaccine containing HepB. The second dose should be administered at age 1–2 months. The final dose should be administered at age ≥24 weeks. It is permissible to administer 4 doses of HepB (e.g., when combination vaccines are given after the birth dose); however, if monovalent HepB is used, a dose at age 4 months is not needed. **Infants born to HBsAg-positive mothers** should be tested for HBsAg and antibody to HBsAg after completion of the HepB series, at age 9–18 months (generally at the next well-child visit after completion of the vaccine series).
2. **Diphtheria and tetanus toxoids and acellular pertussis vaccine (DTaP).** The fourth dose of DTaP may be administered as early as age 12 months, provided 6 months have elapsed since the third dose and the child is unlikely to return at age 15–18 months. The final dose in the series should be given at age ≥4 years. **Tetanus and diphtheria toxoids and acellular pertussis vaccine (Tdap – adolescent preparation)** is recommended at age 11–12 years for those who have completed the recommended childhood DTP/DTaP vaccination series and have not received a Td booster dose. Adolescents 13–18 years who missed the 11–12-year Td/Tdap booster dose should also receive a single dose of Tdap if they have completed the recommended childhood DTP/DTaP vaccination series. Subsequent **tetanus and diphtheria toxoids (Td)** are recommended every 10 years.
3. **Haemophilus influenzae type b conjugate vaccine (Hib).** Three Hib conjugate vaccines are licensed for infant use. If PRP-OMP (PedvaxHIB® or ComVax® [Merck]) is administered at ages 2 and 4 months, a dose at age 6 months is not required. DTaP/Hib combination products should not be used for primary immunization in infants at ages 2, 4 or 6 months but can be used as boosters after any Hib vaccine. The final dose in the series should be administered at age ≥12 months.
4. **Measles, mumps, and rubella vaccine (MMR).** The second dose of MMR is recommended routinely at age 4–6 years but may be administered during any visit, provided at least 4 weeks have elapsed since the first dose and both doses are administered beginning at or after age 12 months. Those who have not previously received the second dose should complete the schedule by age 11–12 years.
5. **Varicella vaccine.** Varicella vaccine is recommended at any visit at or after age 12 months for susceptible children (i.e., those who lack a reliable history of chickenpox). Susceptible persons aged ≥13 years should receive 2 doses administered at least 4 weeks apart.

6. **Meningococcal vaccine (MCV4).** Meningococcal conjugate vaccine (MCV4) should be given to all children at the 11–12 year old visit as well as to unvaccinated adolescents at high school entry (15 years of age). Other adolescents who wish to decrease their risk for meningococcal disease may also be vaccinated. All college freshmen living in dormitories should also be vaccinated, preferably with MCV4, although **meningococcal polysaccharide vaccine (MPSV4)** is an acceptable alternative. Vaccination against invasive meningococcal disease is recommended for children and adolescents aged ≥2 years with terminal complement deficiencies or anatomic or functional asplenia and certain other high risk groups (see *MMWR* 2005;54 [RR-7]:1-21); use MPSV4 for children aged 2–10 years and MCV4 for older children, although MPSV4 is an acceptable alternative.
7. **Pneumococcal vaccine.** The heptavalent **pneumococcal conjugate vaccine (PCV)** is recommended for all children aged 2–23 months and for certain children aged 24–59 months. The final dose in the series should be given at age ≥12 months. **Pneumococcal polysaccharide vaccine (PPV)** is recommended in addition to PCV for certain high-risk groups. See *MMWR* 2000; 49(RR-9):1-35.
8. **Influenza vaccine.** Influenza vaccine is recommended annually for children aged ≥6 months with certain risk factors (including, but not limited to, asthma, cardiac disease, sickle cell disease, human immunodeficiency virus [HIV], diabetes, and conditions that can compromise respiratory function or handling of respiratory secretions or that can increase the risk for aspiration), healthcare workers, and other persons (including household members) in close contact with persons in groups at high risk (see *MMWR* 2005;54[RR-8]:1-55). In addition, healthy children aged 6–23 months and close contacts of healthy children aged 0–5 months are recommended to receive influenza vaccine because children in this age group are at substantially increased risk for influenza-related hospitalizations. For healthy persons aged 5–49 years, the intranasally administered, live, attenuated influenza vaccine (LAIV) is an acceptable alternative to the intramuscular trivalent inactivated influenza vaccine (TIV). See *MMWR* 2005;54(RR-8):1-55. Children receiving TIV should be administered a dosage appropriate for their age (0.25 mL if aged 6–35 months or 0.5 mL if aged ≥3 years). Children aged ≤8 years who are receiving influenza vaccine for the first time should receive 2 doses (separated by at least 4 weeks for TIV and at least 6 weeks for LAIV).
9. **Hepatitis A vaccine (HepA).** HepA is recommended for all children at 1 year of age (i.e., 12–23 months). The 2 doses in the series should be administered at least 6 months apart. States, counties, and communities with existing HepA vaccination programs for children 2–18 years of age are encouraged to maintain these programs. In these areas, new efforts focused on routine vaccination of 1-year-old children should enhance, not replace, ongoing programs directed at a broader population of children. HepA is also recommended for certain high risk groups (see *MMWR* 1999; 48[RR-12]1-37).

Additional information about vaccines, including precautions and contraindications for vaccination and vaccine shortages, is available at http://www.cdc.gov/nip or from the National Immunization Information Hotline, 800-232-2522 (English) or 800-232-0233 (Spanish). Approved by the **Advisory Committee on Immunization Practices** (http://www.cdc.gov/nip/acip), the **American Academy of Pediatrics** (http://www.aap.org), and the **American Academy of Family Physicians** (http://www.aafp.org).

Immunization Protects Children

Regular checkups at your pediatrician's office or local health clinic are an important way to keep children healthy.

By making sure that your child gets immunized on time, you can provide the best available defense against many dangerous childhood diseases. Immunizations protect children against hepatitis B, polio, measles, mumps, rubella (German measles), pertussis (whooping cough), diphtheria, tetanus (lockjaw), *Haemophilus influenzae* type b, pneumococcal infections, and chickenpox. All of these immunizations need to be given before children are 2 years old in order for them to be protected during their most vulnerable period. Are your child's immunizations up to date?

The chart on the other side of this fact sheet includes immunization recommendations from the American Academy of Pediatrics. Remember to keep track of your child's immunizations—it's the only way you can be sure your child is up to date. Also, check with your pediatrician or health clinic at each visit to find out if your child needs any booster shots or if any new vaccines have been recommended since this schedule was prepared.

If you don't have a pediatrician, call your local health department. Public health clinics usually have supplies of vaccine and may give shots free.

American Academy of Pediatrics

DEDICATED TO THE HEALTH OF ALL CHILDREN™

3-4E0106

DTaP Vaccines. At her two-month checkup, your child should receive her first DTaP vaccine, immunizing her against diphtheria (D), tetanus (T), and pertussis (whooping cough) (aP). This vaccine is given in five injections, the first three at two, four, and six months. A fourth dose is given six to twelve months after the third dose, usually around eighteen months of age. Then your child will receive another injection before she enters school, between four and six years. This "booster" shot raises your child's immunity against these diseases to higher levels.

Within the first twenty-four hours after the shot, your baby may be irritable and less energetic than usual. The area where the vaccine was injected may be red and sensitive, and she may have a low-grade fever (less than 102 degrees Fahrenheit [38.9 degrees Celsius]). These normal reactions should last no more than forty-eight hours. They can be treated with acetaminophen given every four hours. (See the chart on page 636 for appropriate doses.) Do not use aspirin.

Notify your pediatrician if your child displays any of these less common reactions:

- Constant, inconsolable crying for more than three hours

- Unusual, high-pitched crying

- Excessive sleepiness or difficulty in waking up

- Limpness or paleness

- Temperature of 105 degrees Fahrenheit (40.6 degrees Celsius) or higher

- Convulsion (usually resulting from a high fever)

While these more serious side effects may sound alarming, there is less than a 1 percent chance that your child will have any of them. If your baby is not immunized, her risk of getting one of these diseases increases greatly. Diphtheria, tetanus, and pertussis (whooping cough) are dangerous diseases. (See Chapter 27, "Immunizations.")

The dangers include:

- Two out of ten people who get tetanus die from it.

- Before this vaccine was available, one out of fifteen people who got diphtheria died from it.

- One out of one hundred babies under two months who get pertussis (whooping cough) die from it. (The overall death rate is one in one thousand, including older infants.)

- Many infants who get pertussis require hospitalization, and one out of five develops pneumonia.

- Infants and children with pertussis may cough for about a hundred days.

The newer acellular DTaP vaccine has replaced the DTP vaccine because it is less likely to cause side effects. Because the benefits so far outweigh the risks, *the American Academy of Pediatrics strongly recommends routine use of DTaP beginning at age two months.*

There are, however, some children who should have these vaccinations postponed and an occasional child who should not receive them at all. These include children who have one or more of the following problems:

- A severe reaction to the initial immunization (allergic reaction or inflammation of the brain called encephalopathy)

- A previous convulsion, or the suspicion of having a progressive disease of the nervous system

If your child has any of these difficulties, make sure that your pediatrician is aware of them before DTaP immunization is given.

Polio Vaccine. Polio is a viral disease that can paralyze some muscles of the body. The illness may be mild to very serious, depending on the muscles involved and the severity of the involvement. Fortunately, disease due to naturally occurring polio virus has been eliminated from the United States, the entire western hemisphere, and most of the rest of the world because effective vaccines have been used to prevent the infection.

Vaccination is the only way to protect against polio. Children should receive four doses of this "inactivated" polio vaccine (IPV) before they enter school. The vaccine is given as an injection in the leg or arm. Polio vaccine is given at two, four, six to eighteen months, and again between four and six years. The American Academy of Pediatrics no longer recommends the oral polio vaccine because of a small risk of vaccine-associated paralytic polio (VAPP), and IPV has been used exclusively since the year 2000.

IPV provides excellent protection against polio and has not been shown to cause any major problems except mild soreness at the site of the injection. IPV protects the child who receives the injection and, because it is made with an inactivated polio virus, does not cause VAPP.

MMR Vaccine. At twelve to fifteen months, your child will receive a single injection immunizing her against mumps, measles, and rubella (German measles). Although these diseases are best known for the rashes (measles and rubella) and glandular swelling (mumps) they produce, each also may cause serious medical complications. (See *Mumps,* page 658; *Rubella* (German Measles) page 706, *Measles,* page 702.) Immunizations against these diseases rarely cause any serious side effects, but your child may experience the following reactions, beginning five to ten days after the injection:

- A mild rash

- Slight swelling of the lymph nodes in the neck or diaper area

- Low-grade fever

- Sleepiness

If your toddler is allergic to eggs, a reaction to the vaccine may rarely occur (because eggs are used in the process of manufacturing it), so you should alert your pediatrician to the fact. Also, if your child is taking any medication that interferes with the immune system, or if her immune system is weakened for any reason, she should not be given the MMR. Because not all children are immune to these diseases after one vaccination and in order to give additional protection, a second MMR is recommended prior to the twelfth birthday. Many states recommend giving this second dose earlier (four to six years of age), so you must check with your pediatrician.

Chickenpox Vaccine. A vaccine to protect against chickenpox is recommended for all healthy children between twelve and eighteen months of age who have never had the disease. Although chickenpox vaccine will not cause complications in most healthy children, a small number will experience pain or redness at the injection site, a mild rash, or a fever.

***Haemophilus Influenzae* Type B Vaccine (Hib).** A vaccine against bacterial infections caused by the bacteria *Haemophilus influenzae* type b is recommended for children beginning at two months of age. (See also *Epiglottitis,* page 585; *Meningitis,* page 655.) Vaccination has markedly reduced the number of children who suffer diseases caused by this bacteria.

Pneumococcal Vaccine. A vaccine against the most common types of pneumococcal bacteria infections (caused by *Streptococcus pneumoniae*) was licensed in 2000. This is called a conjugated vaccine and is different from the older pneumococcal vaccines. The conjugated pneumoccocal vaccine is recommended for all children at ages two to twenty-three months (and certain children ages twenty-four to fifty-nine months).

Hepatitis B Vaccine. A vaccine to prevent hepatitis B is recommended to be given to all children. Hepatitis B is a viral illness that affects the liver. It can occur at any age, including the newborn period. It can be passed from an infected mother to her infant at the time of birth or from one household member to another. It also can be spread through sexual intercourse or contact with infected blood from needles.

Infants and young children can contract the disease and have mild to no symptoms until sometime later, when they may develop chronic liver problems including cancer. Since the disease seems to be increasing and contact cannot always be predicted or avoided, health authorities, including the American Academy of Pediatrics, have recommended immunization in early infancy.

The vaccine is given in three doses beginning shortly after birth and before hospital discharge, with a second dose one or two months later and a booster dose at six to eighteen months of age.

Older children, adolescents, and adults also should be immunized. Many child care providers and public school systems require proof of vaccination for hepatitis B prior to school entry.

WHERE WE STAND

The American Academy of Pediatrics believes that the benefits of immunization far outweigh the risks incurred by childhood diseases, as well as any risks of the vaccines themselves. Despite highly publicized cases of severe adverse effects associated with the vaccines—particularly the pertussis component of the original DTaP (diphtheria, tetanus, and pertussis) immunization—these unfortunate outcomes are very rare; the DTaP vaccine has replaced the older DTP vaccine, and the latter is used only uncommonly (the "a" in the updated DTaP vaccine stands for "acellular" pertussis, meaning that only a portion of the pertussis bacteria is used in the vaccine. The Academy believes that immunizations are the safest and most cost-effective way of preventing disease, disability, and death, and it urges parents to ensure that their children are immunized against dangerous childhood diseases. For more information on immunizations, see Chapter 27.

There have been no serious reactions to the vaccine. However, minor side effects such as fussiness and soreness, redness, or swelling at the site of the injection may be noted. The vaccine is contraindicated only in those persons severely allergic to yeast (rare in children).

Other vaccines are available and recommended for children who fall into particular groups.

- The influenza (or flu) vaccine is recommended for children six months of age or older who fall into certain categories—such as those with asthma, heart disease, diabetes, HIV, and sickle cell disease. It is also recommended in *healthy* children ages six through twenty-three months, because these youngsters have a greater likelihood of developing influenza-related problems that require hospitalization. No matter what the age of the child, the vaccine must be given annually. For children who are eight years old or less, and are receiving the influenza vaccine for the first time, it should be administered in two doses given at least four or six weeks apart, depending on the product.

- The hepatitis A vaccine is recommended in children in selected states and regions of the country, as well as in youngsters who fall into particular high-risk categories. Talk to your pediatrician about whether this vaccine is appropriate for your child. It is a two-dose series, with the doses given six or more months apart.

This chapter has dealt in a general way with the topic of infant care. Your baby is a unique individual, however, so you will have some questions specific to him and him alone. These are best answered by your own pediatrician. Also see Chapter 27, "Immunizations" (pages 673–677).

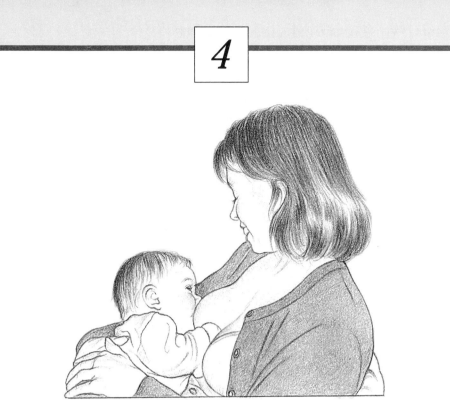

FEEDING YOUR BABY:
BREAST AND BOTTLE

*Y*our baby's nutritional needs during the rapid-growth period of infancy are greater than at any other time in his life. He will approximately triple his birth weight during his first year.

Feeding your infant provides more than just good nutrition. It also gives you a chance to hold your newborn close, cuddle him, and make eye contact. These are relaxing and enjoyable moments for you both, and they bring you closer together emotionally.

Before your baby arrives, you should decide on the type of feeding you are going to use—breast or bottle. All major medical groups worldwide agree that breastfeeding is best for mother and baby. This chapter will provide the basic information you need to learn more about infant feeding and to feel comfortable with your feeding decision.

Because of its nutritional composition, human milk is the ideal food for human infants. Babies who are breastfed are at reduced risk of acquiring ear infections and severe diarrhea and of developing allergic reactions. Formula-fed babies are slightly more likely to need hospitalization for one of these problems. Recent information indicates that breastfeeding plays a small but significant role in the prevention of overweight and diabetes, both in childhood and in later years. In addition, there is some evidence that for mothers, breastfeeding reduces the incidence of certain types of cancer and may prevent hip fractures later in life. As a result, most pediatricians urge expectant mothers to breastfeed.

But it's important not to feel guilty if you decide to bottle-feed your baby. Many women are uncertain about breastfeeding for various reasons. Try to get more information from your prenatal care provider. Be sure someone knowledgeable discusses your specific concerns, doubts, or fears with you. If for some reason you decide not to breastfeed, infant formula is an acceptable and nutritious alternative to human milk. Whatever your reason for not breastfeeding (and it could simply be that you don't want to), this is your choice. However, it's important that you give it serious consideration before your baby arrives, because starting with formula and then switching to breastmilk can be difficult or even impossible if you wait too long. The production of milk by the breast (the process is called lactation) is most successful if breastfeeding begins immediately after delivery. If you begin breastfeeding and then, for any reason, decide that it's not right for you, you can always switch to formula.

The American Academy of Pediatrics, the World Health Organization (WHO), and many other experts encourage women to breastfeed as long as possible,

WHERE WE STAND

The American Academy of Pediatrics believes that breastfeeding is the optimal source of nutrition through the first year of life. We recommend exclusively breastfeeding for four to six months,* and then gradually adding solid foods while continuing breastfeeding until at least the baby's first birthday. Thereafter, breastfeeding can be continued for as long as both mother and baby desire it.

Breastfeeding should begin as soon as possible after birth, usually within the first hour. Newborns should be nursed whenever they show signs of hunger—approximately eight to twelve times every twenty-four hours. The amount of time for each feeding varies widely for each mother-baby pair: It may be anywhere from ten to forty-five minutes in the first few weeks.

* Note: There is a difference of opinion among Academy experts on this matter. The Section on Breastfeeding supports exclusive breastfeeding for about six months. The Committee on Nutrition supports the introduction of complementary foods between four and six months of age where safe and nutritious complementary foods are available.

one year or even longer, because breastmilk provides optimal nutrition and protection against infections. Approximately 7 out of 10 newborns in the United States are breastfed at birth. By six months, only about 3 out of 10 are being breastfed. This means that many women switch from breast to formula feeding, so they need to learn something about proper formula feeding when they make the change.

ADVANTAGES AND DISADVANTAGES OF BREASTFEEDING

As we've already mentioned, human milk is the best possible food for any infant. Its major ingredients are sugar (lactose), easily digestible protein (whey and casein), and fat (digestible fatty acids)—all properly balanced to suit your baby and protect against such conditions as ear infections (otitis media), allergies, vomiting, diarrhea, pneumonia, wheezing, bronchiolitis, and meningitis. In addition, breastmilk contains numerous minerals and vitamins, as well as enzymes that aid the digestive and absorptive process. Formulas only approximate this combination of nutrients and don't provide the enzymes, antibodies, and many other valuable ingredients of breastmilk.

There are many practical reasons to breastfeed, or nurse, your baby. Human milk is relatively low in cost. While maintaining a balanced diet yourself, you should increase your own caloric intake, but that costs less than half of what you'd have to spend for formula. Also, human milk needs no preparation and is instantly available at any time, wherever you may be. As an added advantage to the nursing mother, breastfeeding makes it much easier to get back into shape physically after giving birth, by using up about 500 calories a day and by helping the uterus tighten up and return more quickly to its normal size.

The psychological and emotional advantages of breastfeeding are just as compelling, for both mother and child, as the physical benefits. Nursing provides direct skin-to-skin contact, which is soothing for your baby and pleasant for you. The same hormones that stimulate milk production and milk release also may promote feelings that enhance mothering. Almost all nursing mothers find that the experience makes them feel more attached and protective toward their babies and more confident about their own abilities to nurture and care for their children. When breastfeeding is going well, it has no known disadvantages for the baby. The breastfeeding mother may feel that there is some increased demand on her time. Actually, studies show that breastfeeding and formula feeding take about the same total amount of time, but in breastfeeding all the time is spent with the baby. In bottle-feeding, some time is spent shopping, preparing formula, and cleaning feeding utensils. Time spent with the baby is an important component of infant nurturing and development and is pleasurable to mothers. Other family members can assist by assuming the responsibility for household tasks, and after a few weeks these changes in routine will tend to become accepted as normal.

Keep in mind that other family members can actively share in all aspects of caring for the baby even though they do not directly feed milk to her. Remain sensitive to the needs of fathers and siblings. In fact, other members of the family can feel involved in breastfeeding—enjoying holding the baby during burping, for example. For the father of the breastfed infant, nonnutritive cuddling plays an important role. A father is invaluable when comforting is necessary for baby and mother. He can hold, diaper, bathe, and carry the baby, and he may handle the feeding if the family decides that an occasional bottle of expressed milk or formula is desirable or necessary.

The best protection against miscommunication about matters surrounding feeding is for parents to discuss these issues openly and make sure both mother and father understand and support the choice before the baby arrives. Most fathers want their children to receive the best possible nutrition from the start, and without question, that is mother's milk. Once breastfeeding is well established (usually between three to six weeks of age), if mothers are away from the baby for a period of time (to return to work, for example, or to go shopping or pursue social activities), they can continue to provide their milk to the baby by pumping and collecting breastmilk for frozen storage and bottle-feeding by the father, other family members, or child care workers.

In rare medical circumstances, breastfeeding may be inadvisable. A mother who is extremely ill may not have the energy or stamina to breastfeed without interfering with her own recovery. She also may be taking certain medications that would pass into her milk and be dangerous to her infant, although the great majority of medications are safe for breastfeeding.

If you are taking medications for any reason (prescription drugs or over-the-counter medications), let your pediatrician know before you start breastfeeding. She can advise you whether any of these drugs can pass through breastmilk and cause problems for your baby. Sometimes medicines can be switched to safer ones.

While breastfeeding may be uncomfortable at first, significant early discomfort or latching problems are not normal. Seek help early in the first week from an experienced health professional (pediatrician, nurse, or lactation specialist). Occasionally some mothers have breastfeeding problems that lead to untimely weaning from the breast (before the mother had intended). Most women feel disappointed and sad when breastfeeding did not work out as they had planned. Making compromises (i.e., giving bottles) may be necessary to make the feeding experience positive for both mother and baby. Over time the disappointment and sadness will gradually lessen.

BREASTFEEDING YOUR BABY

Developing the Right Attitude

You can do it! This should be your attitude about breastfeeding from the beginning. There's plenty of help available, and you should take advantage of the expert advice, counseling, classes, and group meetings that are available. For example, you can:

- Talk to your obstetrician and pediatrician. They can provide not only medical information but also encouragement and support when you need it most.

- Talk to your prenatal instructors and attend a breastfeeding class.

- Talk to women who have or are breastfeeding successfully and ask their advice. Sisters-in-law, cousins, office mates, yoga instructors, fellow congregants at your place of worship are precious resources.

- Talk to members of La Leche League or other mother-to-mother support groups in your community. La Leche League is a worldwide organization dedicated to helping families learn about and enjoy the experience of breastfeeding. Ask your pediatrician for information about how to contact La Leche League.

- Read about breastfeeding. A recommended book is the *American Academy of Pediatrics New Mother's Guide to Breastfeeding,* by J. Y. Meek, editor-in-chief, and S. Tippins (Bantam); and the booklet "Breastfeeding Your Baby: Answers to Common Questions" available at www.aap.org.

Getting Started: Preparing the Breasts for Lactation

Your body starts preparing to breastfeed as soon as you become pregnant. The area surrounding the nipples—the areola—becomes darker. The breasts themselves enlarge as the cells that will manufacture the milk multiply, and the ducts that will carry the milk to the nipple develop. Meanwhile, your body starts storing excess fat in other areas to provide the extra energy needed for pregnancy and lactation.

As early as the sixteenth week of pregnancy, the breasts are ready to produce milk as soon as the infant is born. Early milk, called colostrum, is a rich, somewhat thick-appearing, orange-yellow solution that is produced for several days after delivery. Colostrum contains more protein, salt, antibodies, and other protective properties than later breastmilk, but less fat and calories. Your body will

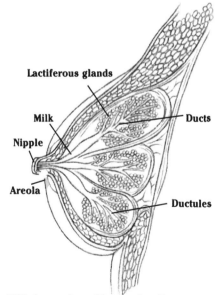

Milk is produced by the lactiferous glands. The milk then passes through the ductules into the ducts and out the nipple.

Preparing Inverted Nipples for Breastfeeding

Normally, when you press the areola (the darkened area around your nipple) between two fingers, the nipple should protrude and become erect. If the nipple seems to pull inward and disappear instead, it is said to be "inverted" or "tied." Inverted nipples are a normal variation. They may begin to move out more as the pregnancy progresses. If you have questions about your nipples, discuss the issue with your prenatal professional or with a lactation specialist.

At times, inverted nipples may be noticed only at the time of delivery. In this case, the postpartum staff will assist you with early feedings.

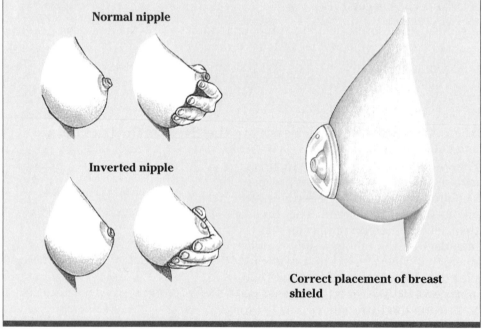

Normal nipple

Inverted nipple

Correct placement of breast shield

produce colostrum for several days after delivery, as it gradually changes into mature milk. Colostrum is a form of milk, even though people commonly say that the "milk comes in" two to five days after delivery. At this time, colostrum increases rapidly in volume, becomes milklike in color and thinner in consistency, and continues to adjust to the baby's needs for the rest of the time that you breastfeed. The nutritional qualities of breastmilk change to match the changing needs of your growing infant.

As your body naturally prepares for breastfeeding, there is very little that you need to do. You don't have to stretch, pull, roll, or buff the nipples toward the

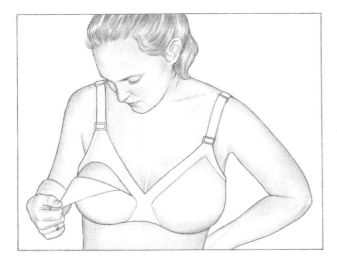

Nursing bras have flaps that allow easy access to the breast. If you wear a nursing bra, make sure it fits properly and is not constricting.

end of pregnancy. The nipples do not need to be "toughened up" to withstand your baby's sucking. In fact, some of these tactics actually may interfere with normal lactation by harming the tiny glands in the areola that secrete a milky fluid that lubricates the nipples in preparation for breastfeeding.

Normal bathing and gentle drying is the best way to care for your breasts during pregnancy. Although many women rub lotions and ointments on their breasts to soften them, these are not necessary and may clog the skin pores. Salves, particularly those containing vitamins or hormones, are unnecessary and could cause problems for your baby if used while breastfeeding.

Some women start wearing nursing bras during pregnancy. They are more adjustable and roomier than normal bras, and are more comfortable as the breast size increases. Nursing bras also have flaps that can be opened for breastfeeding or expressing milk.

Letting Down and Latching On

After your baby is born, your breasts are ready to produce milk. As he nurses, your infant's actions will let your body know when to start and stop the flow of milk. The process begins with the baby getting a good grip on the areola, not the nipple, and starting to suck. This is called latching on. He should do this instinctively as soon as he feels the breast against his mouth. You can help him get started by holding him so that he squarely faces the breast and then stroking his lower lip or cheek with the nipple. Doing this stimulates the reflex that causes him to search for the nipple with his mouth (the rooting reflex). It will result in the infant opening the mouth widely, and at that moment the baby should be moved toward the breast.

As your baby takes the breast into his mouth, his jaws should close around the areola, *not* the nipple. His lips will separate and the gums will encircle the areola. His tongue will form a trough around the nipple and, in a wavelike mo-

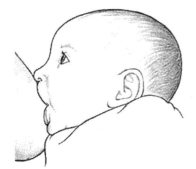

The baby has latched on to the breast correctly. The nose, lips, and chin are all close to the breast allowing for effective breastfeeding.

Most of the areola and nipple are in his mouth.

tion, compress the milk reservoirs and empty the milk ducts. Putting your baby to the breast in the first hour after delivery will establish good breastfeeding patterns at a time when infants are usually alert and vigorous. Later in the first day he may get sleepy, but if he began nursing in the first hour, he is more likely to be a successful breastfeeder.

In some cases an infant will have trouble latching on. This occurs most often in newborns who have been given bottles or pacifiers. Suckling from the breast is different from sucking the nipple on a bottle or pacifier, and some infants are very sensitive to the difference. These babies may simply lick, nibble, or chew with their jaws instead of using the tongue. Others may show frustration, pulling away or crying. This sensitivity has been called nipple confusion or nipple preference. Although nipple confusion has been considered controversial, there is now good evidence to show that starting artificial nipples early on is associated with decreased exclusive breastfeeding and decreased duration of breastfeeding. We are still uncertain if the artificial nipples are the cause of breastfeeding problems or are just a response to a breastfeeding problem that already existed. Experts generally recommend that you avoid bottles and pacifiers for the first several weeks until you feel that breastfeeding is going well. During that time, if the baby seems to need more sucking, offer the breast again, or help him to find his own hand or fingers to soothe himself.

Once your baby is sucking efficiently, his movements will stimulate the nerve fibers in the nipple. In turn, the emptying of the breast and the release of the hormone prolactin from the pituitary gland (see box on page 87) will release hormones that prompt the breasts to make more milk. Breast stimulation also starts milk flowing through the milk ducts in what is known as the let-down reflex, due to the release of another pituitary hormone, oxytocin.

This hormone also causes the muscles of the uterus to contract. So, in the first days or weeks after delivery, you may feel "after pains," or cramping of the uterus, each time you nurse. Although this may be annoying and occasionally painful, it helps the uterus return quickly to its normal size and condition and reduces postpartum blood loss. It also indicates that breastfeeding is going well. Use some deep-breathing techniques or pain medication (ibuprofen is commonly prescribed after delivery) to ease the pain.

Once lactation has begun, it usually takes just a brief period of sucking before

The Let-down Process

As your baby sucks, several different hormones work together to produce milk and release it for feeding. From the moment she starts to nurse, here is what happens within your body:

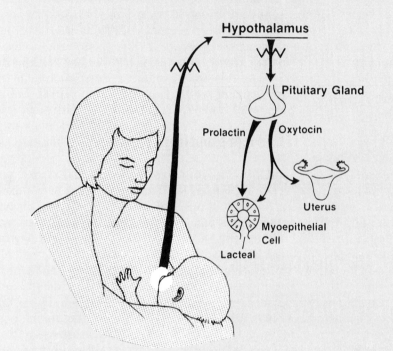

1. Her sucking movements stimulate nerve fibers in the nipple.

2. These nerve fibers carry the request for milk up the spinal column to the pituitary gland in your brain.

3. The pituitary gland responds to this message by releasing the hormones prolactin and oxytocin.

4. Prolactin stimulates the breasts to produce more milk.

5. Oxytocin stimulates contractions of the tiny muscles surrounding the ducts in the breasts. These contractions squeeze the ducts and eject the milk into the reservoir under the areola.

the milk lets down (begins to flow). Just hearing your baby cry actually may be enough to trigger milk flow.

The signs that let-down is occurring vary from woman to woman and change with the volume of milk the baby demands. Some women feel a subtle tingling sensation, while others experience a buildup of pressure that feels as if their breasts are swelling and overfull—sensations that are quickly relieved as the milk starts to flow. Some women never feel these sensations, even though they are nursing successfully and the infant is getting plenty of milk. The way the milk flows also varies widely. It may spray, gush, trickle, or flow. Some women have leakage of milk with let-down or between feedings and others don't; either case can be normal. Flow or leakage also may be quite different in each breast—perhaps gushing on one side and trickling on the other. This is due to slight differences in the ducts on either side and is no cause for concern, as long as the baby is getting adequate milk and growing well.

The First Feeding

If you had a normal delivery, and you and your baby are alert and awake, you should nurse him as soon as he's born. If there were complications with the delivery, or if your newborn needs immediate medical attention, you may have to wait a few hours. If the first feeding takes place within the first day or two, you should have no physical difficulty nursing. If nursing has to be delayed beyond that time, the nursing staff will assist you with pumping and hand expression.

If you do nurse immediately after delivery, you may find it most comfortable to lie on your side, with the baby lying facing you, opposite the breast. If you'd rather sit up, use pillows to help support your arms and cradle the baby slightly below breast level, making sure his entire body, not just his head, is facing your body. Following a cesarean delivery, the most comfortable position may be a side hold, or what's also called a football hold, in which you sit up and the baby lies at your side facing you. Curl your arm underneath him and support and hold his head at your breast. This position keeps the baby's weight off your abdomen, but the infant must squarely face the breast for the proper grasp.

If you stroke your newborn's lower lip with the nipple, he'll instinctively open his mouth wide, latch on, and begin to suck. He's been practicing this for some time by sucking his hand, fingers, and possibly even his feet in utero. (Some babies actually are born with blisters on their fingers caused by this prenatal sucking.) It takes little encouragement to get him to nurse, but you may need to help him properly grasp the areola. You can hold the breast with your thumb above the areola and your fingers and palm underneath it. Some gentle compression may be helpful to form a surface for latch-on. Then, when the baby opens his mouth very wide, pull him onto the breast. It is important to keep fingers behind the areola and be sure the nipple is level or pointed slightly up. No matter which technique you try, you need to keep your fingers clear of the areola so the baby can grasp it. Be sure your fingers are no closer than two inches from the base of the nipple. Let your baby nurse at the first side as long as he wishes,

Whichever position you choose, make sure his entire body, not just his head, is facing your body.

then put him on the other side if he is still interested in feeding. It is more important to complete a feeding on one breast than to have brief feedings from both breasts. The longer your baby feeds, the more fat and calories he will consume. Let-down, uterine cramping, swallowing sounds, and return to sound sleep by the baby are all signs of successful breastfeeding. In the beginning, it may take one to two minutes for let-down to occur. Within a week or so, let-down will take place much more rapidly and your milk supply will increase dramatically.

If you are not sure you are letting down, just watch your baby. He should be swallowing after every few sucks at the start of the feeding. After five or ten minutes, he may switch to what's called nonnutritive sucking—a more relaxed sucking that provides emotional comfort along with small amounts of creamier, fat-rich *hindmilk*. Other signs of let-down vary from woman to woman and already have been discussed: uterine cramps the first few days after delivery; sensations of let-down; leakage of milk from the opposite breast during breastfeeding; breast feels full before and soft after feeding; or the appearance of milk in or around the baby's mouth after feeding.

The more relaxed and confident you feel, the quicker your milk will let down. The first feedings in the hospital may be difficult because of excitement or, perhaps, your uncertainty about what to do. Breastfeeding should not cause sustained pain in the nipple, areola, or breast. If there is pain for more than a few moments at the beginning, ask the doctor, nurse, or lactation specialist to evaluate the breastfeeding and suggest changes. Ask the hospital staff for help; they are usually very experienced at assisting nursing mothers and babies.

Once you are back home, try the following suggestions to help the let-down reflex.

- Apply moist heat (i.e., warm wet washcloths) to the breast several minutes before starting the feeding.

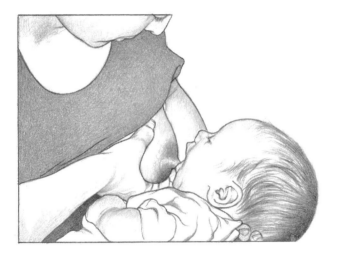

If you stroke your newborn's cheek or lower lip with your finger or with the nipple, he'll instinctively turn, latch on, and begin to suck.

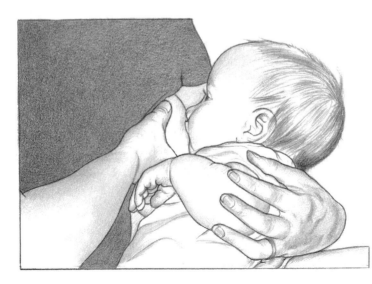

You may need to help him properly grasp the areola.

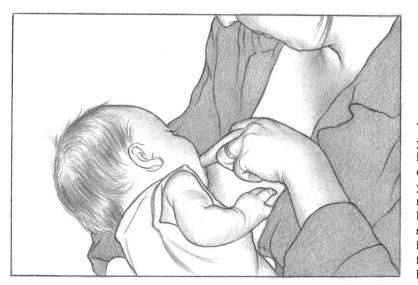

You can slide your finger into the corner of your baby's mouth, breaking his suction to see if there is a flow from the breast.

- Sit in a comfortable chair, with good support for your back and arms. (Many nursing mothers recommend rocking chairs.)

- Make sure the baby is positioned so the baby squarely faces the breast and is well latched on, as described earlier.

- Use some relaxation techniques, such as deep breathing or visual imagery.

- Listen to soothing music and sip a nutritious drink during feedings.

- If your household is very busy, find a quiet corner or room where you won't be disturbed during feedings.

- Do not smoke and avoid second-hand smoke. Do not consume alcohol, or use illegal drugs (i.e., marijuana, cocaine, heroin, ecstasy, etc.), as all contain substances that can interfere with let-down and affect the content of breastmilk and be harmful to the baby. Check with your obstetrician or pediatrician about any prescription or nonprescription drugs you may be taking.

If you still are not letting down after trying these suggestions, contact your pediatrician for additional help. If you continue to have difficulties, ask to be referred to a lactation expert.

When Your Milk Comes In

For the first few days after delivery, your breasts will be soft to the touch; but as the blood supply increases and milk-producing cells start to function efficiently, the breasts will become firmer. By the second to fifth day following delivery, your breasts should be producing transitional milk (the milk that follows colostrum) and may feel very full. At the end of the baby's first week, you will see creamy white breastmilk; after ten to fourteen days, your milk may initially look like skimmed milk, but as the feeding continues, the amount of fat in the milk will increase and the milk will look creamier. This is normal and does not mean there is anything wrong with your milk. Nursing your baby frequently and massaging your breasts prior to and during feeding may help minimize the fullness.

Engorgement occurs when the breasts become overfilled with milk and excess body fluids. This can be very uncomfortable and at times painful. The best solution to this problem is to nurse your baby whenever she is hungry, draining both breasts about every two hours. Sometimes the breasts are so engorged that the baby has trouble latching on. If that happens, you can apply moist heat to soften the breasts, and if necessary, manually express some milk or use a mechanical breast pump before you start to nurse. Doing this may help the baby get a better grasp and nurse more efficiently. (See page 98 regarding milk expression.) You also can try several techniques to ease the pain of engorgement, such as the following.

- Soak a cloth in warm water and put it on your breasts. Or take a warm shower. These techniques, when used just before breastfeeding or expressing milk, will encourage milk flow.

- Warmth may not help cases of severe engorgement. In this case, you may want to use cool compresses in between or just after feeding.

- Express milk or pump just enough milk for comfort's sake.

- Try feeding your baby in more than one position. Begin by sitting up, then lying down. This changes the segments of the breast that are drained most optimally at each feeding.

- Gently massage your breasts from under the arm and down the nipple. This will help reduce soreness and ease milk flow.

- The use of ibuprofen has been shown to be safe and effective for the treatment of engorgement. Take the dosage recommended by your doctor. Do not take any other medications without your doctor's approval.

Fortunately, engorgement lasts only a few days while lactation is getting established. However, it can occur anytime when feedings are skipped and the breasts are not emptied frequently.

The volume of milk produced by the breasts increases dramatically over the first week. You may produce as little as 1 teaspoon (5 ml) at each feeding in the first couple of days. But by the fourth or fifth day, the volume may be up to 1 ounce (30 ml), and by the end of the week—depending on the size and appetite of the baby and the length of feedings—you may be producing 2 to 6 ounces (60–180 ml) at each feeding. At the end of your baby's first month, she should be

Breastfeeding Twins

Twins present a unique challenge to the nursing mother. At first it may be easier to feed them one at a time, but after lactation is established, often it's more convenient to feed them simultaneously in order to save time. You can do this using the "football hold" to position one at each side, or cradle them both in front of you with their bodies crossing each other. Books and support groups for parents of twins can provide further information.

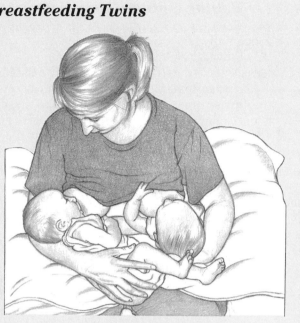

receiving an average of 24 ounces (720 ml) of milk a day. See pages 96–97 for information on how to tell if your baby is getting enough.

How Often and How Long?

Breastfed babies vary greatly in their feeding behaviors. They generally eat more frequently than formula-fed infants. Once the milk has come in, breastfed newborns typically will feed eight to twelve or more times per twenty-four hours. As they get older, some may be able to go longer between feedings, because their stomach capacity enlarges and their mothers' milk production increases. Others will continue to prefer frequent, smaller feeds.

What's the best feeding schedule for a breastfed baby? It's the one she designs herself. Your baby lets you know when she's hungry by waking and looking alert, putting hands toward her mouth, making sucking motions, whimpering and flexing arms and hands, moving fists to her mouth, becoming more active, and nuzzling against your breast. (She can smell its location even through your clothing.) It is best to start nursing the baby before crying starts. Crying is a late sign of hunger. Whenever possible, use these signals rather than

Getting to Know Your Baby's Feeding Patterns

Each baby has a particular style of eating. Years ago researchers at Yale University playfully attached names to five common eating patterns. See if you recognize your baby's dining behavior among them:

Barracudas get right down to business. As soon as they're put to the breast, they grasp the areola and suck energetically for ten to twenty minutes. They usually become less eager as time goes on.

Excited Ineffectives become frantic at the sight of the breast. In a frenzied cycle they grasp it, lose it, and start screaming in frustration. They must be calmed down several times during each feeding. The key to nourishing this type of baby is to feed him as soon as he wakes up, before he gets desperately hungry. Also, if the milk tends to spray from the breast as the baby struggles, it may help to manually express a few drops first to slow the stream.

Procrastinators can't be bothered with nursing until the milk comes in. These babies shouldn't be given bottles of water or formula. Continue to put them to the breast regularly, whenever they appear alert or make mouthing movements. Reluctant nursers sometimes benefit from being placed naked on the reclining mother's bare abdomen and chest for a period of time. They may spontaneously move toward the breast, or they can be placed on the breast after a time. You may find advice on improved positioning and attachment from a lactation spe-

the clock to decide when to nurse her. This way, you'll ensure that she's hungry when she eats. In the process, she'll stimulate the breast more efficiently to produce milk.

For the healthy mother and infant, breastfeeding is generally most successful when you start nursing immediately after delivery (in the first hour), keep the baby with you as much as possible (rooming in with her in the hospital), and respond promptly to cues of hunger (a practice called demand feeding). If you remain in the hospital for several days and she sleeps in the nursery, her feeding schedule may be determined more by the needs of the staff than her own hunger pangs. Once you're finally home, it may take several days for her to reset her internal clock. In the meantime, try feeding her every two to three hours even if she doesn't cry for nourishment. Sleepy babies should be awakened to feed after every three to four hours during the first few weeks of life, so that they have a minimum of eight feedings in twenty-four hours.

Allow your baby to continue nursing on the first breast as long as desired. When she spontaneously stops for a prolonged period or withdraws from the breast, burp her. If your baby seems sleepy after the first breast, you may want to wake her up a bit by changing her diaper or playing with her a little before switching her to the second side. Since your infant sucks more efficiently on the

cialist helpful. For a baby who resists nursing for the first few days, you can use an electric or manual pump between feedings to stimulate milk production. (See pages 98–101.) Just don't give up! Contact your pediatrician's office for assistance or referral to a lactation specialist.

Gourmets or Mouthers insist on playing with the nipple, tasting the milk first and smacking their lips before digging in. If hurried or prodded, they become furious and scream in protest. The best solution is tolerance. After a few minutes of playing, they do settle down and nurse well. Just be sure the lips and gums are on the areola and not on the nipple.

Resters prefer to nurse for a few minutes, rest a few minutes, and resume nursing. Some fall asleep on the breast, nap for half an hour or so, and then awake ready for dessert. This pattern can be confusing, but these babies cannot be hurried. The solution? It's best just to schedule extra time for feedings and remain as flexible as possible.

Learning your own baby's eating patterns is one of your biggest challenges in the first few weeks after delivery. Once you understand his patterns, you'll find it much easier to determine when he's hungry, when he's had enough, how often he needs to eat, and how much time is required for feedings. It is generally best to initiate a feeding at the earliest signs of hunger and before the baby cries. Babies also have unique positions that they prefer and will even show preference for one breast over the other.

first breast she uses, you should alternate from feeding to feeding the one she uses first. Some women place a safety pin or an extra nursing pad on the side where the baby last nursed as a reminder to start first on the other side at the next feeding. Or you can start on the breast that feels the fullest.

Initially your newborn probably will nurse every couple of hours, regardless of whether it's day or night. By six to eight weeks of age, many newborns have one sleep period of four to five hours. Establish nighttime sleep patterns by keeping the room dark, warm, and quiet. Don't turn on the light for the 2:00 A.M. feeding. If soiled or wet, change her diaper quickly and without fanfare before this feeding and put her right back to sleep afterward. By four months, many— but not all—babies are sleeping six hours or more at a stretch without awakening during the night. However, some breastfed babies may continue to awaken more frequently for feedings at night. (See *Helping Your Baby Sleep,* page 45.)

You'll also find that your infant may require long feedings at certain times of the day and be satisfied quickly at others. She'll let you know when she's finished by letting go or drifting off to sleep between spurts of nonnutritive sucking. A few babies want to nurse around the clock. If your baby falls into this category, check with your pediatrician's office. You may be referred to a lactation specialist. There are several reasons why infants behave this way, and the sooner the situation is evaluated, the easier it is to address the cause. Once evaluated, if breastfeeding is going well, your milk supply is well established, and the baby is gaining weight well, you may decide to provide a pacifier for extra sucking. Be aware that the use of pacifiers is associated with a shorter duration of breastfeeding.

How Do You Know If Your Baby Is Getting Enough?

Your baby's diapers will provide clues about whether he is getting enough to eat. During the first month, after your milk supply increases and if his diet is adequate, he should wet six or more times a day and generally have three to four or more bowel movements daily (usually one little one after each feeding). Later he may have less frequent bowel movements, and there may even be a day or more between them. If the bowel movements are soft, and your baby is otherwise thriving, this is quite normal. Another clue about intake is whether you can hear your baby swallow, usually after several sucks in a row. Appearing satisfied for a couple of hours right after a feeding is also a sign that he is getting enough. On the other hand, a baby who is not getting enough to eat over several days may become very sleepy and seem "easy" to care for. In the early weeks, a baby who sleeps for four hours or more at a time should be seen by the pediatrician.

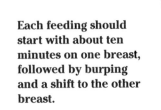

Each feeding should start with about ten minutes on one breast, followed by burping and a shift to the other breast.

Another way to judge your baby's intake over time is by checking her weight gain. We now recommend that babies be examined by a care provider at the third to fifth day of life, which provides an opportunity to check her weight, feeding, and head circumference. During the first week of life, your baby may lose up to 7 to 10 percent of her birth weight (that's about 8 ounces [226 grams] in an approximately 7½-pound [3.4 kg] full-term baby), but after that she should gain fairly steadily. By the end of her second week, she ought to be back to her birth weight. If you've breastfed other children, lactation probably will get established more quickly this time around, so the new baby may lose little weight and return to her birth weight within days.

Once your milk supply is established, your baby should gain between ½ and 1 ounce (14–28 grams) a day during his first three months. Between three and six months, his weight gain will taper off to about ½ ounce (14 grams) a day, and after six months, it will drop even further. Your pediatrician typically will weigh the baby at every visit. If you have concerns between visits, call to schedule an appointment to have the baby weighed; don't depend on a home scale, which is not very reliable for young infants.

What About Bottles?

It is usually best to try to breastfeed your newborn around the clock. Having your baby with you in your hospital room as much as possible (called rooming-in at most hospitals) makes this much easier. You might be tempted to have your baby sleep in the nursery for one night so you can get an uninterrupted night's sleep. But research has shown that those mothers who keep their babies with them in their hospital room twenty-four hours per day sleep just as long in total as mothers whose babies are returned to the nursery. Also, if your baby is always with you, you can avoid any water or formula supplementation, which may interfere with your ability to have a successful breastfeeding experience.

If circumstances keep you away from your baby, you will need to express breastmilk, manually or mechanically, in order to stimulate continued milk production. Only rarely are there serious situations where mother's milk may not be used. If you use bottles of formula when you are away, your baby receives less breastmilk and fewer benefits of breastfeeding. Avoiding formula may be particularly important in babies from families with a history of allergy. Always check with your pediatrician or other expert before you stop giving your milk to your baby.

Once breastfeeding is going well and the milk supply is established, usually three or four weeks after delivery, you may decide to use an occasional bottle so you can be away during some feedings. But you won't need to substitute formula: If you express breastmilk in advance and store it, your baby can continue to receive the benefits of your milk by bottle. In addition, using expressed breastmilk will maintain your body's full milk production for your baby. An occasional bottle at this stage probably won't interfere with your baby's nursing habits, but it may cause another problem: Your breasts may become engorged, and they can leak milk. You can relieve the engorgement by expressing milk to drain the breasts; store this milk to replace the breastmilk that was used while you were away. Wearing nursing pads will help you manage the problem of leakage. (Some women need to wear nursing pads constantly during the first month or two of lactation.)

Milk Expression and Storage

Milk can be expressed either by hand or by pump. In either case, you must have the let-down reflex in order to get the milk out of the breast. Manual expression is easier to learn if someone shows you, rather than just reading about it. Manual expression can be quick and effective once it is learned, but it requires practice.

Initially breast pumps seem easier to use than learning hand expression, but quality of pumps varies widely. A poor-quality breast pump will not remove milk effectively, resulting in engorgement or a gradually lower milk supply over time. Poor-quality breast pumps also may be painful.

If you choose to express manually, wash your hands and use a clean container to collect the milk. Place your thumb on the breast, above the areola, and your fingers underneath. Gently but firmly roll the thumb and fingers toward each other while compressing the breast tissue and pushing toward the chest wall. Do not slide your fingers toward your nipple as this can cause soreness. Transfer the milk into a clean bottle, rigid plastic container, or specially made plastic bag for storage in the freezer. (See page 100.) If your baby is hospitalized, the hospital may give you more specific and detailed information about milk collection and storage.

Hand pumps are available at most drug and baby stores. Avoid pumps that re-

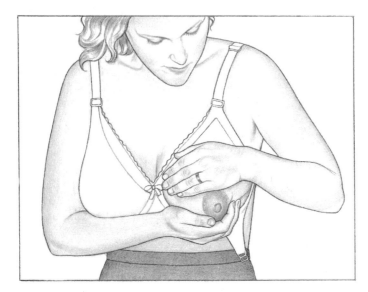

Expressing milk is easier if you stimulate the breast first by massaging it gently.

semble a bicycle horn, an inefficient design that allows pumped milk to flow back into the rubber bulb, which is virtually impossible to clean properly. The milk can become contaminated as a result.

A better choice is a popular pump that consists of two cylinders, one inside the other, attached to a rigid device that looks like a funnel that fits over the breast. As you slide the outer cylinder up and down, negative pressure is created over the nipple area and milk collects in the bottom of the cylinder. This collecting cylinder can be used with a special nipple to feed your baby without transferring the milk, and the entire pump can be cleaned in the dishwasher. Several different companies manufacture variations on this basic design.

Some pumps use a handle to create negative pressure and draw the milk into a bottle, and they work well for some women. They have a soft, pliable flange that fits around the nipple and produces a milking action on the areola while pumping.

Good-quality electric pumps stimulate the breast more effectively than manual expression or hand pumps. These pumps have regulated pressures and are self-cycling for efficient milk removal. They are used primarily to induce or maintain lactation when a mother is unable to feed her infant directly for several days or more, or when the mother returns to work or school. Electric pumps are easier and more efficient than hand pumps, but they're vastly more expensive. The more elaborate ones cost over $1,000 apiece; if you will need the pump for only a limited period, it's much more economical to rent one from a medical supply store, hospital, or a lactation rental agency. Small portable electric pumps sell for around $250 to $300. If you have a hospitalized newborn or return to work shortly after your baby is born and want to continue breastfeeding, obtaining a breast pump is essential.

When shopping for an electric pump to buy or rent, make sure it creates a steady milking action with variable pressure and is not simply a suction device.

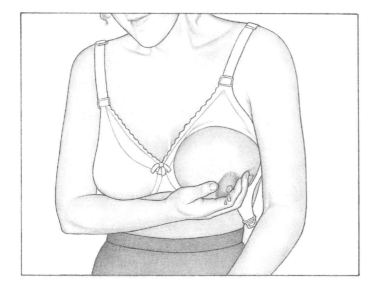

To express manually, hold the breast with the thumb and index finger at the edge of the areola on opposite sides of the breast, then press toward the chest wall with a rhythmic motion. Rotate position of fingers so all parts of the breast are emptied.

Hand pumps are available at most drug and baby stores.

You also may want to consider a pump that expresses both breasts at the same time; such a pump will increase your milk volume as well as save time. Whenever using a pump, wash your hands immediately before pumping. No matter which type of pump you choose, make sure all parts that come in contact with skin or milk can be removed for proper cleaning. (See page 98.)

Store breastmilk in clean containers, preferably glass or rigid plastic containers or special plastic bags. (Sterilization is not required for pumps and containers for a healthy baby. Washing them well with hot soapy water is fine, as is running them through the dishwasher.) Baby bottle insert bags are not sufficiently strong or thick enough to protect the milk from contamination. If the milk is to be given to the baby within forty-eight hours, it should be sealed and cooled immediately. If this refrigerated milk goes unused for more than forty-eight hours, it should be discarded. It may be frozen after up to twenty-four hours of refrigeration.

If you know in advance that the milk won't be used within two days, freeze it immediately. Breastmilk will safely keep in your freezer for at least one month. Store it in the back of the freezer. If you have a separate deep freeze, it can be kept for about three to six months. (Because the fats in human milk begin to break down over time, use the frozen milk as soon as possible.)

It's a good idea to place a label with the date on each container so you can use the oldest milk first. It's useful to freeze milk in quantities of about 3 to 4 ounces (90–120 ml)—the amount of a single feeding. You also can freeze some 1- to 2-ounce portions (30–60 ml); these will come in handy if the baby wants a little extra at any feeding.

When it's time to use this stored milk, keep in mind that your baby is accustomed to breastmilk at body temperature, so the milk should be heated to at least room temperature (68 to 72 degrees Fahrenheit [20–22 degrees Celsius]) for feeding. The easiest way to warm refrigerated or frozen milk is to place the container in warm water and rotate it frequently. To speed up this process, place the container in a pan of warm water or thaw it in the refrigerator.

Do not heat bottles in a microwave oven. Microwaving overheats the milk in the center of the container. Even if the bottle feels comfortably warm to your touch, the superheated milk in the center can scald your baby's mouth. Also, the bottle itself can explode if left in the microwave too long. Bear in mind that heat also can destroy some of the anti-infectious and protective properties of breastmilk.

Incidentally, once milk is thawed, its fat may separate, but it is still safe to drink. Just shake the container gently until the milk returns to a uniform consistency. Thawed milk should be used within twenty-four hours. Never refreeze it. Do not save unfinished milk from a partially consumed bottle to use at another feeding.

Not all breastfed babies react to the bottle the same way. Some accept it easily, regardless of when it is first introduced. Others are willing to take an occasional bottle, but not from the mother or when the mother is in the house.

You can increase the likelihood that your baby will accept a bottle the first few times if someone other than the mother offers it, and she is out of sight at the time. Once familiar with the bottle, he may be willing to take it in his mother's presence, possibly even from the mother herself. If your breastfed baby refuses a bottle, try using a cup or "sippie cup" instead. Even premature newborns are able to cup feed. Some breastfed babies go from breast to cup without ever using a bottle.

Mothers' Possible Nursing Problems and Questions

For some babies and mothers, nursing goes well from the start and there are never any problems. But breastfeeding can have its ups and downs, especially in the beginning. Fortunately, many of the most common difficulties can be prevented with proper positioning and latch-on, along with frequent feedings. Once problems crop up, many may resolve quickly if you seek advice right away. Don't hesitate to ask your pediatrician's office for help with the following problems.

Sore and Cracked Nipples. Breastfeeding may produce some initial soreness, especially with latch-on in the first week or so. But breastfeeding should not cause sustained pain, discomfort, or open cracks. Proper latch-on is the most important factor in preventing sore and cracked nipples. If your nipple or other areas of the breast are painful, you should seek advice from your lactation expert.

During your bath or shower, wash your breasts only with water, not soap. Creams, lotions, and more vigorous rubbing actually may aggravate the problem. Also, try varying the baby's position at each feeding.

In humid climates, the best treatments for cracked nipples are dryness, sunlight, and heat. Don't wear plastic breast shields or plastic-lined nursing pads, which hold in moisture; instead, expose your breasts to the air as much as possible. Also, after nursing, express a little milk from your breasts and let it dry on the nipples. This dried milk will leave a protective coating that may help the healing process. In a dry climate, you might want to apply purified hypoallergenic lanolin. If these measures do not solve the problem, consult your doctor for further advice; you might have a yeast or bacterial infection of the nipple.

Engorgement. As we've already mentioned, your breasts can become severely engorged if your baby doesn't nurse often or efficiently during the first few days after your milk comes in. While some engorgement is to be expected when you

Supplemental Nurser

(Infant Feeding Device)

The amount of milk your breasts produce depends on the amount of milk that is removed from them. If you miss too many feedings, your body automatically will decrease milk production. This can occur even if you express milk during missed feedings, because pumps do not stimulate or empty the breasts nearly as efficiently as your baby's sucking.

If you miss a number of feedings because of illness or because your baby is unable to nurse for some reason, you may be able to keep your baby well fed while reestablishing your milk supply with the help of a device called a supplemental nurser (also known as a sup-

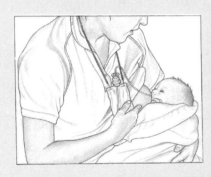

plementer tube, infant feeding device, or nursing trainer). Unlike a bottle, which trains the baby away from the breast, this device provides supplemental formula while the infant is at the breast.

The supplemental nurser also is used for premature infants or to train babies with feeding problems. It even can help stimulate lactation in adoptive mothers, or in mothers who have stopped breastfeeding for a prolonged period and wish to start again.

The device consists of a small plastic container that holds formula or expressed breastmilk and hangs from a ribbon around your neck. The container has a thin flexible tube that is held or taped along the breast with its tip adjacent to the nipple and placed in the corner of the baby's mouth as she sucks. Her suction draws the formula from the container into her mouth, so that even if you aren't producing much milk, she still will be getting a full meal. This process reinforces her desire to nurse at the breast. At the same time, her sucking stimulates your body to step up milk production.

Supplemental nursers are available from lactation specialists, medical supply stores, some pharmacies, or mail order. If possible, purchase the device from someone who can help you use it for the first time and show you how to clean it. Most mothers and babies need a few days of practice to get comfortable with the device. Using a supplemental nurser requires commitment and dedication, as it may take weeks or months to rebuild the milk supply and the breastfeeding relationship.

start lactation, extreme engorgement causes swelling of the milk ducts in the breasts and of blood vessels across the entire chest area. The best treatment is to feed your baby frequently; express milk between feedings, either manually or with a pump; and make sure the baby nurses at both breasts at every feeding. Since warmth encourages milk flow, standing in a warm shower as you manually express the milk may help, or use warm compresses. You also may get some relief with the use of warm compresses during nursing and cool compresses between nursing.

If you have very severe engorgement, however, warmth may aggravate the situation because it increases blood flow to the area. If this is the case, try using cool compresses between feedings. The engorgement should subside in a few days. Ibuprofen has been shown to be safe and effective in the treatment of engorgement. Use the same dose that your doctor recommends for uterine cramping.

Mastitis. Mastitis is an infection of the breast tissue caused by bacteria. Mastitis causes flulike symptoms of fever, chills, headache, nausea, dizziness, and lack of energy. These general symptoms occur along with local breast symptoms of redness, tenderness, swelling, heat, and pain. If you experience any of these symptoms, continue breastfeeding and call your doctor at once. The infection is treated with milk removal (by feeding or pumping), rest, fluids, antibiotics, and pain medicine if needed. Your doctor will prescribe an antibiotic that is safe during breastfeeding. Be sure to take all the antibiotics even if you feel better. Do not stop nursing; doing so will worsen the mastitis and cause increased pain. The milk itself is *not* infected. Your baby will not be harmed by nursing during mastitis, and mastitis and the antibiotics will not cause changes in the composition of your milk.

Mastitis may be a sign that your body's immune defenses are down. Bed rest, sleep, and decreased activity will help you recover your stamina. Rarely, a woman may find that it's too painful to have the baby nurse on the infected breast; in that case, open up both sides of your bra and let the milk flow from that breast onto a towel or absorbent cloth such as a clean diaper, relieving the pressure as you feed the baby on the opposite side. Then she can finish the feeding on the infected side with less discomfort. Some women with severe pain find that it is more comfortable to pump the breast than it is to feed the baby. The pumped milk can be stored or can be fed to the baby.

Infant Fussiness. There are a number of reasons for a breastfed baby to be unusually fussy. These range from normal variations in "personality" to a serious illness. Although most "fussy babies" do not have a serious medical problem, their constant crying can become extremely difficult for parents. The fussy baby is a drain on Mom and Dad's energy, time, and enjoyment of their young infant. Here are some general causes for excessive crying in the breastfed baby and suggestions for working with your pediatrician to pinpoint and treat the problem.

- **Hunger:** If your newborn infant feeds constantly and is never satisfied after coming off the breast, your breastfeeding needs to be evaluated by an experienced health care provider. He will weigh your baby, examine your breast and nipples, examine the baby herself, and observe an entire breastfeeding session. The solution may be as simple as improving the baby's positioning and latch-on. It may be more complicated, however, particularly if the baby has lost too much weight.

- **Growth spurt:** A rapid growth phase often happens at two to three weeks of age, again around six weeks, and once more at about three months. During these growth spurts, babies will want to nurse *constantly*. Remember, this is normal, and it is only temporary, usually lasting about four to five days. Many women are tempted to give supplemental bottles at this time, because they do not understand why the baby is eating all the time. Keep breastfeeding very often, and do not give other liquids. If the growth spurt lasts longer than five days, or if you are tempted to start your baby on bottles, call your pediatrician's office for assistance. He should see the baby, check her weight, and evaluate the feeding process (or refer you to a lactation specialist if needed).

- **Hyperalert or high-needs infants:** These babies require more of everything, except sleep. They cry around the clock. They are not very regular in their eating, sleeping, or reactions to others. They need lots of holding, carrying, and usually motion, like rocking. Sometimes swaddling in a blanket helps them, but at other times it makes them worse. They tend to "snack" at the breast frequently and sleep in cat naps, brief fifteen- to thirty-minute naps while someone is holding or carrying them. Slings or other baby carriers, as well as swings, are good to try to help calm these babies. In spite of their fussiness, they should be gaining weight normally.

- **Colic:** Colic begins around two weeks of age. Colicky babies generally have one period of time each day when they appear to be in pain with their legs drawn up, crying hard, and turning red. They may act hungry during these times, but then pull back and refuse the breast. Your baby's doctor probably will have lots of suggestions for managing colic. (See Chapter 6, page 152.)

- **Oversupply or overactive let-down of breastmilk:** This could begin at almost any time in the first month. Your breast will feel very full, and you may experience lots of leaking and spraying. Your baby will be gulping down milk very fast, sometimes pulling away to catch his breath. This rapid drinking causes the baby to swallow lots of air and milk. Later, gas bubbles will form, causing plenty of discomfort and tummy rumbling. Your pediatrician may guide you to a lactation consultant to assist with this problem. On the positive side, these babies usually gain weight very rapidly. (Also see *Engorgement,* page 101.)

- **Reflux (also called gastroesophageal reflux):** Most newborns spit up after feeding. When spitting up results in problems for the baby, such as pain or weight loss, he should be evaluated by your pediatrician. (See page 196.)

- **Food sensitivities:** Occasionally a particular food (including caffeinated beverages) that you're eating may cause problems in your breastfed baby. If you think this might be the case, avoid that food for one week to see if the symptoms go away. Then you may try the food again carefully to see if the symptoms return.

- **Allergies:** Although infant crying often is blamed on food allergies, such allergies are less common than some other reasons for fussiness. Allergies occur more often in babies from families where mother, father, or siblings are affected by asthma, eczema, or other allergic diseases. In the breastfed baby, the mother's diet is the source of these allergies. It can be difficult to pinpoint the precise food, however, and allergic symptoms can linger for more than a week after the food has been removed from the mother's diet. Food allergies can be very serious, with blood in the stools, wheezing, hives, or shock (collapse). True food allergies definitely require the attention of your pediatrician.

- **Serious illness:** Other serious illnesses may not be related to feeding and may cause babies to cry endlessly, unable to be comforted. If this occurs suddenly or seems unusually severe, call your pediatrician or seek emergency care immediately.

The Cancer Question. Some studies indicate that breastfeeding offers some protection against breast cancer. If a woman has been diagnosed with cancer or has had a malignant tumor removed, but is no longer getting chemotherapy or radiation treatment, breastfeeding should be acceptable. (Check with your physician.) Most doctors feel that breastfeeding is safe even if a woman has had a benign (noncancerous) lump or cyst removed.

Breastfeeding After Plastic Surgery on the Breasts. Plastic surgery to enlarge the breasts should not interfere with breastfeeding—provided that the breasts were normal to begin with and that the nipples have not been moved and no ducts have been cut. Women with silicone implants may worry about leakage of silicone causing problems for their baby. But most authorities recommend breastfeeding even after implant surgery and feel that it does not pose any dangers to the baby.

The course of breastfeeding after breast reduction surgery is highly individual. Plastic surgery to reduce the size of the breasts typically involves disruption of normal breast tissue and movement of the entire nipple and areola. Surgeons often make blanket statements, such as "You will not be able to breastfeed" or just the opposite, "We did the surgery so that you will be able to breastfeed." Each mother-baby pair must be helped and followed individually.

Your baby's weight should be checked at least twice a week for the first few weeks, until the baby is gaining well. It is worth trying to breastfeed so that you can provide some breastmilk for your baby, even if you don't have a full supply.

Make sure you discuss all your concerns with your doctor. Your baby's pediatrician needs to be aware of previous breast surgery that you've had so your infant can be followed closely.

For additional difficulties such as jaundice and worries about milk supply, refer to pages 139 and 96.

ADVANTAGES AND DISADVANTAGES OF BOTTLE-FEEDING

While recognizing the benefits of breastfeeding, mothers, and fathers, too, may feel that bottle-feeding gives the mother more freedom and time for duties other than those involving baby care. Dad, grandparents, sitters, and even older siblings can feed an infant breastmilk or formula in a bottle. This may give some mothers more flexibility.

There are other reasons why some parents feel more comfortable with bottle-feeding. They know exactly how much food the baby is getting, and there's no need to worry about the mother's diet or medications that might affect the milk.

Formula manufacturers have not yet found a way to reproduce the components that make human milk so unique. Although formula does provide the nutrients an infant needs, it lacks the antibodies and other components that only mother's milk contains.

Formula-feeding is also costly and may be inconvenient for some families. The formula must be bought and prepared (unless you use the more expensive, ready-to-use types). This means trips to the kitchen in the middle of the night, as well as extra bottles, nipples, and other equipment. Unintended contamination of formula also must be considered a potential risk.

BOTTLE-FEEDING YOUR BABY

If you have decided to bottle-feed your baby, you'll have to start by selecting a formula. Your pediatrician will help you pick one based on your baby's needs. Twenty or thirty years ago, the majority of mothers made their own formula—a mixture of evaporated cow's milk, water, and sugar. However, the American Academy of Pediatrics no longer recommends homemade baby formulas, since they tend to be deficient in vitamins and other important nutrients. Also, only a small error in mixing the ingredients for the formula can have serious negative effects on your baby's well-being. Today there are several varieties and brands of commercial formulas from which to choose.

Why Formula Instead of Cow's Milk?

Many parents ask why they can't just feed their baby regular cow's milk. The answer is simple: Young infants cannot fully digest cow's milk as completely or easily as they digest formula. Also, cow's milk contains high concentrations of protein and minerals, which can stress a newborn's immature kidneys and can cause severe illness at times of heat stress, fever, or diarrhea. In addition, cow's milk lacks the proper amounts of iron and vitamin C that infants need. It may even cause iron-deficiency anemia in some babies, since protein can irritate the lining of the stomach and intestine, leading to loss of blood into the stools. For these reasons, your baby should not receive any regular cow's milk for the first twelve months of life.

Once your baby is past one year old, you may give him whole cow's milk, provided he has a balanced diet of solid foods (cereals, vegetables, fruits, and meats). But limit his intake of milk to one quart (946 ml) per day. More than one quart can provide too many calories and may decrease his appetite for the other foods he needs. If he is not yet eating a broad range of solid foods, give him iron-fortified formula instead of cow's milk.

Do not give your baby any reduced-fat milk (2 percent, 1 percent, or skimmed) before his second birthday. He needs the higher fat content of whole milk to maintain normal weight gain, and his body absorbs vitamins A and D better from whole milk. Also, nonfat, or skimmed, milk provides too high a concentration of protein and minerals and should not be given to infants or toddlers under age two. After two years of age, you should discuss your child's nutritional needs, including choice of milk products, with your pediatrician.

Choosing a Formula

An act of Congress governs the contents of infant formula, and the Food and Drug Administration monitors all formulas. When shopping for infant formula, you'll find three basic types.

Cow's milk–based formulas account for about 80 percent of the formula sold today. Although cow's milk is the basis for such formulas, the milk has been changed dramatically to make it safe for infants. It is treated by heating and other methods to make the protein more digestible. More milk sugar (lactose) is added to make the concentration equal to that of breastmilk, and the fat (butterfat) is removed and replaced with vegetable oils and other fats that infants can more easily digest.

Cow's milk formulas are available with added iron. These iron-fortified formulas have dramatically reduced the rate of iron-deficiency anemia in infancy in recent decades. Some infants do not have enough natural reserves of iron, a mineral necessary for normal human growth and development, to meet their needs. For that reason, the American Academy of Pediatrics currently recommends that iron-fortified formula be used for all infants who are not breastfed, or who are only partially breastfed, from birth to one year of age. Additional

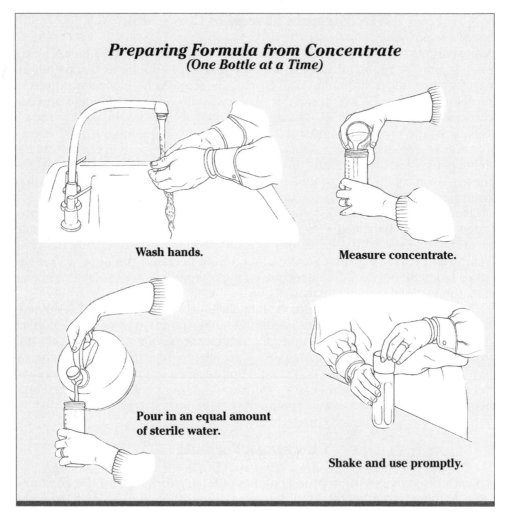

Preparing Formula from Concentrate
(One Bottle at a Time)

Wash hands.

Measure concentrate.

Pour in an equal amount of sterile water.

Shake and use promptly.

iron is available in many baby foods, especially iron-fortified cereals. Low-iron formulas should not be used, since they do not provide enough iron to optimally support your baby's growth and development.

Soy formulas contain a protein (soy) and carbohydrate (glucose polymers or sucrose) different from milk-based formulas. They are recommended most commonly for babies unable to digest lactose, the main carbohydrate in cow's milk formula, although lactose-free cow's milk–based formula now is also available. Many infants have brief periods when they cannot digest lactose, particularly following bouts of diarrhea, which can damage the digestive enzymes in the lining of the intestines. Your pediatrician may suggest a lactose-free formula when diarrhea occurs. This lactose-free formula will not negatively affect your baby's health.

Another (and far less common) reason for placing an infant on soy formula is milk allergy, which can cause colic, failure to thrive, and even bloody diarrhea.

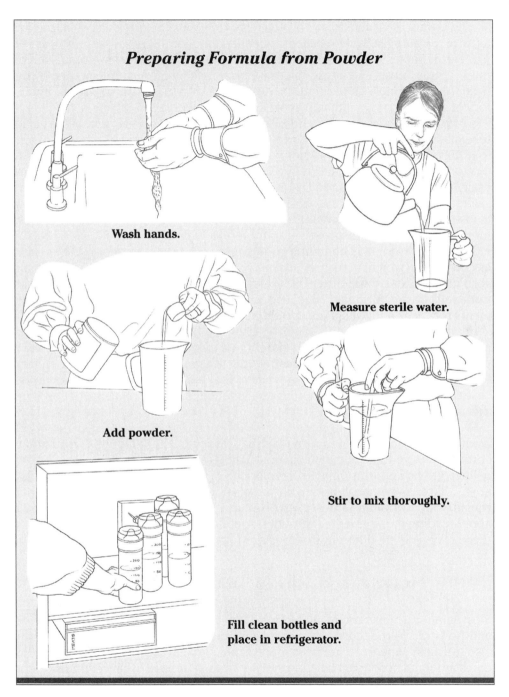

Preparing Formula from Powder

Wash hands.

Measure sterile water.

Add powder.

Stir to mix thoroughly.

Fill clean bottles and place in refrigerator.

This reaction can be so dangerous to a newborn that some doctors prescribe soy formula from birth as a preventive measure when there is a strong family history of allergies to cow's milk. Unfortunately, as many as half the infants who have milk allergy are also sensitive to soy protein, and they must be given a specialized formula or breastmilk. The so-called hypoallergenic formulas will help at least 90 percent of babies who have food allergies, which can cause symptoms such as hives, a runny nose, and intestinal problems. Breastfeeding, supplemented by hypoallergenic formula, is particularly desirable when there is a strong family history of allergies, and could help avoid some food allergies in infants.

Soy formula also is recommended for infants with a rare disorder called galactosemia. These babies have an intolerance to galactose, one of the two sugars that make up lactose. The carbohydrates used to replace lactose in most soy formulas are sucrose and corn syrup (or a combination of the two). Both are easily digested and absorbed by infants. Most of these formulas cost about the same as milk-based formulas and are supplemented with iron. Most states include the galactosemia test in the newborn screening. Infants with the classic form of this very rare disorder cannot tolerate breastmilk either.

Today's soy formulas contain a good source of protein, but not quite as good as cow's milk (which, in turn, is inferior to human milk). Also, your baby will absorb calcium and some other minerals less efficiently from soy formulas than from milk-based formulas. Because premature infants have higher requirements for these minerals, they should not be given soy formula at all.

Healthy full-term infants should be given soy formula only when medically necessary. Some strict vegetarian parents choose to use soy formula because it contains no animal products. Breastfeeding is a good option for vegetarian families. Also, although some parents believe that a soy formula might prevent or ease the symptoms of colic, there is no evidence to support its effectiveness for this purpose.

Specialized formulas are manufactured for infants with particular disorders or diseases. There are also formulas made specifically for premature babies. Formulas with added docosahexaenoic acid (DHA) and arachidonic acid (ARA), believed to be important for the development of the baby's brain and eyes, also are available. Whether your newborn has special needs or not, ask your pediatrician which formula is best. Also be sure to check the package for details about feeding requirements (amounts, scheduling, special preparations), since these may be quite different from regular formulas.

Preparing, Sterilizing, and Storing Formula

Most infant formulas are available in ready-to-feed liquid forms, concentrates, and powders. Although ready-to-feed formulas are very convenient, they are also the most expensive. Formula made from concentrate is prepared by mixing equal amounts of concentrate and sterile water. If the entire can is not used, the remaining concentrate may be covered and left in the refrigerator for no more than forty-eight hours. Powder, the least expensive form, comes either in premeasured packets or in a can with a measuring scoop. To prepare most formula, you'll add one level scoop of powder for every 2 ounces (60 ml) of water, and then mix thoroughly to make sure there are no clumps of undissolved powder in the bottle. The solution will mix more easily and the lumps will dissolve faster if you use slightly warmed water. Always read the label to make sure you are mixing the formula properly.

Aside from the price, one advantage of the powder is its light weight and portability. You can place a couple of scoops of powder in a bottle when you are going out with your baby and then add water just before feeding. The powder will not spoil, even if it stays in the bottle several days before you add water. If you choose a formula that requires preparation, be sure to follow the manufacturer's directions exactly. If you add too much water, your baby won't get the calories and nutrients she needs for proper growth; and if you add too little water, the high concentration of formula could cause diarrhea or dehydration and will give your infant more calories than she needs.

If you use well water or are concerned about the safety of your tap water, boil it for approximately one minute before you add it to the formula. You also can use bottled water with fluoride in preparing formulas.

Make sure all bottles, nipples, and other utensils you use to prepare formula—or to feed your baby—are clean. If the water in your home is chlorinated, you can simply use your dishwasher or wash the utensils in hot tap water with dishwashing detergent and then rinse them in hot tap water. For nonchlorinated water, place the utensils in boiling water for five to ten minutes.

Store any formula you prepare in advance in the refrigerator to discourage bacterial growth. If you don't use refrigerated formula within twenty-four hours, discard it. Refrigerated formula doesn't necessarily have to be warmed for your baby, but most infants prefer it at least at room temperature. You can either leave the bottle out for an hour so it can reach room temperature, or warm it in a pan of hot water. (Again, do not use a microwave.) If you warm it, test it in advance to make sure it's not too hot for your child. The easiest way to test the temperature is to shake a few drops on the inside of your wrist.

The bottles you use may be glass, plastic, or plastic with a soft plastic liner.

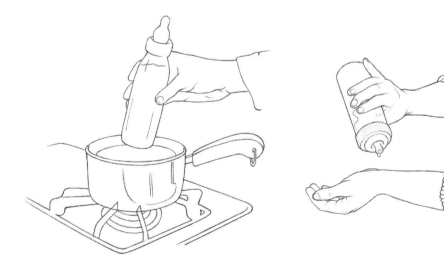

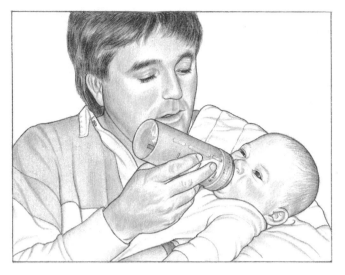

Hold the bottle so that formula fills the neck of the bottle and covers the nipple. This will prevent your baby from swallowing air as she sucks.

These inner liners are convenient to use and may help prevent your baby from swallowing too much air as she sucks, but they are also the most expensive. As your baby gets older and begins holding the bottle herself, avoid using breakable glass bottles. Also, bottles that are designed to promote self-feeding are not recommended, as they may contribute to nursing-bottle tooth decay by promoting constant feeding and exposure of the teeth to sugars throughout the day and night. When milk collects behind the teeth, bacterial growth occurs. Self-feeding in a supine position (lying down on the back) has been shown to contribute occasionally to ear infections. (See *Middle Ear Infections,* page 580.) Infants and older children should not receive a bottle to suck on during the night. If you give your baby a feeding at bedtime, take away the bottle right after she falls asleep.

Ask your pediatrician which type of nipple she recommends. She'll choose from among the standard rubber nipples, orthodontic ones, and special designs for premature infants and babies with cleft palates. You may need to try several nipples before finding the one your baby prefers. Whichever type you use, always check the size of the hole. If it's too small, your baby may suck so hard that she swallows too much air; if it's too big, the formula may flow so fast that she chokes. Ideally, formula should flow at a rate of one drop per second when you first turn the bottle upside down. (It should stop dripping after a few seconds.) Many parents find that a nipple with a single small hole is adequate for feeding water but that they need one with a larger hole or with several holes when feeding formula.

The Feeding Process

Feeding times should be relaxing, comforting, and enjoyable for both you and your baby. They provide opportunities to show your love and to get to know each other. If you are calm and content, your infant will respond in kind. If you

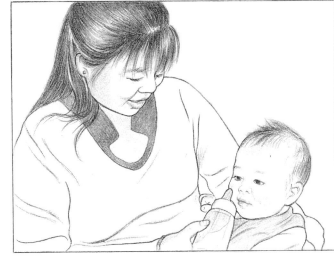

Hold baby closely for formula feeding. Encourage her to open widely and root for the nipple by touching it to the lower lip.

are nervous or uninterested, he may pick up these negative feelings and a feeding problem can result.

You probably will be most comfortable in a chair with arms or in one with pillows that let you prop up your own arms as you feed your infant. Cradle him in a semiupright position and support his head. Don't feed him when he's lying down totally flat, because this will increase the risk of choking; it also may cause formula to flow into the middle ear, where it can lead to an infection.

Hold the bottle so that formula fills the neck of the bottle and covers the nipple. This will prevent your baby from swallowing air as he sucks. To get him to open his mouth and grasp the nipple, stimulate his rooting reflex by stroking the nipple against the lower lip or cheek. Once the nipple is in his mouth, he will begin to suck and swallow naturally.

Amount and Schedule of Formula Feedings

Your formula-fed newborn will take from 2 to 3 ounces (60–90 ml) of formula per feeding and will eat every three to four hours on average during her first few weeks. Breastfed infants usually take smaller, more frequent feedings than formula-fed infants. During the first month, if your baby sleeps longer than four to five hours and starts missing feedings, wake her up and offer a bottle. By the end of her first month, she'll be up to at least 4 ounces (120 ml) per feeding, with a fairly predictable schedule of feedings about every four hours. By six months, your baby will consume 6 to 8 ounces (180–240 ml) at each of four or five feedings in twenty-four hours.

On average, your baby should take in about 2½ ounces (75 ml) of formula a day for every pound (453 grams) of body weight. But he probably will regulate his intake from day to day to meet his own specific needs. So instead of going by fixed amounts, let him tell you when he's had enough. If he becomes fidgety or easily distracted during a feeding, he's probably finished. If he drains the bottle and still continues smacking his lips, he's probably still hungry. There are high and low limits, however. Most babies are satisfied with 3 to 4 ounces (90–120 ml) per feeding during the first month and increase that amount by 1 ounce (30 ml) per month until they reach 8 ounces (240 ml). If your baby consistently seems to want more or less than this, discuss it with your pediatrician. Your baby should drink no more than 32 ounces (960 ml) of formula in 24 hours.

Initially it is best to feed your formula-fed newborn on demand, or whenever he cries because he's hungry. As time passes, he'll begin to develop a fairly regular timetable of his own. As you become familiar with his signals and needs, you'll be able to schedule his feedings around his routine.

By two months (or 12 pounds [5.4 kg]), most babies no longer need a middle-of-the-night feeding, because they're consuming more during the day and their sleeping patterns have become more regular, but this varies considerably from baby to baby. Their stomach capacity has increased, too, which means they can go longer between daytime feedings—up to four or five hours at a time. If your baby still seems to want more frequent feedings at this age, try distracting him with play and an occasional bottle of water between scheduled feedings. This should make him hungrier for the next feeding, so he'll eat more at that time and be satisfied for a longer period.

The most important thing to remember, whether you breastfeed or bottle-feed, is that your baby's feeding needs are unique. No book can tell you precisely how much or how often he needs to be fed or exactly how you should handle him during feedings. You will discover these things for yourself as you and your baby get to know each other.

SUPPLEMENTATION FOR BREASTFED AND BOTTLE-FED INFANTS

Vitamin Supplements

Human milk contains a natural balance of vitamins, especially C, E, and the B vitamins, so if you and your baby are both healthy, and you are well nourished, your child may not require any supplements of these vitamins.

Breastfed infants need supplemental vitamin D. This vitamin is naturally manufactured by the skin when it is exposed to sunlight. However, the American Academy of Pediatrics feels strongly that all children should wear sunscreen while in the sun, and sunscreen keeps the skin from manufacturing vitamin D. For that reason, talk to your pediatrician about the need for supplemental vitamin D drops at 200 IU (International Units) per day for your breastfed baby beginning by two months of age. (Prepared formula has vitamin D added to it.) Your baby also will need vitamin supplements if he was born prematurely or has certain other medical problems. Discuss this issue with your doctor after your baby is born.

A regular, well-balanced diet should provide all the vitamins necessary for both nursing mothers and their babies. However, some pediatricians recommend that mothers continue taking a daily prenatal vitamin supplement just to ensure the proper nutritional balance. If you are on a strict vegetarian diet, you need to take an extra B-complex supplement, since certain B vitamins are available only from meat, poultry, or fish products. If your baby is on infant formula, he generally will receive adequate vitamins because formula has added vitamins.

WHERE WE STAND

The American Academy of Pediatrics believes that healthy children receiving a normal, well-balanced diet do not need vitamin supplementation over and above the recommended dietary allowances. Megadoses of vitamins—for example, large amounts of vitamins A, C, or D—can produce toxic symptoms, ranging from nausea to rashes to headaches and sometimes to even more severe adverse effects. Talk with your pediatrician before giving vitamin supplements to your child.

Iron Supplements

Most babies are born with sufficient reserves of iron that will protect them from anemia. If your baby is breastfed, there is sufficient, well-absorbed iron to give her an adequate supply so that no additional supplement is necessary. When she is between four and six months old,* you should be starting your breastfed infant on baby foods that contain supplemental iron (cereals, meats, green vegetables), which should further guarantee sufficient iron for proper growth.

If you are bottle-feeding your baby, it is now recommended that you use iron-fortified formula (containing from 4.0 to 12 mg of iron) from birth through the entire first year of life.

Water and Juice

Until your baby starts eating solid foods, he'll get all the water he needs from breastmilk or formula. In the first six months, additional water or juice is generally unnecessary for breastfed or bottle-fed infants. After a bottle-fed baby is six months old, you may offer him water between feedings but don't force it on him

---

* Note: There is a difference of opinion among Academy experts on this matter. The Section on Breastfeeding supports exclusive breastfeeding for about six months. The Committee on Nutrition supports the introduction of complementary foods between four and six months of age where safe and nutritious complementary foods are available.

or worry if he rejects it. He may prefer to get the extra liquid from more frequent feedings. Breastfed infants generally do not need extra water if they are permitted adequate access to the breast for feeding.

WHERE WE STAND

The American Academy of Pediatrics recommends that fruit juice not be given to infants under six months of age since it offers no nutritional benefit to babies in this age group. After six months of age, infants may have limited amounts of juice each day. For youngsters older than six months, fruit juice offers no nutritional benefits over whole fruit. Infants also should not be given fruit juice at bedtime, nor as a treatment of dehydration or management of diarrhea. For children ages one to six, limit fruit juice consumption to 4 to 6 ounces (120–180 ml) each day.

Mean Carbohydrate (Sugar) Content (Grams per 100 grams [1 oz. = 28 grams]) of Fruits and Fruit Juices

Fruit/Fruit Juice	Fructose	Glucose	Sucrose	Sorbitol
Prune	14.0	23.0	0.6	12.7
Pear	6.6	1.7	1.7	2.1
Sweet Cherry	7.0	7.8	0.2	1.4
Peach	1.1	1.0	6.0	0.9
Apple	6.0	2.3	2.5	0.5
Grape	6.5	6.7	0.6	trace
Strawberry	2.2	2.3	0.9	0.0
Raspberry	2.0	1.9	1.9	0.0
Blackberry	3.4	3.2	0.2	0.0
Pineapple	1.4	2.3	7.9	0.0
Orange	2.4	2.4	4.7	0.0

The table shows how many grams of different kinds of sugars are in different juices. When the child is recovering from diarrhea, juices high in sorbitol should probably be avoided, as this sugar may increase loose stools.

Juices containing sorbitol may be beneficial for a baby who has hard stools.

Once your baby is eating solid foods, his need for liquid will increase. About 9 out of 10 of all infants consume fruit juice by the time they are one year of age. The most common fruit juices are apple juice, grape juice, and, more recently, pear juice. Fruit juice has been recommended by pediatricians to provide extra water for normal infants and young children. However, if a child drinks too much juice, sometimes it can't be digested properly, and can result in gas or diarrhea. Some fruit juices, such as white grape juice, may be digested more easily than others because they contain a balance of carbohydrates and no sorbitol, a natural sugar.

Make sure your child's daily juice intake does not exceed 4 to 6 ounces (120–180 ml). To help regulate the amount of fruit juice your child drinks, offer juice with food to slow down the rate at which it's absorbed, and serve a combination of one-half juice and one-half water (see the table outlining fruit juices). If you offer him extra milk, formula, or juice at mealtimes, you may curb his appetite for solid foods. In fact, infants who drink too much fruit juice may become malnourished as a result of the juice replacing formula or human milk. Many fruit juices do not contain any significant amount of protein, fat, minerals, or vitamins other than vitamin C. So rather than giving your child juice in excess, try giving him water with his meals.

Your baby also may need extra water when he's ill, especially when he has a fever. Ask your pediatrician to help you determine how much water your baby needs at these times. The best fluid for a breastfed infant who is ill is breastmilk.

Fluoride Supplements

Babies do not require fluoride supplementation during the first six months of life, whether they are breastfed or formula-fed. After that time, breastfed and formula-fed infants need fluoride supplementation if local drinking water contains less than 0.3 parts per million (ppm) of fluoride. Your pediatrician or pediatric dentist can advise you on the need for fluoride drops for your baby.

Formula-fed infants receive some fluoride from their formula if the drinking water is fluoridated in their community or if it is made with bottled water with fluoride. The American Academy of Pediatrics recommends that you check with your pediatrician to find out if any additional fluoride supplements are necessary.

BURPING, HICCUPS, AND SPITTING UP

Burping

Young babies naturally fuss and get cranky when they swallow air during feedings. Although this occurs in both breastfed and bottle-fed infants, it's seen more often with the bottle. When it happens, you're better off stopping the feeding than letting your infant fuss and nurse at the same time. This continued fuss-

How Do You Burp a Baby?

Here are a few tried-and-true techniques. After a little experimentation, you'll find which ones work best for your child.

1. Hold the baby upright with his head on your shoulder, supporting his head and back while you gently pat his back with your other hand.

2. Sit the baby on your lap, supporting his chest and head with one hand while patting his back with your other hand.

3. Lay the baby on your lap with his back up. Support his head so it is higher than his chest, and gently pat or rotate your hand on his back.

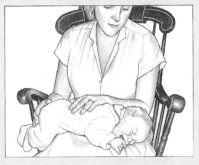

If he still hasn't burped after several minutes, continue feeding him and don't worry; no baby burps every time. When he's finished, burp him again and keep him in an upright position for ten to fifteen minutes so he doesn't spit up.

ing will cause her to swallow even more air, which will only increase her discomfort and may make her spit up.

A much better strategy is to burp her frequently, even if she shows no discomfort. The pause and the change of position alone will slow her gulping and reduce the amount of air she takes in. If she's bottle-feeding, burp her after every 2 to 3 ounces (60–90 ml). If she's nursing, burp her when she switches breasts. Some breastfed babies don't swallow very much air, and therefore they may not need to burp frequently.

Hiccups

Most babies hiccup from time to time. Usually this bothers parents more than the infant, but if hiccups occur during a feeding, change his position, try to get him to burp, or help him relax. Wait until the hiccups are gone to resume feeding. If they don't disappear on their own in five to ten minutes, try to resume feeding for a few minutes. Doing this usually stops them. If your baby gets hiccups often, try to feed him when he's calm and before he's extremely hungry. This will usually reduce the likelihood of hiccups occurring during the feeding.

Spitting Up

Spitting up is another common occurrence during infancy. Sometimes spitting up means the baby has eaten more than her stomach can hold; sometimes she spits up while burping or drooling. Although it may be a bit messy, it's usually no cause for concern. It almost never involves choking, coughing, discomfort, or danger to your child, even if it occurs while she's sleeping.

Some babies spit up more than others, but most are out of this phase by the time they are sitting. A few "heavy spitters" will continue until they start to walk or are weaned to a cup. Some may continue throughout their first year.

You should be able to tell the difference easily between normal spitting up and true vomiting. Unlike spitting up, which most babies don't even seem to notice, vomiting is forceful and usually causes great distress and discomfort for your child. It generally occurs soon after a meal and produces a much greater volume than spitting up. If your baby vomits on a regular basis (one or more times a day), consult your pediatrician. (See *Vomiting,* pages 175 and 522.)

While it is practically impossible to prevent all spitting up, the following steps will help you decrease the frequency of these episodes and the amount spit up.

1. Make each feeding calm, quiet, and leisurely.

2. Avoid interruptions, sudden noises, bright lights, and other distractions during feedings.

3. Burp your bottle-fed baby at least every three to five minutes during feedings.

4. Avoid feeding while your infant is lying down.

5. Place the baby in an upright position in an infant seat or stroller immediately after feeding.

6. Do not jostle or play vigorously with the baby immediately after feeding.

7. Try to feed her before she gets frantically hungry.

8. If bottle-feeding, make sure the hole in the nipple is neither too big (which lets the formula flow too fast) nor too small (which frustrates your baby and causes her to gulp air). If the hole is the proper size, a few drops should come out when you invert the bottle, and then stop.

9. Elevate the head of the entire crib with blocks (don't use a pillow) and put her to sleep on her back. This keeps her head higher than her stomach and prevents her from choking in case she spits up while sleeping.

As you can tell from the length and detail of this chapter, feeding your baby is one of the most important and, at times, confusing challenges you'll face as a parent. The recommendations in this section apply to infants in general. Please remember that your child is unique and may have special needs. If you have questions that these pages have not answered to your satisfaction, ask your pediatrician to help you find the answers that apply specifically to you and your infant.

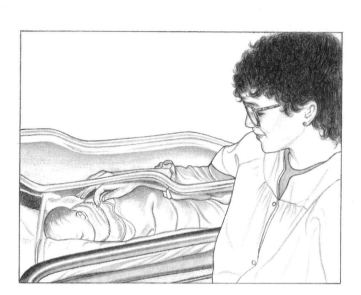

YOUR BABY'S FIRST DAYS

*A*fter all the months of pregnancy, you may believe that you already know your baby. You've felt her kicks, monitored her quiet and active periods during the day, and run your hands over your abdomen as she nestled in the womb. Although all of this does bring you closer to her, nothing can prepare you for the sight of her face and the grip of her fingers around yours.

For the first few days after her birth, you probably won't be able to take your eyes off her. Watching her, you may see hints of yourself or other members of the family reflected in her features. But for the most part, she is unlike anyone else. And she'll have a definite temperament of her own that will start making itself known immediately. As she turns and stretches, only she knows what she wants and feels. She may, for example, protest wet or messy diapers from the first day after birth, complaining loudly until she is changed and fed and rocked back to sleep. Infants who behave like this not only tend to spend more time awake than other babies, but they also may cry and eat more. Other newborns may not seem to notice when their diapers are dirty and may object to having their bottoms exposed to the cold air during changes. These babies probably sleep a lot and eat less frequently than the more sensitive infants. Such individual differences are early hints of your child's future personality.

Some mothers say that after so many months of literally "possessing" her in the womb, it becomes difficult to view the baby as a separate human being, with thoughts, emotions, and desires of her own. Making this adjustment and respecting her individuality, however, are important parts of being a parent. If you can welcome her uniqueness now at birth, you'll have a much easier time accepting the person she becomes in the years ahead.

YOUR NEWBORN'S FIRST DAYS

How Your Newborn Looks

As you relax with your baby in your own room, unwrap his blankets and examine him from head to toe. You'll notice many details that escaped you in the first moments after birth. For instance, when he opens his eyes, you'll see their color. Many Caucasian newborns have blue eyes, but they may change over the next year. Generally infants with dark-skinned heritage have brown eyes at birth, and they remain that color throughout life. If his eyes are going to turn brown, they'll probably become "muddy" during the first six months; if they're still blue at that time, they'll probably remain so.

You may notice a blood spot in the white area of one or both eyes. This, and the general puffiness of his face, are caused by pressures exerted during labor, but both will fade in a few days. If he was delivered by C-section, he won't have this puffiness and the whites of his eyes should be clear.

Bathed and dry, your baby's skin will seem very delicate. If he was born after his due date, he probably already lost his protective covering of vernix, and his skin would have been wrinkled and peeling at birth. If he was born on time or early, he may peel a little now because of the sudden exposure to air after the vernix is washed away. This is a normal process and requires no treatment. All babies, including those with a dark-skin heritage, have lighter appearing skin at birth. This gradually darkens as the child becomes older.

As you examine your baby's shoulders and back, you may notice some fine hair, called lanugo. Like the vernix, this hair is produced toward the end of pregnancy; however, it's usually shed before birth or soon thereafter. If your baby was born before his due date, he is more likely to still have this hair, and it may take a couple of weeks to disappear.

You also may notice a lot of pink spots and marks on your baby's skin. Some, like those that appear around the edges of his diaper, are simply due to pressure. Mottled or blotchy-looking patches are caused by exposure to cool air and will disappear quickly if you cover him again. If you find scratches, particularly

on his face, trim his finger-nails. (Check with the nursery nurse on how to do this, and keep his hands covered until you have a chance to do so.) Otherwise, he'll continue to scratch himself as he randomly moves his hands and arms.

Your baby also may have rashes and birthmarks. Most will fade quickly without treatment, but some may be permanent. These are the most common newborn rashes and birthmarks:

Salmon Patches or "Stork Bites." Patches of deep pink, usually located on the bridge of the nose, lower forehead, upper eyelids, back of the head, or neck. The most common birthmark, especially in light-skinned babies, they disappear over the first few months.

Mongolian Spots. Large, flat areas containing extra pigment, which appear green or blue (like a bruise) on the back or buttocks. Very common, especially in dark-skinned babies. They usually disappear by school age and are of no significance.

Pustular Melanosis. Small blisters that quickly dry and peel away, leaving dark spots like freckles. Some babies have only the spots, indicating that they had the rash before birth. The spots disappear in several weeks.

Milia. Tiny white bumps or yellow spots across the tip of the nose or chin, caused by skin gland secretion. They appear raised but are nearly flat and smooth to the touch. They disappear in the first two to three weeks of life.

Miliaria. A raised rash consisting of small fluid-filled blisters. The fluid is normal skin secretion and may be clear or milky white. Miliaria usually disappears with normal skin cleansing.

Erythema Toxicum. A rash of red splotches with yellowish-white bumps in the centers. They generally appear only during the first day after birth and disappear without treatment within the first week or so.

Capillary or Strawberry Hemangiomas. Raised red spots with a rough texture. For the first week or so, they may appear white or pale, then turn red later. Caused by dilated blood vessels in the top layers of the skin, they enlarge during the first few months, then gradually shrink and disappear without treatment.

Port Wine Stain. Large, flat, irregularly shaped red or purple areas. They're caused by a surplus of blood vessels under the skin. They won't disappear without treatment, which can be performed when the child is older by either a plastic surgeon or a pediatric dermatologist.

(See also *Birthmarks and Hemangiomas,* page 689.)

If your baby was born vaginally, in addition to the elongated shape of her head, there also may be some scalp swelling in the area that was pushed out first during birth. If you press on this area, your finger may even leave a small indentation. This swelling is not serious and should disappear in a few days.

Swelling under the scalp also sometimes is visible several hours after birth, probably due to bleeding. (The bleeding occurs outside the skull bones, not inside the brain.) This swelling often is present on only one side of the head, and will seem to spring right back after you press on it. This swelling, too, is caused by the intense pressure on the head during labor. It is not serious, although it usually takes six to ten weeks to disappear.

All babies have two soft spots, or fontanelles, on the top of the head. These are the areas where the immature bones of the skull are still growing together. The larger opening is on the top of the head toward the front; a smaller one is at the back. You needn't be afraid to touch these areas gently. They are covered by a thick, durable membrane that protects the brain.

All infants are born with hair but the amount, texture, and color varies from child to child. This "baby hair" falls out during the first six months of life as it is being replaced by mature hair. The color and texture of the mature hair may be quite different from the "baby hair."

Babies are affected by the large amount of hormones manufactured by their mothers during pregnancy. As a result, your baby's breasts may be enlarged temporarily and might even secrete a few drops of milk. This is equally likely in boy and girl babies, and normally lasts less than a week, although it can last several weeks. Don't try to compress or manipulate the breasts, since this won't reduce the swelling and could cause infection.

As you examine your baby's abdomen, it will seem prominent, and you may notice spaces between the abdominal muscles where the skin protrudes during crying spells. The spaces may be in a line down the center of the abdomen or in a circle at the base of the umbilical cord. This is normal and disappears within about one year.

The stub of the umbilical cord is white, translucent, and shiny right after birth. If it was painted with antibacterial dye in the hospital when she was born, it may look blue. The stub quickly will begin to dry and shrink. It should fall off within three weeks.

The genitals of newborn babies are often reddish and seem quite large for bodies so small. Girls may have clear, white, or slightly bloody vaginal discharge, caused by exposure to their mother's hormones during pregnancy. The

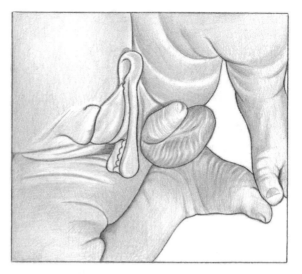

The stub of the umbilical cord is white, translucent, and shiny right after birth. The genitals of newborn babies often seem quite large for bodies so small.

scrotum of a baby boy may be smooth and barely big enough to hold the testicles; or it might be large and wrinkled. The testicles can move in and out of the scrotum. Sometimes they will retract as far as the base of the penis or even to the crease at the top of the thigh. As long as they are located in the scrotum most of the time, this is normal.

Some boys have a buildup of fluid in a sac called a hydrocele (see page 514) inside the scrotum. This buildup will shrink gradually without treatment over several months as the fluid is reabsorbed by the body. If the scrotum swells up suddenly or gets larger when the baby cries, notify your pediatrician; this could be a sign of an inguinal hernia, which requires treatment.

At birth the foreskin is attached to the head, or glans, of the penis, and cannot be pushed back as it can in older boys and men. There is a small opening at the tip through which urine flows. If you have your son circumcised, the connections between the foreskin and the glans are artificially separated and the foreskin is removed, leaving the glans visible. Without a circumcision, the foreskin will separate from the glans naturally during the first few years.

While you're still in the hospital, the staff will watch carefully for your baby's first urination and bowel movement to make sure she has no problem with elimination. These may occur right after birth or up to a day later. The first bowel movement or two will be dark black-green and very slimy. They contain meconium, a substance that fills the infant's intestines during pregnancy and that must be eliminated before normal digestion and passage of new stool can take place. If meconium is not passed within the baby's first forty-eight hours, it could mean that a problem exists in the lower bowel.

If you notice a little blood in the bowel movements during these first few days, it probably means that the infant swallowed some of your blood during birth or while nursing if she is breastfed. Although the baby won't be harmed by this in any way, it's best to let your pediatrician know about it so he can make

Care of the Penis

Caring for the Circumcised Penis. If you choose to have your son circumcised, the procedure probably will be performed on the second or third day after birth, unless it is delayed for religious reasons. Afterward, a light dressing such as gauze with petroleum jelly will be placed over the head of the penis. The next time the baby urinates, this dressing usually will come off. Some pediatricians recommend keeping a clean dressing on until the penis is fully healed, while others advise leaving it off. The important thing is to keep the area as clean as possible. If particles of stool get on the penis, wipe it gently with soap and water during diaper changes.

The tip of the penis may look quite red for the first few days, and you may notice a yellow secretion. Both indicate that the area is healing normally. The redness and secretion should disappear gradually within a week. If the redness persists or there is swelling or crusted yellow sores that contain cloudy fluid, there may be an infection. This does not happen very often, but if you suspect that infection is present, consult your pediatrician.

Usually, after the circumcision has healed, the penis requires no additional care. Occasionally a small piece of the foreskin remains. You should pull back this skin gently each time the child is bathed. Examine the groove around the head of the penis and make sure it's clean.

Occasionally circumcision must be postponed because of prematurity or other medical problems. If it is not performed within the baby's first week, it is usually put off for several weeks or months. Your pediatrician will determine the best time for the circumcision. The follow-up care is the same, whenever it is performed.

sure this is really the reason behind it; if the actual cause is internal bleeding, immediate treatment will be necessary.

Your Baby's Birth Weight and Measurements

Did your baby weigh more or less than you had anticipated? His birth weight may have been affected by a number of factors, including:

- Length of pregnancy before delivery: The later in the nine-month cycle he was born, the larger he may be.

- Parents' size: If both Mom and Dad are unusually large or small, the baby may follow suit.

Caring for the Uncircumcised Penis. In the first few months, you should simply clean and bathe your baby's uncircumcised penis with soap and water, like the rest of the diaper area. Initially, the foreskin is connected by tissue to the glans, or head, of the penis, so you shouldn't try to retract it. No cleansing of the penis with cotton swabs or antiseptics is necessary, but you should watch your baby urinate occasionally to make sure that the hole in the foreskin is large enough to permit a normal stream. If the stream consistently is no more than a trickle, or if your baby seems to have some discomfort while urinating, consult your pediatrician.

The doctor will tell you when the foreskin has separated and can be retracted safely. This will not be for several months to years, and should never be forced; if you were to force the foreskin to retract before it is ready, you could cause painful bleeding and tears in the skin. After this separation occurs, retract the foreskin occasionally to gently cleanse the end of the penis underneath.

Once your son is out of diapers, you'll need to teach him what he must do in order to urinate and wash his penis. Teach him to clean his foreskin by:

- Gently pulling it back away from the head of the penis.

- Rinsing the head of the penis and inside fold of the foreskin with soap and warm water.

- Pulling the foreskin back over the head of the penis.

- Complications during pregnancy: If the mother's blood pressure was high or she had certain other illnesses during pregnancy, the baby might be small. If she had diabetes during pregnancy, however, the baby might be larger than expected.

- Nutrition during pregnancy: If the baby was not getting enough nourishment while inside the uterus, either because the mother's diet was very poor or because of a medical problem with pregnancy, she might be smaller than expected.

- Mother's smoking or alcohol or drug usage during pregnancy.

If your baby is either much larger or much smaller than average, he's more likely to have problems adjusting to life outside the womb. To determine how

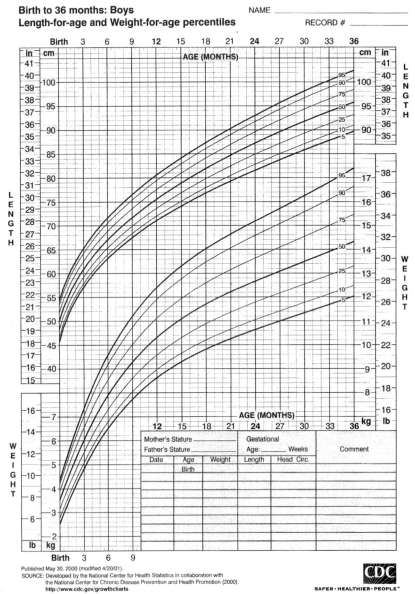

Birth to 36 months: Boys
Length-for-age and Weight-for-age percentiles

NAME _____

RECORD # _____

Published May 30, 2000 (modified 4/20/01).
SOURCE: Developed by the National Center for Health Statistics in collaboration with
the National Center for Chronic Disease Prevention and Health Promotion (2000).
http://www.cdc.gov/growthcharts

CDC
SAFER · HEALTHIER · PEOPLE™

his measurements compare with those of other babies born after the same length of pregnancy, your pediatrician will refer to one of the growth charts on the following pages.

The first two growth charts examine length and weight in boys and girls, from birth to thirty-six months. They are followed by body mass index for age charts for boys and girls, ages two to twenty years. (Body mass index, or BMI, is a measure of weight in relation to height.)

As you can see in the first two charts, eighty out of every one hundred babies born at forty weeks of pregnancy, or full term, weigh between 5 pounds 11½

Birth to 36 months: Girls
Length-for-age and Weight-for-age percentiles

NAME _____

RECORD # _____

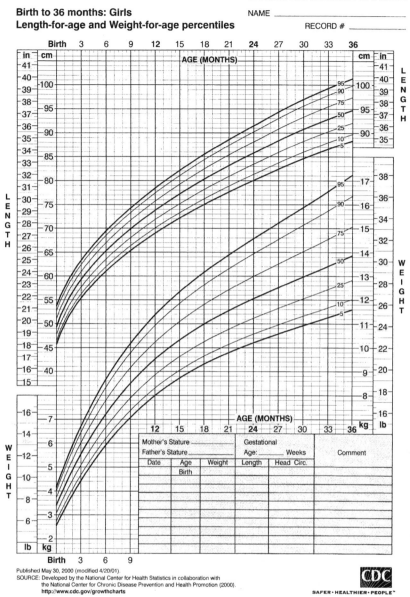

Published May 30, 2000 (modified 4/20/01).
SOURCE: Developed by the National Center for Health Statistics in collaboration with
the National Center for Chronic Disease Prevention and Health Promotion (2000).
http://www.cdc.gov/growthcharts

CDC
SAFER·HEALTHIER·PEOPLE™

ounces (2.6 kg) and 8 pounds 5¾ ounces (3.8 kg). This is a healthy average. Those above the ninetieth percentile on the chart are considered large, and those below the tenth percentile are regarded as small. Initially some large babies may have difficulty regulating their blood-sugar levels and may require extra feedings to prevent hypoglycemia (low blood sugar). Small babies may have problems feeding or regulating their body temperature. Incidentally, these early weight designations (large or small) do not predict whether your child will be above or below average when he grows up; but they do help the hospital staff determine whether he needs extra attention during the first few days after birth.

2 to 20 years: Boys
Body mass index-for-age percentiles

NAME _____

RECORD # _____

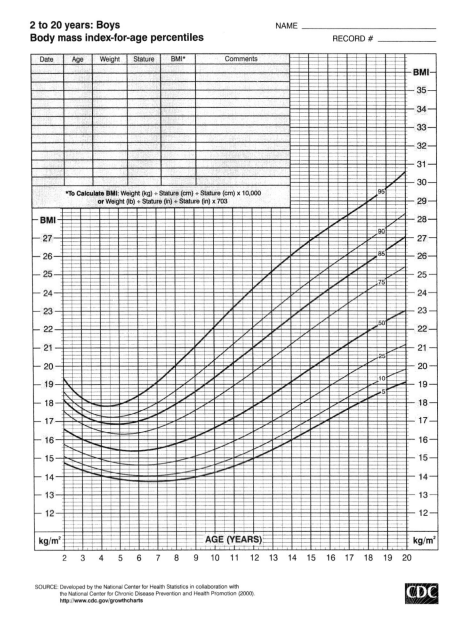

SOURCE: Developed by the National Center for Health Statistics in collaboration with
the National Center for Chronic Disease Prevention and Health Promotion (2000).
http://www.cdc.gov/growthcharts

At every physical exam, beginning with the first one after birth, your pediatrician will take certain measurements. She'll routinely measure your baby's length, weight, and head circumference (the distance around his head) and will plot them on growth charts similar to the ones on these pages. In a healthy, well-nourished infant, these three measurements should increase at a predictable rate. Any interruption in this rate can help the doctor detect feeding, developmental, or medical problems.

2 to 20 years: Girls
Body mass index-for-age percentiles

NAME _____

RECORD # _____

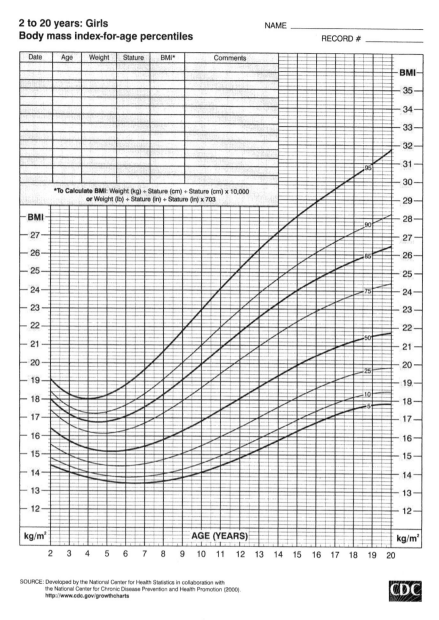

*To Calculate BMI: Weight (kg) ÷ Stature (cm) ÷ Stature (cm) x 10,000
or Weight (lb) ÷ Stature (in) ÷ Stature (in) x 703

SOURCE: Developed by the National Center for Health Statistics in collaboration with
the National Center for Chronic Disease Prevention and Health Promotion (2000).
http://www.cdc.gov/growthcharts

How Your Newborn Behaves

Lying in your arms or in the crib beside you, your newborn makes a tight little bundle. Just as he did in the womb, he'll keep his arms and legs bent up close to his body and his fingers tightly clenched, although you should be able to straighten them gently with your hands. His feet will naturally curve inward. It may take several weeks for his body to unfold from this preferred fetal position.

You'll have to wait even longer for him to make the cooing or babbling sounds

we generally think of as "baby talk." However, from the beginning he'll be very noisy. Besides crying when something is wrong, he'll have a wide variety of grunts, squeaks, sighs, sneezes, and hiccups. (You may even remember the hiccups from pregnancy!) Most of these sounds, just like his sudden movements, are reactions to disturbances around him; a shrill sound or a strong odor may be all it takes for him to jump or cry.

These reactions, as well as more subtle ones, are signs of how well your baby's senses are functioning at birth. After all those months in the womb, he'll quickly recognize his mother's voice (and possibly his father's, as well). If you play soothing music, he may become quiet as he listens or move gently in time with it.

By using his senses of smell and taste, he can distinguish breastmilk from any other liquid. Born with a sweet tooth, he'll prefer sugar water to plain water and will wrinkle his nose at sour or bitter scents and tastes.

Your baby's vision will be best within an 8- to 12-inch (20.3 to 30.5 cm) range, which means he can see your face perfectly as you hold and feed him. But when you are farther away, his eyes may wander, giving him a cross-eyed or wall-eyed appearance. Don't worry about this. As his eye muscles mature and his vision improves, both eyes will remain focused on the same thing at the same time. This usually occurs between two and three months of age. If it does not, check with your child's pediatrician.

While your infant will be able to distinguish light from dark at birth, he will not yet see the full range of colors. If you show him a pattern of black and white or sharply contrasting dark red and pale yellow, he probably will study it with interest; but if you show him a picture with lots of closely related colors, he may not respond at all.

Perhaps the newborn's most important sense is touch. After months of being bathed in warm fluid, his skin will now be exposed to all sorts of new sensations—some harsh, some wonderfully comforting. While he may cringe at a sudden gust of cold air, he'll love the feel of a soft blanket and the warmth of your arms around him. Holding your baby will give him as much pleasure as it does you. It will give him a sense of security and comfort, and it will tell him he is loved. Research shows it actually will promote his growth and development.

Going Home

If your baby is born in an alternative birthing center, you probably will go home within twenty-four hours. By contrast, you might spend up to three days in a hospital if yours was a routine delivery and up to a week if you had a C-section or an especially difficult delivery. Recently, however, even full-term babies who are well go home with their mothers within forty-eight hours after delivery.

From an emotional and physical standpoint, there are arguments for both a short and a long stay. Many women simply dislike being in the hospital; these women tend to feel more comfortable and relaxed at home. As soon as mother and baby are proclaimed healthy and able to travel, they're eager to leave. By keeping the hospital stay short, they'll certainly save themselves—or their insurance company—money. However, new mothers often cannot get as much rest at home as in the hospital—especially if there are older children clamoring for attention. Nor is there the support of the hospital nurses during the first days of breastfeeding and baby care. You should weigh these advantages and disadvantages carefully prior to making your decision about when to go home. If a newborn does leave the hospital early, he should be seen by his pediatrician twenty-four to forty-eight hours after discharge. Of course, the doctor should be called immediately if the baby appears listless or is feverish, vomiting, or develops a yellow color to his skin (jaundice).

Before you do leave the hospital, your home and car should be equipped with at least the bare essentials. At home you'll need a safe place for the baby to sleep, some diapers, and enough clothing and blankets to keep her warm and protected. If you're bottle-feeding, you'll also need a supply of formula. Finally, make sure you have a federally approved car safety seat in which your baby can ride on her trip home. The car safety seat should be placed in the backseat of your automobile, securely attached by the car seat belt. Follow installation instructions carefully. (For more information on the choice and proper use of car safety seats, see pages 447–460.)

WHERE WE STAND

The timing of discharge of a newborn from the hospital should be a mutual decision between the physician caring for the infant and the parents. The American Academy of Pediatrics believes that the health and well-being of the mother and her baby should take precedence over financial considerations. Academy policy has established minimum criteria for early discharge of a mother and her baby, which include term delivery, appropriate growth, and normal physical examination, and states that it is unlikely that all of its criteria can be met in less than forty-eight hours. The Academy supports state and federal legislation based on AAP guidelines as long as physicians, in consultation with parents, have the final authority in determining when to discharge the patient.

PARENTING ISSUES

Mother's Feelings

If you're like most new mothers, your first few days with your baby will be a mixture of delight, pain, utter exhaustion, and—especially if this is your first child—some apprehension about your capabilities as a parent. When the anxiety levels peak, it will be difficult to believe that you'll ever be an expert on baby care. But rest assured. As soon as you're home, things will start to fall into place. Instead of worrying while in the hospital, take advantage of the time to rest and let your body recover.

Quite often, women are so excited about their new arrival that they don't even notice how tired and sore they are. In spite of the fatigue, it still may be difficult to relax enough to fall asleep. Your rooming-in arrangements may add to the problem; however, if you imagine that every crying baby you hear is your own, having your baby sleep in the nursery may not give you the peace you thought it would. You can solve these problems by letting him sleep in his hospital-supplied bassinet next to you, so you can sleep when he does and hold him when he awakens.

On the other hand, particularly if you had a long, hard labor or a cesarean section, you simply may not have the strength to keep the baby with you full time. After having a C-section, you may find it uncomfortable to lift your baby for a few weeks; you may have to try different positions for holding and nursing him that put less strain on your stitches. These obstacles may make you feel that you're not bonding with your baby as you imagined you would; and you may feel especially disappointed if you had planned for a problem-free, natural delivery. Fortunately, your child's major preoccupation during these first few days also will be sleeping and recuperating, and he won't much care where he does it as long as he's warm, dry, and fed when he's hungry. So for the moment,

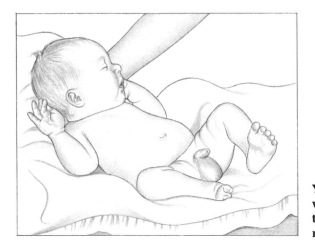

You have just given birth to a wonderful new being, but also to a new and awesome responsibility.

the hospital nursery will suit him fine. You will have plenty of time to form a secure bond with each other after your physical recoveries are complete.

If this is not your first child, there may be some questions on your mind, such as:

▪ Will this new baby come between you and an older child?

This needn't happen if you make a point of spending time separately with each child. As you develop a routine during your first weeks home with the new baby, make sure to include special times with your older child.

▪ Will you be able to give the same intensity of love to the new child?

In fact, each child is special and will draw out different responses and feelings from you. Even the birth order of your children may influence the way you relate to each of them.

▪ How can you avoid comparing one to another?

You may find yourself thinking that the new baby is not as beautiful or as alert as another child was right after birth, or you may worry because he's more attractive and attentive. In the beginning, these comparisons are inevitable, but as the new baby's own unique qualities begin to emerge, you'll become as proud of your children's differences as you are of their similarities.

On a more practical note, the prospect of taking care of two or more young children may worry you—and with good reason. Greater time demands and sibling rivalry loom before you, presenting a new, awesome challenge. Don't let yourself get overwhelmed by it. Given time and patience, all of you will adjust and learn to be a family.

If the newness, fatigue, and seemingly unanswerable questions push you to tears, don't feel bad. You won't be the first new mother to cry—or the last. If it makes you feel any better, your hormones are at least partly responsible for your fragile state.

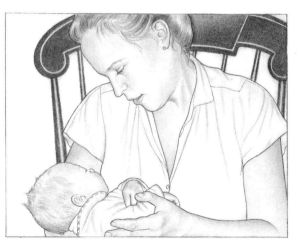

Do not be afraid to ask for help if your concerns seem too great for you to handle.

The hormonal changes you went through as an adolescent or experience during your menstrual cycle are minor compared to the hormonal overhaul you're undergoing after giving birth. Blame it on the hormones, and rest assured that this, too, shall pass.

In addition to the hormonal effects, significant emotional changes are taking place. You have just given birth not only to a wonderful new human being, but also to a new and awesome responsibility. There are significant changes taking place in your family life and your relationship with your husband. It is normal to think about these things and easy to attach too much importance to them.

The emotional changes of this time often lead to feelings of sadness, fear, irritability, or anxiety—or sometimes even anger toward your baby—feelings doctors call the postpartum blues or baby blues. About three out of four new mothers experience these baby blues a few days after birth. Fortunately, these feelings tend to subside on their own as quickly as they develop, typically lasting no more than several days.

Some new mothers, however, have such severe feelings of sadness, emptiness, apathy, and even despair that doctors categorize them as having postpartum depression. They also may experience feelings of inadequacy, and they may begin to withdraw from family and friends. These feelings may develop a few weeks after the baby is born and affect about one out of ten new mothers. The symptoms can last for many months (or even for more than a year), worsen with time, and become so intense that these mothers may feel helpless and incapable of caring for their baby and their other children. If they don't receive care for their postpartum depression, the condition may worsen with time, and in some cases they may worry about harming themselves or their baby. If you are breastfeeding, and medications for postpartum depression are recommended, check with your pediatrician as to their safety.

You should discuss your feelings with your husband and close friends and try to reduce your stress and anxiety by getting some exercise and as much rest as possible. If these feelings haven't subsided in about two weeks, talk to your obstetrician or pediatrician, or seek help from a mental health professional; counseling and/or antidepressant medications may be recommended. Do not be afraid to ask for help from professionals if your concerns seem too great for you to handle, or if you feel increasingly depressed. Although a certain amount of postdelivery depression may be normal, it should not be overwhelming or last more than a few days.

Father's Feelings

As a new dad, your role is no less complicated than your wife's. No, you didn't have to carry the baby for nine months, but you did have to make adjustments physically and emotionally as the due date approached and preparations for the baby became all important. On one hand, you may have felt as if you had nothing to do with this birth; but on the other, this is very much your baby, too.

When the baby finally arrived, you may have been tremendously relieved as well as excited and somewhat awed. In witnessing your baby's birth, feelings of commitment and love may have surfaced that you had worried you might never feel for this child. You also may experience a greater admiration and love for your wife than you ever felt before. At the same time, contemplating the responsibility of caring for this child for the next twenty years can be more than a little unnerving.

So how should you deal with all these conflicting emotions? The best approach is to become as actively involved in fathering as possible. For example, depending on the hospital and your own schedule, you may be able to room in with mother and/or child until it's time to take the baby home. This will help you feel less like a bystander and more like a key participant. You'll get to know your baby right from the start. It also will allow you to share an intense emotional experience with your wife.

Once the entire family is home, you can—and should—help feed (if bottle fed), diaper, bathe, and comfort your baby. Contrary to old-fashioned stereotypes, these jobs are not exclusively "woman's work." They are wonderful opportunities for all of you—mother, father, and even older siblings—to get to know and love this new family member.

Sibling's Feelings

Older children may greet a new baby with either open arms or closed minds. Their reaction will depend largely on their age and developmental level. Consider a toddler, for instance. There's little you can do to prepare her in advance for the changes that will come with a new sibling. To begin with, she'll be confused by the sudden disappearance of her parents when the baby is born. Upon visiting the hospital, she may be frightened by the sight of her mother in bed, perhaps attached to intravenous tubing.

She also may be jealous that her parents are holding someone else instead of

Let the older sibling know frequently that there's enough room and love in your heart for both children.

her, and she may misbehave or begin acting younger—for example, by insisting on wearing diapers or suddenly having accidents several months after being toilet-trained. These are normal responses to stress and change, and don't deserve discipline. Instead of punishing her or insisting that she share your love for the new baby, give her extra love and reassurance. Her attachment to the baby will build gradually and naturally over time.

If your older child is a preschooler, she'll be better able to understand what's happening. By preparing her during the pregnancy, you can help ease her confusion, if not her jealousy. She can understand the basic facts of the situation ("The baby is in Mommy's tummy"; "The baby will sleep in my old crib"), and she probably will be very curious about this mysterious person.

Once the baby is born, the older sibling still will miss her parents and resent the infant for being the new center of attention. But praising her for helping out and acting "grown-up" will let her know that she, too, has an important new role to play. Make sure she still gets some time to be the important one and is allowed to be the baby when she needs to. And let her know frequently that there's enough room and love in your heart for both children.

If your older child is of school age, she shouldn't feel threatened by the newcomer in the family. She'll probably be fascinated by the process of pregnancy and childbirth and be eager to meet the new baby. Once the infant arrives, you can expect the older child to be very proud and protective. Let her help take care of the little one, but don't forget that she still needs time and attention herself. Even if she doesn't demand it, set aside some time each day to spend with her alone.

(If you're the grandparent of a newborn, see Chapter 6 [pages 168–169] for some thoughts about your new role now that your new grandson or granddaughter has arrived.)

HEALTH WATCH

Some physical conditions are especially common during the first couple of weeks after birth. If you notice any of the following in your baby, contact your pediatrician.

Abdominal Distension. Most babies' abdomens normally stick out, especially after a large feeding. Between feedings, however, the belly should feel quite soft. If your child's abdomen feels swollen and hard, and if he has not had a bowel movement for more than one or two days or is vomiting, call your pediatrician. Most likely the problem is due to gas or constipation, but it also could signal a more serious intestinal problem.

Birth Injuries. The baby can be injured during birth if labor is particularly long or difficult, or if she is very large. Quite often the injury is a broken collarbone, which will heal quickly if the arm on that side is kept relatively motionless; your pediatrician will advise you how to do this. Incidentally, after a few weeks a small lump may form at the site of the fracture, but don't be alarmed; this is a positive sign that new bone is forming to mend the injury.

Muscle weakness is another common birth injury, caused during labor by pressure or stretching of the nerves attached to the muscles. These muscles, usually weakened on one side of the face or one shoulder or arm, generally return to normal after several weeks. In the meantime, ask your pediatrician to show you how to nurse and hold the baby to promote healing.

Blue Baby. Blue hands and feet are nothing to worry about in a newborn. His face, tongue, and lips may turn a little blue occasionally when crying hard, but once he becomes calm, his color in these areas should quickly return to normal. Likewise, if his hands and feet turn a bit blue from cold, they should return to pink as soon as they are warm. Persistently blue skin coloring is a sign that the heart or lungs are not operating properly, and the baby is not getting enough oxygen in the blood. Immediate medical attention is essential.

Coughing. If your baby eats very fast or is trying to drink water for the first time, she may choke, cough, and sputter a bit; but the coughing should stop as soon as she adjusts to a familiar feeding routine. If she coughs persistently or routinely chokes during feedings, consult your pediatrician. These symptoms could indicate an underlying problem in the lungs or digestive tract.

Excessive Crying. All newborns cry, often for no apparent reason. If you've made sure that your baby is fed, burped, warm, and dressed in a clean diaper, the best tactic is probably to hold him and talk or sing to him until he stops. You cannot "spoil" a baby this age by giving him too much attention. If this doesn't work, wrap him snugly in a blanket or try some of the tactics listed on pages 43–44.

You'll become accustomed to your baby's normal pattern of crying. If it ever sounds peculiar—for example, like shrieks of pain—or if it persists for an unusual length of time, it could mean a medical problem. Call the pediatrician and ask for advice.

Forceps Marks. When forceps are used to help during a delivery, the baby may have red marks or even superficial scrapes on her face and head where the metal pressed against her skin. These should disappear within a few days. Sometimes a firm, flat lump develops in one of these areas because of minor damage to the tissue under the skin, but this, too, usually will go away within two months.

Jaundice. Most normal, healthy infants develop a yellowish tinge to their skin in the first few days of life. This condition, called jaundice, occurs when a chemical known as bilirubin builds up in the baby's blood. Bilirubin is formed from the body's normal breakdown of red blood cells, and it is usually cleared very quickly from the blood. Newborns tend to have higher bilirubin levels because their immature liver is not very good at removing it, and they produce more of it than the liver can handle.

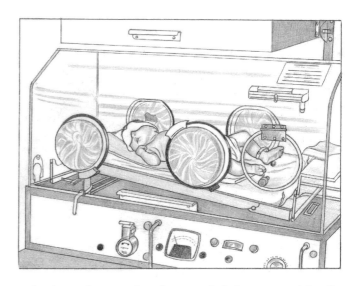

In phototherapy treatment for jaundice, the baby is placed under fluorescent-type lights for a day or two.

Jaundice appears first on the face, then on the chest and abdomen, and finally on the arms and legs. Typically, after worsening for a few days, the jaundice subsides without treatment. If the bilirubin level is extremely high and does not decline, there's a risk of damage to the nervous system. Your doctor will order blood tests to determine the cause and may recommend treatment with phototherapy. In this procedure, the baby is placed under special lights for a day or two until the liver matures enough to handle the bilirubin load. His eyes will be covered during the treatments to protect them from the light. Normal daylight has a similar effect, but is not intense enough to help. Direct sunlight is not more effective, and should be avoided because of the danger of sunburn.

Breastmilk, incidentally, sometimes interferes with the liver's ability to process bilirubin, so breastfeeding may prolong jaundice in some newborns. When that happens, your pediatrician may recommend that you consider halting breastfeeding briefly (for no more than forty-eight hours) to help decrease the bilirubin levels. This approach will be taken only when absolutely necessary, since the baby's frequent sucking at the breast during these first few days is crucial to stimulate the mother's milk supply. Or your pediatrician may recommend that you supplement with formula after breastfeeding for a day or two to help increase bilirubin excretion. As soon as the bilirubin level begins to decrease, your doctor will advise you to return solely to breastfeeding. (For additional information about jaundice, see pages 38 and 174.)

Lethargy and Sleepiness. Every newborn spends most of his time sleeping. As long as he wakes up every few hours, eats well, seems content, and is alert part of the day, it's perfectly normal for him to sleep the rest of the time. But if he's rarely alert, does not wake up on his own for feedings, or seems too tired or uninterested to eat, you should consult your pediatrician. This lethargy—especially if it's a sudden change in his usual pattern—may be a symptom of a serious illness.

Respiratory Distress. It may take your baby a few hours after birth to form a normal pattern of breathing, but then she should have no further difficulties. If she does show any of the following warning signs, however, notify your pediatrician immediately:

- Fast breathing (more than sixty breaths in one minute)
- Retractions (sucking in the muscles between the ribs with each breath, so that her ribs stick out)
- Flaring of her nose
- Grunting while breathing
- Persistent blue skin coloring

Umbilical Cord. You'll need to keep the stump of the umbilical cord clean and dry as it shrivels and, within a few weeks, eventually falls off. At each diaper change, use a cotton swab (soaked in rubbing alcohol and then squeezed) to clean away the wet, sticky material that sometimes collects where the base of the stump meets the skin. This will help dry the cord, as will exposing it to air. Also keep the diaper folded below the cord to keep urine from soaking it. You may notice a few drops of blood on the diaper around the time the stump falls off; this is normal. If the stump becomes infected, however, it will require medical treatment, so alert your pediatrician if you notice any of these signs of infection:

- Pus at the base of the cord
- Red skin around the base of the cord
- Crying when you touch the cord or the skin next to it. (If your baby cries when the alcohol is applied, that is normal, because it's cold, but crying at the touch of your finger is not.)

Umbilical Granuloma. Occasionally, after the umbilical cord has fallen off, the remaining area will continue to be moist and may swell slightly. This is called an umbilical granuloma. If it is small, your pediatrician will treat it by applying a drying medication called silver nitrate. If this is not successful, or if the area continues to enlarge or ooze, it may have to be tied off and surgically removed. This is a minor procedure that does not require anesthetic or a hospital stay.

Umbilical Hernia. If your baby's umbilical cord area seems to push outward when he cries, he may have an umbilical hernia—a small hole in the muscular part of the abdominal wall that allows tissue to bulge out when there's pressure inside the abdomen (e.g., when the baby cries). This is not a serious condition, and it usually heals by itself in the first twelve to eighteen months. (For unknown reasons it takes longer to heal in African American babies.) In the unlikely event that it doesn't heal, the hole may need to be surgically closed.

YOUR NEWBORN'S FIRST PHYSICAL EXAMS

Your baby should have one thorough physical examination within her first twenty-four hours and a follow-up at some point before you and she leave the hospital. If you take your baby home early (less than twenty-four hours after delivery), your pediatrician should see the baby again in her office twenty-four to forty-eight hours after discharge for follow-up. The purpose of this visit is to assess the baby's general health, identify any new problems, discuss issues such as the baby's stool and urine patterns, and review feeding techniques, including those associated with breastfeeding (adequate position, latch-on, and swallowing). The American Academy of Pediatrics also recommends that you and your baby schedule a doctor's visit when he's age two to four weeks. As we described in Chapter 3 (pages 71–72), your doctor will physically examine your baby and take measurements such as his length, weight, and head circumference. She'll listen to your baby's heart and lungs to ensure that they are normal; look into his eyes, ears, and mouth; feel his abdomen for tenderness; evaluate the healing of the navel and a baby boy's circumcision; check his reflexes; and examine other parts of the body, from head to toe. She'll ask about your baby's feedings (breast or formula), and urine and stool habits. She'll inquire about how your baby is sleeping (and whether you place him on his back for sleep).

These early visits to the pediatrician are also opportunities to ask questions about baby care and relieve any worries you may have. Don't hesitate to ask questions that sound unimportant; the answers may provide valuable information and be reassuring to you.

Blood Tests

While your baby was in the hospital, he should have undergone a series of newborn screening tests. In all states, in fact, newborns are required to be screened for certain serious congenital diseases. (See page 40 for a discussion of these newborn screening tests.) For example, one of these tests detects phenylketonuria (PKU); this condition, which causes mental retardation, can be prevented if the problem is detected early and treated with a special diet. Screening tests also are done for congenital hypothyroidism (a problem that can lead to mental retardation) and, in some states, for sickle-cell anemia (a blood disease found chiefly among African Americans) and other disorders.

These tests involve pricking the baby's heel to obtain a small blood sample on which the laboratory work can be performed. The PKU test is best done as close as possible to the time of discharge from the nursery. If the test is done before twenty-four hours of age, it may not be accurate and you will have to visit your pediatrician to have it done a second time. The repeat test should be completed no later than the third week of life.

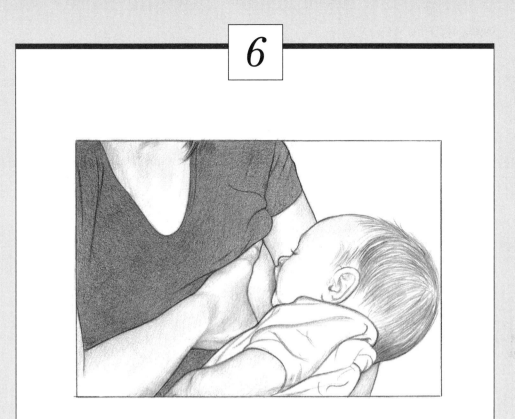

6

THE FIRST MONTH

GROWTH AND DEVELOPMENT

*I*n the very beginning, it may seem that your baby does nothing but eat, sleep, cry, and fill his diapers. By the end of the first month, he'll be much more alert and responsive. Gradually he'll begin moving his body more smoothly and with much greater coordination—especially in getting his hand to his mouth. You'll realize that he listens when you speak, watches you as you hold him, and occasionally moves his own body to respond to you or attract your attention. But before we explore his expanding capabilities, let's look at the changes that will occur in his physical appearance during the first month.

Physical Appearance and Growth

When your baby was born, her birth weight included excess body fluid, which she lost during her first few days. Most babies lose about one-tenth of their birth weight during the first five days, then regain it over the next five, so that by about day 10 they usually are back to their original birth weight. You can plot your own infant's growth on the charts on pages 128 to 131.

Most babies grow very rapidly after regaining their birth weight, especially during growth spurts, which occur around seven to ten days and again between three and six weeks. The average newborn gains weight at a rate of ⅔ of an ounce (20–30 grams) per day and by one month weighs about 9 pounds (4 kg). She grows between 1 and 1½ inches (2.5 to 4 cm) during this month. Boys tend to weigh slightly more than girls (by less than 1 pound, or approximately 400 grams). They also tend to be slightly longer than girls at this age (by about ½ inch, or 1.25 cm).

Your pediatrician will pay particular attention to your child's head growth, because it reflects the growth of her brain. The skull should grow faster during the first four months than at any other time in her life. The average newborn's head circumference measures about 13¾ inches (35 cm), growing to about 14¾ inches (37.5 cm) by one month. Because boys tend to be slightly larger than girls, their heads are larger, though the average difference is less than ⅓ inch (1 cm).

During these first weeks your baby's body gradually will straighten from the tightly curled position she held inside the uterus during the final months of pregnancy. She'll begin to stretch her arms and legs and may arch her back from time to time. Her legs and feet may continue to rotate inward, giving her a bowlegged look. This condition usually will correct itself gradually over the next five to six months. If the bowlegged appearance is particularly severe or associated with pronounced curving of the front part of the foot, your pediatrician may suggest a splint or a cast to correct it, but these circumstances are extremely unusual. (See *Bowlegs and Knock-Knees,* page 683; *Pigeon Toes [Intoeing],* page 686.)

If your baby was born vaginally and her skull appeared misshapen at birth, it soon will resume its normal shape. Any bruising of the scalp or swelling of the eyelids that occurred during birth will be gone by the end of the first week or two. Any red spots in the eyes will disappear in about three weeks.

To your dismay, you may discover that the fine hair that covered your child's head when she was born soon begins falling out. If she rubs the back of her head on her bedding, she may develop a temporary bald spot there, even if the rest of her hair remains. This loss is insignificant. The bare spots will be covered with new hair in a few months.

Another normal development is baby acne—pimples that break out on the face, usually during the fourth or fifth week of life. They are thought to be due to stimulation of oil glands in the skin by hormones passed across the placenta during pregnancy. This condition may be made worse if the baby lies in sheets laundered in harsh detergents or soiled by milk that she's spit up. If your baby does have baby acne, place a soft, clean receiving blanket under her head while she's awake and wash her face gently once a day with a mild baby soap to remove milk or detergent residue.

Your newborn's skin also may look blotchy, ranging in color from pink to blue. Her hands and feet in particular may be colder and bluer than the rest of her body. The blood vessels leading to these areas are more sensitive to temperature changes and tend to shrink in response to cold. As a result, less blood gets to the exposed skin, causing it to look pale or bluish. If you move her arms and legs, however, you'll notice that they quickly turn pink again.

Your baby's internal "thermostat," which causes her to perspire when she's too hot or shiver when she's too cold, won't be working properly for some time. Also, in these early weeks, she'll lack the insulating layer of fat that will protect her from sudden temperature shifts later on. For these reasons, it's important for you to dress her properly—warmly in cool weather and lightly when it's hot. Don't automatically bundle her up just because she's a baby.

By the third week, the stump from the umbilical cord should have dried and fallen off, leaving behind a clean, well-healed area. Occasionally a raw spot is left after the stump is gone. It may even ooze a little blood-tinged fluid. Just keep it clean and dry, and it will heal by itself. If it is not completely closed and dry in two weeks, consult your doctor.

Reflexes

Much of your baby's activity in his first weeks of life is reflexive. For instance, when you put your finger in his mouth, he doesn't think about what to do, but sucks by reflex. When confronted by a bright light, he will tightly shut his eyes, because that's what his reflexes make him do. He's born with many of these automatic responses, some of which remain with him for months, while others vanish in weeks.

In some cases, reflexes change into voluntary behavior. For example, your baby is born with a "rooting" reflex that prompts him to turn his head toward your hand if you stroke his cheek or mouth. This helps him find the nipple at feeding time. At first he'll root from side to side, turning his head toward the nipple and then away in decreasing arcs. But by about three weeks he'll simply turn his head and move his mouth into position to suck.

Sucking is another survival reflex present even before birth. If you had an ultrasound test done during pregnancy, you may have seen your baby sucking his thumb. After birth, when a nipple (either breast or bottle) is placed in your baby's mouth and touches the roof of his mouth, he automatically begins to suck. This motion actually takes place in two stages: First, he places his lips around the areola and squeezes the nipple between his tongue and palate. (Called expression, this action forces out the milk.) Then comes the second phase, or the milking action, in which the tongue moves from the areola to the nipple. This whole process is helped by the negative pressure, or suction, that secures the breast in the baby's mouth.

Coordinating these rhythmic sucking movements with breathing and swallowing is a relatively complicated task for a newborn. So even though this is a reflexive action, not all babies suck efficiently at first. With practice, however, the reflex becomes a skill that they all manage well.

As rooting, sucking, and bringing his hand to his mouth become less reflexive

Newborn Reflexes

The following are some of the normal inborn reflexes you will see your baby perform during her first weeks. Not all infants acquire and lose these reflexes at exactly the same time, but this table will give you a general idea of what to expect.

Reflex	Age When Reflex Appears	Age When Reflex Disappears
Moro reflex	Birth	2 months
Walking/stepping	Birth	2 months
Rooting	Birth	4 months
Tonic neck reflex	Birth	5–7 months
Palmar grasp	Birth	5–6 months
Plantar grasp	Birth	9–12 months

and more directed, your infant will start to use these movements to console himself. Have you already seen him nestling into his blanket or gnawing on his hand when he's tired? You may want to encourage these consoling techniques by giving him a pacifier or helping him find his thumb.

Another, more dramatic reflex present during these first few weeks is called the Moro reflex. If your baby's head shifts positions abruptly or falls backward, or he is startled by something loud or abrupt, he will react by throwing out his arms and legs and extending his neck, then rapidly bringing his arms together as he cries loudly. The Moro reflex peaks during the first month and then disappears after two months.

One of the more interesting automatic responses is the tonic neck reflex, otherwise known as the fencing posture. You may notice that when your baby's head turns to one side, his arm on that side will straighten, with the opposite arm bent as if he's fencing. Do not be surprised if you don't see this response, however. It is subtle, and if your baby is disturbed or crying, he may not perform it. It disappears at five to seven months of age.

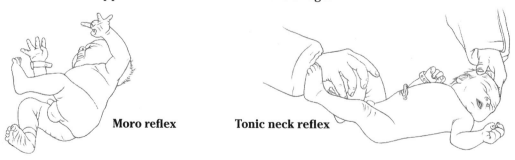

Moro reflex   **Tonic neck reflex**

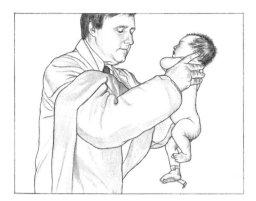

Walking/stepping reflex

You'll see still another reflex when you stroke the palm of your baby's hand and watch him immediately grip your finger. Or stroke the sole of his foot, and watch it flex as the toes curl tightly. In the first few days after birth, your baby's grasp will be so strong that it seem he can hold his own weight—but don't try it. He has no control over this response and may let go suddenly.

Aside from his "herculean" strength, your baby's other special talent is stepping. He can't support his own weight, of course, but if you hold him under the arms (being careful to support his head, as well) and let his soles touch a flat surface, he'll place one foot in front of the other and "walk." This reflex will disappear after two months, then recur as the learned voluntary behavior of walking toward the end of the first year.

Although you may think of your baby as utterly defenseless, he actually has several protective reflexes. For instance, if a blanket or a pillow falls over his eyes, nose, or mouth, he'll shake his head from side to side and flail his arms to push it away so he can breathe and see. Or if an object comes straight toward him, he'll turn his head and try to squirm out of its way. (Amazingly, if the object is on a path that would make it a near miss instead of a collision, he will calmly watch it approach without flinching.) Yes, he's dependent on you, but he's not totally defenseless.

States of Consciousness

As you get to know your baby, you'll soon realize that there are times when he's very alert and active, times when he's watchful but rather passive, and times when he's tired and irritable. You may even try to schedule your daily activities to capitalize on his "up" times and avoid overextending him during the "down" periods. Don't count on this schedule, however. These so-called states of consciousness will change dramatically in this first month.

There are actually six states of consciousness through which your baby cycles several times a day. Two are sleep states; the others are waking states.

State 1 is deep sleep, when the baby lies quietly without moving and is relatively unresponsive. If you shake a rattle loudly in his ear, he may stir a little, but not much. During lighter, more active sleep (State 2), the same noise will startle him and may awaken him. During this light sleep, you also can see the rapid movements of his eyes beneath his closed eyelids. He will alternate between these two sleep states, cycling through both of them within a given hour. Sometimes he'll retreat into these sleep states when he's overstimulated, as well as when he's physically tired.

Early Brain Development

As a parent, you know that your actions affect your child. You laugh, she laughs. You praise him, he gloats. You frown at her misbehavior, she saddens. You are at the center of your child's universe.

Research shows that during the first three years of a baby's life, the brain grows and develops significantly and patterns of thinking and responding are established. What does this mean for you as a parent? It means that you have a very special opportunity to help your baby develop appropriately and thrive socially, physically, and cognitively throughout her life. The first years last forever.

For years, people have mistakenly believed that the baby's brain is an exact replica of the genetic codes of her parents. For example, if the mother is a good artist, then the baby has more potential to possess the same artistic skills when she grows up. While genetics does play a role in determining your child's skills and abilities, new research highlights the equally significant role that environment plays. Recently neuroscientists realized that the experiences that fill a baby's first days, months, and years have a great impact on how the brain develops. Both nature and nurture work hand in hand in the development of young children.

Studies have shown that children need certain elements in the early stages of life to grow and develop to their full potential:

- A child needs to feel special, loved, and valued.

- She needs to feel safe.

- She needs to feel confident about what to expect from her environment.

- She needs guidance.

- She needs a balanced experience of freedom and limits.

- She needs to be exposed to a diverse environment filled with language, play, exploration, books, music, and appropriate toys.

While it may seem that what goes on in a baby's brain would be relatively simple compared to an adult's, in fact, a baby's brain is twice as active as an adult's brain. Neuroscientists are focusing especially on the first three years of a baby's life because they have identified these as times of special importance. During these years, the human brain has the greatest potential for learning. Not only is learning occurring rapidly, but basic ways of thinking, responding, and solving problems are established. For example, notice how easy it is for a child to pick up words from a foreign language. How difficult is that same task for an adult?

What does this mean for you as a parent? It means that you and the environment that you create for your baby will influence the way she deals with her emotions, the way she interacts with people, the way she thinks, and the way she grows physically. By creating an appropriate environment for your child, you are allowing normal brain development to take place. You may wonder what is considered an "appropriate" environment. It's one that is "child-centered" and provides opportunities for learning that are geared to your child's development, interests, and personality. Fortunately, the components of a good environment include basic things that many parents want to provide for their children: proper nutrition; a warm, responsive, and loving family as well as other caregivers; fun playtime; consistent positive reinforcement; engaging conversation; good books to read and to listen to; music to stimulate brain activities; and the freedom to explore and learn from their surroundings.

Review the following elements of children's health and how each one contributes to a child's brain development:

- *Language.* Direct face-to-face communication between parents and other caregivers and their young children supports language development, as does reading to them.

- *Early identification of developmental problems.* Many developmental and medical problems can be treated if detected early. Children with disabilities and other special health care needs also can greatly benefit from close monitoring of early brain development.

- *Stimulating environment.* Exploring and problem solving in a variety of safe places promote learning.

- *Positive parenting.* Raising a child in a loving, supportive, and respectful environment enhances self-esteem and self-confidence, and has a great impact on the child's development.

More and more behavioral researchers are discovering how much the environment plays a role in shaping a baby's life. This new science helps us understand exactly how significant our role is in the development of the child's brain. How nurturing and responsive to your infant you are as a parent will play a critical role in shaping your baby's future.

To build a positive environment for your baby in your home and in your community, follow these suggestions:

- **Get good prenatal care.** Since brain development begins in the womb, good prenatal care can help ensure the healthy development of your child's brain. Start prenatal care early, see your doctor regularly, and be sure to follow her instructions. Eating a balanced, healthy diet and avoiding drugs, alcohol, and tobacco are just a few steps you can take to contribute to your child's future health.

- **Try to create a "village" around you.** Since it's hard to raise a child on your own, seek support from your family, friends, and community. Talk to your pediatrician about parent-support groups and activities.

- **Interact with your child as much as possible.** Talk with your child, read, listen to music, draw pictures, and play together. These kinds of activities allow you to spend time focused on your child's thoughts and interests. This, in turn, can make your child feel special and important. You also can teach the language of communication that your child will use to form healthy relationships over a lifetime.

- **Give your child plenty of love and attention.** A warm and loving environment helps children feel safe, competent, and cared for, as well as helping them feel concern for others.

- **Provide consistent guidelines and rules.** Be sure you and other caregivers are working with the same rules. Also, be sure your own rules and guidelines are consistent while taking into account your child's growing competency. Consistency helps children feel confident about what to expect from their environment.

As your baby wakes up or starts to fall asleep, he'll go through State 3. His eyes will roll back under drooping eyelids and he may stretch, yawn, or jerk his arms and legs. Once awake, he'll move into one of the three remaining states. He may be wide awake, happy, and alert but relatively motionless (State 4). Or he may be alert, happy, and very active (State 5). Or he may cry and flail about (State 6).

If you shake a rattle by your baby's ear when he's happy and alert (States 4 and 5), he'll probably become quiet and turn his face to look for the source of this strange sound. This is the time when he'll appear most responsive to you and the activity around him, and be most attentive and involved in play.

In general, it's a mistake to expect much attention from a baby who is crying. At these times, he's not receptive to new information or sensations; what he wants instead is comforting. The same rattle that enchanted him when he was

Your Baby's States of Consciousness		
State	**Description**	**What Your Baby Does**
State 1	Deep sleep	Lies quietly without moving
State 2	Light sleep	Moves while sleeping; startles at noises
State 3	Drowsiness	Eyes start to close; may doze
State 4	Quiet alert	Eyes open wide, face is bright; body is quiet
State 5	Active alert	Face and body move actively
State 6	Crying	Cries, perhaps screams; body moves in very disorganized ways

happy five minutes earlier will only irritate him and make him more upset when he's crying. As he gets older, sometimes you may be able to distract him with an attractive object or sound so that he stops crying, but at this young age, the best way to comfort him usually is to pick him up and hold him. (See *Responding to Your Baby's Cries,* page 42.)

As your baby's nervous system becomes more developed, he'll begin to settle into a pattern of crying, sleeping, eating, and playing that matches your own daily schedule. He still may need to eat every three to four hours, but by the end of the month he'll be awake for longer periods during the day and be more alert and responsive at those times.

Colic

Does your infant have a regular fussy period each day when it seems you can do nothing to comfort her? This is quite common, particularly between 6:00 P.M. and midnight—just when you, too, are feeling tired from the day's trials and tribulations. These periods of crankiness may feel like torture, especially if you have other demanding children or work to do, but fortunately they don't last long. The length of this fussing usually peaks at about three hours a day by six weeks and then declines to one or two hours a day by three to four months. As long as the baby calms within a few hours and is relatively peaceful the rest of the day, there's no reason for alarm.

If the crying does not stop, but intensifies and persists throughout the day or night, it may be caused by colic. About one-fifth of all babies develop colic, usually between the second and fourth weeks. They cry inconsolably, often screaming, extending or pulling up their legs, and passing gas. Their stomachs may be enlarged or distended with gas. The crying spells can occur around the clock, although they often become worse in the early evening.

Unfortunately, there is no definite explanation for why this happens. Most often, colic means simply that the child is unusually sensitive to stimulation. As she matures, it will decrease, and generally it stops by three months. Sometimes, in breastfeeding babies, colic is a sign of sensitivity to a food in the mother's diet. The discomfort is caused only rarely by sensitivity to milk protein in formula. Colicky behavior also may signal a medical problem, such as a hernia or some type of illness.

Perhaps you'll find it reassuring that there's a time limit to this problem, but that doesn't stop the crying now. Although you simply may have to wait it out, several things might be worth trying. First, of course, consult your pediatrician to rule out any medical reason for the crying. Then ask which of the following would be most helpful.

- If you're nursing, eliminate milk products, caffeine, onions, cabbage, and any other potentially irritating foods from your diet. If you're bottle-feeding, try a hypoallergenic formula. If food sensitivity is causing the discomfort, the colic should decrease within a day or two of these changes.

- Walk your baby in a body carrier to soothe her. The motion and body contact will reassure her, even if her discomfort persists.

- Rock her, run the vacuum in the next room, or place her where she can hear the clothes dryer. Steady rhythmic motion and sound may help her fall asleep. However, be sure to never place your child on the washer/dryer.

- Introduce a pacifier. While some breastfed babies will actively refuse it, it will provide instant relief for others. (See page 162.)

- Lay your baby tummy-down across your knees and gently rub her back. The pressure against her abdomen may help relieve her pain.

- Swaddle her in a blanket so that she feels secure and warm.

- If you or your spouse smoke, try to quit smoking or at least smoke outside the house.

- For future pregnancies, do not smoke during the pregnancy.

- When you're feeling tense and anxious, have someone else look after the baby—and get out of the house. Even an hour or two away will help you maintain a positive attitude. No matter how impatient or angry you feel, do not shake the baby. Shaking an infant hard can cause blindness, brain damage, or even death (see sidebar *Shaken Baby Syndrome,* page 155).

The First Smile

One of the most important developments during this month is the appearance of your baby's first smiles and giggles. These start during sleep, for reasons that are not understood. They may be a signal that the baby feels aroused in some way or is responding to some internal impulse. While it's great fun to watch a newborn smile his way through a nap, the real joy comes near the end of this month when he begins to grin back at you during his alert periods.

Those first loving smiles will help you tune in even more closely to each other, and you'll soon discover that you can predict when your baby will smile, look at you, make sounds, and, equally important, pause for time out from play. Gradually you'll recognize each other's patterns of responsiveness so that your play together becomes a kind of dance in which you take turns leading and following. By identifying and responding to your child's subtle signals, even at this young age, you are telling him that his thoughts and feelings are important and that he can affect the world around him. These messages are vital to his developing self-esteem.

Movement

For the first week or two, your baby's movements will be very jerky. Her chin may quiver and her hands may tremble. She'll startle easily when moved suddenly or when she hears a loud sound, and the startling may lead to crying. If these movements are very pronounced or disturbing, you can contain them by holding the baby tightly against your body or swaddling her in a blanket. But by the end of the first month, as her nervous system matures and her muscle control improves, these shakes and quivers will give way to much smoother arm and leg movements that look almost as if she's riding a bicycle. Lay her on her stomach now and she will make crawling motions with her legs and may even push up on her arms.

The baby's neck muscles also will develop rapidly, giving her much more control over her head movements by the end of this month. Lying on her stomach, she may lift her head and turn it from one side to the other. However, she won't be able to hold her head securely until about three months, so make sure you support it whenever you're holding her.

Your baby's hands, a source of endless fascination throughout much of this first year, will catch her eyes during these weeks. Her finger movements are limited, since her hands are clenched in tight fists most of the time. But she can flex her arms and bring her hands to her mouth and into her line of vision. While she can't control her hands precisely, she'll watch them closely as long as they're in view.

***Movement Milestones
by the End of This Period***

- **Makes jerky, quivering arm thrusts**
- **Brings hands within range of eyes and mouth**
- **Moves head from side to side while lying on stomach**
- **Head flops backward if unsupported**
- **Keeps hands in tight fists**
- **Strong reflex movements**

Vision

Your baby's vision will go through many changes this first month. He was born with peripheral vision (the ability to see to the sides), and he'll gradually acquire the ability to focus closely on a single point in the center of his visual field. He likes to look at objects held about 8 to 15 inches (20.3 to 38.1 cm) in front of him, but by one month he'll focus briefly on things as far away as 3 feet (91.4 cm).

At the same time, he'll learn to follow, or track, moving objects. To help him practice this skill, you can play tracking games with him. For example, move your head slowly from side to side as you hold him facing you; or pass a patterned object up and down or side to side in front of him (making sure it's within his range of focus). At first he may only be able to follow large objects moving

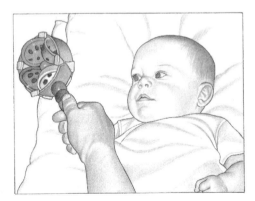

Your baby likes to look at objects held about 8 to 15 inches (20.3 to 38.1 cm) in front of him.

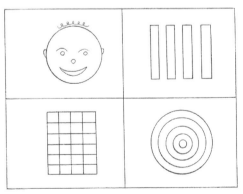

He is most attentive to black-and-white pictures or high-contrast patterns, such as sharply contrasting stripes, bull's-eyes, checks, and very simple faces.

Shaken Baby Syndrome

Shaking a baby is a serious form of child abuse that occurs mostly in infants in the first year of life. The act of severely or violently shaking a baby—often the result of a parent's or caregiver's frustration or anger in response to a baby's or toddler's constant crying or irritability—can cause serious physical and mental damage, even death.

As the young child is shaken, his fragile brain moves back and forth within the skull. Serious injuries associated with this so-called shaken baby syndrome may include blindness or eye injuries, brain damage, damage to the spinal cord, and delay in normal development. Signs and symptoms may include irritability, lethargy (difficulty staying awake), tremors (shakiness), vomiting, seizures, difficulty breathing, and coma.

The American Academy of Pediatrics feels strongly that it is *never* okay to shake your baby. If you suspect that a caregiver, such as a babysitter, has shaken your baby—or if you or your spouse have done so in a moment of frustration—take your baby to the pediatrician or an emergency room immediately. Any brain damage that might have occurred will only get worse without treatment. Don't let embarrassment or fear keep you from getting treatment for your baby.

If you feel as if you might lose control when caring for your baby:

- Take a deep breath and count to 10.

- Put your baby in her crib or another safe place, leave the room, and let her cry alone.

- Call a friend or relative for emotional support.

- Give your pediatrician a call. Perhaps there's a medical reason why your baby is crying.

slowly through an extremely limited range, but soon he'll be tracking even small, speedy movements.

At birth your baby was extremely sensitive to bright light, and his pupils were constricted (small) to limit the amount of light that entered his eyes. At two weeks of age, his pupils will begin to enlarge, allowing him to experience a broader range of shades of light and dark. As his retina (the light-sensitive tissue inside the eyeball) develops, his ability to see and recognize patterns also will improve.

The more contrast there is in a pattern, the more it will attract his attention, which is why he is most attentive to black-and-white pictures or high-contrast

Visual Milestones by the End of This Period

- **Focuses 8 to 12 inches (20.3 to 30.4 cm) away**
- **Eyes wander and occasionally cross**
- **Prefers black-and-white or high-contrast patterns**
- **Prefers the human face to all other patterns**

patterns, such as sharply contrasting stripes, bull's-eyes, checks, and very simple faces.

If you show your infant three identical toys—one blue, one yellow, one red—he probably will look longest at the red one, although no one yet understands why. Is it the color red itself? Or is it the brightness of this color that attracts newborn babies? We do know that color vision doesn't fully mature before about four months, so if you show your baby two related colors, such as green and turquoise, he probably can't tell the difference at this age.

Hearing

Your baby may have had a hearing test shortly after birth; in fact, the American Academy of Pediatrics recommends that newborn hearing screenings occur prior to every baby's discharge from the hospital, and parents should be told the results. (See "Hearing Loss," pages 569–572.)

Assuming your infant's hearing is fine, she will pay close attention to human voices during the first month, especially high-pitched ones speaking "baby talk." When you talk to her, she'll turn her head to search for you and listen closely as you sound out different syllables and words. Watch carefully and you may even see her make subtle movements of her arms and legs in time with your speech.

Your infant also will be sensitive to noise levels. If you make a loud clicking sound in her ear or bring her into a noisy, crowded room, she may "shut down," becoming as unresponsive as if she had heard nothing. Or she may be so sensitive that she startles, erupts into crying, and turns her entire body away from the noise. (Extremely sensitive babies also will cry when exposed to a very bright light.) Substitute the sound of a soft rattle or quiet music and she'll become alert and turn her head and eyes to locate the source of this interesting sound.

Not only does your baby hear well, but even at this age, she'll remember some of the sounds she hears. Some mothers who repeatedly read a story aloud during late pregnancy have found that their babies seem to recognize the story when it was read to them again after birth—the babies became quiet and looked more attentive. Try reading your favorite children's story aloud for several days in a row at times when your baby is alert and attentive. Then wait a day or two and read it again. Does she seem to recognize it?

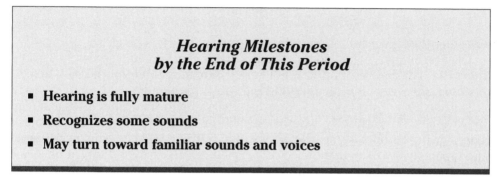

Hearing Milestones by the End of This Period

- **Hearing is fully mature**
- **Recognizes some sounds**
- **May turn toward familiar sounds and voices**

Smell and Touch

Just as he prefers certain patterns and sounds, your baby is very particular about tastes and smells. He will breathe deeply to catch a whiff of milk, vanilla, banana, or sugar, but will turn up his nose at the smell of alcohol or vinegar. By the end of his first week, if he's nursing, he'll turn toward his own mother's breast pad but will ignore the pads of other nursing mothers. This radarlike system helps direct him at feeding times and warns him away from substances that could harm him.

Your baby is equally sensitive to touch and the way you handle him. He'll nestle into a soft piece of flannel or satin, but pull away from scratchy burlap or coarse sandpaper. Stroke him gently with your palm, and he'll relax and become quiet. If you pick him up roughly, he'll probably take offense and start to cry. If you pick him up gently and rock him slowly, he'll become quiet and attentive. Holding, stroking, rocking, and cuddling will calm him when he's upset and

Smell and Touch Milestones by the End of This Period

- **Prefers sweet smells**
- **Avoids bitter or acidic smells**
- **Recognizes the scent of his own mother's breastmilk**
- **Prefers soft to coarse sensations**
- **Dislikes rough or abrupt handling**

make him more alert when he's drowsy. It also sends a clear message of your love and affection for him. Long before he understands a word you say, he'll understand your moods and feelings from the way you touch him.

Temperament

Consider these two babies, both from the same family, both girls:

The first infant is calm and quiet, happy to play by herself. She watches everything that happens around her, but rarely demands attention herself. Left on her own, she sleeps for long periods and eats infrequently.

The second baby is fussy and startles easily. She thrashes her arms and legs, moving almost constantly whether awake or asleep. While most newborns sleep fourteen hours a day, she sleeps only ten, and wakens whenever there's the slightest activity nearby. She seems in a hurry to do everything at once and even eats in a rush, gulping her feedings and swallowing so much air that she needs frequent burping.

Both these babies are absolutely normal and healthy. One is no "better" than the other, but because their personalities are so far apart, the two will be treated very differently, right from birth.

Like these babies, your infant will demonstrate many unique personality traits from the earliest weeks of life. Discovering these traits is one of the most exciting parts of having a new baby. Is she very active and intense, or relatively slow-going? Is she timid when faced with a new situation, such as the first bath, or does she enjoy it? You'll find clues to her personality in everything she does, from falling asleep to crying. The more you pay attention to these signals and learn to respond appropriately to her unique personality, the calmer and more predictable your life will be in the months to come.

While most of these early character traits are built into the newborn's hereditary makeup, their appearance may be delayed if your baby is born quite prematurely. Premature babies don't express their needs—such as hunger, fatigue, or discomfort—as clearly as other newborns. They may be extra sensitive to light, sound, and touch for several months. Even playful conversation may be too intense for them and cause them to become fussy and look away. When this happens, it's up to the parent to stop and wait until the baby is alert and ready for more attention. Eventually most of these early reactions will fade away, and the baby's own natural character traits will become more evident.

Babies who are underweight at birth (less than 5.5 pounds or 2.5 kg), even if they're full term, also may be less responsive than other newborns. At first they may be very sleepy and not seem very alert. After a few weeks they seem to wake up, eating eagerly but still remaining irritable and hypersensitive to stimulation between feedings. This irritability may last until they grow and mature further. The more they are protected from overstimulation and comforted through this fussy period, the more quickly it will pass.

From the very beginning, your baby's temperamental traits will influence the

Developmental Health Watch

If, during the second, third, or fourth weeks of your baby's life, she shows any of the following signs of developmental delay, notify your pediatrician.

- Sucks poorly and feeds slowly
- Doesn't blink when shown a bright light
- Doesn't focus and follow a nearby object moving side to side
- Rarely moves arms and legs; seems stiff
- Seems excessively loose in the limbs, or floppy
- Lower jaw trembles constantly, even when not crying or excited
- Doesn't respond to loud sounds

way you treat her and feel about her. If you had specific ideas about child rearing before she was born, reevaluate them now to see if they're really in tune with her character. The same goes for expert advice—from books, articles, and especially from well-meaning relatives and friends—about the "right way" to raise a child. The truth is, there is no right way that works for every child. You have to create your own guidelines based on your child's unique personality, your own beliefs, and the circumstances of your family life. The important thing is to remain responsive to your baby's individuality. Don't try to box her into some previously set mold or pattern. Your baby's uniqueness is her strength, and respecting that strength from the start will help lay the best possible foundation for her high self-esteem and for loving relationships with others.

Toys Appropriate for Your Baby's First Month

- **Mobile with highly contrasting colors and patterns**
- **Unbreakable mirror attached securely to inside of crib**
- **Music boxes and record or CD players with soft music**
- **Soft, brightly colored and patterned toys that make gentle sounds**

BASIC CARE

Feeding and Nutrition

(see Chapter 4 for additional information)

Breastmilk or formula should be your child's basic source of nutrition for the first twelve months. But while you don't have to worry much about his diet, you need to pay attention to his pattern of feedings and make sure that he's getting enough calories for growth.

Establishing a pattern of feedings does not mean setting a rigid timetable and insisting that he breastfeed for a set amount of time or eat a full 4 ounces (120 ml) at each feeding. It's much more important to listen to your baby's signals and work around his needs. If he is bottle-fed, he probably will cry at the end of his feeding if he is not getting enough. On the other hand, if he is getting an adequate amount in the first ten minutes, he may stop and fall asleep. Breastfed babies behave a little differently in that they do not always cry when they are hungry, and the best way to be sure yours is getting enough milk is to watch his weight gain. Also, he should be fed at least every two to three hours and not allowed to sleep through a feeding until at least four weeks of age.

Growth spurts can occur at different times for different babies. At the beginning of the second week and again between three and six weeks, your baby may go through growth spurts that may make him hungrier than usual. Even if you don't notice any outward growth, his body is changing in important ways and needs extra calories during these times. Be prepared to feed him more often if he's breastfed, and if he's bottle-fed, try giving him slightly more at each feeding.

If your baby has a nutritional problem, he's likely to start losing weight or not gain adequately. There are some signals that may help you detect such a problem.

If he's breastfeeding, one warning signal is a lack of fullness in your breasts after one week. If they don't drip milk at the start of each feeding, the baby may not be providing enough stimulation when he sucks. Some other trouble signs are listed below. These also may be signs of medical problems that are unrelated to your baby's nutrition. You should call your pediatrician if they persist.

Too Much Feeding:

- If bottle-fed, the baby is consuming more than 4 to 6 ounces (120 to 180 ml) per feeding.

- He vomits most or all the food after a complete feeding.

- Stools are loose and very watery, eight or more times a day. (Breastfed babies may have more stools.)

Too Little Feeding:

- If breastfed, the baby stops feeding after ten minutes or less.
- He wets fewer than four diapers per day.
- His skin remains wrinkled beyond the first week.
- He does not develop a rounded face by about three weeks.
- He appears hungry, searching for something to suck shortly after feedings.
- He becomes more yellow, instead of less, during the first week.

Feeding Allergy or Digestive Disturbance:

- Your baby vomits most or all food after a complete feeding.
- He produces loose and very watery stools eight or more times a day.

Most babies this age begin to spit up occasionally after feedings. That's because the muscular valve between the esophagus (the passage between throat and stomach) and the stomach is immature. Instead of closing tightly, it remains open enough to allow the contents of the stomach to come back up and gently spill out of the mouth. This is normal, won't harm your baby, and resolves as your baby grows, usually by one year of age.

Carrying Your Baby

A newborn or very young infant who has not developed head control needs to be carried in a way that keeps her head from flopping from side to side or snapping from front to back. This is done by cradling the head when carrying the baby in a lying position and supporting the head and neck with your hand when carrying the baby upright.

A very young infant who has not developed head control needs to be carried in a way that keeps her head from flopping from side to side or snapping from front to back.

Pacifiers

Many parents have strong feelings about pacifiers. Some oppose their use because of the way they look, or they resent the notion of "pacifying" a baby with an object. Others believe—incorrectly—that using a pacifier can harm a baby. Pacifiers do not cause any medical or psychological problems. If your baby wants to suck beyond what nursing or bottle-feeding provides, a pacifier will satisfy that need.

A pacifier is meant to satisfy your baby's noneating sucking needs, not to replace or delay meals. So offer a pacifier to your baby only after or between feedings, when you are sure he is not hungry. If he is hungry, and you offer a pacifier as a substitute, he may become so angry that it interferes with feeding. Remember, the pacifier is for your baby's benefit, not your convenience, so let him decide whether and when to use it.

Some babies use a pacifier to fall asleep. The trouble is, they often wake up when it falls out of their mouth. Once your baby is older and has the hand coordination to find and replace it, there is no problem. However, when he's younger, he may cry for you to do this for him. Babies who suck their fingers or hands have a real advantage here, because their hands are always readily available.

When shopping for a pacifier, look for a one-piece model that has a soft nipple. (Some models can break into two pieces.) It should be dishwasher-safe so you can either boil it or run it through the dishwasher before your baby uses it. Until he's six months old, you should clean the pacifier this way frequently, so he's not exposed to any increased risk of infection, as his immune system is still maturing. After that, the likelihood of his picking up an infection in that way is minimal, so you can just wash it with soap and rinse it in clear water.

Pacifiers are available in two sizes, one for the first six months and another for children after that age. You'll also find a variety of nipple shapes, from squarish "orthodontic" versions to the standard bottle type. Once you decide which your baby prefers, buy some extras. Pacifiers have a way of disappearing or falling on the floor or street when you need them most. However, never try to solve this problem by fastening the pacifier with a cord around your baby's neck. That could interfere with his breathing or choke him. Also, for safety reasons, do not make your own pacifiers out of a bottle nipple. Babies have pulled the nipple out of such homemade pacifiers and choked on them.

Going Outside

Fresh air and a change of surroundings are good for both you and your baby, even in her first month, so take her out for walks when the weather is nice. Be sure to dress her properly for these outings, however. Her internal temperature control isn't fully mature until the end of her first year. This makes it difficult for her to regulate her body temperature when she's exposed to excessive heat or cold. Her clothing must do some of this work for her by keeping heat in when she is in a cold location and letting heat escape when she's in a very warm place. In general, she should wear one more layer than you do.

Your infant's skin also is extremely susceptible to sunburn during the first six months, so it's important to keep her out of direct and reflected sunlight (e.g., off of water, sand, or concrete) as much as possible. If you must take her out in the sun, dress her in lightweight and light-colored clothing, with a bonnet or hat to shade her face. If she is lying or sitting in one place, make sure it is shady, and adjust her position to keep her in the shade as the sun moves. Sunscreen is generally not recommended for infants under six months of age, although this is a topic of controversy. Some dermatologists believe that when other forms of protection aren't available—such as adequate clothing, hats, and shade—sunscreen can be used on small areas of the baby's skin (i.e., the face and the back of the hands). This is a topic to discuss with your pediatrician.

Another warning for the hot-weather months: Do not let baby equipment (car safety seats, strollers) sit in the sun for a long period of time. When that happens, the plastic and metal parts can get hot enough to burn your child. Check the surface temperature of any such equipment before you allow your baby to come in contact with it.

In uncomfortably cold or rainy weather, keep your baby inside as much as possible. If you have to go out, bundle her up in warm sweaters over her other clothes, and use a warm hat to cover her head and ears. You can shield her face from the cold with a blanket when you're outside.

To check whether she's clothed well enough, feel her hands and feet and the skin on her chest. Her hands and feet should be slightly cooler than her body, but not cold. Her chest should feel warm. If her hands, feet, and chest feel cold, take her to a warm room, unwrap her, and feed her something warm or hold her close so the heat from your body warms her. Until her temperature is back to normal, extra layers of clothing will just trap the cold, so use these other methods to warm her body before wrapping her in additional blankets or clothing.

Finding Temporary Child Care Help

Most mothers need some help when they bring a new baby home. If Dad can take a few days off from work during the first week or two, this will help a lot. If he cannot, and if the family finances won't allow you to hire help, the next best choice is a close relative or friend. It is wise to make these arrangements in advance rather than waiting until after the delivery to seek help.

Some communities have a visiting nurse or homemaking service. This will not solve your middle-of-the-night problems, but it will give you an hour or two during the day to catch up on work or simply rest a little. These arrangements, too, should be made in advance.

Be selective about the help you seek. Look for assistance from those who will really support you. Your goal is to reduce the stress level in your home, not add to it.

Before you start interviewing or asking friends or family for assistance, decide exactly what kind of help will work best for you. Ask yourself the following questions:

- Do you want someone who can help you tend the baby, or do the housework or cook meals—or a little bit of everything?

- During what hours do you want help?

- Do you need someone who can drive (to pick up other children at school, shop for groceries, run errands, and the like)?

Once you know what you need, make sure the person you choose to help out understands and agrees to meet your needs.

Your Baby's First Sitter. Sometime in the first month or two, you'll probably need to leave your baby for the first time. The more confidence you have in your babysitter, the easier this experience will be for you. Therefore, you may want to have your first sitter be someone very close and trusted—a grandparent, close friend, or relative who's familiar with both you and the child.

After you've survived the first separation, you may want to look for a regular babysitter. Start by asking your friends, neighbors, and coworkers for recommendations, or see if your pediatrician or nurse practitioner can refer you to someone. If they have no suggestions, ask your pediatrician if she knows of any local child care agencies or referral services. If that still doesn't yield any names, contact the placement services at local colleges for a listing of child development or early education students who babysit. You also can find the names of sitters in community newspapers, telephone directories, and church and grocery store bulletin boards, but remember that no one screens the people in these listings. It is absolutely essential that you check references—inquiring about the sitter's responsibility, maturity, and ability to adhere to instructions—particularly for someone you've only recently met or don't know well.

Interview every candidate in person and with your baby present. You should be looking for someone who is affectionate, capable, and supports your views about child care. If you feel comfortable with the individual after you've talked awhile, let her hold the baby so you can see how she handles him. Ask if she's had experience caring for infants. Although experience, references, and good health are important, the best way to judge a babysitter is by giving her a trial run while you're home. It will give your baby and the babysitter a chance to get to know each other before they're alone together, and it will give you an opportunity to make sure you feel comfortable with the sitter.

Whenever you leave your child with a sitter, give her a list of all emergency phone numbers, including those where you or other close family members can be contacted if problems arise; she should know where you'll be and how to reach you at all times. Establish clear guidelines about what to do in an emergency, and remind her about calling 911 for emergency help. Show her where all exits to your home are located, as well as smoke detectors and fire extinguishers. Make sure the sitter knows how to treat a child who is choking or not breathing. (See *Cardiopulmonary Resuscitation* and *Mouth-to-Mouth Resuscitation,* page 478; *Choking,* page 481); in fact, see if the the local YMCA or American Red Cross chapter can provide a list of babysitters who have taken their CPR or babysitting safety courses. Give her any other guidelines that you feel are important (e.g., she should never open the door to strangers, including delivery people). Ask the sitter to jot down any notes or questions she has about your child. Let friends and neighbors know about your arrangement so they can help if there's an emergency, and ask them to tell you if they suspect any problems in your absence.

Traveling with Your Baby

Traveling with your baby during her infancy is probably the easiest traveling the two of you will ever do. For the first few months, all she cares about is her own comfort, which amounts to a full stomach, a clean diaper, and a comfortable place to sit or lie. If you can satisfy these basic needs, your baby probably will travel with minimum protest. The key is to maintain her normal patterns as much as possible.

Long trips involving a change of time zones can disturb your baby's sleep schedule. (See *Traveling by Plane,* page 383.) So do your best to plan your activities according to the schedule your child is on and allow several days for her to adjust to a time change if possible. If she awakens very early in the morning, plan to start your own activities earlier. Be ready to stop earlier, too, because your little one will be getting tired and cranky long before the clock says it's time to go to bed. Always remember to perform a safety inspection of any cribs when checking into a hotel. (See *Cribs,* page 430.)

If you're going to remain in a new time zone for more than two or three days, your baby's internal time clock gradually will shift to coincide with the time zone you're in. You'll have to adjust mealtimes to match the times when her body is telling her she's hungry. Mom and Dad—and even older children—may be able to postpone meals to fit the new time zone, but a baby isn't able to make those adjustments as easily.

Your baby will adapt to her new environment more quickly if you bring some familiar things from home. If she has a favorite blanket that she always sleeps with, make sure it goes with you on your trip. A few familiar rattles and toys will provide some comfort and reassurance, too. Use her regular soap, a familiar towel, and bring along one of her tub toys to make her more at ease during baths. At meals give her familiar foods. This is not the time to try out a new formula or introduce her to strange tastes.

When packing for a trip with your baby, it's usually best to use a separate bag for her things. This makes it easier to find items quickly when you want them and reduces the chance that you'll forget an important one. You'll also need a large diaper bag for bottles, small toys, snacks, lotion, diapers, and baby wipes. Keep this bag with you at all times.

When traveling by automobile, make sure your child is safely strapped into her car safety seat. For more information on car safety seats, see page 447. The backseat is the safest place for children to ride. Rear-facing seats should never be placed in the front seat of a car with a passenger-side airbag. At this age a baby always should ride in the rear-facing position. If you're renting an automobile, reserve a car safety seat ahead of time or bring your own with you. If a rented car seat seems too large, you can use rolled-up diapers to center your baby.

Always use a car safety seat on planes and trains, as well. If you're not sure how to secure your baby safely on a plane or train, ask a flight attendant or a conductor to help you. As we'll describe in Chapter 12, unless you buy a ticket for the baby, you'll be expected to carry her on your lap, which the Academy strongly discourages, believing that all children should travel with proper restraints on an aircraft. When there is extra room on board, you may be able to get a separate seat for the baby without paying for it.

If your baby is bottle-fed, bring not only enough formula for the expected travel time, but some extra in case any unexpected delays occur. The attendant or conductor will help you refrigerate the formula until it is needed. If you're nursing and are concerned about privacy, ask for some blankets you can use as a screen.

A bottle (or pacifier) may have other benefits when traveling with a baby by plane. The rapid changes in air pressure associated with air travel can cause discomfort in the baby's middle ear. Babies cannot intentionally "pop" their ears as adults can (by swallowing or yawning), but this relief within the ear may occur when they suck on a bottle or pacifier. To reduce the risk of pain, feed your baby during the flight, and do not let him fall asleep during the plane's descent.

THE FAMILY

A Special Message to Mothers

One reason why this first month can be especially difficult is that you are still recovering physically from the stress of pregnancy and delivery. It may take weeks before your body is back to normal, your incisions (if you had an episiotomy or C-section) have healed, and you're able to resume everyday activities. You also may experience strong mood swings due to changes in the amount of hormones in your body. These changes can prompt sudden crying episodes for no apparent reason or feelings of mild depression for the first few weeks. These emotions may be intensified by the exhaustion that comes with waking up every two or three hours at night to feed and change the baby.

If you experience these so-called postpartum blues, they may make you feel a little "crazy," embarrassed, or even that you're a "bad mother." Difficult as it may be, try to keep these emotions in perspective by reminding yourself that they're normal after pregnancy and delivery. Even fathers sometimes feel sad and unusually emotional after a new baby arrives (possibly a response to the psychological intensity of the experience). To keep the blues from dominating your life—and your enjoyment of your new baby—avoid isolating yourself in these early weeks. Try to nap when your baby does, so you don't get overtired.

If these feelings persist past a few weeks or become severe, consult your pediatrician or your own physician about getting extra help. (For more information about the postpartum blues, also see Chapter 5, pages 134–136.)

Visitors often can help you combat the blues by celebrating the baby's arrival with you. They may bring welcome gifts for the baby or—even better during these early weeks—offer food or household help. But they also can be exhausting for you and overwhelming for the baby, and may expose him to infection. It is wise to strictly limit the number of visitors during the first couple of weeks, and keep anyone with a cough, cold, or contagious disease away from your newborn. Ask all visitors to call in advance, wash their hands before holding the baby, and keep their visits brief until you're back to a regular schedule. If the baby seems unsettled by all the attention, don't let anyone outside the family hold or come close to him.

If you become overwhelmed with phone calls, and you have a telephone answering machine, use it to give yourself a little peace. Record a message that gives the baby's sex, name, birth date, time, weight, and length. Then turn on the machine and turn off the phone's ringing mechanism. That allows you to return the calls on your own schedule without feeling stressed or guilty every time the bell rings. If you don't have an answering machine, unplug the phone or muffle the sound of the bell with a pillow.

With a new baby, constant visitors, an aching body, unpredictable mood swings, and, in some cases, other siblings demanding attention, it's no wonder the housework gets neglected. Resign yourself ahead of time to knowing that the wash may not get done as often as it should, the house will get dustier than usual, and a lot of meals will be frozen or take-out. You always can catch up next month. For now, concentrate on recuperating and enjoying your new baby.

A Special Message to Fathers

This can be a very stressful time for parenting couples. It's almost impossible to find time—much less energy—for each other, between the seemingly constant demands of the baby, the needs of other children, household chores, and the father's work schedule. (In our society, not

Become as involved as possible in caring for and playing with the new baby. You'll get just as emotionally attached to her as her mother will.

all fathers have the option of taking paternity leaves, which can help reduce these tensions.) Nights spent feeding, diapering, and walking the floor with a crying baby quickly take their toll in fatigue. If both parents don't make up for this by relieving each other and taking naps, exhaustion can drive a large and unnecessary wedge between them.

At this time, some fathers also feel shut off from the child and from the mother's attention and affections, especially if the baby is breastfed. The problem is not helped by the fact that the obstetrician usually prohibits sexual intercourse for these first few weeks. Even if it were allowed, many women simply aren't interested in sexual activity for a while after delivery because of the physical exhaustion and emotional stress they may be experiencing now.

This conflict and the jealous feelings that may arise at this time are temporary. Life soon settles into a fairly regular routine that will once again give you some time to yourselves and restore your sex life and social activities to normal. Meanwhile, make an effort for just the two of you to spend some time together each day, and remember, you're entitled to hold, hug, cuddle, and kiss each other as well as the baby.

A positive way for men to deal with these issues is to become as involved as possible in caring for and playing with the new baby. When you spend this extra time with your child, you'll get just as emotionally attached to her as her mother will.

This is not to say that moms and dads play with babies the same way. In general, fathers play to arouse and excite their babies, while mothers generally concentrate on more low-key stimulation such as gentle rocking, quiet interactive games, singing, and soothing activities. Fathers tend to roughhouse more, making lots of noise, and move the baby about more vigorously. The babies respond in kind, laughing and moving more with Dad than they do with Mom. From the baby's viewpoint, both play styles are equally valuable and complement each other beautifully, which is another reason why it's so important to have both of you involved in the care of the baby.

A Special Message to Grandparents

The first time you gaze into the eyes of your new grandchild, you probably will be overwhelmed by many feelings: love, wonder, amazement, and joy, among many other emotions. You might find yourself reflecting back on when your own children were born and feel enormous pride now that your own adult child is raising a family of her own.

Depending on your other responsibilities and how close you live to your grandchild, you can and should play as active a role as possible in the life of the new baby. Research shows that children who have grandparents participating in their lives fare better throughout childhood and later in life. You have plenty of love and lots of hugs to give, and they can make a difference. As you spend time with your grandchild, you'll form and strengthen a lasting bond and become an invaluable source of nurturing and guidance.

If you live in the same city as your new grandchild, make frequent visits at times deemed appropriate by your adult child. (Don't show up uninvited on the doorstep, and of course know when to leave.) At the same time, also encourage their family to visit you at your home. (Make sure that your home is child-proofed in the ways recommended in this book.) Minimize the advice and certainly the criticism you offer the new parents; instead, give them support, respect their opinions, and be patient. They may have approaches to child rearing that are somewhat different than yours were, but remember that they're the parents now. If they should ask, "Mom, what do you think I should do about...?" then of course provide some input. Share your point of view, but don't try to impose your beliefs on them. Remember, it's been a while since you were raising your own babies, and although much may be the same, much has changed, as well. Ask how you can support the new parents in the child-rearing process, and take your lead from them on how, when, and how often to get involved. For example, you might focus on basic baby care, including feeding and changing diapers, but don't try to take over. Also, offer them a break from time to time by giving them a night out (or, at some point, perhaps a weekend away). No matter how often you visit, however, make regular phone calls, not only during your grandchild's infancy, but also in the upcoming years when you're actually able to have a conversation with her.

Later, as your grandchild grows, tell her stories of what her own mother or father was like during childhood. (Sharing the family history and teaching family values are important contributions you can make as your grandchild becomes older.) In the meantime, consider keeping your own scrapbook of photos and other mementoes of your grandchild that you can share with her someday; as part of that scrapbook, create a family tree that the entire family can contribute to. Make it a priority to get together on holidays, attend birthday parties, and, later on, go to as many soccer matches and Little League games as possible.

If you live hundreds of miles away, and thus can't be as much of a presence in your grandchild's life as you'd like, you still can be an excellent long-distance grandparent. One option: E-mail is a wonderful way to stay in touch. If the new parents have a digital camera, ask them to e-mail photographs of your grandchild to you that you can view on your computer. Maybe they can make and share videotapes of your grandchild, as well. Make some videos of you and your spouse that your children can share with your grandchild when she is older.

Siblings

With all the excitement over the new baby's arrival, siblings often feel neglected. They still may be a little upset over their mother's hospitalization, especially if this was their first prolonged separation from her. Even after Mom returns home, they may have trouble understanding that she's tired and cannot play with them as much as they're used to. Compound this with the attention she's now devoting to the baby—attention that just a couple of weeks ago belonged to them!—and it's no wonder that they may feel jealous and left out. It's up to both parents to find ways to reassure the siblings that they're still very much loved and valued, and to help them come to terms with their new "competition."

Here are some suggestions to help soothe your older children and make them feel more involved during the first month home with your new baby.

1. If possible, have the siblings visit mother and baby in the hospital.

2. When Mom comes home from the hospital, bring each sibling a special gift to celebrate.

3. Set aside a special time to spend alone with each sibling every day. Make sure that both Mom and Dad have time with each child, individually and together.

4. While you're taking pictures of the new baby, take some of the older children—alone and with the baby.

5. Ask the grandparents or other close relatives to take the older children on a special outing—to the zoo, a movie, or just dinner. This special attention may help them through moments when they feel abandoned.

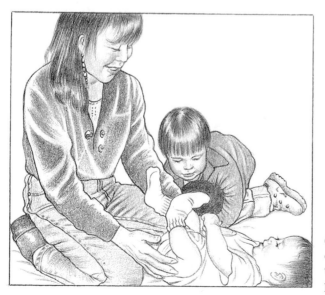

Once the infant arrives, you can expect your older child to be very proud and protective.

6. Have some small gifts for the older child and present them when friends come with gifts for the baby.

7. Especially during the first month, when the baby needs to eat so often, older children can get very jealous of the intimacy you have with the baby during feedings. Show them that you can share this intimacy by turning feeding times into story times. Reading stories that specifically deal with issues of jealousy encourages a toddler or preschooler to voice his feelings so that you can help him become more accepting.

HEALTH WATCH

The following medical problems are of particular concern to parents during the first month. (For problems that occur generally throughout childhood, check the listings in Part II.)

Breathing Difficulties. Normally, your baby should take from twenty to forty breaths per minute. This pattern is most regular when he is asleep and healthy. When awake, occasionally he may breathe rapidly for a short period, then take a brief pause (less than ten seconds) before returning to normal breathing. If he has a fever, his breathing may increase by about two breaths per minute for each degree of temperature elevation. A runny nose may interfere with breathing because his nasal passages are narrow and fill easily. This condition is eased by using a cool-mist humidifier and gently suctioning the nose with a rubber aspirating bulb (ordinarily given to you by the hospital; for its use, see page 198). Occasionally mild salt-solution nose drops are used to help thin the mucus and clear the nasal passages.

Diarrhea. A baby has diarrhea if she produces loose, very watery stools more than six to eight times a day. Diarrhea usually is caused by a viral infection. The danger, especially at this young age, is of losing too much water and becoming dehydrated. The first signs of dehydration are a dry mouth and a significant decrease in the number of wet diapers. But don't wait for dehydration to occur. Call your pediatrician if the stools are very loose or occur more often than after each feeding (six to eight per day).

Excessive Sleepiness. Since each infant requires a different amount of sleep, it's difficult to tell when a baby is excessively drowsy. If your infant starts sleeping much more than usual, it might indicate the presence of an infection, so notify your pediatrician. Also, if you are nursing and your baby sleeps more than five hours without a feeding in the first month, you must consider the possibility that he is not getting enough milk or perhaps is being affected, through the breastmilk, by a medication that you are taking.

Eye Infections. (See also *Tear Production Problems,* page 605.) Some babies are born with one or both tear ducts partially or totally blocked. They typically open by about two weeks, when tear production begins. If they don't, the blockage may cause a watery or mucus tearing. In this case, the tears will back up and flow over the eyelids instead of draining through the nose. This is not harmful, and the ducts generally will open without treatment. You also may help open them by gently massaging the inner corner of the eye and down the side of the nose. However, do this only at the direction of your pediatrician.

If the ducts remain blocked, thus keeping the tears from draining properly, infection can occur easily. These infections produce a white discharge in the corner of the eye. The eyelashes become sticky and may dry together at night so the eyelid can't open. Such infections usually are treated with special drops or ointment that your doctor will prescribe after examining the eye. Sometimes all that's needed is a gentle cleansing with sterile water. When the lashes are sticky, dip a cotton ball in sterile water, and use it to gently wipe from the part of the lid nearest the nose to the outside. Use each cotton ball just once, then discard it. Use as many cotton balls as you need to clean the eye thoroughly.

Although this type of mild infection may recur several times during your baby's first months, it will not damage the eye and she probably will outgrow it, even without more serious treatment. Only rarely does this tear-duct blockage require surgical care.

If the eye itself is bloodshot or pinkish, there probably is a more serious infection, called conjunctivitis, and you should notify your pediatrician at once.

Fever. Whenever your child is unusually cranky or feels warm, take his temperature. (See *Taking a Rectal Temperature,* page 66.) If his rectal temperature reads higher than 100.4 degrees Fahrenheit (38 degrees Celsius) on two separate readings, and he's not overly bundled up, call your pediatrician at once. Fever in these first few weeks can signal an infection, and babies this age can become seriously ill quickly.

Floppiness. Newborn infants all seem somewhat floppy because their muscles are still developing, but if your baby feels exceptionally loose or loses muscle tone, it could be a sign of a more serious problem, such as an infection. Consult your pediatrician immediately.

Hearing. Pay attention to the way your baby responds to sounds even if she passed her newborn hearing screening. Does she startle at loud or sudden noises? Does she become quiet or turn toward you when you talk to her? If she does not respond normally to sounds around her, ask your pediatrician about formal hearing testing. (See *Hearing Loss,* pages 569–572.) This testing might be particularly appropriate if your infant was extremely premature, if she was deprived of oxygen or had a severe infection at birth, or if your family has a history of hearing loss in early childhood. If there is any suspicion of hearing loss, your infant should be tested as early as possible, as a delay in diagnosis and treatment is likely to interfere with normal language development.

Sudden Infant Death Syndrome (SIDS)

Approximately one newborn out of every two thousand die in their sleep, for no apparent reason, between the fourth and sixteenth weeks of life. These babies generally are well cared for and show no obvious symptoms of illness. Their autopsies turn up no identifiable cause of death, so the terms *sudden infant death syndrome (SIDS)* or *crib death* are used.

SIDS occurs most often in winter among males who had a low birth weight. Premature infants and babies with a family history of SIDS, and babies of mothers who smoke and those who sleep in the prone (stomach) position (see page 45) also appear to be at increased risk. There are many theories about the cause of SIDS, but none has been proven. Infection, milk allergy, pneumonia, and child abuse all have been disproven as causes. The most believable theory at this time is that there is a delay in maturation of arousal centers in the brains of certain babies, which predisposes them to stop breathing under certain conditions.

If your baby occasionally stops breathing or turns blue, your pediatrician probably will want to hospitalize him to make sure there are no treatable causes for the episodes and to assess the severity of the condition. If the spells are severe, you may be advised to learn cardiopulmonary resuscitation (CPR) and use a home monitor while the baby sleeps. This device measures his respiration rate and sounds an alarm if it goes too low. If your baby was born prematurely, the pediatrician may choose to control the condition with medications such as caffeine or theophylline, which stimulate respiration.

Along with the normal feelings of grief and depression, many parents who lose a child to SIDS feel guilty and become extremely protective of older siblings or any babies born afterward. Help for parents is available through local groups or through the National SIDS Alliance in Maryland. Ask your pediatrician about resources in your area. At this time, the best preventive measure that parents can take is to place their baby to sleep on his back. Since 1992, the American Academy of Pediatrics has recommended that babies always be placed in this sleep position. Before this recommendation was made, more than 5,000 babies died from SIDS every year in the United States. But today, with the decrease in the number of babies sleeping on their stomach, the deaths from SIDS have declined to less than 3,000 per year. Each of these deaths is tragic, and campaigns are continuing to promote a back-to-sleep message to parents and others who care for young children.

Jaundice. Jaundice, the yellow color that often appears in the skin shortly after birth, sometimes persists into the second week of life in a baby who is breast-fed. (See page 140.) Sometimes breastfeeding must be stopped for twenty-four to forty-eight hours in order to clear the jaundice. Once it disappears, you may resume breastfeeding, because this type of jaundice rarely recurs. If it does, a second interruption of breastfeeding might be recommended, or the baby might be changed to formula-feeding. Your pediatrician will help you make this decision. (For additional information about jaundice, see Chapter 5, page 139.)

Jitters. Many newborns have quivery chins and shaky hands, but if your baby's whole body seems to be shaking, it could be a sign of low blood sugar or calcium levels, or some type of seizure disorder. Notify your pediatrician so he can determine the cause.

Rashes and Infections. Common newborn rashes include the following:

- **Cradle cap (seborrheic dermatitis)** appears as scaly patches on the scalp. Washing the hair and brushing out the scales daily helps control this condition. It usually disappears on its own within the first few months, but may have to be treated with a special shampoo. (See *Cradle Cap and Seborrheic Dermatitis,* page 692.)

- **Fingernail or toenail infections** will appear as a redness around the edge of the toenail or fingernail, which may seem to hurt when touched. These infections may respond to warm compresses, but usually need to be examined by a doctor and may require medication.

- **Umbilical infections** often appear as redness around the umbilical stump. They should be examined by your pediatrician. If your baby has an umbilical infection, he may need antibiotics or hospitalization.

- **Diaper rash.** See instructions for handling this problem on pages 54–55.

Thrush. White patches in the mouth may indicate that your baby has thrush, a common yeast infection. This condition is treated with an oral antifungal medication prescribed by your pediatrician.

Vision. Watch how your baby looks at you when she is alert. When you're about 8 to 15 inches (20.3 to 38.1 cm) from her face, do her eyes follow you? Will she follow a light or small toy passing before her at the same distance? At this age, the eyes may appear crossed, or one eye occasionally may drift inward or outward. This is because the muscles controlling eye movement are still developing. Both eyes should be able to move equally and together in all directions, however, and she should be able to track slowly moving objects at close range. If she can't, or if she was born severely premature or needed oxygen as a newborn, your pediatrician may refer you to an eye specialist for further examination.

Vomiting. If your baby starts forcefully vomiting (shooting out several inches rather than dribbling from the mouth), contact your pediatrician at once to make sure he does not have an obstruction of the valve between the stomach and the small intestine (hypertrophic pyloric stenosis; see page 522). Any vomiting that persists for more than twelve hours or is accompanied by diarrhea or fever also should be evaluated by your pediatrician.

Weight Gain. Your baby should be gaining weight rapidly (½ to 1 ounce per day [14 to 28 grams]) by the middle of this month. If he isn't, your pediatrician will want to make sure that he's getting adequate calories in his feedings and that he is absorbing them properly. Be prepared to answer these questions.

- How often does the baby eat?

- How much does he eat at a feeding, if bottle-feeding? How long does he nurse, if breastfeeding?

- How many bowel movements does the baby have each day?

- What is the amount and thinness or thickness of the stools?

- How often does the baby urinate?

If your baby is eating well and the contents of his diapers are normal in amount and consistency, there is probably no cause for alarm. Your baby may just be getting off to a slow start, or his weight could even have been measured wrong. Your pediatrician may want to schedule another office visit in two or three days to reevaluate the situation.

SAFETY CHECK

Car Safety Seats

- Your baby should ride in a properly installed, federally approved car safety seat *every time* she is in the car. At this age, she should ride in the rear-facing position, in the backseat. Never place a baby in the front seat of a car with a passenger-side air bag.

Bathing

- When bathing the baby in the sink, seat him on a washcloth to prevent slipping, and hold him under the arms. Never run the dishwasher at the same time that your baby is being bathed in the sink; otherwise, you may risk scald burns from the dishwasher's hot water.

- Adjust the temperature of your water heater to 120 degrees Fahrenheit (48.9 degrees Celsius) or lower so hot water can't scald him.

Changing Table

- Never leave your baby unattended on any surface above the floor. Even at this young age, she can suddenly extend her body and flip over the edge.

Suffocation Prevention

- Do not use baby or talcum powders on the baby. If inhaled, powders can cause severe lung damage and breathing problems in babies.
- Keep the crib free of all small objects (safety pins, small parts of toys, etc.) that he could swallow.
- Never leave plastic bags or wrappings where your baby can reach them.

Fire Prevention

- Dress your baby in flame-resistant clothing.
- Install smoke detectors in the proper places throughout your home.

Supervision

- Never leave your baby alone in the house, yard, or car.

Necklaces and Cords

- Do not let strings or cords dangle in the crib.
- Don't attach pacifiers, medallions, or other objects to the crib or body with a cord.
- Don't place a string or necklace around the baby's neck.
- Don't use clothing with drawstrings.

Jiggling

- Be careful not to jiggle or shake the baby's head too vigorously.
- Always support the baby's head and neck when moving her body.

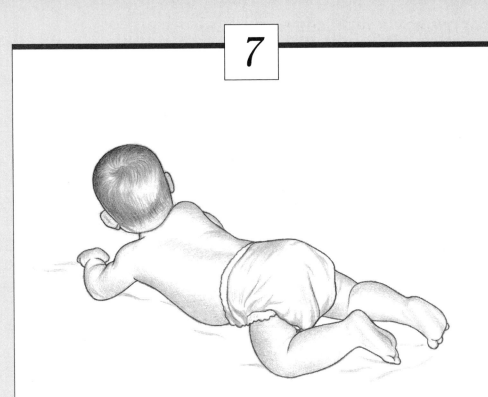

7

Age One Month Through
Three Months

*B*y the beginning of your baby's second month, much of the awe, exhaustion, and uncertainty that you felt immediately after her birth has given way to self-confidence. You probably have settled into a fairly routine (if still grueling) schedule around her feedings and naps. You've adjusted to having a new member of the family and are beginning to understand her general temperament. And you probably already have received the crowning reward that makes all the sacrifice worthwhile: her first true smile. This smile is just a glimmer of the delights in store over the next three months.

Between one and four months, your baby will undergo a dramatic transformation from a totally dependent newborn to an active and responsive infant. She'll lose many of her newborn reflexes while acquiring more voluntary control of her body. You'll find her spending hours inspecting her hands and watching their movements. She'll

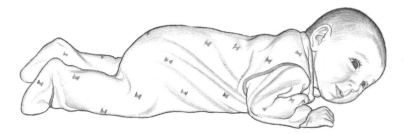

also become increasingly interested in her surroundings, especially the people close to her. She'll quickly learn to recognize your face and voice, and often will smile when she sees or hears you. Sometime during her second or third month, she'll even begin "talking" back to you in gentle but intentional coos and gurgles. With each of her new discoveries or achievements, you'll see a new part of your child's personality emerging.

Occasionally there will be moments in which your baby's development seems to be going backward. For example, she may have been sleeping through the night for several weeks—and then suddenly starts waking up every three hours again. What should you make of this? It's probably a sign that she's about to take a major developmental leap forward. In a week or two, she'll probably be sleeping through the night again and taking fewer naps, and she'll be considerably more alert and responsive to people and events around her. Developmental progress like this often is preceded by what appears to be a slight setback. As frustrating as it may be at first, you'll soon learn to read the signals, anticipate, and appreciate these periods of change.

GROWTH AND DEVELOPMENT

Physical Appearance and Growth

From months one through four, your baby will continue growing at the same rate he established during his first few weeks of life. Each month he'll probably gain between 1½ and 2 pounds (0.7 to 0.9 kg) and grow 1 to 1½ inches (2.5 to 4 cm). His head size probably will increase in circumference by about ½ inch (1.25 cm) each month. These figures are only averages, however, so you shouldn't be concerned as long as your child's development matches one of the normal curves on the growth charts on pages 128–129.

At two months, the soft spots on your baby's head should still be open and flat, but by two to three months, the soft spot at the back should be closed. Also, his head may seem out of proportion, because it is growing faster than the rest of his body. This is quite normal; his body will soon catch up.

At two months, your baby will look round and chubby, but as he starts using his arms and legs more actively, muscles will develop and fat will begin to disappear. His bones also will grow rapidly, and as his arms and legs "loosen up," his body and limbs will seem to stretch out, making him appear taller and leaner.

Movement

Many of your baby's movements still will be reflexive at the beginning of this period. For example, she may assume a "fencing" position every time her head turns (tonic neck reflex; see page 146) and throw out her arms if she hears a loud noise or feels that she's falling (Moro reflex, page 146). But as we've mentioned, most of these newborn reflexes will peak and begin to fade by the second or third month. She may temporarily seem less active after the reflexes have diminished, but now her movements, however subtle, are intentional ones and will build steadily toward mature activity.

One of the most important developments of these early months will be your baby's increasing neck strength. Try placing her on her stomach and see what happens. Before two months, she'll struggle to raise her head to look around. Even if she succeeds for only a second or two, that will allow her to turn for a slightly different view of the world and to move her nose and mouth away from any pillows or blankets that might be in the way. These momentary "exercises" also will strengthen the muscles in the back of her neck so that, by her four-month birthday, she'll be able to hold up her head and chest as she supports herself on her elbows. This is a major accomplishment, giving her the freedom and control to look all around at will, instead of just staring at her crib mattress or the mobile directly overhead.

For you, it's also a welcome development because you no longer have to support her head quite so much when carrying her. If you use a front or back carrier, she'll now be able to hold her own head up and look around as you walk.

A baby's control over the front neck muscles and abdominal muscles develops more gradually, so it will take a little longer for your baby to be able to raise her head when lying on her back. At one month, if you gently pull your baby by the arms to a sitting position, her head will flop backward; by four months, however, she'll be able to hold it steady in all directions.

Your child's legs also will become stronger and more active. During the second month, they'll start to straighten from their inward-curving newborn posi-

By her four-month birthday, your baby will be able to hold up her head and chest as she supports herself on her elbows.

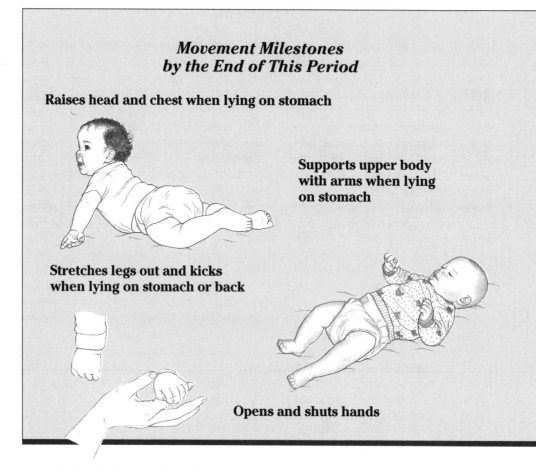

***Movement Milestones
by the End of This Period***

Raises head and chest when lying on stomach

**Supports upper body
with arms when lying
on stomach**

**Stretches legs out and kicks
when lying on stomach or back**

Opens and shuts hands

tion. Although her kicks will remain mostly reflexive for some time, they'll quickly gather force, and by the end of the third month, she might even kick herself over from front to back. (She probably won't roll from back to front until she's about six months old.) Since you cannot predict when she'll begin rolling over, you'll need to be especially vigilant whenever she's on the changing table or any other surface above floor level.

The newborn stepping reflex will disappear at about six weeks, and you may not see your baby step again until she's ready to walk. By three or four months, however, she'll be able to flex and straighten her legs at will. Lift her upright with her feet on the floor and she'll push down and straighten her legs so that she's virtually standing by herself (except for the balance you're providing). Then she'll try bending her knees and discover that she can bounce herself.

Your baby's hand and arm movements also will develop rapidly during these three months. In the beginning, her hands will be tightly clenched with her thumb curled inside her fingers; if you uncoil the fingers and place a rattle in her palm, she'll grasp it automatically, yet she won't be able to shake it or bring it to her mouth. She'll gaze at her hands with interest when they come into view by

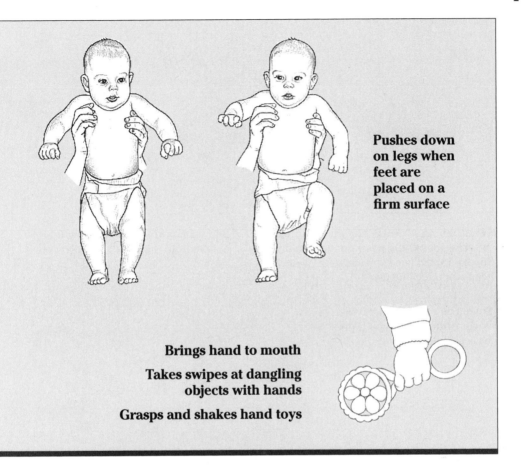

Pushes down on legs when feet are placed on a firm surface

Brings hand to mouth

Takes swipes at dangling objects with hands

Grasps and shakes hand toys

chance or because of reflexive movements, but she probably won't be able to bring them to her face on her own.

However, many changes will occur within just a month or two. Suddenly your baby's hands will seem to relax and her arms will open outward. During the third month, her hands will be half open most of the time, and you'll notice her carefully opening and shutting them. Try placing a rattle in her palm and she'll grip it, perhaps bring it to her mouth, and then drop it only after she's explored it fully. (The more lightweight the toy, the better she'll be able to control it.) She'll never seem to grow bored with her hands themselves; just staring at her fingers will amuse her for long stretches of time.

Your baby's attempts to bring her hands to her mouth will be persistent, but mostly in vain at first. Even if her fingers occasionally reach their destination, they'll quickly fall away. By four months, however, she'll probably have finally mastered this game and be able to get her thumb to her mouth and keep it there whenever she wishes. Put a rattle in her palm now and she'll clench it tightly, shake it, mouth it, and maybe even transfer it from hand to hand.

Your baby also will be able to reach accurately and quickly—not only with

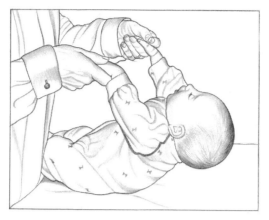

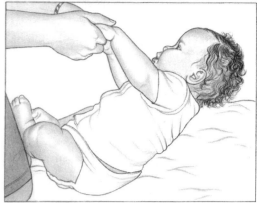

At one month, if you gently pull your baby by the arms to a sitting position, her head will flop backward (so always support your baby's head when picking her up).

By four months, however, she'll be able to hold it steady in all directions.

Since you can't predict when she'll begin rolling over, you'll need to be especially vigilant.

both hands but with her entire body. Hang a toy overhead and she'll reach up eagerly with arms and legs to bat at it and grab for it. Her face will tense in concentration, and she may even lift her head toward her target. It's as if every part of her body shares in her excitement as she masters these new skills.

Vision

At one month your baby still can't see very clearly beyond 12 inches (30.4 cm) or so, but he'll closely study anything within this range: the corner of his crib, the play of lights, the shadows on the wall, the shapes of his mobile. The human face is his favorite image, however. As you hold him in your arms, his attention is drawn automatically to your face, particularly your eyes. Often the mere sight of your eyes will make him smile. Gradually his visual span will broaden so that he can take in your whole face instead of just a single feature like your eyes. As this happens he'll be much more responsive to facial expressions involving your mouth, jaw, and cheeks. He'll also love flirting with himself in the mirror.

By two months, your baby's eyes are more coordinated and can work together to move and focus at the same time.

Buy an unbreakable mirror that's specially made to attach inside cribs and playpens, so he can entertain himself when you're not nearby.

In his early weeks, your baby will have a hard time tracking movement. If you wave a ball or toy quickly in front of him, he'll seem to stare through it, or if you shake your head, he'll lose his focus on your eyes. But this will change dramatically by two months, when his eyes are more coordinated and can work together to move and focus at the same time. Soon he'll be able to track an object moving through an entire half-circle in front of him. This increased visual coordination also will give him the depth perception he needs to track objects as they move toward and away from him. By three months, he'll also have the arm and hand control needed to bat at objects as they move above or in front of him; his aim won't be very good for a long time to come, but the practice will help him develop his hand-eye coordination. However, if your baby's eyes aren't tracking together by three months of age, talk to your pediatrician.

Your baby's distance vision also is developing at this time. You may notice at three months that he's smiling at you halfway across the room, or studying a toy several feet away. By four months, you'll catch him staring at the distant television screen or looking out the window. These are clues that his distance vision is developing properly.

Your infant's color vision will mature at about the same rate. At one month, he'll be quite sensitive to the brightness or intensity of color; consequently, he'll prefer to look at bold patterns in sharply contrasting colors or in black-and-white. Young infants do not appreciate the soothing pastels we usually associate with a newborn's nursery because of the babies' limited color vision. By about four months, your baby finally will be responsive to the full range of colors and their many shades.

As his eyesight develops, your infant naturally will seek out more stimulating things to see. Around one month, his favorite patterns will be simple linear images, such as big stripes or a checkerboard. By three months, he'll be much more interested in circular patterns (bull's-eyes, spirals). This is one reason why faces, which are full of circles and curves, are so appealing to him.

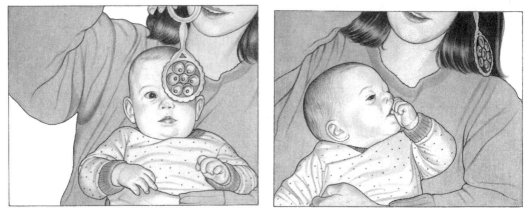

Soon he'll be able to track an object moving through an entire half-circle in front of him.

Hearing and Making Sounds

Just as your baby naturally prefers the human face over any other visual pattern, she also prefers the human voice to other sounds. Her mother's voice is her absolute favorite, because she associates it with warmth, food, and comfort. Babies like the high-pitched voices of women in general—a fact that most adults seem to understand intuitively and respond to accordingly, without even realizing it.

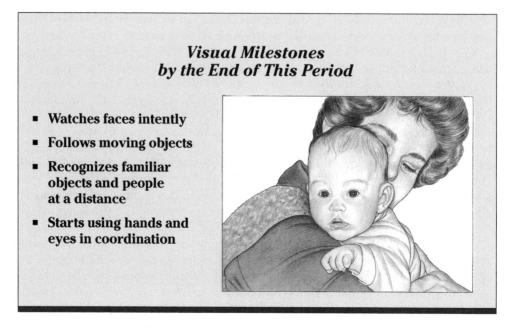

Visual Milestones by the End of This Period

- **Watches faces intently**
- **Follows moving objects**
- **Recognizes familiar objects and people at a distance**
- **Starts using hands and eyes in coordination**

Just listen to yourself the next time you talk to your baby. You'll probably notice that you raise the pitch of your voice, slow your rate of speech, exaggerate certain syllables, and widen your eyes and mouth more than normal. This dramatic approach is guaranteed to capture almost any baby's attention—and usually make her smile.

By listening to you and others talk to her, your baby will discover the importance of speech long before she understands or repeats any specific words herself. By one month, she'll be able to identify you by voice, even if you're in another room, and as you talk to her, she'll be reassured, comforted, and entertained. When she smiles and gurgles back at you, she'll see the delight on your face and realize that talk is a two-way process. These first conversations will teach her many of the subtle rules of communication, such as turn-taking, vocal tone, imitation and pacing, and speed of verbal interaction.

At about two months, you may begin hearing your infant repeat some vowel sounds (ah-ah-ah, ooh-ooh-ooh), especially if you've been talking to her often with clear, simple words and phrases. Along the way, it's easy to fall into a habit of baby talk, but you should try to mix your conversations with adult language and phase out the baby talk after she's six months old.

By four months, your infant will babble routinely, often amusing herself for long periods by producing strange new sounds (muh-muh, bah-bah). She'll also be more sensitive to your tone of voice and the emphasis you put on certain words or phrases. As you move through each day together, she'll learn from your voice when you're going to feed her, change her diapers, go out for a walk, or put her down to sleep. The way you talk will tell her a great deal about your mood and personality, and the way she responds will tell you a lot about her. If you speak in an upbeat or comforting way, she may smile or coo. Yell or talk angrily, and she'll probably startle or cry.

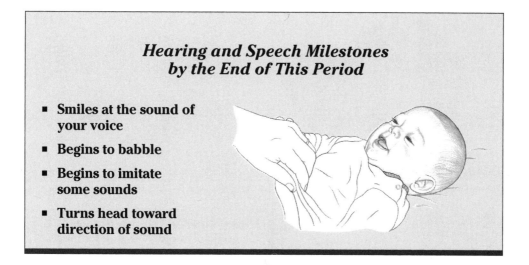

Hearing and Speech Milestones by the End of This Period

- **Smiles at the sound of your voice**
- **Begins to babble**
- **Begins to imitate some sounds**
- **Turns head toward direction of sound**

Emotional and Social Development

By the second month, your baby will spend much of each day watching and listening to the people around him. He learns that they will entertain and soothe him, feed him, and make him comfortable. He feels good when they smile at him, and he seems to know instinctively that he can smile, too. Even during his first month, he'll experiment with primitive grins and grimaces. Then, during the second month, these movements will turn to genuine signals of pleasure and friendliness.

Have you experienced his first true smile yet? It's a major turning point for both you and your infant. In case there was any doubt in your mind, all the sleepless nights and erratic days of these first weeks suddenly seem worthwhile at the sight of that first grin, and you'll do everything in your power to keep those smiles coming. For his part, your baby suddenly will discover that just by moving his lips he can have two-way "conversations" with you, as his grins bring him even more attention than usual and make him feel good. Smiling also will give him another way besides crying to express his needs and exert some control over what happens to him.

At first your baby actually may seem to smile past you without meeting your gaze, but don't let this disturb you. Looking away from you gives him some control and protects him from being overwhelmed by you. It's his way of taking in the total picture without being "caught" by your eyes. In this way, he can pay equal attention to your facial expressions, the sound of your voice, the warmth of your body, and the way you're holding him. As you get to know each other, he'll gradually hold your gaze for longer and longer periods, and you'll find ways to increase his "tolerance"—perhaps by holding him at a certain distance, adjusting the level of your voice, or modifying your expressions.

By three months, your baby will be a master of "smile talk." Sometimes he'll start a "conversation" by aiming a broad smile at you and gurgling to catch your

As you get to know each other, he'll gradually hold your gaze for longer and longer periods.

attention. At other times he'll lie in wait, watching your face until you give the first smile and then beaming back his enthusiastic response. His whole body will participate in these dialogues. His hands will open wide, one or both arms will lift up, and his arms and legs will move in time with the rhythms of your speech. His facial movements also may mirror yours. As you talk he may open his mouth and widen his eyes, and if you stick out your tongue, he may do the same!

Of course, your baby probably won't act this friendly with everyone. Like adults, your infant will prefer certain people to others. And his favorites, naturally, will be his parents. Then, at about three or four months, he'll become intrigued by other children. If he has brothers or sisters, you'll see him beaming as soon as they start talking to him. If he hears children's voices down the street or on television, he may turn to find them. This fascination with children will increase as he gets older.

Grandparents or familiar sitters may receive a hesitant smile at first, followed by coos and body talk once they've played with your baby awhile. By contrast, strangers may receive no more than a curious stare or a fleeting smile. This selective behavior tells you that even at this young age, he's starting to sort out who's who in his life. Although the signals are subtle, there's no doubt that he's becoming very attached to the people closest to him.

This unspoken give-and-take may seem like no more than a game, but these early exchanges play an important part in his social and emotional development. By responding quickly and enthusiastically to his smiles and engaging him often in these "conversations," you'll let him know that he's important to you, that he can trust you, and that he has a certain amount of control in his life. By recognizing his cues and not interrupting or looking away when he's "talking," you'll also show him that you are interested in him and value him. This contributes to his developing self-esteem.

As your baby grows, the way the two of you communicate will vary with his needs and desires. On a day-to-day basis you'll find that he has three general levels of need, each of which shows a different side of his personality:

1. When his needs are urgent—when he's very hungry or in pain, for instance—he'll let you know in his own special way, perhaps by screaming, whimpering, or using desperate body language. In time you'll learn to recognize these signals so quickly that you usually can satisfy him almost before he himself knows what he wants.

2. While your baby is peacefully asleep, or when he's alert and entertaining himself, you'll feel reassured that you've met all his needs for the moment. This will give you a welcome opportunity to rest or take care of other business. The times when he's playing by himself provide you with wonderful opportunities to observe—from a distance—how he is developing new skills such as reaching, tracking objects, or manipulating his hands.

3. Each day there will be periods when your baby's obvious needs are met but he's still fussy or fitful. He may let you know this with a whine, agitated movements, or spurts of aimless activity between moments of calm. He probably won't even know what he wants, and any of several responses might help calm him. Playing, talking, singing, rocking, and walking may work sometimes; on other occasions, simply repositioning him or letting him "fuss it out" may be the most successful strategies. You also may find that while a particular response calms him down momentarily, he'll soon become even fussier and demand more attention. This cycle may not break until you either let him cry a few minutes or distract him by doing something different—for example, taking him outside or feeding him. As trying as these spells can be, you'll both learn a lot about each other because of them. You'll discover how your baby likes to be rocked, what funny faces or voices he most enjoys, and what he most likes to look at. He'll find out what he has to do to get you to respond, how hard you'll try to please him, and where your limits of tolerance lie.

Over time your baby's periods of acute need will decrease, and he'll be able to entertain himself for longer stretches. In part, this is because you're learning to anticipate and care for many of his problems before he's uncomfortable. But also, his nervous system will be maturing, and, as a result, he'll be better able to cope with everyday stresses by himself. With greater control over his body, he'll be able to do more things to amuse himself and he'll experience fewer frustrations. The periods when he seems most difficult to satisfy probably won't disappear entirely for a few years, but as he becomes more active, it will be easier to distract him. Ultimately he should learn to overcome these spells on his own.

During these early months, don't worry about spoiling your baby with too much attention. Observe him closely and respond promptly when he needs you. You may not be able to calm him down every time, but it never hurts to show him that you care. In fact, the more promptly and consistently you comfort your baby's fussing in the first six months, the less demanding he's likely to be when he's older. At this age, he needs frequent reassurance in order to feel secure about himself and about you. By helping him establish this sense of security now, you're laying a foundation for the confidence and trust that will allow him gradually to separate from you and become a strong, independent person.

BASIC CARE

Feeding

Ideally, your baby will continue on his diet of exclusive breastmilk or formula until four to six months.* The amount he consumes at each

* There is a difference of opinion among Academy experts on this matter. The Section on Breastfeeding supports exclusive breastfeeding for about six months. The Committee on Nutrition supports the introduction of complementary foods between four and six months of age where safe and nutritious complementary foods are available.

> ## Social/Emotional Milestones by the End of This Period
>
> - **Begins to develop a social smile**
> - **Enjoys playing with other people and may cry when playing stops**
> - **Becomes more communicative and expressive with face and body**
> - **Imitates some movements and facial expressions**

feeding should increase gradually from about 4 or 5 ounces (120 to 150 ml) during the second month, to 5 or 6 ounces (150 to 180 ml) by four months. His daily intake should reach about 30 ounces (900 ml) by four months. Ordinarily, this will supply all his nutritional needs at this age. If your baby seems persistently hungry after what you think are adequate feedings, consult your pediatrician for advice. When a breastfeeding infant is not gaining weight, your milk supply may have decreased. A variety of techniques can be used to increase supply and intake. If it's clear that he's getting enough milk but is still hungry, the doctor may advise you to start solid foods. Solids should be introduced only near the end of this period, however, because younger babies have a tendency to push the food out with their tongues, which makes spoon-feeding difficult. Also, young infants may not be able to tolerate certain solid foods. If you do need to introduce solids, start with the least allergenic food, which is rice cereal, and thin it as much as possible with breastmilk or formula. (For more information about introducing solids, see Chapter 8.)

Even if you don't make any additions to your baby's diet, you'll probably notice a change in his bowel movements during these months. His intestines can hold more now and absorb a greater amount of nutrients from the milk, so his stools will tend to be more solid. The gastrocolic reflex is also diminishing, so he should no longer have a bowel movement after each feeding. (See *Bowel Movements,* page 56.) In fact, between two and three months, the frequency of stools in both breastfed and bottle-fed babies may decrease dramatically; some breastfed babies have only one bowel movement every three or four days, and a few perfectly healthy breastfed infants have just one a week. As long as your baby is eating well, gaining weight, and his stools are not too hard or dry, there's no reason to be alarmed by this drop in frequency.

Sleeping

By two months, your baby will be more alert and social and will spend more time awake during the day. This will make her a little more tired during the dark, quiet hours when no one is around to entertain her. Meanwhile, her stomach

Developmental Health Watch

Although each baby develops in her own individual way and at her own rate, failure to reach certain milestones may signal medical or developmental problems requiring special attention. If you notice any of the following warning signs in your infant at this age, discuss them with your pediatrician.

- Still has Moro reflex after four months
- Doesn't seem to respond to loud sounds
- Doesn't notice her hands by two months
- Doesn't smile at the sound of your voice by two months
- Doesn't follow moving objects with her eyes by two to three months
- Doesn't grasp and hold objects by three months
- Doesn't smile at people by three months
- Cannot support her head well at three months
- Doesn't reach for and grasp toys by three to four months
- Doesn't babble by three to four months
- Doesn't bring objects to her mouth by four months
- Begins babbling, but doesn't try to imitate any of your sounds by four months
- Doesn't push down with her legs when her feet are placed on a firm surface by four months
- Has trouble moving one or both eyes in all directions
- Crosses her eyes most of the time (Occasional crossing of the eyes is normal in these first months.)
- Doesn't pay attention to new faces, or seems very frightened by new faces or surroundings
- Still has the tonic neck reflex at four to five months

capacity will be growing, so that she needs less frequent feedings; as a result, she may start skipping one middle-of-the-night feeding and sleep from around 10:00 P.M. through to daylight. By three months, most (but not all) infants consistently sleep through the night (seven or eight hours without interruption).

Toys and Activities Appropriate for a One- to Three-Month-Old

- **Images or books with high-contrast patterns**
- **Bright, varied mobile**
- **Unbreakable mirror attached to inside of crib**
- **Rattles**
- **Singing to your baby**
- **Playing varied music from music boxes, CDs, records, or tapes**

If your child does not start sleeping through the night by three months, you may need to give her some encouragement by keeping her awake longer in the afternoon and early evening. Play with her actively at these times, or let her join the rest of the family in the kitchen or living room so she's not tempted to drift to sleep before bedtime. Increase the amount of her feeding right before bed, as well (if she's breastfeeding, increase the amount of time she nurses), so she doesn't wake up too early because she's hungry.

Even after your baby has established a fairly regular and reasonable sleep pattern, problems can develop. For example, it's common for babies at this age to get their days and nights mixed up so that they're doing most of their sleeping during the day. Although this situation may seem to occur without warning, it usually develops over several days. The baby begins by sleeping more during the day, which causes her to sleep less at night. If she's fed and comforted when she wakes up at night, she'll adopt this new sleep cycle quite naturally. To prevent or break this habit, induce your baby to go back to sleep as quickly as possible during the night. Don't turn up the lights, talk, or play with her. If you need to feed and change her, try to disturb her as little as possible when doing so. Then keep her awake as much as possible during the day, and don't put her down for the night before 10:00 or 11:00 P.M. *Remember, at this age, children should be put to sleep on their back* (although be sure to give her some "tummy time" during her waking hours, which is good for her normal physical development). If you're patient and consistent, her sleep pattern will start to respond soon. (See *Helping Your Baby Sleep,* page 45.)

Many infants also wake up too early in the morning to suit their parents. Sometimes this problem can be solved by putting shades on the windows to block out the morning sun; then when the baby awakens, perhaps after a few minutes of fussing, she may fall back to sleep. If this doesn't work, however, it may help to keep her up an extra hour at night. Unfortunately, not all infants are able to sleep late in the morning; some wake up automatically and are ready to

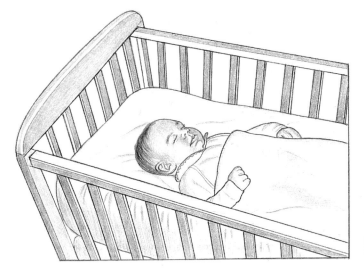

After three months, most (but not all) infants consistently sleep through the night.

start the day at dawn. If that's your own baby's pattern, you really have little choice but to adapt to her schedule. As she gets older (age six to eight months), having favorite toys in her crib may keep her occupied so you can have a few more minutes to sleep.

Sometimes you may think your baby is waking up when she's actually going through a phase of very light slumber. She could be squirming, startling, fussing, or even crying—and still be asleep. Or she may be awake but on the verge of drifting off again if left alone. Don't make the mistake of trying to comfort her during these moments; you'll only awaken her further and delay her going back to sleep. Instead, if you let her fuss and even cry for a few minutes, she'll learn to get herself to sleep without relying on you. Some babies actually need to let off energy by crying in order to settle into sleep or rouse themselves out of it. As much as fifteen to twenty minutes of fussing won't do your child any harm. Just be sure she's not crying out of hunger or pain, or because her diaper is wet. Although it may be difficult just to let her cry for even a minute or two, you and she will be much better off in the long run.

Siblings

By the second month, although you may be used to having a new baby in the house, your older children still may be having a hard time adjusting. Especially if the baby is your second child, your first probably resents giving up the central place in the household. No longer the primary focus of the family, he may do everything in his power to recapture that position—and that usually involves misbehaving.

Sometimes your older child might display his frustration by talking back, doing something he knows is forbidden, or literally shouting for attention. He also might regress, suddenly wetting his bed or having daytime accidents even

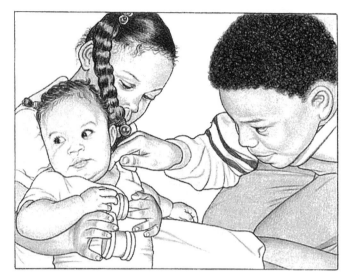

Invite older siblings to play with the baby.

though he's been toilet-trained for months. Having each parent take time with him alone each day should help resolve these problems.

However, if the older child takes out his anger on the baby—pulling away his bottle or even hitting him—you'll need to take more direct action. Sit down and talk with him, and be prepared to hear things such as "I wish that baby had never come here." Try to keep these and his other feelings in mind as you confront him. Reassure him that you still love him very much, but explain firmly that he must not hurt the baby. Make an extra effort to include him in all family activities, and invite him to play with the newborn. Make him feel like an important "big kid" by giving him specific baby-related jobs, such as carrying the diaper bag, putting away toys, or helping dress the baby. At the same time, set clear and consistent rules, such as never picking up the baby without permission.

Set clear and consistent rules, such as never picking up the baby without permission.

For the Grandparents

As a grandparent, your role can be especially important in the lives of not only your newborn grandchild and his parents, but also the other children in the family. Make sure you pay plenty of attention to the older youngsters, who might feel a little neglected with all the attention showered on the baby. You can serve as a "pinch hitter" when the new parents are adjusting to their infant by planning some special activities just for you and the baby's older brother(s) or sister(s). For example, make time for the sibling(s) with:

- Trips to the store or other activities

- Car rides

- Appropriate stimulating times with music or reading stories

- Sleepovers at Grandma's house

As we've suggested elsewhere in the book (see pages 168, 224, and 262), you can play other important roles to help your daughter or son adjust to the new addition to their family. Help them with cleaning, shopping, and other errands. At the same time, without being overly intrusive, pass along some of your own wisdom and reassurances about baby care—perhaps explaining the "normalness" of crying, the color of bowel movements, the little rashes or other changes in skin color, and a host of other occurrences in the early months. For example, there will be times of frustration for the new parents, such as when the baby is crying excessively and is difficult to console. Provide support and encouragement for the parents—and give them a breather, if possible, by taking the baby out for a stroll in the carriage. The insights and assistance of both grandfathers and grandmothers can have a calming and "life-saving" effect on new parents.

HEALTH WATCH

The following medical problems are common between the ages of two months and four months. Check Part II of this book for other illnesses and conditions that occur throughout childhood.

Diarrhea (see also *Diarrhea,* page 505). If your baby has a vomiting spell followed a day or two later by diarrhea, she probably has a viral infection in her intestinal tract. If you're breastfeeding, your pediatrician probably will suggest that you continue nursing her as usual. If you're bottle-feeding, in most cases

Stimulating Infant Brain Growth: Age One Month Through Three Months

- Provide healthful nutrition as your baby grows; have periodic check-ups and timely immunizations from a regular source of medical care.

- Give consistent, warm, physical contact—hugging, skin-to-skin, body-to-body contact—to establish your infant's sense of security and well-being. Talk or sing to your baby during dressing, bathing, feeding, playing, walking, and driving. Use simple, lively phrases and address your baby by name. Respond to his gestures, as well as to the faces and the sounds he makes.

- Be attentive to your baby's rhythms and moods. Learn to read her cues and respond to her when she is upset as well as when she is happy. Babies cannot be spoiled.

- Provide colorful objects of different shapes, sizes, and textures that he can play with. Show her children's picture books and family photographs.

- Your face is by far the most interesting visual object at this age. Play peekaboo with your baby.

- Place a child-safe mirror in your infant's crib so he can look at his own face.

- If you speak a foreign language, use it at home.

- Avoid subjecting your baby to stressful or traumatic experiences, physical or psychological.

- Make sure other people who provide care and supervision for your baby understand the importance of forming a loving and comforting relationship with your child and also provide consistent care.

you can continue formula-feeding. In some instances your pediatrician may advise you to limit the baby's intake to a special solution containing electrolytes (i.e., salt and potassium) and sugar. You may be advised to use a soy formula for a few days when you return to formula-feeding. This is because diarrhea washes out the enzymes needed to digest the sugar in cow's milk.

Ear Infections (see also *Middle Ear Infections,* page 580). Although ear infections are more common in older babies, occasionally they occur in infants under three months. Babies are prone to ear infections because the tube that connects the nasal passages to the middle ear is very short, making it easy for a cold in the nose to spread to the ear. If the infection becomes severe or is not treated, the eardrum may break and the infected fluid will pass through it and out the ear canal. With proper treatment, however, the eardrum will heal with no permanent damage.

The first sign of an ear infection is usually irritability, especially at night. Your baby also may use his hand to pull or swipe at his ear. As the infection advances, it may produce a fever. If you suspect that your child has an ear infection, call the doctor as soon as possible. If an ear examination confirms that an infection is present, the doctor may recommend giving liquid acetaminophen to your baby in an appropriate dose. (Do *not* give him aspirin; it can cause a serious brain disorder called Reye syndrome; see page 520.) Your pediatrician also may prescribe a course of antibiotics, although antibiotics are being used with more care than in the past.

Eye Infections. In infants, conjunctivitis, or "pink eye," usually is caused by a viral or bacterial infection. In babies, the infection often is associated with chlamydia, acquired as the newborn moves through the birth canal. The eyedrops or ointments that all babies receive in the delivery room may not clear this infection in the eyes nor do they prevent it from spreading to the nose and throat and from there to the lungs, causing pneumonia. Because of this danger, babies who have been exposed to chlamydia during the birthing process are treated with an oral antibiotic called erythromycin.

Any signs of eye infection such as eye swelling, redness, or discharge during the first few weeks of life should be immediately reported to your pediatrician. (For more information, see *Eye Infections,* page 604.)

Gastroesophageal Reflux. This condition occurs when contents from the stomach make their way back into the esophagus (the tube through which food and liquids are transported from the throat to the stomach). This so-called reflux takes place when the sphincter (the valve separating the stomach and the esophagus) is weak or relaxes so the food can flow upward in the direction from which it came.

Recent research shows that gastroesophageal reflux is more common in children than was once believed, beginning as early as infancy. Not long after eating, an infant with this condition may vomit, have periods of coughing, become irritable, have difficulty swallowing, and may be underweight. To minimize the problem, burp your baby several times while he is feeding, as well as afterward. Because the condition can worsen when your infant is lying flat, try keeping him in an upright position for about half an hour following each feeding. Babies may experience fewer symptoms when lying on their back than their stomach, and because of concerns about SIDS (sudden infant death syndrome) when babies sleep, it's best not to place them in a prone position (on stomach) for sleep or to help their reflux symptoms.

To ease the condition, your doctor might recommend switching to a hypoallergenic formula if your baby is consuming a formula; he'll ask you to check to see if symptoms improve in the next week or two. At times, infants who vomit have an allergy to cow's milk, and this switch in formulas may help.

Rashes and Skin Conditions. Many of the rashes seen in the first month may persist through the second or third. In addition, eczema may occur anytime after one month. Eczema, or atopic dermatitis (see also *Eczema,* page 693), produces dry, scaly, and often red patches, usually on the face, in the bends of the elbows, and behind the knees. In young infants, elbows and knees are the most common locations. The patches are extremely itchy, which may make your baby irritable. Ask your pediatrician to prescribe treatment. Don't use any over-the-counter lotions or creams unless he specifically recommends them. To prevent a recurrence of the rash, make sure you use only the mildest of soaps to wash your baby and her clothes, and dress her only in soft clothing (no wool or rough weaves). Bathe her no more than three times a week, since frequent baths may further dry her skin.

Respiratory Syncytial Virus (RSV) Infections. Although many parents have never heard of RSV, it is the most common cause of lower respiratory tract infections in children. Infecting the lungs and breathing passages, it is frequently responsible for bronchiolitis and pneumonia in youngsters under age one. In fact, the highest incidence of RSV illness occurs in infants from two months to eight months of age. RSV is also the most common reason that infants under one year of age are hospitalized.

RSV is a highly contagious infection, occurring most often during the months from fall through spring. It causes symptoms similar to those of the common cold, including a runny or stuffy nose, a sore throat, a mild cough, and a fever, although in a condition like bronchiolitis, the symptoms also may include abnormally rapid breathing and wheezing.

If your baby was born prematurely, or has chronic lung disease, he has a higher risk of developing an RSV infection. Premature babies frequently have underdeveloped lungs, and may not have received enough antibodies from their mother to help them combat RSV if they encounter it.

If your own baby falls into the high-risk category, you can reduce his chances of developing an RSV infection by:

- Washing your hands with warm water and soap before picking up and holding your baby

- Reducing your contact with your baby when you have a cold or a fever

- Discouraging your baby's siblings from spending time with your infant when they have a cold

- Keeping your baby away from crowded areas, such as shopping malls

- Avoiding smoking around your baby

If your pediatrician determines that your baby has developed bronchiolitis or another RSV infection, she may recommend symptomatic treatment, such as the use of acetaminophen to lower your infant's fever. Severe pneumonia or bronchiolitis can require hospitalization so humidified oxygen and medications can be administered to help your child breathe more easily. (For more information about RSV infections, see *Bronchiolitis,* page 546.)

Upper Respiratory Infections (URI) (see also *Colds/Upper Respiratory Infection,* page 577). Many babies have their first cold during these months. Breastfeeding provides some immunity, but it is not complete protection by any means, especially if another member of the family has a respiratory illness. The infection can spread easily through droplets in the air or by hand contact. (Exposure to cold temperatures or drafts does not cause colds.) Washing hands, covering mouths while sneezing or coughing, and refraining from kissing when you have a cold will help prevent the infection from spreading to others.

Most respiratory infections in young babies are mild, producing a cough, runny nose, and slightly elevated temperature, but rarely a high fever. A runny nose, however, can be troublesome for an infant. He cannot blow his nose, so the mucus blocks the nasal passages. Before three or four months of age, an infant doesn't breathe well through his mouth, so this blockage of his nose causes more discomfort for him than for older children. A congested nose also often disturbs his sleep because he wakes up when he's not able to breathe. It can interfere with feeding, too, since he must interrupt sucking in order to breathe through his mouth.

To help reduce this problem, use a cool-mist humidifier in his room. If congestion does occur, use a bulb syringe to suction the mucus from his nose, especially before feedings and when it's obviously blocked. Put a few drops of normal saline (prescribed by your pediatrician) into his nose first to thin the mucus, making it easier to suction. Squeeze the bulb first; then insert the tip gently into the nostril and slowly release the bulb. Although acetaminophen will lower an elevated temperature and calm him if he's irritable, you should give it to a baby this age *only* on your pediatrician's advice. *Do not use aspirin.* (See *Reye Syndrome,* page 520; *Medication,* page 635.)

Ordinarily, you won't need to take your baby to the doctor when he has an upper respiratory infection. You should call, however, if any of the following occurs.

- He develops a persistent cough.

- He loses his appetite and refuses several feedings.

- He runs a fever: *Contact your pediatrician anytime a baby under three months of age has a rectal temperature higher than 101 degrees Fahrenheit (38.3 Celsius).*

- He seems excessively irritable.

- He seems unusually sleepy or hard to awaken.

IMMUNIZATION ALERT

Your baby should receive the Hepatitis B vaccine soon after birth and before your baby is discharged from the hospital, and again at least four weeks after the first dose.

At two months, and again at four months, your baby should receive:

- DTaP vaccine

- Inactivated polio vaccine

- Hib vaccine (This vaccine may cause a slight fever and some soreness where it's injected. The vaccine helps prevent meningitis, pneumonia, and joint infection caused by *Haemophilus influenzae* type b bacteria.)

- Pneumococcal vaccine

(For detailed information, see pages 72–77 and Chapter 27, "Immunizations.")

SAFETY CHECK

Falls

- Never place the baby in an infant seat on a table, chair, or any other surface above floor level.

- Never leave your baby unattended on a bed, couch, changing table, or chair. When purchasing a changing table, look for one with two-inch guardrails. Don't place it near a window. (For more information about changing tables, see page 433.)

- Use safety straps that are part of high chairs and changing tables.

Burns

- Never hold your baby while smoking, drinking a hot liquid, or cooking by a hot stove or oven.

- Never allow anyone to smoke around your baby.

- Before placing your baby in the bath, always test the water temperature with the inside of your wrist or forearm.

- Never heat your baby's milk (or, later on, food) in a microwave oven.

Choking

- Routinely check all toys for sharp edges or small parts that could be pulled or broken off.

- If you use a crib gym or other suspended toys for the crib, make sure they are fastened securely and tightly so the baby cannot pull them down or entangle herself in them.

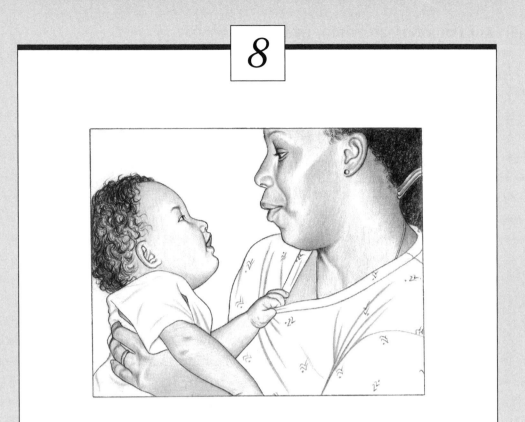

8

AGE FOUR MONTHS
THROUGH SEVEN MONTHS

*B*y your infant's four-month birthday, you'll probably have a daily routine for his feeding, napping, bathing, and going to sleep at night. This routine will provide a predictability that will help your baby feel secure while allowing you to budget your time and activities. The schedule should be flexible, however, to allow for spur-of-the-moment fun. Short strolls when the sun finally appears on a dreary day, an unexpected lunch visit from grandparents, or a family excursion to the zoo or park are all wonderful excuses to break the routine. Being open to impulse will make your life together more enjoyable and help your baby learn to adapt to all the changes facing him in his life ahead.

For the time being, the most important changes are taking place within him. This is the period when he'll learn to coordinate his emerging perceptive abilities (the use of senses like vision, touch, and hearing) and his increasing motor abilities to develop skills like grasping, rolling over, sitting up, and possibly even crawling. The control that's evident in his budding motor skills will extend to every part of his life. Instead of reacting primarily by reflex, as he did during his earlier months, he'll now choose what he will and won't do. For example, as a newborn, he sucked on almost anything placed in his mouth, but now he has definite favorites. Although in the past he merely looked at a strange new toy, now he mouths, manipulates, and explores every one of its qualities.

Your baby will be better able to communicate his emotions and desires now, and he'll voice them frequently. For example, he'll cry not only when he's hungry or uncomfortable, but also when he wants a different toy or a change in activity.

You may find that your five- or six-month-old also occasionally cries when you leave the room or when he's suddenly confronted by a stranger. This is because he's developing a strong attachment for you and the other people who regularly care for him. He now associates you with his own well-being and can distinguish you from other people. Even if he doesn't cry out for you, he will signal this new awareness by curiously and carefully studying a stranger's face. By eight or nine months, he may openly object to strangers who come too close. This signals the start of a normal developmental stage known as stranger anxiety.

During these months before stranger anxiety hits full force, however, your child probably will go through a period of delightful show-offmanship, smiling and playing with everyone he meets. His personality will be coming out in full bloom, and even people meeting him for the first time will notice many of his unique character traits. Take advantage of his sociability to acquaint him with people who will help care for him in the future, such as babysitters, relatives, or child care workers. This won't guarantee clear sailing through the stranger-anxiety period, but it may help smooth the waters.

You'll also learn during these months, if you haven't before, that there is no formula for raising an ideal child. You and your baby are each unique, and the relationship between the two of you is unique, as well. So what works for one baby may not for another. You have to discover what succeeds for you through trial and error. While your neighbor's child may fall asleep easily and sleep through the night, your baby may need some extra holding and cuddling to settle him down at bedtime and again in the middle of the night. While your first child might have needed a great deal of hugging and comforting, your second might prefer more time alone. These individual differences don't necessarily indicate that your parenting is "right" or "wrong"; they just mean that each baby is unique. Over these first months and years, you will get to know your child's individual traits and you'll develop patterns of activity and interaction that are designed especially for him. If you remain flexible and open to his special traits, he'll help steer your actions as a parent in the right direction.

GROWTH AND DEVELOPMENT

Physical Appearance and Growth

Between four and seven months, your baby will continue to gain approximately 1 to 1¼ pounds (0.45 to 0.56 kg) a month. By the time she reaches her eighth-month birthday, she probably will weigh about two and a half times what she did at birth. Her bones also will continue to grow at a rapid rate. As a result, during these months her length will increase by about 2 inches (5 cm) and her head circumference by about 1 inch (2.5 cm).

Your child's specific weight and height are not as important as her rate of growth. By now you should have established her position on the growth curve on pages 128–129. Continue to plot her measurements at regular intervals to make sure she keeps growing at the same rate. If you find that she's beginning to follow a different curve or gaining weight or height unusually slowly, discuss it with your pediatrician.

Movement

In his first four months, your baby established the muscle control he needed to move both his eyes and his head so he could follow interesting objects. Now he'll take on an even greater challenge: sitting up. He'll accomplish this in small steps as his back and neck muscles gradually strengthen and he develops better balance in his trunk, head, and neck. First he'll learn to raise his head and hold it up while lying on his stomach. You can encourage this by placing him on his stomach and extending his arms forward; then hold a rattle or other attractive toy in front of him to get his attention and coax him to hold his head up and look at you. This also is a good way to check his hearing and vision.

Once he's able to lift his head, your baby will start pushing up on his arms and arching his back to lift his chest. This strengthens his upper body so he can

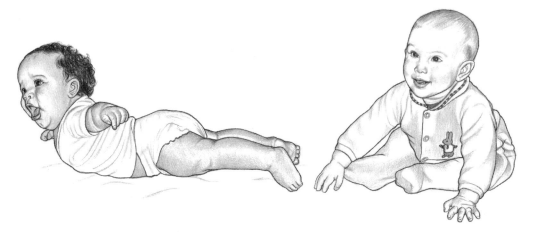

remain steady and upright when sitting. At the same time he may rock on his stomach, kick his legs, and "swim" with his arms. These abilities, which usually appear at about five months, are necessary for rolling over and crawling. By the end of this period, he'll probably be able to roll over in both directions. Most children are able to roll first from the stomach to the back and later in the opposite direction, although doing it in the opposite sequence is perfectly normal.

Once your baby is strong enough to raise his chest, you can help him practice sitting up. Hold him up or support his back with pillows or a couch corner as he learns to balance himself. Soon he'll learn to "tripod," leaning forward as he extends his arms to balance his upper body. Bright, interesting toys placed in front of him will give him something to focus on as he gains his balance. It will be some time before he can maneuver himself into a sitting posture without your assistance, but by six to eight months, if you position him upright, he'll be able to remain sitting without leaning forward on his arms. Then he can discover all the wonderful things that can be done with his hands as he views the

world from this new vantage point.

By the fourth month, your baby can easily bring interesting objects to his mouth. During his next four months, he'll begin to use his fingers and thumbs together in a mitten or clawlike grip or raking motion, and he'll manage to pick up many things. He won't develop the pincer grasp using his index finger and thumb until he's about

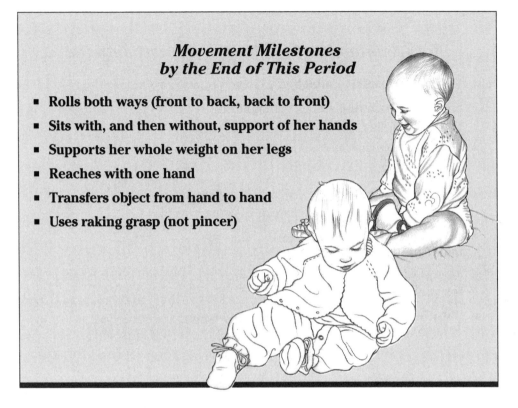

Movement Milestones by the End of This Period

- **Rolls both ways (front to back, back to front)**
- **Sits with, and then without, support of her hands**
- **Supports her whole weight on her legs**
- **Reaches with one hand**
- **Transfers object from hand to hand**
- **Uses raking grasp (not pincer)**

nine months old, but by the sixth to eighth month, he'll learn how to transfer objects from hand to hand, turn them from side to side, and twist them upside down.

As his physical coordination improves, your baby will discover parts of his body that he never knew existed. Lying on his back, he can now grab his feet and toes and bring them to his mouth. While being diapered, he may reach down to touch his genitals. When sitting up, he may slap his knee or thigh. Through these explorations he'll discover many new and interesting sensations. He'll also start to understand the function of each body part. For example, when you place his newly found feet on the floor, he may first curl his toes and stroke the carpet or wood surface, but soon he'll discover he can use his feet and legs to practice "walking" or just to bounce up and down. Watch out! These are all preparations for the next major milestones: crawling and standing.

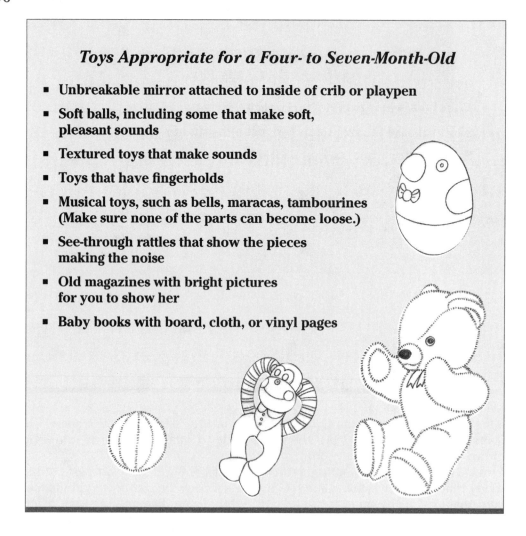

Toys Appropriate for a Four- to Seven-Month-Old

- Unbreakable mirror attached to inside of crib or playpen
- Soft balls, including some that make soft, pleasant sounds
- Textured toys that make sounds
- Toys that have fingerholds
- Musical toys, such as bells, maracas, tambourines (Make sure none of the parts can become loose.)
- See-through rattles that show the pieces making the noise
- Old magazines with bright pictures for you to show her
- Baby books with board, cloth, or vinyl pages

Vision

As your baby works on her important motor skills, have you noticed how closely she watches everything she's doing? The concentration with which she reaches for a toy may remind you of a scientist engrossed in research. It's obvious that her good vision is playing a key role in her early motor and cognitive development. Conveniently, her eyes become fully functional just when she needs them most.

Although your baby was able to see at birth, her total visual ability has taken months to develop fully. Only now can she distinguish subtle shades of reds, blues, and yellows. Don't be surprised if you notice that she prefers red or blue to other colors; these seem to be favorites among many infants this age. Most babies also like increasingly complex patterns and shapes as they get older—

By four months, your baby will begin noticing not only the way you talk but the individual sounds you make.

something to keep in mind when you're shopping for picture books or posters for your child's nursery.

By four months, your baby's range of vision has increased to several feet (meters) or more, and it will continue to expand until, at about seven months, her eyesight will be more nearly mature. At the same time, she'll learn to follow faster and faster movements with her eyes. In the early months, when you rolled a ball across the room, she couldn't coordinate her eyes well enough to track it, but now she'll follow the path of moving objects easily. As her hand-to-eye coordination improves, she'll be able to grab these objects as well.

A mobile hung over the crib or in front of the infant seat is an ideal way to stimulate a young baby's vision. However, by about five months, your baby will quickly get bored and search for other things to watch. Also by this age, she may be sitting up and might pull down or tangle herself in a mobile. *For this reason, remove mobiles from cribs or playpens as soon as your baby is able to pull or hold herself upright.*

Still another way to hold your baby's visual interest is to keep her moving—around your home, down the block, to the store, or out on special excursions. Help her find things to look at that she's never seen before, and name each one out loud for her.

A mirror is another source of endless fascination for babies this age. The reflected image is constantly changing, and, even more important, it responds directly to your child's own movements. This is her clue that the person in the mirror is actually herself. It may take your baby a while to come to this realization, but it probably will register during this period.

In general, then, your child's visual awareness should clearly increase during these four months. Watch how she responds as you introduce her to new shapes, colors, and objects. If she doesn't seem to be interested in looking at new things, or if one or both eyes turn in or out, inform your pediatrician. (See also Chapter 21, "Eyes.")

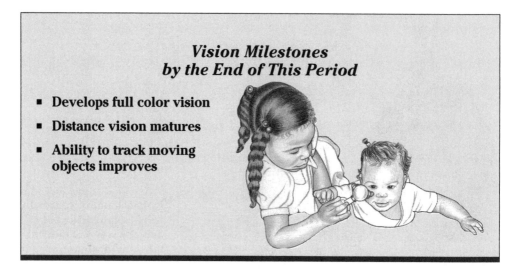

**Vision Milestones
by the End of This Period**

- **Develops full color vision**
- **Distance vision matures**
- **Ability to track moving objects improves**

Language Development

Your baby learns language in stages. From birth, he receives information about language by hearing people make sounds and watching how they communicate with one another. At first he is most interested in the pitch and level of your voice. When you talk to him in a soothing way, he'll stop crying because he hears that you want to comfort him. By contrast, if you shout out in anger, he probably will cry, because your voice is telling him something is wrong. By four months, he'll begin noticing not only the way you talk but the individual sounds you make. He'll listen to the vowels and consonants and begin to notice the way these combine into syllables, words, and sentences.

Besides receiving sounds, your baby also has been producing them from the very beginning, first in the form of cries and then as coos. At about four months, he'll start to babble, using many of the rhythms and characteristics of his native language. Although it may sound like gibberish, if you listen closely, you'll hear him raise and drop his voice as if he were making a statement or asking a question. Encourage him by talking to him throughout the day. When he says a recognizable syllable, repeat it back to him and then say some simple words that contain that sound. For example, if his sound of the day is "bah," introduce him to "bottle," "box," "bonnet," and "Baa, Baa, Black Sheep."

Your participation in your child's language development will become even more important after six or seven months, when he begins actively imitating the sounds of speech. Up to that point, he might repeat one sound for a whole day or even days at a stretch before trying another. But now he'll become much more responsive to the sounds he hears you make, and he'll try to follow your lead. So introduce him to simple syllables and words such as "baby," "cat," "dog," "go," "hot," "cold," and "walk," as well as "Mama" and "Dada." Although it

Language Milestones by the End of This Period

- **Responds to own name**
- **Begins to respond to "no"**
- **Distinguishes emotions by tone of voice**
- **Responds to sound by making sounds**
- **Uses voice to express joy and displeasure**
- **Babbles chains of consonants**

may be as much as a year before you can interpret any of his babbling, your baby can understand many of your words well before his first birthday.

If he doesn't babble or imitate any sounds by his seventh month, it could mean a problem with his hearing or speech development. A baby with a partial hearing loss still can be startled by loud noises or will turn his head in their direction, and he may even respond to your voice. But he will have difficulty imitating speech. If your child does not babble or produce a variety of sounds, alert your pediatrician. If he has had frequent ear infections, he might have some fluid remaining in his inner ear, and this could interfere with his hearing.

Special equipment is used to check a very young baby's hearing. All newborns should be tested for hearing loss. Your observations are the early warning system that tells whether further testing is needed. If you suspect a problem, you might ask your pediatrician for a referral to a children's hearing specialist.

Cognitive Development

During your baby's first four months, did you have doubts that she really understood much that was happening around her? This parental reaction is not surprising. After all, although you knew when she was comfortable and uncomfortable, she probably showed few signs of actually thinking. Now, as her memory and attention span increase, you'll start to see evidence that she's not only absorbing information but also applying it to her day-to-day activities.

During this period, one of the most important concepts she'll refine is the principle of cause and effect. She'll probably stumble on this notion by accident somewhere between four and five months. Perhaps while kicking her mattress, she'll notice the crib shaking. Or maybe she'll realize that her rattle makes a noise when she hits or waves it. Once she understands that she can cause these

When she bangs certain things on the table or drops them on the floor, she'll start a chain of responses from her audience.

interesting reactions, she'll continue to experiment with other ways to make things happen.

Your baby will quickly discover that some things, such as bells and keys, make interesting sounds when moved or shaken. When she bangs certain things on the table or drops them on the floor, she'll start a chain of responses from her audience, including funny faces, groans, and other reactions that may lead to the reappearance—or disappearance—of the object. Before long, she'll begin dropping things intentionally to see you pick them up. As annoying as this may be at times, it's one important way for her to learn about cause and effect and her personal ability to influence her environment.

It's important that you give your child the objects she needs for these experiments and encourage her to test her "theories." But make sure that everything you give her to play with is unbreakable, lightweight, and large enough that she can't possibly swallow it. If you run out of the usual toys or she loses interest in them, plastic or wooden spoons, unbreakable cups, and jar or bowl lids and boxes are endlessly entertaining and inexpensive.

Another major discovery that your baby will make during this period is that objects continue to exist when they're out of her sight—a principle called object

Cognitive Milestones by the End of This Period

- **Finds partially hidden object**
- **Explores with hands and mouth**
- **Struggles to get objects that are out of reach**

permanence. During her first few months, she assumed that the world consisted only of things that she could see. When you left her room, she assumed you vanished; when you returned, you were a whole new person to her. In much the same way, when you hid a toy under a cloth or a box, she thought it was gone for good and wouldn't bother looking for it. But sometime after four months, she'll begin to realize that the world is more permanent than she thought. You're the same person who greets her every morning. Her teddy bear on the floor is the same one that was in bed with her the night before. The block that you hid under the can did not actually vanish after all. By playing hiding games and observing the comings and goings of people and things around her, your baby will continue to learn about object permanence for many months to come.

Emotional Development

Between four and seven months, your baby may undergo a dramatic change in personality. At the beginning of this period, she may seem relatively passive and preoccupied with getting enough food, sleep, and affection. But as she learns to sit up, use her hands, and move about, she's likely to become increasingly assertive and more attentive to the world outside. She'll be eager to reach out and touch everything she sees, and if she can't manage on her own, she'll demand your help by yelling, banging, or dropping the nearest object at hand. Once you've come to her rescue, she'll probably forget what she was doing and concentrate on you—smiling, laughing, babbling, and imitating you for many minutes at a stretch. While she'll quickly get bored with even the most engaging toy, she'll never tire of your attention.

The more subtle aspects of your baby's personality are determined largely by her constitutional makeup or temperament. Is she rambunctious or gentle? Easygoing or easily upset? Headstrong or compliant? To a large extent, these are inborn character traits, and they'll become increasingly apparent during these months. You won't necessarily find all of these characteristics enjoyable all the time—especially not when your determined six-month-old is screaming in frustration as she lunges for the family cat. But in the long run, adapting to her natural personality is best for both of you.

Strong-willed and high-strung babies require an extra dose of patience and gentle guidance. They often don't adapt to changing surroundings as easily as calmer babies, and will become increasingly upset if pushed to move or perform before they're ready. Language and cuddling sometimes will do wonders to calm the nerves of an irritable child. Distracting her also often can help refocus her energy. For instance, if she screams because you won't retrieve the toy she dropped for the tenth time, move her to the floor so she can reach the toy herself.

The shy or "sensitive" child also requires special attention, particularly if you have more boisterous children in the household who overshadow her. When a baby is quiet and undemanding, it's easy to assume she's content, or if she doesn't laugh or smile a lot, you may lose interest in playing with her. But a baby

Developmental Health Watch

Because each baby develops in his own particular manner, it's impossible to tell exactly when or how your child will perfect a given skill. The developmental milestones listed in this book will give you a general idea of the changes you can expect, but don't be alarmed if your own baby's development takes a slightly different course. Alert your pediatrician, however, if your baby displays any of the following signs of possible developmental delay for this age range.

- Seems very stiff, with tight muscles
- Seems very floppy, like a rag doll
- Head still flops back when body is pulled up to a sitting position
- Reaches with one hand only
- Refuses to cuddle
- Shows no affection for the person who cares for him
- Doesn't seem to enjoy being around people
- One or both eyes consistently turn in or out
- Persistent tearing, eye drainage, or sensitivity to light
- Does not respond to sounds around him

like this often needs personal contact even more than other children. She may be overwhelmed easily and needs you to show her how to be assertive and become involved in the activities around her. How should you do this? Give her plenty of time to warm up to any situation, and make sure that other people approach her slowly. Let her sit on the sidelines before attempting to involve her

Social/Emotional Milestones by the End of This Period

- **Enjoys social play**
- **Interested in mirror images**
- **Responds to other people's expressions of emotion and appears joyful often**

- Has difficulty getting objects to his mouth
- Does not turn his head to locate sounds by four months
- Doesn't roll over in either direction (front to back or back to front) by five months
- Seems inconsolable at night after five months
- Doesn't smile spontaneously by five months
- Cannot sit with help by six months
- Does not laugh or make squealing sounds by six months
- Does not actively reach for objects by six to seven months
- Doesn't follow objects with both eyes at near (1 foot) [30 cm] and far (6 feet) [180 cm] ranges by seven months
- Does not bear some weight on legs by seven months
- Does not try to attract attention through actions by seven months
- Does not babble by eight months
- Shows no interest in games of peekaboo by eight months

directly with other children. Once she feels secure, gradually she'll become more responsive to the people around her.

Also let your pediatrician know if you have any concerns about your baby's emotional development. Your pediatrician can help if she knows there are problems, but they can be difficult to detect in a routine office visit. That's why it's important for you to call the doctor's attention to your concerns and describe your day-to-day observations. Write them down so you don't forget them.

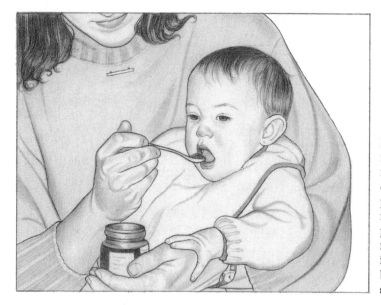

Do not feed directly from the jar but rather from a small dish into which a portion of the jar of food has been placed. Any remaining portion in the dish should be discarded, not saved.

BASIC CARE

Introducing Solid Foods

At four months, your baby's diet should consist of breastmilk and/or formula (with added vitamins or iron if your pediatrician recommends it), but by four to six months,* you can begin adding solid foods. Some babies are ready for solids as early as three months, but most have not lost their tongue-thrust reflex at that age. Because of this reflex, the young infant will push his tongue against a spoon or anything else inserted into his mouth, including food. Most babies lose this reflex at about four months. Coincidentally, the baby's energy needs increase around this age, making it an ideal time to start adding different calories through solids.

You may start solid food at whichever feedings during the day are most acceptable to you and your baby. However, remember that as he gets older, he will want to eat with the other family members. To minimize the chances of choking, make sure your baby is sitting up, either in your lap or in an infant seat, when you introduce solids. If he cries or turns away when you try to feed him, don't force the issue. It's more important that you both enjoy his mealtimes than for him to start these foods by a specific date. Go back to nursing or bottle-feeding exclusively for a week or two, then try again.

Always use a spoon to feed your baby solids unless, at your pediatrician's

---

* Note: There is a difference of opinion among Academy experts on this matter. The Section on Breast-feeding supports exclusive breastfeeding for about six months. The Committee on Nutrition supports the introduction of complementary foods between four and six months of age where safe and nutritious complementary foods are available.

recommendation, you are thickening the formula for an infant with gastro-esophageal reflux (spitting up stomach contents). Some parents try putting solid foods in a bottle or infant feeder with a nipple, but feeding a baby this way can drastically increase the amount of food he takes in at each feeding and lead to excessive weight gain. Besides, it's important for your baby to get used to the process of eating—sitting up, taking bites from a spoon, resting between bites, and stopping when he's full. This early experience will help lay the foundation for good eating habits throughout his life.

Even standard baby spoons may be too wide for a child this young, but a small coffee spoon will work well. Start with half a spoonful or less (about a quarter of a teaspoonful), and talk your baby through the process ("Mmm, see how good this is"). He probably won't know what to do the first time or two. He may look confused or insulted, wrinkle his nose, and roll the food around his mouth or reject it entirely. This is an understandable reaction, considering how different his feedings have been up to this point.

One way to ease the transition to solids is to give your infant a little breast-milk or formula first, then switch to very small half-spoonfuls of food, and finally finish off with more breastmilk or formula. This will prevent him from being overly frustrated when he's very hungry, and it will link the satisfaction of nursing with this new experience of spoon-feeding.

No matter what you do, most of the first few solid-food feedings are sure to wind up outside his mouth on his face and bib, so increase the size of his feedings very gradually, starting with just a teaspoonful or two, until he gets the idea of swallowing solids.

For most babies, the first solid food is rice cereal, followed by oatmeal and barley. Generally, it's a good idea to introduce wheat and mixed cereals last, since they may cause allergic reactions in very young babies.

You may use premixed baby cereals in a jar or dry varieties to which you add formula, breastmilk, or water. However, meats are richest in iron and zinc, which are nutrients that babies need. Meats also can be introduced as the first solid food. The prepared cereals are convenient, but the dry ones are richer in iron and can be varied in consistency to suit your baby. Whichever you choose, make sure that it's made for babies. This assures you that it contains the extra nutrients your child needs at this age.

If you started with cereal and your baby has accepted it, you can start introducing him to other foods slowly. One possible order is meat, vegetables, and fruit. Give your baby just one new food at a time, and wait at least two to three days before starting another. After each new food, watch for allergic responses such as diarrhea, rash, or vomiting. If any of these occur, eliminate the suspect food from his diet until you've consulted your pediatrician. Within two or three months, your baby's daily diet should include breastmilk or formula, cereal, vegetables, meats, and fruits, distributed among three meals. Because it frequently is associated with allergy, egg is started last.

Once your baby sits up, you can give him finger foods to help him learn to feed himself. Make sure anything you give him is soft, easy to swallow, and breaks down into small pieces that can't possibly choke him. Well-cooked cut-up green

Do Not Home-Prepare These Foods

Beets, Turnips, Carrots, Collard Greens, Spinach. In some parts of the country, these vegetables contain large amounts of nitrates, a chemical that can cause an unusual type of anemia (low blood count) in young infants. Baby-food companies are aware of this problem and screen the produce they buy for nitrates; they also avoid buying these vegetables in parts of the country where nitrates have been detected. Since you cannot test for this chemical yourself, it's safer to use commercially prepared forms of these foods, especially while your child is an infant. If you choose to prepare them at home anyway, serve them fresh and don't store them. Storage of these foods actually may increase the amount of nitrates in them.

beans, peas, potatoes, and small pieces of wafer-type cookies or crackers are good examples. Don't give him any food that requires chewing at this age.

At each of his three daily meals, your six month old baby should be eating about 4 ounces (120 ml) of strained baby food. (Because canned adult-type foods generally contain added salt and preservatives, they should not be fed to babies.)

When feeding solid foods, do not feed directly from the jar but rather from a small dish into which a portion of the jar of food has been placed. This will prevent the jar of food from becoming contaminated from the introduction of bacteria from the baby's mouth. The portion in the dish also should be discarded, not saved.

Do not offer fruit juice until your baby is at least six months old. Because of the nonabsorbed carbohydrates in juices, large amounts of fruit juice can increase the frequency of stools and make them looser. These more frequent loose stools can cause diaper rash that is bright red and painful when the baby is wiped during his diaper change. Contact with air and the application of a heavy, protective diaper ointment usually will heal the rash. You also should decrease the fruit juice intake.

If your infant seems to be thirsty between feedings, put him to the breast or offer him extra formula. During the hot months when he's losing fluid through perspiration, 2 to 4 ounces (60–120 ml) of water or extra feedings of breastmilk or formula will help prevent dehydration.

What if you want your baby to have fresh food instead of canned or dehydrated? In that case, use a blender or food processor, or just mash softer foods with a fork. Everything should be soft, unsalted, well cooked, and unseasoned. Cooked fresh vegetables and stewed fruits (see the box above for exceptions) are the easiest to prepare. Although you can feed your baby mashed raw bananas, all other fruits should be cooked until soft. Refrigerate any food you don't use immediately, and then inspect it carefully for signs of spoilage before giving it to your baby. Unlike commercial foods, your own are not bacteria-free, so they will spoil more quickly.

By the time your baby is six or seven months old, he'll probably sit up well enough to use a high chair during mealtime. To ensure his comfort, the seat of the chair should be covered with a pad that's removable and washable, so you can clean out the food that probably will accumulate there. Also, when shopping for a high chair, look for one with a detachable tray with raised rims. (See page 440 for safety recommendations.) The rims will help keep dishes and food from sliding off during your baby's more rambunctious feeding sessions. The detachable tray can be carried straight to the sink for cleaning, a feature you're bound to appreciate in the months to come. (There still may be days when the only solution is to put the entire chair in the shower for a complete wipe-down!)

As your child's diet expands and he begins feeding himself more regularly, discuss his personal nutritional needs with your pediatrician. Poor eating habits established in infancy can lead to health problems later on.

Your pediatrician will help you determine whether your baby is overfed, not eating enough, or eating too many of the wrong kinds of foods. By familiarizing yourself with the caloric and nutritional contents of what he eats, you can make sure he's eating a proper diet. Be aware of the food habits of others in your family. As your baby eats more and more "table foods" (this usually starts at eight to ten months in quantities similar to those used for baby foods), he'll imitate the way you eat—including using the salt shaker and nibbling on salty snacks and processed foods. For his sake as well as your own, cut your salt use to a minimum.

What if you're concerned that your baby is *already* overweight? Even when infants are at this young age, some parents are already worried that their babies are gaining too much weight. On one hand, there *is* a rise in childhood obesity and all of its potential complications (such as diabetes), and thus it's wise to be sensitive to the problem, no matter what age your child is. Some evidence indicates that bottle-fed infants gain weight more rapidly than breast-fed babies, perhaps because some parents encourage their infant to finish a bottle feeding. However, *don't let any anxiety over obesity lead you to underfeed your infant during the first year.* Get your pediatrician's advice before making any dietary adjustments. During these months of rapid growth, your infant needs the proper balance of fat, carbohydrates, and protein. It's not wise to switch a baby this age to skim milk, for example, or to other low-fat substitutes for breastmilk or formula.

As soon as you start giving your child solid foods, his stools will become more solid and variable in color. Due to the added sugars and fats, they'll also have a much stronger odor. Peas and other green vegetables may turn the stool deep green; beets may make it red. (Beets sometimes make urine red, as well.) If his meals aren't strained, his stools may contain undigested particles of food, especially hulls of peas or corn, and the skin of tomatoes or other vegetables.

All of this is perfectly normal. If the stools are extremely loose, watery, or full of mucus, however, it may mean his digestive tract is irritated. In this case, consult your pediatrician to determine if your infant or child has a digestive problem.

Dietary Supplements

Although the American Academy of Pediatrics recommends breastfeeding your baby for the first twelve months of his life, human milk does not contain sufficient vitamin D to prevent a deficiency of this vitamin, which can produce diseases like rickets (the severe form of vitamin D deficiency characterized by the softening of bones). Even though sunlight stimulates the skin to manufacture vitamin D, all children should wear sunscreen when they're outdoors, and sunscreen prevents the skin from making vitamin D.

As a result, the Academy recommends that if you are breastfeeding your baby, you need to provide her with supplemental vitamin D, beginning within the first two months of life. Vitamin D supplements of 200 IU (International Units) per day are recommended for breastfed babies unless they are weaned to at least 16.9 ounces (500 ml) of vitamin D–fortified formula or milk, and for all nonbreastfed infants who are consuming less than 16.9 ounces (500 ml) per day of vitamin D–fortified formula or milk. You should discuss this issue with your pediatrician. Formula supplies all the vitamin D that is necessary in formula-fed infants, and thus no supplementation is required.

What about iron? For the first four to six months, your breastfed baby needs no additional iron. The iron she had in her body at birth was enough to see her through her initial growth. But now the reserves will be running low and her need for iron will increase as her growth speeds up. The Academy believes that babies who are not breastfed or are only partially breastfed should receive an iron-fortified formula (containing between 4 and 12 mg of iron) from birth through twelve months of age. We discourage the use of low-iron infant formulas.

Fortunately, once you start your baby on solid foods, she'll also receive iron from iron-fortified baby cereals, meats, and green vegetables. For example, four level tablespoons of fortified cereal, diluted with breastmilk or formula, provides 7 mg of iron; meat is another very good source of iron. (See also *Supplementation for Breastfed and Bottle-fed Infants,* page 114.)

Weaning from Breast to Bottle

Mothers wean their babies for a variety of reasons. The weaning process begins when the baby first receives anything in the diet besides breastmilk.

In any event, you should continue to breastfeed or provide infant formula until your baby is one year old. After that, whole cow's milk can be given. Many breastfed babies never use a bottle, but wean directly to a cup. If you plan to introduce bottle-feedings of formula or expressed milk, don't expect smooth sailing if your baby has never been given a bottle before. He probably will object to it the first few times, especially if his mother tries to give it to him. By this age, he associates his mother with nursing, so it's understandable if he's confused and annoyed when there's a sudden change in the routine. Things may go more smoothly if his father or another family member feeds him—and Mom stays out of the room. After he's gotten used to the idea, then she can take over, but he should get lots of cuddling, stroking, and encouragement to make up for the lost skin-to-skin contact.

Once your baby has learned to take an occasional bottle, it should be relatively easy to wean him from the breast if you desire to do so. The time needed to wean him, however, will vary, depending on the emotional and physical needs of both child and mother. If your baby adapts well to change and you're ready for the transition, you can make a total switch in one or two weeks. For the first two days, substitute one bottle of formula for one breastfeeding per day. (Don't express milk during this time.) On the third day, use a bottle for two feedings. By the fifth day, you can jump to three or four bottle-feedings.

Once you've stopped breastfeeding entirely, breastmilk production will cease very quickly. In the meantime, if your breasts should become engorged, you may need to express milk for the first two or three days to relieve the discomfort. Gradual weaning by eliminating one feeding at a time will help to minimize engorgement. Within a week, the discomfort should subside.

Many women prefer to wean more slowly, even when their babies cooperate fully. Breastfeeding provides a closeness between mother and child that's hard to duplicate any other way, and, understandably, you may be reluctant to give up such intimacy. In this case, you can continue to offer a combination of the breast and the bottle for up to one year, or beyond. Some babies lose interest between nine and twelve months, or when they learn to drink from a cup. It's important for you to remember that this is not a personal rejection, but a sign of your child's growing independence. However, breastfeeding can continue as part of the routine feeding beyond the first year of life.

Sleeping

Most babies this age still need at least two naps a day, of from one to three hours each, one in the morning and the other in the afternoon. In general, it's best to let your baby sleep as long as she wants, unless she has trouble falling asleep at her normal nightly bedtime. If this becomes a problem, wake her up earlier from her afternoon nap.

By four months, your baby should be sleeping through at least one nighttime feeding and perhaps through the entire night. "Through the night" could mean from 7:00 P.M. to 7:00 A.M., or from 10:00 P.M. to 6:00 A.M., depending on your baby's own internal clock; but at this age she should be able to go at least eight hours without being fed.

Because your child is more alert and active now, she may have trouble winding down at the end of the day. A consistent bedtime routine will help. Experiment to see what works best, taking into consideration both the activities in the rest of the household and your baby's temperament. A warm bath, a massage, rocking, a story or lullaby, soft music, and a breast- or bottle-feeding will all help relax her and put her in a bedtime mood. Eventually she'll associate these activities with going to sleep, and that will help relax and soothe her.

Instead of letting your baby fall asleep during this ritual, settle her in her crib while she's still awake so she learns to fall asleep on her own. Gently put her head down, whisper your good-night, and leave the room. If she cries, don't rush back in. She may calm down after a few minutes and fall asleep on her own.

But what if she's still crying lustily at the end of five minutes? Go in and comfort her for about a minute, without picking her up, and then leave. Let her know that you love her and are available if she needs you, but don't stay in the room. If she continues to cry, wait a little longer than five minutes before going back in again to repeat the sequence. Be consistent and firm. As hard as this is on you, it's harder on your baby if she senses you are wavering. The real reward will come when she awakens in the middle of the night and goes back to sleep without your help.

Many babies cry some every night, leading parents to wonder if the prolonged crying can hurt them psychologically. If you actually time your baby's crying, you may find that it doesn't last that long—it just *seems* forever. If parents are steadfast, most babies will cry less each night until they finally go to sleep with only a token protest. But even if your child cries for a long time (twenty to thirty minutes), there is no evidence that she'll be hurt by it.

Crying that goes on for more than twenty minutes may need to be checked to see if there is not some problem (i.e., a hair wrapped around the baby's toe), but such interruptions should be short. Do not stop to play. The important thing is for you to keep your perfectly natural feelings of frustration and, perhaps, anger in check, so you can be firm in a calm and loving way when your baby resists sleep.

When your child awakens in the middle of the night, give her a few minutes to fall back to sleep before you go to her. If she continues to cry, talk to her and comfort her, but don't bring her to your bed. Also, unless you have reason to believe she's really hungry (e.g., if she fell asleep earlier than usual and missed a feeding), don't feed her. As tempting as it may be to calm her down with food or cuddling in your bed, she'll soon come to expect these responses when she wakes up at night, and she won't go back to sleep without them.

When a baby wakes up more than once a night, there may be something disturbing her sleep. If the child is still sleeping in your room by six months, it's time to move her out; she may be waking up because she hears you or senses your presence when you're nearby. If she's still in a bassinet, she's probably feeling cramped; by this age, she needs room to stretch and move in her sleep, and she should be in a full-size crib with bumpers to cushion her when she rolls to the sides. Still another problem may be a room that's too dark. She needs enough light to reassure herself that she's in familiar surroundings. A simple night-light can solve this problem.

Teething

Teething usually starts during these months. The two bottom front teeth (central incisors) usually appear first, followed about four to eight weeks later by the four upper teeth (central and lateral incisors), and then about one month later by the two lower incisors. The first molars come in next, followed by the canine or eye teeth.

If your child doesn't show any teeth until much later, don't worry. Timing of teething may be determined by heredity, and it doesn't mean that anything is wrong.

Teething *occasionally* may cause mild irritability, crying, low-grade temperature (but not over 101 degrees Fahrenheit or 38.3 degrees Celsius), excessive drooling, and a desire to chew on something hard. More often, the gums around the new teeth will swell and be tender. To ease your baby's discomfort, try gently rubbing or massaging the gums with one of your fingers. Teething rings are helpful, too, but they should be made of firm rubber. (The teethers that you freeze tend to get too hard and can cause more harm than good.) Pain relievers and medications that you rub on the gums are not necessary or useful since they wash out of the baby's mouth within minutes. If your child seems particularly miserable or has a fever higher than 101 degrees Fahrenheit (38.3 degrees Celsius), it's probably not because he's teething, and you should consult your pediatrician.

How should you clean the new teeth? Simply brush them with a soft child's toothbrush, or wipe them with gauze at the end of the day. To prevent cavities, never let your baby fall asleep with a bottle, either at nap time or at night. By avoiding this situation, you'll keep milk from pooling around the teeth and creating a breeding ground for decay.

Swings and Playpens

Many parents find that mechanical swings, especially those with cradle attachments, can calm a crying baby when nothing else seems to work. If you use one of these devices, don't put your baby in the seat of the swing until she can sit on her own (usually between seven and nine months). Use only swings that stand firmly on the floor, not the ones that hang suspended from door frames. Also, don't use a swing more than half an hour twice a day; while it may quiet your baby, it is no substitute for your attention. Secure your baby properly with a safety strap at all times. Also, be sure the product you're considering buying has not been recalled. Check the Consumer Product Safety Commission website (www.cpsc.gov) for recalled products.

Once your baby starts to move about, you may need to start using a playpen (also called a play yard). But even before she crawls or walks, a playpen offers a protected place where she can lie or sit outdoors as well as in rooms where you have no crib or bassinet. (See *Playpens,* page 442, for specific recommenda-

Stimulating Infant Brain Growth: Age Four Months Through Seven Months

Many connections are being made in your baby's brain during this time in her young life, reflected in her behaviors, such as showing strong attachments to you and others who regularly take care of her, crying when you leave the room or when she is approached suddenly by a stranger, or crying when she wants a particular toy or a change in activity. She is becoming more interested in the world around her and is better able to communicate her emotions and desires—all the while developing new skills such as grasping, rolling over, and sitting up.

Without overstimulating your baby, try these activities to help strengthen the connections in her developing brain:

- Provide a stimulating, safe environment where your baby can begin to explore and roam freely.

- Give consistent, warm, physical contact—hugging, skin-to-skin, body-to-body contact—to establish your infant's sense of security and well-being.

- Be attentive to your baby's rhythms and moods. Respond to her when she is upset as well as when she is happy.

- Talk and sing to your baby during dressing, bathing, feeding, playing, walking, and driving. She may not yet understand the language, but as she hears it all the time, her language skills will develop. Check with your pediatrician if your baby doesn't seem to hear sounds or doesn't imitate your words.

- Engage your child in face-to-face talk. Mimic her sounds to show interest.

tions.) Remember never to leave the side of the playpen down. If the baby gets used to a playpen now, she may be more willing to stay in it as she gets older. Don't count on this, though; while some babies don't mind being enclosed, others resist it vigorously.

- Read books to your baby every day. She'll love the sound of your voice, and before long she'll enjoy looking at the pictures and "reading" on her own.

- If you speak a foreign language, use it at home.

- Engage in rhythmic movement with your child, such as dancing together with music.

- Avoid subjecting your baby to stressful or traumatic experiences, physical or psychological.

- Introduce your child to other children and parents; this is a very special period for infants. Be sensitive to cues indicating that she is ready to meet new people.

- Encourage your child to reach for toys. Give her baby blocks and soft toys that can stimulate her eye-hand coordination and her fine motor skills.

- Make sure other people who provide care and supervision for your baby understand the importance of forming a loving and comforting relationship with your child.

- Encourage your child to begin to sleep for extended periods at night; if you need advice about this important step in your infant's development, ask your pediatrician.

- Spend time on the floor playing with your child every day.

- Choose quality child care that is affectionate, responsive, educational, and safe. Visit your child care provider frequently and share your ideas about positive caregiving.

BEHAVIOR

Discipline

As your baby becomes more mobile and inquisitive, he'll naturally become more assertive, as well. This is wonderful for his self-esteem and should be encouraged as much as possible. When he wants to do something that's dangerous or disrupts the rest of the family, however, you'll need to take charge.

For the first six months or so, the best way to deal with such conflicts is to distract him with an alternative toy or activity. Standard discipline won't work

A Word for Grandparents

As a grandparent, you thoroughly love watching your grandchild develop. During this time of his life (ages four to seven months), he's continuing to discover the world around him and has more physical skills and cognitive abilities to engage and enjoy his environment.

As sights and sounds take on more meaning for your grandchild, and as laughter abounds, these are great months for both of you. Smiles, interactive play, and recognition of familiar objects, sounds, people, and names will become part of these discovery months. His vision is better, his hand transfer is more efficient, and his curiosity is nonstoppable. Be sure to reinforce these early learning milestones that are occurring along the way.

Your grandchild also is beginning to move during this time. Although it is a wondrous period of life, you need to be particularly vigilant as he begins to sit. While he will be upright more frequently, he is also likely to tip over.

You have an important role to play as a grandparent, and can make the most of it—enjoying your time with him and stimulating his parents' development—by taking these steps:

- Follow your own child's lead with respect to activities to do with your grandchild, adding some special things of your own when appropriate. Special names you share ("Nana," "Grandpa Stan"), places that the two of you go, and books or music CDs that you share can be unique to his experiences with you. Also consider inviting other grandparents and their grandchildren to join you from time to time, which can be a special treat for your own grandchild.

- When buying gifts for your grandchild, choose age-appropriate books, as well as toys that encourage creative play.

- Make yourself available as a babysitter as often as possible when your son or daughter requests it. These times spent alone with your grandchild will be special moments that you'll always treasure. Take him on field trips (to the park or the zoo), and as the years pass, help him develop hobbies that you can do together.

- You will get a better idea of your grandchild's temperament as he moves through this time of life. Inevitably, you will make comparisons as to who she is really like in the family. Some of her own likes and dislikes will start to emerge, and it is best to respect them. If your grandchild is particularly boisterous and active, you may need extra patience at times to fully enjoy her company. Give her some space, let her be the person she is—but rein her in if she gets too far out of bounds. The same with a shy child; don't expect him to break free of his bashfulness the moment you show up. Enjoy him for who he is.

- Diaper changing is often an exercise in controlling the "wiggly monster," and you may need all of your strength just to keep the baby from rolling onto the floor. Switching from the changing table to the bed is often a good idea; remember to keep all of the diapering paraphernalia close by and within reach.

- When it comes to discipline, discuss it with the baby's parents, and make sure your own approach is consistent with their wishes.

- Consider investing in a grandchild-appropriate crib and other furniture for your home. A high chair certainly will come in handy if she occasionally (or frequently) eats meals at your home. A stroller and a car safety seat may be very useful, as well. And keep some everyday medications at your home (for a fever, diaper rash, etc.), and a few toys that she can enjoy.

- Your grandchild's eating has become more regular, and by the end of this time period, he will be on solid foods (i.e., infant cereal and pureed vegetables, fruits, and meats). When you're caring for your grandchild, again follow the guidance of his parents on what and when to feed him. If they're on his menu, let him explore your own versions of "junior foods," such as fruit, pureed vegetables, and meats. Stay away from adult-type canned foods. Avoid giving him food chunks that are too large and could cause choking. If your grandchild is still breastfeeding, keep some frozen breastmilk in your freezer.

- Your grandchild should be sleeping through the night, so "overnighters" will be more enjoyable and less disruptive of your own schedule. When she spends the night at your home, you and your spouse can take turns on who's going to take the early morning shift if the baby awakens before you normally would.

- Make your home a safe environment for your grandchild. Follow the guidelines in Chapter 14 to baby-proof your home, from placing protective covers on unused electrical outlets, to ensuring that matches are nowhere where the baby can reach them.

- At times, having your grandchild and her siblings staying at your home at the same time may be too much for you to handle. Try caring for one youngster at a time, especially at first. Doing this will allow you to tailor-make the activities you do, while still providing much-needed relief to your own child, who can then focus her energies on the child(ren) she has remaining at her home. Your continued, valued role in assisting your child to become the most effective parent possible remains the core purpose for all that you do.

- You can promote your grandchild's development now and in the future by taking family pictures and movies, creating photo albums, and putting family stories down on paper (accompanied by old and new photos).

until his memory span increases around the end of his seventh month. Only then can you use a variety of techniques to discourage undesired behavior.

When you finally begin to discipline your child, it should never be harsh. Often the most successful approach is simply to reward desired behavior and withhold rewards when he does not behave as desired. For example, if he cries for no apparent reason, make sure there's nothing wrong physically; then when he stops, reward him with extra attention, kind words, and hugs. If he starts up again, wait a little longer before turning your attention to him, and use a firm tone of voice as you talk to him. This time, don't reward him with extra attention or hugs.

The main goal of discipline is to teach a child limits, so try to help him understand exactly what he's doing wrong when he breaks a rule. If you notice him doing something that's not allowed, such as pulling your hair, let him know that it's wrong by calmly saying "no," stopping him, and redirecting his attention to an acceptable activity.

If your child is touching or trying to put something in his mouth that he shouldn't, gently pull his hand away as you tell him this particular object is off limits. But since you do want to encourage him to touch *other* things, avoid saying "Don't touch." More pointed phrases, such as "Don't eat the flowers" or "No eating leaves," will convey the message without confusing him.

Because it's still relatively easy to modify his behavior at this age, this is a good time to establish your authority. Be careful not to overreact, however. He's still not old enough to misbehave intentionally and won't understand if you punish him or raise your voice. Instead, remain calm, firm, consistent, and loving in your approach. If he learns now that you have the final word, it may make life much more comfortable for both of you later on, when he naturally becomes more headstrong.

Siblings

If your baby has a big brother or sister, you may start to see increasing signs of rivalry at about this time. Earlier, the baby was more dependent, slept a lot, and didn't require your constant attention. But now that she's becoming more demanding, you'll need to ration your time and energy so you have enough for each child individually as well as all of them together. This rationing is even more important—and more difficult—if you go back to work.

One way to give some extra attention to your older child is to set aside special "big brother" or "big sister" chores that don't involve the baby. Doing this allows you to spend some time together and get the housework done. Be sure to show the child how much you appreciate this help.

You also might help sibling relations by including the older child in activities with the baby. If the two of you sing a song or read a story, the baby will enjoy listening. The older child also can help take care of the baby to some extent, assisting you at bathtime or changing time. But unless the child is at least ten, don't leave him alone with the baby, even if he's trying to be helpful. Younger children can easily drop or injure an infant without realizing what they're doing.

HEALTH WATCH

Don't be surprised if your baby catches his first cold or ear infection soon after his four-month birthday. Now that he can actively reach for objects, he'll come into physical contact with many more things and people, so he'll be much more likely to contract contagious diseases.

The first line of defense is to keep your child away from anyone you know is sick. Be especially careful of infectious diseases such as chickenpox, measles, or mumps (see *Mumps,* page 658; *Chickenpox,* page 691; *Measles,* page 702). If someone in your playgroup has caught one of these diseases, keep your child out of the group until you're sure no one else is infected.

No matter how you try to protect your baby, of course, there will be times when he gets sick. This is an inevitable part of growing up, and will happen more frequently as he has more direct contact with other children. It's not always easy to tell when a baby is ill, but there are some signs that will tip you off. Does he look pale or have dark circles under his eyes? Is he acting less energetic or more irritable than usual? If he has an infectious disease, he'll probably have a fever (see Chapter 23, "Fever"), and he may be losing weight due to loss of appetite, diarrhea, or vomiting. Some difficult-to-detect infections of the kidneys or lungs also can prevent weight gain in babies. At this age, weight loss could mean that the baby has some digestive problem, such as an allergy to wheat or milk protein (see *Celiac Disease,* page 502; *Milk Allergy,* page 517) or lacks the digestive enzymes needed to digest certain solid foods. If you suspect that your child may be ill but can't identify the exact problem, or if you have any concerns about what is happening, call your pediatrician and describe the symptoms that worry you.

Your Child and Antibiotics

Antibiotics are among the most powerful and important medicines known. When used properly, they can save lives, but when used improperly, antibiotics actually can harm your child.

Two main types of germs—viruses and bacteria—cause most infections. Viruses cause all colds and most coughs and sore throats. Antibiotics never cure common viral infections. Your child recovers from these common viral infections when the illness has run its course. *Antibiotics should not be used to treat viral infections.*

Antibiotics can be used to treat bacterial infections, but some strains of bacteria have become resistant to certain antibiotics. If your child is infected with resistant bacteria, she might need a different antibiotic or even need to be treated in the hospital with more powerful medicines given by vein (intravenously [by IV]). A few new strains of bacteria are already untreatable. To protect your child from antibiotic-resistant bacteria, use antibiotics only when your pediatrician has determined that they might be effective, since repeated or improper use of antibiotics contributes to the increase in resistant bacteria.

- **When are antibiotics needed? When are they not needed?**
These complicated questions are best answered by your pediatrician, as the answer depends on the specific diagnosis. If you think your child might need treatment, contact your pediatrician.

The following illnesses are the most common ones that occur at this age. (All are described in Part II of this book.)

Bronchiolitis	Diarrhea	Viral Infections
Colds (URIs)	Earache/Ear Infection	Vomiting
Conjunctivitis	Fever	
Croup	Pneumonia	

IMMUNIZATION ALERT

At four months, your baby should receive:

- Second DTaP vaccine
- Second polio vaccine
- Second Hib (*Haemophilus influenzae* type b) vaccine

- *Ear infections:* Some types need antibiotics and some do not.

- *Sinus infections:* Some long-lasting or severe cases need antibiotic treatment, but just because your child's mucus is yellow or green does not mean that he has a bacterial infection. It is normal for the mucus to get thick and change color during a viral cold.

- *Bronchitis:* Children rarely need antibiotics for bronchitis.

- *Sore throat:* Most cases are caused by viruses. Only strep throat, which must be diagnosed by a laboratory test, requires antibiotics.

- *Colds:* Colds are caused by viruses and sometimes can last for two weeks or more. Antibiotics have no effect on colds. Your pediatrician may have suggestions for comfort measures while the cold runs its course.

Viral infections sometimes may lead to bacterial infections. But treating viral infections with antibiotics to prevent bacterial infections does not work and may lead to infection with resistant bacteria. Keep your pediatrician informed if the illness gets worse or lasts a long time, so that proper treatment can be given as needed.

If an antibiotic is prescribed, make sure your child takes the entire course, even if she's feeling better before all of the pills or liquid are gone. Never save antibiotics for later use or let other family members use a prescription that wasn't intended for them.

- Second pneumococcal vaccine
- Second Hepatitis B vaccine (may be given between one and four months)

And at six months:

- Third DTaP vaccine
- Third polio vaccine (which can be given between six and eighteen months)
- Third pneumococcal vaccine
- Third Hib vaccine (depending on vaccine type given for doses one and two)
- Third Hepatitis B vaccine, given between six and eighteen months

SAFETY CHECK

Car Safety Seats

- Buckle the baby into an approved, properly installed infant car safety seat before you start the car. It should be equipped with a three-point or a five-point harness. Keep the seat rear-facing. You can continue placing your baby into this seat until she weighs at least 20 pounds (9 kg) and is at least one year of age. (Some infant-only seats can be used up to 22 pounds (10 kg); check the guidelines that were provided with the seat.) When your child reaches the top weight (or height) allowed by her infant-only car safety seat, she will need to use a convertible car safety seat, which is bigger and heavier than an infant seat and can accommodate larger children.

- The American Academy of Pediatrics recommends that children ride rear-facing as long as possible, preferably to the highest weight or height allowed by the car safety seat. The backseat is the safest place for all children to ride. Never place a rear-facing car seat in the front seat of a car that has a passenger-side air bag.

Drowning

- **Never leave a baby alone even for a moment in a bath or near a pool of water, no matter how shallow it is. Infants can drown in just a few inches of water. Baby bath seats or supporting rings are not a substitute for adult supervision.**

Falls

- Never leave the baby unattended in high places, such as on a tabletop or in a crib with the sides down. If she does fall and seems to be acting abnormally in any way, call the pediatrician immediately.

Burns

- Never smoke or eat, drink, or carry anything hot while holding a baby.

- Prevent scalding by reducing the water heater setting to 120 degrees Fahrenheit (48.9 degrees Celsius) or lower.

Choking

- Never give a baby any food or small object that could cause choking. All foods should be mashed, ground, or soft enough to swallow without chewing.

9

AGE EIGHT MONTHS
THROUGH TWELVE MONTHS

*D*uring these months, your baby is becoming increasingly mobile, a development that will thrill and challenge both of you. Being able to move from place to place gives your child a delicious sense of power and control—her first real taste of physical independence. And while this is quite exhilarating for her, it's also frightening, since it comes at the time when she's most likely to be upset by separation from you. So as eager as she is to move out on her own and explore the farthest reaches of her domain, she may wail if she wanders out of your sight or you move too far from her.

From your point of view, your baby's mobility is a source of considerable concern as well as great pride. Crawling and walking are signals that she's developing right on target, but these achievements also mean that you'll have your hands full keeping her safe. If you haven't already fully child-proofed your home, do it now. (Read Chapter 14, on safety.) At this age, your baby has no concept of danger and only a limited memory for your warnings. The only way to protect her from the hundreds of hazards in your home is to secure cupboards and drawers, place dangerous and precious objects out of her reach, and make perilous rooms such as the bathroom inaccessible unless she's supervised.

By child-proofing your home, you'll also give your baby a greater sense of freedom. After all, fewer areas will be off limits, and thus you can let her make her own discoveries without your intervention or assistance. These personal accomplishments will promote her emerging self-esteem; you might even think of ways of facilitating them—for example:

1. Fill a low kitchen cupboard with safe objects and let your baby discover it herself.

2. Place some kiddie gardening tools in a corner of the garden for her to find when she's in the yard with you.

3. Equip your home with cushions of assorted shapes and sizes and let her experiment with the different ways she can move over and around them.

Knowing when to guide a child and when to let her do things for herself is part of the art of parenting. At this age, your child is extremely expressive and will give you the cues you need to decide when to intervene. When she's acting frustrated rather than challenged, for instance, don't let her struggle alone. If she's crying because her ball is wedged under the sofa out of her reach, or if she's climbed up the stairs and can't get down, she needs your help. At other times, however, it's important to let her solve her own problems. Don't let your own impatience cause you to intervene any more than absolutely necessary. You may be tempted to feed your nine-month-old, for instance, because it's faster and less messy than letting her feed herself. However, that also deprives her of a chance to learn a valuable new skill. The more opportunities you can give her to discover, test, and strengthen her new capabilities, the more confident and adventurous she'll be.

GROWTH AND DEVELOPMENT

Physical Appearance and Growth

Your baby will continue to grow rapidly during these months. The typical eight-month-old boy weighs between 14½ and 17½ pounds (6½ to 8 kg). Girls tend to weigh half a pound less. By his first birthday, the average child has tripled his birth weight and is 28 to 32 inches (71 to 81 cm) tall. Head growth between eight and twelve months slows down a bit from the first six months. Typical head size at eight months is 17½ inches (45 cm) in circumference; by one year, it's 18 inches (47 cm). Each baby grows at his own rate, however, so you should check your child's height and weight curves on the growth charts on pages 128–129 to make sure he's following the pattern established in his first eight months.

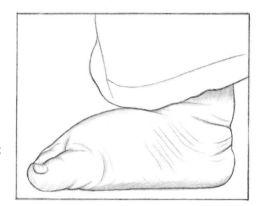

At this age your child's feet will seem flat because the arch is hidden by a pad of fat. But in two to three years this fat will disappear and his arch will be evident.

When your child first stands, you may be surprised by his posture. His belly will protrude, his rear end will stick out, and his back will have a forward sway to it. It may look unusual, but this stance is perfectly normal from the time he starts to stand until he develops a confident sense of balance sometime in the second year.

Your child's feet also may look a little odd to you. When he lies on his back, his toes may turn inward so that he appears pigeon-toed. This common condition usually disappears by eighteen months. If it persists, your pediatrician may show you some foot or leg exercises to do with your baby. If the problem is severe, your pediatrician may refer you to a pediatric orthopedist. (See *Pigeon Toes,* page 686.)

When your child takes his first teetering steps, you may notice quite a different appearance—his feet may turn outward. This occurs because the ligaments of his hips are still so loose that his legs naturally rotate outward. During the first six months of his second year, the ligaments will tighten and then his feet should point nearly straight.

At this age, your child's feet will seem flat because the arch is hidden by a pad of fat. In two to three years, this fat will disappear and his arch will be evident.

Movement

At eight months, your baby probably will be sitting without support. Although she may topple over from time to time, she'll usually catch herself with her arms. As the muscles in her trunk grow stronger, she'll also start leaning over to pick up toys. Eventually she'll figure out how to roll down onto her stomach and get back up to a sitting position.

When she's lying on a flat surface, your baby is now in constant motion. When on her stomach, she'll arch her neck so she can look around, and when on her back, she'll grab her feet (or anything else nearby) and pull them to her mouth. But she won't be content to stay on her back for long. She can turn over at will now and flip without a moment's notice. This can be especially dangerous during diaper changes, so you may want to retire her changing table, using instead the floor or a bed from which she's less likely to fall. Never leave her alone for an instant at any time.

All this activity strengthens muscles for crawling, a skill that usually is mastered between seven and ten months. For a while she simply may rock on her hands and knees. Since her arm muscles are better developed than her legs, she may even push herself backward instead of forward. But with time and practice she'll discover that, by digging with her knees and pushing off, she can propel herself forward across the room toward the target of her choice.

A few children never do crawl. Instead, they use alternative movement methods, such as scooting on their bottoms or slithering on their stomachs. As long as your baby is learning to coordinate each side of her body and is using each arm and leg equally, there's no cause for concern. The important thing is that she's able to explore her surroundings on her own and is strengthening her body in preparation for walking. If you feel your child is not moving normally, discuss your concern with the pediatrician.

How can you encourage your child to crawl? Try presenting her with intriguing objects placed just beyond her reach. As she becomes more agile, create miniature obstacle courses using pillows, boxes, and sofa cushions for her to crawl over and between. Join in the game by hiding behind one of the obstacles and surprising her with a "peekaboo!" Don't ever leave your baby unsupervised among these props, though. If she falls between pillows or under a box, she might not be able to pull herself out. This is bound to frighten her, and she could even smother.

Stairs are another ready-made—but potentially dangerous—obstacle course. Although your baby needs to learn how to go up and down stairs, you should not allow her to play on them alone during this time. If you have a staircase in your home, she'll probably head straight for it every chance she gets, so place sturdy gates at both the top and the bottom to close off her access. The gates should have small openings and a solid piece across the top; old-fashioned accordion gates can strangle children who get their heads caught in the openings. (See illustration in Chapter 14, page 439.)

As a substitute for real stairs, let your baby practice climbing up and down steps constructed of heavy-duty foam blocks or sturdy cardboard cartons covered in fabric. At about a year of age, when your baby has become a competent crawler, teach her to go down real stairs backward. She may take a few tumbles before she understands the logic of going feetfirst instead of headfirst, so practice on carpeted steps and let her climb only the first few. If your home doesn't have carpeted stairs, let her perfect this skill when you visit a home that does.

Although crawling makes a huge difference in how your baby sees the world and what she can do in it, don't expect her to be content with that for long. She'll see everyone else around her walking, and that's what she'll want to do too. In preparation for this big step, she'll pull herself to a standing position every chance she gets—although when she first starts, she may not know how to get down. If she cries for your help, physically show her how to bend her knees so she can lower herself to the floor without falling. Teaching her this skill will save you many extra trips to her room at night when she's standing in her crib and crying because she doesn't know how to sit down.

Once your baby feels secure standing, she'll try some tentative steps while holding on to a support. For instance, when your hands aren't available, she'll "cruise" alongside furniture. Just make sure that whatever she uses for support has no sharp edges and is properly weighted or securely attached to the floor so it won't fall on her.

As her balance improves, occasionally she may let go, only to grab for support when she feels herself totter. The first time she continues forth on her own, her steps will be shaky. At first, she may take only one step before dropping, either in surprise or relief. Soon, however, she'll manage to keep herself up and moving until you catch her several steps later. As miraculous as it may seem, most children advance from these first steps to quite confident walking in a matter of days.

Although both of you will feel excited over this dramatic development, you'll also find yourself unnerved at times, especially when she stumbles and falls. But even if you take pains to provide a safe and soft environment, it's almost impossible to avoid bumps and bruises. Just be matter-of-fact about these accidents. Offer a quick hug or a reassuring word and send your little one on her way again. She won't be unduly upset by these falls if you're not.

Although your baby needs to learn how to go up and down stairs, you should not allow her to play on them alone during this time.

Soon he'll manage to keep himself up and moving until you catch him several steps later.

At this stage, or even earlier, many parents start using a baby walker. Contrary to what the name suggests, these devices do not help the process of learning to walk. While they strengthen the muscles in the lower legs, they don't do a good job of strengthening muscles in the upper legs and hips, which are used most in walking and need the workout. These walkers actually eliminate the desire to walk, since they allow the baby to get around too easily. To make matters worse, they present a serious safety hazard because they can tip over easily when the child bumps into an obstacle, such as a small toy or a throw rug. Children in walkers also are more likely to fall down stairs and get into dangerous places that would otherwise be beyond their reach. For these reasons, *the American Academy of Pediatrics strongly urges parents not to use baby walkers.*

A sturdy wagon or a "kiddie push car" is a better choice. Be sure the toy has a bar she can push and that it's weighted so it won't tip over when she pulls herself up on it.

As your child begins to walk, she'll need shoes to protect her feet. Wedges, inserts, high backs, reinforced heels, special arches, and other features designed to shape and support the feet make shoes more expensive but have no proven benefit for the average child. Look instead for comfortable shoes with nonskid soles that will help your baby avoid slipping on smooth floors; sneakers are fine. Her feet will grow rapidly during these months, and her shoes will have to

Movement Milestones
by the End of This Period

- **Gets to sitting position without assistance**
- **Crawls forward on belly by pulling with arms and pushing with legs**
- **Assumes hands-and-knees position**
- **Creeps on hands and knees supporting trunk on hands and knees**
- **Gets from sitting to crawling or prone (lying on stomach) position**
- **Pulls self up to stand**
- **Walks holding on to furniture**

- **Stands momentarily without support**
- **May walk two or three steps without support**

keep pace. Her first pair of shoes probably will last two to three months, but you should check the fit of her shoes as often as monthly during this formative period.

Many babies' first steps are taken around their first birthday, although it's perfectly normal for children to start walking a little earlier or later. At first, your child will walk with her feet wide apart to improve her shaky sense of balance. During those initial days and weeks, she accidentally may get going too fast and fall when she tries to stop. As she becomes more confident, she'll learn how to stop and change directions. Before long, she'll be able to squat to pick something up and then stand again. When she reaches this level of accomplishment, she'll get enormous pleasure from push-pull toys—the noisier the better.

Hand and Finger Skills

Your baby's mastery of crawling, standing, and walking are bound to be his most dramatic accomplishments during these months, but don't overlook all the wonderful things he's learning to do with his hands. At the beginning of this period, he'll still clumsily "rake" things toward himself, but by the end, he'll grasp accurately with his thumb and first or second finger. You'll find him practicing this pincer movement on any small object, from dust balls to cereal, and he may even try to snap his fingers if you show him how.

As your baby learns to open his fingers at will, he'll delight in dropping and throwing things. If you leave small toys on the tray of his high chair or in his playpen, he'll fling them down and then call loudly for someone to retrieve them so he can do it again. If he throws hard objects such as blocks, he might do some damage and probably will increase the noise level in your household considerably. Your life will be a little calmer if you redirect him toward softer objects, such as balls of various sizes, colors, and textures. (Include some with beads or chimes inside so they make a sound as they roll.) One activity that not only is fun but allows you to observe your child's developing skills is to sit on the floor and roll a large ball toward him. At first, he'll slap randomly at it, but eventually he'll learn to swat it so it rolls back in your direction.

With his improved coordination, your baby can now investigate the objects he encounters more thoroughly. He'll pick them up, shake them, bang them, and pass them from hand to hand. He'll be particularly intrigued by toys with moving parts—wheels that spin, levers that can be moved, hinges that open and close. Holes also are fascinating because he can poke his fingers in them and, when he becomes a little more skilled, drop things through them.

Blocks are another favorite toy at this age. In fact, nothing motivates a baby to crawl quite as much as a tower waiting to be toppled. Toward the end of this period, your child may even start to build towers of his own by stacking one block on top of another.

Language Development

Toward the end of the first year, your baby will begin to communicate what she wants by pointing, crawling, or gesturing toward her target. She'll also imitate many of the gestures she sees adults make as they talk. This nonverbal communication is only a temporary measure, however, while she learns how to phrase her messages in words.

Do you notice the coos, gurgles, and screeches of earlier months now giving way to recognizable syllables, such as "ba," "da," "ga," and "ma"? Your child may even stumble on words such as "mama" and "bye-bye" quite accidentally, and when you get excited she'll realize she's said something meaningful. Before long she'll start using "mama" to summon you or attract your attention. At this age, she may also say "mama" throughout the day just to practice saying the word. Ultimately, however, she'll use words only when she wants to communicate their meanings.

Even though you've been talking to your baby from birth, she now under-

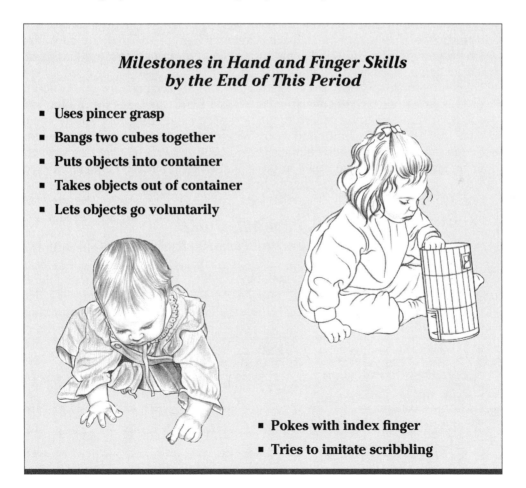

Milestones in Hand and Finger Skills by the End of This Period

- **Uses pincer grasp**
- **Bangs two cubes together**
- **Puts objects into container**
- **Takes objects out of container**
- **Lets objects go voluntarily**

- **Pokes with index finger**
- **Tries to imitate scribbling**

stands more language, and thus your conversations will take on new significance. Before she can say many, if any, words, she'll probably be comprehending more than you suspect. For example, watch how she responds when you mention a favorite toy across the room. If she looks toward it, she's telling you she understands. To help her increase her understanding, keep talking to her as much as possible. Tell her what's happening around her, particularly as you bathe, change, and feed her. Make your language simple and specific: "I'm drying you with the big blue towel. How soft it feels!" Verbally label familiar toys and objects for her, and try to be as consistent as possible—that is, if you call the family pet a cat today, don't call it a kitty tomorrow.

Picture books can enhance this entire process by reinforcing her budding understanding that everything has a name. Choose books with large board, cloth, or vinyl pages that she can turn herself. Also look for simple but colorful illustrations of things your child will recognize.

Whether you're reading or talking to her, give her plenty of opportunities to join in. Ask questions and wait for a response. Or let her take the lead. If she says "Gaagaagaa," repeat it back and see what she does. Yes, these exchanges may seem meaningless, but they tell your baby that communication is two-way and that she's a welcome participant. Paying attention to what she says also will help you identify the words she understands and make it more likely that you'll recognize her first spoken words.

These first words, incidentally, often aren't proper English. For your child, a "word" is any sound that consistently refers to the same person, object, or event. So if she says "mog" every time she wants milk, you should treat "mog" with all the respect of a legitimate word. When you speak back to her, however, use "milk," and eventually she'll make the correction herself.

There's a tremendous variance in the age at which children begin to say rec-

Language Milestones by the End of This Period

- **Pays increasing attention to speech**
- **Responds to simple verbal requests**
- **Responds to "no"**
- **Uses simple gestures, such as shaking head for "no"**
- **Babbles with inflection**
- **Says "dada" and "mama"**
- **Uses exclamations, such as "oh-oh!"**
- **Tries to imitate words**

ognizable words. Some have a vocabulary of two to three words by their first birthday. More likely, your baby's speech at twelve months will consist of a sort of gibberish that has the tones and variations of intelligible speech. As long as she's experimenting with sounds that vary in intensity, pitch, and quality, she's getting ready to talk. The more you respond to her as if she were speaking, the more you'll stimulate her urge to communicate.

Bilingual Babies

If you speak a second language in your home, don't be concerned that your child is going to become confused by hearing two languages. Millions of American families speak not only English but also another language in their daily lives. Research and parental experience show that when children are exposed to two (or even more) languages at a very young age, particularly when they hear both of them consistently, they are able to learn both languages simultaneously. Yes, during the child's normal language development, he may be more proficient in one or the other language, and at times he may interject words from one language when speaking the other. But with time, the two languages will become distinct and separate, and he should be able to communicate in both. (Some studies suggest that while he may be able to understand both languages, he will speak one of them better than the other for a time.)

Certainly you should encourage your child to become bilingual. It's an asset and a skill that will benefit him for the rest of his life. In general, the younger he is when both languages are introduced, the more proficiently he'll learn them; by contrast, he may have a little more difficulty learning the second language if he is introduced to it during the preschool years only after learning and speaking the first language exclusively.

Cognitive Development

An eight-month-old is curious about everything, but he also has a very short attention span and will move rapidly from one activity to the next. Two to three minutes is the most he'll spend with a single toy, and then he'll turn to something new. By twelve months, he may be willing to sit for as long as fifteen minutes with a particularly interesting plaything, but most of the time he'll still be a body in motion, and you shouldn't expect him to be any different.

Ironically, although toy stores are brimming with one expensive plaything after another, the toys that fascinate children most at this age are ordinary household objects such as wooden spoons, egg cartons, and plastic containers of all

Variations of Peekaboo

The possible variations of peekaboo are almost endless. As your child becomes more mobile and alert, create games that let her take the lead. Here are some suggestions.

1. Drape a soft cloth over her head and ask, "Where's the baby?" Once she understands the game, she'll pull the cloth away and pop up grinning.

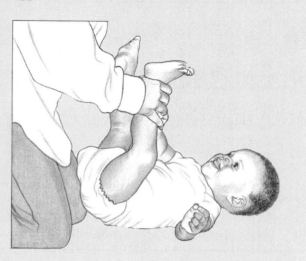

2. With baby on her back facing toward you, lift both her legs together—"Up, up, up"—until they conceal your face from her. Then open them wide: "Peeka-boo!" As she gets the idea, she'll move her legs herself. (This is a great game at diaper-changing time.)

3. Hide behind a door or a piece of furniture, leaving a foot or arm in her view as a clue. She'll be delighted to come find you.

4. Take turns with your baby "hiding" your head under a large towel and letting her pull the towel off and then putting it over her head and pulling it off.

shapes and sizes. Your baby will be especially interested in things that differ just a bit from what he already knows, so if he's bored with the oatmeal box he's been playing with, you can renew his interest by putting a ball inside or turning it into a pull toy by tying a string to it. These small changes will help him learn to detect small differences between the familiar and the unfamiliar. Also, when you choose playthings, remember that objects too much like what he's seen before will be given a quick once-over and dismissed, while things that are too foreign may be confusing or frightening. Look instead for objects and toys that gradually help him expand his horizons.

Often your baby won't need your help to discover objects that fall into this middle ground of newness. In fact, as soon as he can crawl, he'll be off in search

Cognitive Milestones by the End of This Period

- Explores objects in many different ways (shaking, banging, throwing, dropping)

- Finds hidden objects easily

- Looks at correct picture when the image is named

- Imitates gestures

- Begins to use objects correctly (drinking from cup, brushing hair, dialing phone, listening to receiver)

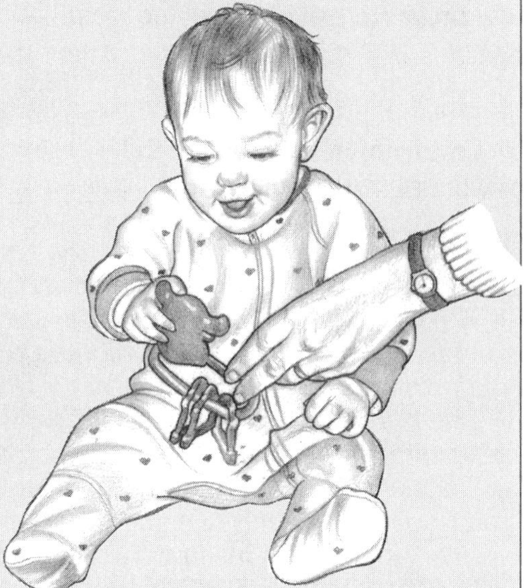

of new things to conquer. He'll rummage through your drawers, empty out wastebaskets, ransack kitchen cabinets, and conduct elaborate experiments on everything he finds. (Make sure there's nothing that can hurt him in those containers, and keep an eye on him whenever he's into these things.) He'll never tire of dropping, rolling, throwing, submerging, or waving objects to find out how they behave. This may look like random play to you, but it's your child's way of finding out how the world works. Like any good scientist, he's observing the properties of objects, and from his observations, he'll develop ideas about shapes (some things roll and others don't), textures (things can be scratchy, soft, or smooth), and sizes (some things fit inside each other). He'll even begin to understand that some things are edible and others aren't, although he'll still put everything into his mouth just to be sure. (Again, make sure there's nothing dangerous lying around that he can put in his mouth.)

His continuing observations during these months also will help him understand that objects exist even when they're out of his sight. This concept is called object permanence. At eight months, when you hide a toy under a scarf, he'll pick up the scarf and search for the toy underneath—a response that wouldn't have occurred three months earlier. Try hiding the toy under the scarf and then removing it when he's not looking, however, and your eight-month-old will be puzzled. By ten months, he'll be so certain that the toy still exists that he'll continue looking for it. To help your baby learn object permanence, play peekaboo with him. By switching from one variation of this game to another, you'll maintain his interest almost indefinitely.

As he approaches his first birthday, your child will become increasingly conscious that things not only have names but that they also have particular functions. You'll see this new awareness weave itself into his play as a very early form of fantasy. For example, instead of treating a toy telephone as an interesting object to be chewed, poked, and banged, he'll put the receiver to his ear just as he's seen you do. You can encourage important developmental activities like this by offering him suggestive props—a hairbrush, toothbrush, cup, or spoon—and by being an enthusiastic audience for his performances.

Brain Development

As you've read in this chapter and the ones that preceded it, the early months of your child's life are crucial to her brain development. The environment to which you expose her and the experiences that she has at this time in life will have a powerful influence on the way her brain grows.

You have opportunities every day to nurture your child's brain. You can provide her with intellectual stimulation just by talking with her and by encouraging her to say words that she's learning. You can give her a comfortable and safe environment in which to explore the world around her. You can provide her with simple toys that challenge her brain to develop. You can play games with her that encourage her to stretch her memory.

In the box on page 245, you'll find some suggestions that can be used day by

Stimulating Infant Brain Growth: Age Eight Months Through Twelve Months

- Talk to your baby during dressing, bathing, feeding, playing, walking, and driving, using adult talk; check with your pediatrician if your baby does not seem to respond to sound or if syllables and words are not developing.
- Be attentive to your baby's rhythms and moods. Respond to her when she is upset as well as when she is happy.
- Encourage your baby to play with blocks and soft toys, which helps her develop eye-hand coordination, fine-motor skills, and a sense of competence.
- Provide a stimulating, safe environment where your baby can begin to explore and roam.
- Give consistent warm, physical contact—hugging, skin-to-skin, body-to-body contact—to establish your child's sense of security and well-being.
- Read to your baby every day.
- If you speak a foreign language, use it at home.
- Avoid subjecting your child to stressful or traumatic experiences, physical or psychological.
- Play games like peekaboo and pattycake to stimulate your baby's memory skills.
- Introduce your child to other children and parents.
- Provide age- and developmentally appropriate toys that are safe and inexpensive. Toys do not need to be costly—ordinary household objects will do just fine. Remember, it's much more important to give your child more attention than more toys.
- Teach your baby to wave "bye-bye" and to shake her head "yes" and "no."
- Make sure other people who provide care and supervision for your baby understand the importance of forming a loving and comforting relationship with her.
- Respect your baby's periodic discomfort around people who may not be her primary caregivers.
- Spend time on the floor playing with your child every day.
- Choose quality child care that is affectionate, responsive, educational, and safe. Visit your child care provider frequently and share your ideas about positive caregiving.

day as your baby progresses from ages eight to twelve months. They really can make a difference in your child's life, and not only now—they'll build a foundation for brain growth for years to come.

Emotional Development

During these four months, your child sometimes may seem like two separate babies. First there's the one who's open, affectionate, and outgoing with you. But then there's another who's anxious, clinging, and easily frightened around unfamiliar people or objects. Some people may tell you that your child is fearful or shy because you're "spoiling" her, but don't believe it. Her widely diverse behavior patterns aren't caused by you or your parenting style; they occur because she's now, for the first time, able to tell the difference between familiar and unfamiliar situations. If anything, the predictable anxieties of this period are evidence of her healthy relationship with you.

Anxiety around strangers is usually one of the first emotional milestones your baby will reach. You may think something is wrong when this child of yours who, at the age of three months, interacted calmly with people she didn't know is now beginning to tense up when strangers come too close. This is normal for this age, and you need not worry. Even relatives and frequent babysitters with whom your baby was once comfortable may prompt her to hide or cry now, especially if they approach her hastily.

At about the same time, she'll become much more "clutchy" about leaving you. This is the start of separation anxiety. Just as she's starting to realize that each object is unique and permanent, she'll also discover that there's only one of you. When you're out of her sight, she'll know you're somewhere, but not with her, and this will cause her great distress. She'll have so little sense of time that she won't know when—or even whether—you'll be coming back. Once she gets a little

The predictable anxieties of this period are evidence of your child's healthy relationship with you.

Social/Emotional Milestones by the End of This Period

- Shy or anxious with strangers
- Cries when mother or father leaves
- Enjoys imitating people in play
- Shows specific preferences for certain people and toys
- Tests parental responses to his actions during feedings (What do you do when he refuses a food?)
- Tests parental responses to his behavior (What do you do if he cries after you leave the room?)
- May be fearful in some situations
- Prefers mother and/or regular caregiver over all others
- Repeats sounds or gestures for attention
- Finger-feeds himself
- Extends arm or leg to help when being dressed

older, her memory of past experiences with you will comfort her when you're gone, and she'll be able to anticipate a reunion. But for now she's only aware of the present, so every time you leave her sight—even to go to the next room—she'll fuss and cry. When you leave her with someone else, she may scream as though her heart will break. At bedtime, she'll refuse to leave you to go to sleep, and then she may wake up searching for you in the middle of the night.

How long should you expect this separation anxiety to last? It usually peaks between ten and eighteen months and then fades during the last half of the second year. In some ways, this phase of your child's emotional development will be especially tender for both of you, while in others, it will be painful. After all, her desire to be with you is a sign of her attachment to her first and greatest love—namely you. The intensity of her feeling as she hurtles into your arms is irresistible, especially when you realize that no one—including your child herself—will ever again think you are quite as perfect as she does at this age. On the other hand, you may feel suffocated by her constant clinging, while experiencing guilt whenever you leave her crying for you. Fortunately, this emotional roller coaster eventually will subside along with her separation anxiety. But in the meantime, try to downplay your leave-taking as much as possible. Here are some suggestions that may help.

Acquainting Your Baby with a Sitter

Is your baby about to have a new babysitter for a few hours? Whenever possible, let your child get to know this new person while you're there. Ideally, have the sitter spend time with him on several successive days before you leave them alone. If this isn't possible, allow yourself an extra hour or two for this get-acquainted period before you have to go out.

During this first meeting, the sitter and your baby should get to know each other very gradually, using the following steps.

1. Hold the baby on your lap while you and the sitter talk. Watch for clues that your child is at ease before you have the sitter make eye contact with him. Wait until the baby is looking at her or playing contentedly by himself.

2. Have the sitter talk to the baby while he stays on your lap. She should not reach toward the child or try to touch him yet.

3. Once the baby seems comfortable with the conversation, put him on the floor with a favorite toy, across from the sitter. Invite the sitter to slowly come closer and play with the toy. As the baby warms up to her, you can move back gradually.

4. See what happens when you leave the room. If your baby doesn't notice you're missing, the introduction has gone well.

You can use leisurely introduction with anyone who hasn't seen the child in the past few days, including relatives and friends. Adults often overwhelm babies of this age by coming close and making funny noises or, worse yet, trying to take them from their mothers. You have to intervene when this occurs. Explain to these well-meaning people that your baby needs time to warm up to strangers and that he's more likely to respond well if they go slowly.

1. Your baby is more susceptible to separation anxiety when she's tired, hungry, or sick. If you know you're going to go out, schedule your departure so that it occurs after she's napped and eaten. And try to stay with her as much as possible when she's sick.

2. Don't make a fuss over your leaving. Instead, have the person staying with her create a distraction (a new toy, a visit to the mirror, a bath). Then say good-bye and slip away quickly.

3. Remember that her tears will subside within minutes of your departure. Her outbursts are for your benefit, to persuade you to stay. With you out of sight, she'll soon turn her attention to the person staying with her.

4. Help her learn to cope with separation through short practice sessions at home. Separation will be easier on her when she initiates it, so when she crawls to another room (one that's baby-proofed), don't follow her right away; wait for one or two minutes. When you have to go to another room for a few seconds, tell her where you're going and that you'll return. If she fusses, call to her instead of running back. Gradually she'll learn that nothing terrible happens when you're gone and, just as important, that you always come back when you say you will.

5. If you take your child to a sitter's home or a child care center, don't just drop her off and leave. Spend a few extra minutes playing with her in this new environment. When you do leave, reassure her that you'll be back later.

If your child has a strong, healthy attachment to you, her separation anxiety probably will occur earlier than in other babies, and she'll pass through it more quickly. Instead of resenting her possessiveness during these months, maintain as much warmth and good humor as you can. Through your actions, you're showing her how to express and return love. This is the emotional base she'll rely on in years to come.

From the beginning, you've considered your baby to be a unique person with specific character traits and preferences. She, however, has had only a dim notion of herself as a person separate from you. Now her sense of identity is coming into bloom. As she develops a growing sense of herself as an individual, she'll also become increasingly conscious of you as a separate person.

One of the clearest signs of her own self-awareness is the way your baby watches herself in the mirror at this age. Up to about eight months, she treated the mirror as just another fascinating object. Perhaps, she thought, the reflection was another baby, or maybe it was a magical surface of lights and shadows. But now her responses will change, indicating she understands that one of the images belongs to her. While watching the mirror, for example, she may touch a smudge on her own nose or pull on a stray lock of her hair. You can reinforce her sense of identity by playing mirror games. When you're looking in the mirror together, touch different body parts: "This is Jenny's nose. This is Mommy's nose." Or move in and out of the mirror, playing peekaboo with the reflections. Or make faces and verbally label the emotions you are conveying.

Toys Appropriate for an Eight- to Twelve-Month-Old

- **Stacking toys in different sizes, shapes, colors**
- **Cups, pails, and other unbreakable containers**
- **Unbreakable mirrors of various sizes**
- **Bath toys that float, squirt, or hold water**
- **Large building blocks**
- **"Busy boxes" that push, open, squeak, and move**
- **Squeeze toys**
- **Large dolls and puppets**
- **Cars, trucks, and other vehicle toys made of flexible plastic, with no sharp edges or removable parts**
- **Balls of all sizes (but not small enough to fit in the mouth)**
- **Cardboard books with large pictures**
- **CDs, tapes, music boxes, and musical toys**
- **Push-pull toys**
- **Toy telephones**
- **Paper tubes, empty boxes, old magazines, egg cartons, empty plastic soda/ juice/milk bottles (well rinsed)**

As the months pass and your child's self-concept becomes more secure, she'll have less trouble meeting strangers and separating from you. She'll also become more assertive. Before, you could count on her to be relatively compliant as long as she was comfortable. But now, more often than not, she'll want things her own particular way. For instance, don't be surprised if she turns up her nose at certain foods or objects when you place them in front of her. Also, as she becomes more mobile, you'll find yourself frequently saying "no," to warn her away from things she shouldn't touch. But even after she understands the

Developmental Health Watch

Each baby develops in his own manner, so it's impossible to tell exactly when your child will perfect a given skill. Although the developmental milestones listed in this book will give you a general idea of the changes you can expect as your child gets older, don't be alarmed if his development takes a slightly different course. Alert your pediatrician if your baby displays any of the following signs of *possible* developmental delay in the eight- to twelve-month age range.

- Does not crawl
- Drags one side of body while crawling (for over one month)
- Cannot stand when supported
- Does not search for objects that are hidden while he watches
- Says no single words ("mama" or "dada")
- Does not learn to use gestures, such as waving or shaking head
- Does not point to objects or pictures

word, she may touch anyway. Just wait—this is only a forerunner of power struggles to come.

Your baby also may become afraid of objects and situations that she used to take in stride. At this age, fears of the dark, thunder, and loud appliances such as vacuum cleaners are common. Later you'll be able to subdue these fears by talking about them, but for now, the only solution is to eliminate the source of the fears as much as possible: Put a night-light in her room, or vacuum when she's not around. And when you can't shield her from something that frightens her, try to anticipate her reaction and be close by so she can turn to you. Comfort her, but stay calm so she understands that you are not afraid. If you reassure her every time she hears a clap of thunder or the roar of a jet overhead, her fear gradually will subside until all she has to do is look at you to feel safe.

BASIC CARE

Feeding

At this age, your baby needs between 750 and 900 calories each day, about 400 to 500 of which should come from breastmilk or formula (approximately 24

Transitional Objects

Almost everyone knows about the Charles Schulz character Linus and his blanket. He drags it around wherever he goes, nibbling on its corner or curling up with it when the going gets tough. Security objects such as blankets are part of the emotional support system every child needs in his early years.

Your child may not choose a blanket, of course. He may prefer a soft toy or even the satin trim on Mom's bathrobe. Chances are, he'll make his choice between months eight and twelve, and he'll keep it with him for years to come. When he's tired, it will help him get to sleep. When he's separated from you, it will reassure him. When he's frightened or upset, it will comfort him. When he's in a strange place, it will help him feel at home.

These special comforts are called transitional objects, because they help children make the emotional transition from dependence to independence. They work, in part, because they feel good: They're soft, cuddly, and nice to touch. They're also effective because of their familiarity. This so-called lovey has your child's scent on it, and it reminds him of the comfort and security of his own room. It makes him feel that everything is going to be okay.

Despite myths to the contrary, transitional objects are not a sign of

ounces [720 ml] a day). But don't be surprised if her appetite is less robust now than it was during the first eight months. This is because her rate of growth is slowing, and she also has so many new and interesting activities to distract her.

At about eight months, you may want to introduce "junior" foods. These are slightly coarser than strained foods and are packaged in larger jars—usually 6 to 8 ounces (180 to 240 ml). They require more chewing than baby foods. You also can expand your baby's diet to include soft foods such as puddings, mashed potatoes, yogurt, and gelatin. Eggs are an excellent source of protein, but feed her only the yolks at first, since their nutritional value is higher and they're less likely to cause allergies than the whites. In one or two months you can give her the whole egg. As always, introduce one food at a time, then wait two or three days before trying something else to be sure your child doesn't develop an allergic reaction.

At about eight to nine months, as your baby's ability to use her hands improves, give her a spoon of her own and let her play with it at mealtimes. Once she's figured out how to hold it, dip it in her food and let her try to feed herself. But don't expect much in the beginning, when more food is bound to go on the floor and high chair than into her mouth. A plastic cloth under her chair will help minimize some of the cleanup.

Be patient, and resist the temptation to grab the spoon away from her. She

weakness or insecurity, and there's no reason to keep your child from using one. In fact, a transitional object can be so helpful that you may want to help him choose one and build it into his nighttime ritual. From early infancy, you might try keeping a small, soft blanket or toy in his crib. He may ignore it at first, but if it's always there, he'll probably take to it eventually.

You also can make things easier for yourself by having two identical security objects. Doing this will allow you to wash one while the other is being used, thus sparing your baby (and yourself) a potential emotional crisis and a very bedraggled "lovey." If your baby chooses a large blanket for his security object, you can easily turn it into two by cutting it in half. He has little sense of size and won't notice the change. If he's chosen a toy instead, try to find a duplicate as soon as possible. If you don't start rotating them early, your child may refuse the second one because it feels too new and foreign.

Parents often worry that transitional objects promote thumb sucking, and in fact they sometimes (but not always) do. But it's important to remember that thumb or finger sucking is a normal, natural way for a young child to comfort himself. He'll gradually give up both the transitional object and the sucking as he matures and finds other ways to cope with stress.

needs not only the practice but also the knowledge that you have confidence in her ability to feed herself. For a while you may want to alternate bites from her spoon with bites from a spoon that you hold. Once she consistently gets her own spoon to her mouth (which might not be until after her first birthday), you may keep filling her spoon for her to decrease the mess and waste, but leave the actual feeding to her.

In the early weeks of self-feeding, things may go more smoothly when she's really hungry and is more interested in eating than playing. Although your baby now eats three meals, just like the rest of the family, you may not want to impose her somewhat disorderly eating behavior on everyone else's dinnertime. Many families compromise by feeding the baby most of her meal in advance and then letting her occupy herself with finger foods while the others eat their meal.

Finger foods for babies include crunchy toast, well-cooked pasta, small pieces of chicken, scrambled eggs, cereals, and chunks of banana. Try to offer a selection of

flavors, shapes, colors, and textures, but always watch her for choking in case she bites off a piece too big to swallow. (See *Choking,* page 481.) Also, because she's likely to swallow without chewing, never offer a young child spoonfuls of peanut butter, large pieces of raw carrot, nuts, grapes, popcorn, uncooked peas, celery, hard candies, or other hard round foods. Choking can happen with hot dogs or meat sticks (baby-food "hot dogs"), so these always should be cut lengthwise and then into smaller pieces before being fed to a child of this age.

Weaning to a Cup

Once your baby is feeding himself more often, it's a natural time to introduce him to drinking from a cup. To get started, give him a trainer cup that has two handles and a snap-on lid with a spout, or use small plastic juice glasses. Either option will minimize spillage as he experiments with different ways to hold (and most likely to throw) the cup.

In the beginning, fill the cup with water and offer it to him at just one meal a day. Show him how to maneuver it to his mouth and tip it so he can drink. Don't become dismayed, however, if he treats the cup as a plaything for several weeks; most babies do. Just be patient until he's finally able to get most of the

In the early weeks of self-feeding, things may go more smoothly when she's really hungry and is more interested in eating than playing.

liquid down his throat—not dribbling down his chin or flying around the room—before you fill the cup with juice or milk or give it to him at other meals.

There are advantages to drinking from a cup: It will improve your child's hand-to-mouth coordination, and it will begin to prepare him for the weaning process, which frequently occurs around this age. Remember, the American

WHERE WE STAND

Childhood overweight and obesity is becoming an increasingly prevalent problem. Prevalence has doubled in children and tripled among adolescents in the United States over the past two decades. Throughout a child's lifetime, chronic obesity can lead to potentially serious health problems, including diabetes and high blood pressure. It also can cause psychological stresses associated with feeling different from his peers, leading to depression and low self-esteem.

The American Academy of Pediatrics believes that both parents and pediatricians need to take steps to prevent the development of overweight problems in children. Your pediatrician can monitor annually your child's weight gain from age one and help make sure that it remains within normal guidelines as he grows. Your doctor will calculate your youngster's body mass index (BMI), which is the weight in pounds divided by the height in inches squared, and then multiplied by 703 (or, weight in kilograms divided by height in meters squared). A child with a BMI between the 85th and 95th percentile for age and sex is considered at risk of being overweight; when the BMI is at or above the 95th percentile, he is considered overweight or obese. (See *Growth Charts,* Chapter 5, pages 130–131.)

Some youngsters are more prone to gain extra weight because of family history, but in many instances eating and exercise behaviors can contribute to obesity. Talk to your pediatrician about ways to develop healthy eating habits that should begin in infancy and continue throughout childhood and adulthood. Bear in mind that, as a parent, you have an enormous impact not only on your youngster's lifelong food choices, but also on other factors that can contribute to or prevent obesity. Early on, encourage your child to eat moderate portions of nutritious foods and to lead an active lifestyle at home, in child care settings, and in school. When he begins eating snacks, choose nutritious ones for him, including vegetables, fruits, low-fat dairy foods, and whole grains. Because children are inactive and tend to snack while watching television, the Academy recommends that youngsters limit their viewing of TV and other media to a maximum of two hours per day.

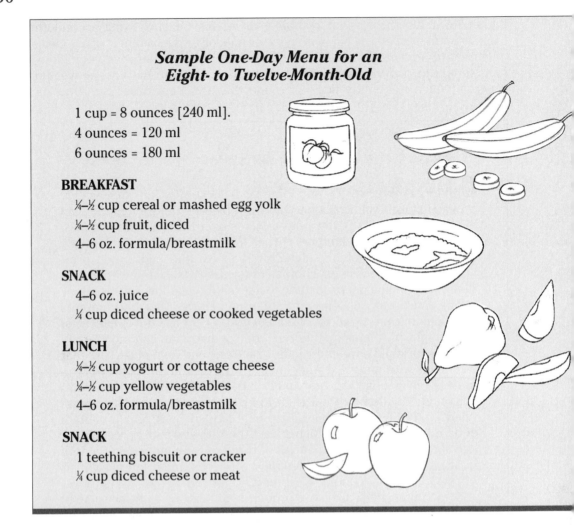

Sample One-Day Menu for an Eight- to Twelve-Month-Old

1 cup = 8 ounces [240 ml].
4 ounces = 120 ml
6 ounces = 180 ml

BREAKFAST
¼–½ cup cereal or mashed egg yolk
¼–½ cup fruit, diced
4–6 oz. formula/breastmilk

SNACK
4–6 oz. juice
¼ cup diced cheese or cooked vegetables

LUNCH
¼–½ cup yogurt or cottage cheese
¼–½ cup yellow vegetables
4–6 oz. formula/breastmilk

SNACK
1 teething biscuit or cracker
¼ cup diced cheese or meat

Academy of Pediatrics believes that breastfeeding is the best source of nutrition for babies through at least their first birthday. But as you gradually transition him to receiving other types of liquids, your baby's readiness for drinking from a cup will be signaled by his:

1. Looking around while nursing or taking the bottle

2. Mouthing the nipple without sucking

3. Trying to slide off your lap before the feeding is finished

Even under the best of circumstances, weaning may not take place overnight. Six months may pass before your baby is willing to take all his liquid from a cup. Even so, you can start the process and proceed gradually, letting his interest and willingness guide you. You'll probably find it easiest at first to substitute a cup for the bottle or breast at the midday feeding. Once he's adjusted to this

DINNER

¼ cup diced poultry, meat, or tofu

¼–½ cup green vegetables

¼ cup noodles, pasta, rice, or potato

¼ cup fruit

4–6 oz. formula/breastmilk

BEFORE BEDTIME

6–8 oz. formula/breastmilk or water (If formula or breastmilk, follow with water or brush teeth afterward.)

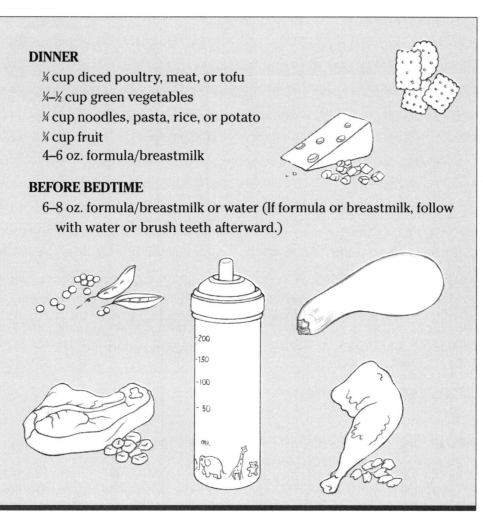

change, try doing the same in the morning. The bedtime feeding probably will be the last one abandoned, and for good reason: Your baby has become accustomed to this source of nighttime comfort and calming, and it will take him some time to give it up. If he's sleeping through the night and not waking up hungry, he doesn't physically need the extra nourishment from bedtime breast- or bottle-feeding. In this case, you might break the habit in stages, first by substituting a bedtime bottle with water instead of milk and then by switching to a drink of water from a cup.

During this process, you may be tempted to put milk or juice in his bottle to help him go to sleep, but don't do it. If he falls asleep while feeding, the milk or juice will pool around his teeth, and this can cause his incoming teeth to decay—a condition known as nursing-bottle syndrome. To make matters worse, drinking while lying flat on his back can contribute to middle ear infections, since the liquid may flow through the eustachian tube into the middle ear.

**Six months may pass before your baby is
willing to take all his liquid from a cup.**

There's still one more disadvantage to prolonged bottle-feeding: The bottle can become a security object, particularly if your baby keeps it beyond about age one. To avoid this, don't let him carry or drink from a bottle while playing. Restrict the use of a bottle to feedings when he's sitting down or being held. At all other times, give him a cup. If you never allow him to take the bottle with him, he won't realize that bringing it along is even an option. Don't relent once this decision has been made, or it could prompt him to demand a bottle again long after he has "officially" been weaned.

Sleeping

At eight months, your baby probably still takes two regular naps, one in the morning and one in the afternoon. She's also likely to sleep as much as twelve hours at night without needing a middle-of-the-night feeding. But be aware of some possible problems ahead: As her separation anxieties intensify in the next few months, she may start to resist going to bed, and she may wake up more often looking for you.

During this difficult period, you may need to experiment with several strategies to find those that help your baby sleep. For example, some children go to sleep more easily with the door open (so they can hear you); others develop consoling habits, such as sucking their thumbs or rocking. As previously mentioned, your child also might adopt a special blanket or stuffed animal as a transitional object, which comforts her when you're not nearby. Anything that's soft and huggable and can be stroked or sucked will serve this purpose. You can encourage your child to use a transitional object by providing her with an assortment of small blankets or soft toys. But avoid resorting to a pacifier unless she is old enough to retrieve it herself. Otherwise, she'll cry for you to retrieve it for her each time it falls out of her mouth during the night.

Once your baby dozes off, her sleep patterns will be quite predictable. After one or two hours of deep sleep, she'll move into a stage of lighter snoozing, and she may partially awaken before returning to deeper sleep. For the rest of the night, there will be alternating periods of deeper and then lighter sleep. During the lighter periods, which may occur four to six times a night, she may even open her eyes, look around, and cry for you. This can be an exasperating experience, particularly if you've just become used to getting a full night's sleep. However, take comfort in the fact that most babies go through this stage largely because of separation anxiety. She just needs to be reassured that you're still there when she wakes up. She also must learn to put herself back to sleep, and it's up to you to teach her. To do so, use the same techniques you relied on to get her to sleep in the first place. (See *Helping Your Baby Sleep,* page 45.) Handled properly, this period of nighttime awakenings should last no more than a few weeks.

Here are some additional suggestions to help this stage pass more quickly. First of all, don't do anything that will reward your baby for calling you in the middle of the night. Go to her side to make sure she's all right, and tell her that you're nearby if she really needs you; but don't turn on the light, rock her, or walk with her. You might offer her a drink of water, but don't feed her, and certainly don't take her to your bed. If she's suffering from separation anxiety, taking her to your bed will only make it harder for her to return to her own crib.

When you do check on her, try to make her as comfortable as possible. If she's gotten tangled in her blanket or stuck in a corner of her crib, rearrange her. Also make sure she isn't sick. Some problems, such as ear infections or the croup, can come on suddenly in the night. Once you're sure there's no sign of illness, then check her diaper, changing her only if she's had a bowel movement or if her diaper is uncomfortably wet. Do the change as quickly as possible in dim light and then settle her back in her crib under her blanket—and on her back. Before leaving the room, whisper a few comforting words about how it's time to sleep. If she continues to cry, wait five minutes, then go back in and comfort her for a short time. Continue to return briefly every five to ten minutes until she's asleep.

To repeat, this period can be extremely difficult for parents. After all, it's emotionally and physically exhausting to listen to your child cry, and you'll probably respond with a combination of pity, anger, worry, and resentment. But remember, her behavior is not deliberate. Instead, she's reacting to anxieties and stresses that are natural at her age. If you stay calm and follow a consistent pattern from one night to the next, she'll soon be putting herself to sleep. Keep this objective in sight as you struggle through the "training" nights. Doing so ultimately will make life much easier for both of you.

BEHAVIOR

Discipline

Your baby's desire to explore is almost impossible to satisfy. As a result, he'll want to touch, taste, and manipulate everything he can get into his hands. In the process, he's bound to find his way into places and situations that are off limits. Although his curiosity is vital to his overall development and shouldn't be discouraged unnecessarily, he can't be allowed to jeopardize his own safety or to damage valuable objects. Whether he's investigating the burners on your stove or pulling up plants in your flower bed, you need to help him stop these activities.

Keep in mind that the way you handle these early incidents will lay the foundation for future discipline. Learning not to do something that he very much wants to do is a major first step toward self-control. The better he learns this lesson now, the less you'll have to intervene in years to come.

What's your best strategy? As we suggested earlier, distraction usually can deal effectively with undesirable behavior. Your baby's memory is still short, and thus you can shift his focus with minimal resistance. If he's headed for something he shouldn't get in to, you don't necessarily have to say "no." Overusing that word will blunt its effect in the long run. Instead, pick him up and direct him toward something he can play with. Look for a compromise that will keep him interested and active without squelching his natural curiosity.

You should reserve your serious discipline for those situations where your child's activities can expose him to real danger—for example, playing with electric cords. This is the time to say "no" firmly and remove him from the situation. But don't expect him to learn from just one or two incidents. Because of his short memory, you'll have to repeat the scene over and over before he finally recognizes and responds to your directions.

To improve the effectiveness of your discipline, consistency is absolutely critical. Make sure that everyone responsible for caring for your baby understands what the child is and isn't allowed to do. Keep the rules to a minimum, preferably limited to situations that are potentially dangerous to the child. Then make sure he hears "no" every time he strays into forbidden territory.

Immediacy is another important component of good discipline. React as soon as you see your baby heading into trouble, not five minutes later. If you delay your reprimand, he won't understand the reason you're angry and the lesson will be lost. Likewise, don't be too quick to comfort him after he's been scolded. Yes, he may cry, sometimes as much in surprise as distress; but wait a minute or two before you reassure him. Otherwise, he won't know whether he really did something wrong.

In the next chapter, we'll describe in some detail the importance of refraining from spanking or striking your child in any way when disciplining him. No matter what your youngster's age, or what his behavior has been, physical punishment is always an inappropriate way for you to respond. Spanking only teaches a child to act aggressively when he's upset. Yes, it may relieve your own frustration temporarily, and for the moment you actually might believe that it will do some good. But there is *no less effective way* of disciplining your child, and it certainly doesn't teach your youngster any alternative way for him to act. It also undermines effective communication between the two of you, as well as weakening his own sense of security.

What's the alternative? The American Academy of Pediatrics recommends using "time-outs" instead of spankings—putting a child who has misbehaved in a quiet place for a few minutes, away from other people, TV, or books. When the time-out is over, explain to him exactly why his behavior was unacceptable. (For more information about spanking and more appropriate ways to discipline, see pages 289–292.)

As you refine your own disciplinary skills, don't overlook the importance of responding in a positive way to your baby's *good* behavior. This kind of reaction is equally important in helping him learn self-control. If he hesitates before reaching for the stove, notice his restraint and tell him how pleased you are. And give him a hug when he does something nice for another person. As he grows older, his good behavior will depend, in large part, on his desire to please you. If you make him aware now of how much you appreciate the good things he does, he'll be less likely to misbehave just to get your attention.

Some parents worry about spoiling a child this age by giving him too much attention, but you needn't be concerned about that. At eight to twelve months, your baby still has a limited ability to be manipulative. You should assume that when he cries, it's not for effect but because he has real needs that aren't being met.

These needs gradually will become more complex, and as they do, you'll notice more variation in your baby's cries—and in the way you react to them. For example, you'll come running when you hear the shattering wail that means something is seriously wrong. By contrast, you may finish what you're doing before you answer the shrill come-here-I-want-you cry. You'll also probably soon recognize a whiny, muffled cry that means something like "I could fall asleep now if everyone would leave me alone." By responding appropriately to the hidden message behind your baby's cries, you'll let him know that his needs are important, but you'll only respond to deserving calls for attention.

Incidentally, there probably will be times when you won't be able to figure out exactly why your baby is crying. In these cases, he himself may not even know what's bothering him. The best response is some comfort from you, combined with consoling techniques that he chooses for himself. For instance, try holding him while he cuddles his favorite stuffed animal or special blanket, or take time to play a game or read a story with him. Both of you will feel better when he's cheered up. Remember that his need for attention and affection is just as real as his need for food and clean diapers.

Siblings

As your baby becomes more mobile, she'll be better able to play with her siblings, and those brothers and sisters usually will be glad to cooperate. Older children, particularly six- to ten-year-olds, often love to build towers for an eight-month-old to destroy. Or they'll lend a finger to an eleven-month-old just learning to walk. A baby this age can be a wonderful playmate to her siblings.

However, while the baby's mobility can turn her into a more active participant in games with her brothers and sisters, it also will make her more likely to invade their private territory. This may violate their budding sense of ownership and privacy, and it can present a serious safety hazard for the baby, since

A baby this age can be a wonderful play-mate to his siblings.

the toys of older children often contain small, easily swallowed pieces. You can ensure that everyone is protected by giving older siblings an enclosed place where they can keep and play with their belongings without fear of a "baby invasion."

Also, now that the baby can reach and grab just about everything in sight, sharing is another issue that must be dealt with. Children under three just aren't capable of sharing without lots of adult prodding and, in most cases, direct intervention. As much as possible, try to sidestep the issue by encouraging both children to play with their own toys, even if they're doing so side by side. When they do play together, suggest looking at books or listening to music, rolling a ball back and forth, or playing hide-and-seek games—in other words, activities requiring limited cooperation.

Grandparents

This childhood age (eight to twelve months) is a wonderful time to enjoy your grandchild. She is now much more physically active and has more language expressions and emotional enthusiasm. However, babies of this age also may experience stranger anxiety, and could be reluctant to go to Grandma and Grandpa with much eagerness. Don't take this personally; it's part of normal development. Simply hang in there, and continue to provide all of the love and attention that you always have, but don't feel you must overdo it in the midst of these pulling-back episodes by the baby. Be patient, and the apparent standoffishness will resolve over time.

In your activities with your grandchild, you can take advantage of her developmental progress in the following areas.

Crawling. Get down on the floor with your grandchild as much as you physically can. This "floor time" is both fun and reassuring for the baby. She'll show delight if you use yourself as her crawling target or object of exploration. Remember, though, to check the floor carefully for possible hazards, since babies will pick up every object within reach and put it in their mouth.

Fine Motor Skills. Develop your own set of fine motor "games" with your grandchild—for example, opening and closing items, dumping out and putting back games and toys, and operating latches. Expect plenty of repetition since babies seem tireless doing the same activity, over and over.

Language. Read books, and listen to music, tapes, and CDs with your grandchild. All the while, keep the language interactive. If you speak a language that's different from the one in which your grandchild is becoming proficient, don't be afraid to speak it to her. (Be sure her parents agree.) For more information on bilingualism, see page 241.

Basic Care. When it comes to feeding and sleeping, consistency of routines is important in this age group. Keep "junior foods" in your home. You also can establish "Grandma's Special Menus" that your grandchild can come to expect. When the baby is staying at your home, nap times and nighttime sleep schedules should be maintained as close as possible to those at her own home. Changes of routine sometimes can create confusion for babies.

Safety. Follow the safety check items in your own home that are described at the end of this chapter to ensure your grandchild's well-being. Keep gates on the top and the bottom of stairways. Place soft, protective coverings around sharp or round edges. Don't use walkers. Also, since babies of this age can have a strong nature and are wiggly, changing diapers should be a two-person operation if possible; change the diapers on carpeted floors or sofas to minimize the risk that your grandchild will twist off the changing table. While you're changing the baby, try distracting her with something she can manipulate.

IMMUNIZATION ALERT

At one year of age (or in the months immediately after your baby's first birthday), she should receive the measles, mumps, rubella vaccine (MMR). This vaccine will protect your baby from three serious diseases that can cause fever, rash, and other symptoms, and potentially lead to serious complications (pneumonia in children with measles, and hearing impairment in children with mumps). The current recommendation is to have your child receive the first MMR vaccine between twelve and fifteen months of age.

The varicella vaccine, which protects your child against chickenpox, should be given at or after twelve months of age if she is susceptible to the disease—that is, if she has not already had the chickenpox.

The third Hepatitis B vaccine will also be given between six and eighteen months of age.

SAFETY CHECK
Car Safety Seats

- Buckle the baby into an approved, properly installed car safety seat before you start the car. Be sure to keep him rear-facing until he weighs at least 20 pounds (9 kg) and is at least one year of age. The American Academy of Pediatrics recommends that children ride rear-facing as long as possible, preferably to the maximum weight allowed by the seat (as long as the top of the child's head is below the top of the seat back).

Falls

- Use gates at the top and bottom of stairways, and to doors of rooms with furniture or other objects that the baby might climb on or that have sharp or hard edges against which he might fall.

- Do not allow an infant to climb on a narrow-based ladder-back chair, since the child will try to climb the ladder and the chair will tip over, resulting in head injury and possible leg or arm fractures.

Burns

- Never smoke or carry hot liquids or foods near your baby or while you're holding him.

- Never leave containers of hot liquids or foods near the edges of tables or counters.

- Do not allow your baby to crawl around hot stoves, floor heaters, or furnace vents.

Drowning

- Never leave your baby alone in a bath or around containers of water, such as buckets, wading pools, sinks, or open toilets. Remove all water from containers immediately after use.

Poisoning and Choking

- Never leave small objects in your baby's crawling area.

- Do not give your baby hard pieces of food.

- Store all medicines and household cleaning products high and out of his reach.

- Use safety latches on drawers and cupboards that contain objects that might be dangerous to him.

10

THE SECOND YEAR

*Y*our baby enters her second year and becomes a toddler, crawling vigorously, starting to walk, even talking a little. As she becomes more and more independent, the days of her unquestioning adoration and dependency on you are becoming numbered.

This realization probably makes you feel both sad and excited—not to mention a little nervous as you think about the coming clashes between her will and yours. In fact, you may already be getting some glimpses of these struggles. For instance, try to take something away from her and she may scream in protest. Or pull her away from a dangerous swinging door and she may quickly return to it, ignoring your warnings. Or offer her one of her favorite meals of cereal and bananas and she may reject it unexpectedly. These are her early experiments with control—testing your limits and discovering her own.

Exploring the boundaries established by your rules and her own physical and developmental limits will occupy much of her time for the next few years. Fortunately, this testing will begin slowly, giving both of you time to adjust to her emerging independence. As a toddler just learning to walk, she'll be most interested in finding out what the world looks like from an upright position. This curiosity, however, is bound to lead her into some forbidden situations. Remember, she's not consciously trying to be mischievous. She still very much counts on you to show her what's OK and what's not, and she'll look to you frequently for reassurance and security.

But as she becomes more confident on her feet, she'll also start showing more signs of assertiveness. By eighteen months, she'll probably have chosen "no" as her favorite word, and as she nears age two, she may throw a tantrum when you ask her to come with you against her will.

Your toddler also may be showing more signs of possessiveness with belongings and people close to her. Upon seeing you pick up another baby, she may react with an outpouring of tears. If another child grabs an attractive toy, she may engage in a strenuous tug-of-war for possession. In a few months, as her vocabulary grows, "mine" will become another of her favorite words.

For now, her vocabulary is still limited, although expanding rapidly. She understands much of what you say to her, provided you speak in clear, simple words, and you probably can decipher some of what she says to you. Hard as it may be to believe, in a year you'll be having running conversations.

GROWTH AND DEVELOPMENT

Physical Appearance and Growth

By the end of her first year, your baby's growth rate will begin to slow. From now until her next growth spurt (which occurs during early adolescence), her height and weight should increase steadily, but not as rapidly as during those first months of life. As an infant, she may have gained 4 pounds (1.8 kg) in four months or less, but during the entire second year, 3 to 5 pounds (1.4–2.3 kg) probably will be her total weight gain. Continue to plot her measurements every few months on the growth charts on pages 128–129 to make sure she's generally following the normal growth curve. As you'll see, there's now a much broader range of what's "normal" than there was at earlier ages.

At fifteen months, the average girl weighs about 22 pounds (10 kg) and is almost 31 inches (77.5 cm) tall; the average boy weighs about 24 pounds (10.4 kg) and is 31 inches (78 cm) tall. Over the next three months, they'll each gain approximately 1½ pounds (0.7 kg) and grow about an inch (2.5 cm). By two, she'll be about 34 inches (about 86 cm) tall and weigh 27 pounds (12.2 kg); he'll reach 36 inches (88 cm) and almost 28 pounds (12.6 kg).

Your baby's head growth also will slow dramatically during the second year. Although she'll probably gain only about 1 inch (2.5 cm) in head circumference this entire year, by age two she'll have attained about 90 percent of her adult head size.

Your toddler's looks, however, probably will change more than her size. At twelve months, she still looked like a baby, even though she may have been walking and saying a few words. Her head and abdomen were still the largest parts of her body, her belly stuck out when she was upright, and her buttocks, by comparison, seemed small—at least when her diaper was off. Her arms and legs were still relatively short and soft, rather than muscular, and her face had softly rounded contours.

All this will change as she becomes more active, developing her muscles and trimming away some of her baby fat. Her arms and legs will lengthen gradually, and her feet will start to point forward as she walks, instead of out to the sides. Her face will become more angular and her jawline better defined. By her second birthday, it will be hard to remember how she looked as an infant.

Movement

If your baby hasn't started walking before his first birthday, he should within the next six months. In fact, perfecting this skill will be the major physical accomplishment of his second year. Even if he's already begun walking, it may take another full month or two before he can stand up and start moving smoothly without support. However, don't expect him to get up the way you would. Instead, his technique may be to spread his hands on the floor, straighten his arms, and lift his bottom in the air as he pulls his legs under him. Finally, while straightening his legs, he'll unbend at the waist and be off.

In the beginning, he really is toddling, which is quite different from mature walking. Instead of striding, he'll plant his legs wide apart, toes pointing outward, and lurch from side to side as he moves forward. As slow and painstaking as the process may seem in the beginning, he'll quickly pick up speed. In fact, don't be surprised if very soon you're running to keep up with him.

An inevitable part of this toddling, of course, is falling. In particular, walking on uneven surfaces will remain a challenge for some time. At first he'll trip on even small irregularities, such as a wrinkle in the carpet surface or an incline into another room. It will be months before he can walk up and down stairs, or turn corners without falling.

Also, at the beginning, don't expect him to use his hands during walking. While he'll use his arms for balance (bent and held at shoulder level in the "high guard" position), using his hands to carry, play with, or pick up a toy will be out of the question for a time. After he's been walking for two to three months, however, he'll have the entire process under control: Not only will he be stooping to pick up and carry a toy across the room, but he'll

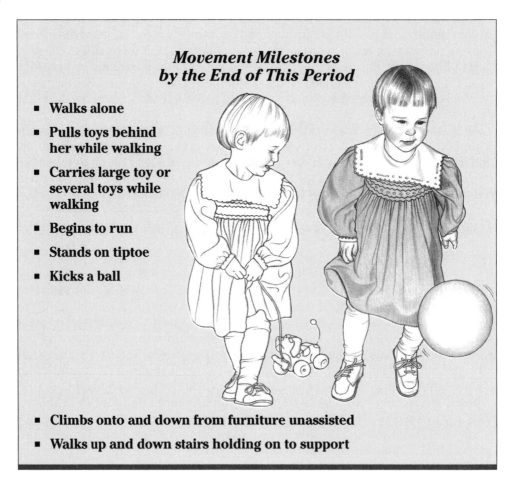

**Movement Milestones
by the End of This Period**

- **Walks alone**
- **Pulls toys behind her while walking**
- **Carries large toy or several toys while walking**
- **Begins to run**
- **Stands on tiptoe**
- **Kicks a ball**

- **Climbs onto and down from furniture unassisted**
- **Walks up and down stairs holding on to support**

be able to push or pull a toy wagon, step sideways or backward, and even throw a ball while walking.

About six months after he takes his first steps, your baby's walking style will become much more mature. He'll keep his feet close together as he moves, making his gait much smoother. With your help he may even walk up and down stairs. However, when he tries this on his own, he'll crawl up on his hands and knees and back down one stair at a time on his stomach. Soon he'll take his first short, stiff runs straight ahead, though he probably won't run well until his third year. By his second birthday, your child will be moving with great efficiency. To think—just a year ago he could barely walk!

Hand and Finger Skills

Given all the large motor skills your one-year-old is mastering, it's easy to overlook the more subtle changes in her ability to use her hands, both alone and in coordination with her eyes. These developments will allow her much more control and precision as she examines objects and tries new movements. They also will greatly expand her ability to explore and learn about the world around her.

At twelve months, it's still a challenge for her to pick up very small objects between her thumb and forefinger, but by the middle of her second year, this task will be simple. Watch how she'll manipulate small objects at will, exploring all the ways they can be combined and changed. Some of her favorite games might include:

- Building towers of up to four blocks, then knocking them down

- Covering and uncovering boxes or other containers

- Picking up balls or other objects in motion

- Turning knobs and pages

- Putting round pegs into holes

- Scribbling and painting

These activities not only will help her develop hand skills but also will teach her spatial concepts, such as "in," "on," "under," and "around." As she nears two

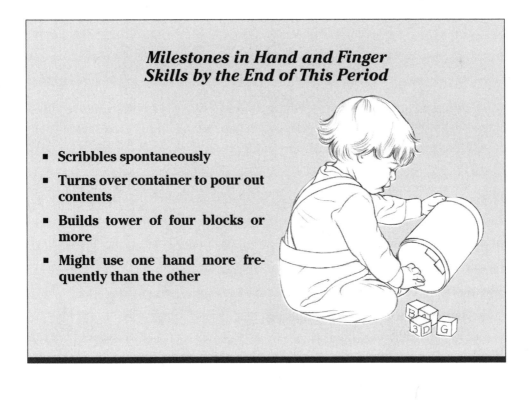

Milestones in Hand and Finger Skills by the End of This Period

- **Scribbles spontaneously**
- **Turns over container to pour out contents**
- **Builds tower of four blocks or more**
- **Might use one hand more frequently than the other**

years and her physical coordination improves, she'll be able to try more complex games, such as:

- Folding paper (if you show her how)
- Putting large square pegs into matching holes (which is more difficult than it is with round pegs, because it involves matching angles)
- Stacking up to five or six blocks
- Taking toys apart and putting them back together
- Making shapes from clay

By her second birthday, your toddler may demonstrate a clear tendency toward right- or left-handedness. However, many children don't show this preference for several years. Other children are ambidextrous, being able to use both hands equally well. They may never establish a clear preference. There's no reason to pressure your toddler to use one hand over the other or to rush the natural process that leads her to this preference.

Language Development

Early in the second year, your toddler will suddenly seem to understand everything you say. You'll announce lunchtime and he'll be waiting by his high chair.

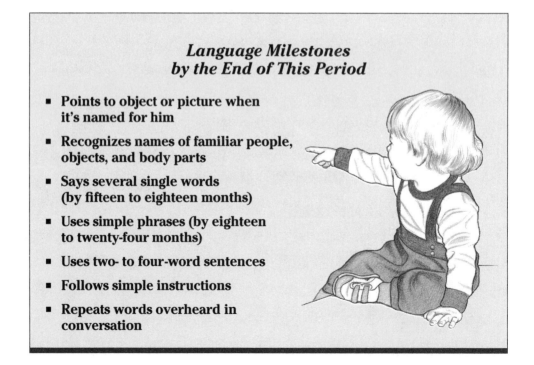

Language Milestones by the End of This Period

- **Points to object or picture when it's named for him**
- **Recognizes names of familiar people, objects, and body parts**
- **Says several single words (by fifteen to eighteen months)**
- **Uses simple phrases (by eighteen to twenty-four months)**
- **Uses two- to four-word sentences**
- **Follows simple instructions**
- **Repeats words overheard in conversation**

You'll tell him you've lost your shoe and he'll find it. At first, his rapid response may seem a little unusual. Did he really understand, or is this just a dream? Rest assured, it's not your imagination. He's developing his language and comprehension skills right on schedule.

This giant developmental leap probably will alter the way you now talk to him and converse with others when he's around. For example, you may edit conversations held within his earshot, perhaps spelling out words you'd rather he didn't understand (as in, "Should we stop for I-C-E C-R-E-A-M?"). At the same time, you'll probably feel more enthusiastic about talking to him, because he's so responsive.

You may find yourself using less baby talk, no longer needing high-pitched singsong monologues to get his attention. Instead, try speaking slowly and clearly, using simple words and short sentences. Teach him the correct names of objects and body parts, and stop using cute substitutes such as "piggies" when you really mean "toes." By providing a good language model, you'll help him learn to talk with a minimum of confusion.

Most toddlers master at least fifty spoken words by the end of the second year and can talk in short sentences, although there are differences among children. Even among those with normal hearing and intelligence, some don't talk much during the second year. Boys generally develop language skills more slowly than girls. Whenever your child begins to speak, his first few words probably will include the names of familiar people, his favorite possessions, and parts of his body. You may be the only person who understands these early words, since he'll omit or change certain sounds. For example, he might get the first consonant *(b, d, t)* and vowel *(a, e, i, o, u)* sounds right, but drop the end of the word. Or he may substitute sounds he can pronounce, such as *d* or *b,* for more difficult ones.

You'll learn to understand what he's saying over time and with the help of his gestures. By all means, don't ridicule his language mistakes. Give him as much time as he needs to finish what he wants to say without hurrying, and then answer with a correct pronunciation of the word ("That's right, it's a ball!"). If you're patient and responsive, his pronunciation will improve gradually.

By midyear, he'll use a few active verbs, such as "go" and "jump," and words of direction, such as "up," "down," "in," and "out." By his second birthday, he'll have mastered the words "me" and "you" and use them all the time.

At first, he'll make his own version of a whole sentence by combining a single word with a gesture or grunt. He might point and say "ball"—his way of telling you he wants you to roll him the ball. Or he might shape a question by saying "Out?" or "Up?"—raising his voice at the end. Soon he'll begin to combine verbs or prepositions with nouns, to make statements like "Ball up" or "Drink milk," and questions like "What that?" By the end of the year, or soon thereafter, he'll begin to use two-word sentences.

Cognitive Development

As you watch your toddler at play, have you noticed how hard she concentrates on everything she does? Each game or task is a learning proposition, and she'll gather all sorts of information about the way things work. She'll also now be able to draw on facts she's already learned in order to make decisions and find solutions to play-related challenges. However, she'll be interested in solving only those problems that are appropriate for her developmental and learning level, so hand her a toy that fascinated her at eleven months and she may walk away bored. Or suggest a game that's too advanced and she'll object. She'll be especially attracted to mechanical devices, such as wind-up toys, switches, buttons, and knobs. It may be difficult for you to judge exactly what she can and can't handle at this age, but it's not hard for her to decide. Provide her with a range of activities, and she'll select the ones that are challenging but not completely beyond her abilities.

Imitation is a big part of her learning process at this age. Instead of simply manipulating household objects, as she did during her first year, she'll actually use a brush on her hair, babble into the phone, turn the steering wheel of her toy car, and push it back and forth. At first, she'll be the only one involved in these activities, but gradually she'll include other players. She might brush her doll's hair, "read" to you from her book, offer a playmate a pretend drink, or hold her toy phone to your ear.

Well before her second birthday, your toddler will excel at hiding games, remembering where hidden objects are long after they leave her sight. If you pocket her ball or cracker while she's playing, you may forget all about it, but she won't!

As she masters hide-and-seek, she'll also become more understanding about separations from you. Just as she knows that a hidden object is somewhere, even when she can't see it, she'll now recognize that you always come back, even when you're away from her a whole day. If you actually show her where you go when you leave her—to work or to the grocery store, for example—she'll form a mental image of you there. This may make the separation even easier for her.

At this age, your toddler is very much the director; she lets you know what role she wants you to play in her activities. Sometimes she'll bring you a toy so you can help her make it work; other times she'll pull it away from you to try it by herself. Often, when she knows she's done something special, she'll pause and wait for your applause. By responding to these cues, you'll provide the support and encouragement she needs to keep learning.

You also must supply the judgment that she still lacks. Yes, she now understands how certain things behave, but—because she can't see how one thing affects another—she doesn't yet grasp the full notion of consequences. So even though she may understand that her toy wagon will roll downhill, she can't predict what will happen when it lands in the middle of the busy street below. Although she knows that a door swings open and shut, she doesn't know that she has to keep her hand from getting caught in it. And even if she's found out the

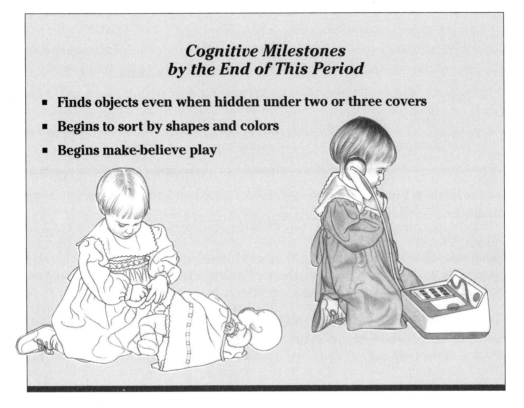

**Cognitive Milestones
by the End of This Period**

- **Finds objects even when hidden under two or three covers**
- **Begins to sort by shapes and colors**
- **Begins make-believe play**

hard way once, don't assume she's learned her lesson. Chances are she doesn't associate her pain with the chain of events that led up to it, and she almost certainly won't remember this sequence the next time. Until she develops her own common sense, she'll need your vigilance to keep her safe.

Social Development

During his second year, your toddler will develop a very specific image of his social world, friends, and acquaintances. He is at its center, and while you may be close at hand, he is most concerned about where things are in relation to himself. He knows that other people exist, and they vaguely interest him, but he has no idea how they think or what they feel. As far as he's concerned, everyone thinks as he does.

As you can imagine, his view of the world (technically, some experts call it egocentric or self-centered) often makes it difficult for him to play with other children in a truly social sense. He'll play alongside and compete for toys, but he doesn't play cooperative games easily. He'll enjoy watching and being around other children, especially if they're slightly older. He may imitate them or treat them the way he does dolls, for example, trying to brush their hair, but he's usually surprised and resists when they try to do the same thing to him. He

> ## Social Milestones
> ## by the End of This Period
>
> - **Imitates behavior of others, especially adults and older children**
> - **Increasingly aware of herself as separate from others**
> - **Increasingly enthusiastic about company of other children**

may offer them toys or things to eat but may get upset if they respond by taking what he's offered them.

Sharing is a meaningless term to a child this age. Every toddler believes that he alone deserves the spotlight. Unfortunately, most are also as assertive as they are self-centered, and competition for toys and attention frequently erupts into hitting and tears. How can you minimize the combat when your child's "friends" are over? Try providing plenty of toys for everyone and be prepared to referee.

As we've suggested earlier, your child also may start to show possessiveness over toys that he knows belong to him. If another child even touches the plaything, he may rush over and snatch it away. Try reassuring him that the other child is "only looking at it" and that "it's okay for him to have a turn with it." But also acknowledge that "yes, it's your toy, and he's not going to take it away from you." It may help to select a couple of particularly prized items and make them off limits to everyone else. Sometimes this helps toddlers feel they have some control over their world and makes them less possessive about other belongings.

Because children this age have so little awareness of the feelings of others, they can be very physical in their responses to the children around them. Even when just exploring or showing affection, they may poke each other's eyes or pat a little too hard. (The same is true of their treatment of animals.) When they're upset, they can hit or slap without realizing they are hurting the other child. For this reason, be alert whenever your toddler is among playmates, and pull him back as soon as this physical aggressiveness occurs. Tell him, "Don't hit," and redirect all the children to friendlier play.

Fortunately, your toddler will show his self-awareness in less aggressive ways, as well. By eighteen months, he'll be able to say his own name. At about the same time, he'll identify his reflection in the mirror and start showing a greater interest in caring for him-

Gender Identification

If you were to take a group of one-year-olds, dress them alike, and let them loose on a playground, could you tell the boys from the girls? Probably not, because except for minor variations in size, there are very few differences between the sexes at this age. Boys and girls develop skills at about the same rate (although girls tend to talk earlier than boys), and they enjoy the same activities. Some studies have found boys to be more active than girls, but the differences in these first years are negligible.

Although parents generally treat boys and girls this age very similarly, they often encourage different toys and games for each sex. But aside from tradition, there's no basis for pushing girls toward dolls and boys toward trucks. Left to their own devices, both sexes are equally attracted to all toys, and they'll benefit developmentally if allowed to play with both "boy" and "girl" toys.

Incidentally, young children learn to identify themselves as boys or girls by associating with other members of their own sex. But this process takes years. Dressing your girl exclusively in frills or taking your boy to baseball games won't make much of a difference at this age. What does matter is the love and respect you give your child as a person, regardless of sex. This will lay the foundation for high self-esteem.

Masturbation

As your toddler explores the many parts of his body, he'll naturally discover his genitals. Since touching them will produce pleasant sensations, he'll do it often when his diaper is off. Although this may be accompanied by penile erections in boys, it's neither a sexual nor an emotional experience for toddlers. It just feels good. There's no reason to discourage it, worry, or call any attention to it. If you show a strong negative reaction when he touches his genitals, you're suggesting to him that there is something wrong or bad about these body parts. He may even interpret this to mean there's something wrong or bad about him. Wait until he's older to teach him about privacy and modesty. For now, accept his behavior as normal curiosity.

The Shy Child

Some children are naturally fearful about new people and situations. They hold back, watching and waiting before joining a group activity. If pushed to try something different, they resist, and when faced with someone new, they cling. For a parent trying to encourage boldness and independence, this behavior can be very frustrating. But challenging or ridiculing it will only make a shy child more insecure.

The best solution is to allow your child to move at her own individual pace. Give her the time she needs to adapt to new situations and let her hold your hand when she needs some extra assurance. If you take her behavior in stride, outsiders will be less likely to ridicule her, and she'll develop self-confidence much more quickly. If she continues this kind of behavior, discuss it with your pediatrician. She will be able to give you some individual advice and can, if necessary, refer you to a pediatric psychologist or child psychiatrist.

self. As he approaches age two, he may be able to brush his teeth and wash his hands if shown how to do it. He'll also help dress and, especially, undress himself. Many times a day you may find him busily removing his shoes and socks even in the middle of a store or the park.

Because your toddler is a great imitator, he will eagerly participate in anything you're doing around the house. Whether you're reading the paper, sweeping the floors, mowing the lawn, or making dinner, he'll want to "help." Even though it may take longer with him doing so, try to turn it into a game. If you're doing something he can't help with because it's dangerous or you're in a hurry, look for another "chore" he *can* do. By all means don't discourage these wonderful impulses to be helpful. Helping, like sharing, is a vital social skill, and the sooner he develops it, the more pleasant life will be for everyone.

Emotional Development

Throughout her second year, your child will swing back and forth constantly between fierce independence and clinging to you. Now that she can walk and do things for herself physically, she has the power to move away from you and test

The Aggressive Child

Some children are naturally aggressive in ways that begin to show during the second year. They want to take charge and control everything that goes on around them. When they don't get what they want, they may turn their energy toward violent behavior, such as kicking, biting, or hitting.

Does your toddler fit this description? If so, you'll need to watch him closely and set firm, consistent limits. Give him plenty of positive outlets for his energy through physical play and exercise. But when he's with other children, supervise him carefully to prevent serious trouble, and be sure to praise him when he gets through a play session without a problem.

In some families, aggressiveness is encouraged, especially in boys. Parents proudly call their little child "tough," which he may take to mean that he has to kick and bite in order to win their approval. In other families, a toddler's aggressive outbursts are considered an omen of future delinquency. Believing they have to come down hard on this behavior as soon as it appears, the parents spank or hit the child as punishment. However, a child treated this way can begin to believe that this is the correct way to handle people when you don't like their behavior, so this reaction may just reinforce his aggressiveness toward others. The best way to teach your child how to hold his aggressive impulses in check is to be firm and consistent when he misbehaves. Also, give him a good example to imitate with your own behavior and that of his siblings. (See also *Anger, Aggression, and Biting,* page 525.)

her new skills. But at the same time, she's not yet entirely comfortable with the idea that she's an individual, separate from you and everyone else in the world. Especially when she's tired, sick, or scared, she'll want you there to comfort her and fend off loneliness.

It's impossible to predict when she'll turn her back on you and when she'll come running for shelter. She may seem to change from one moment to the next, or she may seem mature and independent for several whole days before suddenly regressing. You may feel mixed reactions to this, as well: While there are moments when it feels wonderful to have your baby back, there are bound to be other times when her fussing and whining is the last thing you need. Some people call this period the first adolescence. It reflects some of your child's mixed feelings about growing up and leaving you, and it's absolutely normal. Remember that the best way to help her regain her composure is to give her attention and reassurance when she needs it. Snapping at her to "act like a big girl" will only make her feel and act more insecure and needy.

Brief separations from you may help your toddler become more independent. She'll still suffer some separation anxiety and, perhaps, put up a fuss when you leave her—even if it's just for a few minutes. But the protest will be brief. Chances are, you may be more upset by these separations than she is, but try not to let her know that. Instead, leave her with a kiss and a promise to return. And when you do come back, greet her enthusiastically and devote your full attention to her for a while before moving on to other chores or business. When your child understands that you always return and continue to love her, she'll feel more secure.

BASIC CARE

Feeding and Nutrition

You'll probably notice a sharp drop in your toddler's appetite after his first birthday. Suddenly he's picky about what he eats, turns his head away after

Stimulating Child Brain Growth: Second Year

- **Your child learns through play. Choose toys that encourage creativity. By selecting simple toys, you'll encourage your child to develop his own imagination.**

- **Encourage playing with blocks and soft toys, which helps your child develop eye-hand coordination, fine motor skills, and a sense of competence.**

- **Give consistent warm, physical contact—hugging, skin-to-skin, body-to-body contact—to establish your toddler's sense of security and well-being.**

- **Be attentive to your child's rhythms and moods. Respond to her when she is upset as well as when she is happy. Be encouraging and supportive, with firm discipline as appropriate, but without yelling or hitting; provide consistent guidelines.**

- **Talk or sing to your child during dressing, bathing, feeding, playing, walking, and driving, using adult talk. Speak slowly and give your child time to respond. Try not to reply with "uh-huh," because your child will recognize when you're not listening; instead, expand on your child's phrases.**

- **Be consistent and predictable; establish routines for mealtimes, naps, and bedtime.**

- **Develop word associations by naming everyday objects and activities.**

just a few bites, or resists coming to the table at mealtimes. It may seem as if he should be eating more now that he's so active, but there's a good reason for the change. His growth rate has slowed, and he really doesn't require as much food now.

Your toddler needs about 1,000 calories a day to meet his needs for growth, energy, and good nutrition. If you've ever been on a 1,000-calorie diet, you know it's not a lot of food. But your child will do just fine with it, divided among three small meals and two snacks a day. Don't count on his always eating it that way, however, because the eating habits of toddlers are erratic and unpredictable from one day to the next. He may eat everything in sight at breakfast but almost nothing else for the rest of the day. Or he may eat only his favorite food for three days in a row, then reject it entirely. Or he may eat 1,000 calories one day, but then eat noticeably more or less on the subsequent day or two. Your child's needs will vary, depending on his activity level, his growth rate, and his metabolism.

As a general rule, it's a real mistake to turn mealtimes into sparring matches to get him to eat a balanced diet. He's not rejecting you when he turns down the

---

- **Read to your child every day. Choose books that encourage touching and pointing to objects, and read rhymes, jingles, and nursery stories.**

- **If you speak a foreign language, use it at home.**

- **Play fun, calm, and melodic music for your child.**

- **Listen to and answer your child's questions. Also ask questions to stimulate decision-making processes.**

- **Begin to explain safety in simple terms; for example, feeling the heat from the stove teaches the meaning and danger of hot objects.**

- **Make sure other people who provide care and supervision for your child understand the importance of forming a loving and comforting relationship with her.**

- **Encourage your child to look at books and to draw.**

- **Help your child use words to describe emotions and to express feelings such as happiness, joy, anger, and fear ("glad," "mad," and "sad").**

- **Spend time on the floor playing with your child every day.**

- **Choose quality child care that is affectionate, responsive, educational, and safe. Visit your child care provider frequently and share your ideas about positive caregiving.**

Developmental Health Watch

Because each child develops at his own particular pace, it's impossible to tell exactly when yours will perfect a given skill. The developmental milestones listed in this book will give you a general idea of the changes you can expect as your child gets older, but don't be alarmed if he takes a slightly different course. Alert your pediatrician, however, if he displays any of the following signs of possible developmental delay for this age range.

- Cannot walk by eighteen months
- Fails to develop a mature heel-toe walking pattern after several months of walking, or walks exclusively on his toes
- Does not speak at least fifteen words by eighteen months
- Does not use two-word sentences by age two
- Does not seem to know the function of common household objects (brush, telephone, bell, fork, spoon) by fifteen months
- Does not imitate actions or words by the end of this period
- Does not follow simple instructions by age two
- Cannot push a wheeled toy by age two

Emotional Milestones by the End of This Period

- **Demonstrates increasing independence**
- **Begins to show defiant behavior**
- **Increasing episodes of separation anxiety toward midyear, then they fade**

food you prepared, so don't take it personally. Besides, the harder you push him to eat, the less likely he is to comply. Instead, offer him a selection of nutritious foods at each sitting, and let him choose what he wants. Vary the tastes and consistencies as much as you can.

If he rejects everything, you might try saving the plate for later when he's hungry. However, don't allow him to fill up on cookies or sweets after refusing his meal, since that will just fuel his interest in empty-calorie foods (those that are high in calories but relatively low in important nutrients, such as vitamins and minerals) and diminish his appetite for nutritious ones. Hard as it may be to believe, your child's diet will balance out over several days if you make a range of wholesome foods available and don't pressure him to eat a particular one at any given time.

Your toddler needs foods from the same four basic nutrition groups that you do:

1. Meat, fish, poultry, eggs

2. Dairy products

3. Fruits and vegetables

4. Cereal grains, potatoes, rice, breads, pasta

When planning your child's menu, remember that cholesterol and other fats are very important for his normal growth and development, so they should not be restricted during this period. Babies and young toddlers should get about half of their calories from fat. You can gradually decrease the fat consumption once your child has reached the age of two (lowering it to about one-third of daily calories by ages four to five). While you should not lose sight of the fact that childhood obesity is a growing problem, youngsters in the second year of life need dietary fat. If you keep your child's caloric intake at about 1,000 calories a day, you shouldn't have to worry about overfeeding him and putting him at risk of gaining too much weight.

By his first birthday, your child should be able to handle most of the foods you serve the rest of the family—but with a few precautions. First, be sure the food is cool enough so that it won't burn his mouth. Test the temperature yourself, because he'll dig in without considering the heat. Also, don't give him foods that are heavily spiced, salted, buttered, or sweetened. These additions prevent your child from experiencing the natural taste of foods, and they may

Adult eating preferences are developed now.

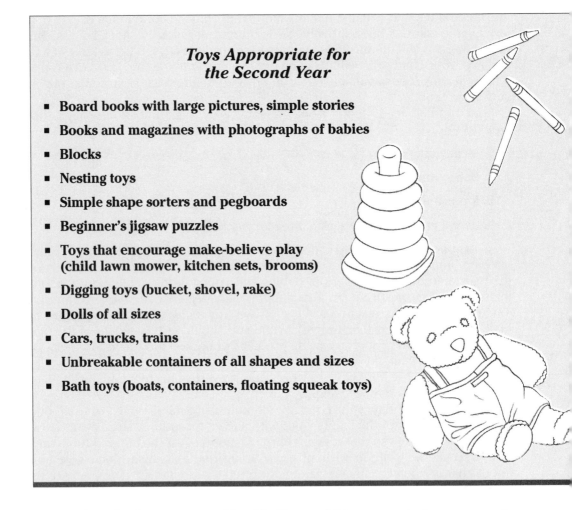

Toys Appropriate for the Second Year

- Board books with large pictures, simple stories
- Books and magazines with photographs of babies
- Blocks
- Nesting toys
- Simple shape sorters and pegboards
- Beginner's jigsaw puzzles
- Toys that encourage make-believe play (child lawn mower, kitchen sets, brooms)
- Digging toys (bucket, shovel, rake)
- Dolls of all sizes
- Cars, trucks, trains
- Unbreakable containers of all shapes and sizes
- Bath toys (boats, containers, floating squeak toys)

be harmful to his long-term good health. Young children seem to be more sensitive than adults to these flavorings and may reject heavily spiced foods.

Your little one can still choke on chunks of food that are hard and large enough to plug his airway. Keep in mind that children don't learn to chew with a grinding motion until they're about four years old. In his second year of life, make sure anything you give him is mashed or cut into small, easily chewable pieces. Never offer him peanuts, whole grapes, cherry tomatoes (unless they're cut in quarters), carrots, seeds (i.e., processed pumpkin or sunflower seeds), whole or large sections of hot dogs, meat sticks, or hard candies (including jelly beans), or chunks of peanut butter (it's fine to thinly spread peanut butter on a cracker or bread). Hot dogs and carrots in particular should be quartered lengthwise and then sliced into small pieces. Also make sure your toddler eats only while seated and supervised by an adult. Although he may want to do everything at once, "eating on the run" or while talking increases his risk of choking. Teach him as early as possible to finish a mouthful prior to speaking.

- Balls of all shapes and sizes
- Push and pull toys
- Outdoor toys (slides, swings, sandbox)
- Beginner's tricycle
- Connecting toys (links, large stringing beads, S-shapes)
- Stuffed animals
- Child keyboard and other musical instruments
- Large crayons
- Toy telephone
- Unbreakable mirrors of all sizes
- Dress-up clothes
- Wooden spoons, old magazines, baskets, cardboard boxes and tubes, other similar safe, unbreakable items she "finds" around the house (i.e., pots and pans)

By his first birthday or soon thereafter, your toddler should drink his liquids from a cup. He'll need less milk now, since he'll get most of his calories from solid foods.

Dietary Supplements. Despite the claims of advertising and promotions, preschool children don't need vitamin supplements. If you provide your child with selections from each of the four basic food groups and let her experiment with a wide variety of tastes, colors, and textures, she should be eating a balanced diet with plenty of vitamins. Some vitamins, such as the water-soluble vitamins (A and D), may even pose risks; they're stored in the tissues when consumed in excess, and at very high levels could make your child sick. High doses of minerals such as zinc and iron taken over an extended time can have negative effects, as well.

For some children, however, supplementation may be important. Your youngster may need some vitamin and/or mineral supplementation if your family's dietary practices limit the food groups available to her. For example, if your

Cutting Down on Sweets

Almost everyone naturally enjoys sweets, and your toddler is no different. Like other human beings, she was born with a taste for sugar, and she's already quite sensitive to different concentrations of sweetness. Offer her a yam and a baked potato, and she'll take the yam every time. Give her a choice between the yam and a cookie, and the cookie will win. Rest assured, it's not your fault if she makes a beeline for the candy and ice cream when you'd rather she take a piece of cheese. But it is your responsibility to limit her access to sweets and to provide a diet made up primarily of more nutritious foods that promote growth, not tooth decay.

Fortunately, when sweets are out of your toddler's sight, they won't be on her mind, so either don't bring them into the house or keep them hidden. Also avoid adding sugar to her food, and don't make dessert an everyday event. As for snacks, instead of giving her sweet or fatty ones, let her have small portions of fruit, bread, crackers, and cheese. In other words, start encouraging good eating habits that can last a lifetime.

household is strictly vegetarian, with no eggs or dairy products (which is not a diet recommended for children), she may need supplements of vitamins B12 and D as well as riboflavin and calcium. Rickets, for example, is a disease in which the bones soften, and it is associated with inadequate vitamin D intake and decreased exposure to sunlight; although uncommon in the United States, it continues to be reported. Consult your pediatrician about which supplements are needed and the amounts.

Iron deficiency does occur among some young children and can lead to anemia (a condition that limits the ability of the blood to carry oxygen). In some cases the problem is dietary. Toddlers need to receive at least 15 milligrams of iron a day in their food, but many fail to do so. (See table of iron-rich foods, page 287.) Drinking large quantities of milk may lead to iron deficiency anemia, as the child will be less interested in other foods, some of which are potential sources of iron.

If your child is drinking 24 to 32 ounces (720–960 ml) of milk or less each day, there's little cause for concern. If she drinks much more than that and you can't get her to eat more iron-rich foods, consult your pediatrician about adding an iron supplement to her diet. In the meantime, decrease her milk intake and keep offering her a wide variety of iron-rich foods so that, eventually, supplementation won't be necessary.

Self-Feeding. At twelve months, your baby was just getting used to drinking from a cup and feeding himself with a spoon and his fingers. By fifteen months,

Sample One-Day Menu for a One-Year-Old

This menu is planned for a one-year-old child who weighs approximately 21 pounds (9.5 kg).

1 teaspoon = ⅓ tablespoon (5 ml)
1 tablespoon = ½ ounce (15 ml)
1 cup = 8 ounces (240 ml)
1 oz = 30 ml

BREAKFAST

½ cup iron-fortified breakfast cereal or 1 cooked egg (not more than
   3 eggs per week)
¼ cup whole milk (with cereal)
4–6 oz. juice
Add to cereal one of the following:
   ½ banana, sliced
   2–3 large sliced strawberries

SNACK

1 slice toast or whole wheat muffin
1–2 tablespoons cream cheese or peanut butter
1 cup whole milk

LUNCH

½ sandwich—tuna, egg salad, peanut butter, or cold cuts
½ cup cooked green vegetables

SNACK

1–2 ounces cubed cheese, or 2–3 tablespoons pitted and diced dates
1 cup whole milk

DINNER

2–3 ounces cooked meat, ground or diced
½ cup cooked yellow or orange vegetables
½ cup pasta, rice, or potato
½ cup whole milk

Discontinuing the Bottle

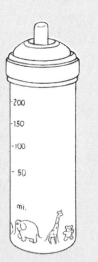

Most pediatricians recommend that the bottle be given up entirely at around age one and almost certainly by eighteen months. As long as your baby is drinking from a cup, he doesn't need to take liquids from a bottle anymore. Unfortunately, weaning your baby from the bottle is not as easy as it sounds. To help things along, eliminate the midday bottle first, then the evening and morning ones; save the bedtime bottle for last, since it's often the most difficult for your youngster to give up.

It's easy to get into the habit of using food or a bottle to comfort a child who has trouble falling asleep or who wakes up at night. But at this age, he no longer needs anything to eat or drink during the night. If you are still feeding him at that time, you should stop. Even if he demands a bottle and drinks thirstily, midnight feedings are a comfort rather than a nutritional necessity. The bottle soon turns into a crutch and prevents his learning to fall back to sleep on his own. If he cries for only a short time, try letting him cry himself back to sleep. After a few nights he'll probably forget all about the bottle. If this doesn't happen, consult your pediatrician and read the other sections on sleep in this book. (See, for example, page 45 and page 219.)

Incidentally, giving your toddler a drink or other snack before bedtime is perfectly fine. In fact, it may help him fall asleep. A short breastfeeding, a drink of cow's milk or other liquid, or even some fruit or another nutritious food will do. If the snack is a bottle, gradually phase it out by substituting a cup.

Whatever the snack, have your child finish it before brushing his teeth. Otherwise the food or liquid will remain in his mouth all night, promoting tooth decay. If he needs some comfort to get to sleep, let him use a cuddly toy, blanket, or his thumb—but not a bottle.

he'll be much more in control, getting food into his mouth with relative ease when he wants to and flinging it about the room when that seems like more fun. He'll be able to fill his spoon and get it to his mouth consistently, although occasionally it will tip the wrong way and spill at the last second. Unbreakable dishes, cups, and glasses are essential, since they, too, may go flying when he's bored with their contents. Such behavior should be discouraged by a firm reprimand and replacement of the utensils in the proper location.

Make sure your toddler eats only while seated and supervised by an adult.

Sources of Iron

Excellent

Liver	Oysters	Blackstrap molasses
40% bran flakes	Clams	

Good

Hamburger	Shrimp	Potato, baked in skin	Dried apricots
Lean beef	Frankfurter	Navy beans	Raisins
Chicken	Egg, egg yolks	Kidney beans	Prunes, prune juice
Tuna	Spinach, mustard greens	Soybeans	Strawberries
Ham	Asparagus	Split peas	Tomato juice

Adequate

Enriched rice	Avocado	Broccoli	Green peas
Enriched pasta, noodles	Cranberry juice	Tomato	Bacon
Enriched bread	Orange	Carrots	Peanut butter
Banana	Apple	Green beans	

By eighteen months, your toddler can use a spoon, fork, and unbreakable glass or cup when he wants to, but he may not always want to. There will be times when he'd rather fingerpaint with his pudding or turn his plate into a soaring airplane. Some children get over this chaotic eating behavior by their second birthday, at which time they actually may become upset when they spill or get even a little smudge of food on their hands. Others, however, will remain very messy eaters well into their third year.

Getting Ready for Toilet Training

As your child approaches age two, you'll begin to think about toilet training. Perhaps the grandparents will urge you to start, or you may be considering a child care or preschool program that requires her to be trained. Before you launch your campaign, however, be forewarned that toilet training generally becomes easier and is accomplished more quickly when your child is older. Yes, early training is possible—but not necessarily preferred. It may even place unnecessary pressure on your young toddler. She may not have the necessary bowel or bladder control or the motor skills needed to remove her clothes quickly and reliably before using the toilet.

Many children are ready to be toilet trained after their second birthday (boys often slightly later than girls), but your toddler might be ready earlier. If so, you'll see the following signals.

1. Her bowel movements occur on a fairly regular and predictable schedule.

2. Her diaper is not always wet, staying dry at least two hours at a time during the day, or is dry after naps. This indicates that her bladder is able to store urine.

3. She can and will follow simple instructions.

4. She shows an interest in imitating other family members or friends in the bathroom.

5. Through words, facial expressions, posture, or a change in activity, she shows you that she knows when her bladder is full or when she's about to have a bowel movement.

6. She can walk to and from the bathroom and can help undress herself.

If your toddler is ready to be toilet trained, turn to page 321 for complete details. Even if she's not quite ready, you still can familiarize her with the process by keeping her potty chair handy and explaining, in very simple terms, how it works. The more familiar she is with the process, the less scary and confusing it will seem when you begin training her.

Sleeping

No toddler looks forward to going to sleep. After all, it means missing out on the action, separating from you, and facing the nighttime on his own. If you let him, your youngster probably will spend the entire evening putting off bedtime. One more story, one more kiss, one more drink of water—he'll use any trick he can think of to keep you with him. As he becomes more verbal, his requests and delaying tactics will become more contrived and elaborate. And once he becomes bigger and stronger, he may even climb out of his crib and come to get you himself.

Sometimes it's tempting just to give up and let your child fall asleep in his tracks when he's overcome by exhaustion. But that will only make the problem worse. Instead, watch the clock to see when he shows signs of sleepiness, and then make that his regular bedtime. Devise a quiet bedtime ritual and discuss it with your toddler. Whether you include a bath, story, or song, the routine should end with him quiet, but awake, in his crib, ready for your good-night kiss before you leave the room. If he cries continuously, use the method described in Chapter 9 to teach him to fall asleep on his own.

Unfortunately, resistance at bedtime isn't the only sleep struggle you'll have with your youngster. Remember the first time he slept through the night as a baby and you thought sleep problems were over? As the parent of a toddler, you now know the unhappy truth: You can never depend on your child to sleep through the night—at least not in these early years. He may go for a few days, weeks, or even months sleeping like an angel, then begin waking up almost as frequently as a newborn.

A change in routine is a common cause of nighttime awakening. Changing rooms or beds, losing a favorite cuddly toy or blanket, or taking a trip away from home may all disrupt his sleep. If he's ill or cutting a tooth, he might wake up more often. Also, between twelve and fourteen months, he'll begin actively dreaming, which can startle or frighten him awake. These are all valid reasons for him to wake up—but not for you to pick him up or take him to your room. He needs to put himself back to sleep, even if it means crying a bit first. The strategies outlined in Chapter 9 still apply.

But what if your toddler is used to getting lots of nighttime attention? In this case, you'll need to retrain him gradually. Let's say you've been giving him milk when he wakes up. It's time to change first to water and soon after stop it entirely. If you've been turning on the light and playing with him, try to soothe him in the dark instead. If you've been picking him up, restrict yourself to calming him with only your voice from a distance. Above all, don't get angry with him if he continues to protest. You'll need to show him some compassion, even as you remain firm. It's not easy, but in the long run it will improve your sleep as well as his.

BEHAVIOR

Discipline

Having a toddler is a humbling experience and presents new challenges, adventures, and opportunities for fulfillment. Before your child was born, or even when she was a baby, it was easy for you to watch someone else's toddler throwing a temper tantrum and say, "My child will never do that." Now you realize there are times when any child acts up unexpectedly. You can guide your child and teach her what's right, and that will work most of the time. But you can't force her to act exactly as you want. So face the facts: There are bound to be times when the unruly child everyone is staring at is yours!

At this age, your toddler has a limited idea of what "good" and "bad" mean, and she does not fully understand the concept of rules or warnings. You may say, "If you pull the cat's tail, she'll bite you," but it may make no sense to her at all. Even "Be nice to kitty" may not be clear to her. So whether she's running into the street or turning her face away from Grandma's kiss, she's not deliberately behaving badly, nor do her actions mean that you've failed as a parent. She's simply acting on the impulses of the moment. It will take years of firm but gentle guidance before she fully understands what you expect from her and has the self-control to meet those expectations.

Many people think of discipline as punishment. While punishment may be part of it, a much more important aspect of discipline is love. Affection and caring form the core of your relationship with your child, and they play a powerful role in shaping her behavior. Your love and respect will teach her to care about others as well as herself. Your own daily example of honesty, dedication, and trust will teach her to become honest, hardworking, and trustworthy herself. Also, the control you show in helping her to learn right from wrong will serve as a model for the self-discipline she develops later on. In short, if you want her to behave well, you need to act that way toward her.

If you were keeping a running tally, you'd want displays of affection to greatly outnumber punishments and criticisms. Even a quick hug or kiss, or a bit of good-natured roughhousing, will reassure your child that you love her. And on a day when your toddler is getting into everything and you find yourself being especially snappy with her, make sure you go out of your way when she does behave well to give her a hug and tell her she's doing a good job. Especially during this second year, pleasing you is very important to your toddler, so praise and attention are powerful rewards that can motivate her to obey the reasonable rules you set for her.

It's important to have realistic expectations for your child's behavior. They should reflect her own temperament and personality, not your fantasies. She may be much more active and inquisitive than you would like her to be, but insisting that she spend long stretches in the playpen or confined in her high chair will only make her more resistant and frustrated.

Even if your toddler is a "model" child, she still has to learn what you expect. No matter how obvious it may seem to you, she won't automatically know that it's wrong to eat dirt or run into the street or pull her friend's hair. And telling her once won't get the message across. She'll have to learn by trial and error (often, several errors) before she understands the rule.

One other important reminder. If you load too much on your child at this early age, you'll be frustrated, and she'll be hurt and bewildered. Make things easier for both of you by establishing some priorities and then building your list of rules gradually. Give precedence to limits that keep her safe. As your youngster learns to walk (between nine and sixteen months of age), safety should be the most important discipline issue, giving her the freedom to explore in safe ways, while making sure that child-proof locks are on cabinets that contain heavy dishes or pots. Also be certain that she understands that there are prohibitions against hitting, biting, and kicking. Once she masters these rules, you can turn your attention to nuisance behavior, such as screaming in public, throwing food, writing on the wall, and removing her clothing at unexpected moments. Plan to save the finer points of polite social behavior for the next few years. It's too much to ask an eighteen-month-old to be nice when Grandma's kissing her at a time she'd rather be outside playing.

At this age, since your toddler can't understand everything that you say, it's also only fair to eliminate as many temptations as possible. She needs freedom to explore. Cluttering your home with "no-nos" will deprive her of this freedom and create more restrictions than she can possibly absorb. It also will frustrate her. While you can't get rid of the oven, you can lock away the china and place your houseplants out of reach.

To prevent further unwanted behavior, pay extra attention to your toddler when she's tired, hungry, sick, or is in an unfamiliar setting—in other words, when she's most likely to be stressed. Also try to keep your own daily routine as flexible as possible so she doesn't feel extra pressure. If the two of you are at the grocery store during her nap time, don't be surprised if she acts up.

Despite all your attempts at prevention, sometimes your toddler will violate one or more of your top ten rules. When that happens, alert her with your facial expression and the displeased sound of your voice. Then move her to a different place. Sometimes this will be enough, but just as often, other measures still may be required. It's best to decide on these responses now, while your toddler is young. Otherwise, when she becomes naturally more mischievous in the next few years, you may be more prone to lose your temper and do something you'll regret.

Here's an important pact to make with yourself. *Never* resort to punishments that physically or emotionally hurt your child. While you need to let her know that she's done something wrong, this doesn't mean you have to inflict pain. Spanking, slapping, beating, and screaming at children of any age do far more harm than good. Here are some of the main reasons why this is true.

1. Even if it stops the child from misbehaving at the moment, it also teaches her that it's OK to hit and yell when she's upset or angry. Think of the mother busily whacking her child as she yells at her: "I told you not to hit!" It's absurd, isn't it? But it's also tragically common, and has an equally tragic result: Children who are hit often become hitters themselves, having learned that violence is an acceptable way to express anger and to discipline.

2. Physical punishment can harm your child. If a little spank doesn't work, many parents will slap even harder as they become angrier and more frustrated.

3. Physical punishment makes the child angry at and resentful of the parent. So instead of developing self-discipline, the youngster is much more likely to try to get back at the parent by continuing to misbehave, but without getting caught.

4. Physical punishment gives a child a very extreme form of attention. Although it's unpleasant, even painful, it tells the child that she's gotten through to her parent. If the mother or father is usually too busy or preoccupied to pay much attention to her, the child may decide that the bad behavior and the punishment that follows it is worth it to get parental attention.

Physical punishment is harmful emotionally to both parent and child. It is the least effective way to discipline. So if spanking and yelling are wrong, what approach should you take? As difficult as it may be, the best way to deal with your misbehaving toddler is to isolate her briefly. No attention. No toys. No fun. This strategy, known as time-out, works like this:

1. You've told your toddler not to open the oven door, but she persists.

2. Without raising your voice, again say firmly, "No. Don't open the oven door," and pick her up with her back toward you.

3. Put her in her playpen and empty it of everything else. Then leave the room.

4. Wait a minute or two, or until her crying subsides, before returning to her.

The keys to this form of discipline—or to any other, for that matter—are consistency and calmness. As hard as it may be, try to respond immediately every time your child breaks an important rule, but don't let your irritation get the better of you. If you're like most parents, you won't succeed 100 percent of the time, but an occasional slip-up won't make much difference. Just try to be as consistent as you can.

When you do feel yourself losing your temper, take a few deep breaths, count to ten, and, if possible, get someone else to watch your child while you leave the room. Remind yourself that you are older and should be wiser than your toddler. You know that at her age she's not deliberately trying to annoy or embarrass you, so keep your own ego out of it. In the end, the more self-discipline you exercise, the more effective you'll be at disciplining your child.

Coping with Temper Tantrums

While you're busily planning the rules and regulations by which your toddler must live, he's attempting to master his own destiny, and it's inevitable that you'll clash from time to time. Your first sign of this collision course will come when your one-year-old shakes his head and emphatically says "No!" after you've asked him to do something. By year's end, his protests may have escalated to screaming fits or full-blown tantrums in which he throws himself onto his back on the floor, clenches his teeth, kicks and screams, pounds his fists on the floor, and perhaps even holds his breath. As difficult as these performances may be for you to tolerate, they are a normal (even healthy) way for your toddler to deal with conflict at this age.

Look at the situation from his point of view. Like all young toddlers, he believes that the world revolves around him. He's trying hard to be independent, and most of the time you're encouraging him to be strong and assertive. Yet every now and then, when he's trying to do something he very much wants to do, you pull him away or ask him to do something else. He can't understand why you're getting in his way, nor can he verbally tell you how upset he is. The only way he can express his frustration is by acting it out.

Outbursts, then, are all but inevitable, and your child's general temperament will set the tone for most of them. If he's very adaptable, easygoing, generally positive, and easily distracted, he may never kick and scream. Instead, he might pout, say "no," or simply head in an opposite direction when you try to guide him. The negativism is there, but it's low key. On the other hand, if your child has been very active, intense, and persistent from infancy, he'll probably channel the same intensity into his tantrums. You'll need to remind yourself over and over that this is neither good nor bad, and it has nothing to do with your skill as a parent. Your child is not consciously trying to thwart you, but is simply going through a normal stage of development that soon (but perhaps not soon enough to suit you) will pass.

Here are some important points to keep in mind about living with temper tantrums.

- You may have an easier time coping with your toddler's outbursts if you think of them as performances. This will help remind you of what you have to do to stop them: namely, eliminate the audience. Since you are the only audience that matters to your child, leave the room. If he follows, call time-out and put him in his playpen. Also, if he kicks or bites at any time during the tantrum, call time-out immediately. While it's normal for him to try out this kind of superaggressive behavior, you shouldn't let him get away with it.

- When a tantrum takes place away from home, it's much more difficult to remain calm. Especially when you're out in public, you can't just leave him and go to another room. And because you're trapped and embarrassed, you're much more likely to spank or snap at him. But that's not going to work any better here than it does at home, and it has the added disadvan-

WHERE WE STAND

The American Academy of Pediatrics strongly opposes striking a child. If the spanking is spontaneous, parents should later explain calmly why they did it, the specific behavior that provoked it, and how angry they felt. They might apologize to their child for their loss of control, because that usually helps the youngster understand and accept the spanking.

Preventing Temper Tantrums
(*see also* Temper Tantrums, *page 538*)

When it comes to discipline, you have several distinct advantages over your child. First of all, because you know that there inevitably will be conflicts between you (you can probably even predict which issues are likely to spark them), you can plan your strategy in advance to prevent friction as much as possible.

Use the following guidelines to help you minimize your child's temper tantrums, both in number and in intensity. Make sure everyone who takes care of her understands and follows these policies consistently.

1. When you ask your toddler to do something, use a friendly tone of voice and phrase your request like an invitation instead of a command. It also helps to say "please" and "thank you."

2. Don't overreact when she says "no." For quite some time, she may automatically say "no" to *any* request or instruction. She'll even say "no" to ice cream and cake at this stage! What she really means is something like "I'd like to be in control here, so I'll say 'no' until I think it through or until I see if you're serious." Instead of jumping on her, answer her hidden challenge by repeating your request calmly and clearly. Don't punish her for saying "no."

3. Choose your battles carefully. She won't throw a temper tantrum unless you push her first, so don't push unless there's something worth fighting for. For example, keeping her safely buckled into her car seat while the automobile is moving is a priority item. Making sure she eats her peas before her applesauce is not. So while she's

tage of making you look even worse than your child. Rather than lashing out or letting him have his way—either of which will only encourage his tantrums—calmly carry him to a restroom or out to the car, so he can finish his performance away from onlookers. Also, sometimes in public a big, immobilizing hug and calming voice will soothe and quiet such a child.

- When the tantrum or the time-out is over, don't dwell on it. Instead, if a request from you had triggered his outburst initially, calmly repeat it. Remain composed and determined, and he'll soon realize that acting out is a waste of his time as well as yours.

- He may hold his breath during a severe temper tantrum. Sometimes this might last long enough to cause him to faint for a very short period of time. This can be very frightening when it occurs, but he will awaken in thirty to

saying "no" to everything all day long, you should be saying "no" only the few times a day when it's absolutely necessary.

4. Don't offer choices where none exist, and don't make deals. Issues like bathing, bedtime, and staying out of the street are nonnegotiable. She doesn't deserve an extra cookie or trip to the park for cooperating with these rules. Bribery will only teach her to break the rule whenever you forget to give her the agreed-on reward.

5. Do offer limited choices whenever possible. Let her decide which pajamas to wear, which story to read, which toys to play with. If you encourage her independence in these areas, she'll be much more likely to comply when it counts.

6. Anticipate situations that are likely to trigger a tantrum, and avoid them whenever possible. If she always makes a scene in the grocery store, arrange to leave her with a sitter the next few times you go shopping. If one of her playmates always seems to get her keyed up and irritable, separate the children for a few days or weeks and see if the dynamics improve when they're older.

7. Reward her good behavior with plenty of praise and attention. Even if you just sit with her while she looks at her books, your companionship shows her you approve of this quiet activity.

8. Keep your sense of humor. While it's not a good idea to laugh at your toddler as she kicks and screams (that just plays to her performance), it can be very therapeutic to laugh and talk about it with friends or older family members when she's out of earshot.

sixty seconds. Just keep him safe and protected during this brief episode and try not to overreact yourself, since this tends to reinforce tantrum breath-holding behavior. If not reinforced, this type of activity usually will disappear after a short period of time.

Family Relationships

Because your toddler is so self-centered, her older brothers and sisters might find her very taxing. Not only does she still consume the bulk of your time and attention, but with increasing frequency she will deliberately invade her siblings' territory and possessions. When they throw her out, she may respond with a tantrum. Even if the older siblings were tolerant and affectionate toward her as an infant, they are bound to display some antagonistic feelings toward her now—at least occasionally.

It will help keep the peace if you enforce off-limits rules to protect the older children's privacy, and you set aside time to spend just with them. No matter how old they are, all your children want your affection and attention. Whether they're preparing for the preschool picnic, planning a second-grade science project, trying out for the junior high soccer team, or fretting over a date for the junior prom, they need you as much as your toddler does.

If your toddler is the older sibling, the rivalry may be much more intense. (See *Sibling Rivalry,* page 621.) The normal feelings of jealousy are heightened by her self-centeredness, and she doesn't have the reasoning abilities to cope with them. Despite her drive for independence, there are many times each day when she'll want to be the baby, and she isn't about to wait her turn.

It's important to begin preparing your toddler before the new baby arrives. She'll recognize the changes quite early in pregnancy, so don't try to hide anything from her. When she asks, tell her that a new baby is coming, but don't stress that it will be a brother or sister. Otherwise she'll expect a playmate instead of an infant. Also, try not to overemphasize the arrival of the new brother or sister far in advance of your delivery; your toddler is concerned only with events that happen in the immediate future.

As tempting as it may be to have her toilet trained before the new baby arrives—so you don't have two in diapers at the same time—it's not worth it if you have to pressure her to make it happen. (See Chapter 1, page 23.) Such efforts probably will backfire, and the added stress may make her resent the new baby. If major changes must be made, such as moving her to a new room, make them well in advance of the baby's due date. The less pressure you place on your toddler at this time, the better everyone will fare.

After the new baby comes home, include your toddler as much as possible in your activities with the infant. Although she definitely can't be trusted alone with the infant, invite her to "help" as you feed, bathe, change, and dress her new sibling. Take advantage of the baby's naps to spend time alone with your toddler, and stress her importance to you and to the baby.

It's also essential to recognize that you can't satisfy the needs of both of them all the time, especially not by yourself. When you're feeling especially overwhelmed, "divide and conquer" by handing one child to your spouse, relative, or a close friend while you attend to the other. If possible, arrange for your toddler to go on special outings during this time, even if just to a park or the zoo. If the children get these occasional breaks from each other, everyone will feel less competitive—and a little more comfortable.

IMMUNIZATION ALERT

Between twelve and fifteen months, your toddler will need booster doses of the Hib and pneumococcal conjugate vaccines. These vaccines help prevent meningitis, pneumonia, and joint infection caused by *Haemophilus influenzae* type b and several strains of *Streptococcus pneumoniae* bacteria. Your toddler also should receive her first measles, mumps, rubella vaccine (MMR) during these months. At twelve to eighteen months, your toddler also will require:

- The fourth dose of the DTaP vaccine (This can be administered as early as twelve months, but is recommended at fifteen to eighteen months of age.)

- The third dose of the "inactivated" polio vaccine

- The chickenpox (varicella) vaccine, if your child hasn't already had the chickenpox

SAFETY CHECK

Sleeping Safety

- Keep the crib mattress at the lowest setting.

- Keep the crib free of any objects that your toddler could stack and climb on to get out.

- If your toddler can climb out of his crib, move him to a low bed.

- Keep the crib away from all drapery and electrical and other cords.

- Be sure all cradle gyms and hanging toys have been removed from the crib.

Toy Safety

- Do not give your toddler any toy that has to be plugged into an electrical outlet.

- Do not give her a motorized riding toy.

A Message for Grandparents

You have an ongoing role to play in your grandchild's nurturing and development. During this time of his young life, here are some activities in which you can participate and some things to keep in mind as you do:

Motor Skills

Help your grandchild practice skills that tie in with your own likes and preferences. For example:

- **Involve him in physical activities (such as sweeping, dusting or arranging items) around the house in which you can lend a helping hand to ensure his success and safety.**

- **Devise and initiate outdoor games and exercises that you and he can enjoy together.**

Cognitive Milestones

To help your grandchild develop cognitively:

- **Read special books to him**

- **Play music and sing songs with him**

- **Assist him as he begins to learn his numbers**

- **Play hiding games like hide-and-seek and peekaboo**

- **Mix fantasy play with real play**

Water Safety

- Never leave your toddler, *even for a few seconds,* in or near any body of water without supervision. This includes a bathtub, toilet, wading pool, swimming pool, fishpond, whirlpool, hot tub, lake, or ocean.

Auto Safety

- The safest place for all children to ride is in their car safety seat in the backseat.

- Never let your toddler climb out of his car safety seat while the car is moving.

- Never leave him alone in the car, even if it is locked and in your driveway.

Social Development

- Encourage your grandchild to interact with his peers, but keep in mind that egocentric behavior is normal for this age.

- Don't overreact to selfishness or disregarding the feelings of others. Just reinforce that he should be sensitive to the feelings of other children.

- Keep in mind that this period of self-centeredness will taper off by the age of three.

- Nurture his self-esteem at every opportunity, but not at the expense of others.

Emotional Development

- Repeatedly tell your grandchild how special he is to you. Tell him how important your time together is to you.

- Don't overreact to the mood swings he goes through—clinging one moment, independent the next, and defiant after that.

- Don't reinforce his aggressiveness if it becomes abusive. Set limits, but do not physically restrain or punish him. Read the section on brain growth of children this age (pages 278–279). Follow your own inclinations about the activities or areas that can promote his development.

Home Safety

- Protect any open windows with screens or barriers that your toddler cannot possibly push out or open. Screens do not prevent falls out of windows.

- Make sure all electrical outlets have caps or plugs on them and all cabinets that contain cleaning fluids or other dangerous items have safety locks on them.

- Install ground-fault circuit interrupters (GFCIs) to prevent electrocution.

- Keep electrical cords out of reach.

- Guns should not be in the home of any child. The best way to protect children from firearm-related injuries is to remove guns from homes and communities. When children come across an unsupervised gun, or another child with a gun, they should not touch the gun and should immediately get help from a parent or trusted adult. If you must have guns, keep them unloaded and locked out of sight. Lock ammunition in a separate location.

Outdoor Safety

- Install door locks, barriers, and alarms to prevent your child from accessing pools, driveways, and streets without your knowledge.

- Hold on to your toddler whenever you're near streets, parking lots, and driveways, even in quiet neighborhoods.

- Set up fences or other barriers to make sure she stays within her outside play area and away from the street, pools, and other hazards.

- Make sure there is sand, wood chips, or other soft surfaces under outdoor play equipment.

11

AGE TWO TO
THREE YEARS

*Y*our baby is now advancing from infancy into the preschool years. During this time, her physical growth and motor development will slow, but you can expect to see some tremendous intellectual, social, and emotional changes. Her vocabulary will grow, she'll try to increase her independence from the other members of her family, and—upon discovering that society has certain rules that she is expected to observe—she'll begin to develop some real self-control.

These changes will present an emotional challenge for both you and your child. After all, these are the "terrible twos," when her every other word seems to be "no." This period will seem like a constant tug-of-war between her continuing reliance on you and her need to assert her independence. She may flip-flop between these extremes, clinging to you when you try to leave her and running in the opposite direction when you want her to obey you. You may find yourself longing for the cuddly infant she used to be while at the same time pushing her to behave like a "big kid." It's no wonder you occasionally lose patience with each other.

By acknowledging and accepting these changes, you'll make it easier for both of you through the next few hectic years. Largely through your responses to her—the encouragement and respect you show her, your appreciation for her accomplishments, the warmth and security you offer her—she'll learn to feel comfortable, capable, and special.

These feelings will help in later years as she goes to school and meets new people. Most important, they'll make her proud of herself as a person.

GROWTH AND DEVELOPMENT

Physical Appearance and Growth

Although your toddler's growth rate will slow between his second and third birthdays, nevertheless he will continue his remarkable physical transformation from baby to child. The most dramatic change will occur in his bodily proportions. As an infant, he had a relatively large head and short legs and arms; now his head growth will slow, from ¾ inch (2 cm) in his second year alone to ¾ to 1¼ inches (2–3 cm) over the next ten years. At the same time, his height will increase, primarily because his legs and, to some degree, his trunk will be growing quickly. With these changes in the rates of growth, his body and legs will look much more in proportion. By measuring his "sitting height," you'll get a good sense of these proportional changes.

"Sitting height" is the distance from the top of a child's head to the surface on which he's seated. It accounts for approximately three-fourths of a newborn's total body length, mainly because of his proportionately large head. But by age two, sitting height declines to about two-thirds of total body length, decreasing to about one-half by age thirteen or fourteen.

The baby fat that seemed to make your infant so cuddly in the first months of life gradually will disappear during the preschool years. The percentage of fat, which reached a peak at age one, will steadily decrease to approximately half that by his fifth birthday. Notice how his arms and thighs become more slender and his face less round. Even the pads of fat under the arches, which have until now given the appearance of flat feet, will disappear.

His posture will change, as well, during this time. His pudgy, babyish look as a toddler has been partly due to his posture, particularly his protruding abdomen and inwardly curving lower back. But as his muscle tone improves and his posture becomes more erect, he'll develop a longer, leaner, stronger appearance.

Although it will happen more slowly now, your child will continue to grow steadily. Preschoolers grow an average of 2½ inches (6 cm) annually and gain about 4 pounds (2 kg) each year. Plot your child's height and weight on the growth charts on pages 128–129 to compare his rate of growth to the average for this age. If you should notice a pronounced lapse in growth, discuss it with your pediatrician. He probably will tell you there is no need to become overly concerned, as some healthy children just may not grow as quickly during their second and third years as their playmates seem to do. By age three, their growth rate usually does return to normal, although they may not reach normal height for their age until adolescence. Also, because of this slowdown in growth, such youngsters often enter puberty at a later age. Even though their adolescent growth spurt may come later than usual, most of these children eventually achieve normal adult height.

Less commonly, this pause in growth during the toddler or preschool years may signal something else—perhaps a chronic health problem, such as kidney or liver disease, or a recurrent infection. In rare cases, slow growth may be due to a disorder of one of the hormone glands or to gastrointestinal complications of some chronic illnesses. Your pediatrician will take all of these things into consideration when he examines your child.

Remember that after age two, children of the same age begin to vary much more in size and weight, so try not to spend too much time comparing your child's measurements with those of his playmates. As long as he's maintaining his own individual rate of growth, there's no reason to worry.

Don't be surprised if your child is eating less than you think he should. Children need fewer calories at this time because they're growing more slowly. Even though he's eating less, he still can remain well nourished as long as you make a variety of healthy food available to him. At the same time, if he seems overly preoccupied with food and appears to be accumulating excess weight, talk to your pediatrician about ways to help manage his weight. Early eating behaviors can influence the risk of obesity throughout life, so managing your child's weight in childhood is as important as it is at any stage of life.

Movement

At this age, your child will seem to be continually on the go—running, kicking, climbing, jumping. Her attention span, which was never particularly long, may now seem even shorter. Try starting a game with her, and she'll immediately change to a different one. Head in one direction, and she'll quickly detour to another. This yearlong energy spurt between ages two and three certainly will keep you on the go. But take heart—her activity level will strengthen her body and develop her coordination.

In the months ahead, her running will become smoother and more coordinated. She'll also learn to kick and direct the motion of a ball, walk up and down steps by herself while holding on, and seat herself confidently in a child-size chair. With a little help, she'll even be able to stand on one leg.

Watch your two-year-old walk, and you'll see how she has cast aside the stiff, spread-legged gait of a young toddler, replacing it with a more adult, heel-to-toe motion. In the process, she has become much more adept at maneuvering her body, capable of walking backward and turning corners that are not too sharp.

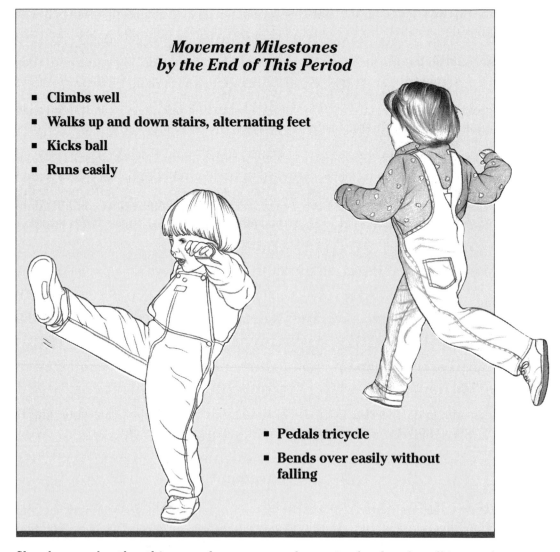

Movement Milestones by the End of This Period

- **Climbs well**
- **Walks up and down stairs, alternating feet**
- **Kicks ball**
- **Runs easily**

- **Pedals tricycle**
- **Bends over easily without falling**

She also can do other things as she moves, such as using her hands, talking, and looking around.

Don't worry about finding activities that will help your child develop her motor skills. She'll probably be able to do that herself. When you are able to join in the fun, bear in mind that children this age love piggyback rides, rolling on mats, going down small slides, and climbing with help on the floor-level balance beam. The more running and climbing your games involve, the better.

If you can, set aside specific times during the day when she can go outside to run, play, and explore. This will help minimize wear and tear on the inside of the house as well as on your nerves. It's also safer for her to run around in the open than to bump into walls and furniture inside. While outdoors, let her use the yard, playground, or park—whichever is most available and safe for her. But be aware that since her self-control and judgment lag considerably behind her motor skills, you must remain vigilant and keep safety and injury prevention high on your priority list at all times.

Hand and Finger Skills

At age two, your child will be able to manipulate small objects with ease. He'll turn the pages of a book, build a tower six blocks high, pull off his shoes, and unzip a large zipper. He'll also coordinate the movements of his wrist, fingers,

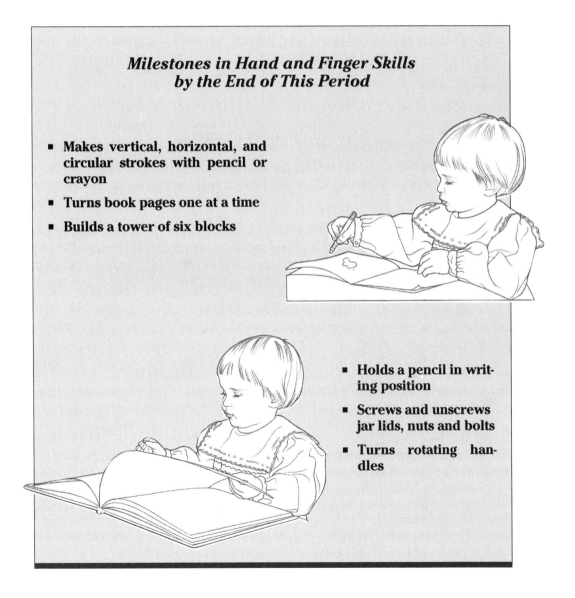

Milestones in Hand and Finger Skills by the End of This Period

- **Makes vertical, horizontal, and circular strokes with pencil or crayon**
- **Turns book pages one at a time**
- **Builds a tower of six blocks**

- **Holds a pencil in writing position**
- **Screws and unscrews jar lids, nuts and bolts**
- **Turns rotating handles**

and palm so well that he can turn a doorknob, unscrew a jar lid, use a cup with one hand, and unwrap paper from a candy.

One of his major accomplishments this year will be learning to "draw." Hand him a crayon and watch what happens: He'll place his thumb on one side of it and his fingers on the other, then awkwardly try to extend his index or middle finger toward the point. Clumsy as this grip may seem, it will give him enough control to create his first artistic masterpieces, using sweeping vertical and circular strokes.

Fortunately, your child's quiet play at this age will be much more focused than it was at eighteen months, when he was into everything. His attention span is longer, and now that he can turn pages, he'll be an active participant as you look at books or magazines together. He'll also be interested in activities such as drawing, building, or manipulating objects, so blocks and interlocking construction sets may keep him entertained for long periods. And if you let him loose with a box of crayons or a set of fingerpaints, his creative impulses will flourish.

Language Development

Your two-year-old not only understands most of what you say to her, but also speaks with a rapidly growing vocabulary of fifty or more words. Over the course of this year, she'll graduate from two- or three-word sentences ("Drink juice," "Mommy want cookie") to those with four, five, or even six words ("Where's the ball, Daddy?" "Dolly sit in my lap"). She's also beginning to use pronouns (I, you, me, we, they) and understands the concept of "mine" ("I want my cup," "I see my mommy"). Pay attention to how she also is using language to describe ideas and information and to express her physical or emotional needs and desires.

It's human nature to measure your toddler's verbal abilities against those of other children her age, but you should try to avoid this. At this time, there's more variation in language development than in any other area. While some preschoolers develop language skills at a steady rate, others seem to master words in an uneven manner. And some children are naturally more talkative than others. This doesn't mean that the more verbal children are necessarily smarter or more advanced than the quieter ones, nor does it even mean that they have richer vocabularies. In fact, the quiet child may know just as many words but be choosier about speaking them. As a general rule, boys start talking later than girls, but this variation—like most others mentioned above—tends to even out as children reach school age.

Without any formal instruction, just by listening and practicing, your child will master many of the basic rules of grammar by the time she enters school. You can help enrich her vocabulary and language skills by making reading a part of your everyday routine. At this age, she can follow a story line and will understand and remember many ideas and pieces of information presented in books. Even so, because she may have a hard time sitting still for too long, the books you read to her should be short. To keep her attention, choose activity-oriented books that encourage her to touch, point, and name objects or to repeat certain phrases. Toward the end of this year, as her language skills become more advanced, she'll also have fun with poems, puns, or jokes that play with language by repeating funny sounds or using nonsense phrases.

For some youngsters, however, this language-development process does not run smoothly. In fact, about one in every ten to fifteen children has trouble with language comprehension and/or speech. For some children, the problem is caused by hearing difficulty, low intelligence, lack of verbal stimulation at home, or a family history of speech delays. In most cases, though, the cause is unknown. If your pediatrician suspects your child has difficulty with language, she'll conduct a thorough physical exam and hearing test and, if necessary, refer you to a speech/language or early-childhood specialist for further evaluation. Early detection and identification of language delay or hearing impairment is critically important, so treatment can begin before the problem interferes with learning in other areas. Unless you and your pediatrician identify the difficulty and do something about it, your child may have continuous trouble with classroom learning.

Language Milestones by the End of This Period

- **Follows a two- or three-part command, such as "Go to your room and bring back the teddy bear and the dog"**
- **Recognizes and identifies almost all common objects and pictures**
- **Understands most sentences**
- **Understands physical relationships ("on," "in," "under")**
- **Uses four- and five-word sentences**
- **Can say name, age, and sex**
- **Uses pronouns (I, you, me, we, they) and some plurals (cars, dogs, cats)**
- **Strangers can understand most of her words**

Cognitive Development

Think back to your child's infancy and early toddler months. That was a time when he learned about the world by touching, looking, manipulating, and listening. Now the learning process has become more thoughtful. His grasp of language is increasing, and he's beginning to form mental images for things, actions, and concepts. He also can solve some problems in his head, performing mental trial-and-error instead of having to manipulate objects physically. And as his memory and intellectual abilities develop, he'll begin to understand simple time concepts, such as "You can play *after* you finish eating."

Your toddler also is starting to understand the relationship between objects. For instance, he'll be able to match similar shapes when you give him shape-sorting toys and simple jigsaw puzzles. He'll also begin to recognize the pur-

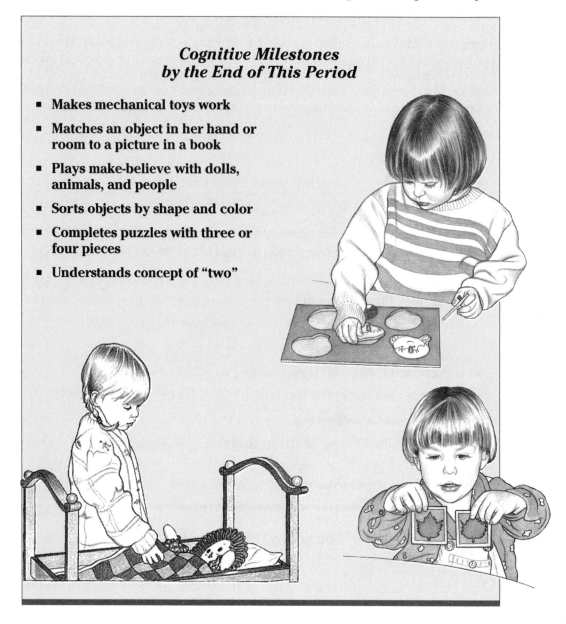

Cognitive Milestones by the End of This Period

- Makes mechanical toys work
- Matches an object in her hand or room to a picture in a book
- Plays make-believe with dolls, animals, and people
- Sorts objects by shape and color
- Completes puzzles with three or four pieces
- Understands concept of "two"

pose of numbers in counting objects—especially the number 2. And as his understanding of cause and effect develops, he'll become much more interested in winding up toys and turning lights and appliances on and off.

You'll also notice your toddler's play growing more complex. Most noticeably, he'll start stringing together different activities to create a logical sequence. Instead of drifting randomly from one toy to another, he may first put a doll to bed and then cover it up. Or he may pretend to feed several dolls, one after the other. Over the next few years, he'll put together longer and more elaborate sequences of make-believe, acting out much of his own daily routine, from getting up in the morning to taking a bath and going to bed at night.

If we were to single out the major intellectual limitation at this age, it would be your child's feeling that everything that happens in his world is the result of something he has done. With a belief like this, it becomes very difficult for him to understand correctly such concepts as death, divorce, or illness, without feeling that he played some role in it. So if parents separate or a family member gets sick, children often feel responsible. (See discussion in Chapter 22, "Family Issues.")

Reasoning with your two-year-old is often difficult. After all, he views everything in extremely simple terms. He still often confuses fantasy with reality unless he's actively playing make-believe. For example, a wonderful story from Selma Fraiberg's *The Magic Years* talks about parents telling their two-and-a-half-year-old that they soon would be flying to Europe. With a worried look on his face, the little boy said, "But my arms aren't strong enough to fly." Therefore, during this stage, be sure to choose your own words carefully: Comments that you think are funny or playful—such as "If you eat more ice cream, you'll explode"—actually may panic him, since he won't know you're joking.

Social Development

By nature, children this age can be more concerned about their own needs and even act selfishly. Often they refuse to share anything that interests them, and they do not easily interact with other children, even when playing side by side, unless it's to let a playmate know that they would like a toy or object for themselves. There may be times when your child's behavior may make you upset, but if you take a close look, you'll notice that all the other toddlers in the play-group probably are acting the same way.

At age two, children view the world almost exclusively through their own needs and desires. Because they can't yet understand how others might feel in the same situation, they assume that everyone thinks and feels exactly as they do. And on those occasions when they realize they're out of line, they may not be able to control themselves. For these reasons, it's useless to try to shape your child's behavior using statements such as "How would you like it if she did that to you?" Save these comments until your child is older; then she'll be able really to understand how other people think and feel and be capable of responding to such reasoning.

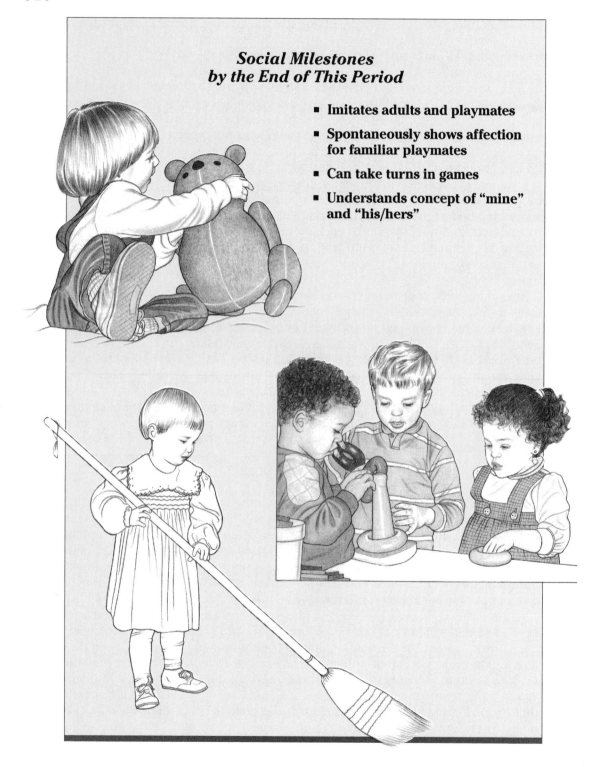

Social Milestones by the End of This Period

- Imitates adults and playmates
- Spontaneously shows affection for familiar playmates
- Can take turns in games
- Understands concept of "mine" and "his/hers"

Because your two-year-old's behavior seems only self-directed, you also may find yourself worrying that she's spoiled or out of control. In all likelihood, your fears are unfounded, and she'll pass through this phase in time. Highly active, aggressive children who push and shove usually are just as "normal" as quiet, shy ones who never seem to act out their thoughts and feelings.

Ironically, despite your child's being most interested in herself, much of her playtime will be spent imitating other people's mannerisms and activities. Imitation and "pretend" are favorite games at this age. So as your two-year-old puts her teddy to bed or feeds her doll, you may hear her use exactly the same words and tone of voice you use when telling her to go to sleep or eat her vegetables. No matter how she resists your instructions at other times, when she moves over into the parent role, she imitates you exactly. These play activities help her learn what it's like to be in someone else's shoes, and they serve as valuable rehearsals for future social encounters. They'll also help you appreciate the importance of being a good role model, by demonstrating that children often do as we do, not as we say.

The best way for your child to learn how to behave around other people is to be given plenty of trial runs. Don't let her relatively antisocial behavior discourage you from getting playgroups together. At first it may be wise to limit the groups to two or three children. And although you'll need to monitor their activities closely to be sure that no one gets hurt or overly upset, you should let the children guide themselves as much as possible. They need to learn how to play with one another, not with one another's parents.

Emotional Development

It's so difficult to follow the ups and downs of a two-year-old. One moment he's beaming and friendly; the next he's sullen and weepy—and often for no apparent reason. These mood swings, however, are just part of growing up. They are signs of the emotional changes taking place as your child struggles to take control of actions, impulses, feelings, and his body.

At this age, your child wants to explore the world and seek adventure. As a result, he'll spend most of his time testing limits—his own, yours, and his environment's. Unfortunately, he still lacks many of the skills required for the safe accomplishment of everything he needs to do, and he often will need you to protect him.

When he oversteps a limit and is pulled back, he often reacts with anger and frustration, possibly with a temper tantrum or sullen rage. He may even strike back by hitting, biting, or kicking. At this age, he just doesn't have much control over his emotional impulses, so his anger and frustration tend to erupt suddenly in the form of crying, hitting, or screaming. It's his only way of dealing with the difficult realities of life. He may even act out in ways that unintentionally harm himself or others. It's all part of being two.

Have sitters or relatives ever told you that your child never behaves badly when they're caring for him? It's not uncommon for toddlers to be angels when

Holding the Line on Tantrums

Frustration, anger, and an occasional tantrum are inevitable for all two-year-olds. As a parent, you should allow your toddler to express her emotions but, at the same time, try to help her channel her anger away from violent or overly aggressive behavior. Here are some suggestions.

1. When you see your child starting to get worked up, try to turn her energy and attention to a new activity that is more acceptable.

you're not around, because they don't trust these other people enough to test their limits. But with you, your toddler will be willing to try things that may be dangerous or difficult, because he knows you'll rescue him if he gets into trouble.

Whatever protest pattern he has developed around the end of his first year probably will persist for some time. For instance, when you're about to leave him with a sitter, he may become angry and throw a tantrum in anticipation of the separation. Or he may whimper, or whine and cling to you. Or he simply could become subdued and silent. Whatever his behavior, try not to overreact by scolding or punishing him. The best tactic is to reassure him before you leave that you will be back and, when you return, to praise him for being so patient while you were gone. Take solace in the fact that separations should be much easier by the time he's three years old.

The more confident and secure your two-year-old feels, the more indepen-

2. If you can't distract your toddler, ignore her. Every time you react to one of her outbursts in any way, you're rewarding her negative behavior with extra attention. Even scolding, punishing, or trying to reason with her may encourage her to act up more.

3. If you're in a public place where her behavior is embarrassing you, simply remove her without discussion or fuss. Wait until she's calmed down before you return or continue with your activities.

4. If the tantrum involves hitting, biting, or some other potentially harmful behavior, you can't ignore it. But overreacting won't help your child. Instead, tell her immediately and clearly that she is not to behave this way, and move her off by herself for a few minutes. She can't understand complicated explanations, so don't try to reason with her. Just make sure she understands what she was doing wrong and dole out your punishment then and there. If you wait an hour, she won't connect the punishment with the "crime." (See *Temper Tantrums,* page 538.)

5. Do not use physical punishment to discipline your child. If you do, she may assume that aggression is an acceptable way to respond when she doesn't get her way.

6. Monitor her television viewing. (See *Television,* page 533.) Preschool children may behave more aggressively if they watch violent programs on TV.

dent and well behaved he's likely to be. You can help him develop these positive feelings by encouraging him to behave more maturely. To do this, consistently set reasonable limits that allow him to explore and exercise his curiosity, but that draw the line at dangerous or antisocial behavior. With these guidelines, he'll begin to sense what's acceptable and what's not. To repeat, the key is consistency. Praise him every time he plays well with another child, or whenever he feeds, dresses, or undresses himself without your help, or when you help him to start with the activity and he completes it by himself. As you do, he'll start to feel good about these accomplishments and himself. With his self-esteem on the rise, he'll also develop an image of himself as someone who behaves a certain way—the way that you have encouraged—and negative behavior will fade.

Since two-year-olds normally express a broad range of emotions, be prepared for everything from delight to rage. However, you should consult your pediatri-

Hyperactivity

By adult standards, many two-year-olds seem "hyperactive." But it's perfectly normal for a child this age to prefer running, jumping, and climbing to walking slowly or sitting still. He also may speak so fast that it's hard to understand him, and you may worry about his short attention span, but be patient. This excess energy usually subsides by the time he reaches school age.

While the energy level is high, it makes more sense for parents to adjust than to try to force the child to slow down. If your toddler is a "mover," adjust your expectations accordingly. Don't expect him to stay seated through a long community meeting or restaurant meal. If you take him shopping, be prepared to move at his pace, not yours. In general, avoid putting him in confining situations where you know you'll both be frustrated, and give him plenty of opportunities to release his excess energy through games involving running, jumping, climbing, and throwing or kicking a ball.

Without strong guidance, a very active child's energy easily can turn toward aggressive or destructive behavior. To avoid this, you need to establish clear and logical rules and enforce them consistently. You also can encourage more low-keyed behavior by praising him whenever he plays quietly or looks at a book for more than a few minutes at a time. It helps, too, to keep his routine of bedtime, mealtimes, baths, and naps as regular as possible so that he has a sense of structure to his day.

A small number of preschool children have problems with hyperactivity and short attention spans that persist beyond the preschool years. Only if these problems interfere with school performance or social behavior do they warrant special treatment. (See *Hyperactivity and the Distractible Child,* page 531.) If you suspect that your child may be having difficulties in these areas, ask your pediatrician to evaluate him.

cian if your child seems very passive or withdrawn, perpetually sad, or highly demanding and unsatisfied most of the time. These could be signs of depression, caused either by some kind of hidden stress or biological problems. If your doctor suspects depression, he'll probably refer your child to a mental health professional for a consultation.

Developmental Health Watch

The developmental milestones listed in this book give you a general idea of the changes you can expect as your child gets older, but don't be alarmed if her development takes a slightly different course. Each child develops at her own pace. Do consult your pediatrician, however, if your child displays any of the following signs of possible developmental delay for this age range.

- **Frequent falling and difficulty with stairs**
- **Persistent drooling or very unclear speech**
- **Inability to build a tower of more than four blocks**
- **Difficulty manipulating small objects**
- **Inability to copy a circle by age three**
- **Inability to communicate in short phrases**
- **No involvement in "pretend" play**
- **Failure to understand simple instructions**
- **Little interest in other children**
- **Extreme difficulty separating from mother**
- **Poor eye contact**
- **Limited interest in toys**

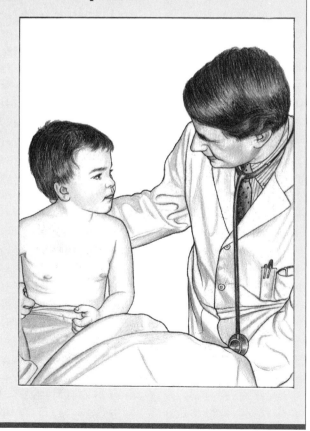

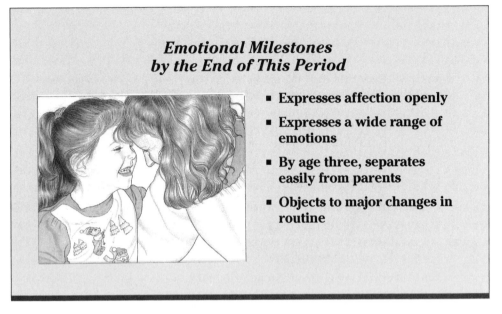

Emotional Milestones by the End of This Period

- Expresses affection openly
- Expresses a wide range of emotions
- By age three, separates easily from parents
- Objects to major changes in routine

BASIC CARE

Feeding and Nutrition

By age two, your toddler should be eating three meals a day, plus one or two snacks. She can eat the same food as the rest of the family. With her improved language and social skills, she'll become an active participant at mealtimes if given the chance to eat with everyone else.

Fortunately, your child's feeding skills have become relatively "civilized" by now. At age two, she can use a spoon, drink from a cup with just one hand, and feed herself a wide variety of finger foods. By age three, she also should be able to use a fork and feed herself independently, spilling between the plate and her mouth only occasionally. But while she can eat properly, she's still learning to chew and swallow efficiently, and may gulp her food when she's in a hurry to get on with playing. For that reason, the risk of choking is high, so avoid the following foods, which could be swallowed whole and block the windpipe.

hot dogs (unless sliced lengthwise, then across)	spoonfuls of peanut butter
	whole raw carrots
nuts (especially peanuts)	raw cherries with pits
round, hard candies	raw celery
whole grapes	

Ideally, your child will eat from each of the basic four food groups each day:

1. Meat, fish, poultry, eggs

2. Milk, cheese, and other dairy products

3. Fruits and vegetables

4. Cereals, potatoes, rice, flour products

Don't be alarmed, however, if she doesn't meet this ideal. Many toddlers resist eating certain foods, or for long periods insist on eating only one or two favorite foods. The more you struggle with your child over her eating preferences, the more determined she'll be to defy you. As we suggested earlier, if you offer her a variety of foods and leave the choices to her, she'll eventually consume a balanced diet on her own. She may be more interested in healthful foods if she can feed them to herself. So, whenever possible, offer her finger foods (i.e., fruits or raw vegetables other than carrots and celery) instead of cooked ones that require a fork or spoon to eat.

Dietary Supplements. Vitamin supplements are rarely necessary for toddlers who eat a varied diet. However, supplemental iron may be needed if your child eats very little meat, iron-fortified cereal, or vegetables rich in iron. Large quantities of milk (more than 32 ounces [960 ml] per day) also may interfere with the proper absorption of iron, thus increasing the risk of iron deficiency. Your child should drink between 16 and 32 ounces (480 and 960 ml) of milk each day. This will provide most of the calcium he needs for bone growth and still not interfere with his appetite for other foods, particularly those that provide iron.

A vitamin D supplement of 200 IU per day is important for children who are not regularly exposed to sunlight, do not consume adequate vitamin D–fortified milk, or do not take a daily multivitamin supplement containing at least 200 IU of vitamin D. This amount of vitamin D can prevent rickets.

Sample One-Day Menu for a Two-Year-Old

This menu is planned for a two-year-old child who weighs approximately 27 pounds (12.5 kg).

1 teaspoon = ⅓ tablespoon (5 ml)
1 tablespoon = ½ ounce (15 ml)
1 ounce = 30 ml
1 cup = 8 ounces (240 ml)

BREAKFAST
¾ cup 2 percent milk
½ cup iron-fortified cereal or 1 egg
½ cup citrus or tomato juice or ⅓ cup cantaloupe or strawberries
½ slice toast
½ teaspoon margarine or butter
1 teaspoon jelly

SNACK
1 ounce cream cheese
4 crackers
½ cup juice

Teething and Dental Hygiene

By age two and a half, your child should have all her primary (or baby) teeth, including the second molars, which usually erupt between twenty and thirty months. Her secondary (or permanent) teeth probably won't start coming in until she's six or seven, although it's quite normal for them to arrive a little earlier or later than this.

As you might guess, the number-one dental problem among preschoolers is tooth decay. Approximately one out of ten two-year-olds already have one or more cavities; by age three, 25 percent of children do; by age five, nearly 50 percent of children do. Many parents assume that cavities in baby teeth don't matter, because they'll be lost anyway. But that's a risky assumption. Dental decay can progress to a painful abscess, and if primary teeth are lost too early because of decay or infection, the secondary teeth won't be ready to replace them. When that happens, the other primary teeth shift position to fill in the gap, so by the time the permanent teeth finally break through, there's no room for them.

LUNCH

½ cup 2 percent milk

½ sandwich—1 slice whole wheat bread, 1 teaspoon margarine (or butter) or 2 teaspoons salad dressing, and 1 ounce meat

2–3 carrot sticks or 2 tablespoons other dark-yellow or dark-green vegetable

1 small (½ ounce) low-fat oatmeal cookie

SNACK

½ cup 2 percent milk

½ apple (sliced), 3 dates, ⅓ cup grapes (cut up), or ½ orange

DINNER

½ cup 2 percent milk

2 ounces meat

⅓ cup pasta, rice, or potato

2 tablespoons vegetable

1 teaspoon margarine (or butter) or 2 teaspoons salad dressing

The best way to protect your child's teeth is to teach her good dental habits. With the proper coaching she'll quickly adopt good oral hygiene as a part of her daily routine. By age two, she should have her teeth brushed at least twice a day. However, while she may be an enthusiastic participant, she won't yet have the control or concentration to brush her teeth all by herself. You'll need to supervise and help her so that the brush removes all the plaque—the soft, sticky, bacteria-containing deposits that accumulate on the teeth, causing tooth decay.

While you should have used a piece of gauze or a damp cloth to wipe your child's teeth when she was younger, change to a toothbrush with a fluoride toothpaste as she becomes older. (Fluoride in the toothpaste is absorbed into the tooth enamel and helps prevent tooth decay.) Be sure to use a soft, multi-tufted nylon-bristle brush. Also use only a small (pea-size) amount of toothpaste on the brush; it's difficult to keep her from swallowing some of the toothpaste, and ingesting too much fluoride can cause permanent white tooth stains (mottling). If she doesn't like the taste of one type of toothpaste, try another or just use plain water for a while. The brushing and rinsing are more important than the toothpaste.

You'll hear all kinds of advice on whether the best brushing motion is up and down, back and forth, or around in circles. The truth is that the direction really doesn't matter. What's important is to clean each tooth thoroughly, top and bottom, inside and out. This is where you'll encounter resistance from your child, who probably will concentrate on only the front teeth that she can see. It may help to turn it into a game of "find the hidden teeth."

Besides regular toothbrushing, your child's diet will play a key role in her dental health. And, of course, sugar is the big villain. The longer and more frequently her teeth are exposed to sugar, the greater the risk of cavities. This means that a giant piece of cake will do virtually no harm if she brushes her teeth immediately after eating it; but sticky caramel, toffee, gum, and dried fruit—particularly when it stays in her mouth and bathes her teeth in sugar for hours—could do serious damage. Discourage these "sticky sugar" foods, especially as between-meal snacks, and do not allow your child to have any sugar-containing liquid in a sippy cup for a prolonged period.

During regular well-child visits, the pediatrician will check your child's teeth and gums to ensure their health. If he notices problems, he may refer your child to a pediatric dentist (pedodontist) or a general dentist with an interest in treating the dental needs of children. Younger than age one, the following circumstances would warrant a trip to the dentist:

- Your child chips or injures a tooth, or experiences an injury to the face or mouth.

- Your child's teeth appear discolored (which might be an indication of tooth decay).

- Your child complains of a painful tooth or is sensitive to hot or cold foods or liquids. (This also might be a sign of tooth decay.)

Children should begin seeing a dentist for regular checkups during the early toddler years. The dentist will make sure her teeth have come in normally and that there are no dental problems. He also may apply a topical fluoride solution to provide extra protection against cavities. If you live in an area where the water is not fluoridated, he may prescribe fluoride drops or chewable tablets for your toddler. For more guidance on fluoride supplements, talk to your pediatrician, and see Chapter 4 ("Feeding Your Baby"), page 117.

Toilet Training

By the time your toddler is two years old, you probably can hardly wait for him to be toilet trained. The pressure to reach that goal may be particularly intense if you want him to enter a nursery school or child care program that requires the children to be trained. Be forewarned, though, that pushing him too early, before he is ready, actually may prolong the process.

In general, you won't cause any damage if you start the training prior to eighteen months of age—as long as you keep your expectations for your child's success realistic and don't punish him if he has difficulty following instructions or has accidents. However, most experts think that toilet training is most effective if it is delayed until the child himself can control much of the process. Studies indicate that many children who begin training before eighteen months are not completely trained until after age four. By contrast, most of those who start around age two are completely trained before their third birthday. The average age of complete training is a little over two and a half years.

Chances are, toilet training won't be very successful until your child is past the extreme negativism and resistance to it that occurs in early toddlerhood. He must want to take this major step. He'll be ready when he seems eager to please and imitate you, but also wants to become more independent. Since he needs to be independent, it is important to avoid power struggles, which will always delay training. Most children reach this stage sometime between eighteen and twenty-four months, but it's also normal for it to occur a little later.

Once your toddler is ready to begin this process, things should proceed smoothly as long as you maintain a relaxed, unpressured attitude. Praise him for his successes, and do not even mention his mistakes along the way. Punish-

For the first few weeks, let him sit on the potty fully clothed while you tell him about the toilet, what it's for, and when to use it.

ing him or making him feel bad when he has an "accident" will only add an unnecessary element of stress, which is bound to hinder his progress.

How should you introduce your toddler to the concept of using the toilet? The best way is to let him watch other family members of his sex. (Watching people of the opposite sex simply may confuse him.) Also talk to him frequently about the process.

The first goal is bowel training. Urination usually occurs with the bowel movement, so at first it is difficult for the child to separate the two acts. Once bowel training is established, however, most children (especially girls) quickly will relate the two. Boys usually learn to empty their bladders in the sitting position but gradually transfer to the standing one, particularly after watching older boys do it that way.

The first step in training is to obtain a potty chair and place it in your child's room or in the nearest or most convenient bathroom. Then do the following:

1. For the first few weeks, let him sit on the potty fully clothed while you tell him about the toilet, what it's for, and when to use it.

2. Once he sits on it willingly, let him try it with his diaper off. Show him how to keep his feet planted solidly on the floor, since this will be important when he's having a bowel movement. Make the potty part of his routine, gradually increasing sitting on it from once to several times each day.

3. When he's comfortable with this pattern, try changing his diaper while he's seated, and actually drop the contents of the dirty diaper into the pot under him to let him know that this is the chair's real purpose.

4. Once your child grasps how this process works, he'll probably be more interested in using the potty properly. To encourage this, let him play near the chair without a diaper and remind him to use the potty when he needs to. He's bound to forget or miss at first, but don't show your disappointment. Instead, wait until he succeeds and reward him with excitement and praise.

5. After he is using the potty chair regularly, gradually switch over from diapers to training pants during the day. At this point, most boys quickly learn to urinate into an adult toilet by imitating their fathers or older boys. Both girls and boys may be able to use adult toilets outfitted with training seats.

Like most children, your own toddler probably will take a little longer to complete nap- and nighttime toilet training. Even so, encourage these steps along with daytime training, and stress them even more after he's routinely using the potty. The best approach is to encourage your toddler to use the potty immediately before going to bed and as soon as he wakes up. Using training pants rather than diapers at nap time and bedtime may also help. Yes, there will be a few accidents, but a plastic sheet under the cloth one will minimize the cleanup. Reassure your toddler that all children have these accidents, and praise him whenever he makes it through the nap or night without wetting. Also tell him that if he wakes up in the middle of the night and needs to use the toilet, he can either go by himself or call for you to help him.

Your goal is to make this entire process as positive, natural, and nonthreatening as possible so he's not afraid to make the effort on his own. If nap-time or nighttime wetting is still a consistent problem one year after daytime training is complete, discuss the situation with your pediatrician.

Sleeping

Between ages two and three, your child may sleep from nine to thirteen hours a day. Most toddlers take a two- to three-hour nap around lunchtime, but some continue to take two shorter naps instead. Others give up napping entirely during this period. Unless she routinely becomes irritable and overtired from lack of sleep, there's no reason to force a nap schedule on your child.

At bedtime, your toddler may become downright rigid about her going-to-sleep ritual. She now knows that at a certain time each day she changes into her nightclothes, brushes her teeth, listens to a story, and takes her favorite blanket, doll, or stuffed animal to bed. If you change this routine, she may complain or even have trouble going to sleep.

However, even with a completely predictable bedtime routine, some children between the ages of two and three resist going to sleep. If they're still in a crib, they may cry when left alone or even climb out to look for Mom and Dad. If they've graduated to a bed, they may get up again and again, insisting that they're not tired (even when they're clearly exhausted) or asking to join in whatever else is going on in the household. Part of this pattern is due to the typical negativism of this age—that is, the refusal to do anything Mom and Dad want them to do—and part is due to lingering separation anxiety. Despite their insistence on independence, they still feel uneasy when parents are out of their sight—especially if they're left alone in the dark.

To give a child like this a feeling of control, let her make as many of the

At bedtime, put your toddler in a good frame of mind for sleep by playing quietly or reading a pleasant story.

choices as possible at bedtime—for example, which pajamas to wear, what story she wants to hear, and which stuffed animals to take to bed. Also, leave a night-light on (she may even be more comfortable with the room light on), and let her sleep with her security objects (see *Transitional Objects,* pages 252–253) to help take the edge off her separation anxiety. If she still cries after you leave, give her ten minutes or so to stop on her own before you go in to settle her down again; then leave for another ten minutes, and repeat the process. Don't scold or punish her, but also don't reward her behavior by feeding or staying with her.

For some children, this bedtime battle is actually an attempt to attract attention. If your toddler climbs out of bed night after night and comes looking for you, immediately return her to bed and tell her: "It's time to go to sleep." Don't reprimand or talk to her any further, and leave as soon as she's lying down again. She'll probably push you to your limits, getting up over and over for many nights in a row; but if you keep calm and remain consistent, she'll eventually realize she has nothing to gain by fighting you, and she'll start going to sleep more willingly.

Occasionally your child may wake up from a nightmare. Bad dreams are common among toddlers, who still cannot distinguish between imagination and reality. Often if they hear a scary story or see violence on television, the images will stay in their minds, later cropping up as nightmares. And if they remember dreaming about a "monster," they may believe the monster is real.

When a nightmare awakens your toddler, the best response is to hold and comfort her. Let her tell you about the dream if she can, and stay with her until she's calm enough to fall asleep.

Your child will have nightmares more frequently when she's anxious or under stress. If she has bad dreams often, see if you can determine what's worrying her in order to ease her anxiety. For example, if she's having nightmares during the period when she's being toilet trained, relax the pressure to use the potty and give her more opportunities to be messy through fingerpainting or playing with her food. Also try talking with her (to the extent she can) about issues that might be bothering her. Some of her anxieties may involve her separation from you, time spent in child care, or changes at home. Talking sometimes can help prevent these stressful feelings from building up.

As a general precaution against nightmares, carefully select television programs for your toddler, and don't allow her to watch TV right before bed. Even programs you consider innocent may contain images that are frightening to her. During the rest of the day, restrict her viewing to educational or nature programs geared to her age level. Don't let her watch violent programs of any kind, including many cartoons.

At bedtime, put your toddler in a good frame of mind for sleep by playing quietly with her or by reading her a pleasant story. Soothing music also may help calm her as she falls asleep, and a night-light will help reassure her if she wakes up.

Discipline

What's the greatest challenge facing you as a parent during this and the next few years? Without a doubt, it's discipline. As you'll see, your child will develop the ability to control his impulses very gradually. At ages two and three, he'll still be very physical, using temper tantrums, pushing, shoving, and quarreling to get his own way. Most of these reactions are very impulsive; although he doesn't plan to behave this way, he cannot control himself yet. Whether he consciously understands it or not, the whole point of his misbehavior is to find not only his limits but yours, as well.

How you choose to establish and enforce these limits is a very personal issue. Some parents are quite strict, punishing their children whenever they violate a household rule; others are more lenient, preferring reason to punishment. Whatever approach you choose, if it's going to work, it must suit your child's temperament, and you also must feel comfortable enough with it to use it consistently. You'll find other helpful suggestions in *Some Golden Rules of Preschool Discipline* on pages 326–327.

Preparing for School

Kindergarten usually is considered the "official" start of school. But many children get a taste of school much earlier, through preschool, nursery school, or group child care programs that may accept children as young as two or three. These programs generally are not designed to begin your child's academic or book-learning education, but they will help her get used to the idea of leaving home for a period of time each day and introduce her to the idea of learning in a group. They'll also give her a chance to improve her social skills by meeting and playing with other children and adults, as well as introducing her to more formal rules than you may have established at home. A preschool program may be especially beneficial if your child doesn't have many opportunities to meet other youngsters or adults, or if she has unusual talents or developmental problems that might benefit from special attention.

Aside from these advantages for your child, a preschool or child care program may help you meet some of your own needs. Perhaps you're going back to work now, or have a new baby at home. Maybe you just want a few hours to yourself each day. At this stage of your child's development, the separation can be good for both of you.

If you've never regularly spent much time apart from your child, you may feel sad or guilty about this new separation. You also may feel a little jealous if she becomes attached to her preschool teacher, especially if—in a moment of anger—she insists she likes her teacher better than you. But face it: You know very well that her teacher can't replace you, any more than preschool can replace your child's home life. These new relationships help her learn that there's a world of caring people in addition to her family. This is an important lesson for her to learn as she gets ready for the much larger world of primary school.

Some Golden Rules of Preschool Discipline

Whether you're a strict disciplinarian or use a more easygoing approach, the following guidelines should help you shape a strategy of discipline that ultimately will benefit both you and your child.

1. Always encourage and reward good behavior and punish the bad. Whenever you have a choice, take the positive route. For example, let's say your two-year-old is moving toward the stove; you should try to distract him with a safe activity instead of waiting for him to get into trouble. And when you notice that he has independently chosen to do something acceptable instead of misbehaving, congratulate him on making the right decision. By showing that you're proud of him, you'll make him feel good about himself and encourage him to behave the same way in the future.

2. Map out rules that help your child learn to control his impulsiveness and behave well socially without impairing his drive for independence. If your rules are overly restrictive, he may be afraid to explore on his own or try out new skills.

3. Always keep your child's developmental level in mind when you set limits, and don't expect more than he's capable of achieving. For example, a two- or three-year-old can't control the impulse to touch things that attract him, so it's unrealistic for you to expect him not to touch displays at the grocery or toy store.

4. Set the punishment to your child's developmental level. For example, if you decide to send your toddler to his room for misbe-

When you're hit by pangs of sadness, guilt, or jealousy, remind yourself that these structured separations will help your child become more independent, experienced, and mature, and also give you valuable time to pursue your own interests and needs. In the end, this time apart actually will strengthen the bond between the two of you.

Ideally, every preschool or nursery school program should offer children a safe and stimulating environment supervised by attentive, supportive adults. Unfortunately, not all programs meet these basic requirements. How can you distinguish the good from the bad? Here are some things to look for.

1. The school should have stated goals with which you agree. A good preschool tries to help children gain self-confidence, become more independent, and develop interpersonal skills. Be wary of programs that claim to teach academic skills or "speed up" children's intellectual development. From a de-

having, don't keep him there for more than about five minutes; any longer, and he'll forget why he's there. If you prefer to reason with him, keep the discussion simple and practical. Never use hypothetical statements such as "How would you like it if I did that to you?" No preschooler can understand this kind of reasoning.

5. Don't change the rules or the punishments at random. That will only confuse your child. As he grows older, you naturally will expect more mature behavior, but when you change the rules at that time, tell him why. For example, you may tolerate his pulling on your clothes to get your attention when he's two, but by the time he's four, you may want him to find more grown-up ways of approaching you. Once you make the decision to change a rule, explain it to him before you start to enforce it.

6. Make sure that all the adults in the house and other caregivers agree to and understand the limits and punishments used to discipline your child. If one parent says something is OK and the other forbids it, the child is bound to be confused. Eventually he'll figure out that he can get his way by playing one adult against the other, which will make your lives miserable now and in the future. You can prevent this game-playing by presenting a united front.

7. Remember that you are a key role model for your child. The more even-handed and controlled your behavior, the more likely your child will be to pattern himself after you. If, on the other hand, you hit or spank him every time he breaks a rule, you're teaching him that it's OK to solve problems through violence.

velopmental standpoint, most preschoolers are not yet ready to begin formal education, and pushing them will only prejudice them against learning. If you suspect that your child is ready to take on more educational challenges, ask your pediatrician to evaluate her or refer her to a child development specialist. If testing supports your suspicions, look for a program that will nurture her natural curiosity and talents without pressuring her to perform.

2. For a child with special needs—such as language or hearing impairment, behavioral or developmental problems—contact the director of special education in your local school system for a referral to appropriate programs in your area. Many neighborhood programs are not equipped to provide special therapy or counseling, and may make your child feel "behind" or out of place among the other children.

Extinction

Extinction is a disciplinary technique that is most effective with two- and three-year-olds, although it can be useful into the school years. The idea is to ignore the child systematically whenever he breaks a certain rule. As you might guess, this method should be used for misbehavior that's annoying or undesirable but not dangerous or destructive; the latter needs the more direct, immediate approach already discussed.

Here's how "extinction" works.

1. Define exactly what your child is doing wrong. Does he scream for attention in public? Does he cling to you when you're trying to do something else? Be very specific about the behavior and the circumstances in which it occurs.

2. Keep track of how often your child does this, and what you do in response. Do you try to pacify him? Do you stop what you're doing to pay attention to him? If so, you're unwittingly encouraging him to keep misbehaving over and over.

3. Keep recording the frequency of his misbehavior as you begin to ignore it. Remember, the key is consistency. Even if every person in the grocery store is glaring at you, do not show your child that you hear him screaming. Just keep doing what you're doing. At first, he'll probably act out more intensely and more frequently to test your will, but eventually he'll realize that you mean business.

4. When your child acts properly in a situation where he usually misbehaves, be sure to compliment him. If, instead of screaming when you refuse to buy him a candy bar, he talks to you in a normal voice, praise him for acting so grown up.

5. If you manage to extinguish the misbehavior for a while and then it reappears, start the process over again. It probably won't take as long the second time.

3. Look for programs with a relatively small class size. Two- to three-year-olds do best in classes of eight to ten children, with close adult supervision. By age four, your child will need slightly less direct supervision and thus may enjoy a group of up to sixteen. Here are the American Academy of Pediatrics standards for the ratio of child-to-staff:

Age	Maximum Child: Staff Ratio	Maximum Group Size
13–30 mos.	4:1	8
31–35 mos.	5:1	10
3-year-olds	7:1	14
4-year-olds	8:1	16

4. Teachers and aides should be trained in early-childhood development or education. Be suspicious of schools with an extremely high turnover rate among the staff. Not only does this reflect poorly on the school's appeal to good teachers, but it also makes it difficult to find people who know anything about the teachers who are now there.

5. Make sure you agree with the disciplinary methods used. Limit-setting should be firm and consistent without discouraging each child's need to explore. Rules should reflect the developmental level of the children in the program, and teachers should be supportive and helpful without stifling creativity and independent learning.

6. You should be welcome to observe your child at any time. While it may disrupt the daily routine to have parents coming and going, this openness reassures you that the program is consistent and the school has nothing to hide.

7. The school and grounds should be thoroughly child-proofed. (See Chapter 14 on safety.) Make sure there's an adult present at all times who knows basic first aid, including cardiopulmonary resuscitation (CPR—emergency breathing and heart stimulation techniques to revive a person who has stopped breathing or whose heart has stopped beating) and how to care for a child who's choking.

A preschool program may be especially beneficial if your child doesn't have many opportunities to meet other youngsters or adults.

Stimulating Child Brain Growth: Third Year

The third year of your child's life is an important time in the development of his brain. As we described earlier, your child's physical growth may slow during this time, but his brain and his intellectual growth are moving full speed ahead. Just as you've made an effort to stimulate his brain growth from birth, you should continue doing so during this crucial year. Here are some suggestions:

- Encourage creative play, building, and drawing. Provide the time and tools for playful learning.

- Be attentive to your child's rhythms and moods. Respond to her when she is upset as well as when she is happy. Be encouraging and supportive, with firm discipline as appropriate, but without yelling, hitting, or shaking. Provide consistent guidelines and rules.

- Give consistent warm, physical contact—hugging, skin-to-skin, body-to-body contact—to establish your child's sense of security and well-being.

- Talk to or sing to your child during dressing, bathing, feeding, playing, walking, and driving, using adult talk. Speak slowly and give your child time to respond. Try not to reply with "uh-huh" because your child will recognize when you're not listening; instead, expand on your child's phrases.

- Read to your child every day. Choose books that encourage touching and pointing to objects, and read rhymes, jingles, and nursery stories.

- If you speak a foreign language, use it at home.

- Introduce your child to musical instruments (toy pianos, drums, etc.). Musical skills can influence math and problem-solving skills.

8. There should be a clear policy about illness among the children. In general, children with a fever should be excluded whenever the fever is accompanied by behavioral changes or by symptoms of illness that may need a doctor's attention; children whose symptoms indicate an infectious disease should be sent home. At the same time, keep in mind that the presence of a fever alone should not keep a child from participating in child care, since the fever itself isn't particularly relevant to whether the disease will spread to other children.

- Play calm and melodic music for your child.

- Listen to and answer your child's questions.

- Spend one-on-one personal time with your child each day.

- Offer your child simple choices in appropriate situations throughout the day (Peanut butter or cheese? Red T-shirt or yellow?).

- Help your child use words to describe emotions and to express feelings such as happiness, joy, anger, and fear.

- Limit your child's television viewing and video time; avoid violent cartoons. Monitor what your child does watch and discuss programs with your child. Don't use the TV as a babysitter.

- Promote out-of-home social experiences such as preschool programs and play groups in which your child can play and interact with other children.

- Acknowledge desirable behavior frequently (e.g., "I like it when the two of you play together").

- Make sure other people who provide care and supervision for your child understand the importance of forming a loving and comforting relationship with her.

- Spend time on the floor playing with your child every day.

- Choose quality child care that is affectionate, responsive, educational, and safe; visit your child care provider frequently and share your ideas about positive caregiving.

9. Hygiene is very important to minimize the spread of infectious illness among the children. Make sure there are child-height sinks and that children are encouraged to wash their hands when appropriate, especially after using the toilet. If the school accepts youngsters who are not yet toilet trained, a diaper-changing area isolated from child activity and eating areas is absolutely necessary to control the spread of infectious disease.

10. Be certain you agree with the program's overall philosophy. Find out ahead of time how the school's philosophy affects the curriculum, and decide

Programs for Children with Potential Learning Difficulties

Some young children who regularly fail to meet the developmental milestones for their age are at greater risk of having trouble learning in school. Early identification and intervention for such children may prevent later problems in school and may help you deal with the day-to-day difficulties you might be experiencing. (See *Hyperactivity and the Distractible Child,* page 531.)

If your pediatrician shares your concern, and the teacher (an invaluable source of information) also agrees, an additional professional evaluation may be suggested. But don't be alarmed. A learning disability is just a difficulty that any child could experience while trying to learn new information. It may only mean a problem with reading or understanding what is said to him.

Federal law (the Individuals with Disabilities Education Act [IDEA]) encourages the establishment of state-supported services for infants and preschoolers who need special help to promote their early development and prepare them for school. Although the actual way in which this law has been put into action varies from state to state, most states provide services for children who are at least three years old, and some provide programs beginning in early infancy. Children may be referred to these programs by their parents, pediatricians, preschool teachers, or any concerned adult. Recommendations for assistance are based on the child's needs and the available programs. Most of these services involve some form of nursery school or specialized preschool. (See also Chapter 19, "Developmental Disabilities.")

---

whether this is right for your family. Many preschools are connected with churches, synagogues, or other religious organizations. Children do not generally have to be members of the congregation in order to attend the program, but they may be exposed to certain rituals of faith.

For more information about child care and preschool programs, see Chapter 13.

A Message for Grandparents

The second year of a child's life, encompassing the so-called terrible twos, is often a challenging one for parents and therefore for grandparents, as well. A youngster at this age is showing increased physical activity, greater mood swings, frequent tantrums or demanding behavior, and testing the limits of all adults.

As a grandparent, you may have forgotten what two-year-olds are like; after all, it's been many years since you raised your own children through this age. Here are some guidelines to keep in mind when you spend time with your two-year-old grandchild (although some of these steps are more easily said than done).

- Make an effort to "keep your cool." Don't overreact to outbursts. Try to take them in stride, and realize that much of this behavior is designed to get you to react. Maintain a flexible but firm response.

- Be consistent in your approach to discipline, and make sure it's consistent with the disciplinary style of the youngster's parents. *Never use physical punishment.*

- Reinforce good behaviors with praise and compliments. Become a role model of the way you would like your grandchild to act.

- Try to encourage self-control.

- Always be affectionate.

- Recognize that children of this age are very egocentric (i.e., they are thinking mostly of "me," not of the others in their life), so don't take their lack of interest in you personally. This is normal for a two-year-old, and it won't last forever.

Toilet training will be one of your grandchild's most important accomplishments at this age. Talk to his parents about the stage of training he's in, and how you can reinforce what he has already achieved, particularly when you're caring for him—babysitting on a Saturday afternoon or caring for him for the weekend. If he spends time in your home, purchase some extra training pants and have a potty chair identical to the one he is accustomed to at home.

Finally, always remember to place your grandchild in a car safety seat in the backseat for every trip in the automobile.

FAMILY RELATIONSHIPS

A New Baby

During this year, if you decide to have another baby, you can expect your toddler to greet this news with considerable jealousy. After all, at this age he doesn't yet understand the concept of sharing time, possessions, or your affection. Nor is he eager to have someone else become the center of the family's attention.

The best way to minimize his jealousy is to start preparing him several months before the new baby is born. Let him help shop for clothes and equipment for the infant. If your hospital offers a sibling preparation class, take him there during the last month of pregnancy so he can see where the baby will be born and where he can visit you. Discuss what it will be like having a new member of the family and how he can help his little brother or sister. (See *Preparing Your Other Children for the Baby's Arrival*, page 23.)

Once the baby is home, encourage your toddler to help and play with the newborn, but don't force him. If he shows an interest, give him some tasks that will make him feel like a big brother, such as disposing of dirty diapers and picking out the baby's clothes or bath toys. And when you're playing with the baby, invite him to join you and show him how to hold and move the baby. Make sure he understands, however, that he's not to do these things unless you or another adult is present. Remember to reserve special time for older siblings.

Hero Worship

Does your preschooler have older siblings? If so, you'll probably start seeing signs of hero worship around age two. In the young child's eyes, older brothers

If he shows an interest, give the older sibling some tasks that will make him feel like a big brother.

In the young child's eyes, his older brother or sister can do no wrong.

or sisters can do no wrong. They are perfect role models—people who are strong and independent, but still play like kids.

This kind of relationship has both benefits and drawbacks. Your preschooler probably will follow her older sibling around like a lapdog. This will give you some freedom, and it's usually fun for both children for a while. But before long, your older youngster will want his freedom back, which is bound to cause some disappointment—and perhaps tears or misbehavior—from your little one. Nevertheless, it's up to you to make sure that she doesn't overstay her welcome with big brother or sister. If you don't step in, their relationship will become strained.

If the older child is eight or more, he probably already has a fairly independent life, with friends and activities outside the home. Given the chance, your preschooler will tag along with him everywhere he goes. You shouldn't allow this unless the older child desires it or you, too, are going along and can keep the little one from becoming a pest. If the older child is of babysitting age, compensating him for taking care of your preschooler when you're out will help prevent resentment.

Pressures and rivalries are inevitable between siblings, but if there's a healthy balance between comradeship and independence, the bond between your children should grow and contribute to the self-esteem of both of them. Through her older sibling, your preschooler will get a sense of family values as well as a preview of what it's like to be a "big kid." The older child, meanwhile, will discover what it means to be a hero in his own home.

Being a role model for a younger brother or sister is a big responsibility, of course, and if you point this out to your older child, it may prompt an improvement in behavior. If you feel he's a bad influence on his younger sibling, however, and he doesn't improve, you have no choice but to separate the two whenever he's misbehaving. Otherwise, your preschooler will mimic him and soon pick up bad habits. Don't embarrass the older child by punishing him in front of the preschooler, but make sure the younger one understands the difference between "good" and "bad" behavior.

VISIT TO THE PEDIATRICIAN

Beginning at twenty-four months of age, your child should see the pediatrician for a routine examination once a year. In addition to the screening tests performed during his earlier examinations, he may undergo the following laboratory tests.

- A *blood test* to check for lead poisoning.

- A *urinalysis* to check for infection and kidney and metabolic diseases. If the results of the first urinalysis are normal, it may not be repeated at future visits unless there are symptoms of a urinary-tract infection or related problems. However, some pediatricians do "dipstick" tests for sugar and protein at each regular checkup.

- A *skin test for tuberculosis* may be given annually, depending on the risk of possible exposure.

IMMUNIZATION ALERT

By age two, your child should have received most of her childhood immunizations. These include the hepatitis B series, the Hib vaccine series against *Haemophilus influenzae* type b, the vaccine series against pneumococcus, the first three doses of the polio vaccine, the first four doses of DTaP, the first dose of the measles, mumps, rubella (MMR) vaccine, and the chickenpox (varicella) vaccine. Certain states have an increased incidence of infections caused by hepatitis A, and your pediatrician may recommend starting a two-dose series. Also remember to have your child obtain booster doses for DTaP, polio, and MMR at school entry or four to six years of age.

WHERE WE STAND

When children have a chronic, serious illness or disability, their parents often turn to complementary and alternative medicine as an adjunct to the conventional care their child is receiving from their pediatrician or other mainstream practitioner, even when they're happy with this traditional care. In some cases, they may have become frustrated with what mainstream medicine offered their youngster, and they've turned to alternative treatment, which continues to increase in popularity.

If you've made the decision to seek alternative approaches for your child's care, involve your pediatrician in the process. Your doctor may be able to help you better understand these therapies, whether they have scientific merit, whether claims about them are accurate or exaggerated, and whether they pose any risks to your child's well-being. Keep in mind that a "natural" treatment does not always mean a "safe" one. Your pediatrician can help you determine whether there is a risk of interactions with your youngster's other medications.

The American Academy of Pediatrics has encouraged pediatricians to evaluate the scientific merits of alternative treatments, determine whether they might cause any direct or indirect harm, and advise parents on the full range of treatment options. If you decide to use an alternative therapy, your pediatrician also may be able to assist in evaluating your child's response to that treatment.

SAFETY CHECK

Your preschooler is now able to run, jump, and ride a tricycle. His natural curiosity will drive him to explore many new things, including some dangerous places. Unfortunately, his self-control and ability to rescue himself are not yet fully developed, so he still needs careful supervision. (See Chapter 14 for additional information on safety.)

Falls

- Lock doors to any dangerous areas and hide the keys.

- Install stairway gates and window guards.

Burns

- Keep her away from kitchen appliances, irons, and wall or floor heaters.
- Place plug covers on all outlets.
- Keep electrical cords out of reach.

Poisonings

- Keep all medicines in child-resistant containers and locked up high and out of reach.
- Store only those household products and medicines that are used regularly, and keep them in a locked cabinet.
- Post the universal Poison Control Center phone number—1–800–222–1222 in the United States—next to every telephone.

Car Safety

- Supervise your child closely whenever he's playing in the driveway or near the street.
- Use approved and properly installed car safety seats or booster seats for every ride.

12

AGE THREE TO FIVE YEARS

W ith your child's third birthday, the "terrible twos" are officially over and the "magic years" of three and four begin—a time when your child's world will be dominated by fantasy and vivid imagination. No longer a toddler, he is becoming more independent and, at the same time, more responsive to other children. This is a perfect age to introduce him to nursery school or an organized play group, where he can stretch his skills while learning to socialize.

During the next two years, he'll mature in many areas, including toilet training and learning how to take proper care of his body. Since he can control and direct his movements now, he'll be able to play more organized games and sports. He also has mastered the basic rules of language and has built an impressive vocabulary that will increase daily as he experiments with words. Language will play an important role in his behavior, too, as he learns to express his desires and feelings verbally instead of through physical actions such as grabbing, hitting, or crying. Helping him put all his new skills together so he feels confident and capable is one of the most important ways you can guide his self-discipline during this period.

Your relationship with your child will change dramatically during this time. Emotionally, he is now able to view you as a separate person, with feelings and needs he's beginning to understand. When you're sad, he may render some sympathy or offer to solve your problems. If you become angry at another person, he may announce that he, too, "hates" that individual. He wants very much to please you at this age, and knows that he must do certain things and behave in certain ways to do so. At the same time, though, he wants to please himself, so he'll often try to bargain with you: "If I do this for you, will you do that for me?" At times when you simply want him to behave as you desire, this attempt at bargaining may be irritating, but it's a healthy sign of independence, and it shows that he has a clear sense of justice.

By his fifth birthday, your "baby" will be ready to tackle "real" school—the major occupation of childhood. This enormous step demonstrates that he's able to behave within the limits expected by school and society and has the skills to take on increasingly complex learning challenges. It also means that he's able to separate comfortably from you and move out on his own. Not only can he now share and show concern for others, but also he has learned to value friends—both children and adults—outside his own family.

GROWTH AND DEVELOPMENT

Physical Appearance and Growth

Your child's body should continue to lose baby fat and gain muscle during this time, giving her a stronger and more mature appearance. Her arms and legs will become more slender and her upper body more narrow and tapered. In some children, gains in height occur so much more quickly than gains in weight and muscle that they may begin to look quite skinny and fragile. But this doesn't mean they are unhealthy or that anything is wrong; such children fill out gradually as their muscles develop.

Your preschooler's growth gradually will slow from about 5 pounds (2.3 kg) and 3½ inches (8.9 cm) during the third year to about 4½ pounds (2 kg) and 2½ inches (6.4 cm) during the fifth. Measure your child twice a year and record her measurements on her growth charts on pages 128–129. If her weight seems to be rising much faster than her height, she may be getting too fat, or if her height does not increase at all in six months, she may have a growth problem. In either case, discuss this with your pediatrician.

Your child's face also will mature during these years. The length of her skull will increase slightly, and the lower jaw will become more pronounced. At the same time, the upper jaw will widen to make room for her permanent teeth. As a result, her face actually will become larger and her features more distinct.

How to Measure Your Child

Although your child may visit the doctor only once a year during the preschool period, you might want to measure and weigh him every six months. But you'll need his cooperation to get an accurate measurement of his height, so make it a special event. Start by establishing a special place where you can record the height. For example, you may want to make or buy a measuring scroll that can be fastened to the wall or the back of a door. Such a scroll usually is illustrated and has measurements marked up to about five feet. Space is available to note the child's height along with his age and the date. Alternatively, you can use a doorframe or wall. If you record the measurements there over a period of years, however, you'll have to be careful not to paint over it during remodeling. It's great fun for both you and your child to look back and see how he's grown.

To take the measurement, have him back up against the wall, bare feet flat on the floor. His head should be straight so that he's looking directly in front of him. Then use a ruler, book, or other firm, flat device to accurately line up the top of his head before making the mark on the wall.

AGE THREE TO FOUR YEARS

Movement

At age three, your preschooler no longer has to concentrate on the mechanics of standing, running, jumping, or walking. His movements are now quite agile, whether he's going forward, backward, or up and down stairs. While walking he stands erect, shoulders pulled back and belly held in by firm abdominal muscles. He uses a regular heel-toe motion, taking steps of the same length, width, and speed. He also can ride a tricycle with great ease.

However, not everything comes easily yet. Your child still may need to make a conscious effort while standing on tiptoes or on one foot, while getting up from a squatting position, or while catching a ball. But if he keeps his arms extended and stiffly forward, he can catch a large ball as well as throw a smaller one overhand quite smoothly.

Your three-year-old still may be as active as he was at two, but he'll probably be more interested in structured games at this age. Instead of running aimlessly or flitting from one activity to another, he'll probably ride his tricycle or play in the sandbox for long periods at a time. He also may enjoy active games such as tag, catch, or playing ball with other children.

Your preschooler may seem to be in constant motion much of the time. This is because he uses his body to convey thoughts and emotions that he still can't describe through language. Moving his body also helps him better understand many words and concepts that are new to him. For example, if you start talking about an airplane, he may spread his wings and "fly" around the room. While at times this level of activity may be annoying and distracting for you, it's a necessary part of his learning process and his fun.

Because your child's self-control, judgment, and coordination are still developing, adult supervision remains essential to prevent injuries. However, it's a mistake to fuss too much over him. A few bumps and bruises are inevitable and even necessary to help him discover his limits in physical activity. As a general rule, usually you can leave him alone when he's playing by himself in his room. He'll play at his own pace, attempting only those tasks that are within his abilities. Your concern and attention should be reserved for situations when he's around other children, hazardous equipment or machinery, and especially traffic. Other children may tease or tempt him to do things that are dangerous, while machines, equipment, and traffic defy his ability to predict their actions or speed. And he still cannot anticipate the consequences of actions such as chasing a ball into traffic or sticking his hand into the spokes of his tricycle, so you'll have to protect him in these situations.

Movement Milestones
by the End of This Period

- **Hops and stands on one foot up to five seconds**
- **Goes upstairs and downstairs without support**
- **Kicks ball forward**
- **Throws ball overhand**
- **Catches bounced ball most of the time**
- **Moves forward and backward with agility**

Hand and Finger Skills

At age three, your child is developing both the muscular control and the concentration she needs to master many precision finger and hand movements. You'll notice that now she can move each of her fingers independently or together, which means that instead of grasping her crayon in her fist she can hold it like an adult, with thumb on one side and fingers on the other. Now she will be able to trace a square, copy a circle, or scribble freely.

Because her spatial awareness has developed quite a bit, she's more sensitive to the relationships among objects, so she'll position her toys with great care during play and control the way she holds utensils and tools to perform specific tasks. This increased sensitivity and control will allow her to build a tower of nine or more cubes, feed herself without spilling very much, pour water from a pitcher into a cup (using two hands), unbutton clothes, and possibly put large buttons into buttonholes.

She's also extremely interested in discovering what she can do with tools such as scissors and paper and with materials such as clay, paint, and crayons. She now has the skill to manipulate these objects and is beginning to experiment with using them to make other things. At first she'll play randomly with craft materials, perhaps identifying the end product only after it's completed. Looking at her scribbles, for example, she might decide they look like a dog. But soon this will change, and she'll decide what she wants to make before starting

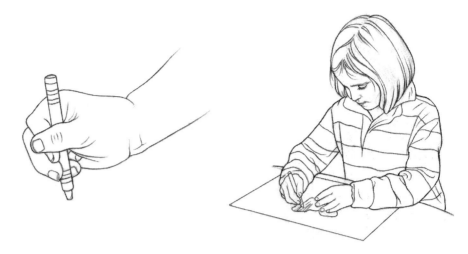

to work on it. This change in approach will motivate her to develop even more precision in moving and using her hands.

Quiet-time activities that can help improve your child's hand abilities include:

- Building with blocks
- Solving simple jigsaw puzzles (four or five large pieces)
- Playing with pegboards
- Stringing large wooden beads
- Coloring with crayons or chalk
- Building sand castles
- Pouring water into containers of various sizes
- Dressing and undressing dolls in clothing with large zippers, snaps, and laces

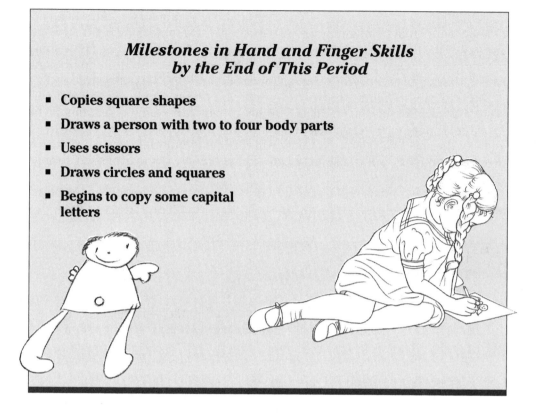

Milestones in Hand and Finger Skills by the End of This Period

- **Copies square shapes**
- **Draws a person with two to four body parts**
- **Uses scissors**
- **Draws circles and squares**
- **Begins to copy some capital letters**

You can encourage your child to use her hands by teaching her to use certain adult tools. She'll be thrilled to progress to a real screwdriver, a lightweight hammer, an eggbeater, or gardening tools. You'll need to supervise closely, of course, but if you let her help as you work, you may be surprised how much of the job she can do herself.

Language Development

At age three, your child should have an active vocabulary of three hundred or more words. He'll be able to talk in sentences of five or six words and imitate most adult speech sounds. At times he'll seem to be chattering constantly—a phenomenon that sometimes may disturb you but that is essential to his learning of new words and gaining experience in using and thinking with them. Language allows him to express his thoughts, and the more advanced he is in speaking and understanding words, the more tools he'll have for thinking, creating, and telling you about it.

You should be able to see how your child uses language to help him understand and participate in the things going on around him. For instance, he can name most familiar objects, and he'll freely ask "What's this?" when he can't call something by name. You can help him expand his vocabulary by providing additional words that he might not even request. For example, if he points to a car and says, "Big car," you might answer, "Yes, that's a big gray car. Look how shiny the surface is." Or if he's helping you pick flowers, describe each one he collects: "That's a beautiful white-and-yellow daisy, and that's a pink geranium."

You also can help him use words to describe things and ideas he can't see. When he's describing the "monster" in his dream, for example, ask him if the monster is angry or friendly. Ask him about the monster's color, where he lives, and whether he has friends. Not only will this help your child use words to express his thoughts, but it also may help him overcome his fear of such strange and frightening images.

Your three-year-old is still learning to use pronouns such as "I," "me," "mine," and "you." As simple as these words seem, they're difficult ideas to grasp be-

Stuttering

Many parents experience anxiety over their child's stuttering, even though such concern is usually unnecessary. After all, it's quite common for children to repeat syllables, sounds, or words occasionally, or to hesitate between words at around age two or three. Most of them never realize they're talking incorrectly, and they grow out of it without any special help. Only when this pattern persists over a long period of time (greater than two to three months) and interferes with communication is it considered actual stuttering.

About one in twenty preschool children stutter at some point, most often between the ages of two and six, when language is being developed, with a threefold greater incidence in boys than in girls. The cause is unknown. Some children may have trouble learning the normal timing and rhythm of speech, but most have no medical or developmental problems. Stuttering may increase when a child is anxious, tired, ill, or when he gets excited and tries to talk too rapidly. Some children stutter when learning too many new words at once. At other times, the child's thoughts are running ahead of his speech and he loses track of what he is saying in midsentence. Repeating a sound or word allows him to catch up. In some youngsters who stutter, the pitch of their voice may rise as they repeat syllables or sounds; or they may open their mouth to speak but nothing comes out for a few moments.

The more frustrated a child becomes about his stuttering, the more trouble he will have with it. Thus the best approach for parents is simply to ignore the stuttering. Listen when he speaks, but don't correct him. Don't interrupt him or finish sentences for him, and make it

cause they indicate where his body, possessions, or authority ends and someone else's begins. And to complicate matters, the terms change depending on
who's talking. Often he may use his name instead of saying "I" or "me." Or when
talking to you, he may say "Mommy" instead of "you." If you try to correct him
(e.g., by suggesting, "Say 'I would like a cookie' "), you'll only confuse him more,
because he'll think you're talking about yourself. Instead, use these pronouns
correctly in your own speech. So, for instance, say "I would like you to come" instead of "Mommy would like you to come." Not only will this help him learn the
correct use of these words, but it also will help him establish a sense of you as
an individual apart from your role as Mommy.

At this age, your child's speech should be clear enough that even strangers
can understand most of what he says. Even so, he still may mispronounce as
many as half the speech sounds he uses. For example, he may use *w* for *r* ("wab-

clear through your body language that you're interested in listening
to him. At the same time, you can set a good example by talking
calmly and correctly, and using simple language when addressing the
child. It also may help him if you slow the entire pace of your household, including the speed at which you (and other family members)
speak; your own slower rate of speech will be more helpful than
telling your youngster that he needs to talk more slowly.

You also should set aside some relaxed time each day to play and
talk quietly with your youngster, giving him all of your attention free
of distractions, and letting him decide the activities that you'll do together. You can build his self-esteem and confidence by praising him
for all the activities he's doing correctly, while not drawing attention
to his speech difficulties. Don't show any signs that you're annoyed,
frustrated, or embarrassed by his stuttering (avoid statements like
"Talk slower!" "Say it again more clearly this time!" or "Relax!"), and
demonstrate that you are accepting of him. Reinforce the things that
he does well. In an environment of acceptance, the anxiety associated
with stuttering will be reduced, which will help him conquer the
problem. With your support, usually he can overcome his true stuttering difficulty before entering school.

When a child's stuttering is severe, speech therapy may be necessary to help avoid a long-term problem. If your child frequently repeats sounds or parts of words, is very self-conscious, and shows
obvious signs of tension (i.e., facial twitches or grimaces), let your
pediatrician know. Also inform her of any family history of serious
stuttering. She'll probably refer you to a speech and language specialist.

If the question is "Why can't the dog talk to me?" you can invite your child to look into the question further by finding a book about dogs.

bit," "wice," "wose"), *d* for *th* ("dis," "dat," "den"), or *t* for any sounds he has trouble with ("tee" for "three," "tik" for "six"). The sounds *b, p, m, w,* and *h* will only begin to emerge midway through this year, and it may take months after that for him to perfect his use of them.

Language Milestones by the End of This Period

- **Understands the concepts of "same" and "different"**
- **Has mastered some basic rules of grammar**
- **Speaks in sentences of five to six words**
- **Speaks clearly enough for strangers to understand**
- **Tells stories**

Cognitive Development

Your three-year-old will spend most of her waking hours questioning everything that happens around her. She loves to ask "Why do I have to . . . ?" and she'll pay close attention to your answers as long as they're simple and to the point. Don't feel that you have to explain your rules fully; she can't yet understand such reasoning and isn't interested in it anyway. If you try to have this kind of "serious" conversation, you'll see her stare into space or turn her attention to more entertaining matters, such as a toy across the room or a truck passing outside the window. Instead, telling her to do something "because it's good for you" or "so you don't get hurt" will make more sense to her than a detailed explanation.

Your child's more abstract "why" questions may be more difficult, partly because there may be hundreds of them each day and also because some of them have no answers—or none that you know. If the question is "Why does the sun shine?" or "Why can't the dog talk to me?" you can answer that you don't know, or invite her to look into the question further by finding a book about the sun or about dogs. Be sure to take these questions seriously. As you do, you help broaden your child's knowledge, feed her curiosity, and teach her to think more clearly.

When your three-year-old is faced with specific learning challenges, you'll find her reasoning still rather one-sided. She can't yet see an issue from two angles, nor can she solve problems that require her to look at more than one factor at the same time. For example, if you take two equal cups of water and pour one into a short, fat container and the other into a tall, skinny one, she'll probably say the tall container holds more water than the short. Even if she sees the

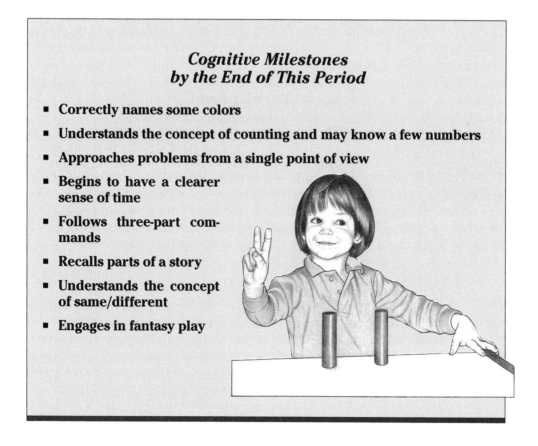

Cognitive Milestones by the End of This Period

- **Correctly names some colors**
- **Understands the concept of counting and may know a few numbers**
- **Approaches problems from a single point of view**
- **Begins to have a clearer sense of time**
- **Follows three-part commands**
- **Recalls parts of a story**
- **Understands the concept of same/different**
- **Engages in fantasy play**

two equal cups to start with and watches you pour, she'll come up with the same answer. By her logic, the taller container is "bigger" and therefore must hold more. At around age seven, children finally understand that they have to look at multiple aspects of a problem before arriving at an answer.

At about three years of age, your child's sense of time will become much clearer. Now she'll know her own daily routine and will try hard to figure out the routines of others. For example, she may eagerly watch for the mail carrier who arrives every day, but be perplexed that trash is picked up only one day out of seven. She'll understand that certain special events, such as holidays and birthdays, occur every once in a while, but even if she can tell you how old she is, she'll have no real sense of the length of a year.

Although it's almost human nature to try to measure your child's intellectual progress, beware of over- or underestimating her reasoning or thinking ability without formal testing. It's easy to convince yourself that your friendly, happy, highly verbal three-year-old is brilliant, while the quieter, more laid-back youngster playing next to her is not as bright. This may or may not be true, but the only way to know for sure is to have the child evaluated professionally. All pediatricians are familiar with these developmental evaluations, and some actually conduct formal assessments themselves. Many pediatricians prefer to refer children to testing specialists. So, if you believe your child is either gifted or lagging behind, ask your doctor about such testing. If your suspicions prove true, you may want to enter her in a special program geared to her individual needs and abilities.

Social Development

At age three, your child will be much less selfish than he was at two. He'll also be less dependent on you, a sign that his own sense of identity is stronger and more secure. Now he'll actually play with other children, interacting instead of just playing side by side. In the process, he'll recognize that not everyone thinks exactly as he does and that each of his playmates has many unique qualities, some attractive and some not. You'll also find him drifting toward certain children and starting to develop friendships with them. As he creates these friendships, he'll discover that he, too, has special qualities that make him likable—a revelation that will give a vital boost to his self-esteem.

There's some more good news about your child's development at this age: As he becomes more aware of and sensitive to the feelings and actions of others, he'll gradually stop competing and will learn to cooperate when playing with his friends. He'll be capable of taking turns and sharing toys in small groups, even if he doesn't always do it. Instead of grabbing, whining, or screaming for something, he'll actually ask politely much of the time. As a result, you can look forward to less aggressive behavior and calmer play sessions. Often three-year-olds are able to work out their own solutions to disputes by taking turns or trading toys.

However, particularly in the beginning, you'll need to encourage this type of cooperation. For instance, you might suggest that he "use his words" to deal with problems instead of violent actions. Also, remind him that when two children are sharing a toy, each gets an equal turn. Suggest ways to reach a simple solution when he and another child want the same toy, perhaps drawing for the first turn or finding another toy or activity. This doesn't work all the time, but it's worth a try. Also, help him with the appropriate words to describe his feelings and desires so that he doesn't feel frustrated. Above all, show him by your own example how to cope peacefully with conflicts. If you have an explosive temper, try to tone down your reactions in his presence. Otherwise, he'll mimic your behavior whenever he's under stress.

No matter what you do, however, there probably will be times when your child's anger or frustration becomes physical. When that happens, restrain him from hurting others, and if he doesn't calm down quickly, move him away from the other children. Talk to him about his feelings and try to determine why he's so upset. Let him know that you understand and accept his feelings, but make it clear that physically attacking another child is not a good way to express these emotions.

Help him see the situation from the other child's point of view by reminding him of a time when someone hit or screamed at him, and then suggest more peaceful ways to resolve his conflicts. Finally, once he understands what he's done wrong—but not before—ask him to apologize to the other child. However, simply saying "I'm sorry" may not help your child correct his behavior; he also needs to know why he's apologizing. He may not understand right away, but by age four these explanations will begin to mean something to him.

Actually, the normal interests of three-year-olds will help keep fights to a minimum. They spend much of their playtime in fantasy activity, which tends to be more cooperative than play that's focused on toys or games. As you've probably already seen, your preschooler and his playmates enjoy assigning different roles to one another and then launching into an elaborate game of make-believe using imaginary or household objects. This type of play helps them develop important social skills, such as taking turns, paying attention, communicating (through actions and expressions as well as words), and responding to one another's actions. And there's still another benefit: Because pretend play allows children to slip into any role they wish—including He-Man, Wonder Woman, Superman, or the Fairy Godmother—it also helps them explore more complex social ideas, such as power, wealth, compassion, cruelty, and sexuality.

By watching the role-playing that goes on during your child's make-believe games, you'll also see that he's beginning to identify with his own sex. While playing house, boys naturally will adopt the father's role and girls the mother's, reflecting whatever differences they've noticed in their own families and in the world around them. At this age, your son also may be fascinated by his father, older brothers, or other boys in the neighborhood, while your daughter will be drawn to her mother, older sisters, and other girls.

Research shows that a few of the developmental and behavioral differences that typically distinguish boys from girls are biologically determined. For instance, the average preschool boy tends to be more aggressive, while girls generally are more verbal. However, most gender-related characteristics at this age

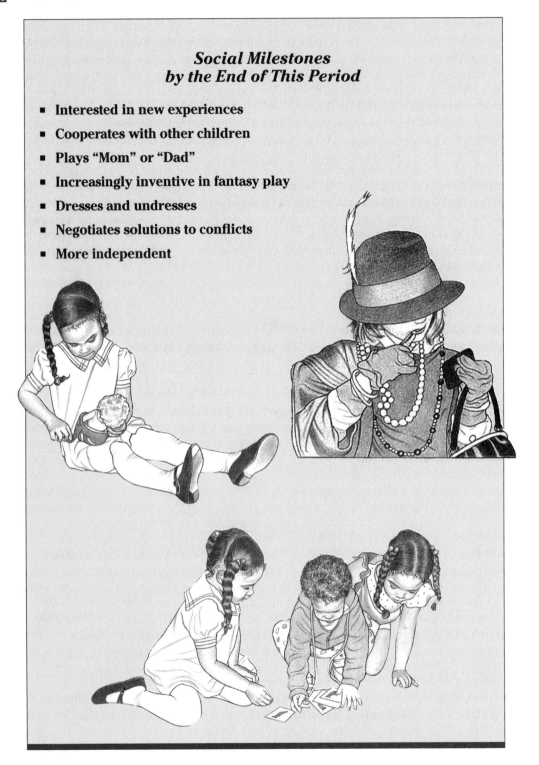

Social Milestones
by the End of This Period

- Interested in new experiences
- Cooperates with other children
- Plays "Mom" or "Dad"
- Increasingly inventive in fantasy play
- Dresses and undresses
- Negotiates solutions to conflicts
- More independent

are more likely to be shaped by cultural and family influences. Even if both parents work and share family responsibilities equally, your child still will find conventional male and female role models in television, magazines, books, billboards, and the families of friends and neighbors. Your daughter, for example, may be encouraged to play with dolls by advertisements, gifts from well-meaning relatives, and the approving comments of adults and other children. Boys, meanwhile, are generally guided away from dolls (although most enjoy them during the toddler years) in favor of more rough-and-tumble games and sports. The girl who likes to roughhouse is called a tomboy, but the boy who plays that way is called tough or assertive. Not surprisingly, children sense the approval and disapproval in these labels and adjust their behavior accordingly. Thus, by the time they enter kindergarten, children's gender identities are well established.

Children this age often will take this identification process to an extreme. Girls will insist on wearing dresses, nail polish, and makeup to school or to the playground. Boys will strut, be overly assertive, and carry pretend guns wherever they go. This behavior reinforces their sense of being male or female.

As your child develops his own identity during these early years, he's bound to experiment with attitudes and behaviors of both sexes. There's rarely any reason to discourage such impulses, except when the child is resisting or rejecting strongly established cultural standards. For instance, if your son wanted to wear dresses every day, you should gently persuade him to take a more conventional course. If he persists, however, discuss the issue with your pediatrician.

Your child also may imitate certain types of behavior that adults consider sexual, such as flirting. If he's very dramatic and expressive, you may be put off by these "suggestive" looks and movements, but the suggestions are all in your head, not his. At this age, he has no mature sexual intentions, and his mannerisms are merely playful mimicry, so don't worry. If, however, his imitation of sexual behavior is very explicit or otherwise indicates that he may have been personally exposed to sexual acts, you should discuss this with your pediatrician, as it could be a sign of sexual abuse.

Emotional Development

Your three-year-old's vivid fantasy life will help her explore and come to terms with a wide range of emotions, from love and dependency to anger, protest, and fear. She'll not only take on various identities herself, but also she'll often assign living qualities and emotions to inanimate objects, such as a tree, a clock, a truck, or the moon. Ask her why the moon comes out at night, for example, and she might reply, "To say hello to me."

From time to time, expect your preschooler to introduce you to one of her imaginary friends. Some children have a single make-believe companion for as long as six months; some change pretend playmates every day, while still others never have one at all or prefer imaginary animals instead. Don't be concerned that these phantom friends may signal loneliness or emotional upset;

Developmental Health Watch

Because each child develops in his own particular manner, it's impossible to tell exactly when or how he'll perfect a given skill. The developmental milestones listed in this book will give you a general idea of the changes you can expect as your child gets older, but don't be alarmed if his development takes a slightly different course. Alert your pediatrician, however, if your child displays any of the following signs of possible developmental delay for this age range.

- **Cannot throw a ball overhand**
- **Cannot jump in place**
- **Cannot ride a tricycle**
- **Cannot grasp a crayon between thumb and fingers**
- **Has difficulty scribbling**
- **Cannot stack four blocks**
- **Still clings or cries whenever his parents leave him**
- **Shows no interest in interactive games**
- **Ignores other children**
- **Doesn't respond to people outside the family**
- **Doesn't engage in fantasy play**
- **Resists dressing, sleeping, using the toilet**
- **Lashes out without any self-control when angry or upset**
- **Cannot copy a circle**
- **Doesn't use sentences of more than three words**
- **Doesn't use "me" and "you" appropriately**

they're actually a very creative way for your child to sample different activities, lines of conversation, behavior, and emotions.

You'll also notice that, throughout the day, your preschooler will move back and forth freely between fantasy and reality. At times she may become so involved in her make-believe world that she can't tell where it ends and reality begins. Her play experience may even spill over into real life. One night she'll come to the dinner table convinced she's Cinderella; another day she may come to you sobbing after hearing a ghost story that she believes is true.

While it's important to reassure your child when she's frightened or upset by an imaginary incident, be careful not to belittle or make fun of her. This stage in emotional development is normal and necessary and should not be discouraged. Above all, never joke with her about "locking her up if she doesn't eat her dinner" or "leaving her behind if she doesn't hurry up." She's liable to believe you and feel terrified the rest of the day—or longer.

From time to time, try to join your child in her fantasy play. By doing so, you can help her find new ways to express her emotions and even work through some problems. For example, you might suggest "sending her doll to school" to see how she feels about going to nursery school. Don't insist on participating in these fantasies, however. Part of the joy of fantasy for her is being able to control these imaginary dramas, so if you plant an idea for make-believe, stand back and let her make of it what she will. If she then asks you to play a part, keep your performance low key. Let the world of pretend be the one place where *she* runs the show.

Back in real life, let your preschooler know that you're proud of her new independence and creativity. Talk with her, listen to what she says, and show her that her opinions matter. Give her choices whenever possible—in the foods she eats, the clothes she wears, the games you play together. Doing this will give her a sense of importance and help her learn to make decisions. Keep her options simple, however. When you go to a restaurant, for example, narrow her choices down to two or three items. Otherwise she may be overwhelmed and unable to decide. (A trip to an ice cream store that sells twenty flavors can be agonizing if you don't limit her choices.)

What's the best approach? Despite what we've already said, one of the best ways to nurture her independence is to maintain fairly firm control over all parts of her life, while at the same time giving her some freedom. Let her know that you're still in charge and that you don't expect her to make the big decisions. When her friend is daring her to climb a tree, and she's afraid, it will be comforting to have you say no, so that she doesn't have to admit her fears. As she conquers many of her early anxieties and becomes more responsible in making her own decisions, you'll naturally give her more control. In the meantime, it's important that she feels safe and secure.

Emotional Milestones
by the End of This Period

- **Imagines that many unfamiliar images may be "monsters"**
- **Views self as a whole person involving body, mind, and feelings**
- **Often cannot distinguish between fantasy and reality**

Especially for Grandparents

A three- to five-year-old child is becoming more of a real person. As that happens, your grandparent-grandchild relationship will become more meaningful and unique and will present many opportunities for additional growth for both of you.

These years are often known as "the magic years" for children. They are becoming more sociable, they engage in more make-believe and fantasy play, and they may have an "imaginary friend" for a while. As a grandparent, your role is to be part of his activities, play along, enjoy his creative mind at work, and develop favorite play scenarios with him that you can return to whenever you're with him.

Make time for adventures or parties at your house. Take him on sightseeing trips and visits to the museum or park. (Be sure to follow all of the travel rules and advice that appear in this chapter.)

You'll probably notice a little change in your grandchild's personality as he moves from a four-year-old to the more independent five-year-old. He may test your authority, show aggressiveness, be bossy, and at times even use "imitated" foul language. But fear not. Keep calm, knowing that this stage is only a stepping-stone to gaining greater mastery over his surroundings. Discipline him firmly but not harshly, and don't overreact to language you may find surprising and perhaps even offensive.

During this period in your grandchild's young life, he also will be developing larger social networks and some "best friends." You can expand this network even further if you can locate some other children nearby. Set up some play dates with these other children of your neighbors or friends as well as with nearby cousins.

What if you live many miles from your grandchild, and frequent vis-

AGE FOUR TO FIVE YEARS

Before you know it, the somewhat calm child of three becomes a dynamo of energy, drive, bossiness, belligerence, and generally out-of-bounds behavior. You may be reminded of the earlier trials and tribulations you went through when he was two, but your child is now taking different directions. Although he may seem to be chasing off in all directions at the same time, he is learning from all these experiences. Eventually this will let up (just when you thought you couldn't take it for another day), and gradually a more confident, calm child will emerge around his fifth birthday.

Meanwhile, this is a difficult age to handle. Each day there are new challenges to deal with. The emotional highs and lows will have him appearing secure and

its are not possible? There are many long-distance strategies for grandparents, taking advantage of the fact that children of this age are now quite verbal. Here are some suggestions.

- The telephone is an obvious option. Establish a regular time when your grandchild can count on you to call. During these phone calls, talk about his activities. Ask questions about what he's doing and who his friends are. Preschool activities and "events" are often first on his mind. Keep notes so you can refer to his friends or special places by name in later conversations.

- If video phones become more available at a reasonable cost, consider investing in one, especially if you don't get to see your grandchild very often. If the two of you can view each other during a phone call, it's worth a thousand words.

- Children *love* to get mail. Sending cards and playful mementos of trips you have been on can keep the connection real.

- Exchanging family pictures, movies, and audiotapes can mean a lot.

- Phone and send a card to arrive on birthdays or holidays when you can't be there. It is important to make some contact on special occasions.

- Despite the distance, visits should become a priority. As important as the above suggestions are, nothing replaces actually being there with your grandchild. Even if it's only for a weekend, repeated contact and familiarity are keys to a meaningful relationship for both grandchild and grandparent.

bragging one minute and insecure and whining the next. In addition, four-year-olds become set in some of their routines, not wanting to change for fear they will not know what to do. This fixation reveals some of the insecurity they are feeling during these months.

Their out-of-bounds behavior also is seen in the language they use. They enjoy using four-letter words, and they love to watch your expression when they say them. They use these words more to get a response out of you than for any other reason, so don't overreact to them.

This energy machine of yours still has little sense of property. To him, all things are his. Four-year-olds are not thieves or liars, though. They simply believe that possession means ownership.

Also obvious during this year is the tremendous spurt of imaginative ideas that spring from children's minds and mouths. The "monsters" they talked with at school or the "dragon" who helped them across the street represent the normal tall tales told by four- to five-year-olds. They reflect the fact that children of this age are trying to distinguish fact from fantasy, and their fantasies sometimes get a bit out of control. All of this behavior and thinking will help your youngster build a secure foundation as he emerges into the world of kindergarten.

Movement

Your preschooler now has the coordination and balance of an adult. Watch her walk and run with long, swinging, confident strides, go up and down stairs without holding the handrail, stand on her tiptoes, whirl herself in a circle, and pump herself on a swing. She also has the muscular strength to perform challenging activities such as turning somersaults and doing a standing broad jump. It will be a toss-up as to who is excited more by her progress—you or she.

In your child's eagerness to prove just how capable and independent she is, she'll often run ahead of you when out on a walk. Her motor skills are still way ahead of her judgment, however, so you'll need to remind her frequently to wait and hold your hand when crossing the street. The need for vigilance is just as important when she is anywhere near water. Even if she can swim, she probably can't swim well or consistently. And should she accidentally go under, she may become frightened and forget how to keep herself afloat. So never leave her alone in a pool or in the water at the beach.

Movement Milestones
by the End of This Period

- **Stands on one foot for ten seconds or longer**
- **Hops, somersaults**
- **Swings, climbs**
- **May be able to skip**

Hand and Finger Skills

Your four-year-old's coordination and ability to use his hands are almost fully developed. As a result, he's becoming able to take care of himself. He now can brush his teeth and get dressed with little assistance, and he may even be able to lace up his shoes.

Notice how he uses his hands with far more care and attention when he draws now. He'll decide in advance what he wants to create and then go ahead with it. His figures may or may not have a body, and the legs may be sticking out of the head. But now they'll have eyes, a nose, and a mouth, and, most important to your child, they are people.

Because of this growing control over his hands, arts and crafts in general are becoming more exciting for him now. His favorite activities may include:

- Writing and drawing, holding the paper with one hand and the pencil or crayon with the other

- Tracing and copying geometric patterns, such as a star or diamond

- Card and board games

- Painting with a brush and finger painting

- Clay modeling

- Cutting and pasting

- Building complex structures with many blocks

These kinds of activities will not only permit him to use and improve many of his emerging skills, but he'll also discover the fun of creating. In addition, because of the success he'll feel with these activities, his self-esteem will grow. You may even notice certain "talents" emerging through his work, but at this age it's not advisable to push him in one direction over another. Just be sure to provide a broad range of opportunities so he can exercise all his abilities. He'll take the direction he enjoys most.

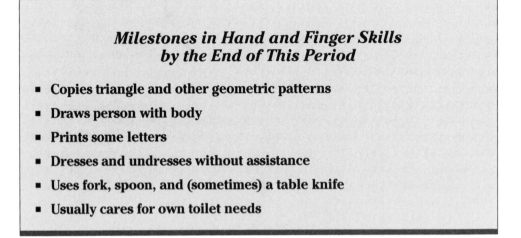

Milestones in Hand and Finger Skills by the End of This Period

- Copies triangle and other geometric patterns
- Draws person with body
- Prints some letters
- Dresses and undresses without assistance
- Uses fork, spoon, and (sometimes) a table knife
- Usually cares for own toilet needs

Language Development

At about age four your child's language skills will blossom. She'll now be able to pronounce most of the sounds in the English language, with the following exceptions: *f, v, s,* and *z* probably will remain difficult for her until midway through age five, and she may not fully master *sh, l, th,* and *r* until age six or later.

Your preschooler's vocabulary will have expanded to around 1,500 words by now, and it will grow by another 1,000 or so over the course of this year. She now can tell elaborate stories using relatively complex sentences of up to eight words. And she will tell you not only about things that happen to her and things she wants, but also about her dreams and fantasies.

Don't be surprised, however, if some of the words she uses are not ones you want to hear. After all, by now she's learned how powerful words can be, and she'll enthusiastically explore this power, for better and for worse. Thus, if your four-year-old is like most others, she'll be very bossy at times, perhaps commanding you and your spouse to "stop talking" or her playmates to "come here now." To help counteract this, teach your child how to use "please" and "thank you." But also review the way you and other adults in the family address her and each other. Chances are, she's repeating many of the commands she most often hears.

Your child also will probably pick up many swear words at this age. From her point of view, these are the most powerful words of all. She hears adults say them when they are most angry or emotional, and whenever she uses them herself, she gets quite a reaction. What's the best way to stop this behavior? Be a good role model and make a conscious effort not to use these words, even when you are stressed. In addition, try to minimize your child's use of these words without drawing too much attention to them. She probably has no idea what these words really mean; she just enjoys their energy.

When your child's upset, you may find she'll use words as insults. This is certainly preferable to physical violence, although it can be quite disturbing to you. Remember, though, that when your child uses these words, she's disturbed, too. If she says "I hate you!" what she really means is "I am very angry, and I want you to help me sort out my feelings." By getting angry and shouting back at her, you'll only make her feel more hurt and confused. Instead, remain calm and tell her you know she doesn't really hate you. Then let her know that it's OK to feel angry, and talk about the events leading up to her outburst. Try giving her the words that will allow her to tell you how she feels.

If the insults she chooses are mild ones, the best response may be a joke. For example, let's presume she calls you a "wicked witch"; you might laugh and respond: "And I'm just boiling up a pot of bat's wings and frog's eyes. Care to join me for supper?" This kind of humor is an excellent way to take the edge off her anger as well as your own.

Language Milestones by the End of This Period

- **Recalls part of a story**
- **Speaks sentences of more than five words**
- **Uses future tense**
- **Tells longer stories**
- **Says name and address**

Of course, sometimes your preschooler doesn't have to say anything offensive to try your patience—her constant chatter can do it just as quickly. One solution at these moments is to redirect her verbal energy. For instance, instead of allowing her to chant mindless sound rhymes, teach her some limericks or songs, or take time out to read some poems. This will help her learn to pay more attention to the words she speaks and will boost her appreciation for the written language, as well.

Learning to Read

Is your child interested in learning the names of letters? Does he look through books and magazines on his own? Does he like to "write" with a pencil or pen? Does he listen attentively during story time? If the answer is yes, he may be ready to learn some of the basics of reading. If not, he's like most preschoolers, and will take another year or two to develop the language skills, visual perception, and memory he needs to begin formal reading.

Although a few four-year-olds sincerely want to learn to read and will begin to recognize certain familiar words, there's no need to push your child to do so. Even if you succeed in giving him this head start, he may not maintain it once school begins. Most early readers lose their advantage over other children during the second or third grade, when the other students acquire the same basic skills.

The crucial factor that determines whether a student will do well or poorly in school is not how aggressively he was pushed early on, but rather his own enthusiasm for learning. This passion cannot be forced on a child by teaching him to read at age four. To the contrary, many so-called early learning programs interfere with the child's nat-

Cognitive Development

By age four, your child is beginning to explore many basic concepts that will be taught in greater detail in school. For example, she now understands that the day is divided into morning, afternoon, and night and that there are different seasons. By the time she enters kindergarten, she may know some days of the week and that each day is measured in hours and minutes. She also may comprehend the essential ideas of counting, the alphabet, size relationships (big versus small), and the names of geometric shapes.

There are many good children's books that illustrate these concepts, but don't feel compelled to rush things. There's no advantage to her learning them this early, and if she feels pressured to perform now, she actually may resist learning when she gets to school.

The best approach is to offer your child a wide range of learning opportunities. For instance, this is the perfect age to introduce her to zoos and museums, if you haven't done so already. Many museums have special sections designed for children, where she can actively experience the learning process.

At the same time, you should respect her special interests and talents. If your child seems very artistic, take her to art museums and galleries, or let her try a preschool art class. Also, if you know an artist, take her for a visit so she can see what a studio is like. If she's most interested in machines and diural enthusiasm by forcing him to concentrate on tasks for which he's not yet ready.

What's the most successful approach to early learning? Let your child set his own pace and have fun at whatever he's doing. Don't drill him on letters, numbers, colors, shapes, or words. Instead, encourage his curiosity and tendencies to explore on his own. Read him books that he enjoys, but don't push him to learn the words. Provide him with educational experiences, but make sure they're also entertaining.

When your child is ready to learn to read, there are plenty of valuable tools to help him—educational television, games, songs, and even some of the latest computer teaching programs. But don't expect them to do the job alone. You need to be involved, too. If he's watching *Sesame Street* or other educational TV programs, for example, sit with him and talk about the concepts and information being presented. If he's playing with a computer program, do it with him so you can make sure it's appropriate for his abilities. If the game is too frustrating for him, it may diminish some of his enthusiasm and defeat the whole purpose. Active learning in a warm, supportive environment is the key to success.

nosaurs, take her to the natural history museum, help her learn to build models, and provide her with construction kits that allow her to create her own machines. Whatever her interests, you can use books to help answer her questions and open her horizons even further. At this age, then, your child should be discovering the joy of learning so that she will be self-motivated when her formal education begins.

You'll also find that, in addition to exploring practical ideas, your four-year-

Cognitive Milestones by the End of This Period

- **Can count ten or more objects**
- **Correctly names at least four colors**
- **Better understands the concept of time**
- **Knows about things used every day in the home (money, food, appliances)**

old probably will ask many "universal" questions about subjects such as the origin of the world, death and dying, and the composition of the sun and the sky. Now, for example, is when you'll hear the classic question "Why is the sky blue?" Like so many other parents, you may have trouble answering these questions, particularly in simple language your child will understand. As you grapple with these issues, don't make up answers; rely instead on children's books that deal with them. Your local library should be able to recommend age-appropriate books to help you.

Social Development

By age four, your child should have an active social life filled with friends, and he may even have a "best friend" (usually, but not always, of his own sex). Ideally, he'll have friends in the neighborhood or in his nursery school or preschool whom he sees routinely.

But what if your child is not enrolled in preschool and doesn't live near other families? And what if the neighborhood children are too old or too young for him? In these cases, you'll want to arrange play sessions with other preschoolers. Parks, playgrounds, and preschool activity programs all provide excellent opportunities to meet other children.

Once your preschooler has found playmates he seems to enjoy, you need to take some initiative to encourage their relationships. More than anything, encourage him to invite these friends to your home. It's important for him to "show off" his home, family, and possessions to other children. This will help him establish a sense of self-pride. Incidentally, to generate this pride, his home needn't be luxurious or filled with expensive toys; it needs only to be warm and welcoming.

It's also important to recognize that at this age his friends are not just playmates. They also actively influence his thinking and behavior. He'll desperately want to be just like them, even during those times when their actions violate rules and standards you've taught him from birth. He now realizes that there are other values and opinions besides yours, and he may test this new discovery by demanding things that you've never allowed him—certain toys, foods, clothing, or permission to watch certain TV programs.

Don't despair if your child's relationship with you changes dramatically in light of these new friendships. For instance, he may be rude to you for the first time in his life. When you tell him to do something that he objects to, he may occasionally tell you to "shut up" or even swear at you. Hard as it may be to accept, this sassiness actually is a positive sign that he's learning to challenge authority and test the limits of his independence. Once again, the best way to deal with it is to express disapproval, and you might want to discuss with him what he really means or feels. The more emotionally you react, the more you'll encourage him to continue behaving badly. But if the subdued approach doesn't work, and he persists in talking back to you, a time-out is the most effective form of punishment (see page 378).

Bear in mind that even though your child is exploring the concepts of good and bad at this age, he still has an extremely simplified sense of morality. Thus, when he obeys rules rigidly, it's not necessarily because he understands or agrees with them, but more likely because he wants to avoid punishment. In his mind, consequences count but not intentions. When he breaks something of value, for instance, he probably assumes he's bad, whether he did it on purpose or not. But he needs to be taught the difference between accidents and misbehaving.

To help him learn this difference, you need to separate him—as a person—from his behavior. When he does or says something that calls for punishment, make sure he understands that he's being punished for a particular act that he's done, not because he's "bad." Instead of telling him that he is bad, describe specifically what he did wrong, clearly separating the person from the behavior. For example, if he is picking on a younger sibling, explain that it's wrong to make someone else feel bad, rather than just saying "You're bad." When he accidentally does something wrong, comfort him and tell him you understand it was unintentional. Try not to get upset yourself, or he'll think you're angry at him rather than about what he did.

It's also important to give your preschooler tasks that you know he can perform and then praise him when he does them well. He's quite ready for simple responsibilities, such as helping to set the table or cleaning his room. When you go on family outings, explain that you expect him to behave well, and congratulate him when he does so. Along with the responsibilities, give him ample opportunities to play with other children, and tell him how proud you are when he shares or is helpful to another youngster.

Social Milestones by the End of This Period

- **Wants to please friends**
- **Wants to be like her friends**
- **More likely to agree to rules**
- **Likes to sing, dance, and act**
- **Shows more independence and may even visit a next-door neighbor by herself**

Emotional Development

Just as it was when she was three, your four-year-old's fantasy life will remain very active. However, she's now learning to distinguish between reality and make-believe, and she'll be able to move back and forth between the two without confusing them as much.

As her games of pretend become more advanced, don't be surprised if she experiments with make-believe games involving some form of violence. War games, dragon-slaying, and even games like tag all fall into this category. Some parents forbid their children to play with store-bought toy guns, only to find them cutting, pasting, and using cardboard guns or simply pointing a finger and shouting "bang bang." Parents shouldn't panic over these activities. This is not evidence that these youngsters are "violent." A child has no idea what it is to kill or die. For her, toy guns are an innocent and entertaining way to be competitive and boost her self-esteem.

If you want a gauge of your child's developing self-confidence, listen to the way she talks to adults. Instead of hanging back, as she may have done at two or

Developmental Health Watch

Because each child develops in her own particular manner, it's impossible to predict exactly when or how your own preschooler will perfect a given skill. The developmental milestones listed in this book will give you a general idea of the changes you can expect as your child gets older, but don't be alarmed if her development takes a slightly different course. Alert your pediatrician, however, if your child displays any of the following signs of possible developmental delay for this age range.

- Exhibits extremely fearful or timid behavior
- Exhibits extremely aggressive behavior
- Is unable to separate from parents without major protest
- Is easily distracted and unable to concentrate on any single activity for more than five minutes
- Shows little interest in playing with other children
- Refuses to respond to people in general, or responds only superficially
- Rarely uses fantasy or imitation in play
- Seems unhappy or sad much of the time

three, she now probably is friendly, talkative, and curious. She also is likely to be especially sensitive to the feelings of others—adults and children alike—and to enjoy making people happy. When she sees they're hurt or sad, she'll show sympathy and concern. This probably will come out as a desire to hug or "kiss the hurt," because this is what she most wants when she's in pain or unhappy.

At about this age, your preschooler also may begin to show an avid interest in basic sexuality, both her own and that of the opposite sex. She may ask where babies come from and about the organs involved in reproduction and elimination. She may want to know how boys' and girls' bodies are different. When confronted with these kinds of questions, answer in simple but correct terms. Don't go into a long explanation, and try not to appear overly embarrassed or serious about the matter. Your four-year-old doesn't need to know the details about intercourse, but she should feel free to ask questions, knowing she'll receive direct and accurate answers.

Along with this increased interest in sexuality, she'll probably also play with her own genitals and may even demonstrate an interest in the genitals of other

- Doesn't engage in a variety of activities
- Avoids or seems aloof with other children and adults
- Doesn't express a wide range of emotions
- Has trouble eating, sleeping, or using the toilet
- Can't differentiate between fantasy and reality
- Seems unusually passive
- Cannot understand two-part commands using prepositions ("Put the cup on the table"; "Get the ball under the couch.")
- Can't correctly give her first and last name
- Doesn't use plurals or past tense properly when speaking
- Doesn't talk about her daily activities and experiences
- Cannot build a tower of six to eight blocks
- Seems uncomfortable holding a crayon
- Has trouble taking off her clothing
- Cannot brush her teeth efficiently
- Cannot wash and dry her hands

children. These are not adult sexual activities but signs of normal curiosity and don't warrant scolding or punishment.

At what point should parents set limits on such exploration? This really is a family matter. It's probably best not to overreact to it at this age, since it's normal if done in moderation. However, children need to learn what's socially appropriate and what's not. So, for example, you may decide to tell your child:

- Interest in genital organs is healthy and natural.

- Nudity and sexual play in public are not acceptable.

- No other person, including even close friends and relatives, may touch her "private parts." The exceptions to this rule are doctors and nurses during physical examinations and her own parents when they are trying to find the cause of any pain or discomfort she's feeling in the genital area.

At about this same time, your child also may become fascinated with the parent of the opposite sex. A four-year-old girl can be expected to compete with her mother for her father's attention, just as a boy may be vying for his mother's attention. This so-called oedipal behavior is a normal part of personality development at this age and will disappear in time by itself if the parents take it in stride. There's no need to feel either threatened or jealous because of it.

Emotional Milestones by the End of This Period

- **Aware of sexuality**
- **Able to distinguish fantasy from reality**
- **Sometimes demanding, sometimes eagerly cooperative**

BASIC CARE

Feeding and Nutrition

As a preschooler, your child should have a healthy attitude toward eating. Ideally, by this age he no longer uses eating—or not eating—to demonstrate defiance, nor does he confuse food with love or affection. Generally (although almost certainly not always), he'll now view eating as a natural response to hunger and meals as a pleasant social experience.

Your child also should be good company at meals now and be ready to learn basic table manners. By age four, he'll no longer grip his fork or spoon in his fist, because now he's able to hold them like an adult. With instruction, he also can

Sample One-Day Menu for a Preschooler

This menu is planned for a four-year-old child who weighs approximately 36 pounds (16.5 kg).

1 teaspoon = ⅓ tablespoon (5 ml)

1 tablespoon = ½ ounce (15 ml)

1 ounce = 30 ml

1 cup = 8 ounces (240 ml)

BREAKFAST
½ cup 2 percent milk

½ cup cereal

4–6 oz. citrus or tomato juice or ½ cup cantaloupe or strawberries

SNACK
½ cup 2 percent milk

½ cup banana

1 slice whole wheat bread

1 teaspoon margarine (or butter)

1 teaspoon jelly

LUNCH
¾ cup 2 percent milk

1 sandwich—2 slices whole wheat bread, 1 teaspoon margarine (or butter) or 2 teaspoons salad dressing, and 1 ounce meat or cheese

¼ cup dark-yellow or dark-green vegetable

SNACK
1 teaspoon peanut butter

1 slice whole wheat bread or 5 crackers

DINNER
¾ cup 2 percent milk

2 ounces meat, fish, or chicken

½ cup pasta, rice, or potato

¼ cup vegetable

1 teaspoon margarine (or butter) or 2 teaspoons salad dressing

How Much Is Enough?

Many parents worry whether their children are getting "enough" to eat. Here are some guidelines to help you make sure your child gets enough, but not too much.

1. Offer her small portions, with seconds only if she asks for them. Here are some acceptable "child-size" portions.

1 teaspoon = 5 ml	1 tablespoon = 15 ml
1 ounce = 30 ml	1 cup = 240 ml

4–6 ounces milk or juice	4 tablespoons vegetables
½ cup cottage cheese or yogurt	½ cup cereal
2 ounces hamburger	2 ounces chicken
1 slice toast	1 teaspoon margarine (or butter)

2. Limit snacks to two a day, stressing healthful items in place of such foods as soft drinks, candy, pastries, or salty and greasy items. Not only will additional snacks decrease her appetite for proper meals, but also they'll expose her teeth to cavity-causing foods over an extended period of time. To minimize the risk of cavities and excess calories, encourage nutritious snack foods, such as:

fruit and fruit juices	finger sandwiches
carrot, celery, or cucumber sticks	oatmeal cookies (low-fat)
	bran muffins
yogurt	cheese
toast or crackers	

3. Don't use food as a reward for good behavior.

learn the proper use of a table knife. You can teach him other table manners, as well, such as not talking with his mouth full, using his napkin instead of his sleeve to wipe his mouth, and not reaching across another person's plate. While it's necessary to explain these rules, it's much more important to model them; he'll behave as he sees the rest of the family behaving. He'll also develop better table manners if you have a family custom of eating together. So make at least one meal a day a special and pleasant family time, and have your child set the table or help in some other way in the meal preparation.

Despite your four-year-old's general enthusiasm for eating, he still may have very specific preferences in food, some of which may vary from day to day. As irritating as it may be to have him turn up his nose at a dish he devoured the

4. Make sure your child actually is hungry or thirsty when she asks for food or drink. If what she really wants is attention, talk or play with her, but don't use food as a pacifier.

5. Don't allow her to eat while playing, listening to stories, or watching television. Allowing her to do so will lead to "unconscious" eating well past the point when she's full.

6. Learn the calorie counts for the foods she eats most often and monitor how many calories she consumes on an average day. The total for a child age four to five should be 900 to 1,800, or about 40 calories per pound of body weight.

7. Don't worry if your child's food intake is inconsistent. One day she may seem to eat anything she can get her hands on, and the next she'll grimace at the sight of everything. When she refuses to eat, she may not be hungry because she's been less active than the day before. Also consider the possibility that she's using food as a means of exercising control. Especially during the period when she's being negative about nearly everything, she's bound to resist your efforts to feed her. When that happens, don't force her to eat. Rest assured that even at the height of this negativism, she will not starve herself, and she'll seldom, if ever, lose weight. If, however, a markedly decreased appetite persists for more than one week, or there are other signs of illness, such as fever, nausea, diarrhea, or weight loss, consult your pediatrician.

8. Limit her milk intake. Milk is an important food, mainly because of its calcium content. Too much milk, however, may reduce her appetite for other important foods. Your child needs to drink approximately two cups (16 ounces, or 480 ml) of milk a day to meet her calcium requirement.

day before, it's best not to make an issue of it. Let him eat the other foods on his plate or select something else to eat. As long as he chooses foods that aren't overly sugary, fatty, or salty, don't object. However, encourage him to try new foods by offering him very small amounts to taste, not by insisting that he eat a full portion of an unfamiliar food.

Television advertising, incidentally, can be a serious obstacle to your preschooler's good nutrition. Some studies show that children who watch over twenty-two hours of TV per week have a greater tendency to become obese. Children this age are extremely receptive to ads for sugary cereals and sweets, especially after they've visited other homes where these foods are served. Obesity is a growing problem among children in America. For this reason, you need to be aware of your youngster's eating habits, at home and away, and monitor them to make sure she's eating as healthy as possible.

To combat outside influences, keep your own home as "clean" as possible. Stock up on low-sodium, low-sugar, low-fat products, and reserve sweets for special occasions. Also monitor your child's television viewing and exposure to advertisements. Eventually he'll become accustomed to healthful foods, which may make him less susceptible to the temptation of the more sugary, salty, or greasy ones. (See *Television,* page 533.)

Dietary Supplements. Ordinarily, preschool children don't need any vitamin supplements. However, if your child is extremely selective and refuses to eat a balanced diet, you should consult your pediatrician concerning the need for a multivitamin. (Also see pages 283–284.)

Beyond Toilet Training

By about age three, most children are already fully toilet trained, although as a toddler your child may have used a potty chair rather than a toilet. But now, in preparation for school, he must get used to using toilets both at home and away.

The first step in this process is to position the potty next to the toilet so that your child gets used to "going to the bathroom." When he has fully adjusted to the potty seat, get a child-size toilet seat for the toilet, and provide a sturdy box or stool so he can climb up and down by himself. This also will give him a surface on which to plant his feet while using the toilet. Once he has completely and voluntarily made the transition from potty to toilet, remove the potty.

As preschoolers, little boys begin to copy their fathers, friends, or older brothers, and stand up while urinating.

Little boys generally sit down to urinate during early toilet training, but as preschoolers, they'll begin to copy their fathers, friends, or older brothers, and stand up while urinating. As your son learns to do this, make sure he also lifts the toilet seat beforehand. You'd better be prepared to do some extra cleaning around the toilet bowl for a while, since he probably won't have perfect aim for some time. (Note: Make sure the toilet seat stays in the raised position when put there; falling seats have caused injuries.)

Away from home, teach your child to recognize restroom signs, and encourage him to use public bathrooms whenever necessary. You'll need to accompany and assist him in the beginning, but during his fifth year he should become comfortable enough to manage by himself. Whenever possible, however, an adult or older child should accompany him or at least wait outside the door.

He'll also need to learn that, at times, he'll have to use facilities when they're available, even before he feels a strong need. Doing this will make outings and especially car trips much more pleasant. Sometimes, however, a bathroom will not be available when it's really needed, so you may have to teach your child to urinate outdoors. This isn't a problem for boys, but little girls must learn to squat so their feet and clothing are out of the way. You can help your daughter by showing her the appropriate position and physically supporting her as she squats.

During the entire process just described, you'll need to help your child in the bathroom at first—whether at home or away. Plan not only on wiping, but also on helping him dress and undress. Before he goes to school, however, you must teach him to manage entirely on his own. For a girl, that means teaching her to wipe from front to back, particularly after bowel movements, because contact between feces and the urethra or vagina can lead to urinary tract or vaginal infections. A boy must learn to pull down his pants (if elastic-waisted) or use the fly front. To make this procedure as simple as possible, dress your child in clothes that can be undone easily without help. Although overalls, for example, may be practical in other ways, they're very difficult for a child to get into and out of without help. For children of both sexes, elastic-waisted pants or shorts are generally the most practical clothing at this age. A dress with elastic-waisted underpants will work equally well for girls.

Bed-wetting

All young children occasionally wet their beds while going through nighttime toilet training. Also, even after your preschooler is able to stay dry at night for a number of days or weeks, he may start wetting at night again, perhaps in response to stress or changes occurring around her. When this happens, don't make an issue of it. Simply put him back in training pants at night for a while, and as the stress decreases, he should stop wetting. If it persists, however, check with your pediatrician.

Most children with an ongoing bed-wetting pattern have never been consistently dry at night. Some may have unusually small bladders, even by age four or five, so they can't last a whole night without urinating. In other cases, the processes required for successful bladder control take longer to develop, and the children may not be able to recognize when their bladder is full, awakening them to use the toilet.

If your preschooler persistently wets his bed, the problem probably will disappear gradually as he matures. Medication is not advisable during the preschool years, nor should he be punished or ridiculed. He is not wetting the bed on purpose. Limiting his fluid intake and waking him up to use the bathroom probably won't help the situation much either, but reassuring him that these mishaps are "no big deal" may help him feel less ashamed. Also, make sure he understands that the bed-wetting is not his fault and that it probably will stop as he gets older. If there's a family history of bed-wetting, let him know that, too, in order to further take the burden off his shoulders. Should the bed-wetting continue after age five, your pediatrician may recommend one of several treatment programs. (See *Wetting Problems,* page 649.)

If a child who has been completely toilet trained for six months or longer suddenly begins wetting her bed again, there may be an underlying physical or emotional cause. As mentioned, perhaps stress in your child's life is contributing to this situation, or maybe he's reacting to a new baby in the family, a move to a new neighborhood, or a divorce. If he has frequent accidents during the day as well as at night, "dribbles" urine constantly, or complains of burning or pain while urinating, he may have a urinary tract infection or other medical problem. In any of these cases, see your pediatrician as soon as possible.

Sleeping

For many parents, their child's bedtime is the most dreaded part of the day, and often for good reason: Unless a preschooler is very tired, he may resist going to sleep. This is even more likely to be a particular problem if he has older brothers or sisters who stay up later. The younger one is bound to feel left out and afraid of "missing something" if the rest of the family is up after he's asleep. These feelings are understandable, and there's no harm in granting him some flexibility in his bedtime. But remember that most children at this age need at least ten to twelve hours of sleep each night.

The best way to prepare your preschooler for sleep is by reading him a story. Once the story is over and you've said your good-nights, don't let him stall further, and don't let him talk you into staying with him until he falls asleep. He needs to get used to doing this on his own. Also, don't let him roughhouse or get in-

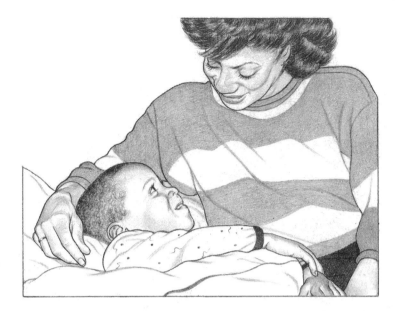

Unless a preschooler is very tired, he may resist going to sleep.

volved in a lengthy play project right before bedtime. The calmer and more comforting the activity that precedes going to bed, the better and the more easily he'll go to sleep.

Most preschoolers sleep through the night, but often rouse several times to check their surroundings before falling back to sleep. There may be nights, however, when your child's very active dreams awaken him. These vivid dreams often represent the way he viewed some of the events of the day. They may reflect some impulse, aggressive feeling, or inner fear that only comes to the surface by way of these frightening images or dreams.

By the time he's five or a little older, he'll be better able to understand that these images are only dreams, but as a preschooler he still may need to be reassured that they're not real. When he wakes up in the middle of the night, afraid and crying, try holding him, talking about the dream, and staying with him until he's calm. For your own peace of mind, don't forget that these are only nightmares and not a serious problem.

To further help your child overcome his nighttime fears, you might read him stories about dreams and sleep. As you talk about these stories together, he'll better understand that everyone has dreams and that he needn't be frightened of them. Some classic children's books on these topics include Maurice Sendak's *In the Night Kitchen,* Russell Hoban's *Bedtime for Frances,* Mercer Mayer's *There's a Nightmare in My Closet,* and Chris van Allsberg's *Ben's Dream.* But always make sure that the books themselves aren't frightening to him.

Occasionally your preschooler will be in bed, appearing to be awake and desperately upset, perhaps screaming and thrashing, eyes wide open and terrified, but he won't respond to you. In this case, he's neither awake nor having a nightmare. Rather, you're witnessing something called a night terror (or sleep terror)—a mysterious and, to parents, distressing form of sleep behavior common

How to Tell a Nightmare from a Night Terror

Sometimes it's difficult to tell the difference between a nightmare and a night terror. This chart should help.

	Nightmare	Night Terror
What is it?	Scary dream followed by complete awakening	Partial arousal from very deep sleep.
When do you become aware of it?	After it's over, when your child wakes up and tells you	During the terror itself, as she screams and thrashes; afterward she is calm.
Time of occurrence	In the second half of the night, when dreaming is most intense	Usually one to four hours after falling asleep.
Appearance and behavior	Crying and fearful after waking	Sitting up, thrashing, bizarre movements; crying, screaming, moaning, talking; bulging eyes, racing heart, sweating. The apparent fear and confusion disappear after awakening.
Responsiveness	After waking, child is aware of and reassured by your presence	Child is not very aware of you, and may physically push you away, screaming and thrashing more if you try to restrain her.
Return to sleep	May have trouble falling back to sleep because of fear.	Returns to sleep rapidly without fully awakening.
Memory of experience	Often remembers dream and may talk about it	No memory of a dream or of yelling or thrashing.

Adapted from *Solve Your Child's Sleep Problems,* by Richard Ferber, M.D.

during the preschool and early school years. Typically, the child falls asleep without difficulty, but wakes up an hour or so later, wide-eyed and terrified. He may have hallucinations, point to imaginary objects, kick, scream, call out ("No, no!" "I can't!"), and generally be inconsolable. Parents find these experiences particularly disturbing because the child looks and acts so differently from her usual self. (These events are much more unsettling for parents than for the child having them.) The only thing you really can do in this situation is hold the child to protect him from hurting himself. Reassure him: "You're fine. Mommy and Daddy are here." Keep the lights dim and speak softly. After ten to thirty minutes of this, he'll settle down and go back to sleep. The next morning, he'll remember nothing about the occurrence.

Some children may have just one episode of night terrors, while others experience them several times. It's not typical, however, for them to recur frequently or for a prolonged period. In cases of very frequent night terrors, sleep medications prescribed by your pediatrician may be helpful, but the best strategy seems to be to wait them out. Since some children have night terrors when they're overtired, try putting your youngster to bed about thirty minutes earlier than usual and see if the episodes diminish in frequency. In any case, they'll disappear naturally as the child grows older.

But what about those instances in which you're sure your child is having neither a nightmare nor a night terror but is nevertheless waking up and calling for you? Simply reassure him that everything is all right, put him back to sleep, and then leave him. Don't reward him for waking up by giving him food or by taking him to your room.

Discipline

By age four, your preschooler will have her unpredictable emotional responses somewhat under control, but still won't be able to manage her feelings of defiance. Thus, at this age, she may openly disobey family rules, talk back, or even swear at you. Often she'll behave badly just to annoy you. As irritating and embarrassing as this behavior may be, it's rarely a sign of emotional illness and usually disappears by school age if you take a relaxed approach to it.

This doesn't mean letting your child control or intimidate you. Believe it or not, even she doesn't want that. On the contrary, she expects you to restrain her when she gets too far out of line, just as she assumes you'll protect her when she does something dangerous. So you must teach her what is acceptable behavior and what isn't. The only way she'll learn to set her own limits later is by having you set reasonable limits for her now. If you are firm and consistent, she will become more secure.

In deciding what limits to set, keep in mind that many of the strategies you used when she was younger also are suitable now. It's still important to reward good behavior more often than punishing bad and to avoid physical punishments. And it's still essential to deal with misbehavior promptly and fairly, not waiting so long that your child forgets why she's being disciplined.

Time-out

Although you can't ignore dangerous or destructive behavior, you can call a time-out. This technique is most successful with three- and four-year-olds, who generally know when they've done something seriously wrong and understand that this is why they're being punished.

Here's how the time-out works:

1. Define the behavior you want to stop, and keep track of how frequently it occurs. Punishment of any kind should be used only when your child is intentionally doing something he knows is forbidden.

2. Warn him that if he continues to do this, he'll be punished.

3. Identify a time-out area, preferably a room that's empty of toys, television, or other attractions—in other words, one that's as boring as possible for the child. If such a room isn't available, use a chair facing the wall in a hall or unoccupied room.

4. When the child does something he knows will result in time-out, send him immediately to the area you have selected and tell him how long he has to stay there. Five minutes is usually sufficient. Place a timer or a clock within view so he can keep track of the time. Start with one minute and increase the time by one minute if the behavior continues (up to five minutes).

5. If he cries or screams, reset the timer for another five minutes. If he leaves the time-out area, return him there and reset the timer.

6. Use a time-out each and every time he violates this particular rule. Also, anytime you notice that he's observing the rule, congratulate him for behaving so well.

At this age, her misconduct tends to be more conscious than it once was. As a toddler, your child acted out of curiosity, trying to find and test her limits; now that she's a preschooler, her misbehavior may be less innocent. A three-year-old whose mother is pregnant or whose parents are separated, for example, may react by doing something that she well knows is forbidden. She may not understand the emotions that are driving her to break the rules, but she certainly realizes that she is breaking them.

To discourage such behavior, help your child learn to express her emotions through words instead of violent or obnoxious actions. The mother whose daughter hits her might say, "Stop it! You are very angry. Please tell me why." If she refuses to stop, a time-out may be necessary.

Sometimes your child won't be able to explain her anger, and it will be up to you to help her. This can be a real test of skill and patience, but is well worth it. Usually the problem will be fairly obvious if you examine the situation from her viewpoint. The pregnant mother just described, for example, can suggest, "You're very angry, but Mommy will help you feel better." This approach is most successful if you encourage your child to talk about her problems and feelings on an ongoing basis.

Preparing for Kindergarten

Kindergarten is a major turning point for your child. Even if he has attended nursery school, he'll be expected to be much more grown up as he enters elementary school, and he'll be given more responsibilities and more independence. "Regular" school is also a much larger and more confusing social setting than any he's known before. Even though his class may be no larger than the one in nursery school, he may spend part of each day mixing with children from older classes. So he must be prepared emotionally not only for the tasks of kindergarten but also for the challenge of being one of the youngest in a big school.

As your child nears school age, you can start the preparations by talking to him about going to kindergarten. Explain how his routine will change when he starts school, and get him involved in choosing his back-to-school clothes. It also will help to drive or walk him by the school occasionally and even go in and show him the classroom so he'll see firsthand what to expect. Many schools open their classrooms before school begins so you can take your child in and introduce him to his teacher. All this preparation will help build his enthusiasm and lessen his anxiety about taking his next big step away from home.

Kindergarten is a major turning point for your child.

Lying

Lying at this age is very common. Preschoolers lie for a variety of reasons. Sometimes it's because they're afraid of punishment, or it may be because they've gotten carried away with their fantasies, or perhaps they're imitating behavior they see among adults. Before you punish your child for not telling the truth, make sure you understand her motives.

When she's lying to avoid punishment, she may have broken one of the household rules. For instance, she may have damaged something she shouldn't have been handling. Or maybe she was too rough and she hurt one of her playmates. In any case, she's concluded that what she did is more serious an offense than lying. If you want her to confess, you must help her understand that lying is the greater misdeed. Save your anger and punishment for times when she conceals the truth, and instead of accusing her when you suspect she's done something wrong, say something like "This is broken. I wonder how it happened?" If she confesses, remain calm and even-tempered, and make the punishment less severe than if she persisted in the lie. This way she may be less afraid to divulge the truth next time.

Telling tall tales is entirely different from lying. This usually is just an expression of your child's imagination at work, and does no harm to anyone. It becomes a problem only if you—or your child—can no longer distinguish truth from fantasy. Although a tall tale doesn't require punishment, it does call for a lesson. Tell her the story of "The Boy Who Cried Wolf" and explain how it could be dangerous for her to keep making up falsehoods. (For example, what if she were hurt or ill, and you didn't know whether to believe her or not?) Make it clear that it's in her own best interests to tell the truth.

When your child's lying is just a copy of your behavior, you can best stop it by eliminating the model. When your child hears you telling "white lies," she may not understand that you're doing it to be tactful or in an effort to avoid hurting another person's feelings. All she knows is that you're not telling the truth—so she feels free to lie, as well. You can try teaching her the difference between outright lies and white lies, but she probably won't understand most of it. You're more likely to succeed by changing your behavior.

Prior to beginning school, your child also should have a thorough physical examination. (Many states require it.) Your doctor will evaluate your child's vision, hearing, and overall physical development, make sure he has had the necessary immunizations, and give him any boosters he needs. (See Chapter 27,

"Immunizations," and the immunization schedule on page 73.) Depending on state law and the likelihood of exposure, she also may administer a test for tuberculosis and may send you to a laboratory for other tests.

In most school systems, children are accepted for kindergarten based on their age, often with a very rigid cutoff date as a guideline. For example, if your child turns five years old by December 31, he may be allowed to start school at age four, but if his birthday is January 1, he probably will have to wait until the following fall. While this approach works well for most children, it's not perfect. Developmental rates vary so widely that one child may be prepared for school at four while another is not mature enough until late in his fifth year.

If you are in doubt about your child's readiness, and your child is attending nursery school, his teacher may be able to help you. She's seen him in action with other children and should be able to tell you if he's ready for a more structured classroom experience. Developmental testing of your child also may help determine whether he has the necessary skills to do well in kindergarten. Your pediatrician can help you make arrangements for such testing. These tests also can be helpful if you feel your child is advanced for his age, and you wish him to start school earlier than normal.

Many public school systems conduct preschool screening tests for all kindergarten-age children to assess their readiness for school. This testing of developmental skills generally is held at the school during the summer before the child is scheduled to enter kindergarten. At the same time, school nursing personnel may collect information about the child's health, making sure he's been fully immunized, and perhaps examining his hearing and vision as well.

Unless there's evidence that your child will do very poorly, the best test may be a trial run when school opens. If there is a serious question about his progress at the end of the year, a decision will have to be made concerning his promotion. This decision will be based largely on his ability to learn, follow directions and routines, and relate to the other children as well as the teacher.

Traveling with Your Preschooler

As your child gets older and more active, traveling will become more challenging. She will be restless when confined to a seat and, with her increasing willfulness, may protest loudly when you insist that she stay put. For safety's sake you will need to be firm, but if you provide enough distractions she actually may forget her restlessness. The specific tricks of traveling will vary somewhat with your mode of transportation.

Traveling by Car. Even on the shortest trips, your child must stay in his car safety seat or booster seat. (See *Car Safety Seats,* page 447, for guidelines on selection and installation of car seats.) Most automobile crashes occur within five miles of home and at speeds under twenty-five miles per hour, so there can be no exceptions to the rule. If your youngster protests, refuse to start the car until he's fastened in. If you are driving and he escapes from his seat, pull over until he is secured again.

Even on the shortest trips, your child must stay in a car safety seat or booster seat.

Travel Activities

If you make car trips fun, your child is less likely to resist the confinement. Here are some suggestions to help pass the time.

- Talk about the passing sights. Ask your child what she sees out her window. Point out interesting sights. When she begins to learn colors, letters, and numbers, ask her to identify them in signs and billboards. Remember to keep your eyes on the road, however.

- Keep a variety of picture books and small toys in the car within reach of her car seat.

- Keep several cassettes of children's songs or stories in the car. Encourage your child to sing along with her favorite tunes.

- For longer trips, take along a small box filled with age-appropriate activity materials, such as coloring or activity books, crayons, paper, stickers, or paper dolls. (Do not allow scissors in the car; they could be hazardous in the event of a sudden stop.) Also take along favorite audiotapes, CDs, videos and DVDs (if there is a rear-seated player), with singalongs, word rhymes, or other entertaining and familiar activities.

- Stop at least every two hours to break up the trip. This will allow your child a chance to stretch, perhaps eat a snack, and have a diaper change or use the toilet.

- If your child is prone to motion sickness, it may help to give her an appropriate dose of Dramamine® one half hour before getting in the car. (See *Motion Sickness,* page 657.)

The trip will be more pleasant and comfortable for everyone if you follow several additional rules consistently, wherever you are.

- Never leave a child alone in the car, even for a minute.

- Don't allow yelling, hitting, biting, or loud noisemaking.

- Don't allow children to touch door handles.

- Remind children to be considerate of other people in the car.

Traveling by Plane. When flying with a young child, choose a direct flight whenever possible to keep travel time to a minimum, and consider flying during your child's nap time or on a "redeye" (overnight) flight. Always let the airlines know in advance that you'll be traveling with one or more children. Special seat-

Tips for Safe Air Travel with Children

- Children younger than two years old are not required to be restrained or secured on aircraft during take-offs, landings, and turbulence; they are permitted to be held on the lap of an adult. However, the American Academy of Pediatrics believes that all children need their own seats on airplanes and strongly recommends that very young children (younger than one year old and weighing less than 20 pounds [9 kg] in body weight) be securely fastened in a rear-facing child safety seat; children older than one year and weighing between 20 to 40 pounds (9 to 18 kg) should be securely fastened in a forward-facing seat. Children who weigh more than 40 pounds can be secured in the aircraft seat belt. These measures will help keep children safe during take-off and landing or in case of turbulence. Shield booster seats should not be used because the aircraft seat-back tends to flex forward from the movement of the passenger behind the seat.

- Ensure that your safety seat has received FAA approval. Check that the label on the restraint reads: "This restraint is certified for use in motor vehicles and aircraft."

- Check the width of your safety seat. While airline seats vary in width, a safety seat no wider than 16 inches (41 cm) should fit in most coach seats. Even if the armrests are moved out of the way, a seat wider than 16 inches is unlikely to fit properly into the frame of the aircraft seat.

- Look into options for making sure that your child has his own seat on the airplane. You may have to buy a ticket for him, so ask the airline reservations agent whether a discounted fare is available. Or select flights that are likely to have empty seats and ask about the airline's policy for a child using a safety seat in an empty seat next to you, without having to pay for your child's travel.

- If you purchase a ticket for your child, reserve adjoining seats. A car seat must be placed in a window seat so it will not block the escape path in an emergency. A car seat may not be placed in an exit row.

- If you need to change planes to make a connecting flight, transporting a car seat, a child, and luggage through a busy airport can be very challenging. You can request assistance from the airlines between connecting flights.

Surviving Your Child's Jet Lag

Nothing can take the fun out of a vacation quicker than a child (and an entire family) dealing with jet lag after a long plane flight. Traveling across time zones can disrupt the body's internal clock, often making chaos of familiar sleep-and-wake cycles (circadian rhythms), and leaving children cranky and lethargic until they become adjusted to the new time zone. Although the change of only one time zone usually doesn't cause a major problem, sleep difficulties are more likely with a time change of two or more hours. In general, people can adapt more easily when travel occurs from east to west.

Some parents find that they can minimize their child's jet lag by trying the following strategies.

- In the days before the trip, gradually put your youngster to sleep at a time closer to the bedtime that coincides with the region to which you'll be traveling. You also can try gradually adjusting mealtimes at home so they're closer to the times that you'll be eating at your travel destination. (Infants, of course, should be fed when they're hungry, no matter what time zone you're in.)

- Once you're at your destination, don't plan a full schedule of activities the day you arrive. Keep things flexible, but do spend some time in outdoor activities in the first few days to expose your child to as much daylight as possible. Daylight will facilitate chemical changes in the body that will help your youngster adapt to the time change.

- Many people become dehydrated on long flights. Make sure your child drinks plenty of water both during the flight and after your arrival to avoid the discomfort of a dry mouth and other symptoms of dehydration, which can contribute to jet lag.

- Although a number of dietary supplements—most notably melatonin—have been widely promoted as effective in combating jet lag, there is no scientific evidence of its benefits, particularly in children. Melatonin is a hormone secreted by the brain's pineal gland, but until more is known about it, the American Academy of Pediatrics strongly advises parents to avoid giving it to children and adolescents.

ing arrangements may be possible, and a selection of "kiddie" meals may be available if you inquire when making your reservations. Do not request seating in an emergency exit row.

Recently airport security procedures have become more rigorous. Be sure to allow your family additional time to move through the security checkpoints. The Federal Aviation Administration (FAA) recommends that when you're traveling with small children, give yourself even more time than usual to negotiate security. Remember, all child-related equipment—including strollers, car seats, infant carriers, and toys—must be visually inspected, as well as pass through an X-ray machine. You'll probably be asked to fold child-related equipment when you reach the X-ray belt so it all can pass through the inspection process more rapidly.

For your child's safety, dress him in bright colors when you travel so you can spot him more easily in a crowd. Tuck a card into his pocket on which you've written his name (and yours), your phone number (including cell phone), your address, and your travel itinerary. Have an up-to-date photograph of your child in your possession. (If possible, have a Polaroid taken the day of your flight, with your child wearing the clothes that he has on the day that you're traveling.)

While it makes sense to ask for preboarding when you're traveling with a baby, keep in mind that preboarding with a toddler or preschooler may not be wise if you think your child will become restless the longer he's on the plane.

One advantage of air travel is that you and your child can take brief walks when the "Fasten Seat Belt" sign is off. This is the best antidote to restlessness, especially if you should meet another preschooler in the aisles.

To amuse your child in her seat, take along an assortment of books and toys similar to those you would pack for a car trip. Also, many airlines offer assortments of activity materials for children. Check with your flight attendant about this.

VISIT TO THE PEDIATRICIAN

Your preschooler should be examined by the pediatrician once a year. Now that she is better able to follow instructions and communicate, some screening procedures are possible that previously weren't. In particular, her maturity will allow more accurate testing of her hearing and vision.

Hearing. By around age four, your child can talk well enough to describe different sounds. A thorough hearing check can be done, using tones at different frequencies. This test should be repeated every year or two, or more often if hearing problems are found.

Vision. By age three or four, your child is able to understand directions and cooperate well enough to have a formal vision test. At this age, her visual acuity should be 20/30 or better. More important than the absolute vision in each eye

is any difference in visual acuity between her two eyes. If you suspect a problem, she'll need to be seen by a pediatric ophthalmologist.

IMMUNIZATION ALERT

During the preschool years, your child should receive a DTaP (diphtheria, tetanus, pertussis) immunization. This DTaP booster is due two and one-half to three and one-half years after receiving the fourth dose of the initial DTaP series. Because the fourth dose of the initial series usually is given at around fifteen to eighteen months of age, the preschool booster is normally due around age four to six years.

Some states also require an MMR (measles, mumps, rubella) booster vaccine for school entry, so check your child's school requirements with your pediatrician.

The fourth dose of the inactivated polio vaccine also is given at four to six years of age.

SAFETY CHECK

Guard Against Falls From

- Play equipment: Watch your child on slides and monkey bars.

- Tricycles: Avoid unstable tricycles, and use the kind that allows the child to be low to the ground. Use a child bicycle helmet that fits your child properly and is certified.

- Stairs: Continue to use gates at the top and bottom of staircases.

- Windows: Continue to use window guards at or above the second floor.

Burns

- Keep matches, cigarette lighters, and hot objects out of your child's reach.

Auto Crashes

- When your child reaches the top weight for his car safety seat, or his ears have reached the top of the car safety seat, he needs a booster seat.

- Your young child is not safe around cars. Keep him away from places where there are cars. Driveways and quiet streets can be dangerous.

- Do not allow children to ride tricycles in the street or near traffic; do not allow them to ride down driveways into the street.

Drowning

- Never leave your preschooler unattended near water, even if he supposedly knows how to swim.

- Children are generally not developmentally ready for formal swimming lessons until after their fourth birthday.

- Swimming lessons are not a strategy for drowning prevention.

13

PART-TIME CARE FOR
YOUR CHILD

*W*ho will care for your child during the hours when you are away? Sooner or later you're bound to face this question. Whether you need someone to care for him a few hours a week or nine hours a day, you'll want to feel confident about the person who does it. But finding the right person to care for your child can be a big challenge. Your top priority should be to ensure the well-being of your child, and that should be the overriding consideration when selecting child care. This chapter provides suggestions to make your search easier. It also contains guidelines for preventing, recognizing, and resolving problems once you've made your choice.

The most important aspect of finding good part-time care is judging the character and abilities of the child care program and of any caregiver involved with your child. Nearly six of every ten families use child care centers for child care. Parents also choose to share

Never entrust your child to anyone until you've taken time to watch her with your child and other children.

care between themselves or have relatives and nonrelatives provide that service. Some children participate in more than one type of child care arrangement at different times of the day or week. If your child's caregiver is not a member of your family, chances are you'll meet this person only a few times before entrusting your child to her. (Many, though not all, caregivers are women.) Even so, you'll want to feel as confident about her as if she were a member of your family. While it's impossible to be absolutely sure about anyone under these circumstances, you can tell a great deal about caregivers by observing them at work for a day or two and carefully checking references. Entrust your child to someone only after you have taken time to watch her with your child and other children, and you feel confident in her abilities and dedication.

WHAT TO LOOK FOR IN A CAREGIVER: GUIDELINES FOR THE TODDLER AND PRESCHOOL CHILD

(For infants, see Chapter 6, page 163.)

Children thrive when they're cared for by supportive adults who are warmly affectionate and help them work out solutions while protecting them from making choices that could lead to serious injury. The following list describes many things you should look for when you're observing someone who might take care of your child. These guidelines apply not only to child care workers but also to babysitters and teachers during the preschool and early primary school years. They're also good to keep in mind as you play with your child yourself or supervise small groups of children. A good caregiver will:

- Listen carefully to children and observe their behavior.

- Set reasonable limits for children and maintain those limits consistently.

- Tell children why certain things are not allowed, and offer acceptable alternatives.

- Deal with difficult situations as they arise and before they get out of control.

- Live up to promises made to the children.

- Join children at play without disrupting their activity.

- Encourage children to think of their own ideas before offering suggestions.

- Reward children's efforts and relieve their "hurts" with an affectionate physical gesture, such as a hug or a pat.

- Talk naturally and conversationally with the children about what they are doing.

- Help children encourage each other by asking them to share their accomplishments.

- Encourage children to complete projects, even if they take longer than the time originally scheduled.

- Limit adult conversations in the children's presence.

- Show respect for the children's ideas and decisions.

- Avoid offering children choices when there is no choice.

- Allow children to make mistakes and learn from them (as long as there is no danger involved in doing so).

CHOICES IN PART-TIME CARE

In addition to the general suggestions just mentioned, you need to identify your specific needs and desires. Your list of questions should include:

- Where do I want my child to be during the day: At home? In someone else's home? In a child care center? If away from home, in what part of town?

- What days and hours do I need part-time care each week?

- How will I handle my child's transportation to and from the program (if it's away from home)?

- What backup arrangements can I make? How will I handle days when my child is sick or when my child's caregiver is unavailable because of illness or personal business? What are the arrangements for holidays, summertime, and vacations?

- What can I realistically afford?

- What size program do I want for my child?

- What qualifications do I want the caregiver(s) to have?

- How do I want my child disciplined?

- What other basic conditions would make me feel comfortable about leaving my child with someone else?

Nearly a quarter of all parents provide all child care themselves. Nearly another quarter involve relatives in child care, mostly grandmothers. Not only are many grandparents caring for children for part of the day, but more and more of them are involved in taking children to and from other child care arrangements.

If you have family members or friends who you would like to care for your child and who live nearby, ask yourself if you would be comfortable with their care and whether they'd be willing to provide part-time care either on a regular basis or as a backup if other arrangements fail. Consider also, when possible, that offering payment for these services makes the arrangement fairer and creates an additional incentive for the person you depend on for child care to help you.

Other options are to bring someone into your own home or to take your child to another person's home or a child care center. Your financial resources, the age and needs of your child, and your own preferences about child rearing will help you decide which choice is best.

In-Home Care

If you are returning to work while your child is still an infant, one choice for child care (often a more expensive one) may be to bring someone into your own home who can look after him and perhaps take some housekeeping duties, as well. This person may come to your home on a regular basis or live with you. You can find such a person by asking your friends for recommendations, scanning or placing ads in the paper (especially local publications for parents), and checking with agencies that specialize in child care.

In-home caregivers are not required to be licensed, so you'll have to check references and monitor the performance of anyone you hire very carefully. This type of care is more popular in some communities than in others, and the extent of use of nonrelatives as caregivers in the child's home is less common now than at other times. Ask each candidate for her work records during the past four or five years and talk to each of her former employers. Ask her for references and detailed and personal questions about whether she's reliable and capable. Also, ask about her approach to discipline, scheduling, feeding, and comforting, to try to determine if she is right for your child and your style of child rearing.

The person you ultimately choose will be a part of your family, so make sure

A Message for Grandparents

As a grandparent, you may become the person providing part-time care for your grandchild. Therefore, many of the guidelines in this chapter would apply to your caregiving. The recommendations about the best environment for the child, safety issues, special needs, and the size of the group (if you care for more than one child) should be considered.

As a grandparent, your role is unique and important. You are not just "another babysitter." You have a fundamental connection, providing the continuity between generations that your grandchild will come to understand and respect. Take advantage of this irreplaceable role. You are the only person who can be called "Grandma" or "Grandpa" in front of your own name. Your involvement with your grandchild, introducing her to your own world, is especially valuable. Treasure it. Make the most of those special days when you are the babysitter, and offer to do it regularly if you're able.

At times, you may not be the actual caregiver for your grandchild, but rather you'll take her to and from a child care center or babysitter. Provide another "set of eyes" to evaluate the quality of the center or sitter, which will help your own child (your grandchild's parent) feel secure in his own choice of a child care setting. Don't hesitate to ask the tough questions about that setting, and be willing to speak up if you disagree with the rest of the family's assessment of the site; if you have reservations of where and with whom your grandchild is spending time, based on your observations, let your concerns be known. After all, you have much more experience in assessing some of the most relevant factors. The information in this chapter will provide some guidelines to better judge the quality of the setting.

By the way, if you've accepted the responsibility of picking up or dropping off your grandchild at regular times, introduce yourself to the responsible person at that site and provide them with your telephone number as a contact person. And remember, when driving with your grandchild, be sure she is placed in a car safety seat at all times.

you hire someone who respects your values, beliefs, and lifestyle. To the extent possible, involve the whole family in the decision, and arrange for a trial period of at least a week when you are at home to watch the caregiver work under your supervision before you make a final commitment.

Arranging for child care at home has the following advantages and disadvantages.

Advantages

1. Your child stays in familiar surroundings and receives individualized care and attention.

2. She isn't exposed to the illnesses and negative behavior of children from other families.

3. When your child is sick, you don't have to stay home from work or make different arrangements to take care of her.

4. Your caregiver may do some light housework and prepare the family meal. (If this is one of your expectations, make that clear from the start.)

5. You needn't worry about transportation for your child (unless you plan for the caregiver to take him on outings).

Disadvantages

1. You may have difficulty finding someone who is willing to accept the wages, benefits, and confinement of working in your home, or you may find the costs of qualified in-home care prohibitive.

2. Since you will be considered an employer, you must meet minimum-wage, Social Security, and tax-reporting requirements. You also should provide health insurance for your employee if she isn't otherwise covered. (If you use a part-time care agency, your costs may be higher, but you won't have to manage the government reporting and tax payments yourself.)

3. The presence of a caregiver may infringe on your family's privacy, especially if she lives in your home. Furthermore, she may bring her own needs and problems with her, which could involve more of your own time and energy than you bargained for.

4. Because the caregiver is alone with your child most of the time, you have no way of knowing exactly how she is performing her job.

5. You are dependent on your caregiver's reliability. If she gets sick, has a family crisis, finds a better job, or wants to take a vacation without warning you, you'll be left frantically searching for a replacement.

Family Child Care

Many people provide informal care in their homes for small groups of children, often looking after their own children or grandchildren at the same time. Some offer evening care or care for children with special needs. Family child care generally is less expensive and more flexible than that offered by child care centers, but over the past decade, the use of family child care has declined sharply. Small family child care homes have less than six children and may have one caregiver. Large family child care homes may have up to twelve children and two or more caregivers.

A minority of these family child care providers are formally licensed and registered. Licensing regulations vary from state to state and can be obtained from the appropriate local authorities. Also, the American Academy of Pediatrics can provide general information on the basic requirements for family child care homes and the national standards for a safe and healthy family child care and child care centers. (Send your request for information to the American Academy of Pediatrics, 141 Northwest Point Boulevard, Elk Grove Village, IL 60007; www.aap.org).

The majority of family child care homes are not inspected, or if they are, usually the inspections are infrequent and superficial. For that reason you must be careful to observe the caregiver's work and check her references and certification before making a decision about such care for your child.

Family child care has the following advantages and disadvantages.

Advantages

1. In good family child care settings, there is a favorable adult/child ratio. The total number of children to adults should be no more than about three children for one adult if some of the children are infants, and no more than two children (a two-to-one ratio) if both are infants.

2. Your child has all the comforts of being in a home and can be involved in many of the same household activities he'd find at your own house.

3. There may be playmates. This provides more opportunities for social stimulation than if your child were cared for alone at home.

4. Family child care is very flexible, so special arrangements usually can be made to meet your child's individual interests and needs.

Disadvantages

1. You cannot observe what happens to your child in your absence. While some providers carefully organize activities that are appropriate for children, others use TV as a babysitter—even letting the children watch shows that are inappropriate for them—while they do housework. (Be aware that the same thing could be true of people who care for your child in your own home.)

2. It may be difficult for you to get satisfactory references for a particular caregiver.

3. Most family child care providers work without supervision or advice from other adults.

4. You need to inquire about and become aware in advance of who else will be in the home while your child is there. The caregiver might share the care of your child with relatives, boyfriends, or other people who might expose your child to injury or disease.

For the names of family child care homes in your area, contact the local agency that licenses or registers them, or use a local referral agency that lists them. Check with these agencies about homes advertised in the paper or on neighborhood bulletin boards, since these may not be licensed. Contact federally supported Child Care Aware at 1–800–424–2246 or www.childcareaware.org for the child care resource and referral agency nearest you. References from parents of children the same age as yours or a little older, who recently had their children at the family child care home you are considering, also can be very helpful.

Before committing to a particular family child care home:

- Check the child care provider's references, licensing or registration by state or local government, accreditation, and inspection status (if any). See if the family child care provider has been accredited by the National Association for Family Child Care. Find out if the provider belongs to a family child care provider association or is a part of a family child care agency.

- Call the parents of children who are in, or recently were in, child care there, and ask about their impression and experiences.

- Find out how many children (including the caregiver's children) actually are cared for in the home at various times of the day and on different days.

In family child care, your child can be involved in many of the same household activities he'd find at your own home.

- Ask about substitute arrangements in case the caregiver (or someone in his family) becomes ill.

- Ask how the caregiver would handle an emergency situation involving one or more of the children or himself.

- Make sure the caregiver and facility (if licensed) complies with standard health and safety requirements such as those of the American Academy of Pediatrics as national standards. You can look up the national standards on the Internet at http://nrc.uchsc.edu. (Also see "Making a Final Selection" on page 399.)

Child Care Centers

Child care centers are also called day care, child development centers, nursery schools, and other similar names. Many child care centers are open from 6:00 or 7:00 A.M. to 6:00 P.M. to meet the needs of most working parents. These facilities usually care for groups of ten or more children, often in a church, community center, school, or office building. Most are licensed for children from two and a half to six years, although many offer care for infants. A growing number of centers participate in accreditation programs. For more information about accreditation of centers, contact the National Association for the Education of Young Children, 1509 16th Street NW, Washington, DC, 20036–1426, 1–800–424–2460, www.naeyc.org.

Child care centers are the fastest-growing form of part-time care in the United States. They can be found in several different versions, each with its own characteristics, strengths, and weaknesses.

Chain centers have become a thriving national industry. Many of the larger ones have a wide variety of activities and programs that appeal to both parents and children (child development programs, structured curricula, and centrally managed personnel and facility routines). Because of centralized management, some do not exhibit unique features found in individually run facilities.

Independent for-profit centers usually are small operations run by a small staff. They generally have no agency, church, or other support, so they must depend on enrollment fees to pay the overhead and earn a narrow profit for the owners. Because many of these programs are built around one or two dedicated people, they can be quite excellent—as long as those individuals remain actively involved with day-to-day operations. Unfortunately, such programs do not always maintain their high standards, because of high costs relative to income, staff turnovers, or ownership changes.

Nonprofit centers often are linked with churches, synagogues, community centers, universities, or organizations like the YMCA or YWCA. They may have access to public funding, permitting discounted fees for lower-income families. Any income earned from enrollment is put back into the program, thus directly benefiting the children. However, these centers are also subject to undesirable changes due to high costs and low income, as well as having to meet the demands of the sponsoring organization. Many also rely on parent involvement for fund-raising events and other aspects of operating the centers.

There are several advantages and disadvantages to child care centers.

Advantages

1. Because local child care centers are easier to regulate and observe, more information generally is available about them than about other child care choices.

2. Many centers have structured programs designed to meet children's developmental needs.

3. Most centers have several caregivers, so you are not dependent on the availability of just one person.

4. Workers in these centers tend to be better supervised than caregivers in other settings.

5. Often you can arrange shorter hours or fewer days of care if you work only part time.

6. Many centers encourage parental involvement so you can help to make the center better while your child is enrolled.

Disadvantages

1. Regulations for child care centers vary widely: Strict standards applied to publicly funded centers may not apply to privately financed ones, and many states exempt church-run facilities from even minimum requirements. To save on personnel costs or to cope with personnel shortages, a center may provide less qualified and less competent adults to care for children than is desirable.

2. Good programs may have waiting lists for admission because they are in such demand.

3. Because these arrangements serve more children and have larger staffs, your child may receive less personalized attention than in smaller programs.

Child care centers generally are listed in the phone book or can be identified by calling your local health or welfare agency. Many communities have resources and referral agencies that help parents find appropriate care. For a resource and referral agency near you, contact federally supported Child Care Aware at 1–800–424–2246 or www.childcareaware.org. Ask your pediatrician or other parents with children in child care to recommend a center from these lists.

MAKING A FINAL SELECTION

When considering a particular child care setting, you need to know all of the rules and practices that would affect your child. If the program is formal enough to have a printed handbook, this may answer many of your questions. Otherwise, ask the program director about the following (some of which apply to in-home or family child care as well).

1. What are the hiring requirements for staff members? In most good programs, caregivers must have at least two years of college, pass minimum health requirements, and receive basic immunizations. Ideally, they will have some background in early child development and perhaps have children themselves. Directors generally must have a college degree or many years of experience qualifying them as experts in both child development and administration.

2. How many staff members are available per child? Although some children need highly personalized attention and others do well with less direct supervision, the general rule to follow is: The younger the child, the more adults there should be in each group. Each child should be assigned to one caregiver as the primary person responsible for that child's care, and that caregiver should provide most of the child's one-on-one care (e.g., feeding, diapering, putting the child to sleep).

How many children are in each group? Generally, smaller groups offer children a better chance to interact with and learn from one another.

While fewer children per adult is usually better, here are maximum ratios and group sizes for each age category:

Age	Child/Staff Ratio	Group Size
Birth–12 mos.	3:1	6
13–30 mos.	4:1	8
31–35 mos.	5:1	10
3-year-olds	7:1	14
4- to 5-year-olds	8:1	16
6- to 8-year-olds	10:1	20
9- to 12-year-olds	12:1	24

3. Is there a problem with frequent staff changes? If so, this may suggest that there are problems with the facility's operations. Ideally, most caregivers should have been with the program for several years. Unfortunately, because of low wages and few benefits for caregivers, a high turnover rate is common.

4. What are the goals of the program? Some are very organized and try to teach children new skills, or attempt to change or mold their behavior and

The younger the child, the more adults there should be in each group.

beliefs. Others are very relaxed, with an emphasis on helping children develop at their own pace. Still others fall somewhere in between. Decide what you want for your child, and make sure the program you choose meets your desires. Avoid those that offer no personalized attention or support for your child. Generally, these care for large groups of children with too few teachers.

5. What are the admission procedures? Quality child care programs require relevant background information on each child. Be prepared for very specific questions about your child's individual needs, developmental level, and health status. You also may be asked about your own child-rearing desires and any other children in your family. You should be asked for a record of your child's routine preventive health care and any health problems your pediatrician has identified. Be concerned if the center does not require that you provide this information.

6. Does the child care provider have a valid license and recent health certificate, and does the provider enforce health and immunization requirements for children in the program? Standard immunizations and regular checkups should be required for all children and staff members.

7. How are illnesses handled? Parents should be notified if a staff member or child contracts a significant communicable disease (not just a cold, but problems like chickenpox or hepatitis). The program also should have a clear policy regarding sick children. You should know when to keep your youngster home and how the center will respond if he becomes ill during the day.

8. What are the costs? How much will you have to pay to start, and how often will you make installment payments? What do the payments cover specifically? Will you need to pay when your child is absent for illness or vacations with the family?

9. What happens on a typical day? Ideally, there should be a mix of physical activity and quiet times. Some activities should be group oriented and others individualized. Times for meals and snacks should be set aside. While a certain amount of structure is desirable, there also should be room for free play and special events.

10. How much parental involvement is expected? Some programs rely heavily on parent participation, while others request very little. At the least, quality programs should welcome your opinions and allow you to visit your child during the day. Do not consider any program that is closed to parents for part or all of the day.

11. What are the general procedures? A well-organized program should have clearly defined rules and regulations regarding:

- Hours of operation

- Transportation of children

- Field trips

- Meals and snacks

- Administration of medication and first aid

- Emergency evacuations

- Notification of child's absence

- Weather cancellations

- Withdrawal of children from the program

- Supplies or equipment that parents must provide

- Special celebrations

- How parents may contact the staff during the day and at night

- Exclusion of children with certain illnesses

- Access of parents to all parts of the facility that their children are using, at any time when their children are being cared for

- Security to be certain that everyone who enters the facility, including outdoor play areas, is screened by child care personnel, that strangers cannot enter the building, and that familiar adults who are acting oddly cannot get into any child care area, indoors or out

Once you've received the basic information, you should inspect the building and grounds during operating hours to see how the caregivers interact with the children. Your first impressions are especially important, since they'll influence all your future dealings with the program. If you sense warmth and a loving approach to the children, you'll probably feel comfortable placing your own child there. If you see a worker spank or restrain one of the youngsters too forcefully,

Napping In Child Care Settings

Sudden infant death syndrome (SIDS) has gotten plenty of attention in recent years, and many parents now know the importance of placing a baby to sleep on her back to minimize the risk of SIDS. Obviously, this same precaution should be followed in child care settings, where 20 percent of all SIDS cases occur. In 2003, when the American Academy of Pediatrics launched a campaign that stressed the importance of using this sleep position to lower the incidence of SIDS during child care, only fifteen states in the United States had licensing regulations mandating that child care facilities place infants on their backs to sleep.

If your baby is going to be napping at his child care site, you must discuss this issue with the caretakers before making a final selection about a facility. Make sure that the child care setting you choose routinely follows this simple procedure. (For more information about SIDS, see page 173.)

you should reconsider sending your own child, even if that's the only sign of abusive behavior you've noticed.

Try to observe the daily routine, paying attention to how the day is organized and what activities are planned for the children. Watch how food is prepared, and find out how often the children are fed. Check how frequently the children are taken to the toilet and/or diapered. While touring the child care home or center, also check to see if the following basic health and safety standards are being met.

- The premises are clean and reasonably neat (without discouraging play by the children).

- There is plenty of play equipment, and it is in good repair.

- The equipment is appropriate for the developmental skills of the children in the program.

- Children are closely supervised when climbing on playthings, roughhousing, or playing with blocks (which are sometimes thrown) and other potentially dangerous toys.

- There are safe indoor and outdoor areas where the children have active (large-muscle) play each day, with cushioning material under and at least 6 feet (1.8 meters) around any climbing equipment indoors or outdoors. Be sure that the surfacing and the equipment meet the guidelines of the Consumer Product Safety Commission. (Visit http://cpsc.gov for more information.)

While touring the child care home or center, also check to see if basic health and safety standards are being met.

- Areas where food is handled are clearly separate from toilets and diaper-changing areas.

- Diaper-changing areas are cleaned and sanitized after being used for each child.

- Handwashing sinks are available where they are needed and are used by the children and staff to wash their hands:

  - Upon arrival for the day

  - When moving from one child care group to another

  - Before and after eating or touching food or food preparation surfaces

  - Before and after giving medication

  - Before and after playing in water that is used by more than one person

  - After diapering

  - After using the toilet or helping children use the toilet

  - After handling any body fluid, such as nasal discharge, blood, vomit, drool, or sores

  - After playing in sandboxes

  - After handling garbage

- Potty (or training) chairs should be avoided because they increase the risk of spreading germs that cause diarrhea.

- Children are supervised by sight and sound at all times, even when napping.

A Child Care Checklist

The following checklist can be used to help you evaluate caregivers and child care programs. Ideally, the answer to every question will be yes, but realistically, there are bound to be a few nos. Look carefully at the questions that receive "no" responses, and decide how important these issues are to you.

For All Children

Does the caregiver:

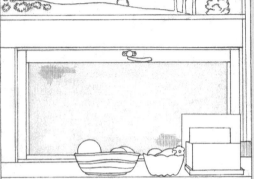

1. feel like someone with whom you can develop an open relationship?

2. impress you as someone your child will enjoy, and who enjoys working with children?

3. agree with your beliefs about child rearing and discipline, and respect your family's cultural and religious values?

4. provide the right activities, materials, and equipment to help children learn and grow?

5. encourage and role-model good health habits, such as washing hands at the appropriate times?

6. know basic first aid?

7. have enough time for each child in his care?

8. help each child to feel good about herself?

9. take time to discuss your child with you regularly?

10. have a regular medical examination?

Does the child care home or center have:

1. an up-to-date license and a recent inspection by health and early childhood education experts?

2. a convenient location near your home or work?

3. an open-door policy allowing parents to visit at any time?

4. enough indoor and outdoor space so children can move freely and safely?

5. an adequate number of caregivers to meet the needs of all the children?

6. equipment that is safe, clean, and suitable for the ages of the children in the program?

7. enough heat, light, and ventilation?

8. a clear policy for the care of sick children, and a separate area to care for sick children? (An isolated area is not necessary, but a quiet place to rest should be available.)

9. acceptable safety standards? These should include:

- Cushioning material in the fall zone of any climbing equipment, indoors or out

- A first-aid kit

- Smoke detectors and enough exits in case of fire

- Covered radiators and protected heaters

- Strong screens or bars on windows above the first floor

- Safety caps on all electrical outlets

- Medicines and poisonous substances stored out of children's reach in a locked cabinet or container

Are there opportunities:

1. to play both quietly and actively, indoors and out?

2. to play both alone and in groups?

3. to use materials and equipment that help develop new skills and abilities?

4. to learn to get along and share with others?

5. to learn about different cultures through art, music, and games?

If Your Child Is an Infant or Toddler (Through Age Three)

Does the caregiver:

1. enjoy cuddling your baby?

2. properly care for your child's physical needs, such as feeding and diapering?

3. spend plenty of time holding, talking, and playing with your child?

4. help your child find interesting things to look at, touch, and hear?

5. cooperate with you in teaching your toddler how to use the toilet?

6. provide a safe environment for children who are beginning to crawl and walk?

Does the child care home or center have:

1. gates at the top and bottom of stairs?

2. special toilet seats or toilets designed for children, and which can be easily cleaned after each use? (Potty or training chairs should not be used, since they are difficult to keep clean and may spread infection.)

3. a clean, safe place to change diapers?

4. cribs with firm mattresses covered in heavy plastic?

5. separate cribs and linens for each baby?

Are there opportunities:

1. to crawl and explore safely?

2. to play with objects and toys that help develop the senses of touch, sight, and hearing (such as mobiles, rattles, crib gyms, nesting toys, balls, and blocks)?

- Where possible, caregivers do not prepare or serve food to the group after being involved in diapering and toileting.

Once you're satisfied that a particular program will provide your child with a safe, loving, healthy environment, let him test it out while you're present. Watch how the caregivers and your child interact, and make sure that all of you are comfortable with the situation.

If Your Child Is a Preschooler (Ages Three to Five)

Does the caregiver:

1. plan a variety of activities for your child?

2. join in activities herself?

3. set consistent and reasonable limits that encourage your child's independence?

4. recognize the value of play and creativity?

5. seem patient and accepting of your child's individuality?

Does the child care home or center have:

1. easy-to-reach handwashing facilities near the toilets?

2. safe, sturdy play equipment inside and outside?

3. a fenced outdoor play area with a gate that can be locked?

4. adequate room for play?

5. educational toys and equipment?

Are there opportunities:

1. to play make-believe using costumes and props?

2. for each child to choose his own activities for part of the day?

3. to take short field trips?

After completing this checklist, if you still are uncertain about your child's care arrangement, discuss your concerns with your pediatrician.

BUILDING A RELATIONSHIP WITH YOUR CHILD'S CAREGIVERS

For your child's sake, you need to develop a good relationship with the person or people who care for her in your absence. The better you get along with her caregiver, the more comfortable your child will feel as she interacts with both of you. The better you communicate with each other about her, the more continuity there will be in her care throughout the day.

One way to build this relationship is by talking with the caregiver—even briefly—each time you leave or return for your child. If something exciting or

Tips to Make It Easier When You Leave Your Child

Just getting the day started is challenging: You have to get the whole family dressed and fed, leaving enough time to get to the child care facility and then to work on schedule. The biggest struggle in all of this comes the moment you leave your child. Separating is hard, whatever your child's age, but it is especially difficult during the first two years of life. Here are some suggestions to make this morning ritual a little easier for both of you.

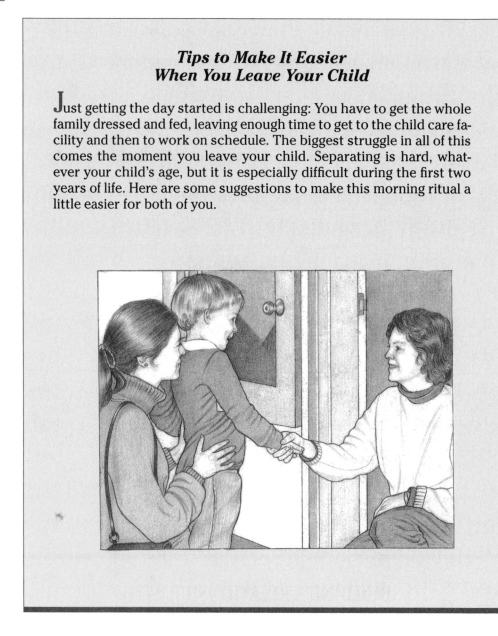

upsetting happened during the early morning, it might affect your child's behavior during the rest of the day, so the caregiver should know about it. When you take her home, you should be told about any important events that occurred in your absence, from a change in bowel movements or eating patterns to a new way of playing or her first steps. Also, if she's showing symptoms of a developing illness, you and the caregiver should discuss the situation and agree on what to do if symptoms get worse.

Your Child's Developmental Stage	Your Response
0 to 7 months In early infancy your baby primarily needs love, comforting, and good basic care to satisfy his physical needs.	Although this period may be a difficult time of separation for you, young infants generally will accommodate well to a consistent child care worker in almost any setting. During the initial settling-in period, your presence should last for up to one hour. This can be shortened by the end of one to two weeks.
7 to 12 months Stranger anxiety normally occurs at this time. Suddenly your baby may be reluctant to stay with anyone outside his family. The unfamiliar setting of a child care center also may upset him.	If possible, do not start child care during this period. If your child is already in a program, take a little extra time each day before you say good-bye. Create a short good-bye ritual, perhaps involving a favorite toy. Above all, be consistent from day to day.
12 to 24 months This is when separation anxiety peaks and your child has the most difficulty with your leaving. He may not believe that you will return, and may weep and cling to you as you try and get out the door.	Be understanding but firm and persistent. Once you have left, do not reappear unless you are prepared to stay or to take your child with you.

A rivalry may develop between you and the caregiver for your child's affection and control of her behavior. For example, you may hear "Funny, she never does that for me" when she misbehaves. Don't take this seriously—children usually save their worst behavior for the people they trust most.

If you treat caregivers as partners, they will feel that you respect them and probably will be more enthusiastic about looking after your child. Here are some ways to build this sense of partnership on a daily basis.

- Show the caregiver something that your child has made at home, or talk about things she's done that are particularly funny or interesting. Explain that sharing this kind of information is important to you, and encourage two-way communication.

- Extend basic courtesy to your child's caregivers.

- Provide materials and suggestions for special projects the caregivers can do with your child and/or the group.

- Help out before you leave your child by spending a few minutes getting her settled. If she's in a child care center, help her put away her things and join an activity. If she is being cared for at home, get her involved in an activity before you depart. Make sure your child always knows you are leaving. Say good-bye before you disappear, but leave without prolonging your departure. Don't just "slip away."

- Help plan and carry out special activities with the caregiver.

Periodically, you and the caregiver also should have longer discussions to review your child's progress, discuss any problems, and plan for future changes in your child's care. Schedule these extended conversations at a time when you won't be rushing to get somewhere and at a place where there won't be distractions. If possible, arrange for someone else to care for your child while you are talking. Allow enough time to discuss all the facts and opinions that both of you have on your minds, and agree on specific objectives and plans.

Most parents find that this discussion goes more smoothly if they've made a list of important topics beforehand. You also should start the conversation on a positive note by talking about some of the things the caregiver is doing that please you. Then move on to your concerns. After presenting your own thoughts, ask for her opinions and listen carefully. Remember, there is little that's strictly right or wrong when it comes to child rearing, and most situations have several "right" approaches. Be open-minded and flexible in your discussions. Close the conversation with a specific plan of action and a date to meet again. Both of you will be more comfortable if something concrete comes out of the meeting, even if it's only a decision to stay on the same course for another month or two.

RESOLVING CONFLICTS THAT ARISE OVER YOUR CHILD'S CARE

Let's assume that you've chosen a child care setting carefully. Does that mean your problems are over? Probably not.

Whenever two or more people share responsibility for a child, conflicts are bound to arise. In many cases you can resolve a disagreement about child care simply by talking through the problem. You may find that the conflict is nothing more than a misunderstanding or a misreading of the situation. Other times, es-

The better you get along with her caregiver, the more comfortable your child will feel as she interacts with both of you.

pecially when several people are involved in the care of your child, you may need a more organized approach to resolving problems. The following step-by-step strategy can help.

1. Define the problem clearly. Make sure you understand who is involved, but avoid blaming anyone. For example, what if your child has been biting other children in her child care program? Find out whom she's bitten and which caregivers were on hand at the time. Ask what they observed before you decide whether the problem is solely your child's. Perhaps she was provoked. Maybe you can suggest an alternate way in which the caregivers can respond if the incident recurs.

2. Listen to everyone's ideas in order to find other possible solutions.

3. Agree on a specific plan of action with clearly defined time limits and assignments to each of the caregivers—including you.

4. Consider everything that could go wrong with the plan you've devised, and decide how these problems might be avoided or handled if they occur.

5. Put the plan into action.

6. Meet again at a specified time to decide whether the plan is working. If it's not, go through the process again to decide what changes need to be made.

WHAT TO DO WHEN YOUR CHILD IS SICK

If your child is like most others, he'll get his share of illnesses, whether he's in a child care program or not. In most cases these illnesses will be colds or other respiratory infections, which tend to occur more often between early fall and late spring. At times he may get one infection right after another and be sick for weeks. If both parents have full-time jobs, this can be a big problem.

Even children who are only mildly ill may be sent home from child care programs, and for good reason. A sick child may be contagious and risks giving his illness to another child. Also, a sick child may need extra care and attention, which most programs are poorly equipped to provide. Few child care workers want to accept the responsibility of caring for a child with anything more than a very minor illness.

Some states have regulations that actually require child care programs to send sick children home. This makes sense, particularly when a child has a fever and is acting sick, is sneezing or coughing, is vomiting, or has diarrhea, since it is under those circumstances that contagious diseases are spread to others.

Respiratory diseases, however, are contagious well before any symptoms appear. By the time anyone realizes the child is sick, he's probably already spread the infection.

Ideally, you'll be able to stay home when your child is sick. However, if you work full time, this may be difficult or not possible. Talk to your employer ahead of time to see if arrangements can be made for you to be home when your child is sick. You might suggest taking your work home with you, or try to identify in advance coworkers who can substitute for you when this situation arises.

If your job and your spouse's require full-time attendance, you'll have to make other arrangements for a sick child. These are days when you might arrange alternate care for him, preferably where both the caregiver and the setting are familiar. If you rely on a relative or hire a sitter to stay with him, make sure the caregiver understands the nature of the illness and how it should be treated.

If your child requires medication, obtain written instructions from your pediatrician and give them to your caregiver, or arrange for someone from the pediatrician's office to review the instructions with your caregiver over the telephone. Don't expect your caregiver to follow your instructions without a pediatrician's authorization. Also, both prescription and over-the-counter medications should have a pharmacy or drugstore label on them, with the child's name, the medication dosage, and the expiration date. Giving medication is a significant burden on caregivers and should be avoided whenever possible.

Tell the caregiver why the medication is being given, how it should be stored and administered (in what doses and at what intervals), what side effects to look for, and what to do if they occur. Explain that medicine should not be disguised as food or described as candy; instead, the child should be told what the medicine is and why he needs to take it. Ask the caregiver to record the time each dose is given. If your child is in a child care center, you should be asked to sign a consent for the staff to administer the medication.

A few communities have services that specialize in care for mildly ill children. These include:

Home-based Programs

- Family child care homes that are equipped to care for both sick and well children. If a child becomes ill in such a program, she can continue attending in a segregated area, if necessary. Not all infections are contagious.

- Family child care homes that care only for sick children. Some of these are associated with well-child care centers.

- Agencies or child care centers that provide caregivers who can work in your home.

Center-based Programs

- Regular child care centers that have trained staff members to care for sick children in the usual child care setting, but apart from the main group of well children.

- Centers that offer a separate "get-well room" for sick children, staffed by a caregiver.

- Sick-child care centers that are set up specifically to care for ill children.

In sick-child programs, caregivers adjust the activity level of the youngsters to the child's ability to participate, and the children receive a lot of cuddling and personal attention. These programs should pay extra attention to hygiene for both caregivers and children. The premises and equipment, especially toys, should be cleaned thoroughly and often. Disposable toys may be necessary in some situations, depending on the nature of the illnesses involved. A pediatrician and public health consultant should be on call for every sick-child care facility.

CONTROLLING INFECTIOUS DISEASES IN CHILD CARE PROGRAMS

Whenever children gather in groups, their risk of getting sick increases. Infants and toddlers are particularly affected, since they tend to place their hands and play objects in their mouths, making it even easier to spread infectious diseases.

It's impossible for adults to keep toys and other objects in the child care center in perfect sanitary condition. However, many precautions and practices can help control the spread of infection. Immunizations, for example, can greatly reduce outbreaks of serious infectious diseases. Centers should require children to be immunized (at appropriate ages) against diphtheria, tetanus, pertussis, polio, measles, mumps, rubella, *Haemophilus influenzae* type b, pneumococcus, hepatitis B, and chickenpox. You also should consider having your child immunized against the influenza (flu) virus. Caregivers' immunity should be checked, and if there is any doubt, they should receive appropriate immunizations, as well.

In addition to requiring immunizations, child care programs should be extremely careful about maintaining good hygiene. Children and teachers should have easy access to sinks. They should be reminded, and children should be assisted if necessary, to wash their hands after using toilets. Staff members also should wash at all the times listed earlier in this chapter, and especially after changing diapers. Both the caregiver's and the child's hands should at least be wiped during diaper changing after removing the soiled diaper, and then both should wash their hands at the end of the diaper change routine. Handwashing after blowing or wiping noses and before handling food or food surfaces can reduce the spread of colds.

If a center cares for infants, toddlers, and toilet-trained youngsters, each group should have a separate area, each with its own accessible sink for handwashing. The facility and all equipment should be cleaned at least daily. Changing tables and toilets should be washed and disinfected.

As a parent, you can help control the spread of disease in your child's center by keeping her at home when she has an illness that's contagious or requires extra attention. (Your center should issue guidelines to help you determine when to do this.) Also notify her caregiver as soon as anyone in your family is diagnosed as having a serious communicable disease, and request that all parents be alerted when any child in the program has a serious or highly contagious infectious illness.

Teach your youngster proper hygiene and handwashing habits so that she's less likely to spread illnesses herself. And finally, educate yourself about the illnesses that are most common in child care settings, so you know what to expect and how to respond if they occur in your child's program. These include the following.

Colds and Flu

The most common infections are caused by viruses that produce the symptoms of a cold or the flu. Most children have six to eight colds each year; children in child care often get more of these infections (up to twelve a year) than do infants cared for at home. However, after infancy, the risk begins to decrease for children in stable child care arrangements. Fortunately, the chances of contracting some of the most severe illnesses can be decreased by immunizing children with vaccines according to the nationally recommended schedule.

Cytomegalovirus (CMV) Infection

Cytomegalovirus usually causes no or only mild possibly flu-like illness in children and adults. However, this virus can be dangerous to a pregnant woman who is not immune to it, because infection sometimes causes serious infection in her unborn child. The infection can be transmitted through direct contact with body fluids (tears, urine, saliva). Fortunately, most adult women are already immune to this disease, but if you are pregnant, have a child in child care, or work in a child care home or center yourself, you have an increased risk of exposure to CMV and should discuss the problem with your obstetrician.

Diarrheal Diseases

Gastrointestinal diseases are less common than respiratory infections. The average child has one or two episodes of diarrhea a year. These illnesses can spread easily in child care homes and centers.

If your child has diarrhea, do not take her to child care unless all of her stool can be controlled by using the toilet. Children with loose stools who wear diapers or who cannot make sure that all of their stool ends up in the toilet should not be in child care unless your pediatrician has determined that the cause is not infectious. If she has a mild form of the illness, then several days away from the center should minimize the chances that she'll transmit it to other children. But if a more serious cause is suspected, further tests to identify the responsible agent (bacteria, virus, or parasite) may need to be done before the child returns. (See *Diarrhea,* page 505.)

Eye and Skin Infections

Conjunctivitis (pinkeye), impetigo, lice, ringworm, scabies, and cold sores are common problems in young children. These afflictions of the skin and mucous membranes can be spread by touching a person on the affected area. Fortunately, these are not serious illnesses, but they are uncomfortable and inconvenient. The child care staff should notify you if this kind of problem occurs in any child in the program, so you can watch for symptoms in your own child. If these symptoms do appear, contact your pediatrician for early diagnosis and possible treatment. (See *Herpes Simplex,* page 586; *Eye Infections,* page 604; *Head Lice,* page 696; *Impetigo,* page 699; *Ringworm,* page 705; *Scabies,* page 707.)

Hepatitis

If a youngster in a child care program gets hepatitis A, a viral infection of the liver, it can spread easily to other children and caregivers. In infants and preschool children, most infections are asymptomatic or cause mild, nonspecific symptoms. Older infected children may have only mild fever, nausea, vomiting, diarrhea, or jaundice (a yellowish skin color). However, adults who contract this illness usually experience these symptoms to a much greater degree. The spread of hepatitis can be controlled by giving injections of gamma globulin, but several staff members and parents may be infected before anyone realizes

Transportation and Car Pool Safety

If you drive children in a car pool, you must be as responsible for every child in the car as you are for your own. This means making sure that everyone is restrained in car safety seats or booster seats appropriate for their size, not overloading the car, disciplining children who disobey safety rules, and checking that your insurance covers everyone on board. In addition, make sure that you and other drivers observe the following precautions, many of which will apply even when you, your spouse, or other family member (e.g., grandparent) are driving only your own youngster to his child care setting.

- Pick up and drop off children only at the curb or in a driveway where the children are protected from other cars.

- If possible, have each child's own parents or another responsible adult buckle her into the car and take her out when she returns home.

- Turn all children over to the direct supervision of a child care staff member.

- Place all hard objects, such as lunch boxes or toys, on the floor.

- Close and lock all car doors, but only after checking that fingers and feet are inside.

- Open passenger window only a few inches, and lock all power window and door controls from the driver's seat if possible.

- Remind children about safety rules and proper behavior before starting out.

- Plan your routes to minimize travel time and avoid hazardous conditions.

- Pull over if any child in the group gets out of control or misbehaves. If any child consistently presents a problem, discuss the difficulty with her parents and exclude her from the car pool until her conduct improves.

- Have available emergency contact information for each child who rides in the car.

- Ideally, equip each vehicle with a fire extinguisher and first-aid kit.

- Be sure that no child is ever left in the car without a supervising adult.

there's a problem. For this reason, whenever hepatitis A is diagnosed in anyone even remotely connected with the program, parents and staff should be alerted and the public health department consulted to decide how best to stop the disease from spreading. (See *Hepatitis,* page 512.) Hepatitis A vaccines are available that are suggested for certain international travelers and certain high-risk conditions. Universal (routine) immunization is recommended in several states where the incidence of infection is highest.

HIV (AIDS Virus) and Hepatitis B

Hepatitis B virus and HIV (the AIDS virus) produce serious chronic infections. HIV infection, when it develops into full-blown AIDS, is a fatal illness. Children who get HIV or hepatitis B infections usually acquire these viruses from their infected mothers during birth. Both diseases can be transmitted from one child to another by passage of blood from an infected child into the body of someone not infected. Because this does not occur in usual child care activities, children with these infections very rarely present a danger to others.

Some parents are hesitant to let people know that their child is HIV positive. The American Academy of Pediatrics believes that the decision on whether to disclose this information should be made by the parent (with the advice of the youngster's pediatrician), and certainly with the child's best interest in mind. There is no need to restrict the placement of an HIV-infected child in a child care setting in the belief that this would protect others.

If an injury in which blood is involved occurs to any child, the caregiver should put on gloves and wash the injury, administer first aid, and apply a bandage. All blood-contaminated surfaces or clothing should be washed and disinfected. Diluted bleach kills both HIV and hepatitis B. All blood should be dealt with as if it were contaminated.

Also, since human milk can transmit HIV and other viruses, be sure that the child care facility has procedures in place to prevent the inadvertent feeding of the milk of one mother to another mother's child. If such an accident occurs, it should follow the national standards (presented in *Caring for Our Children* found at http://nrc.uchsc.edu) to handle the situation.

PREVENTING AND DEALING WITH INJURIES IN CHILD CARE PROGRAMS

Many injuries that occur at home or in child care settings are predictable and preventable. While the staff is largely responsible for your child's safety, you can contribute to the prevention of injuries by helping staff members to identify potential hazards in the facility and by observing the safety practices of caregivers when you leave or return for your child. For instance, you can take "safety walks" through the center, to make sure all equipment is in proper working condition and to find other ways to reduce risks.

Safety Walk Checklist

Next time you walk through your child's child care home or center, use the following checklist to make sure the facility is safe, clean, and in good repair. If there is a problem with any item on the list, bring it to the attention of the director or caregiver and follow up later to be sure it was corrected.

Indoors in All Programs

- Floors are smooth, clean, and have a nonskid surface.

- Climbers are mounted over impact-absorbent surfaces for a distance of 6 feet (1.8 meters) on all sides of the equipment.

- Medicines, cleaning agents, and tools are out of children's reach.

- First-aid kit is fully supplied and out of children's reach.

- Walls and ceilings are clean and in good repair, with no peeling paint or damaged plaster.

- Children are never left unattended.

- Electrical outlets are covered with child-proof caps.

- Electric lights are in good repair, with no frayed or dangling cords.

- Heating pipes and radiators are out of reach or covered so children cannot touch them.

- Hot water is set at or below 120 degrees Fahrenheit (48.9 degrees Celsius) to prevent scalding.

- There are no poisonous plants or disease-bearing animals (i.e., water turtles or iguanas).

- Trash containers are covered.

- Exits are clearly marked and easy to reach.

- No smoking is allowed in the child care facility.

- Windows at or above the second story have operational guards.

Outdoors in All Programs

- Grounds are free of litter, sharp objects, and animal droppings.

- Play equipment is smooth, well anchored, and free of rust, splinters, and sharp corners. All screws and bolts are capped or concealed.

- No play equipment is higher than 6 feet.

- Swing seats are lightweight and flexible, and there are no open or S-shaped hooks.

- Slides have wide, flat, stable steps with good treads, rounded rims along the sides to prevent falls, and a flat area at the end of the slide to help children slow down.

- Metal slides are shaded from the sun.

- Sandboxes are covered when not in use.

- Child-proof barriers keep children out of hazardous areas.

- Playground surfaces are made of 12 inches (30 cm) of wood chips, shredded tires, or other impact-absorbing material for 6 feet (1.8 m) in all directions under and around areas where falls are more likely to occur (under monkey bars, slides).

Infant and Toddler Programs

- Toys do not contain lead or have any signs of chipping paint, rust, or small pieces that could break off. (The weight or softness of the material may provide clues that the toys are made of lead.)

- High chairs have wide bases and safety straps.

- Toddlers are not allowed to walk around with bottles or to take bottles to bed.

- Infant walkers are not used.

- Beds and playpens meet safety standards.

- No recalled products or old products with broken or missing parts are used. Recalled products can be determined by checking the website of the Consumer Product Safety Commission: www.cpsc. gov.

Safety for children (and adults) in and around cars is a special concern. The center should have large, sheltered, and well-marked pickup and drop-off points where children and adults are protected from street traffic. It's best if parents can be protected from stormy weather as they get their children into and out of car seats and seat belts, and the children can be shielded as they walk to and from the building. CHILDREN AT PLAY or similar signs should be placed along the street near the center.

If your child shares a ride to and from child care, be sure the other drivers are using seat restraints for the children. The driver must check the vehicle to be sure that everyone is safely buckled in before pulling away and that everyone has left the vehicle before locking up at the parking spot. Also, care should be taken that the children are released to authorized adults at the child care facility or at day's end at the child's home.

If your child care program includes swimming, make sure appropriate safety precautions are followed. Any pool, lake, creek, or pond used by children should first be checked by public health authorities. If the pool is at or near the child care center itself, it should be surrounded by a five-foot-high child-proof fence with a locked gate. For hygienic reasons, portable wading pools should be avoided.

PART-TIME CARE FOR CHILDREN WITH SPECIAL NEEDS

If your child has a developmental disability or a chronic illness, don't let that keep him out of preschool or child care. In fact, quality part-time care may be good for him and provide a break for you. He is likely to benefit from the social contact, physical exercise, and variety of experiences of a group program.

The time he spends in a child care program will be good for you, too. Tending a child with a disability often is demanding of time, energy, and emotions. It also can be expensive, requiring both parents to work. The challenge is to find an excellent program that encourages normal childhood activities and at the same time meets his special needs.

Federal law (the Individuals with Disabilities Education Act [IDEA], formerly known as the Amendments to the Education for All Handicapped Children Act) requires all states to develop special education programs for preschool (three- to five-year-old) children with developmental disabilities. This act also gives states the option to develop special education programs for infants and toddlers with developmental disabilities or delays. Parents should check with their pediatrician or their state Education or Health Department regarding the availability of these early intervention programs.

Start your search with your pediatrician by asking if your child is capable of participating in a group program and requesting referrals to suitable centers. Sometimes only one choice will be available, but often, especially in larger communities, you will have several from which to choose. The one you select

If your child has a developmental disability or chronic illness, don't let that keep him out of child care.

should meet the same basic requirements outlined earlier for other child care programs, plus the following.

1. The program should include children with and without chronic illnesses and disabilities, to the extent possible. Having relationships with typically developing playmates helps a child with a disability feel more relaxed and confident socially, and helps build his self-esteem. The arrangement also benefits the typically developing child by teaching him to look past the surface differences and helping him develop sensitivity and respect for all people.

2. The staff should be specially trained to provide the specific care your child requires.

3. The program should have at least one physician consultant who is active in the development of policies and procedures affecting the type of special needs present among the children in the group.

4. All children should be encouraged to be as independent as their abilities allow, within the bounds of safety. They should be restricted only in activities that might be dangerous for them or that have been prohibited by doctor's orders.

5. The program should be flexible enough to adapt to slight variations in the children's abilities. For example, this may include altering some equipment or facilities for physically challenged or visually or hearing-impaired children.

6. The program should offer special equipment and activities to meet the special needs of children, such as breathing treatments for children with asthma. The equipment should be in good repair, and the staff should be trained to operate it correctly.

7. The staff should be familiar with each child's medical and developmental status. If a child has a chronic disease, the staff should be able to recognize its symptoms and determine when the child needs medical attention.

8. The staff should know how to reach each child's physician in an emergency and should be qualified to administer any necessary medications.

These are very general recommendations. Because special needs vary so widely, it's impossible to tell you more precisely how to determine the best program for your own child. If you're having trouble deciding among the programs your pediatrician has suggested, go back and discuss your concerns with her. She will work with you to make the right choice.

Whatever your child's special needs, how he will be cared for in your absence is one of the most important decisions you will have to make as a parent. The information you have just read should help you. However, remember that you know your child better than anyone, so rely most heavily on your needs and impressions when choosing or changing a child care arrangement.

KEEPING YOUR CHILD SAFE

Everyday life is full of well-disguised dangers for children: sharp objects, shaky furniture, reachable hot water faucets, pots on burning stoves, hot tubs, swimming pools, and busy streets. By adulthood we've learned to navigate this minefield so well that we no longer think of things like scissors and stoves as hazards. And that's the problem. To protect your child from the dangers she'll encounter in and out of your home, you have to see the world as she does, and you must recognize that she cannot yet distinguish hot from cold or sharp from dull.

Keeping your child physically safe is your most basic responsibility—and a never-ending one. Unintentional injuries are the number-one cause of death and disability in children over the age of one. Each year, at least 2 million children seek medical care because of unintentional injury. Forty to 50,000 suffer permanent damage—and almost 6,000 under the age of fifteen die.

As might be expected, automobile crashes account for a large number of the injuries and deaths. But many children are injured and killed by equipment designed specifically for their use. In one recent twelve-month period, falls from high chairs sent 7,000 children to the hospital. In 2001, toys caused more than 200,000 injuries serious enough to require treatment in hospital emergency rooms in children under the age of fifteen. Even cribs account for about 27 deaths annually.

These are grim statistics, but they are not inevitable. In the past, injuries were called "accidents" because they seemed unpredictable and unavoidable. Today we know that injuries are not random. By understanding how a child grows and develops and the risk of injury at each developmental stage, parents can take precautions that will prevent most, if not all, of those injuries.

WHY CHILDREN GET INJURED

Every childhood injury involves three elements: factors related to the child, the object that causes the injury, and the environment in which it occurs. To keep your child safe, you must be aware of all three.

Let's start with your child. His age makes a tremendous difference in the kind of protection he needs. The three-month-old who sits cooing in an infant seat requires quite different supervision from that needed by the ten-month-old who's started walking or the toddler who has learned to climb. So at each stage of your child's life, you must think again about the hazards that are present and what you can do to eliminate them. Repeatedly, as your child grows, you must ask: How far can he move and how fast? How high can he reach? What objects attract his attention? What can he do today that he couldn't do yesterday? What will he do tomorrow that he can't do today?

During the first six months of life, you can secure your child's safety by never leaving him alone in a dangerous situation. But once he begins to move, he'll create dangers of his own—first by rolling off the bed, then by creeping into places he shouldn't be, and finally by actively seeking out things to touch and taste.

As your child begins to move about, you certainly will tell him "no" whenever he approaches something potentially hazardous, but he will not really understand the significance of your message. Many parents find the ages between six months and eighteen months extremely frustrating, because the child doesn't seem to learn from these reprimands. Even if you tell him twenty times a day to stay away from the toilet, he's still in the bathroom every time you turn your back. At this age your child is not being willfully disobedient; his memory just isn't developed enough for him to recall your warning the next time he's attracted by the forbidden object or activity. What looks like naughtiness is actually the testing and retesting of reality—the normal way of learning for a child of this age.

His curiosity may take him to the bathroom shelf or the refrigerator, into the medicine cabinet, and under the sink.

The second year is also risky for children because their physical abilities exceed their capacities to understand the consequences of their actions. Although your child's judgment will improve, his sense of danger won't be intense enough and his self-control won't be developed enough to make him stop once he's spotted something interesting. At this point, even the things he can't see will interest him, so his curiosity may take him to the bottom shelf of the refrigerator, into the medicine cabinet, and under the sink—to touch things and perhaps to taste.

Young children are extraordinary mimics, so they may try to take medicine just as they've seen Mom doing, or they may play with a razor just like Dad. Unfortunately, their notions of cause and effect aren't as advanced as their motor skills. Yes, your child may realize that tugging on the cord pulled the iron down on his head after it falls, but his ability to anticipate many similar consequences is still months away.

Gradually, between the ages of two and four, your child will develop a more mature sense of himself as a person who makes things happen—he flips a switch, for instance, and the light goes on. Although this thinking eventually will help children avoid dangerous situations, at this age they are so self-involved that they are likely to see only their own part in the action. A two-year-old whose ball rolls into the street will think only about retrieving the ball, not about the danger of being hit by a car.

The risks of this kind of thinking are obvious. And the risks are compounded by something the experts call magical thinking, which means that at this age a child behaves as if his wishes and expectations actually control what happens. A four-year-old, for example, may light a match because he wants to create the beautiful bonfire he saw on television last night. It probably won't occur to him that the fire could get out of control; but even if it did, he might discount the idea because it isn't his idea of what *should* happen.

A Message for Grandparents About Safety

As a grandparent, your grandchild's well-being and safety are extremely important to you. Particularly when she is under your care—at your home, in her own home, in the car, or elsewhere—make sure that you've taken every step possible to ensure that she's safe and secure.

Take the time to read this chapter from beginning to end. It will provide you with guidelines to protect your grandchild in the situations that she's most likely to encounter. Before you have your grandchild visit or stay at your home, make certain that you've reviewed and adopted the recommendations you'll find here.

In this special section, you'll find the most important safety points for grandparents to keep in mind.

Safety Inside the Home

There are plenty of safety measures you should implement in your home to protect your grandchild. To keep some of these guidelines in the forefront of your mind, use the acronym SPEGOS to help remind you of the following:

Smoke detectors should be placed in the proper locations throughout the house.

Pets and pet food should be stored out of a child's reach.

Escape plans should be thought about in advance, and fire extinguishers should be readily available.

Gates should be positioned at the top and bottom of stairs.

Outlet covers should be placed over sockets to prevent your grandchild from putting herself at risk of an electrical shock.

Soft covers or bumpers should be positioned around sharp or solid furniture.

In addition to these general rules, keep the following safety measures in mind for specific areas of your home.

Nursery/Sleeping Area

- If you saved your own child's crib, stored in your attic or garage, perhaps awaiting the arrival of a grandchild someday, review the crib guidelines in this chapter (see pages 430–433). Guidelines for children's furniture and equipment have changed dramatically over the past twenty-five years. There is a good chance the old crib no longer meets today's safety standards and you will need to invest in a new one. (Use the same approach for other saved and aging furniture that could pose risks to children, such as an old playpen.)

- Buy a changing table (see page 433), or use your own bed to change the baby's diapers. As she gets a little older, and she becomes more likely to squirm, you may need a second person to help in changing her diaper.

- Don't allow your grandchild to sleep in your bed.

- Keep the diaper pail emptied.

Kitchen

- Put "kiddy locks" on the cabinets; to be extra safe, move unsafe cleansers and chemicals so they're completely out of reach.

- Remove any dangling cords, such as those from the coffeepot or toaster.

- Take extra precautions before giving your grandchild food prepared in microwave ovens. Microwaves can heat liquids and solids unevenly, and they may be mildly warm on the outside but *very hot* on the inside.

Bathrooms

- Store pills, inhalers, and other prescription or nonprescription medications, as well as medical equipment, locked and out of the reach of your grandchild.

- Put nonslip material in the bathtub to avoid dangerous spills.

- If there are handles and bars in the bathtub for your own use, cover them with soft material if you're going to be bathing the baby there.

- Never leave a child unattended in a tub or sink filled with water.

Baby Equipment

- Never leave your grandchild alone in a high chair or in an infant seat located in high places, such as a table or counter top.

- Do not use baby walkers.

Toys

- Buy new toys for your grandchild that have a variety of sounds, sights, and colors. Simple toys can be just as good as more complex ones. Remember, no matter how fancy the toys may be, your own interaction and play with your grandchild are much more important.

- Toys, music tapes, CDs, and books should be age-appropriate and challenge children at their own developmental level.

- Avoid toys with small parts that the baby could put into her mouth and swallow.

- Because toy boxes can be dangerous, keep them out of your home, or look for one without a top or lid.

Garage/Basement

- Make sure that the automatic reversing mechanism on the garage door is operating.

- Keep all garden chemicals and pesticides as well as tools in a locked cabinet and out of reach.

Safety Outside the Home

Buy a car safety seat that you can keep inside your own automobile. Make sure you install it properly and that you can strap your grandchild into it easily. Experiment with the buckles and clasps before you buy the car seat since their ease of use varies.

This type of self-centered, magical thinking is entirely normal at this age. But because of it, you must be twice as careful about your child's safety until he outgrows this stage. You can't expect your two- to four-year-old to understand fully that his actions can have harmful consequences for himself or for others. He may, for example, throw sand at a playmate partly because it amuses him and partly because he wants it to be fun. Either way, he will find it difficult to understand that his friend is not enjoying the game.

For all these reasons, you must establish and consistently enforce rules related to safety during the early preschool years. Explain the reasons behind the rules: "You can't throw stones, because you'll hurt your friend"; "Never run into the street, because you could be hit by a car." But don't expect these reasons to persuade your child. Repeat the rule itself every time your child is on the edge of breaking it until he understands that unsafe actions are always unacceptable. For most children, it takes dozens of repetitions before even the most fundamental safety rules are remembered. So be patient.

Your child's temperament also may determine his vulnerability. Studies suggest that children who are extremely active and unusually curious have more than their share of injuries. At certain stages of development, your child is likely to be stubborn, easily frustrated, aggressive, or unable to concentrate—all

- Purchase a stroller to use when taking the baby for a walk in your neighborhood.

- On shopping trips, whenever possible choose stores whose shopping carts have child seats built into them. Don't place your own car seat into a shopping cart.

- If you have a tricycle or bicycle at your home for your grandchild, make sure you also have a helmet for her use. Let her choose a helmet in a special design or color.

- Although playgrounds can be fun, they also can be dangerous. Select one that has been designed to keep children as safe as possible; those at schools or at community-sponsored parks are often good choices.

- Inspect your own backyard for anything hazardous or poisonous.

- If you have a backyard swimming pool, or if you take your grandchild to another home or a park where there is a pool, *carefully read the pool safety guidelines in this chapter (see pages 466–468). There should be a four-foot-high fence with a locking gate surrounding the pool.* Make sure that neighbors' pools are enclosed by fences, as well.

characteristics associated with injuries. So when you notice that your child is having a bad day or is going through a difficult phase, be especially alert: That's when he's most likely to test safety rules, even those he ordinarily follows.

Since you can't change your child's age, and you have little influence over his basic temperament, most of your efforts to prevent injury should focus on objects and surroundings. By designing an environment in which the obvious hazards have been removed, you can allow your young child the freedom he needs to explore.

Some parents feel they don't need to "child-proof" their homes because they intend to supervise their children closely. And in fact, with constant vigilance, most injuries *can* be avoided. But even the most conscientious parents can't watch a child every moment. Most injuries occur not when parents are alert and at their best, but when they are under stress. The following situations are often associated with injuries:

- Hunger and fatigue (i.e., the hour or so before dinner)

- Mother's pregnancy

- Illness or death in the family

- Changes in the child's regular caregiver

- Tension between parents

- Sudden changes in the environment, such as moving to a new home or going on vacation

All families experience at least some of these stresses some of the time. Child-proofing eliminates or reduces the opportunities for injury so that even when you are momentarily distracted—for example, by the ring of the telephone or doorbell—your child is less likely to encounter situations and objects that can cause him harm.

The pages that follow include advice about how to minimize dangers in and out of the home. The intention is not to frighten you, but to alert you to hazards—particularly those that, on the surface, might seem harmless—so you can take the sensible precautions that will keep your child safe and allow him the freedom he needs to grow up happy and healthy.

SAFETY INSIDE YOUR HOME

Room to Room

Your lifestyle and the layout of your home will determine which rooms should be child-proofed. Examine every room in which your child spends any time. (For most families, that means the entire house.) It's tempting to exclude a formal dining or living room that remains behind closed doors when not in use; but remember, the rooms that are forbidden to your child are the ones she'll want most to explore as soon as she's old enough. Any areas not child-proofed will require extra vigilance on your part, even if their entrances are normally locked or blocked.

At the very least, your child's room should be a place where everything is as safe as it can be.

Nursery

Cribs. Your baby usually will be unattended when in his crib, so this should be a totally safe environment. Falls are the most common injury associated with cribs, even though they are the easiest to prevent. Children are most likely to fall out of the crib when the mattress is raised too high for their height or when the side rail is left down.

If you use a new crib or one manufactured since 1990, it should meet current safety standards. If you plan to use an older crib, inspect it carefully for the following features.

- Slats should be no more than 2⅜ inches (6 cm) apart so a child's head cannot become trapped between them.

- There should be no cutouts in the headboard or footboard, as your child's head could become trapped in them.

- If the crib has corner posts (sometimes called finials), unscrew them or cut them off. Loose clothing can become snagged on these and choke your baby.

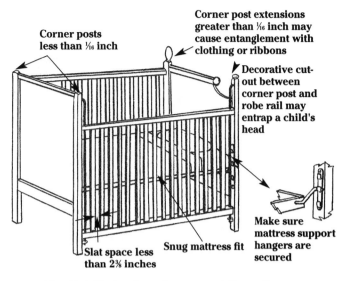

Corner posts less than ¹⁄₁₆ inch

Corner post extensions greater than ¹⁄₁₆ inch may cause entanglement with clothing or ribbons

Decorative cut-out between corner post and robe rail may entrap a child's head

Make sure mattress support hangers are secured

Slat space less than 2⅜ inches

Snug mattress fit

- All screws, bolts, and hardware must be tightly in place to prevent the crib from coming apart. A child's activity can cause the crib to collapse, trapping and suffocating her.

- Before each assembly and weekly thereafter, inspect the crib for damage to hardware, loose joints, missing parts, or sharp edges. Do not use a crib if any parts are missing or broken. Do not substitute parts; instead, obtain replacements from the manufacturer.

Many older cribs were painted with lead-based paint, which can poison children if they gnaw on the crib rails. (It does happen.) As a precaution, strip the old paint and then repaint the crib using high-quality, new enamel. Let it dry thoroughly in a well-ventilated room. Then place plastic strips (available at most children's furniture stores) over the top of the side rails.

You can prevent other crib hazards by observing the following guidelines.

1. The mattress should fit snugly so your child cannot slip into the crack between it and the crib side. If you can insert more than two fingers between the mattress and the sides or ends of the crib, replace the mattress with one that fits snugly.

2. If you purchase a new mattress, remove and destroy all plastic wrapping material that comes with it, because it can suffocate a child. If you cover the mattress with heavy plastic, be sure the cover fits tightly; zippered covers are best.

3. As soon as your baby can sit, lower the mattress of the crib to the level where he cannot fall out either by leaning against the side or by pulling himself over it. Set the mattress at its lowest position by the time your child learns to stand. The most common falls occur when a baby tries to climb out,

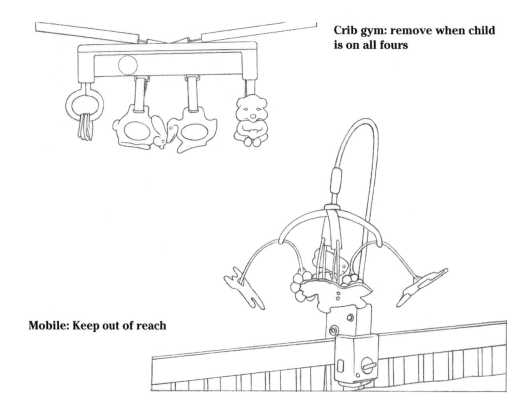

Crib gym: remove when child is on all fours

Mobile: Keep out of reach

so move your child to another bed when he is 35 inches (89 cm) tall, or the height of the side rail is less than three-quarters of his height.

4. When fully lowered, the top of the side rail of the crib should be at least 4 inches (10 cm) above the mattress, even when the mattress is set at its highest position. Be sure the locking latch that holds the side up is sturdy and can't accidentally be released by your child. Always leave the side up when your child is in the crib.

5. Periodically check the crib to be sure there are no rough edges or sharp points on the metal parts, and no splinters or cracks in the wood. If you notice tooth marks on the railing, cover the wood with a plastic strip (available at most children's furniture stores).

6. Use a crib bumper when your child is an infant. Be sure the pad goes all the way around the crib and is secured with at least six straps or ties, to keep the bumper from falling away from the sides. To prevent strangulation, the ties should be no more than 6 inches (15 cm) long.

7. As soon as your child can pull to a standing position, remove crib bumpers.

8. Pillows, quilts, comforters, sheepskins, stuffed animals, and other soft products should not be placed in a crib.

9. If you hang a mobile over your child's crib, be sure it is securely attached to the side rails. Hang it high enough so your baby cannot reach it to pull it down, and remove it when he is able to get up on his hands and knees, or when he reaches five months, whichever comes first.

10. Crib gyms should be removed as soon as your child can get up on all fours. Even though these gyms are designed to withstand a child's grabbing and tugging, he could fall forward onto the gym and become entangled.

11. To prevent the most serious of falls and to keep children from getting caught in cords from hanging windows or blinds or draperies and strangling, don't place a crib—or any other child's bed—beside a window.

Changing Tables. Although a changing table makes it easier to dress and diaper your baby, falls from such a high surface can be serious. Don't trust your vigilance alone to prevent falls, but also consider the following recommendations.

1. Choose a sturdy, stable changing table with a 2-inch (5 cm) guardrail around all four sides.

2. The top of the changing table should be concave, so that the middle is slightly lower than the sides.

3. Don't depend on a safety strap alone to keep your child secure. Never leave a child unattended on a dressing table, even for a moment, even if he is strapped.

4. Keep diapering supplies within your reach, so you don't have to leave your baby's side to get them. Never let him play with a powder container. If he accidentally opens and shakes it, he's likely to inhale particles of powder, which can injure his lungs.

5. If you use disposable diapers, store them out of your child's reach and cover them with clothing when he wears them. Children can suffocate if they tear off pieces of the plastic liner and swallow them.

Bunk Beds. Although children love them, bunk beds pose several dangers: The child on the top bunk can fall out, and the child on the lower bunk can be injured if the top bunk collapses. The bunk beds might be improperly constructed or assembled, causing dangerous structural flaws. Or a mattress that doesn't properly fit could entrap your child. If, despite these warnings, you choose to use bunk beds, take the following precautions.

1. Don't allow a child under six to sleep in the upper bunk. She won't have the coordination she needs to climb safely or to stop herself from falling out.

2. Place the beds in a corner of the room so there are walls on two sides. This provides extra support and blocks two of the possible four sites for falling out.

3. Don't place beds beside a window. This will prevent the most serious of falls and keep children from being strangled by cords from hanging window blinds or draperies.

4. Be sure the top mattress fits snugly and cannot possibly slip over the edge of the frame. If there's a gap, your child might get trapped and suffocate.

5. Attach a ladder to the top bunk bed. Use a night-light so your child can see the ladder.

6. Install a guardrail on the top bunk. The gap between the side rail and guardrail should be no more than 3½ inches (8¾ cm). Be sure your child can't roll under the guardrail when the mattress on the top bunk is compressed by the weight of her body. If her head gets stuck under the guardrail, she may suffocate or be strangled. You may need a thicker mattress to prevent this.

7. Check the supports under the upper mattress. Wires or slats should run directly under the mattress and be fastened in place at both ends. A mattress that is supported only by the frame of the bed or unsecured slats could come crashing down.

8. If you separate bunks into two individual beds, make sure to remove all dowels or connectors.

9. To prevent falls and collapse of the bed, don't allow children to jump or roughhouse on either bunk.

Kitchen

The kitchen is such a dangerous room for young children that some experts recommend they be excluded from it. That's a difficult rule to enforce, because parents spend so much time there and most young children want to be where the action is. While he's with you in the kitchen, sit him in a high chair so he can watch you and others in the room. Keep a toy box in the kitchen to amuse him. It's probably more realistic to eliminate the most serious dangers by taking the following precautions.

1. Store strong cleaners, lye, furniture polish, dishwasher soap, and other dangerous products in a high cabinet, locked and out of sight. If you must store some items under the sink, buy a "kiddy lock" that refastens automatically every time you close the cupboard. (Most hardware and department stores have them.) Never transfer dangerous substances into containers that look as if they might hold food.

2. Keep knives, forks, scissors, and other sharp instruments separate from "safe" kitchen utensils, and in a latched drawer. Store sharp cutting appliances such as food processors out of reach and/or in a locked cupboard.

3. Unplug appliances when they are not in use so your child cannot accidentally turn them on. Don't allow electrical cords to dangle where your child can reach and tug on them, possibly pulling a heavy appliance down on himself.

4. Always turn pot handles toward the back of the stove so your child can't reach up and grab them. Whenever you have to walk with hot liquid—a cup of coffee, a pot of soup—be sure you know where your child is so you don't trip over him.

5. When shopping for an oven, choose one that is well insulated to protect your child from the heat if he touches the oven door. Also, never leave the oven door open.

6. If you have a gas stove, turn the dials firmly to the off position, and if they're easy to remove, do so when you aren't cooking so that your child can't accidentally turn the stove on. If they cannot be removed easily, block the access to the stove as much as possible.

7. Keep matches out of reach and out of sight.

8. Don't warm baby bottles in a microwave oven. The liquid heats unevenly, so there may be pockets of milk hot enough to scald your baby's mouth when he drinks. Also, some overheated baby bottles have exploded when they were removed from the microwave.

9. Keep a fire extinguisher in your kitchen. (If your home has more than one story, mount an extinguisher in a conspicuous place on each floor.)

Bathroom

The simplest way to avoid bathroom injuries is to make this room inaccessible unless your child is accompanied by an adult. This may mean installing a latch on the door at adult height so the child can't get into the bathroom when you aren't around. Also, be sure any lock on the door can be unlocked from the outside, just in case your child accidentally locks himself in.

The following suggestions will prevent injuries when your child is using the bathroom.

1. Children can drown in only a few inches of water, so *never leave a young child alone in the bath, even for a moment.* If you can't ignore the doorbell or the phone, wrap your child in a towel and take him along when you go to answer them. Bath seats and rings are meant to be bathing *aids* and will not prevent drowning if the infant is left unattended.

2. Install no-slip strips on the bottom of the bathtub. Put a cushioned cover over the water faucet so your child won't be hurt if he bumps his head against it.

3. Get in the habit of closing the lid of the toilet, and get a toilet lid lock. A curious toddler who tries to play in the water can lose his balance and fall in.

4. To prevent scalding, set your hot water heater to 120 degrees Fahrenheit (48.9 degrees Celsius) or less. When your child is old enough to turn the faucets, teach him to start the cold water before the hot.

5. Keep all medicines in containers with safety caps. Remember, however, that these caps are child-*resistant,* not child-proof, so store all medicines and cosmetics high and out of reach in a locked cabinet. Don't keep toothpaste, soaps, shampoos, and other frequently used items in the same cabinet. Instead, store them in a hard-to-reach cabinet equipped with a safety latch or locks.

6. If you use electrical appliances in the bathroom, particularly hair dryers and razors, be sure to unplug them and store them in a cabinet with a safety lock when they aren't in use. It is better to use them in another room where there is no water. Your electrician can install special bathroom wall sockets (ground-fault circuit interrupters) that can lessen the likelihood of electrical injury when an appliance falls into the sink or bathwater.

Garage and Basement

Garages and basements tend to be places where potentially lethal tools and chemicals are stored. In almost all homes, these areas should be locked and strictly off limits to children. To minimize the risk on those occasions when children do gain access to the garage and basement:

1. Keep paints, varnishes, thinners, pesticides, and fertilizers in a locked cabinet or locker. Be sure these substances are always kept in their original, labeled containers.

2. Store tools in a safe area out of reach and locked. Be sure power tools are unplugged and locked in a cabinet when you finish using them.

3. Do not allow your child to play near the garage or driveway where cars may be coming and going. Many children are killed when accidentally run over by a car driven by a family member.

4. If you have an automatic garage door opener, be sure your child is nowhere near the door before you open or close it. Keep the opener out of reach and out of sight. Make sure the automatic reversing mechanism is properly adjusted.

5. If, for some reason, you must store an unused refrigerator or freezer, remove the door so that a child cannot become trapped if he crawls inside.

All Rooms

Certain safety rules and preventive actions apply to every room. The following safeguards against commonplace household dangers will protect not only your small child, but your entire family.

1. Install smoke detectors throughout your home, check them monthly to be sure they are working, and change the batteries annually. Develop a fire escape plan and practice it so you'll be prepared if an emergency does occur. (See *Burns,* page 476.)

2. Put safety plugs in all unused electrical outlets so your child can't stick her finger or a toy into the holes. If your child won't stay away from outlets, buy the plastic covers that block unused sockets and make it impossible for her to pull plugs out of sockets that are in use by blocking access to them with furniture. Keep electrical cords out of reach and sight.

3. To prevent slipping, carpet your stairs where possible. Be sure the carpet is firmly tacked down at the edges. When your child is just learning to crawl and walk, install safety gates at both top and bottom of stairs. Avoid accordion-style gates, which can trap an arm or a neck.

4. Certain houseplants may be harmful. Your regional Poison Center will have a list or description of plants to avoid. (See *Poisoning,* page 493.)

5. Check your floors constantly for small objects that a child might swallow, such as coins, buttons, beads, pins, and screws. This is particularly important if someone in the household has a hobby that involves small items, or if there are older children who have small items.

6. If you have hardwood floors, don't let your child run around in stocking feet. Socks make slippery floors even more dangerous.

7. Attach cords for venetian blinds and drapes to floor mounts that hold them taut, or wrap these cords around wall brackets to keep them out of reach. Cords with loops should be cut and equipped with safety tassels. Children can strangle on them if they are left loose.

8. Pay attention to the doors between rooms. Glass doors are particularly dangerous, because a child may run into them, so fasten them open if you can. Swinging doors can knock a small child down, and folding doors can pinch little fingers, so if you have either, consider removing them until your child is old enough to understand how they work.

9. Check your home for furniture pieces with hard edges and sharp corners that could injure your child if she fell against them. (Coffee tables are a particular hazard.) If possible, move this furniture out of traffic areas, particularly when your child is learning to walk. You also can buy cushioned corner and edge protectors that stick onto the furniture.

10. Test the stability of tall pieces of furniture, such as floor lamps and bookshelves. If they seem unsteady, put floor lamps behind other furniture and anchor the bookcases to the wall so your child can't pull them over.

11. Keep computers out of reach so that your child cannot pull them over on herself. Cords should be out of sight and reach.

12. Open windows from the top if possible. If you must open them from the bottom, install operable window guards that only an adult or older child can push out from the inside. Never put chairs, sofas, low tables, or anything else a child might climb on in front of a window. Doing so gives her access to the window and creates an opportunity for a serious fall.

13. Never leave plastic bags lying around the house, and don't store children's clothes or toys in them. Dry-cleaning bags are particularly dangerous. Knot them before you throw them away so that it's impossible for your child to crawl into them or pull them over her head.

14. Think about the potential hazard to your child of anything you put into the trash. Any trash container into which dangerous items will go—for example, spoiled food, discarded razor blades, or batteries—should have a child-resistant cover.

15. To prevent burns, check your heat sources. Fireplaces, woodstoves, and kerosene heaters should be screened so that your child can't get near them. Check electric baseboard heaters, radiators, and even vents from hot-air furnaces to see how hot they get when the heat is on. They, too, may need to be screened.

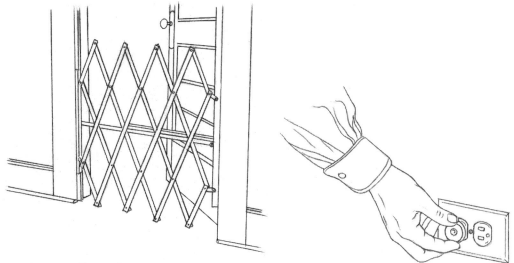

Unsafe, accordion-style gate

Safety plug in unused outlets

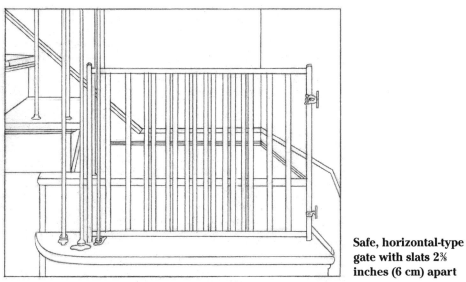

Safe, horizontal-type gate with slats 2⅜ inches (6 cm) apart

16. A firearm should not be kept in the home or environment of a child. If you must keep a firearm in the house, keep it unloaded and locked up. Lock ammunition in a separate location. (Also see *Where We Stand* on the next page.)

17. Alcohol can be very toxic to a young child. Keep all alcoholic beverages in a locked cabinet and remember to empty any unfinished drinks immediately.

WHERE WE STAND

The most effective measure to prevent firearm-related injury to children is the absence of guns from homes and communities. The American Academy of Pediatrics strongly supports gun control legislation. We believe that handguns, deadly air guns, and assault weapons should be banned.

Until handguns are banned, we recommend that handguns and handgun ammunition be regulated, that restrictions be placed on handgun ownership, and that the number of privately owned handguns be reduced. Firearms should be removed from the environments in which children live and play, but if they are not, they *must* be stored locked and unloaded. Loaded firearms and unloaded firearms and ammunition represent a serious danger to children.

Baby Equipment

During the past twenty years, the Consumer Product Safety Commission has taken an active role in setting standards to assure the safety of equipment manufactured for children and infants. Because many of these rules went into effect in the early 1970s, you must pay special attention to the safety of furniture made before then. The following guidelines will help you select the safest possible baby equipment, whether used or new, and utilize it properly.

High Chairs

Falls are the most serious danger associated with high chairs. To minimize the risk of your child falling:

1. Select a chair with a wide base, so it can't be tipped over if someone accidentally bumps against it.

2. If the chair folds, be sure the locking device is secure each time you set it up.

3. Strap your child in with the waist and crotch safety strap whenever he sits in the chair. Never allow him to stand in the high chair.

4. Don't place the high chair near a counter or table or within reach of a hot or dangerous object. Your child may be able to push hard enough against these surfaces to tip the chair over.

5. Never leave a young child unattended in a high chair, and don't allow older children to climb or play on it, as this could cause it to tip over.

6. A high chair that hooks onto a table is *not* a substitute for a more solid one. But if you plan to use such a model when you eat out or when you travel, look for one that locks onto the table. Be sure the table is heavy enough to support your child's weight without tipping. Also, check to see whether his feet can touch a table support. If he can push against it, he may be able to dislodge the seat from the table.

7. Check that all caps or plugs on chair tubing are firmly attached and cannot be pulled off; these could be choking hazards.

Infant Seats

Infant seats are not car safety seats, so not all the same regulations apply. Use care in selecting an infant seat. Check the weight guidelines provided by the manufacturer, and don't use the seat after your baby has outgrown it. Here are some other safety guidelines to follow.

1. Never leave a baby unattended in an infant seat.

2. Never use an infant seat as a substitute for a car safety seat. Infant seats are designed only for propping a baby up, so that she can see or be fed more easily.

3. Always use the safety strap and harness when your baby is in the seat.

4. Choose a seat with an outside frame that allows the infant to sit deeply inside. Be sure the base is wide, so it is difficult to tip over.

5. Look at the bottom of the infant seat to see whether it's covered with a nonskid material. If it isn't, cut thin pieces of rubber, and glue them to the base so that the seat is less likely to slip when it's on a smooth surface.

6. Always carry your baby securely strapped into the seat, and use both your arms under the frame to hold it. Although some infant seats have carrying handles, using them alone will allow the seat to tip if the baby's weight is distributed unevenly. Even with the safety strap on, the weight of her head could pull her down and out.

7. The most serious injuries associated with infant seats occur when a baby falls from a high surface. Even small infants can jiggle a seat or carrier off a surface and fall. Therefore, do not put the seat above floor level. To keep an active, squirming baby from tipping the seat over, place it on a carpeted area near you and away from sharp-edged furniture. Infant seats also may tip over when placed on soft surfaces, such as beds or upholstered furniture; these are not safe places for infant seats.

8. Never place an infant in a car seat on the roof of a car.

Playpens

Most parents depend on playpens (sometimes called play yards) as a safe place to put a baby when Mom or Dad isn't available to watch him every moment. Yet playpens, too, can be dangerous under certain circumstances. To prevent mishaps:

1. Never leave the side of a mesh playpen lowered. An infant who rolls into the pocket created by the slack mesh can become trapped and suffocate.

2. Once your child is able to sit or get up on all fours or when he reaches five months, whichever comes first, remove any toys that have been tied across the top of the playpen, so he cannot become entangled in them.

3. When your child can pull himself to a standing position, remove all boxes and large toys that he could use to help him climb out.

4. Children who are teething often bite off chunks of the vinyl or plastic that cover the top rails, so you should check them periodically for tears and holes. If the tears are small, repair them with heavy-duty cloth tape; if they are more extensive, you may need to replace the rails.

5. Be sure that a playpen's mesh is free of tears, holes,

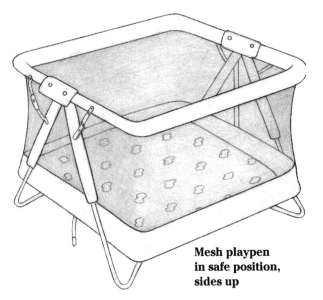

Mesh playpen in safe position, sides up

A Message for Grandparents

Because your grandchild's health and safety are of paramount importance, the information throughout this chapter is as relevant to you as it is to his or her parents. As you've read in these pages, there are critical steps you can take to make your home safer for your grandchild when he visits. You need to child-proof your entire home, just as you did a generation ago with your own youngsters.

Even though all of the information in this chapter is valuable, here are some particularly important points to keep in mind.

- Go room to room through your home, and look for potential hazards. Take the steps recommended to child-proof your living room, bedrooms, kitchen, bathroom, and every other area where your grandchild may be spending time. Note that your special chairs or walking aids could be unstable and present a risk; if possible, move them into the closet or a room that your grandchild won't be able to enter when he visits.

- Insert plug protectors into all unused sockets, using protectors that you (but not a young child) can insert and remove easily.

- Make sure that your medications are placed in a safe location where a curious grandchild cannot get to them.

- Keep important phone numbers by the telephone. In an emergency, you'll not only want to call 911 when appropriate, but certain specific family members.

- Have an exit plan in your home in case of a fire or other emergency.

- If you're going to be transporting your grandchild in your own automobile, make sure you have a car safety seat that you can lift and maneuver easily, and that meets the criteria described on pages 447–449.

or loose threads and that the openings are less than ¼ inch (0.6 cm) across, so that your child cannot get caught in it. The mesh should be securely attached to the top rail and floor plate. If staples are used, they should not be missing, loose, or exposed. Slats on wooden playpens should be no more than 2⅜ inches (6 cm) apart, so your child's head cannot become trapped between them.

6. Circular enclosures made from accordion-style fences are extremely dangerous, because children can get their heads caught in the diamond-shaped openings and the V-shaped border at the top of the gate. Never use such an enclosure, either indoors or out.

How to Report Unsafe Products

If you become aware of an unsafe product used by children—or if your own child suffers an injury related to a particular product—report it to the Consumer Product Safety Commission (CPSC). For more information, go to the CPSC website (www.cpsc.gov), and look for the link for reporting unsafe products. Or call the CPSC's toll-free hotline (1–800–638–2772); when prompted, press ext. 300 to speak with a hotline representative.

Walkers

The American Academy of Pediatrics does not recommend using infant walkers. In a recent year, an estimated 8,800 children younger than fifteen months were treated in U.S. emergency rooms for injuries associated with infant walkers. The vast majority of injuries are from falls down stairs, and head injuries are common. Walkers do not help a child learn to walk, and they can delay normal motor development. If you must use a mobile baby walker, choose a walker that meets internationally agreed-on performance standards to prevent falls down stairs. Such a mobile walker would be labeled ASTM F977–96. Stationary activity centers are a safer alternative to a baby walker with wheels.

Pacifiers

Pacifiers that are improperly constructed can choke an infant if they come apart. For maximum safety:

1. Do not use the top and nipple from a baby bottle as a pacifier, even if you tape them together. If the baby sucks hard, the nipple may pop out of the ring and choke her.

2. Purchase pacifiers that cannot possibly come apart. Those molded of one solid piece of plastic are particularly safe. If you are in doubt, ask your pediatrician for a recommendation.

3. The shield between the nipple and the ring should be at least 1½ inches (3.8 cm) across, so the infant cannot take the entire pacifier into her mouth. Also, the shield should be made of firm plastic with ventilation holes.

4. After retrieving your child's pacifier for the thousandth time, you may think about tying it to her hand or around her neck. Don't. The danger of strangulation is too great.

5. Pacifiers deteriorate over time. Inspect them periodically to see whether the rubber is discolored or torn. If so, replace them.

Toy Boxes and Toy Chests

A toy box can be dangerous for two reasons: A child could become trapped inside, or a hinged lid could fall on your child's head or body while he's searching for a toy. If possible, store toys on open shelves so that your child can get them easily. If you must use a toy box:

1. Look for one with no top, or choose one that has a lightweight removable lid or sliding doors or panels.

2. If you use a toy box with a hinged lid, be sure it has lid support that holds the lid open at any angle to which the lid is opened. If your toy box didn't come with such a support, install one yourself—or remove the lid.

3. Look for a toy box with rounded or padded edges and corners, or add the padding yourself, so your child won't be injured if he falls against it.

4. Children occasionally get trapped inside toy boxes, so be sure your box has ventilation holes or a gap between the lid and the box. Don't block the holes by pushing the box tight against a wall. Be sure the lid doesn't latch.

Toys

Most toy manufacturers are conscientious in trying to produce safe toys, but they cannot always anticipate the way a child might use—or abuse—their products. In a recent year, there were an estimated 255,100 toy-related injuries treated in U.S. hospital emergency rooms. Of these, 30 percent (77,100) involved children under the age of five years. If your child is injured by an unsafe product or if you would like to report a product-related injury, refer to the information in the box on page 444. The Consumer Product Safety Commission keeps a record of complaints and initiates recalls of dangerous toys, so your phone call may protect not only your child but others.

When selecting or using toys, always observe the following safety guidelines.

1. Match all toys to your child's age and abilities. Manufacturers' guidelines can help, but in the end you must decide whether your child is mature and skilled enough to use a plaything safely.

2. Rattles—probably your child's first toys—should be at least 1⅜ inches (4 cm) across. An infant's mouth and throat are very flexible, so one that's smaller than that could cause choking. Also, rattles should have no detachable parts.

3. All toys should be constructed of sturdy materials that won't break or shatter even when a child throws or bangs them.

4. Check squeeze toys to be sure the squeaker can't become detached from the toy.

5. Before giving your child a stuffed animal or a doll, be certain the eyes and nose are firmly attached, and check them periodically. Remove all ribbons. Don't allow your child to suck on a pacifier or any other accessory that comes packaged with a doll and is small enough to be swallowed.

6. Swallowing and/or inhaling small parts of toys are serious dangers to young children. Inspect toys carefully for small parts that could fit in your child's mouth and throat. Look for toys labeled for children three and under, because they must meet federal guidelines requiring that they have no small parts likely to be swallowed or inhaled.

7. Toys with small parts that are purchased for older children should be stored out of the reach of younger ones. Impress on your older child the importance of picking up all the pieces from such toys when she's finished playing with them. You should check that there are no items dangerous for your baby left out.

8. Don't let a child play with balloons; she may inhale a balloon if she tries to blow it up. If a balloon pops, be sure to pick up and discard all the broken pieces.

9. To prevent both burns and electrical shocks, don't give young children (under age ten) a toy that must be plugged into an electrical outlet. Instead, buy toys that are battery-operated. Be sure that the battery cover is securely fastened.

10. Carefully inspect toys with mechanical parts for springs, gears, or hinges that could trap a child's fingers, hair, or clothing.

11. To prevent cuts, check toys before you purchase them to be sure they don't have sharp edges or pointed pieces. Avoid toys with parts made of glass or rigid plastic that could shatter.

12. Don't allow your child to play with very noisy toys, including squeeze toys with unexpectedly loud squeakers. Noise levels at or about 100 decibels—the sound of the typical cap gun at close range—can damage hearing.

13. Projectile toys are not suitable for children, because they can so easily cause eye injuries. Never give your child a toy that actually fires anything except water.

SAFETY OUTSIDE THE HOME

Even if you create the perfect environment for your child inside your home, she'll be spending a lot of time outside, where surroundings are somewhat less controllable. Obviously, your personal supervision will remain the most valuable protection. However, even a well-supervised child will be exposed to many hazards. The information that follows will show you how to eliminate many of these hazards and reduce the risk that your child will ever be injured.

Car Safety Seats

Each year more children between the ages of one and nineteen are killed in car crashes than in any other way. Many of these deaths could be prevented if the children were properly restrained. Contrary to what many people believe, a parent's lap is actually the most perilous place for a child to ride. In case of a car crash, you wouldn't be able to hold on to your child, and your body would crush hers as you were thrown against the dashboard and windshield. The single most important thing you can do to keep your child safe in the car is to buy, install, and use an approved car safety seat, appropriate for the age and size of your child, every time she rides in the car.

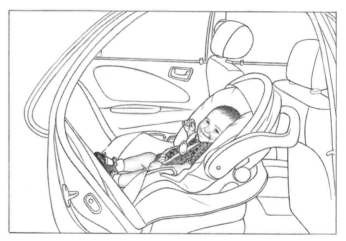

Infant-Only Car Safety Seat

Car safety seats are required by law in all fifty states and U.S. territories. Unfortunately, recent studies show that many parents are not using them properly. The most common mistakes are placing rear-facing seats in front of an air bag, facing car safety seats in the wrong direction, failing to harness the child into the seat, failing to securely fasten the child's car safety seat to the vehicle seat, and not using a booster seat for older children. Also, some parents don't use the seat on short trips. They are not aware that most fatal crashes occur within five miles (8 km) of home and at speeds of less than twenty-five miles (40 km) per hour. For all these reasons, children continue to be at risk. It's not enough to have a car safety seat—you must use it correctly, every time.

Choosing a Car Safety Seat

Here are some guidelines you can use to help you select a car safety seat.

1. The American Academy of Pediatrics annually publishes a list of car safety seats that are available. "Car Safety Seats: A Guide for Families" can be found online at www.aap.org/family/carseatguide.htm.

2. No one seat is "safest" or "best." The "best" car safety seat is one that fits your child's size and weight, and can be installed correctly in your car.

3. Price does not always make a difference. Higher prices can mean added features that may or may not make the seat easier to use.

4. When you find a seat you like, try it out. Put your child in the seat and adjust the harnesses and buckles. Make sure it fits in your car and that the harnesses are easy to adjust when the seat is in your car.

5. Keep in mind that displays or illustrations of seats in stores do not always show them being used correctly.

6. If your baby is born premature, use a car safety seat without a shield. Shields often are too high and too far from the body to fit correctly. A small baby's face could hit a shield in a crash. Before you bring your baby home from the hospital, she should be observed in her car safety seat by hospital staff to make sure the semireclined position does not cause low heart rate, low oxygen, or other breathing problems. If your baby needs to lie flat during

Belt-Positioning Booster Seat

travel, use a crash-tested car bed. If possible, an adult should ride in the backseat next to your baby to watch her closely.

7. Children with special health problems may need other restraint systems. Discuss this with your pediatrician. Easter Seals, Inc., offers programs about car seat safety for children with special health care needs in certain states. More information is available from

Forward-facing car safety seat

Easter Seals, Inc., at 1–800–221–6827, or from the Automotive Safety for Children Program at 1–317–274–2977.

8. Do not use a car safety seat that is too old. Look on the label for the date it was made. If it is more than ten years old, it should not be used. Some manufacturers recommend that seats be used for only five to six years. Check with the manufacturer to find out when the company recommends getting a new seat.

9. If a car safety seat was in a crash, it may have been weakened and should not be used, even if it looks fine. Do not use a seat if you do not know its full history. Call the car safety seat manufacturer if you have questions about the safety of your seat.

10. Do not use a car safety seat that does not have a label with the date of manufacture and seat name or model number. Without these, you cannot check on recalls.

11. Do not use a car safety seat if it does not come with instructions. You need them to know how to use the car safety seat. Do not rely on the former owner's directions. Get a copy of the instruction manual from the manufacturer before you use the seat.

12. Do not use a car safety seat that has any cracks in the frame of the seat or is missing parts.

13. You can find out if your car safety seat has been recalled by calling the manufacturer or the Auto Safety Hot Line at 1–888–DASH–2–DOT (1–888–327–4236), from 8 A.M. to 10 P.M. ET, Monday through Friday. This information is also available on the National Highway Traffic Safety Administration website: www.nhtsa.dot.gov/cars/problems/recalls/index.cfm. If the seat has been recalled, be sure to follow instructions to fix it or get the necessary parts. You also may get a registration card for future recall notices from the hotline.

Types of Car Safety Seats

Infant-only Seats

- Can be used only rear-facing.

- Are used for babies from birth or 5 pounds (2.25 kg) and who weigh up to 20 pounds (9 kg) or 22 pounds (10 kg), depending on the model.

- Are small and portable.

- Come with a three-point harness or a five-point harness.

Infant-only Seat Features

Detachable base
Several infant-only seat models come with detachable bases. The base attaches to the car, and the car safety seat easily snaps into the base. This way you can carry your baby in and out of the car without needing to reinstall the seat. After buckling your baby into the seat, you simply lock the seat into the installed base. Some bases are adjustable to make it easier to recline newborns correctly. These seats also can be installed in the vehicle without the base, or you can buy additional bases for other cars. However, this feature is helpful only if the base fits tightly into your car. In some cases, the seat may fit better without the base.

Higher weight and height limits
Several infant-only seats are available for use up to 22 pounds (10 kg). Many convertible seats also now have higher weight and height limits in the rear-facing position for heavier or taller babies. Keep in mind that some babies may reach the top height limits of the seat before they reach the top weight limits. If your infant's weight or height exceeds the limits of the seat before a year, use an infant-only seat or a rear-facing convertible seat that has a higher limit.

Harness slots
Infant-only seats that come with more than one harness slot provide more room for growing babies. In the rear-facing position, the harness slots usually should be at or below your baby's shoulders. Check the car safety seat manufacturer's instructions to be sure.

Handles
Carrying handles on car safety seats vary greatly in style and ease of use. Check the instructions for how to adjust the handle during travel.

Other features
Angle indicators, built-in angle adjusters, harness adjusters, and head support systems are other features that may make correct installation easier to achieve.

Convertible Seats

- Are bigger and heavier than infant-only seats, but can be used longer and for larger children.

- May not fit newborns as well as some infant-only seats do. Make sure that your baby can recline comfortably in the seat. Check the car safety seat manufacturer's instructions to be sure that harnesses can be adjusted properly.

- Are used rear-facing for infants until they have reached at least one year of age *and* weigh at least 20 pounds (9 kg) (or more depending on model). The American Academy of Pediatrics recommends that babies be kept in rear-facing seats until they reach the maximum weight allowed, as long as the top of the head is below the top of the seat back.

- Can be used forward-facing for toddlers who are at least one year of age *and* weigh at least 20 pounds (9 kg) and not more than 40 pounds (18 kg). When your child is older than one year of age *and* has reached the highest weight or height allowed by the seat for use rear-facing, you may turn the seat forward-facing and make the following three adjustments:

  1. Move the shoulder straps to the slots at or above your child's shoulders (usually the top slots, but check your instructions to make sure).

  2. Move the seat into the upright position. (Check the car safety seat manufacturer's instructions for the recline angle allowed when forward-facing.)

  3. Route the seat belt through the forward-facing belt path.

- Have the following three types of harnesses:

  1. Five-point harness—five straps: two at the shoulders, two at the hips, one at the crotch

  2. Overhead shield—A padded, traylike shield that swings down around the child

  3. T-shield—A padded T-shaped or triangular shield attached to shoulder straps

Note: If you are using a convertible seat for a small infant, the best choice for a more secure fit is the five-point harness. A small baby's face can hit a shield in a crash.

Convertible Seat Features

Adjustable buckles and shields
Many convertible seats have two or more buckle positions to give you extra room for a growing child or bulky clothing. Many overhead shields can be adjusted, as well.

Higher weight limits
Several convertible seats are available with higher rear-facing weight limits for bigger babies. For larger babies, look for a seat that can be used rear-facing up to 30 or 35 pounds (14 kg to 16 kg).

Combination Seats

- Cannot be used rear-facing.

- Are only for children who are at least one year of age *and* weigh at least 20 pounds (9 kg).

- Have an internal harness system for children who weigh 40 pounds (18 kg) or less.

- Convert to belt-positioning boosters (by removing the harnesses) for children who weigh more than 40 pounds (18 kg). This allows the seat to be used longer.

Forward-facing Seats/Restraints

- Cannot be used rear-facing.

- Are only for children who are at least one year of age *and* weigh at least 20 pounds (9 kg).

- Can be used with lap-only belt or lap/shoulder belt.

Booster Seats

When your child reaches the top weight allowed for her car safety seat or her ears have reached the top of her car safety seat, your child needs a belt-positioning booster seat. Booster seats should be used until your child can use a lap/shoulder seat belt correctly. Following are two types of booster seats:

1. Belt-positioning boosters: They are used with lap/shoulder belts. The booster raises your child so that the lap/shoulder belt fits properly. This helps protect your child's upper body and head. Both high-backed and backless models are available.

2. Shield boosters: Based on Federal Motor Vehicle Safety Standards established by the National Highway Transportation Safety Administration (NHTSA), shield boosters have not been certified by their manufacturers for use by children who weigh more than 40 pounds (18 kg). For these children, or for children who are too heavy or too tall to fit in a seat with a full harness, the shield may be removed and the seat used with a lap/shoulder belt as a belt-positioning booster.

Children who weigh 40 pounds or less are best protected in a seat with a full harness. In crashes significant injuries have occurred to children in shield boosters due to ejection, excessive head movement, and shield contact. Although boosters with shields may meet current Federal Motor Vehicle Safety Standards for use by children who weigh 30 to 40 pounds (14 to 18 kg), on the basis of current published peer-reviewed data, the American Academy of Pediatrics does not recommend their use. Children should remain in a convertible, forward-facing, or combination seat with a full harness until they reach the top weight or height allowed by the seat.

Travel Vests

A travel vest may be an option if your car has only lap belts.

Built-in Seats (Integrated Seats)

Built-in seats are available in some cars and vans. They may be used for children who are at least one year of age *and* weigh at least 20 pounds (9 kg). Built-in seats eliminate installation problems. However, weight and height limits vary. Check with vehicle manufacturers for details about built-in seats that are currently available.

Installing a Car Safety Seat

1. Read your vehicle owner's manual for important information on how to install the car safety seat correctly in your vehicle.

2. The safest place for all children to ride is in the backseat.

3. Never place a child in a rear-facing car safety seat in the front seat of a vehicle that has a passenger air bag. Most new cars have air bags. When used with seat belts, air bags work very well to protect older children and adults. However, air bags are very dangerous when used with rear-facing car safety seats. If your car has a passenger air bag, infants in rear-facing seats *must* ride in the backseat. Even in a low-speed crash, the air bag can inflate, strike the car safety seat, and cause serious brain injury and death. Toddlers who ride in forward-facing car safety seats also are at risk from air bag injuries. Remember, *all* children, even through school age, are safest in the backseat. If you must put an older child in the front seat, slide the vehicle seat back as far as it will go. Make sure your child is buckled and stays in the proper position at all times. Doing so will help prevent the air bag from striking your child. For most families, air bag on/off switches are not necessary. Air bags that are turned off cannot protect other passengers riding in the front seat. Air bag on/off switches should be used only if *all* of the following are true:

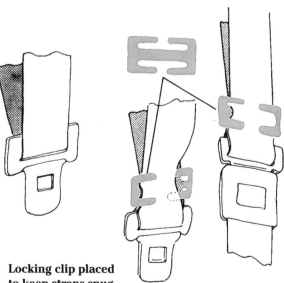

**Locking clip placed
to keep straps snug**

Keeping Your Child Happy and Safe on the Road

As hard as you may try to enforce car safety seat and seat belt use, your child may resist these constraints as he gets older. Here are some tips to keep him occupied and content—and also safe—while the car is in motion.

Birth to Nine Months

- Ensure your newborn's comfort by padding the sides of his car safety seat with rolled diapers or receiving blankets to prevent slouching.

- Place a small rolled-up diaper or receiving blanket between the crotch strap and your baby to prevent his lower body from sliding too far forward.

- If your infant's head flops forward, double-check to see if the seat has been reclined enough. Tilt the seat backward until it is reclined as close as possible to a 45-degree angle, following the manufacturer's instructions. Your seat may have a built-in recline adjuster for this purpose. If not, you may wedge firm padding, such as a rolled towel, under the front of the base of the seat.

Nine Months to Twenty-four Months

- Children this age love to climb, and may want desperately to get out of the car safety seat. If this describes your child, remind yourself that this is only a phase. As mentioned earlier, in a calm

- Your child has special health care needs.

- Your pediatrician recommends constant supervision of your child during travel.

- No other adult is available to ride in the backseat with your child.

On/off switches also must be used if you have a vehicle with no backseat or a backseat that is not made for passengers.

4. Place the seat facing the correct direction for the size and age of your child. Route the seat belt through the correct path on the car safety seat (check your instructions to make sure), and pull it tight. Before each trip, check to make sure the car safety seat is installed tightly enough by pulling on the car

but stern voice, insist that he stay in his seat whenever the car is on the road.

- Entertain your toddler by talking or singing with him as you drive. However, never do this to the point that it distracts you from paying attention to your driving.

Twenty-four Months to Thirty-six Months

- Make driving a learning experience by talking about the things your child sees out the window, as long as this doesn't distract you from your driving.

- Encourage your child to buckle his toy animals or dolls into a seat belt and talk about how safe the toy is now that it's buckled up.

Preschoolers

- Talk about safety as "grown-up" behavior, and praise your child whenever he voluntarily buckles up.

- Encourage your child to accept the car safety seat or booster seat by suggesting make-believe roles, such as astronaut, pilot, or race-car driver.

- Explain why the car safety seat is important: "If we have to stop suddenly, the straps keep you from bumping your head."

- Show him books and pictures with safety messages.

- *Always* wear your seat belt, and make sure everyone else in the car buckles up, too.

safety seat where the seat belt passes through. It should not move easily side to side or toward the front of the car.

5. If your infant's head flops forward, the seat may not be reclined enough. Tilt the seat back until it is reclined as close as possible to a 45-degree angle (according to manufacturer's instructions). Your seat may have a built-in recline adjuster for this purpose. If not, you may wedge firm padding, such as a rolled towel, under the front of the base of the seat.

6. Check the seat belt buckle. Make sure it does not lie just at the point where the belt bends around the car safety seat. If it does, you will not be able to make the belt tight enough. If you cannot get the belt tight, look for another set of belts in the car that can be tightened properly.

7. Many lap/shoulder belts allow passengers to move freely even when they are buckled. Read your car owner's manual to see if your seat belts can be locked into position or if you will need to use a locking clip. Locking clips come with all new car safety seats. (Some have them built in.) Read your instructions for information on how to use the locking clip.

8. Some lap belts need a special, heavy-duty locking clip, available from the vehicle manufacturer. Check your car owner's manual for more information.

9. A new car safety seat attachment system has been developed to make car safety seats easier to use and safer. The system is called LATCH, which stands for *L*ower *A*nchors and *T*ethers for *Ch*ildren. This new anchor system will make correct installation much easier because you will no longer need to use seat belts to secure the car safety seat. Starting in model year 2002, most new vehicles and new safety seats are being equipped with these lower anchors and attachments. However, unless both the vehicle and the car safety seat have this new anchor system, you still will need to secure seat belts to the car safety seat.

10. Most new car safety seats that can be used facing forward come with top tethers, straps that hook the top of the car safety seat to a special permanent anchor in the vehicle. Most anchors are located on the rear window ledge, the back of the vehicle seat, or the floor or ceiling of the vehicle. Tethers give extra protection by keeping the car safety seat from being thrown forward in a crash. Tether kits are available for most older car safety seats. Check with the car safety seat manufacturer to find out how to get a top tether for your seat. Be sure to install it according to instructions. The tether strap may help make some seats that are difficult to install fit more tightly. Since September 2000, all new cars, minivans, and light trucks have been required to have upper tether anchors for securing the tops of car safety seats.

11. For specific information about installing your car safety seat, consult a certified Child Passenger Safety (CPS) Technician. CPS Technicians are certified by the American Automobile Association (AAA). A list of certified CPS Technicians is available by state or ZIP code on the NHTSA website at www.nhtsa.dot.gov/people/injury/childps/Contacts/index.cfm. A list of inspection stations staffed by certified CPS Technicians is also available on the Internet at www.nhtsa.dot.gov/people/injury/childps/CPSFitting/Index.cfm. The information also can be accessed by telephone on the NHTSA Auto Safety Hot Line at 1–888–DASH–2–DOT (1–888–327–4236), from 8 A.M. to 10 P.M. ET, Monday through Friday.

12. Lap belts work fine with infant-only, convertible, and forward-facing seats. They cannot be used with belt-positioning boosters (which are safest for children who weigh more than 40 pounds (18 kg) and who are not big enough to fit in adult seat belts). If your car has lap belts only, use a forward-facing seat with a harness approved for use to higher weights, use a forward-facing restraint, or check with your dealer or the car manufacturer to see if shoulder harnesses can be installed. Some travel vests can be used with lap belts. Or consider buying another car with lap/shoulder belts in the backseat.

13. Avoid driving more children than can be buckled safely in the backseat. However, in an emergency, place the child most likely to sit in the proper forward-facing position in the front seat, with the vehicle seat moved as far back as possible. A child in a forward-facing car safety seat may be the best choice to ride in the front seat, because a child who is in a booster seat or using a regular seat belt can move out of position more easily and be at greater risk for injuries from the air bag.

Use of the Car Safety Seat

1. A car safety seat can protect your child only if she sits in it *every* time she rides in the car—no exceptions, beginning with your baby's first ride home from the hospital. Help your child form a lifelong habit of buckling up by *always* using your own seat belt. If you have two cars, buy two seats or transfer the seat to the car in which your child will be traveling. If you are renting a car, find out if the rental car has a passenger-side air bag. If so, never place a rear-facing car safety seat in the front seat. The safest place for all children to ride is in the back.

2. Read the car safety seat manufacturer's instructions, and always keep them with the car safety seat. If you lose the instructions, call or write the manufacturer and ask for a new set.

3. Most children go through a stage when they protest whenever you put them in the car safety seat. Explain firmly that you cannot drive until everyone is buckled up. Then back up your words with action.

4. Be sure to use the correct harness slots for the child.

5. Be sure the harness straps are snug against your child's body. Dress your baby in clothes that allow the straps to go between her legs. Keep the straps snug by adjusting them to allow for the thickness of your child's clothes, making sure that the harness still holds the child securely. Be certain the straps lie flat and are not twisted.

6. To keep your newborn from slouching, pad the sides of the seat and between the crotch with rolled-up diapers or receiving blankets.

7. In cold weather, tuck blankets around your baby after adjusting the harness straps snugly.

8. In hot weather, drape a towel over the seat when you leave the car in the sun. Before putting your child in the seat, touch the vinyl and the metal buckle with your hand to be sure they aren't hot.

9. No matter how short your errand is, *never* leave an infant or child alone in a car. She might get overheated or too cold, if the outside temperature is extreme, or she may become frightened and panicky when she realizes she's alone. Any child alone in a car is a target for abduction, or an older child may be tempted to play with things such as a cigarette lighter or the gear shift, which could cause her serious injury.

10. Always use your own seat belt. In addition to setting a good example, you'll reduce your own risk of injury or death in a crash by 60 percent.

11. When your child outgrows the booster seat, make certain she uses the seat belt *at all times*. Be sure the seat belts in your car fit your child correctly. The shoulder belt should lie across the chest, and the lap belt should lie low and snug across the thighs. Your child should sit against the vehicle seat back with her feet hanging down when the legs are bent at the knee. Seat belts are made to fit adults, so if the shoulder belt crosses your child's throat or the lap belt crosses the stomach, she is too small for it and should stay in a booster seat. Other points to keep in mind when using seat belts:

- Never tuck the shoulder belt under the child's arm or behind the child's back.

- If only a lap belt is available, make sure it is worn tight and low on the hips, not across the stomach.

Air Bag Safety

An air bag can save your life. However, air bags and young children do not mix. The following information will help keep you and your children safe. (You've already read some of this information, but it's worth repeating.)

- The safest place for all infants and children under twelve years of age to ride is in the backseat.

- Never put an infant under one year of age in the front seat of a car with an air bag.

- Infants always must ride in rear-facing car safety seats in the backseat until they are at least one year of age *and* weigh at least 20 pounds (9 kg).

- All children should be properly secured in car safety seats, booster seats, or shoulder/lap belts correct for their size.

- When purchasing a car, look for one with an air bag on the front passenger side for your family's safety. Keep in mind, however, that young children— as well as children of any age—should ride in the backseat. Even if your baby's safety seat is rear-facing, he can suffer a serious injury from the impact of the air bag against the back of the safety seat. Although the backseat is the safest place for children of any age to ride, all passengers in the front seat should be positioned as far back as possible from the front air bag on the passenger side.

- Side air bags improve safety for adults in side impact crashes. However, children who are seated near a front or rear side airbag can be at risk for serious injury. Refer to your vehicle owner's manual for recommendations that apply to your vehicle.

- Seat belts must be worn correctly at all times by all passengers to provide the best protection.

What Parents Can Do

- Eliminate potential risks of air bags to children by buckling them in the backseat for every ride.

- Plan ahead so that you do not have to drive with more children than can be safely restrained in the backseat.

- For most families, installation of air bag on/off switches is not necessary. Air bags that are turned off provide no protection to older children, teens, parents, or other adults riding in the front seat.

WHERE WE STAND

All fifty states require that children ride in car safety seats. The American Academy of Pediatrics urges that all newborns discharged from hospitals be brought home in infant car safety seats. The AAP has established car safety seat guidelines for low–birth-weight infants, which include riding in a rear-facing seat and supporting the infant with ample padding. A convertible car safety seat is recommended as a child gets older.

Infants and young children always should ride in car safety seats—preferably in the backseat—because it is safest. Never use a rear-facing car safety seat in the front seat of a vehicle equipped with a passenger-side air bag. An infant or child should never ride in an adult's arms. Children age twelve and younger should ride in the rear seat.

Older children should use booster seats until the vehicle safety belt fits well. The shoulder belt should lie across the chest, with the lap belt low and snug across the thighs, and the child should sit against the vehicle's seat back with her feet hanging down when her legs are bent at the knees.

- Air bag on/off switches should be used only if your child has special health care needs, your pediatrician recommends constant observation during travel, and no other adult is available to ride in the backseat with your child. On/off switches must be used if you have a vehicle with no backseat, or if the backseat is not made for passengers.

- If no other arrangement is possible and an older child must ride in the front seat, move the vehicle seat back as far as it can go, away from the air bag. Be sure the child is properly buckled. Keep in mind that your child still may be at risk for injuries from the air bag. The backseat is the safest place for children to ride.

Pedestrian Safety

Although many parents are conscientious about keeping their child as safe as possible when traveling in a car, they may let down their guard when their youngsters are pedestrians. In fact, thousands of pedestrians are killed or injured in the United States each year, many of them children.

From an early age, teach your child rules that will serve him well throughout life. Explain that he should cross streets only at intersections, looking both ways before crossing, and that he should do so only with an adult holding his hand. As soon as he's able to understand, teach him what green and red traffic lights mean and what's meant by "walk" and "don't walk" signs and symbols.

When a sidewalk is available, always use it when walking with your child. When a sidewalk isn't present, walk facing traffic so you can see the oncoming cars.

When you're walking with your child at night, both of you should dress in light clothing. Drivers will have more difficulty seeing you when you're wearing dark clothes.

Baby Carriers—Backpacks and Front Packs

Back and front carriers for infants are very popular, although most babies outgrow front carriers by the age of three months. For your baby's—and your own—comfort and safety, follow these guidelines when purchasing and using baby carriers.

1. Infants born prematurely or with respiratory problems who do not tolerate upright positioning in a car safety seat should not be placed in backpacks or other upright positioning devices.

2. Take your baby with you when you shop for the carrier so that you can match it to his size. Make sure the carrier supports his back and that the leg holes are small enough so he can't possibly slip through. Look for sturdy material.

3. If you buy a backpack, be sure the aluminum frame is padded, so that your baby won't be hurt if he bumps against it.

4. Check the pack periodically for rips and tears in the seams and fasteners.

5. When using a back carrier, be sure to bend at the knees, not the waist, if you need to pick something up. Otherwise, the baby may tip out of the carrier and you may hurt your back.

6. Babies over five months old may become restless in the back carrier, so be sure always to use the restraining straps. Some children will brace their feet against the frame, changing their weight distribution. You should be certain that your child is seated properly before you walk.

Strollers and Baby Carriages

Because children outgrow baby carriages so quickly, many manufacturers now make low carriages that can be converted into strollers when the baby is bigger. Look for safety features and take the following precautions.

1. If you use bumpers in your baby carriage, or if you string toys across it, fasten them securely so they can't fall on top of the baby. Remove such toys as soon as the baby can sit or get on all fours.

2. If the carriage is collapsible, be sure your child cannot reach the release mechanism. This mechanism always should be locked upright before you put your baby in the carriage.

3. Once your child is able to sit alone, stop using the carriage, because falls from them are very common after this point. If you must continue to use the carriage for some reason, or if you have an extremely active baby, harness her and attach the harness to the side of the carriage so she cannot lean out while you're walking.

4. Both carriages and strollers should have brakes that are easy to operate. Use the brake whenever you are stopped, and be sure your child can't reach the release lever. A brake that locks two wheels provides an extra measure of safety.

5. Select a stroller with a wide base, so it won't tip over.

6. Children's fingers can become caught in the hinges that fold the stroller, so keep your child at a safe distance when you open and close it.

7. Don't hang bags or other items from the handles of your stroller—they can make it tip backward. If the stroller has a basket for carrying things, be sure it is placed low and near the rear wheels.

8. The stroller should have a seat belt and harness, and it should be used whenever your child goes for a ride. For infants, use rolled-up baby blankets as bumpers on either side of the seat.

9. Never leave your child unattended in a baby carriage or stroller.

10. If you purchase a twin stroller, be sure the footrest extends all the way across both sitting areas. A child's foot can become trapped between separate footrests.

Shopping Cart Safety

An estimated twenty thousand children under five years old were treated in emergency rooms for shopping cart–related injuries in 1999. The most frequent kinds of injuries were contusions, abrasions, and lacerations, and most injuries are to the head or neck.

The design of shopping carts makes it easier for them to tip over when a child is in the cart or in the seat designed to fit on the cart. Until shopping carts are redesigned, you need to know that seats attached to the top of shopping carts or built into them won't prevent a child from falling out if she isn't properly restrained; these seats also won't prevent the cart from tipping over even if the child is restrained.

If possible, you should seek an alternative to placing your child in a shopping cart. When you must do so, make sure she is restrained at all times. Never allow her to stand up in the cart, be transported in the basket, or ride on the outside of the cart. Never leave a child alone in a shopping cart.

Bicycles and Tricycles

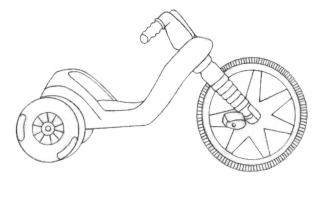

If you like to ride a bicycle, you'll probably consider getting a child carrier that attaches to the back of the bike. You should be aware that even with the best carrier and safety helmet, your child is at risk for serious injury. This can occur when you lose control on an uneven road surface, or if you should happen to strike or be struck by another vehicle. It is wiser to wait to enjoy bicycling together until your child is old enough to ride with you on her own two-wheeler. (See below for further information about child carriers.)

As your child outgrows babyhood, she will want a tricycle of her own, and when she gets one, she'll be exposing herself to a number of hazards. For example, a child on a tricycle is so low to the ground that she can't be seen by a motorist who is backing up. Nevertheless, riding trikes and bikes is almost an essential part of growing up. Here are some safety suggestions that will help you reduce the risk to your child.

1. Don't buy a tricycle until your child is physically able to handle it. Most children are ready around age three.

2. Buy a tricycle that is built low to the ground and has big wheels. This type is safer because it is less likely to tip over.

3. Obtain a properly fitting bicycle helmet, and teach your child to use it every time she rides.

4. Tricycles should be used only in protected places. Don't allow your child to ride near automobiles, driveways, or swimming pools.

5. In general, children don't have the balance and muscle coordination to ride a two-wheel bicycle until around age seven. Most children can safely begin to ride a two-wheeler with training wheels after age six, but not before. Again, to protect your child from injury, make sure she is wearing an approved bicycle helmet (certified on the label that it meets the Consumer Product Safety Commission standards).

6. If you're considering having your child ride as a passenger in a rear-mounted seat on an adult's bike, keep in mind that not only will she make the bike unstable, but she also will increase the braking time and raise the risk of serious injury to both you and your youngster. A much better choice is for your child to ride in a bicycle-towed child trailer. If you must carry your child on a bike, never put her in a seat on the back of your bicycle until she's at least one year old. Children who are old enough (twelve months to four years) to sit well unsupported and whose necks are strong enough to support a lightweight helmet may be carried in a rear-mounted seat, although it is not the preferred choice. *Never* carry infants in backpacks or front packs on a bike.

7. A rear-mounted seat must:

    a. be securely attached over the rear wheel;

    b. have spoke guards to prevent feet and hands from being caught in the wheels; and

    c. have a high back and a sturdy shoulder harness and lap belt that will support a sleeping child.

8. A young passenger always should wear a lightweight infant bike helmet certified for young children to prevent or minimize head injury.

9. The child must be strapped into the bike seat with a sturdy harness.

10. Never ride with a child on the front handlebars or place a seat there.

Playgrounds

Whether it's a swing set in the backyard or the more elaborate apparatus in the park, there are many positive things to say about playground equipment. The use of this equipment encourages children to test and expand their physical abilities. However, there are some inevitable dangers. The risks can be minimized when equipment is well designed and children are taught basic playground manners. Here are some guidelines you can use in selecting playground equipment and sites for your child.

1. Make sure there is sand, wood chips, or rubberized matting under swings, seesaws, and jungle gyms, and that these surfaces are of proper depth and well maintained. On concrete or asphalt, a fall directly on the head can be fatal—even from a height of just a few inches.

2. Wooden structures should be made from all-weather wood, which is less likely to splinter. Examine the surfaces periodically to be sure they are smooth.

3. Conduct a periodic inspection of equipment, looking especially for loose joints, open chains that could come loose, and rusted cotter pins. On metal equipment, check for rusted or exposed bolts as well as sharp edges and points. At home, cover them with protective rubber. In a public playground, report the hazard to the appropriate authorities.

4. Be sure swings are made of soft and flexible material. Insist that your child sit in the middle of the seat, holding on with both hands. Don't allow two children to share the same swing. Teach your child never to walk in front of or behind a swing while another youngster is on it.

5. Be sure children on slides use the ladder instead of climbing up the sliding surface. Don't permit pushing and shoving on the ladder, and have children go up one at a time. Teach your child to leave the bottom of the slide as soon as he reaches it. If a slide has been sitting in the sun for a long time, check the sliding surface to see if it's too hot before letting him use it.

6. Don't allow children under four to use climbing equipment that is taller than they (i.e., jungle gyms) without close supervision.

7. Between the ages of three and five, your child should use a seesaw only with other children of comparable age and weight. Children under three don't have the arm and leg coordination to use the equipment.

8. Children under five should play on equipment separate from older children.

9. Although trampolines often are considered a source of fun for children, about 100,000 people per year are injured on them each year, most often on backyard models. Childhood injuries have included broken bones, head injuries, neck and spinal cord injuries, sprains, and bruises. Parental supervision and protective netting aren't adequate to prevent these injuries. The American Academy of Pediatrics advises parents to take steps to ensure that their children never use trampolines at home, a friend's house, the playground, or in a routine gym class. Older children should use trampolines only in training programs for competitive sports such as gymnastics or diving, and only when supervised by a professional trained in trampoline safety.

Your Backyard

Your backyard can be a sanctuary for your child if you eliminate potential hazards. Here are some suggestions for keeping your yard safe.

1. If you don't have a fenced yard, teach your child the boundaries within which she should play. Always have a responsible person supervise outdoor play.

2. Check your yard for dangerous plants. Among preschoolers, plants are a leading cause of poisoning. If you are unsure about any of the plants in your yard, call your local Poison Center and request a list of poisonous plants common to your area. (The national poison control number is 1–800–222–1222.) If you have any poisonous plants, either replace them or securely fence and lock that area of the yard away from your child.

3. Teach your youngster never to pick and eat anything from a plant, no matter how good it looks, without your permission. This is particularly important if you let her help out in a vegetable garden where there's produce that could be eaten.

4. If you use pesticides or herbicides on your lawn or garden, read the instructions carefully. Don't allow children to play on a treated lawn for at least forty-eight hours.

5. Don't use a power mower to cut the lawn when young children are around. The mower may throw sticks or stones with enough force to injure them. Never have your child on a riding mower even when you are driving.

6. When you cook food outdoors, screen the grill so that your child cannot touch it, and explain that it is hot like the stove in the kitchen. Store propane grills so your child cannot reach the knobs. Be sure charcoal is cold before you dump it.

7. Never allow your child to play unattended near traffic, and do not allow her to cross the street by herself, even if it is just to go to a waiting school bus.

Water Safety

Water is one of the most ominous hazards your child will encounter. Young children can drown in only a few inches of water, even if they've had swimming instruction. Swimming lessons are not a way to prevent drowning. Although swimming classes for young children are widely available, the American Academy of Pediatrics does not recommend them for children until after their fourth birthday for several reasons:

1. You may be lulled into being less cautious because you think your child can swim, and children themselves may unwittingly be encouraged to enter the water without supervision.

2. Young children who are repeatedly immersed in water may swallow so much of it that they develop water intoxication. This can result in convulsions, shock, and even death.

3. Children are generally not developmentally ready for formal swimming lessons until after their fourth birthday. Children can learn swimming skills more quickly once their motor development has reached the five-year-old level.

4. Safety training does not result in a significant increase in poolside safety skills of young children.

If you do enroll a child under four years old in a swimming program, particularly a Daddy- or Mommy-and-me class, think of it primarily as an opportunity to enjoy playing in the water together. Be sure the class you choose adheres to guidelines established by the national YMCA. Among other things, these guidelines forbid submersion of young children and encourage parents to participate

WHERE WE STAND

The American Academy of Pediatrics feels strongly that parents should never—even for a moment—leave children alone near open bodies of water, such as lakes or swimming pools, nor near water in homes (bathtubs, spas). For backyard pools, rigid, motorized pool covers are not a substitute for four-sided fencing, since pool covers are not likely to be used appropriately and consistently. Parents should learn CPR and keep a telephone and emergency equipment (i.e., life preservers) at poolside.

in all activities. When your child reaches age four, you may want him to learn to swim so he'll feel more comfortable in and around water. But remember that even a child who knows how to swim needs to be watched constantly. Whenever your child is near water, follow these safety rules.

1. Be aware of small bodies of water your child might encounter, such as fishponds, ditches, fountains, rain barrels, watering cans—even the bucket you use when you wash the car. Empty containers of water when you're done using them. Children are drawn to places and things like these and need constant supervision to be sure they don't fall in.

2. Children who are swimming—even in a shallow toddler's pool—always should be watched by an adult, preferably one who knows CPR. (See *Cardiopulmonary Resuscitation and Mouth-to-Mouth Resuscitation,* page 478.) The adult should be within an arm's length, providing "touch supervision" whenever infants or toddlers are in or around water. Empty and put away inflatable pools after each play session.

3. Enforce safety rules: no running near the pool and no pushing others underwater.

4. Don't allow your child to use inflatable toys or mattresses to keep him afloat. These toys may deflate suddenly, or your child may slip off them into water that is too deep for him.

5. Be sure the deep and shallow ends of any pool your child swims in are clearly marked. Never allow your child to dive into the shallow end.

6. If you have a swimming pool at home, it should be completely surrounded with at least a 4-foot (1.2 meters) fence that has a self-latching and self-locking gate that opens away from the pool. Check the gate frequently to be sure it is in good working order. Keep the gate closed and locked at all times. Be sure your child cannot manipulate the lock or climb the fence. No opening under the fence or between uprights should be more than 4 inches (10 cm) wide.

7. If your pool has a cover, remove it completely before swimming. Also, never allow your child to walk on the pool cover; water may have accumulated on it, making it as dangerous as the pool itself. Your child also could fall through and become trapped underneath. Do not use a pool cover in place of a four-sided fence because it is not likely to be used appropriately and consistently.

8. Keep a safety ring with a rope beside the pool at all times. If possible, have a phone in the pool area with emergency numbers clearly marked.

9. Spas and hot tubs are dangerous for young children, who can easily drown or become overheated in them. Don't allow young children to use these facilities.

10. Your child should always wear a life preserver when he swims or rides in a boat. A life preserver fits properly if you can't lift it off over your child's head after he's been fastened into it. For the child under age five, particularly the nonswimmer, it also should have a flotation collar to keep the head upright and the face out of the water.

11. Adults should not drink alcohol when they are swimming. It presents a danger for them as well as for any children they might be supervising.

Safety Around Animals

Children are more likely than adults to be bitten by domesticated animals, including your own family pet. This is particularly true when a new baby is brought into the home. At such times, the pet's response should be observed carefully, and it should not be left alone with the infant. After the two- or three-week get-acquainted period, the animal usually ignores or actually enjoys the baby. However, it is always wise to be cautious when the animal is around, regardless of how much your pet seems to enjoy the relationship.

If you are getting a pet as a companion for your child, wait until she is mature enough to handle and care for the animal—usually around age five or six. Younger children have difficulty distinguishing an animal from a toy, so they may inadvertently provoke a bite through teasing or mistreatment. Remember that you have ultimate responsibility for your child's safety around any animal, so take the following precautions.

1. Look for a pet with a gentle disposition. An older animal is often a good choice for a child, because a puppy or kitten may bite out of sheer friskiness. Avoid older pets raised in a home without children, however.

2. Treat your pet humanely so it will enjoy human company. Don't, for example, tie a dog on a short rope or chain, since extreme confinement may make it anxious and aggressive.

3. Never leave a young child alone with an animal. Many bites occur during periods of playful roughhousing, because the child doesn't realize when the animal gets overexcited.

4. Teach your child not to put her face close to an animal.

5. Don't allow your child to tease your pet by pulling its tail or taking away a toy or a bone. Make sure she doesn't disturb the animal when it's sleeping or eating.

6. Have all pets—both dogs and cats—immunized against rabies.

7. Obey local ordinances about licensing and leashing your pet. Be sure your pet is under your control at all times.

8. Find out which neighbors have dogs, so your child can meet the pets with which she's likely to have contact. Teach your child how to greet a dog: The child should stand still while the dog sniffs her; then she can slowly extend her hand to pet the animal.

9. Warn your child to stay away from yards in which dogs seem high-strung or unfriendly. Teach older children the signs of an unsafe dog: rigid body, stiff tail at "half mast," hysterical barking, crouched position, staring expression.

10. Instruct your child to stand still if she is approached or chased by a strange dog. Tell her not to run, ride her bicycle, kick, or make threatening gestures. Your child should face the dog and back away slowly until she's out of reach.

11. Wild animals can carry very serious diseases that may be transmitted to humans. You (and your family pets) need to avoid contact with rodents and other wild animals (raccoons, skunks, foxes) that can carry diseases ranging from hantavirus to plague, from toxoplasmosis to rabies. To avoid bites by wild creatures, notify the health department whenever you see an animal that seems sick or injured, or one that is acting strangely. Don't try to catch the animal or pick it up. Teach your child to avoid all undomesticated animals. Fortunately, most wild animals come out only at night and tend to shy away from humans. A wild animal that is found in your yard or neighborhood during the daylight hours might have an infectious disease like rabies, and you should contact the local health authorities.

PREVENTING KIDNAPPING AND ABDUCTION

Many parents worry about their youngster being kidnapped. Fortunately, child abductions are rare, although they understandably get plenty of media attention when they occur. Most abductions occur when children are taken by non-custodial parents, although a smaller number of stranger abductions do take place each year.

Most hospitals have instituted security measures in newborn nurseries that make abductions of infants very unlikely. Laws throughout the United States mandate that all newborns be footprinted. (In some cases, handprinting must be done, as well.) Identification bracelets are placed on the ankle or arm of infants, and around the wrist of the mother. In some hospitals, babies are fitted with alarm devices that prevent them from being removed from the hospital by unauthorized persons.

Here are some suggestions for reducing the likelihood that your young child will be abducted.

- When you're shopping with your child, keep in mind that he can move quickly and move out of your line of sight in an instant. Keep an eye on him at *all* times.

- When choosing a preschool, look at safety issues as well as the educational program. Make sure a policy is in place where your child can be picked up only by his parent or someone else you designate. If someone he doesn't know talks to him on the playground, instruct him to tell the playground supervisor or teacher on playground duty. (Of course, children should be supervised on the playground at all times.) Many schools now have only one entrance, so that no adult can come onto the campus without being noticed by the front office personnel. If your child's school doesn't take these kinds of steps, check with the administrators and encourage that appropriate changes be made. If these changes are not instituted, you may want to look into other preschools or child care centers that take security more seriously.

- When your child is old enough to understand, make sure he's aware that he should only go with people he knows unless you tell him otherwise. Make sure your child understands that he should never get into a car with someone unfamiliar to him. If a stranger tells him something like "There's a lost puppy in my car; come into the car for a minute and see if you know him," he should emphatically say "no." In fact, tell him to run way as fast as possible from dangers like this and to yell very loudly and find a trusted adult in any situation in which he feels threatened.

- When hiring babysitters, always check references and/or ask for recommendations from friends and family members. Whenever possible, choose a trusted friend or a relative to babysit. Conduct background checks on other people who work in your home, including cleaning crews or handymen.

- Consider having your child fingerprinted. (Most police departments offer fingerprinting programs for children.) Some parents also are placing a lock of their child's hair in a safe place as well as a few of their nail clippings. Also keep a high-quality and current photograph of each of your youngsters.

For more information, see the website of the National Center for Missing & Exploited Children (www.missingkids.com).

When planning ways to keep your child safe, remember that she is constantly changing. Strategies that protect her from danger when she's one year old may no longer be adequate as she becomes stronger, more curious, and more confident in later months and years. Review your family's home and habits often to make sure your safeguards remain appropriate for your child's age.

PART II

15

EMERGENCIES

The information and policies in this section, such as first-aid procedures for the choking child and cardiopulmonary resuscitation (CPR), are constantly changing. Ask your pediatrician or other qualified health professional for the latest information on these procedures.

It is rare for children to become seriously ill with no warning. Based on your child's symptoms, you should usually contact your child's pediatrician for advice. Timely treatment of symptoms can prevent an illness from getting worse or turning into an emergency.

A true emergency is when you believe a severe injury or illness is threatening your child's life or may cause permanent harm. In these cases, a child needs emergency medical treatment immediately. Discuss with your child's pediatrician in advance what you should do in case of a true emergency.

Many true emergencies involve sudden injuries. These injuries are often caused by the following:

- Bicycle or car crashes, falls, or other violent impacts

- Poisoning

- Burns or smoke inhalation

- Choking

- Near drowning

- Firearms or other weapons

- Electric shocks

Other true emergencies can result from either medical illnesses or injuries. Often you can tell that these emergencies are happening if you observe that your child has any of the following symptoms:

- Acting strangely or becoming more withdrawn and less alert

- Increasing trouble with breathing

- Bleeding that does not stop

- Skin or lips that look blue or purple (or gray for darker-skinned children)

- Rhythmical jerking and loss of consciousness (a seizure)

- Unconsciousness

- Very loose or knocked-out teeth, or other major mouth or facial injuries

- Increasing or severe persistent pain

- A cut or burn that is large or deep

- Any loss of consciousness, confusion, a bad headache, or vomiting several times *after a head injury*

- Decreasing responsiveness when you talk to your child

Call your child's pediatrician or the Poison Center at once if your child has swallowed a suspected poison or another person's medication, even if your child has no signs or symptoms.

Always call for help if you are concerned that your child's life may be in danger or your child is seriously hurt.

In Case of a True Emergency

- Stay calm.

- If it is needed and you know how, start rescue breathing or CPR (cardiopulmonary resuscitation).

- If you need immediate help, call 911. If you do not have 911 service in your area, call your local emergency ambulance service or county emergency medical service. Otherwise, call your child's pediatrician's office and state clearly that you have an emergency.

- If there is bleeding, apply continuous pressure to the site with a clean cloth.

- If your child is having a seizure, place her on a carpeted floor with her head turned to the side, and stay with your child until help arrives.

After you arrive at the emergency department, make sure you tell the emergency staff the name of your child's pediatrician, who can work closely with the emergency department and can provide them with additional information about your child. Bring any medication your child is taking and her immunization record with you to the hospital. Also bring any suspected poisons or other medications your child might have taken.

Important Emergency Phone Numbers

Keep the following phone numbers handy by taping them on or near your phone:

- Your home phone and address

- Your cell phone

- A trusted neighbor's phone

- Your child's pediatrician

- Emergency medical services (ambulance) (911 in most areas)

- Police (911 in most areas)

- Fire department (911 in most areas)

- Poison Center

- Hospital

- Dentist

It is important that sitters know where to find emergency phone numbers. If you have 911 service in your area, make sure your older children and your sitter know to dial 911 in case of an emergency. Be sure they know your home address and phone number, since an emergency operator will ask for this information. Always leave your sitter the phone number and address where you can be located.

Remember, for a medical emergency, always call 911, EMS, or your child's pediatrician. If your child is seriously ill or injured, it may be safer for your child to be transported by emergency medical services.

Bites

Animal Bites

Many parents assume that children are most likely to be bitten by strange or wild animals, but in fact most bites are inflicted by animals the child knows, including the family pet. Although the injury often is minor, biting does at times cause serious wounds, facial damage, and emotional problems.

As many as 1 percent of all visits to pediatric emergency centers during the summer months are for the treatment of human or animal bite wounds. An estimated 4.7 million dog bites, 400,000 cat bites, 45,000 snake bites, and 250,000 human bites occur annually in the United States. About six of ten of those bitten by dogs are children. About 50 out of every 100 people bitten by a cat are infected, compared to 15 to 20 of every 100 following dog or human bites.

Treatment

If your child is bleeding from an animal bite, apply firm continuous pressure to the area for five minutes or until the blood flow stops. Then wash the wound gently with soap and water, and consult your pediatrician.

If the wound is very large, or if you cannot stop the bleeding, continue to apply pressure and call your pediatrician to find out where to take your child for treatment. If the wound is so large that the edges won't come together, it probably will need to be sutured (stitched). Although this will help reduce scarring, in an animal bite, it increases the chance of infection, so your doctor may prescribe preventive antibiotics.

Contact your pediatrician whenever your child receives an animal bite that breaks the skin, no matter how minor the injury appears. The doctor will need to check whether your child has been adequately immunized against tetanus (see Immunization Schedule on page 73) or might require protection against rabies. Both of these diseases can be spread by animal bites.

Rabies is a viral infection that can be transmitted by an infected animal. It causes a high fever, difficulty in swallowing, convulsions, and ultimately death. Fortunately, rabies in humans is so rare today that no more than five cases have been reported in the United States each year since 1960; the number of human deaths caused by rabies in this country has declined from one hundred or more each year early in the twentieth century to an average of one or two each year today. Nevertheless, because the disease is so serious and the incidence has been increasing in animals, your pediatrician will carefully evaluate any bite for the risk of contracting this disease. The risk probably depends a great deal on the animal and the circumstances surrounding the bite. Bites from wild animals such as bats, skunks, raccoons, and foxes are much more dangerous than those from tame, immunized (against rabies) dogs and cats. The health of the animal also is important, so if possible, the animal should be captured and confined for later examination by a veterinarian. Talk to your pediatrician about reporting the incident to your local health department. *Do not destroy the animal.* If it has been killed, however, the brain can be examined for rabies, so call your pediatrician immediately for advice on how to handle the situation.

If the risk of rabies is high, your pediatrician immediately will give, or arrange to have given, injections of medications to prevent it. If the biting animal is a healthy dog or cat, he will recommend that it be observed for ten days, initiating your child's treatment only if the animal shows signs of rabies. If the animal is a wild one, commonly identified as a rabies risk if captured, it usually is sacrificed immediately so that its brain can be examined for signs of rabies infection.

Like any other wound, a bite can become infected. Notify your pediatrician immediately if you see any of the following signs of infection.

- Pus or drainage coming from the bite

- The area immediately around the bite becoming swollen and tender (It normally will be red for two or three days, but this in itself is not cause for alarm.)

- Red streaks that appear to spread out from the bite

- Swollen glands above the bite

(See also *Safety Around Animals,* page 468.)

Your pediatrician may recommend antibiotic therapy for a child who has:

- Moderate or severe bite wounds

- Puncture wounds, especially if the bone, tendon, or joint has been penetrated

- Facial bites

- Hand and foot bites

- Genital area bites

Children who are immunocompromised or have no spleen often receive antibiotic treatment.

Your pediatrician may recommend a follow-up visit to inspect any wound for signs of infection within forty-eight hours.

Human Bites

Children often experience a human bite by a sibling or a playmate. If your child is bitten by another person, call your pediatrician immediately to describe the severity of the injury. Doing this can be especially important if the biter's teeth pierced your child's skin or if the injury is large enough to require stitches.

Be sure to wash a serious bite carefully with cool water and soap before going to the pediatrician. Your pediatrician will check your child's tetanus and hepatitis B vaccine status and assess the risk for other infections. For a bite that barely breaks the skin, such as a cut or scrape, a good washing with soap and water, followed by bandaging and close follow-up, is all that is needed. (For more information on human biting, aggressive behavior, or biting in situations with AIDS, see Chapter 17, page 525; Chapter 30, page 726.)

Burns

Burns are divided into three categories, according to their severity. First-degree burns are the mildest and cause redness and perhaps slight swelling of the skin (like most sunburns). Second-degree burns cause blistering and considerable swelling. Third-degree burns may appear white or charred and cause serious injury, not just to the surface but also to the deeper skin layers.

There are many different causes of serious burns in children, including sunburn, hot-water scalds, and those due to fire, electrical contact, or chemicals. All of these can cause permanent injury and scarring to the skin.

Treatment

Your *immediate* treatment of a burn should include the following.

1. As quickly as possible, soak the burn in cool water. Don't hesitate to run cool water over the burn long enough to cool the area and relieve the pain immediately after the injury. *Do not use ice.*

2. Cool any smoldering clothing immediately by soaking with water, then remove any clothing from the burned area unless it is stuck firmly to the skin. In that case, cut away as much clothing as possible.

3. If the injured area is not oozing, cover the burn with a sterile gauze pad.

4. If the burn is oozing, cover it lightly with sterile gauze if available and immediately seek medical attention. If sterile gauze is not available, cover burns with a clean sheet or towel.

5. Do not put butter, grease, or powder on a burn. All of these so-called home remedies actually can make the injury worse.

For anything more serious than a superficial burn, or if redness and pain continue for more than a few hours, consult a physician. *All* electrical burns and burns of the hands, mouth, or genitals should receive immediate medical attention. Chemicals that cause burns also may be absorbed through the skin and cause other symptoms. Call your pediatrician or Poison Center, after washing off all the chemical. (For treatment of a chemical contact to a child's eye, see *Poison in the Eye,* page 496.)

If your physician thinks the burn is not too serious, he may show you how to clean and care for it at home using medicated ointments and dressings. Under the following circumstances, however, hospitalization may be necessary.

- If the burns are third degree

- If 10 percent or more of the body is burned

- If the burn involves the face, hands, feet, or genitals, or involves a moving joint

- If the child is very young or fussy, and therefore too difficult to treat at home

When treating a burn at home, watch for any increase in redness or swelling or the development of a bad odor or discharge. These can be signs of infection, which will require medical attention.

Prevention

Chapter 14, "Keeping Your Child Safe," provides ways to safeguard your child against fire and scalding at home. For added protection, here are a few more suggestions.

- Install smoke detectors in all sleeping rooms, hallways outside sleeping rooms, kitchen, and living rooms, with at least one on every floor of the house. Test them every month to be sure they work. Change batteries at least annually on a specific date that you'll remember (such as the start of daylight saving time).

- Practice home fire drills. Make sure every family member knows how to leave any area of the home safely in case of fire.

- Have several working fire extinguishers readily available.

- Teach your children to crawl to the exits if there's smoke in the room. (They will avoid inhaling the smoke by staying below it.)

- Purchase a safety ladder if your home has a second story, and teach your children how to use it. If you live in a high-rise, teach your children the locations of all exits and make sure they understand never to use the elevator in a fire. (It can become trapped between floors or open on a floor where the fire is burning.)

- Agree on a family meeting point outside the house or apartment so you can make certain everyone has gotten out of the burning area.

- Teach your children to stop, drop, and roll on the ground if their clothing catches fire.

- Lock up flammable liquid in the home.

- Lower the temperature of your hot water heater to below 120 degrees Fahrenheit (48.9 degrees Celsius).

- Don't use inadequate extension cords or old, possibly unsafe electrical equipment.

- Keep matches and lighters away from children.

- Avoid fireworks.

Cardiopulmonary Resuscitation (CPR) and Mouth-to-Mouth Resuscitation

Reading about CPR is not enough to teach you how to perform it. *The American Academy of Pediatrics strongly recommends that all parents and anyone who is responsible for the care of children should complete a course in basic CPR and treatment for choking.* This training is vital if you own a swimming pool or live near water. Contact your local chapter of the American Heart Association or Red Cross to find out where and when certified courses are given in your community.

CPR can save your child's life if his heart stops beating or he has stopped breathing for any reason—drowning, poisoning, suffocation, smoke inhalation, choking, or infections of the respiratory tract. This procedure is most likely to be successful if it is begun immediately after the heart or breathing stops. The following danger signs can alert you that CPR may be needed soon.

- Unresponsiveness, with no evidence of effective breathing

- Extreme difficulty in breathing (i.e., a foreign body in the child's airway)

- Blue lips or skin associated with extreme difficulty in breathing

- Rapid or labored breathing (grunting or pulling in of muscles between the ribs with respirations)

- Severe wheezing

- Drooling, or difficulty in swallowing with trouble breathing

- Extreme paleness

If your child displays any of these signs and you are with someone else, have that person call for emergency help while you begin the following steps. If you are alone, go ahead and follow these steps immediately after shouting or **calling for help.**

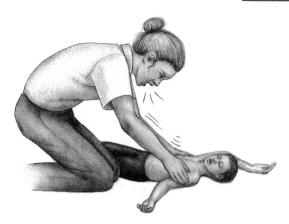

Step 1. Rapidly evaluate your child's condition.

Is he unconscious? Gently tap, or shout as if trying to awaken him. Assume he is unconscious if he doesn't respond after three attempts.

Is he breathing? Place your ear directly over his mouth and listen for breathing. If he is breathing with difficulty, arrange to get him immediately to an emergency medical facility while continuing to monitor his breathing to ensure he has not stopped breathing. If you don't hear breathing, look to see whether his chest is moving up and down.

Step 2. If your child is not breathing, position him on his back on a firm, flat surface.

If you suspect that he has injured his neck or spine (a possibility in a fall or automobile crash), move him carefully so that his neck does not bend or turn. If you find your child facedown, support his head to keep his neck from twisting while you roll him over.

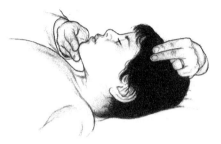

Step 3. Open your child's airway by tilting his head back to lift his chin.

Be careful not to push the head back too far, because that could block the airway in an infant or small child. To clear the tongue from the back of the throat, lift the chin up gently with one hand while pushing down on the forehead with the other hand. A good way to open the airway is to lift the chin by pushing up on the bones at the back of the jaw. In some cases, simply opening the airway will allow your child to breathe on his own. If it doesn't, look into the throat to see whether it is blocked by a foreign object or a piece of food. If so, follow the instructions under *Choking* (see page 481).

Step 4. If your child still is not breathing, and he does not appear to be choking, give mouth-to-mouth resuscitation.

1. Take a deep breath.

2. If your child is an infant, place your mouth over his nose and mouth, making as tight a seal as possible. If your child is older, pinch his nostrils and place your mouth completely over his mouth.

3. Give two breaths (called rescue breaths since you are first getting air into a child who is not breathing), blowing enough air into your child so you can see his chest rise slightly. Then pause, removing your mouth from his so the air can escape, and take another deep breath. *With an infant, be careful not to blow with too much force, because this can be dangerous.* If *no* air seems to be getting into the chest, the airway is still blocked, and you will need to repeat Step 3.

4. If your child's chest does rise as you breathe into his mouth, continue to breathe for him at a rate of approximately one breath every three seconds (twenty per minute), until he is breathing on his own.

5. A child who stops breathing is very likely to vomit, which complicates rescue breathing. If there is no suspected neck injury, turn the child's head to the side to allow fluid to drain out. Wiping deep inside with an absorbent towel may help (do not use much force, to avoid pushing vomit down the windpipe), as may any available equipment to suction the mouth.

Step 5. Assess your child's response to the rescue breathing.

Place your ear next to your child's mouth. Look, listen, and feel for normal breathing (or coughing), and look for body movement.

Step 6. If you can't see, hear, or feel signs of normal breathing, coughing, or movement, begin chest compressions (CPR) to keep the blood circulating to the vital organs.
Proceed as follows (with the child on a flat, firm surface).

1. With an infant, place two or three fingers on the breastbone one finger width below the nipple line. Press down ½ to 1 inch (1.3 to 2.54 cm), at a rate of about one hundred times per minute. *Be careful not to apply too much pressure.*

With an older child, place the heel of one of your hands over the lower third of the breastbone. Press down 1 to 1½ inches (1.3

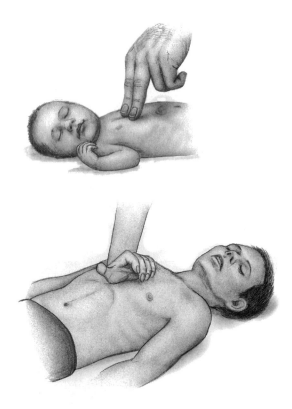

to 3.8 cm) at a rate of eighty to one hundred times per minute.

2. After five compressions, give the child one breath, as described in Step 4. Continue five compressions/one breath, five compressions/one breath. Compress chest one hundred times per minute. Check for signs of normal breathing, coughing, or movement every minute.

Step 7. Get emergency medical help.

If you are alone with your child, call for emergency help immediately or after one minute of CPR. Be sure to give your location and the number of the phone from which you are calling. The paramedics who arrive on the scene will determine your child's condition and treat him appropriately.

Choking

Choking occurs whenever a person inhales something other than air into the windpipe. Among children, choking often is caused by liquid that "goes down the wrong way." The child will cough, wheeze, gasp, and gag until the windpipe is cleared, but this type of choking is usually not harmful.

Choking becomes life-threatening when a child swallows or inhales an object—often food—that blocks the flow of air to the lungs. If this happens, your child will not be able to talk or make normal sounds, and her face will turn from bright red to blue. This is an emergency that calls for immediate first aid. There is no time to call the doctor; you must deal with it immediately. If someone else is available, have him call for medical assistance while you continue your first-aid efforts.

How to Respond

The way to handle a choking incident depends on the condition and age of the child.

Child of Any Age—Coughing but Able to Breathe and Talk

Coughing is the natural mechanism for expelling an object from the throat. Instead of trying some other maneuver that might make the obstruction worse, let your child cough. In particular, don't try to remove the object with your fingers; that could push it farther into the throat and totally block the windpipe.

Baby Under Age One—Cannot Breathe and Is Turning Blue

This situation requires immediate first aid. Because the child's internal organs are fragile, *be gentle,* and use the following steps. (Do not use the Heimlich maneuver recommended for older children and adults.)

1. Place the infant facedown on your forearm in a head-down position with the head and neck stabilized. Rest your forearm firmly against your body for additional support.

For a large infant, you may instead lay the baby facedown over your lap, with her

head lower than her trunk and firmly supported.

2. Give five rapid back blows with the heel of the hand between the shoulder blades.

3. If she still cannot breathe, turn her over onto her back, resting on a firm surface, and deliver five rapid chest compressions over the breastbone, *using only two fingers.*

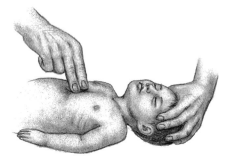

4. If she is still not breathing, open the airway using the tongue-jaw lift technique (see page 479), and attempt to see the foreign body. Do not try to pull out the object unless you can see it. But if you see it, sweep it out with your finger.

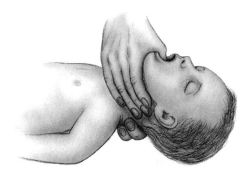

5. If she doesn't start breathing on her own, try to start her breathing by giving two breaths by mouth-to-mouth, or mouth-to-mouth-and-nose, technique (see Step 4, page 479).

6. Continue to repeat Steps 1 through 5 as you call for emergency medical help from your local emergency service.

Child Over One Year—Cannot Breathe or Talk and Is Turning Blue

Step 1. Apply a series of up to five quick abdominal thrusts (Heimlich maneuver) as follows, until the foreign body comes out.

- If the child is small, place her on her back. An older, larger child can be treated while standing, sitting, or lying down.

- Kneel at the child's feet if she is on the floor, or stand at her feet if she is on a table.

- Place the heel of one hand in the center of her body between the navel and the rib cage, your other hand on top of your first.

- Press into the abdomen with a rapid inward and upward thrust. In a small child the thrusts must be applied gently.

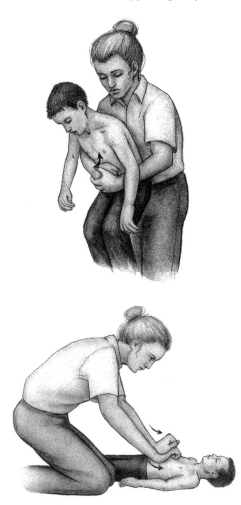

Step 2. If the object does not come out with the Heimlich maneuver, open the child's mouth using the tongue-jaw lift (see page 479); this draws the tongue away from the back of the throat and may help relieve the obstruction. If you can see the object, you may try to sweep it out with your finger. However, blind sweeps may cause further obstruction, so don't attempt this unless you can see the blockage.

Step 3. If your child doesn't start breathing, give mouth-to-mouth resuscitation (see Step 4, page 479). If unsuccessful, repeat a series of five abdominal thrusts.

Step 4. Continue to repeat Steps 1 to 3 as you call for emergency medical help.

If the emergency team arrives before your child has started breathing, they will repeat the steps described above. If this is not successful, she will be taken to the hospital so that further treatment (i.e., insertion of a breathing tube) can be performed.

A child who begins to breathe by herself two or three minutes after a choking incident probably will not suffer any long-term damage. The longer she is deprived of oxygen, however, the greater the risk of permanent injury. In general, when the brain goes without oxygen for more than four minutes, brain damage or even death may occur. Fortunately, most choking incidents do not cause long-term damage and are not even severe enough to require medical attention.

Occasionally a choking episode is followed by persistent coughing, gagging, wheezing, excessive salivation, or difficulty in swallowing or breathing. If this occurs, it may mean that an object is still partially blocking the airway—possibly in the lower breathing tubes. In this case, the object can cause continued breathing difficulty, irritation, and possibly pneumonia. Notify your pediatrician if any symptoms persist, so that further tests, such as chest X rays, can be done. If they show that your child has inhaled something, she probably will need to be admitted to the hospital for an operation to remove the object. (This generally is done under anesthesia by inserting a special instrument through the mouth and into the lungs.)

Prevention

Choking is the most common cause of non-intentional death in children under age one, and the danger remains significant until the age of five. Ask your pediatrician for information about preventing choking and what to do if it should occur. Also see Chapter 14, "Keeping Your Child Safe."

Objects such as safety pins and coins cause choking, but food is responsible for most incidents. You must be particularly watchful when children around the age of one are sampling new foods. Here are some additional suggestions for preventing choking.

- Don't give young children hard, smooth foods (i.e., peanuts, raw vegetables) that must be chewed with a grinding motion. Children don't master that kind of chewing until age four, so they may attempt to swallow the food whole. Do not give peanuts to children until age seven or older.

- Cut or break food into bite-size pieces (no larger than ½ inch [1.27 cm]) and encourage your child to chew thoroughly.

- Supervise mealtime for your infant or young child. Don't let her eat while playing or running. Teach her to chew and swallow her food before talking or laughing.

- Avoid giving your child round, firm foods unless they are chopped completely. These foods include meat sticks, hot dogs, carrot sticks, celery sticks, grapes, and hard candies. All of these can lodge easily in her throat.

- Chewing gum is inappropriate for young children.

- Check under the furniture and between cushions for small food items that children can find and put in their mouths.

Because young children put everything into their mouths, small nonfood objects are also responsible for many choking incidents. Look for age guidelines in selecting toys, but use your own judgment concerning your child. Government regulations specify that toys for children under age three cannot have parts less than 1¼ inches (3.18 cm) in diameter and 2¼ inches (5.72 cm) long. If older siblings have toys with small parts, keep them out of the reach of your younger children. Also, avoid toys that can be compressed to fit entirely into a child's mouth.

Be aware that the following objects have been associated with choking:

- Uninflated balloons and pieces of broken balloon. Children may inhale the rubber when they try to blow them up.

- Baby powder.

- Items from the trash. Be especially alert for eggshells and pop tops from beverage cans.

- Safety pins. Be sure they are closed and out of reach when not in use.

- Coins. Don't give small children coins or other small objects as a reward or treat.

- Marbles and small balls.

- Pen or marker caps.

- Small, button-type batteries.

- Medicine syringes.

Despite these precautions, choking can occur at any time. You must familiarize yourself with the procedure for dealing with it, so that you can act quickly in an emergency. If you feel unsure, seek out an approved first-aid course, such as those sponsored by the American Heart Association or the American Red Cross. To receive a Parent Resource Guide from the American Academy of Pediatrics, send a self-addressed, business-size envelope to: American Academy of Pediatrics, Attn: Dept C-PRG, P.O. Box 927, Elk Grove Village, IL 60009–0927.

Cuts and Scrapes

Your child's natural curiosity and eagerness are likely to produce some scrapes and cuts along the way. His reaction may be far more severe than the actual damage. In most cases, good treatment will require little more than cleansing the injury, protecting it, and providing plenty of reassurance (and perhaps a kiss on the minor bump or bruise).

Scrapes

Most minor injuries in young children are scrapes, or abrasions, which means that the outer layers of skin literally have been scraped off. If the abrasion covers a large area, it may appear to be very bloody, although the actual amount of blood lost is small. The area should be rinsed first with cool water to flush away debris and then washed gently with warm water and soap. Avoid using iodine and other antiseptic solu-

tions. They have little protective value, and can add to the pain and discomfort.

If left alone, most abrasions "scab" over quickly, and this was thought to be the best natural remedy. But scabs actually slow the healing process and can lead to more scarring. Treat large or oozing scrapes with an antibiotic ointment and then cover them with a sterile (germ-free) dressing. These can be obtained at your local pharmacy, either in the form of an adhesive bandage or a separate gauze pad that is held in place by roller gauze or adhesive tape. Antibiotic ointment also helps prevent the dressing from sticking to the healing wound surface. The purpose is to prevent the injury from becoming infected while healing occurs. It is best to keep the bandage in place, except for dressing changes, until the wound heals. Take care that dressings around such areas as fingers or toes are not so tight as to interfere with circulation.

Some dressings are made of materials such as Telfa, which are less likely to adhere to the raw surface of a wound. Examine the wound daily during the dressing change, or whenever it becomes dirty or wet. If a bandage sticks when you try to remove it, soak it off with warm water.

Most wounds require a dressing for only two or three days, but your child may be reluctant to stop applying bandages that quickly, because small children regard bandages as badges or medals. There is no harm in leaving the area loosely covered as long as the bandage is kept dry and clean and the wound is checked daily.

Call your pediatrician if you can't get a wound clean or notice drainage of pus, increasing tenderness or redness around the site, or fever. These are signs that the wound may be infected. If necessary, the doctor can use a local anesthetic to prevent severe pain while cleaning out dirt and debris that you are not able to remove. If the wound is infected, she may prescribe antibiotics by mouth or in the form of an ointment or cream.

Cuts, Lacerations, and Bleeding

A cut or laceration is a wound that breaks through the skin and into the tissues beneath. Because the injury is deeper than a scrape, there are more likely to be problems, such as bleeding, and there is the possibility of damage to nerves and tendons. The following simple guidelines will help you prevent serious bleeding and other problems such as scarring when your child gets a cut.

1. Apply pressure. Almost all active bleeding can be stopped by applying direct pressure with clean gauze or cloth over the site for five or ten minutes. The most common mistake is interrupting the pressure too early in order to peek at the wound. Doing this may result in more bleeding or in the buildup of a clot that can make it harder to control the problem with further pressure. If bleeding starts again after five minutes of continuous pressure, reapply pressure and call your doctor for help. Do *not* use a tourniquet or tie-off on an arm or leg unless you are trained in its use, since this can cause severe damage if left on too long.

2. Stay calm. The sight of blood frightens most people, but this is an important time to stay in control. You'll make better decisions if you are calm, and your child will be less likely to get upset by the situation. Remember, by using direct pressure you will be able to control bleeding from even the most severe lacerations until help can arrive. Relatively minor cuts to the head and face will bleed more than cuts to other parts of the body because of the greater number of small, superficial blood vessels.

3. Seek medical advice for serious cuts. No matter how much (or how little) bleeding occurs, call your doctor if the laceration is deep (through the skin) or more than ½ inch (1.27 cm) long. Deep cuts can severely damage underlying muscles, nerves, and tendons, even if on the surface the wound does not appear serious. Long lacerations and those on the face, chest, and back are more likely to leave disfiguring scars. In these situations, if the wound is properly sutured (stitched), the scar probably will be much less apparent. If in doubt about whether sutures are needed, call your doctor for advice. To reduce unsightly scarring, sutures should be placed within eight hours after injury occurs.

You should be able to treat short, minor cuts yourself, as long as the edges come together by themselves, or with the aid of a "butterfly" bandage, and if there is no numbness beyond the wound and no reduction in sensation or movement. However, have your doctor examine your child if there is any possibility that foreign matter, such as dirt or glass, is trapped in it. Any injury that cannot be managed by you should be seen by your pediatrician or emergency medical services as soon as possible to maximize healing. Your child may not like to let you examine a laceration thoroughly because of the pain involved. The pediatrician, however, can use a local anesthetic, if necessary, to ensure a thorough exam.

4. Cleanse and dress the wound. If you feel comfortable handling the problem, wash the wound with plain water and examine it carefully to be sure it is clean. Apply an antibiotic ointment, then cover it with a sterile dressing. It's easy to underestimate the extent or severity of a laceration, so even if you choose to treat it yourself, don't hesitate to call your pediatrician for advice.

If any redness, swelling, or pus appears around the wound, or if bleeding recurs, consult your physician as soon as possible. Antiseptics such as iodine and alcohol are not necessary and increase the discomfort for your child, so do not use them on cuts. If your child's immunizations are current, tetanus shots are not necessary after most abrasions and lacerations. If your child has not had a tetanus booster within five years, however, your pediatrician may recommend that one be given.

Prevention

It is almost impossible for a curious and active child to avoid some scrapes and minor cuts, but there are things you can do to decrease the number your child will have and to minimize their severity. Keep potentially dangerous objects like sharp knives, easily breakable glass objects, and firearms out of his reach. When he gets old enough to use knives and scissors himself, teach him how to handle them properly and insist that they be used safely. At regular intervals make a safety check of your house, garage, and yard. If you find objects that are potentially dangerous because your child is older and can get into them, store them securely out of his reach. Consider planning for these common injuries of childhood with a well-stocked selection of cleansing materials (sterile gauzes), antibiotic ointment, and bandages.

See also Chapter 14, "Keeping Your Child Safe."

Drowning

Children drown either because they get into water that is too deep or because they get trapped while their faces are submerged. With very young children, this can happen even in only a few inches of water. The natural response in either situation is for the child to panic and struggle, stop breathing, or try to hold her breath. When she finally does breathe, she inhales water and suffocates. *Drowning* refers to death that occurs in this way. When a child is rescued before death occurs, the episode is called a near drowning.

What You Should Do

As soon as your child is out of the water, check to see if she is breathing on her own. If she is not, begin CPR immediately (see page 479). If someone else is present, send him or her to call for emergency medical help, but don't spend precious moments looking for someone, and don't waste time trying to drain water from your child's lungs. Concentrate instead on giving her artificial respiration and CPR until she is breathing on her own. Vomiting of swallowed water is very likely during CPR. Only when the child's breathing has resumed should you stop and seek emergency help. Once the paramedics arrive, they will administer oxygen and continue CPR if necessary. You can then call your pediatrician for further instructions.

Any child who has come close to drowning should be given a complete medical examination, even if she seems all right. If she stopped breathing, inhaled water, or lost consciousness, she should remain under medical observation for at least twenty-four hours to be sure there is no damage to her respiratory or nervous system.

A child's recovery from a near drowning depends on how long she was deprived of oxygen. If she was underwater only briefly, she is likely to recover completely. Longer periods without oxygen can cause damage to the lungs, heart, or brain. A child who doesn't respond quickly to CPR may have more serious problems, but it's important to keep trying, because sustained CPR has revived children who have appeared lifeless or who have been immersed in very cold water for lengthy periods.

Prevention

Toddlers, youngsters with mental retardation, and children with seizure disorders are particularly vulnerable to drowning, but all youngsters are in danger if they play unsupervised in or near water. Even a child who knows how to swim may drown a few feet from safety if she becomes frightened or confused. Therefore, never allow youngsters of any age to swim alone or unsupervised, and watch constantly when small children are near a body of water, such as a swimming pool, lake, or river.

Swimming is not the only opportunity for drowning, however. A toddler's innocent exploration of the toilet or a bucket of water can lead to tragedy. Never leave water standing where your toddler can get to it. Empty or cover plastic wading pools when not in use. Drain wash water promptly from basins. Keep the lid down on the toilet, and, if your toddler is very active and curious, close and latch the bathroom door. Don't leave buckets with even a few inches of water or cleaning solutions where toddlers can explore. Never leave a child under four standing beside a tub while the water is running or alone in a tub filled with water. (For more information on water safety, see page 466.)

Electric Shock

When the human body comes in direct contact with a source of electricity, the current passes through it, producing what's called an electric shock. Depending on the voltage of the current and the length of contact, this shock can cause anything from minor discomfort to serious injury to death.

Young children, particularly toddlers, experience electric shock most often when they bite into electrical cords or poke metal objects such as forks or knives into unprotected outlets or appliances. These injuries also can take place when electric toys, appliances, or tools are used incorrectly, or when electric current makes contact with water in which a child is sitting or standing. Lightning accounts for about 20 percent of the cases that occur. Christmas trees and their lights are a seasonal hazard.

What You Should Do

If your child comes in contact with electricity, *always* try to turn the power off first. In many cases you'll be able to pull the plug or turn off the switch. If this isn't possible, consider an attempt to remove the live wire— but *not with your bare hands,* which would bring you in contact with the current yourself. Instead, try to cut the wire with a wood-handled ax or well-insulated wire cutters or move the wire off the child using a dry stick, a rolled-up magazine or newspaper, a rope, a coat, or another thick, dry object that won't conduct electricity.

If you can't remove the source of the current, try to pull the child away. Again, *do not touch the child with your bare hands* when he's attached to the source of the current, since his body will transmit the electricity to you. Instead, use a nonconducting material such as rubber (or those described above) to shield you while freeing him. (*Caution:* None of these methods can be guaranteed safe unless the power can be shut off.)

As soon as the current is turned off (or the child is removed from it), check the child's breathing, skin color, and ability to respond to you. If his breathing or heartbeat has stopped, or seems very rapid or irregular, immediately use cardiopulmonary resuscitation (CPR; see page 479) to restore it, and have someone call for emergency medical help. At the same time, avoid moving the child needlessly, since such a severe electrical shock may have caused a spinal fracture.

If the child is conscious and it seems the shock was minor, check him for burned skin, especially if his mouth was the point of contact with the current. Then call your pediatrician. Electric shock can cause internal organ damage that may be difficult to detect without a medical examination. For that reason, *all* children who receive a significant electric shock should see a doctor.

In the pediatrician's office, any minor burns resulting from the electricity will be cleansed and dressed. The doctor may order laboratory tests to check for signs of damage to internal organs. If the child has severe burns or any sign of brain or heart damage, he will need to be hospitalized.

Prevention

The best way to prevent electrical injuries is to cover all outlets, make sure all wires are properly insulated, and provide adult supervision whenever children are in an area with potential electrical hazards. Small appliances are a special hazard around bathtubs or pools. (See also Chapter 14, "Keeping Your Child Safe.")

Fingertip Injuries

Children's fingertips get smashed frequently, usually getting caught in closing doors. Too often, those doors are shut by parents unaware that little fingers are in danger. The child is either unable to recognize the poten-

tial danger, or she fails to remove her hand quickly enough. Fingers also sometimes get crushed when youngsters play with a hammer or other heavy object.

Because fingertips are exquisitely sensitive, your child will let you know immediately that she's been injured. Usually the damaged area will be blue and swollen, and there may be a cut or bleeding around the cuticle. The skin, tissues below the skin, and the nail bed—as well as the underlying bone and growth plate—all may be affected. If bleeding occurs underneath the nail, it will turn black or dark blue, and the pressure from the bleeding may be painful.

Home Treatment

When the fingertip is bleeding, wash it with soap and water, and cover it with a soft, sterile dressing. An ice pack or a soaking in cold water may relieve the pain and minimize swelling.

If the swelling is mild and your child is comfortable, you can allow the finger to heal on its own. But be alert for any increase in pain, swelling, redness, or drainage from the injured area, or a fever beginning twenty-four to seventy-two hours after the injury. These may be signs of infection, and you should notify your pediatrician.

When there's excessive swelling, a deep cut, blood under the fingernail, or if the finger looks as if it may be broken, call your doctor immediately. And by all means, do not attempt to straighten a fractured finger on your own.

Professional Treatment

If your doctor suspects a fracture, he may order an X ray. If the X ray confirms a fracture—or if there's damage to the nail bed, where nail growth occurs—an orthopedic consultation may be necessary. A fractured finger can be straightened and set under local anesthesia. An injured nail bed also must be repaired surgically to minimize the possibility of a nail deformity developing as the finger grows. If there's considerable blood under the nail, the pediatrician may drain it by making a small hole in the nail, which should relieve the pain.

Although deep cuts may require stitches, often all that's necessary is sterile adhesive strips (thin adhesive strips similar to butterfly bandages). A fracture underneath a cut is considered an "open" fracture and is susceptible to infection in the bone. In this case, antibiotics will be prescribed. Depending on your child's age and immunization status, the doctor also may order a tetanus booster.

(See also *Fractures/Broken Bones,* below.)

Fractures/Broken Bones

Although the term *fracture* may sound serious, it is just another name for a broken bone. As you probably remember from your own childhood, fractures are very common. In fact, they are the fourth most common injury among children under age six. Falls cause most of the fractures in this age group, but the most serious bone breaks usually result from car crashes.

A broken bone in a child is different from one in an adult, because young bones are more flexible and have a thicker covering, which makes them better able to absorb shock. Children's fractures rarely require surgical repair. They usually just need to be kept free of movement, most often through the use of a molded cast.

Most broken bones in youngsters are either "greenstick" fractures, in which the bone bends like green wood and breaks only on one side, or "torus" fractures, in which the bone is buckled, twisted, and weakened but not completely broken. A "bend" frac-

ture refers to a bone that is bent but not broken, and is also relatively common among youngsters. "Complete" fractures, in which the bone breaks all the way through, also occur in young children.

Because your child's bones are still growing, he is vulnerable to an additional type of fracture that does not occur in adults. This involves damage to the growth plates at the ends of the bones, which regulate future growth. If this part of the bone does not heal properly after the fracture, the bone may grow at an angle or more slowly than the other bones in the body. Unfortunately, the impact on the bone's growth may not be visible for a year or more after the injury, so these fractures must be followed carefully by the pediatrician for twelve to eighteen months to make sure no growth damage has occurred.

Fractures also are classified as "nondisplaced," when the broken ends are still in proper position, or "displaced," when the ends are separated or out of alignment. In an "open" or "compound" fracture, the bone sticks through the skin. If the skin is intact, the fracture is "closed."

Signs and Symptoms

It's not always easy to tell when a bone is broken, especially if your child is too young to describe what he's feeling. Ordinarily with a fracture, you will see swelling and your child will clearly be in pain and unable—or unwilling—to move the injured limb. However, just because your child can move the bone doesn't necessarily rule out a fracture. Anytime you suspect a fracture, notify your pediatrician immediately.

Home Treatment

Until your child can be seen in the pediatrician's office, emergency room, or urgent care center, use an improvised sling or rolled-up newspaper or magazine as a splint to protect the injury from unnecessary movement.

Don't give the child anything by mouth to drink or to relieve pain without first consulting the doctor, but if yours is an older child, you can use an cold pack or a cold towel, placed on the injury site, to decrease pain. Extreme cold can cause injury to the delicate skin of babies and toddlers, so do not use ice with children this young.

If your child has broken his leg, do not try to move him yourself. Call an ambulance, make the child as comfortable as possible, and let the paramedics supervise his transportation.

If part of the injury is open and bleeding, or if bone is protruding through the skin, place firm pressure on the wound (see *Cuts, Lacerations, and Bleeding,* page 486); then cover it with clean (preferably sterile) gauze. Do not try to put the bone back underneath the skin. After this injury has been treated, be alert to any fever, which may indicate that the wound has become infected.

Professional Treatment

After examining the break, the doctor will order X rays to determine the extent of the damage. If the doctor suspects that the bone's growth plate is affected, or if the bones are out of line, an orthopedic consultation will be necessary.

Because children's bones heal rapidly and well, a plaster or fiberglass cast, or sometimes just an immobilizing splint, is all that is needed for most minor fractures. For a displaced fracture, an orthopedic surgeon may have to realign the bones. This may be done as a "closed reduction," in which the surgeon uses local or general anesthesia, manipulates the bones until they're straight, and then applies a cast. An "open reduction"

is a surgical procedure done in an operating room, but this is rarely necessary for children. After the surgical reduction, a cast will be used until the bone has healed, which usually takes about half the time that adult bones require, or less, depending on the child's age. The nice thing about young bones is that they don't have to be in perfect alignment. As long as they are more or less in the right place, they will remodel as they grow. Your pediatrician may order periodic X rays while the bone is healing, just to make sure they are aligning properly.

Usually casting brings rapid relief or at least a decrease in pain. If your child has an increase in pain, numbness, or pale or blue fingers or toes, call your doctor immediately. These are signs that the extremity has swollen and requires more room within the cast. If the cast is not adjusted, the swelling may press on nerves, muscles, and blood vessels, which can produce permanent damage. To relieve the pressure, the doctor may split the cast, open a window in it, or replace it with a larger one.

Also let the doctor know if the cast breaks or becomes very loose, or if the plaster gets wet and soggy. Without a proper, secure fit, the cast will not hold the broken bone in position to mend correctly.

Bones that have been broken often will form a hard knot at the site of the break during the healing process. Especially with a broken collarbone, this may look unsightly, but there is no treatment for this, and the knot will not be permanent. The bone will remodel and resume its normal shape in a few months.

Head Injury/Concussion

It's almost inevitable that your child will hit her head every now and then. Especially when she's a baby, these collisions may upset you, but your anxiety is usually worse than the bump. Most head injuries are minor, causing no serious problems. Even so, it's important to know the difference between a head injury that warrants medical attention and one that needs only a comforting hug.

If your child suffers a brief, temporary loss of consciousness after a hard blow to the head, she is said to have had a concussion. If a child has a concussion, it doesn't necessarily mean that her brain has been damaged, but it does indicate that the brain centers for consciousness have been momentarily disturbed.

Treatment

If a child's head injury has been mild, she'll remain alert and awake after the incident, and her color will be normal. She may cry out due to momentary pain and fright, but the crying should last no more than ten minutes and then she'll go back to playing as usual.

Occasionally a minor head injury also will cause slight dizziness, nausea, and headache, and the child might vomit once or twice. Even so, if the injury seems minor and there's not a significant cut (one that's deep and/or actively bleeding) that might require medical attention or possibly stitches (see *Cuts and Scrapes,* page 485), you can treat your child at home. Just wash the cut with soap and water. If there's a bruise, apply a cold compress. This will help minimize the swelling if you do it in the first few hours after the injury.

Even after a minor head injury, you should observe your child for twenty-four to forty-eight hours to see if she develops any signs that the injury was more severe than it first appeared. Although it's very rare, children can develop a serious brain injury after a seemingly minor bump on the head that causes no immediate obvious problems.

Brain injuries after such an apparently insignificant accident are usually due to internal bleeding and almost always show up within one to two days of the original incident. If your child develops any of the following symptoms, consult your pediatrician immediately or seek prompt attention from the nearest emergency room.

- She seems excessively sleepy or lethargic during her usual wakeful hours, or you cannot awaken her while she's asleep at night. (You should try to awaken her once or twice during the first night if she's had a hard blow to the head.)

- She has a headache that won't go away (even with acetaminophen) or vomits more than once or twice. Headache and vomiting occur commonly after head trauma, but they are usually mild and last only a few hours.

- She's persistently and/or extremely irritable. With an infant who cannot tell you what she's feeling, this may indicate a severe headache.

- Any significant change in your child's mental abilities, coordination, sensation, or strength warrants immediate medical attention. Such worrisome changes would include weakness of arms or legs, clumsy walking, slurred speech, crossed eyes, or difficulty with vision.

- She becomes unconscious again after being awake for a while, or she has a seizure (convulsion) or starts to breathe irregularly. These are signs of disturbed brain activity and may indicate a serious head injury.

If your child loses consciousness *at any time* after hitting her head, notify the pediatrician. If she doesn't awaken within a few minutes, she needs *immediate medical attention.* Call for help while you follow these steps.

1. Move your child as little as possible. *If you suspect that she might have injured her neck, do not attempt to move her. Changing the position of her neck might make her injuries worse.* One exception: Move her only if she's in danger of being injured further where she is (e.g., on a ledge or in a fire), but try to avoid bending or twisting her neck.

2. Check to see if she's breathing. If she isn't, perform CPR (see page 479).

3. If she's bleeding severely from a scalp wound, apply direct pressure with a clean cloth over the wound.

4. If trained ambulance personnel are readily available, it's safer to await their arrival than to try taking your child to the hospital yourself.

Loss of consciousness following a head injury may last only a few seconds or as long as several hours. If you find the child after the injury happened, and you are not sure if she lost consciousness, notify the pediatrician. (An older child who has had a concussion may say that she can't remember what happened just prior to and just after the injury.)

Most children who lose consciousness for more than a few minutes will be hospitalized overnight for observation. Hospitalization is essential for youngsters with severe brain injury and irregular breathing or convulsions. Fortunately, with modern pediatric intensive care, many children who have suffered serious head injury—and even those who have been unconscious for several weeks—eventually may recover completely.

Poisoning

About 2.2 million people swallow or have contact with a poisonous substance each year. More than half of these poison exposures occur in children under six years of age.

Most children who swallow poison are not permanently harmed, particularly if they receive immediate treatment. If you think your child has been poisoned, stay calm and act quickly.

You should suspect poisoning if you ever find your child with an open or empty container of a toxic substance, especially if she is acting strangely in any way. Be alert for these other signs of possible poisoning.

- Unexplained stains on her clothing

- Burns on her lips or mouth

- Unusual drooling, or odd odors on her breath

- Unexplained nausea or vomiting

- Abdominal cramps without fever

- Difficulty in breathing

- Sudden behavior changes, such as unusual sleepiness, irritability, or jumpiness

- Convulsions or unconsciousness (only in very serious cases)

Treatment

Anytime your child has ingested a poison of any kind, you should notify your pediatrician. However, your regional Poison Center will provide the immediate information and guidance you need when you first discover that your child has been poisoned. These centers are staffed twenty-four hours a day with experts who can tell you what to do without delay. The inside cover of your telephone book should list the number of your regional Poison Center. Also write that number on a piece of paper attached to or located near every phone in your home, along with other emergency numbers. Or you can call the national toll-free number for Poison Control Centers—1–800–222–1222—which will provide immediate and free access

---

Poison-proofing Your Home

- Store drugs and medications in a medicine cabinet that is locked or out of reach. Do not keep toothpaste, soap, or shampoo in the same cabinet.

- Buy and keep medications in their own containers with child safety caps. (Remember, however, that these caps are child-resistant, not child-proof, so keep them in a locked cabinet.) Discard leftover prescription medicines by flushing them down the toilet when the illness for which they were prescribed has passed.

- Do not take medicine in front of small children; they may try to imitate you later. Never tell a child that a medicine is candy in order to get him to take it.

- Check the label every time you give medication, to be sure you are giving the right medicine in the correct dosage. Mistakes are most likely to occur in the middle of the night, so always turn on the light when handling any medication.

- Read labels on all household products before you buy them. Try to find the safest ones for the job, and buy only what you need to use immediately.

- Store hazardous products in locked cabinets that are out of your child's reach. Do not keep detergents and other cleaning products under the kitchen or bathroom sink unless they are in a cabinet with a safety latch that locks every time you close the cabinet. (Most hardware stores and department stores sell these safety latches.)

- Never put poisonous or toxic products in containers that were once used for food, especially empty drink bottles, cans, or cups.

- Always open the garage door before starting your car, and never run the car in a closed garage. Be sure that coal, wood, or kerosene stoves are properly maintained. If you smell gas, turn off the stove or gas burner, leave the house and then call the gas company.

- Post the Poison Control number, 1–800–222–1222, near every telephone in your home, along with other emergency numbers. Be sure that your babysitter knows how to use these numbers.

around the clock to your regional Poison Center. *If an emergency exists and you cannot find the number, dial 911 or Directory Assistance and ask for the poison center.*

The immediate action you need to take will vary with the type of poisoning. The Poison Center can give you specific instructions if you know the particular substance your child has swallowed. However, carry out the following instructions before calling them.

Swallowed Poison

First, get the poisonous substance away from your child. If she still has some in her mouth, make her spit it out, or remove it with your fingers. Keep this material along with any other evidence that might help determine what she swallowed.

Next, check for these signs:

- Severe throat pain

- Excessive drooling

- Breathing difficulty

- Convulsions

- Excessive drowsiness

If any of these are present, or if your child is unconscious or has stopped breathing, start emergency procedures and get medical help immediately by calling 911. Take the poison container and remnants of material with you to help the doctor determine what was swallowed. *Do not make your child vomit,* as this may cause further damage, and *do not follow instructions about poisoning on the label* of the container, as these are often out of date or incorrect.

If your child is not showing these serious symptoms, call the poison help line number, 1–800–222–1222, which will direct your call to your regional Poison Center. The person

answering the phone will need the following information in order to help you:

- Your name and phone number.

- Your child's name, age, and weight. Also be sure to mention any serious medical conditions she has or medications she is taking.

- The name of the substance your child swallowed. Read it off the container, and spell it if necessary. If ingredients are listed on the label, read them, too. If your child has swallowed a prescription medicine, and the drug is not named on the label, give the center the name of the pharmacy and its phone number, the date of the prescription, and its number. Try to describe the tablet or capsule, and mention any imprinted numbers on it. If your child swallowed another substance, such as a part of a plant, provide as full a description as possible to help identify it.

- The time your child swallowed this poison (or when you found her), and the amount you think she swallowed.

If the poison is extremely dangerous, or if your child is very young, you may be told to take her directly to the nearest emergency room for medical evaluation. Otherwise, you will be given instructions to follow at home.

Vomiting may be dangerous, so never make a child vomit. Strong acids (i.e., toilet bowl cleaner) or strong alkalis (i.e., lye, drain or oven cleaner, or dishwasher detergent) can burn the throat—and vomiting will only increase the damage. Syrup of ipecac is a drug that was used in the past to make children vomit after they had swallowed a poison; although this may seem to make sense, it is no longer considered a good poison treatment. If you have syrup of ipecac in your home, flush it down the toilet and throw away the container. Do not make a child vomit in any way, whether by giving him syrup of ipecac, making him gag, or giving him saltwater. Instead, you may be advised to have the child drink milk or water.

Poison on the Skin

If your child spills a dangerous chemical substance on her body, remove her clothes and rinse the skin with lukewarm—not hot—water. If the area shows signs of being burned, continue rinsing for at least fifteen minutes, no matter how much your child may protest. Then call the Poison Center for further advice. Do not apply ointments or grease.

Poison in the Eye

Flush your child's eye by holding her eyelid open and pouring a steady stream of lukewarm water into the inner corner. A young child is sure to object to this treatment, so get another adult to hold her while you rinse the eye. If that's not possible, wrap her tightly in a towel and clamp her under one arm so you have one hand free to hold the eyelid open and the other to pour in the water.

Continue flushing the eye for fifteen minutes. Then call the Poison Center, 1–800–222–1222, for further instructions. Do not use an eyecup, eye drops, or ointment unless the Poison Center tells you to do so. If there is any question of continued pain or severe injury, seek emergency assistance immediately.

Poison Fumes

In the home, poisonous fumes are most likely to be produced by an idling automobile in a closed garage; leaky gas vents; wood, coal, or kerosene stoves that are improperly vented or maintained; or space heaters, ovens, stoves, or hot water heaters that use gas. If your child is exposed to fumes or gases from these or other sources, get her into fresh air immediately. If she is breathing, call the Poison Center, 1–800–222–1222, for further instructions. If she has stopped breathing, start CPR (see page 479), and don't stop until she breathes on her own or someone else can take over. If you can, have someone call for emergency medical help immediately; otherwise, try one minute of CPR and then call for emergency assistance.

Prevention

Young children, especially those between ages one and three, are poisoned most commonly by things in the home such as drugs and medications, cleaning products, plants, cosmetics, pesticides, paints, solvents, antifreeze, windshield wiper fluid, gasoline, kerosene, and lamp oil. This happens because tasting and mouthing things is a natural way for children to explore their surroundings, and because they imitate adults without understanding what they are doing.

Most poisonings occur when parents are distracted. If you are ill or under a great deal of stress, you may not watch your child as closely as usual. The hectic routine of getting dinner on the table at the end of the day causes so many lapses in parental attention that late afternoon is known as "the arsenic hour" by Poison Center personnel.

The best way to prevent poisonings is to store all toxic substances in a locked cabinet where your child cannot possibly get to them, even when you are not directly watching her. Also, supervise her even more closely whenever you're visiting a store or home that has not been child-proofed. Be especially attentive when your child is visiting another home, or a grandparent's home, where child-proofing has not been as vigilant.

(See also Chapter 14, "Keeping Your Child Safe.")

16

ABDOMINAL/GASTROINTESTINAL TRACT

Abdominal Pain

Children of all ages experience abdominal pain occasionally, but the causes of such pain in infants tend to be quite different from what they are in older children. So, too, is the way children of different age groups react to the pain. An older youngster may rub her abdomen and tell you she's having a "bellyache" or "tummyache," while a very young infant will show her distress by crying and pulling up her legs or by passing gas (which is usually swallowed air). Vomiting or excessive burping also may accompany the crying in babies.

Fortunately, most stomachaches disappear on their own, and are not serious. However, if your child's complaints continue or worsen over a period of three to five hours, or if she has a fever, severe sore throat, or extreme change in appetite or energy level, you should notify your pediatrician immediately. These symptoms may indicate that a more serious disorder is causing the pain.

Common Causes of Abdominal Pain in Infancy

1. Colic usually occurs in infants between the ages of ten days and three months of age. While no one knows exactly what causes it, colic seems to produce rapid and severe contractions of the intestine that probably are responsible for the baby's pain. The discomfort often is more severe in the late afternoon and early evening, and may be accompanied by inconsolable crying, pulling up of the legs, frequent passage of gas, and general irritability. (See Chapter 7, "Age One Month Through Three Months.")

How should you respond? You may need to try a variety of approaches (detailed on page 152).

2. Constipation often is blamed for abdominal pain, but it's rarely a problem in younger infants. Older babies who have started solid foods, however, sometimes do become constipated and may experience

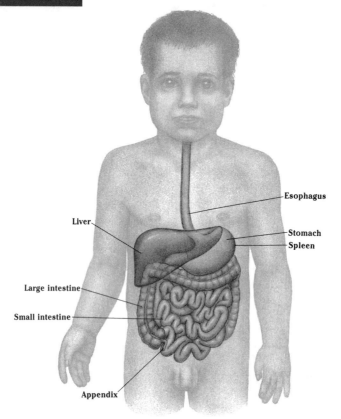

Abdomen/Gastrointestinal Tract

abdominal discomfort while having a bowel movement. If this appears to be your child's problem, try the following.

- Add a small amount of water to the diet.

- Decrease constipating foods, such as rice, banana, or cereal.

If these simple measures don't seem to help, consult the section on *Constipation* (page 503), and talk to your pediatrician. Never give a child laxatives or other types of stool-loosening or -softening medications without first consulting your pediatrician.

3. Intussusception is a rare condition that may be another cause of abdominal pain in young infants (usually less than one year).

This problem occurs when one part of the intestine telescopes or collapses on itself; like a retractable antenna, one part of the intestine slides inside another portion of it, creating an intestinal blockage that causes severe pain. The child will intermittently and abruptly cry and pull her legs toward her stomach. This will be followed by periods without stomach pain, often without any distress. These children also may vomit and have bloody stools, with blood that is somewhat dark and mucusy.

It is important to recognize this cause of abdominal pain and to talk to your pediatrician immediately. She will want to see your child and perhaps order an X ray called an air or barium enema. Sometimes doing this test not only makes the diagnosis but also unblocks the intestine. If the enema does not unblock the intestine, an emergency operation may be necessary to correct the problem.

4. Viral or bacterial infection of the intestine is usually associated with diarrhea and/or vomiting. Infectious gastroenteritis often presents with abdominal pain. If suspected, your pediatrician may perform a culture of the stool, and if bacteria are detected, appropriate treatment will be given. Viral causes require no treatment and will resolve on their own over a week or so.

Causes of Abdominal Pain in Older Children

1. Constipation is a common cause of abdominal pain in older children. It may go unnoticed if the child passes a small stool each day, while a buildup of stool develops in her colon. When the stool hardens, an impaction occurs; the child is unable to have a bowel movement. She complains of pain, especially in the lower part of the abdomen. Children whose diets consist mostly of junk food are prone to such bowel problems. Discuss this with your pediatrician. An initial approach is to increase fiber in the diet, but each child's condition is unique. You and your pediatrician can develop a tailor-made approach to resolve the problem.

2. Urinary tract infections (UTI) can occur during infancy, but they rarely produce abdominal pain at that age. A UTI is much more common among three- to five-year-old girls, where it produces discomfort in the bladder area, as well as some pain and burning when urinating. These children also may urinate more frequently and possibly wet the bed. However, the infection usually does not produce a fever.

If your child complains of these symptoms, take her to the pediatrician, who will examine her and her urine. If an infection is present, an antibiotic will be prescribed. This will eliminate both the infection and the abdominal pain. (See *Urinary Tract Infections,* page 647.)

3. Strep throat is a throat infection caused by bacteria called *streptococci.* It occurs frequently in children over two years of age. The symptoms and signs include a sore throat and a fever. There may be some vomiting and headache, as well. The pediatrician will want to examine your child and take a throat culture. If the culture is positive for strep—results usually take twenty-four hours, although many doctors now are using a test that provides results in less than an hour—your child will need to be treated with an antibiotic. (See *Sore Throat,* page 589.)

4. Appendicitis is very rare in children under age three and uncommon under the age of five. When it does occur, the first sign is often a complaint of constant stomachache in the center of the abdomen. Later the pain moves down and over to the right side, and the child may feel nauseous, have a slight fever, and even vomit. If your child has pain and other symptoms that occur in this pattern, notify your pediatrician at once. The doctor will want to see your child immediately, and may even ask you to go to the emergency room at the hospital for blood tests and X rays. If the diagnosis turns out to be appendicitis, an operation will be performed as quickly as possible to remove the appendix. (See *Appendicitis,* page 500, for more detailed information.)

5. Lead poisoning most often occurs in toddlers living in an older house where lead-base paint has been used. Children in this age group may eat small chips of paint off the walls and woodwork. The lead is then stored in their bodies and can create many serious health problems. Symptoms of lead poisoning include

- Abdominal pain

- Constipation

- Irritability (The child is fussy, crying, difficult to satisfy.)

- Lethargy (She is sleepy, doesn't want to play, has a poor appetite.)

- Convulsions

If your child is exposed to lead paint, or if you know she has eaten paint chips and has any of the above symptoms, call your pediatrician. She can order a blood test for lead and advise you as to what else needs to be done. (See *Lead Poisoning,* page 730.)

6. Intestinal infection (gastroenteritis) is caused most frequently by viruses. However, an intestinal infection also can be caused by bacteria or parasites (organisms—larger than bacteria or viruses—that often are found in unsanitary water or food supplies). When an infection occurs, the child usually has abdominal cramps, diarrhea, and/or vomiting. (See *Diarrhea,* page 505, and *Vomiting,* page 522.) The pain generally lasts one or two days and then disappears. One exception is an infection caused by the *Giardia lamblia* parasite. This infestation may produce periodic recurrent pain not localized to any one part of the abdomen. The pain may persist for a week or more and can lead to a marked loss of appetite and weight. Treatment with appropriate medication can cure this infestation and the abdominal pain that accompanies it.

7. Milk allergy is a reaction to the protein in milk, and can produce cramping abdominal pain. (See *Milk Allergy,* page 517.)

8. Emotional upset in school-age children sometimes causes recurrent abdominal pain that has no other obvious cause. Although this pain rarely occurs before age five, it can happen to a younger child who is under unusual stress. The first clue is pain that tends to come and go, over a period of more than a week. In addition, there are no other associated findings or complaints (fever, vomiting, diarrhea, coughing, lethargy or weakness, urinary tract symptoms, sore throat, or flulike symptoms). There also may be a family history of this type of illness. Finally, your child probably will act either quieter or noisier than usual and have trouble expressing her thoughts or feelings. If this type of behavior occurs with your youngster, find out if there's something troubling her at home or school or with siblings, relatives, or friends. Has she recently lost a close friend or a pet? Has there been a death of a family member, or the divorce or separation of her parents?

Your pediatrician can suggest ways to help your child talk about her troubles. For example, he may advise you to use toys or games to help the youngster act out her problems. If you need additional assistance, the pediatrician may refer you to a child psychologist or psychiatrist.

Appendicitis

The appendix is a narrow, finger-shaped, hollow structure attached to the large intestine. While it serves no purpose in humans, it can cause serious problems when it becomes inflamed. Because of its location, this can happen quite easily; for instance, a piece of food or stool can get trapped inside, causing the appendix to swell and become infected and painfully inflamed. This inflammation—called appendicitis—is most common in youngsters over the age of six, but can occur in younger children. Once infected, the appendix must be removed. Otherwise it may burst, allowing the infection to spread within the abdomen. Since this problem is potentially life-threatening, it's important to know the symptoms of appendicitis so you can tell your pediatrician at the first sign of trouble. In order of appearance, the symptoms are:

1. Abdominal pain: This usually is the first complaint the child will have. Almost always, the pain is felt first around the umbilicus (belly button). After several hours, as the infection worsens, the pain may intensify in the lower right side. Sometimes, if the appendix is not located in the usual position, the discomfort may occur elsewhere in the abdomen or in the back, or there may be urinary symptoms, such as increased frequency or burning. Even when the appendix lies in its normal position and the pain is in the right lower abdomen, it may irritate one of the muscles that leads toward the leg, causing the child to limp or walk bent over.

2. Vomiting: After several hours of pain, vomiting may occur. It is important to remember that a stomachache comes before the vomiting with appendicitis, not after. Abdominal pain that follows vomiting is very commonly seen in viral illnesses such as the flu.

3. Loss of appetite: The absence of hunger occurs shortly after the onset of the pain.

4. Fever: There may be a low-grade fever (100–101 degrees Fahrenheit; 37.8–38.4 degrees Celsius).

Unfortunately, the symptoms associated with appendicitis sometimes may be hidden by a viral or bacterial infection that preceded it. Diarrhea, nausea, vomiting, and fever may appear before the typical pain of appendicitis, making the diagnosis much more difficult.

Also, your child's discomfort may suddenly vanish, thus persuading you that all is well. Unfortunately, this disappearance of pain also could mean that the appendix has

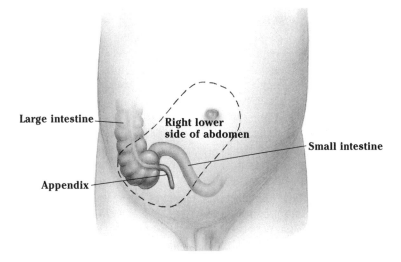

Large intestine

Right lower side of abdomen

Small intestine

Appendix

just broken open. Although the pain may leave for several hours, this is exactly when appendicitis becomes dangerous. The infection will spread to the rest of the abdomen, causing your child to become much more ill, develop a higher fever, and require hospitalization for surgery and intravenous antibiotics. Recovery may take much longer, and there may be more complications than with appendicitis diagnosed and treated earlier.

Treatment

Detecting the signs of appendicitis is not always easy, particularly with children under the age of three, who cannot tell you where it hurts or that the pain is moving to the right side. This is why it's better to act sooner rather than later if you have any suspicion that your child's pain or discomfort seems "different," more severe than usual, or out of the ordinary. While most children with abdominal pain don't have appendicitis, only a physician should diagnose this serious problem. If the abdominal pain persists for more than an hour or two, and if your child also has nausea, vomiting, loss of appetite, and fever, notify your pediatrician immediately. If the doctor is not certain that the problem is appendicitis, she may decide to observe your child closely for several hours, either in or out of the hospital. During this time, she will have performed additional laboratory or X-ray examinations to see if more conclusive signs develop. If there is a strong probability that appendicitis is present, surgery usually will be done as soon as possible.

In almost all cases, the treatment of appendicitis is surgical removal of the appendix. In rare instances, the tissue covering the intestines may enclose the appendix, thus containing the infection. This makes it more difficult to remove the appendix without spreading the infection, so antibiotics may be used, either alone or combined with drainage of the infection by a small tube. But because inflammation can recur even after the initial infection is gone, the appendix usually is removed later.

Celiac Disease

Celiac disease is a problem that causes malabsorption—that is, a failure of the bowels to absorb nutrients. It's caused by an immune reaction to gluten (the protein found in wheat, rye, barley, and perhaps oats) that takes place in the intestine and stimulates the body's immune system to attack and damage the lining of the intestine, preventing nutrients from being absorbed into the system. As a result, food simply passes through the intestines, only partially digested. The result is crampy abdominal pain, foul-smelling stools, diarrhea, weight loss, irritability, and a continuous feeling of being sick.

Treatment

Once your pediatrician has ruled out other possible digestive problems, he'll order certain blood tests that can be used to screen for celiac disease. These tests measure the blood levels of antibodies to gluten. However, to make a definitive diagnosis, a small-bowel biopsy is required, which entails the removal of a small piece of the intestine for laboratory examination. This procedure usually is done by passing a small tube through the mouth and into the small intestine, where the biopsy is obtained.

If the intestinal lining turns out to be damaged, your child will be placed on a gluten-free diet. This means staying away from wheat, rye, barley, and possibly oat products. Your pediatrician will give you a complete list of foods to avoid, but you also need to carefully check the labels of any foods you purchase, since wheat flour is a hidden ingredient in many items. Because rice and rice products do not contain gluten, they'll probably become a major part of your child's diet.

Incidentally, your child may not be able to tolerate milk sugar for as long as several months after the initial diagnosis is made. In this case, you may be advised to eliminate milk temporarily, as well as gluten products, from her diet. During this time she might be given milk treated with enzymes, so that it will be predigested before reaching the intestine. Extra vitamins and minerals also might be necessary.

If your child does have celiac disease, she must remain on a gluten-free diet for her entire life, avoiding completely wheat, rye, barley, and possibly oats.

(See also: *Diarrhea,* page 505; *Malabsorption,* page 516; *Milk Allergy,* page 517; *Anemia,* page 715.)

Constipation

Bowel patterns vary in children just as they do in adults. Because of this, it is sometimes difficult to tell if your child is truly constipated. One child may go two or three days without a bowel movement and still not be constipated, while another might have relatively frequent bowel movements but have difficulty passing the stool. In general, it is best to watch for the following signals before suspecting constipation.

- In a newborn, firm stools less than once a day

- In an older child, stools that are hard and compact, with three or four days between bowel movements

- At any age, stools that are large, hard and dry, and associated with painful bowel movements

- Episodes of abdominal pain relieved after having a large bowel movement

- Blood in or on the outside of the stools

- Soiling between bowel movements

Constipation generally occurs when the muscles at the end of the large intestine tighten, preventing the stool from passing normally. The longer the stool remains there, the firmer and drier it becomes, making it even more difficult to pass without discomfort. Then, because the bowel movement is painful, your child consciously may try to hold it back, making the problem still worse.

The tendency toward constipation seems to run in families. It may start in infancy and remain as a lifetime pattern, becoming worse if the child does not establish regular bowel habits or withholds stool. Stool retention occurs most commonly between the ages of two and five, at a time when the child is coming to terms with independence, control, and toilet training. Older children may resist having bowel movements away from home because they don't want to use an unfamiliar toilet. This, too, can cause constipation or make it worse.

If your child does withhold, he may produce such large stools that his rectum stretches. Then he may no longer feel the urge to defecate until the stool is too big to be passed without the help of an enema, laxative, or other treatment. In some of these cases, soiling occurs when liquid waste leaks around the solid stool. This looks like diarrhea on the child's underpants or diaper. In these severe cases, the rectum must be emptied under a physician's supervision, and the child must be retrained to establish normal bowel patterns.

Treatment

Mild or occasional episodes of constipation may be helped by the following suggestions.

If your constipated child is between six months and twelve months of age and recently has started cow's milk, return to his previous formula. This may be helpful since infant formula tends to be less constipating than unmodified cow's milk. Constipation due to breastmilk is unusual, but if your breastfed infant is constipated, it is probably due to a reason other than diet. Do *not* substitute formula for breastmilk unless your doctor tells you to do so. (Keep in mind that the American Academy of Pediatrics recommends breastfeeding for the first twelve months of life.)

If your child is eating solid foods and has problems with constipation, you may need to add high-fiber foods to his daily diet. These include prunes, apricots, plums, raisins, high-fiber vegetables (peas, beans, broccoli), and whole-grain cereals and bread products. Increasing the daily consumption of water also may help.

In more severe cases, the pediatrician may prescribe a mild laxative or enema. Follow such prescriptions exactly. Never give your child a laxative without your doctor's advice.

Prevention

Parents should become familiar with their children's normal bowel patterns and the typical size and consistency of their stools. Doing this is helpful in determining when constipation occurs and how severe the problem is. If the child does not have regular bowel movements each day or two, or is uncomfortable when they are passed, he may need help in developing proper bowel habits. This may be done by providing a proper diet and establishing a regular bowel routine.

In a child who is not yet toilet trained, the best way to guard against constipation is to provide a high-fiber diet. Increase the amount of fiber as he gets older.

Once the child is mature enough to be toilet trained, he should be urged to sit on the toilet after breakfast every day. A book, puzzle, or toy can occupy him during this time so that he feels relaxed. Encourage him to stay on the toilet until he has a bowel movement, or for about fifteen minutes. Praise him if he is successful; if he is not, encourage him with positive statements. Eventually he should be able to toilet himself without parental guidance.

If the combination of a high-fiber diet and a daily toilet routine does not result in regular bowel movements, the child may consciously be withholding stool. In this case, you should consult the pediatrician. He can supervise the use of stool softeners, laxatives, or suppositories, should they be necessary. Occasionally stool withholding becomes so severe that both the child and the family become upset by the symptoms. Much of each day's interactions focus on bowel movements. Programs have been devised to deal effectively with this problem.

Usually the withholding begins around the time of toilet training. The child is reluctant to move his bowels on the potty or toilet and withholds. The next bowel movement is painful. The child associates pain with bowel movements and now withholds stool because of that. The situation can progress to an all-consuming fear. When such severe symptoms develop the rectum must be cleansed with enemas or rectal suppositories. Following this, a stool softener such as mineral oil is given in amounts large enough to prevent the child from voluntarily withholding stool. Because the bowel movements are now no longer painful, the child

Causes of Diarrhea

In young children, the intestinal damage that produces diarrhea is caused most often by viruses called enteroviruses.

Other causes are:

- Bacteria (salmonella, shigella, *E. coli*, campylobacter)

- Parasitic infections *(Giardia)*

- Food or milk allergy

- Side effects from oral medication (most commonly antibiotics)

- Food poisoning (from things such as mushrooms, shellfish, or contaminated food)

- Infections outside the gastrointestinal tract, including the urinary tract, the respiratory tract, and even the middle ear (If your child is taking an antibiotic for such an infection, the diarrhea may become more severe.)

- Rotavirus infections

---

will start to go on the potty without fear. This treatment may go on for several months while the mineral oil is slowly withdrawn. A diet high in fiber and regular toileting are also part of the routine.

Diarrhea

Normally your child's bowel movements will vary in number and consistency, depending on her age and diet. Breastfed newborns may have up to twelve small bowel movements a day, but by the second or third month, they may have some days without any. Most babies under one year of age produce less than 5 ounces (150 ml) of stool per day, while older children can produce up to 7 ounces (210 ml). By age two, most children will have only one or two large bowel movements a day, but your child can have several smaller ones and still be normal, especially if his diet includes juices and fiber-containing foods, such as prunes or bran.

An occasional loose stool is not cause for alarm. If, however, your child's bowel pattern suddenly changes to loose, watery stools that occur more frequently than usual, he has diarrhea.

Diarrhea occurs when the inner lining of the intestine is injured. The stools become loose because the intestine does not properly digest or absorb the nutrients from the foods that your child eats and drinks. Also, the injured lining tends to leak fluid. Minerals and salt are lost along with the fluid. This loss can be made even worse if your child is fed food or beverages that contain large amounts of sugar, since unabsorbed sugar draws even more water into the intestine, increasing the diarrhea.

When the body loses too much water and salt, dehydration results. This can be prevented by replenishing losses due to the diarrhea with adequate amounts of fluid and salt, as described under *Treatment* (page 506).

The medical term for intestinal inflammation is *enteritis*. When the problem is accompanied by or preceded by vomiting, as it

Signs and Symptoms of Dehydration
(Loss of Significant Amounts of Body Water)

The most important part of treating diarrhea is to prevent your child from becoming dehydrated. Be alert for the following warning signs of dehydration, and notify the pediatrician immediately if any of them develop.

Mild to Moderate Dehydration:

■ Plays less than usual

■ Urinates less frequently (wets fewer than six diapers per day)

■ Parched, dry mouth

■ Fewer tears when crying

■ Sunken soft spot of the head in an infant or toddler

■ Stools will be loose if dehydration is caused by diarrhea; if dehydration is due to other fluid loss (vomiting, lack of fluid intake), there will be decreased bowel movements

Severe Dehydration (in addition to the symptoms and signals listed above):

■ Very fussy

■ Excessively sleepy

■ Sunken eyes

■ Cool, discolored hands and feet

■ Wrinkled skin

■ Voiding only one to two times per day

---

often is, there is usually some stomach and small-intestinal inflammation, as well, and the condition is called *gastroenteritis*.

Children with viral diarrheal illnesses (see the box on page 505) often have symptoms such as vomiting, fever, and irritability, as well. (See *Vomiting*, page 522; Chapter 23, "Fever.") Their stools tend to be greenish yellow in color and have a significant amount of water with them. (If they occur as often as once an hour, they usually won't have any solid material at all.) If the stools appear red or blackish, they might contain blood; this bleeding may arise from the injured lining of the intestine or, more likely, simply may be due to irritation of the rectum by frequent, loose bowel movements. In any event, if you notice this or any other unusual stool color, you should mention it to your pediatrician.

Treatment

There are no effective medications for treating viral intestinal infections, which cause most cases of diarrhea in infants. Prescription medications should be used only to treat certain types of bacterial or parasitic intestinal infections, which are much less common. When the latter conditions are suspected, your pediatrician will ask for stool specimens to test in the laboratory; other tests also may be done.

Over-the-counter antidiarrheal medications are not recommended for children un-

Estimated Oral Fluid and Electrolyte Requirements by Body Weight
1 pound = 0.45 kilograms
1 ounce = 30 ml

Body Weight (in pounds)	Minimum Daily Fluid Requirements (in ounces)*	Electrolyte Solution† Requirements for Mild Diarrhea (in ounces for 24 hours)
6–7	10	16
11	15	23
22	25	40
26	28	44
33	32	51
40	38	61

*NOTE: This is the *smallest* amount of fluid that a normal child requires. Most children drink more than this.
†Commercially available electrolyte solutions include Infalyte®, Pedialyte®, and Rehydralyte®.

der age two and should be used with caution in older children. They often worsen the intestinal injury, and they do not stop the body's loss of water and salt if an infection is present. Instead, they cause the fluid and salt to remain within the intestine. When this occurs, your child can become dehydrated without your being aware of it, and without necessarily showing weight loss, because the diarrhea appears to stop. For this reason, always consult your pediatrician before giving your child any medication for diarrhea.

Mild Diarrhea

If your child has a small amount of diarrhea but is not dehydrated (see the box on page 506 for signs of dehydration), does not have a high fever, and is active and hungry, you may not need to change the diet, and you can continue breastmilk or formula. You should *not* give a "clear liquid diet" consisting solely of sweetened beverages (juices, Jell-O, or soda pop), because their high sugar content and low salt levels may make the diarrhea worse.

If your child has mild diarrhea and is vomiting, substitute a commercially available electrolyte solution for her normal diet. Your pediatrician will recommend these solutions to maintain normal body water and salt levels until the vomiting has stopped. In most cases, they're needed for only one to two days. Once the vomiting has subsided, gradually restart the normal diet.

Never give boiled milk (skimmed or otherwise) to any child with diarrhea. Boiling the milk allows the water to evaporate, leaving the remaining part dangerously high in salt and mineral content. (In fact, you should never give boiled milk even to a well child.)

Significant Diarrhea

If your child has a watery bowel movement every one to two hours, or more frequently, and/or has signs of dehydration (see the box on page 506), consult his pediatrician. She may advise you to withhold all solid foods for at least twenty-four hours and to avoid liquids that are high in sugar (Jell-O, soft drinks, full-strength fruit juices, or artificially sweetened beverages), high in salt (packaged broth), or very low in salt (water and tea). She probably will have you give him only commercially prepared electrolyte solutions, which contain the ideal balance of salt and minerals. (See the table on page 507.) Breastfed babies usually are treated in a similar fashion except in very mild cases, when breastfeeding may be continued.

If your child has diarrhea and you are concerned that he may be becoming dehydrated, call your pediatrician and withhold all foods and milk beverages until she gives you further instructions. *Take your child to the pediatrician or nearest emergency room immediately if you think he is moderately to severely dehydrated.* In the meantime, give your child a commercially prepared electrolyte solution.

For severe dehydration, hospitalization is sometimes necessary so that your child can be rehydrated intravenously. In milder cases, all that may be necessary is to give your child an electrolyte replacement solution according to your pediatrician's directions. The table on page 507 indicates the approximate amount of this solution to be used.

Once your child has been on an electrolyte solution for twelve to twenty-four hours and the diarrhea is decreasing, you gradually may expand the diet to include foods such as applesauce, pears, bananas, and flavored gelatin. Milk can be withheld for one to two days except in the case of young, bottle-fed babies, who can be given half-strength formula to start. (Add an equal volume of water to your child's usual full-strength formula.) If the infant is breastfed, you can continue breastfeeding while giving the electrolyte solution. As the diarrhea improves, an older child may be able to eat small quantities of bland foods such as rice, toast, potatoes, and cereal. You can continue to give the electrolyte replacement solution.

It is usually unnecessary to withhold food for longer than twenty-four hours, as your child will need some normal nutrition to start to regain lost strength. After you have started giving him food again, his stools may remain loose, but that does not necessarily mean that things are not going well. Look for increased activity, better appetite, more frequent urination, and the disappearance of any of the signs of dehydration. When you see these, you will know your child is getting better.

Diarrhea that lasts longer than two weeks (chronic diarrhea) may signify a more serious type of intestinal problem. When diarrhea persists this long, your pediatrician will want to do further tests to determine the cause and to make sure your child is not becoming malnourished. If malnutrition is becoming a problem, the pediatrician may recommend a special diet or special type of formula.

If your child drinks too much fluid, especially too much juice or sweetened beverages, a condition commonly referred to as toddler's diarrhea could develop. This causes ongoing loose stools but shouldn't affect appetite or growth or cause dehydration. Although toddler's diarrhea is not a dangerous condition, the pediatrician may suggest that you limit the amounts of juice and sweetened fluids your child drinks. You can give plain water to children whose thirst does not seem to be satisfied by their normal dietary and milk intake.

When diarrhea occurs in combination with other symptoms, it could mean that there is a more serious medical problem. Notify your pediatrician immediately if the diarrhea is accompanied by any of the following:

- Fever that lasts longer than twenty-four to forty-eight hours

- Bloody stools

- Vomiting that lasts more than twelve to twenty-four hours

- Vomited material that is green-colored, blood-tinged, or like coffee grounds in appearance

- A distended (swollen-appearing) sabdomen

- Refusal to eat or drink

- Severe abdominal pain

- Rash or jaundice (yellow color of skin and eyes)

If your child has another medical condition or is taking medication routinely, it is best to tell your pediatrician about any diarrheal illness that lasts more than twenty-four hours without improvement, or anything else that really worries you.

Prevention

The following guidelines will help lessen the chances that your child will get diarrhea.

1. Most forms of infectious diarrhea are transmitted from direct hand-to-mouth contact following exposure to contaminated fecal (stool) material. This happens most often in children who are not toilet trained. Promote personal hygiene (i.e.,

hand washing after using the toilet or changing diapers and before handling food) and other sanitary measures in your household and in your child's child care center or preschool.

2. Avoid drinking raw (unpasteurized) milk and eating foods that may be contaminated. (See *Food Poisoning,* below.)

3. Avoid the unnecessary use of medications, especially antibiotics.

4. If possible, breastfeed your child through early infancy.

5. Limit the amount of juice and sweetened beverages.

(See also *Abdominal Pain,* page 497; *Celiac Disease,* page 502; *Malabsorption,* page 516; *Milk Allergy,* page 517; and *Vomiting,* page 522.)

Food Poisoning

Food poisoning occurs after eating food contaminated by bacteria. The symptoms of food poisoning are basically the same as those of "stomach flu": abdominal cramps, nausea, vomiting, diarrhea, and fever. But if your child and other people who have eaten the same food all have the same symptoms, the problem is more likely to be food poisoning than the flu. The bacteria that cause food poisoning cannot be seen, smelled, or tasted, so your child won't know when she is eating them. These organisms include:

Staphylococcus aureus (Staph)

Staph contamination is the leading cause of food poisoning. These bacteria ordinarily cause skin infections, such as pimples or boils, and are transferred when foodstuffs are handled by an infected person. If the food temperature is right (100 degrees Fahrenheit [37.8 Celsius] is ideal), the staph bacteria multiply and produce a poison (toxin) that ordinary cooking will not destroy. The symptoms begin one to six hours after eating the contaminated food, and the discomfort usually lasts about one day.

Salmonella

Salmonella bacteria (there are many types) are another major cause of food poisoning in the United States. The most commonly contaminated foods are raw meat (including chicken), raw or undercooked eggs, and unpasteurized milk. Fortunately, salmonella are killed when the food is cooked thoroughly. Symptoms caused by salmonella poisoning start sixteen to forty-eight hours after eating, and may last two to seven days.

Clostridium perfringens

Clostridium perfringens (*C. perfringens*) is a bacterium frequently found in soil, sewage, and the intestines of humans and animals. It usually is transferred by the food handler to the food itself, where it multiplies and produces its toxin. *C. perfringens* often is found in school cafeterias because it thrives in food that is served in quantity and left out for long periods at room temperature or on a steam table. The foods most often involved are cooked beef, poultry, gravy, fish, casseroles, stews, and bean burritos. The symptoms of this type of poisoning start eight to twenty-four hours after eating, and can last from one to several days.

Botulism

This is the deadly food poisoning caused by the bacteria *Clostridium botulinum*. Although these bacteria normally can be found in soil and water, illness from them is extremely rare because they need very special condi-

tions in order to multiply and produce poison. *Clostridium botulinum* grows best without oxygen and in certain chemical conditions, which explains why improperly canned food is most often contaminated and the low-acid vegetables, such as green beans, corn, beets, and peas, are most often involved. Honey also can be contaminated and frequently causes severe illness, particularly in children under one year of age.

Botulism attacks the nervous system and causes double vision, droopy eyelids, and difficulty in swallowing and breathing. It also can cause vomiting, diarrhea, and abdominal pain. The symptoms develop in eighteen to thirty-six hours and can last weeks to months. Without treatment, botulism can cause death. Even with treatment, it can cause nerve damage.

Cryptosporidiosis

In very uncommon situations, watery diarrhea, low-grade fever, and abdominal pain may be caused by an infection known as cryptosporidium. This infection is of special concern in children who do not have a normal immune system.

Other sources of food poisoning include poisonous mushrooms, contaminated fish products, and foods with special seasonings. Young children do not care for most of these foods and so will eat very little of them. However, it still is very important to be aware of the risk. If your child has unusual gastrointestinal symptoms, and there is any chance she might have eaten contaminated or poisonous foods, call your pediatrician.

Treatment

In most cases of food poisoning, all that's necessary is to limit eating and drinking for a while. The problem then usually will resolve itself. Infants can tolerate three to four hours without food or liquids; older young-sters, six to eight. If your child is still vomit-ing or her diarrhea has not decreased significantly during this time, call your pedi-atrician.

Also notify the doctor if your child:

- Shows signs of dehydration: dry lips; no tears when she cries; sunken eyes; doughy-feeling skin; decreased appetite; decreased urination; sleepiness; irritabil-ity

- Has bloody diarrhea

- Has continuous diarrhea with a large vol-ume of water in the stool, or diarrhea al-ternating with constipation

- Was poisoned by mushrooms

- Suddenly becomes weak, numb, con-fused, restless, and feels tingling, acts drunkenly, or has hallucinations or diffi-culty breathing

Tell the doctor the symptoms your child is having, what foods she has eaten recently, and where they were obtained. The treat-ment your pediatrician gives will depend on your child's condition and the type of food poisoning. If she is dehydrated, fluid re-placement will be prescribed. Sometimes antibiotics are helpful, but only if the bacte-ria are known. Antihistamines help if the ill-ness is due to an allergic reaction to a food, toxin, or seasoning. If your child has botu-lism, she will require hospitalization and in-tensive care.

Prevention

Most food poisoning is preventable if you observe the following guidelines.

Cleanliness

- Be especially careful when preparing raw meats and poultry. After you have rinsed the meat thoroughly, wash your hands and all surfaces with hot, sudsy water be-fore continuing your preparation.

- Always wash your hands before prepar-ing meals and after going to the bathroom or changing your child's diaper.

- If you have open cuts or sores on your hands, wear gloves while preparing food.

- Do not prepare food when you are sick, particularly if you have nausea, vomiting, abdominal cramps, or diarrhea.

Food Selection

- Carefully examine any canned food (espe-cially home-canned goods) for signs of bacterial contamination. Look for milky liquid surrounding vegetables (it should be clear), cracked jars, loose lids, and swollen cans or lids. *Don't use canned goods showing any of these signs. Do not even taste them. Throw them away so that nobody else will eat them.* (Wrap them first in plastic and then in a heavy paper bag.)

- Buy all meats and seafood from reputable suppliers.

- Do not use raw (unpasteurized) milk or cheese made from raw milk.

- Do not eat raw meat.

- Do not give honey to a baby under one year of age.

Food Preparation and Serving

- Do not let prepared foods (particularly starchy ones), cooked and cured meats, cheese, or anything with mayonnaise stay at room temperature for more than two hours.

- Do not interrupt the cooking of meat or poultry to finish the cooking later.

- Do not prepare food one day for the next unless it will be frozen or refrigerated right away. (Always put hot food right into the refrigerator. Do not wait for it to cool first.)

- Make sure all foods are cooked thoroughly. Use a meat thermometer for large items like roasts or turkeys, and cut into other pieces of meat to check if they are done.

- When reheating meals, cover them and reheat them thoroughly.

You also may want to write to the U.S. Department of Agriculture, Washington, DC 20250, or contact it via the Internet at www.usda.gov. The department has a number of extremely helpful pamphlets and newsletters, including special ones about cooking on a grill and preparing holiday turkeys.

Hepatitis

Hepatitis is an inflammation of the liver that, in children, is almost always caused by one of several viruses. In some children it may cause no symptoms, while in others it can provoke fever, jaundice (yellow skin), loss of appetite, nausea, and vomiting. There are at least six forms of hepatitis, each categorized according to the type of virus that causes it:

1. Hepatitis A, also called infectious hepatitis or epidemic jaundice

2. Hepatitis B, also known as serum hepatitis or transfusion jaundice

3. Hepatitis C, which is an important cause of chronic hepatitis

4. Hepatitis D, or delta virus hepatitis, which causes disease in persons acutely or chronically ill with hepatitis B

5. Hepatitis E, which causes particularly severe disease in pregnant women

6. Hepatitis G, which is one of the most recently recognized types of hepatitis

Approximately 400,000 cases of hepatitis occur in the United States each year. About one-half of these are caused by hepatitis B; of the remainders, slightly less than one-half are caused by hepatitis A, and nearly all of the remainder are hepatitis C.

Children, especially those in low socioeconomic groups, have the highest incidence of hepatitis A infection. However, because they often have no symptoms, their illnesses may go unrecognized.

Hepatitis A can be transmitted directly from person to person or through contaminated food or water. Commonly, human feces are infected with the virus, so in a child care or household setting, the infection can be spread when hands are not washed after having a bowel movement or after changing the diaper of an infected infant. Anyone who drinks water contaminated with infected human feces or who eats raw shellfish taken from polluted areas also may become infected. A child infected with hepatitis A virus will become ill from two to six weeks after the virus is transmitted. The illness usually disappears within one month after it begins.

Although hepatitis A is rarely transmitted

via contaminated blood or semen, hepatitis B is spread through these body fluids. The incidence of hepatitis B infection is now greatest among adolescents, young adults, and in the newborns of women who are infected with the virus. When a pregnant woman has acute or chronic hepatitis B, she may transmit the infection to her newborn at the time of delivery. Among adults and adolescents, the virus can be transmitted during sexual activity.

In the past, hepatitis C was acquired from contaminated blood transfusions. With screening of all donors using new, sensitive tests, however, blood contaminated with the hepatitis C virus is now discovered and discarded. Hepatitis C also can be acquired by intravenous (IV) drug abusers who use contaminated needles. However, the use of sterile disposable needles and the screening of all blood and blood products has essentially eliminated the risk of transmission of hepatitis B and C in hospitals and doctors' offices.

Infection with the hepatitis C virus commonly produces no symptoms, or only mild symptoms of fatigue and jaundice. In many cases, however, this form of hepatitis may become chronic and can result in severe liver disease, liver failure, cancer of the liver, and death.

Signs and Symptoms

A child could have hepatitis without anyone being aware of it, since many affected children have few, if any, symptoms. In some children the only signs of disease may be malaise and fatigue for several days. In others there will be a fever followed by the appearance of jaundice (the sclera, or whites of the eyes, and the skin develop noticeable yellowish color). This jaundice is due to an abnormal increase in bilirubin (a yellow pigment) in the blood, caused by liver inflammation.

With hepatitis B, fever is less likely to occur, although the child may suffer loss of appetite, nausea, vomiting, abdominal pain, and malaise, in addition to jaundice.

If you suspect that your child has jaundice, notify your pediatrician. She will order blood tests to determine if hepatitis is causing the problem, or if it is due to another condition. You should contact your doctor anytime vomiting and/or abdominal pain persist beyond a few hours, or if appetite loss, nausea, or malaise continue for more than a few days. These may be indicators of hepatitis.

Treatment

In most settings, there is no specific treatment for hepatitis. As with most viral infections, the body's own defense mechanisms usually will overcome the infecting agent. Although you do not need to rigidly restrict the diet or activity of your child, you may need to make adjustments depending on his appetite and energy levels. Avoid aspirin and acetaminophen, because of the risk of toxicity due to inadequate liver function. Also, children on certain medications for long-term illnesses should have their dosages carefully reviewed by the pediatrician, again to avoid the toxicity that might result because the liver is unable to handle the usual medication load.

A few medications are available for patients with hepatitis B and hepatitis C. Most of these drugs are not approved for use in children, however. If your child's hepatitis becomes a chronic condition, your pediatrician will recommend a specialist to help decide on appropriate follow-up care and to consider whether medications should be used.

Most children with hepatitis do not need to be hospitalized. However, if loss of appetite or vomiting is interfering with your child's fluid intake and posing a risk of dehydration, your pediatrician may recommend that he be hospitalized. You should contact your doctor immediately if your youngster appears very lethargic, unresponsive, or delirious, as these may indicate that his illness is worsening and hospitalization is indicated.

Many infants with hepatitis B develop chronic hepatitis. Cirrhosis (scarring of the liver) may follow recovery in some of these children. Death, however, occurs rarely. There is no chronic infection following hepatitis A; in comparison, about ten of every hundred people infected with hepatitis B become chronic carriers of the virus. A much higher percentage of infants who are born to mothers with acute or chronic hepatitis B become chronic carriers if they are not properly immunized with the vaccine developed for protection against the hepatitis B virus. As chronic hepatitis B carriers, they would be at risk for the development of liver cancer many years later.

A vaccine also is now available for protecting your child against hepatitis A. This vaccine, first licensed in 1995, is recommended for certain international travelers, for adults employed in certain high-risk occupations, and for all children living in states where hepatitis A infection is most common. Check with your pediatrician to see if your state is one of these.

Prevention

Handwashing before eating and after using the toilet is the most important preventive measure against hepatitis. Children should be taught as young as possible to wash their hands at these times. If your child is in child care, check to be sure that members of the staff wash their hands after handling diapers and before feeding the children.

Hepatitis is not transmitted simply by being in the same school or room with an infected person, or by talking to him, shaking his hand, or playing a board game with him. A hepatitis A infection can occur if there has been a direct exposure to food or water contaminated with feces from a person infected with hepatitis A. It might be transmitted during kissing, the mouthing of toys, or sharing food or utensils. For hepatitis B, there must be direct contact with the blood or bodily fluids of an infected person.

If you find out that your child has been exposed to a person with hepatitis, immediately contact your pediatrician, who will determine if the exposure has placed your youngster at risk. If there's a chance of infection, the doctor may administer an injection of gamma globulin or a hepatitis vaccine, depending on which hepatitis virus was involved.

Prior to foreign travel with your child, consult your physician to determine the risk of exposure to hepatitis in the countries you plan to visit. In certain situations, gamma globulin and/or a hepatitis A vaccine may be indicated.

It is now recommended that all newborn infants, children, and adolescents be immunized against hepatitis B. (See immunization schedule on page 73.)

Hydrocele (Communicating Hydrocele, Infant Hernia)

The testicles of the developing male grow inside his abdominal cavity, moving down through a tube (the inguinal canal) into the scrotum as birth nears. When this movement takes place, the lining of the abdominal wall (peritoneum) is pulled along with the testes to form a sac connecting the testicle with the abdominal cavity. The opening into the abdominal space usually closes. If it does not, and the passage remains open, the fluid that normally surrounds the abdominal organs will flow through it and collect in the scrotal area. This is called a communicating hydrocele (pronounced hy-dro-seal).

As many as half of all newborn boys have this problem; however, it usually disappears within one year without any treatment. Although most common in newborns, hydroceles also can develop later in childhood, most often in association with a hernia (see below).

If your son has a hydrocele, he probably will not complain, but you or he will notice that one side of his scrotum is swollen. In an infant or young boy, this swelling decreases at night or when he is resting or lying down. When he gets more active or is crying, it increases, then subsides when he quiets again. Your pediatrician will make the final diagnosis by shining a bright light through the scrotum, to show the fluid surrounding the testicle.

If your baby is born with a hydrocele, your pediatrician will examine it at each regular checkup until around one year of age. During this time your child should not feel any discomfort in the scrotum or the surrounding area. If he seems to be tender in this area or has unexplained discomfort, nausea, or vomiting, call the doctor at once. These are signs that a piece of intestine may have entered the scrotal area along with abdominal

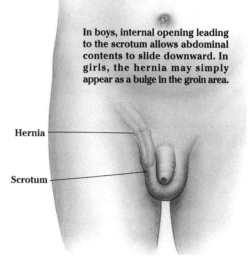

In boys, internal opening leading to the scrotum allows abdominal contents to slide downward. In girls, the hernia may simply appear as a bulge in the groin area.

Hernia

Scrotum

fluid. (See *Inguinal Hernia,* below.) If this occurs and the intestine gets trapped in the scrotum, your son probably will require immediate surgery to release the trapped intestine and close the opening between the abdominal wall and scrotum.

If the hydrocele persists beyond one year without causing pain, a similar surgical procedure may be recommended. In this operation, the excess fluid is removed and the opening into the abdominal cavity closed.

Inguinal Hernia

If you notice a small lump or bulge in your child's groin area or an enlargement of the scrotum, you may have discovered an inguinal hernia. This condition, which is present in five of every hundred children (most commonly in boys), occurs when an opening in the lower abdominal wall allows the child's intestine to squeeze through.

A hernia in a child is due to a failure of normal protrusions from the peritoneum to close properly before birth. The peritoneum is a large, balloonlike sac that surrounds all the organs within the abdomen. Before

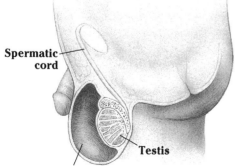

Spermatic cord

Testis

Hydrocele sac with fluid

birth, this sac has two fingerlike projections through the muscle walls that, in boys, lead into the scrotum alongside the testicles and, in girls, lead into the labia. Normally these projections separate from the rest of the peritoneum before birth, producing in boys protective sacs for the testicles inside the scrotum. When these extensions do not close properly, a small portion of the bowel may push through into the groin or scrotum, producing a hernia. If the opening is very small and only abdominal fluid comes down into the sac, it is called a hydrocele (see page 514).

Most hernias do not cause any discomfort, and you or the pediatrician will discover them only by seeing the bulge. Although this kind of hernia must be treated, it is not an emergency condition. You should, however, notify your doctor, who may instruct you to have the child lie down and elevate his legs. Sometimes this will cause the bulge to disappear. However, your doctor will still want to examine the area as soon as possible.

Rarely, a piece of the intestine gets trapped in the hernia, causing swelling and pain. (If you touch the area, it will be tender.) This condition is called an incarcerated (trapped) hernia and does require immediate medical attention.

Treatment

Even if the hernia is not incarcerated, it still needs to be surgically repaired as soon as possible. The surgeon also may check the other side to see if it, too, needs to be corrected, since it is very common for the same defect to be present there.

If the hernia is causing pain, it may indicate that a piece of intestine has become trapped, or incarcerated. In that case, your pediatrician will need to be consulted immediately. He may try to move the trapped piece of intestine out of the sac. Even if this can be done, the hernia still needs to be surgically repaired soon thereafter. If the intestine remains trapped despite the physician's efforts, emergency surgery must be performed to prevent permanent damage to the intestine.

Malabsorption

Sometimes children who eat a balanced diet suffer from malnutrition. The reason for this may be malabsorption, the body's inability to absorb nutrients from the digestive system into the bloodstream.

Normally the digestive process converts nutrients from the diet into small units that pass through the wall of the intestine and into the bloodstream, where they are carried to other cells in the body. If the intestinal wall is damaged by a virus or bacterial infection or by parasites, its surface may change so that digested substances cannot pass through. When this happens, the nutrients will be eliminated through the stool.

Malabsorption commonly occurs in a normal child for a day or two during severe cases of stomach or intestinal flu. It rarely lasts much longer. However, if two or more of the following signs or symptoms seem to persist, notify your pediatrician.

Signs and Symptoms

Possible signs and symptoms of malabsorption include the following:

- Abdominal pain and vomiting

- Frequent, loose, bulky, foul-smelling stools

- Increased susceptibility to infection

- Loss of fat and muscle

- Increase in bruises and bone fractures

- Dry, scaly skin rashes

- Personality changes

- Slowing of growth and weight gain (may not be noticeable for several months)

Not all children who have absorption problems display these symptoms. Some simply consume more food to make up for the nutrients they're losing. In others, the digestive surface of the intestine heals so quickly there is no significant discomfort or damage. In these cases, malabsorption is no cause for concern.

Treatment

When a child suffers from malnutrition, malabsorption is just one of the possible causes. She might be undernourished because she's not getting enough of the right types of food, or she has digestive problems that prevent her body from digesting them. She also might have a combination of these problems. Before prescribing a treatment, the pediatrician must determine the cause. This can be done in one or more of the following ways.

- You may be asked to list the amount and type of food your child eats.

- The pediatrician may test the child's ability to digest and absorb specific nutrients. For example, the doctor might have her drink a solution of milk sugar (lactose) and then measure the level of hydrogen in her breath afterward. This is known as a lactose hydrogen breath test.

- The pediatrician may collect and analyze stool samples. In healthy people, only a small amount of the fat consumed each day is lost through the stool. If too much is found in the stool, it is an indication of malabsorption.

- Collection of sweat from the skin, called a sweat test, may be performed to see if cystic fibrosis (see page 718) is present. In this disease, the body produces insufficient amounts of certain enzymes necessary for proper digestion and an abnormality in the sweat.

- In some cases the pediatrician might request a specialist to take a small piece of the wall of the small intestine (a biopsy) and have it examined under the microscope for signs of infection, inflammation, or other injury.

Ordinarily, these tests are performed before any treatment is begun, although a seriously sick child might be hospitalized in order to receive special feedings while her problem is being evaluated.

Once the physician is sure the problem is malabsorption, she will try to identify a specific reason for its presence. When the reason is infection, the treatment usually will include antibiotics. If malabsorption occurs because the intestine is too active, certain medications may be used to counteract this, so that there's time for the nutrients to be absorbed.

Sometimes there's no clear cause for the problem. In this case, the diet may be changed to include foods or special nutritional formulas that are more easily tolerated and absorbed.

Milk Allergy

Everyone has heard of children who are allergic to ordinary cow's milk. It's actually a rare occurrence. Only two to three of every one hundred children develop a true milk protein allergy. It usually appears in the first few months of life, when an infant's digestive system is still quite immature.

If other family members have allergies, your baby may be more likely to develop a milk allergy. This likelihood will increase further if he's fed cow's milk formula from birth. Breastfeeding will delay if not prevent the onset of a milk allergy. Once in a while a very sensitive breastfed baby may develop this condition because milk products consumed by the mother may be passed to the baby through the breastmilk.

The symptoms of milk allergy may appear anywhere from a few minutes to a few hours after the baby consumes the product, but the most severe symptoms usually occur within half an hour. The most common symptoms are:

- Colic: inconsolable crankiness or fussiness, often interfering with normal sleep (See *Colic,* page 497.)

- Vomiting and/or diarrhea (See pages 522 and 505.)

  Less common symptoms are

- Constipation (See page 503.)

- Bleeding in the digestive tract

If the milk allergy affects the respiratory system, the baby also may have chronic nasal stuffiness, a runny nose, cough, wheezing, or difficulty in breathing. The allergy also can cause eczema, hives, swelling, itching, or a rash around the mouth and on the chin due to contact with milk. (See *Cough,* page 548; *Eczema,* page 693; *Hives,* page 698.)

If you suspect your baby has an allergy to milk, tell your pediatrician, and be sure to mention whether there's a family history of milk allergy. Take your child to the doctor's office or emergency room *immediately* if he

- Has difficulty breathing

- Turns blue

- Is extremely pale or weak

- Has generalized hives

- Develops swelling in the head and neck region

- Has bloody diarrhea

Treatment

If your pediatrician suspects that a milk allergy is present, first he will try eliminating milk and milk products completely for a period of time to see if there is any improvement. If there is, your child may then be given a milk trial—that is, a controlled introduction of milk to the diet. This will reveal whether the symptoms decrease or disappear when milk is avoided and if they reappear when it's introduced again. *This trial of milk should be carried out cautiously and under the supervision of a physician.* Infants who are allergic to milk can become sick quickly, even if exposed to only a small amount.

Your pediatrician can use several appropriate medications to treat the symptoms of milk allergy. These include antihistamines, decongestants, and antiasthma medication (if wheezing is among your child's allergy symptoms). The most important treatment, however, is to eliminate milk and milk products from your child's diet (or from yours if you're breastfeeding). When milk is avoided completely for a long enough period of time, most children eventually will outgrow the allergy. One in two children outgrow it by age one; three in four children outgrow it by age two; and more than eight in ten outgrow a milk allergy by three to four years. This allergy seldom lasts until adolescence.

In the meantime, children with milk allergy must avoid cheese, yogurt, ice cream, and cow's milk formula as well as any food that contains milk. You also must check all processed food labels for casein, caseinate, and whey—they are all milk products and must be avoided, too. A bottle-fed infant will need a milk substitute, such as a soybean formula. If he's also sensitive to soy protein (some infants and children are allergic to both soy and milk), your doctor will suggest still another milk substitute. Do not use goat's milk as a substitute, however; it is too similar to cow's milk. Older children who can eat a wide variety of calcium-containing foods usually don't need a milk substitute.

If your breastfed infant develops a milk allergy, you'll have to have a milk-free diet yourself. (You'll also need to start taking calcium and vitamin supplements.) When you wean your baby, delay feeding him cow's milk as long as possible, and give it very cautiously at first, at the direction of your doctor.

You may be tempted to let your child "cheat" on the milk-free diet once his symptoms lessen or disappear. Don't! If you give your child even small quantities of milk or its products, he may continue to have mild symptoms or an ongoing hidden reaction, and he may even develop other food allergies. In the process, you also may prolong the milk allergy and reduce his chance of outgrowing it.

We can't overemphasize the importance of a milk-free diet for a child with milk allergy. If the diet is ignored, his allergy may lead to potentially serious complications, including dehydration due to severe vomiting or diarrhea; loss of weight from chronic diarrhea; anemia caused by gastrointestinal bleeding; infected eczema; severe difficulty breathing; and occasionally an inflammation of the lungs resembling recurrent pneumonia. The very worst complication, acute shock, is rare but can be fatal.

By the way, be sure to tell all of your child's caregivers (including babysitters and those in child care settings) of your child's milk allergy so he is not given milk by mistake.

Prevention

In general, breastfeeding a baby is the best way to prevent the onset of milk allergy. Particularly if anyone in the immediate family is allergy-prone, you should plan to breastfeed your baby for as long as possible, preferably for six months or more. While doing so, you'll need to minimize or perhaps eliminate your own intake of milk products. And when you eventually introduce other foods to your baby, you'll want to do it gradually (a new one at one- or two-week intervals), watching for the signs of allergy mentioned previously.

If you cannot breastfeed, ask your pediatrician to guide you in selecting an appropriate formula. Use of a protein hydrolysate formula may help prevent food allergy in a child at risk of food allergy.

Pinworms

Fortunately, the most common type of worm infesting children, the pinworm, is essentially harmless. The pinworm is unpleasant to look at and may cause itching and, in girls, vaginal discharge, but it is not responsible for more serious health concerns. Pinworms cause more social concern than medical problems.

Pinworms are spread easily from one child to another by the transfer of eggs. The mature pinworm, which lives in the intestinal tract and around the anal area, lays its eggs on the skin around the anus and buttocks. An infested child may get the tiny eggs on her hand when scratching the area or while wiping after a bowel movement, or the eggs may be left on the toilet seat, to be picked up by the next person who uses it. If the child does not wash the eggs off her hands, she may transfer them to her mouth or to other objects she touches, including the hands or mouth of another person.

Another child picks up the eggs by touching the infested child's hands or objects she handled. She then transfers them to her own mouth by putting her hands in her mouth or mouthing contaminated material.

After the eggs are swallowed, they remain in the small intestine until they hatch, and the small worms travel to the end of the intestine, where they mature and mate. The female then deposits eggs around the anus, and the thirty-five-day life cycle is ready to be repeated. If the new eggs are not ingested, however, the infection ends at this time.

Your child may become aware that she has itching around her behind at night. This may be due to pinworms and the itching occurs when the adult worms move from the rectum to the anus. This movement can cause irritation and, sometimes, intense itching. If the worms crawl into the vaginal area, they may cause pain and a slight discharge. In many children, however, pinworms cause absolutely no discomfort, and may be detected only if the mature worms are seen while depositing their eggs.

The adult worms are whitish gray and threadlike, measuring about ¼ to ½ inch (0.63–1.27 cm) long. You might see them on the skin around the anus, or you or your pediatrician might collect some of the worms and eggs by applying the sticky side of a strip of clear cellophane tape to the skin around the anus. The tape can be examined under a microscope to confirm the presence of the parasite.

Treatment

Pinworms can be treated easily with an oral prescription drug, taken in a single dose and then repeated in one to two weeks. This medication causes the mature pinworms to be expelled through bowel movements. Some pediatricians may advise treating the other family members, as well, since one of them may be a carrier without having any symptoms. None of these medicines is recommended for use in children under two years of age. Also, when the infection is resolved, the child's underclothes, bedclothes, and sheets should be washed carefully to reduce the risk of reinfection.

Prevention

It is very difficult to prevent pinworms, but here are some hints that might be helpful.

- Encourage your child to wash her hands after using the bathroom.

- Encourage her sitter or child care provider to wash the toys frequently, particularly if pinworms have been detected in one or more of the children.

- Encourage your child to wash her hands after playing with a house cat or dog, since these pets can carry the eggs in their fur.

Reye Syndrome

Reye syndrome (often referred to as Reye's syndrome) is a rare but very serious illness that usually occurs in children between the ages of three and twelve. It can affect all organs of the body, but most often injures the brain and the liver. Most children who survive an episode of Reye syndrome do not suffer any lasting consequences. However, this illness can lead to permanent brain damage or death.

Reye syndrome is preceded by a viral infection, such as chickenpox or influenza. However, because it affects only an extremely small number of the children who have these infections, there must be another cause in addition to the infection. Although no one knows exactly what this second cause is, there are three major theories:

1. An unusual reaction to common medications, such as aspirin, which are taken during a viral illness

2. A toxin or poison that is released from inside the body while the susceptible child has a viral illness

3. Chemical changes within the body caused by viral illness in a child who is particularly susceptible

Because so many children were given aspirin during the viral illness that preceded development of Reye syndrome, the first theory is the most widely accepted at this time.

Signs and Symptoms

Whenever your child has a viral illness, be alert for the following pattern, which is typical of Reye syndrome.

1. Your child has had a viral infection, such as influenza, an upper respiratory illness, or chickenpox, and he seems to be improving; his fever is decreasing.

2. Then he abruptly starts to vomit repeatedly and frequently every one or two hours over a twenty-four- to thirty-six-hour period.

3. During that twenty-four- to thirty-six-hour period, he shows variations in his level of consciousness. He may be lethargic or sleepy and then become agitated, delirious, or angry. Then he may become confused or even become unresponsive.

4. If the disease progresses, there is a strong chance he will have seizures and go into a deep coma.

Call your pediatrician as soon as you suspect that your child's illness is following this pattern. If your doctor is not available, take your child to the nearest emergency room. It is very important to diagnose this illness as early as possible. Children with Reye syndrome must be hospitalized. In some cases it may be necessary to transfer the child to a center that specializes in the treatment of this condition.

The diagnosis is made by testing the child's blood and spinal fluid. Because other diseases may resemble Reye syndrome, sometimes it is necessary to examine a specimen of liver tissue under a microscope. If so, a liver biopsy will be performed by inserting a needle through the anesthetized skin into the liver.

Prevention

Because we do not know the exact cause of Reye syndrome, it is difficult to prevent it. However, since the medical community issued a public warning against the use of aspirin during viral illnesses, the number of cases of Reye syndrome has decreased greatly. Therefore, *we strongly recommend that you do not give aspirin or any medications containing aspirin to your child or teenager when he has any viral illness, particularly chickenpox or influenza.* If he needs medication for mild fever or discomfort, give him acetaminophen or ibuprofen (see pages 636 and 638). Ibuprofen is approved for use in children six months of age or older; however, it should never be given to children who are dehydrated or who are vomiting continuously.

Vomiting

Because many common childhood illnesses can cause vomiting, you should expect your child to have this problem several times during these early years. Usually it ends quickly without treatment, but this doesn't make it any easier for you to watch. That feeling of helplessness combined with the fear that something serious might be wrong and the desire to do something to make it better may make you tense and anxious. To help put your mind at ease, learn as much as you can about the causes of vomiting and what you can do to treat your child when it occurs.

First of all, there's a difference between real vomiting and just spitting up. Vomiting is the forceful throwing up of stomach contents through the mouth. Spitting up (most commonly seen in infants under one year of age) is the easy flow of stomach contents out of the mouth, frequently with a burp.

Vomiting occurs when the abdominal muscles and diaphragm contract vigorously while the stomach is relaxed. This reflex action is triggered by the "vomiting center" in the brain after it has been stimulated by:

- Nerves from the stomach and intestine when the gastrointestinal tract is either irritated or swollen by an infection or blockage

- Chemicals in the blood (e.g., drugs)

- Psychological stimuli from disturbing sights or smells

- Stimuli from the middle ear (as in vomiting caused by motion sickness)

The common causes of spitting up or vomiting vary according to age. During the first few months, for instance, most infants will spit up small amounts of formula or breastmilk, usually within the first hour after being fed. This "cheesing," as it is often called, is simply the occasional movement of food from the stomach, through the tube (esophagus) leading to it, and out of the mouth. It will occur less often if a child is burped frequently and if active play is limited right after meals. This spitting up tends to decrease as the baby becomes older, but may persist in a mild form until ten to twelve months of age. Spitting up is not serious and doesn't interfere with normal weight gain. (See *Spitting Up,* page 119.)

Occasional vomiting may occur during the first month. If it appears repeatedly or is unusually forceful, call your pediatrician. It may be just a mild feeding difficulty, but it also could be a sign of something more serious.

Between two weeks and four months of age, persistent forceful vomiting may be caused by a thickening of the muscle at the stomach exit. Known as hypertrophic pyloric stenosis, this thickening prevents food from passing into the intestines. It requires *immediate* medical attention. Surgery usually is required to open the narrowed area. The important sign of this condition is forceful vomiting occurring approximately fifteen to thirty minutes or less after every feeding. Anytime you notice this, call your pediatrician as soon as possible.

Occasionally the spitting up in the first few weeks to months of life gets worse instead of better—that is, even though it's not forceful, it occurs all the time. This happens when the muscles at the lower end of the esophagus become overly relaxed and allow the stomach contents to back up. This condition is known as gastroesophageal reflux disease, or GERD. This condition usually can be controlled by doing the following:

1. Thicken the milk with small amounts of baby cereal.

2. Avoid overfeeding.

3. Burp the baby frequently.

4. Leave the infant in a quiet, upright position for at least thirty minutes following feeding.

If these steps are not successful, your pediatrician may refer you to a gastrointestinal (GI) specialist.

After the first few months of life, the most common cause of vomiting is a stomach or intestinal infection. Viruses are by far the most frequent infecting agents, but occasionally bacteria and even parasites may be the cause. The infection also may produce fever, diarrhea, and sometimes nausea and abdominal pain. The infection is usually contagious; if your child has it, chances are good that some of her playmates also will be affected.

Occasionally infections outside the gastrointestinal tract will cause vomiting. These include infections of the respiratory system, infections of the urinary tract (see page 647), otitis media (see page 580), and pneumonia (see page 553), as well as meningitis (see page 655), appendicitis (see page 500), and Reye syndrome (see page 520). Some of these conditions require immediate medical treatment, so be alert for the following trouble signs, whatever your child's age, and call your pediatrician if they occur.

- Blood or bile (a green-colored material) in the vomitus

- Severe abdominal pain

- Strenuous, repeated vomiting

- Swollen abdomen

- Lethargy or severe irritability

- Convulsions

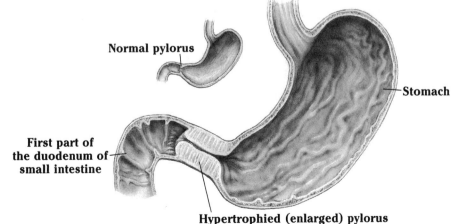

Normal pylorus

Stomach

First part of the duodenum of small intestine

Hypertrophied (enlarged) pylorus muscle with narrowed stomach outlet

- Signs or symptoms of dehydration, including dry mouth, absent tears, depression of the "soft spot," and decreased urination

- Inability to drink adequate amounts of fluid

- Vomiting continuing beyond twenty-four hours

Treatment

In most cases, vomiting will stop without specific medical treatment. You should never use over-the-counter or prescription remedies unless they've been specifically prescribed by your pediatrician for your child and for this particular illness.

When your infant or young child is vomiting, keep her lying on her stomach or side as much as possible. Doing this will minimize the chances of her inhaling vomit into her upper airway and lungs.

When there is continued vomiting, you need to make certain that dehydration doesn't occur. *Dehydration* is a term used when the body loses so much water that it can no longer function efficiently (see *Signs of Dehydration,* page 506). If allowed to reach a severe degree, it can be serious and life-threatening. To prevent this from happening, make sure your child consumes enough extra fluids to restore what has been lost through throwing up. If she vomits these fluids, notify your pediatrician.

For the first twenty-four hours or so of any illness that causes vomiting, keep your child off solid foods, and encourage her to suck or drink clear fluids, such as water, sugar water (½ teaspoon [2.5 ml] sugar in 4 ounces [120 ml] of water), Popsicles, gelatin water (1 teaspoon [5 ml] of flavored gelatin in 4 ounces

of water), or preferably an electrolyte solution (ask your pediatrician which one), instead of eating. Liquids not only help to prevent dehydration, but also are less likely than solid foods to stimulate further vomiting.

Here are some guidelines to follow for giving your child fluids *after* she has vomited.

1. Wait for two to three hours after the last vomiting episode, and then give 1 to 2 ounces (30–60 ml) of cool water every half hour to one hour for four feedings.

2. If she retains this, give 2 ounces (60 ml) of electrolyte solution alternated with 2 ounces of clear liquids every half hour.

3. If this is retained for two feedings, add half-strength formula or milk (depending on age), and continue increasing the quantity slowly to 3 to 4 ounces (90–120 ml) every three or four hours.

4. After twelve to twenty-four hours with no additional vomiting, gradually return your child to her normal diet, but continue to give her plenty of clear fluids.

In most cases, your child will just need to stay at home and receive a liquid diet for twelve to twenty-four hours. Your pediatrician usually won't prescribe a drug to treat the vomiting.

If your child also has diarrhea (see page 505), ask your pediatrician for instructions on giving liquids and restoring solids to her diet.

If she can't retain any clear liquids or if the symptoms become more severe, notify your pediatrician. She will examine your child and may order blood and urine tests or X rays to make a diagnosis. Occasionally hospital care may be necessary.

17

BEHAVIOR

Anger, Aggression, and Biting

We all have feelings of anger and aggression, and so does your child. These impulses are normal and healthy. As a toddler or preschooler, your youngster may lack the self-control to express his anger peacefully. Instead, he may naturally lash out, perhaps hitting or biting in frustration. When this happens, he needs you to take control for him and to help him develop judgment, self-discipline, and the other tools he needs in order to express his feelings in more acceptable and age-appropriate ways.

While occasional outbursts are normal in youngsters, especially during temper tantrums, it is not normal for a child to have frequent rages in which he attacks others or himself. Most children usually get angry at others only when they are provoked. Unless they are very tired or overstressed, they usually can be distracted or consoled, and

will quickly forget their anger. They may cry, argue, or yell, but they resort to violence only when they are extremely frustrated.

Some children are supersensitive, easily offended, and quickly angered. Many of these youngsters have been tense and unusually active since birth. They are often more difficult to soothe and settle as infants. Beginning in the preschool years, they show signs of becoming aggressive toward other children, adults, even animals. They often lash out suddenly and for no apparent reason, and may seem to be touchy or irritable most of the time. Even if they hurt someone in their anger, they may or may not feel sorry and may not feel responsible for the incident. Instead, they blame the other child for "making me angry," as if this excuses their own actions.

Your child might go through a brief period of this kind of behavior if he's particularly worried, tired, or overstressed, but if it continues for more than a few weeks, and is especially aggressive, consult your pediatrician. If it becomes a routine daily pattern for more than three to six months, it should be viewed as a serious problem.

This extreme form of aggressive behavior can lead to serious social and emotional problems if allowed to continue. The child eventually loses all his friends, which makes him even more tense and irritable, and seriously damages his self-esteem. There is always the danger that he will seriously injure himself or others, and the problems will multiply when he reaches school age. Then his aggressive behavior may cause him to be suspended or expelled from school. Because he has so little self-esteem, he may later become self-destructive, abuse drugs or alcohol, become accident-prone, or even attempt suicide.

No one knows exactly what causes conduct disorder. The problem may lie in the child's biological makeup, the relationships within the family, or a combination of the two. In many cases, other members of the child's family behave aggressively, and the atmosphere within the family is tense and stressful. In some cases, however, there is no clear explanation for the child's behavior.

What You Can Do

The best way to prevent aggressive behavior is to give your child a stable, secure home life with firm, loving discipline and full-time supervision during the toddler and preschool years. Everyone who cares for your child should be a good role model and agree on the rules he's expected to observe as well as the response to use if he disobeys. Whenever he breaks an important rule, he should be reprimanded *immediately* so that he understands exactly what he's done wrong.

Your youngster has little natural self-control. He needs you to teach him not to kick, hit, or bite when he is angry, but in-

stead to express his feelings through words. It's important for him to learn the difference between real and imagined insults and between appropriately standing up for his rights and attacking out of anger.

The best way to teach these lessons is to supervise your child carefully when he's involved in disputes with his playmates. As long as a disagreement is minor, you can keep your distance and let the youngsters solve it on their own. However, you must intervene when children get into a physical fight that continues even after they're told to stop, or when one child seems to be in an uncontrollable rage and is assaulting or biting the other. Pull the children apart and keep them separate until they have calmed down. If the fight is extremely violent, you may have to end the play session. Make it clear that it doesn't matter who "started it." There is no excuse for trying to hurt each other.

To avoid or minimize "high-risk" situations, teach your child ways to deal with his anger without resorting to aggressive behavior. Teach him to say "no" in a firm tone of voice, to turn his back, or to find compromises instead of fighting with his body. Through example, teach him that settling differences with words is more effective—and more civilized—than with physical violence. Praise him on his appropriate behavior and help explain to him how "grown-up" he is acting whenever he uses these tactics instead of hitting, kicking, or biting.

Always watch your own behavior around your child. One of the best ways to teach him appropriate behavior is to control your own temper. If you express your anger in quiet, peaceful ways, he probably will follow your example. If you must discipline him, do not feel guilty about it and certainly don't apologize. If he senses your mixed feelings, he may convince himself that he was in the right all along and you are the "bad" one. Although disciplining your child is never pleasant, it is a necessary part of parenthood, and there is no reason to feel guilty about it. Your child needs to understand when he is in the wrong so that he will take responsibility for his actions and be willing to accept the consequences.

When to Call the Pediatrician

If your child seems to be unusually aggressive for longer than a few weeks, and you cannot cope with his behavior on your own, consult your pediatrician. Other warning signs include:

- Physical injury to himself or others (teeth marks, bruises, head injuries)

- Attacks on you or other adults

- Being sent home or barred from play by neighbors or school

- Your own fear for the safety of those around him

The most important warning sign is the frequency of outbursts. Sometimes children with conduct disorders will go for several days or a week or two without incident, and may even act quite charming during this time, but few can go an entire month without getting into trouble at least once.

Your pediatrician can suggest ways to discipline your child and will help you determine if he has a true conduct disorder. If this is the problem, you probably will not be able to resolve it on your own, and your pediatrician will advise appropriate mental health intervention.

The pediatrician or other mental health specialist will interview both you and your child and may observe your youngster in different situations (home, preschool, with adults and other children). A behav-

ior management program will be outlined. Not all methods work on all children, so there will be a certain amount of trial and reassessment.

Once several effective ways are found to reward good behavior and discourage bad, they can be used in establishing an approach that works both at home and away. The progress may be slow, but such programs usually are successful if started when the disorder is just beginning to develop.

(See also *Temper Tantrums,* page 538, and the sections on discipline in Chapters 9 through 12.)

Computers and the Internet

The use of computers and the availability of the Internet have given both children and adults unprecedented access to knowledge and information. The Internet can provide your child with the ability to explore virtually any topic right at her fingertips. It is an invaluable and vast resource of information about the world around her.

In a fast-changing, increasingly technological world, it is important for youngsters to become skilled at using computers. Even if you don't have a computer in your own home, your child probably has access to one at school, the library, or in child care settings. Certainly even young children can find age-appropriate activities, pictures, and information on the Internet. As children become older, the Internet can become a wonderful resource for helping them with homework assignments. Encyclopedias and many other reference materials are available online. So are databases with news, photos, and important documents.

As a parent, you should be involved in your child's use of the Internet. She needs your experience, judgment, and supervision to help guide her along the Information Superhighway. Not only does she need your help in finding websites that interest her—whether it's pictures of dinosaurs or stories about trips to the moon—but also you need to help her avoid material that may be inappropriate for kids. As her parent, you can offer guidance in a way that no one else can and ensure that her use of the computer is educational, enjoyable, and safe.

While the Internet is a source of unlimited information, some of it may be inappropriate for children. Your child may encounter hate-filled and violent material quite inadvertently. There are also sexually explicit photographs and information about the use of alcohol, tobacco products, and illegal drugs. Keep in mind that child pornography in particular is illegal and should be reported to your local law enforcement agency or the National Center for Missing and Exploited Children (1–800–843–5678; www.missingkids.org).

Consider installing software or use your internet service provider's software to block or filter out offensive websites and material. Contact your Internet service provider, and ask about parental controls and website blocking.

Guidelines for Computer Use

Use of the computer can and should be a family activity. Take the time to explore the Internet with your child, talk about what you've discovered together, answer her questions, and help her begin to develop the skills to become a discriminating Internet user. At the same time, don't let use of the computer become an all-consuming activity; make sure she has plenty of time for play and physical activity, as well.

The American Academy of Pediatrics believes that it's important to create clear rules for your child's Internet experiences. For example:

- Your child should use the Internet only when you're sitting at the computer with her or are close by and can supervise her online activities.

- Set and enforce a daily or weekly time limit for your child's use of the Internet.

- Even at a young age, make sure that your child understands that she should never

---

Special-Needs Children and Computers

If your child has special needs, you can obtain equipment that makes it easier for her to use computers. For example, special screens, keyboards, joysticks, and computerized voice programs allow children with disabilities to enjoy using a computer.

For additional information, contact:

- The ERIC Clearinghouse on Disabilities and Gifted Education (1–800–328–0272; www.ericec.org). This

clearinghouse disseminates many types of information and literature about individuals who have disabilities and/or who are gifted.

- The Starbright Foundation (1–310–479–1212; www.starbright.org) is another excellent resource. It is an organization dedicated to developing projects that empower seriously ill children to face their day-to-day challenges.

give out her name, age, or other personal information over the Internet. Websites aimed at children should never request this kind of information without a parent's permission.

Be particularly cautious about letting your child become involved in so-called chat rooms. These are places where several individuals can communicate with one another in "real time," sending messages that are instantaneously posted on the computer screens of others who are also visiting that particular chat room.

Chat rooms might be an opportunity for children to "meet" other youngsters and find online pen pals from other cultures and parts of the world. But sexual predators also use the Internet to target and entice children—making connections, forming "friendships," and perhaps trying to arrange in-person contact with children. Make sure your child understands that she should not respond to someone who is sending her offensive messages and should let you know about such messages at once. As a warning for the future, if you're going to let your child visit chat rooms, do so cautiously and only with your constant supervision. From the very beginning your child should clearly understand the following:

- People online are not always who they say they are; they may not be the "friends" they claim to be.

- Your child should not open or read e-mails from someone she does not know; she should tell you or a trusted adult about them.

- She should never respond to messages that make her feel uncomfortable or confused, or appear harassing. She should tell a parent immediately.

- She should never arrange a face-to-face meeting with anyone she meets online,

unless you approve and go with her to a public place for the meeting.

- She should never use a credit card online without parental permission.

- She should never share passwords with anyone, including friends.

Remember, a parent's constant supervision of a child's activities on the computer is essential. If you have a computer at home, keep it in the family room or other public area.

Coping with Disasters and Terrorism

Disastrous events—earthquakes, hurricanes, tornadoes, floods, and fires—can be frightening and traumatic for both children and adults. Events like these have always demanded that parents be available to talk with and reassure their children and be particularly sensitive to their youngsters' needs. More recently, since the tragic events of September 11, 2001, parents have been understandably concerned about the effects of terrorism on their children, including the effects of the media's coverage of those events.

What to Expect

Even if terrorism, natural disasters, or other traumatic events occur hundreds or thousands of miles from you and your child, television and newspaper coverage can make the aftermath traumatizing.

If the disaster actually has occurred in your own community, it can be especially frightening for your youngster.

In the aftermath of such a crisis, children may experience posttraumatic stress disorder (PTSD), something comparable to "shell shock" with symptoms that may vary from child to child, depending in part on his age. A youngster up to age five:

- May have difficulty sleeping

- May exhibit a decreased appetite

- May cry and become cranky

- May show defiance, have tantrums, and exhibit hostility toward siblings

- May cling to you, "shadowing" you as you move from one room of the house to another, and show anxiety on leaving your side

- May have nightmares and refuse to sleep in his own bed

- May have bed-wetting episodes, if he's toilet-trained

- May develop physical symptoms, such as stomachaches and headaches

- Might refuse to go to the preschool that he had attended enthusiastically for months or years

What You Can Do

Remember that children tend to personalize events. They may think that a terrorist attack or disaster is going to strike them or their family members. One of your primary goals as a parent is to talk with your child and make him feel secure. Your words and actions can be very powerful in comforting your child and making him feel safe. Talking to him about the events won't increase his fear and anxiety. As you interact with him, speak to him at a level he can understand. Here are some guidelines to keep in mind.

- Listen to what your child says to you. Help him use age-appropriate words to describe his feelings—perhaps "sad," "mad" or "scared." Don't make assumptions, and don't downplay what he's saying. Accept what he's feeling.

- If your child has difficulty expressing himself, encourage him to get his feelings out in other ways—perhaps by drawing pictures or playing with toys.

- At his age, your youngster may not need a lot of information about the events that have happened. Don't be surprised if he asks the same questions over and over. While you should be honest about what you tell him, don't overload him with information.

- If a terrorist attack has happened, explain that there are "bad" people in the world, and bad people do bad things. But make sure he understands that most people are not bad and that most people of all ethnic and religious groups are good. Use this event to teach tolerance to your youngster.

- For an event like a terrorist attack that occurred elsewhere in the country, let him know that the violence was isolated to particular areas, and not in your community.

- Although you always should monitor what your child watches on television, this advice is *particularly* important when coverage of terrorism or other disasters are filling the screen. No matter what your child's age, he can be traumatized by what he sees on television, so restrict his viewing. When he does watch TV, make sure you are there with him, and talk about what you've seen.

- If you appear particularly anxious over what has happened, he'll feel it and find coping more difficult. Try to stay as calm as possible in his presence, and maintain as many of the routines of the family's life as you can. If your child has been going to preschool, for example, the structure of continuing to do so can be comforting to him.

If your youngster has been particularly traumatized by the events that have happened, talk with your pediatrician. She may suggest seeking the help of a mental health professional who specializes in treating children in tough emotional times.

Hyperactivity and the Distractible Child

Almost every child has days when she seems "hyperactive," but true hyperactivity is a condition that affects only about one in twenty children under age twelve. Children who are hyperactive move about a great deal, have trouble sleeping, and cannot sit still for more than a few minutes at a time. They usually are easily distracted, often act on impulse, and have difficulty paying attention when listening or watching events around them. Physicians call this condition of combined hyperactivity and distractibility attention deficit hyperactivity disorder, or ADHD.

Particularly when your child is a toddler, you may worry that she shows signs of hyperactivity, but if you compare her with others her age, you probably will discover that she's normal. Around ages two and three, children naturally are very active and impulsive and have a short attention span. All children occasionally seem overactive or easily distractible—for example, when they're very tired, excited about doing something "spe-

cial," or anxious about being in a strange place or among strangers.

Truly hyperactive children, however, are noticeably *more* active, *more* easily distracted, and *more* excitable than their peers. Most important of all, these children never seem to be calm from one day to the next, nor does their behavior improve as they get older.

Although most have normal intelligence, they may seem like slow learners, because they can't pay attention or follow instructions through to completion. They also are slower to develop control over their impulses and emotions and slower in developing the age-appropriate ability to concentrate and pay attention. They tend to be more talkative, emotional, demanding, disobedient, and noncompliant than others their age. Their behavior often remains immature throughout childhood and adolescence, and may lead to problems in school, among friends, and in some cases with the law. Without support and treatment, children who are truly hyperactive have difficulty developing the self-esteem they need to lead healthy, productive lives.

No one knows exactly what causes hyperactivity. Sometimes the condition can be traced to illnesses affecting the brain or nervous system, such as meningitis, encephalitis, fetal alcohol syndrome, or severe prematurity. Most hyperactive children have never had such an illness, however, and most children who do suffer these ailments do not become hyperactive. Many children with this disorder do have close relatives with similar problems, which suggests that it may be at least partially inherited. Also, boys are four to seven times more likely than girls to develop this problem. In part, this is because boys naturally tend to mature more slowly in these areas of behavior control and regulation, but no one knows precisely why these differences exist. Although there has also been much speculation that certain foods and food additives might be linked to ADHD, extensive research has failed to show conclusively any such link. Children with these problems tend to elicit negative, punitive, and controlling responses from adults or parents who may not understand the true nature of hyperactivity. These children, when subjected to much criticism, only see their self-esteem and self-image more negatively.

Whatever the source of hyperactivity, the way the problem is perceived, understood, and treated and the way parents and teachers respond tends to determine the outcome for the child. Parents who are emotionally healthy and who discipline with gentle firmness, consistency, love, and reward produce the best changes.

When to Call the Pediatrician

Observing your child alongside others her age over a period of days or weeks is the best way to determine if she is hyperactive. For this reason, those who care for her at nursery school or child care may be your best source of information. They can tell you how she behaves in a group and whether she is acting normally for her age. Specific signs of hyperactivity include:

- Difficulty paying attention to activities that interest other children her age

- Difficulty following simple instructions

- Repeated running into the street, interrupting other children's play, racing through off-limit areas without considering consequences

- Unnecessarily hurried activity, such as running, touching, and jumping without periods of rest

- Sudden emotional outbursts, such as crying, angry yelling, hitting, or frustration that seems inappropriate

- Persistent misbehavior despite being told "no" many times

If you and others observe three or more of these warning signs on a continuing basis, consult your pediatrician. The doctor will examine your child to rule out any medical cause for the behavior and then either conduct a further evaluation or refer you to a psychologist or child psychiatrist. The evaluation of hyperactivity ordinarily consists of three parts. The doctor or therapist will ask questions about past behavior and may consult the nursery school or child care providers to see if there's a pattern of behavior over time and in different settings. Developmental testing will determine whether your child is maturing normally mentally and physically. Finally, a play session will reveal whether her emotional development is normal for her age.

If this evaluation suggests that your preschooler is hyperactive, the doctor or therapist probably will recommend some specific behavior strategies for managing her behavior and may even refer you to a special nursery school. Unless the behavior is extremely unmanageable, medication probably won't be prescribed because of possible side effects in a child this young and because many diagnoses of hyperactivity made before age five are uncertain. Toddlers and preschoolers change so rapidly and so dramatically that what might seem like a behavioral problem at one point could disappear a few months later. For this reason, most physicians prefer to watch the child's development over a period of months or even years before prescribing medication for treatment.

Medications are used in severe cases of attention deficit disorder among older children. No medications are recommended for hyperactivity among children under age three.

As a parent of a hyperactive child, you may hear about alternative treatments, some of which are still unproven and some of which have been proven ineffective. Controversial therapies that may be useful in some cases include:

- Play therapy. This approach helps the child to overcome inhibitions and anxieties, but these are not the key problems among most hyperactive children.

- Special physical exercises. These generally are intended to improve motor coordination and increase the child's tolerance for stimulation. Most hyperactive children do have difficulty in these areas, but this is not the cause of the disorder. While such exercises may benefit a hyperactive child, they seem to work mostly because they cause the parents to pay more attention to the child, and this increases her self-esteem.

- Special diets. These are based on the assumption that certain foods produce undesirable behavior. Each diet targets a different group of foods or substances, such as artificial additives, sugar, or common allergenic foods (corn, nuts, chocolate, shellfish, wheat). Scientific evidence to support such diets is weak; however, many parents believe they help. Most of these food plans are healthy and will not cause harm unless the child's eating habits become a source of conflict within the family, or unless they are used instead of other methods for modifying her behavior. No special diet alone can solve the problem of hyperactivity.

Treatments that have been disproven and may be dangerous include:

- Megavitamin therapy

- Special vitamin and mineral supplements

How to Respond

If your child shows signs of hyperactivity, it may mean that she cannot control her behavior on her own. In her hurry and excitement, she may be accident-prone and may be destructive to property. You will have to help her learn to control herself and to pay attention to what she is doing.

To discipline a hyperactive child, you need to respond both "effectively" and "constructively." If your actions are "effective," your child's behavior will improve as a result. If they are "constructive," they also will help develop her self-esteem and make her more personable. The box provides some examples of effective and constructive responses to common problems among hyperactive children.

It is important to respond immediately whenever your child misbehaves and to make sure that everyone caring for her responds to these incidents in the same way. Punishment that hurts, such as spanking or slapping, may stop her temporarily but does not encourage her to control herself and may encourage a continued negative self-image. To the contrary, this approach tells her that it's OK to hurt other people. Loving, appropriate attention is far more effective in the long run.

Television

Your child may view his first television program during infancy and by his third year will have several favorite ones. If you own a TV set and DVD and/or VCR, they will become an important part of his life and will teach him many lessons, some good and some bad.

During the preschool years, your youngster can benefit a great deal from watching educational programming such as *Sesame Street, Mister Rogers' Neighborhood,* nature programs, and broadcasts of concerts or dance. Educational television is not a substitute for reading or playing, but it can enrich your child's life. Such viewing introduces young children to letters, numbers, and experiences they could not have any other way.

Unfortunately, most television programming is not good for youngsters. Even if your child watches only cartoons, he'll see characters hitting, shooting, or otherwise harming each other at a rate of about twenty times per hour. This violence usually occurs without any reasonable explanation, and the victims rarely seem to suffer any pain or have any permanent injuries. Both the heroes and the villains attack one another with lethal weapons, then reappear to fight again. The message to children is that violence is an acceptable way to deal with problems and that it does no real harm. This encourages them to behave more violently and discourages them from objecting when they see others in physical fights. Children viewing many hours per week of violent TV may become numb to violence and may begin to view the world as a scary place.

Television also exposes children to sexuality, drugs, and alcohol use at a time when they are too young to understand the consequences of these issues. Soap operas, prime-time television, music videos, and many other programs inevitably allow your child to see people engaged in or talking about sex, using or selling drugs, smoking, and drinking alcohol. Often these actions are portrayed as if they were exciting, fun things that all adults do. Your child will not see people getting sick, pregnant, or dying as a result of these actions, and will come away with a distorted view of how to handle these issues in his own life. In addition, a great deal of TV perpetuates myths and stereotypes of certain gender tasks and racial associations that will serve as poor influences on children.

Children tend to believe what they see and hear, and they do not understand the concept of a sales pitch. Just as a child believes that the cartoon characters are real creatures, he believes the children in the ads really love the sugar-coated cereals they eat and that the toys shown on TV will be as big and lifelike as they appear. Cartoon programs based on toy products are specifically intended to be attractive, increasing a child's desire to have the full range of characters and equipment.

Furthermore, because your child will see commercials for so many products, he may assume he is deprived if he isn't constantly acquiring new possessions. You will feel this pressure keenly every time you take him shopping and he begs for something that he "has to have" because he's seen it on TV.

Food commercials also can have an undesirable impact on your child's eating habits. Many of these ads push heavily sugared or salted products such as cereals, soft drinks, and snack foods. Less than 5 percent of food ads during the daytime are for more nutritious foods such as fruits and vegetables. As a result, your child gets a very distorted view of what he should be eating. The more commercial television he watches, the more he will demand snack items and the less interested he'll be in healthful foods.

Children who watch a great deal of television are more likely to become obese than are children who tend to be more physically active. One reason is that advertising tends to encourage them to eat more frequently and to select more fattening foods. Another is that much of the time they spend sitting in front of the TV would otherwise be spent actively playing and burning up calories.

All children need active play, not only for the physical exercise but also for proper mental and social development. Watching

TV is passive. It does not help your child acquire the most important skills and experiences he needs at this age, such as communication, creativity, fantasy, judgment, and experimentation. The more time your child spends in front of a TV set, the less he'll have left for other, more worthwhile activities.

What You Can Do

Media-wise children and families are well equipped to enjoy the positive benefits of television and to minimize the negative effects. Media education includes smart, limited use of TV in your home, plus an understanding of how TV programming and advertising work. If you do not make a conscious effort to control your child's television viewing, it could become one of the most important negative influences in his life.

For many youngsters, TV serves as a substitute for friends, babysitters, teachers, and even parents. It is the easiest way to be entertained and quickly becomes habit-forming unless limits are set.

As a general policy, your child should watch no more than one to two hours of quality television programming a day (which compares to about four hours of TV viewing per day for the average child in the United States); the American Academy of Pediatrics recommends *no* television watching at all for children ages two years old and younger (see box below). The one- to two-hour limit includes not only television, but also videos, movies, computer games, and surfing the Internet.

It is easy to enforce these viewing guidelines when your child is an infant or a toddler, but it becomes more difficult as he grows older and more independent, so you should start early. If your child limits his TV watching to no more than two hours a day beginning in early childhood, he shouldn't develop a habit that may be difficult to break later in life. Parents should help children choose shows to watch. When the show is over, the TV should be turned off. To make enforcement easier, keep TV sets, VCRs or DVDs, video games, and computers out of your child's bedroom; instead, place them where you can be involved and monitor your youngster's viewing.

Distraction is the best way to get your

WHERE WE STAND

The first two years of your child's life are especially important in the growth and development of his brain. During this time, children need positive interaction with other youngsters and adults. Too much television can negatively affect early brain development. This is especially true at younger ages, when learning to talk and play with others is so important.

Until more research is done about the effects of TV on very young children, the American Academy of Pediatrics does not recommend television for children ages two years old or younger. For older children, the Academy advises no more than one to two hours per day of educational, nonviolent programs.

child away from television. Invite him to join you in enjoyable but constructive activities such as reading, playing board or outdoor games, coloring, cooking, building, or visits with playmates. Praise him when he entertains himself without relying on television, and present a good model by restricting your own viewing. Do not use television as a reward or withhold it as a punishment. Doing so will only make it seem more enticing.

If these tactics are not effective and your child "sneaks" TV time behind your back, you may need to take more forceful measures, such as removing the television or installing a lockout device so he cannot view certain channels. Since the year 2000, the V-chip device has been installed in every new TV set with a screen 13 inches or larger, giving parents one more tool to control TV viewing in the home. If you're purchasing a new TV set, learn to use the V-chip technology to block programs

A ratings system—called *TV Parental Guidelines*—is also available to alert you to programs that contain violence, sexual situations, and adult language, and help you find programs appropriate for your children. These ratings are generally available for all TV programs except news and sports. Sometimes they are listed in local program logs, and they appear on the TV screen for fifteen seconds at the start of each program.

Even an hour or two of television can be harmful if your child chooses to watch programs that are violent or otherwise inappropriate. Teach him to plan his viewing so you both know in advance what he'll be watching.

Help him find programs that encourage positive behavior instead of violence. If you forbid him to watch a particular show, give him a clear, concise explanation so he understands why. Then make sure the set goes off as soon as his chosen program is over, so he doesn't get involved in the show that follows. Never allow the television set to become a babysitter. Plan a TV-viewing schedule weekly, choosing shows carefully with your child. Be a good role model. If you watch nonstop TV during the evening, your child will not learn to control his viewing.

To help your youngster get the most out of the programs he does watch, view them with him. Even "bad" shows can be educational if you discuss them with him. Keep in mind that children under eight years old cannot differentiate between fantasy and reality, and thus when they see violence on TV, they may not be able to separate "make-believe" from real life, and realize that violence hurts and kills people. So help him understand that the violence he sees on the screen is not actually happening, and that if it were, the characters would be severely injured. Explain that TV shows are "made up" and that the characters are really actors playing imaginary roles. Criticize the characters who drink alcohol, smoke, use drugs, or ride in cars without wearing seat belts. If he knows that you disapprove of these characters, he will start to think about their behavior and question it instead of accepting it automatically. Discuss negative or misleading stereotypes of different people on television; ethnic, gender, religious, or cultural stereotypes teach powerful lessons to young viewers. A wise parent can use TV programming or portrayals to teach and transmit positive values.

When watching television with your child, you also can educate him about advertising. Teach him that commercials are not the same as programs and that their sole purpose is to make him want something he doesn't have. This is not an easy lesson for a preschooler, but if you explain the difference between "healthy" and "unhealthy" foods and good- and poor-quality playthings, it will help him become a more critical viewer. Pointing out any advertised products that he's tried and rejected will help him realize how misleading commercials can be.

Where We Stand

Although the American Academy of Pediatrics does not hold television solely responsible for violence in our society, we believe that televised violence has a clear effect on the behavior of children and contributes to the frequency with which violence is used to resolve conflict. The absence of consequences of the TV violence that children see and the rapidity with which difficulties are resolved by the use of violence increase the likelihood that violence will be among the first strategies that a child selects, rather than the last.

Together, parents, broadcasters, and advertisers must be held responsible for the television that children see. We urge parents to limit the amount of TV that their children view, to monitor what their children are watching, and to watch TV with them to help them learn from what they see.

The American Academy of Pediatrics strongly supports legislative efforts to improve the quality of children's programming.

The primary goal of commercial children's television is to sell products—from toys to junk food—to youngsters. Young children in particular cannot distinguish between programs and their commercials, nor do they fully understand that commercials are designed to sell them (and their parents) something.

Television is also guilty of distorting reality on matters such as drugs, alcohol, tobacco, sexuality, family relations, and sex roles.

You also can help improve television programming for children by contacting the networks, commercial sponsors, or local broadcasters. Voice your complaints and your preferences. If there is a program you especially like, be sure to let the local station manager know, because quality programs often have low ratings, and your support can help keep them on the air.

Become involved in local advocacy groups for better children's TV; join local, community-based coalitions for "Turn Off the Violence" events; and urge local schools to teach media literacy.

Other forms of media, including rock music and music videos, film, video games and computer games, and the Internet, present more of the same challenges to families as does television. As children spend more and more time in front of screens or listening to music, powerful lessons about violence, sexuality, substance abuse, relationships, and the world are taught and absorbed. You should supervise your child when he uses the Internet or any of these other forms of the media. Parents should be aware of the media consumed by their children and should set time limits, co-view or co-listen with children, and discuss content and portrayals. Media-educated families and children are in the best position to resist the negative influences of the media.

Temper Tantrums

Temper tantrums are not fun for you or your child, but they are a normal part of life with most preschoolers. The first time your child screams and kicks because she can't have her way, you may feel angry, frustrated, humiliated, or frightened. You may wonder where you've gone wrong as a parent to produce such a miserable child. Rest assured, you are not responsible for this behavior, and tantrums are not ordinarily a sign of severe emotional or personality disorders. Almost all youngsters have these episodes occasionally, especially around ages two and three. If handled successfully, they usually diminish in intensity and frequency by age four or five.

In the developmental stage of separating from their parents, the "no" is a perfectly understandable and normal expression of children's emerging need for some autonomy. Tantrums are often an expression of frustration. Preschoolers are very eager to take control. They want to be more independent than their skills and safety allow, and they don't appreciate their limits. They want to make decisions, but they don't know how to compromise, and they don't deal well with disappointment or restraint. They also can't express their feelings well in words, so instead they act out their anger and frustration by crying or withdrawing, and sometimes by having temper tantrums. Although these emotional displays are unpleasant, they rarely are dangerous.

You often can tell when a temper tantrum is coming. For some time before it begins, the child may seem more sullen or irritable than usual, and neither gentle affection nor playing with her will change her moodiness. She may be tired, hungry, or lonely. Then she tries, or is expected, to do something beyond her capabilities, or asks for something she can't have. She begins to whimper or whine and becomes more demanding. Nothing will distract or comfort her, and finally she starts to cry. As the crying increases, she begins to flail her arms and kick her legs. She may fall to the ground or hold her breath—some children actually hold their breath until they turn blue or faint. As frightening as it is to watch these breath-holding spells, the child's normal breathing resumes as soon as she faints, and she will recover quickly and completely. (Also see the box on page 539.)

Don't be surprised if your child has tantrums only when you are present—most children act up only around their parents or other family members, seldom when with outsiders. She is also testing your rules and limits, whereas she wouldn't dare do this with someone she knows less well. When her challenge goes too far and you restrain her, she may respond with a tantrum. She's not consciously trying to make your life miserable, and she certainly doesn't prefer strangers to you. Don't take tantrums personally. Try to remain calm and understand the behavior. Ironically, her occasional outbursts are actually a sign that she trusts you.

This emotional explosion serves as a kind of energy release, which often exhausts the child so that she falls asleep soon afterward. When she awakens she usually is calm and her behavior is quiet and pleasant. If she is ill or there is a great deal of tension among the people around her, however, the frustration may start building all over again. Children who are anxious, ill, or temperamental, who get too little rest, or who live in very stressful households tend to have tantrums more frequently.

Prevention

You can't prevent every tantrum, but you may be able to decrease the number, dura-

Effective Parenting

Child's Behavior*	Your Responses	
	Effective	*Constructive*
Temper tantrum	Walk away.	Discuss the incident when child is calm.
Overexcitement	Distract with another activity.	Talk about his behavior when he's calm.
Hitting or biting	Immediately remove him from situation or in anticipation of this behavior.	Discuss consequences of his actions (pain, damage, bad feelings) to himself and others. Try time-out after brief one-word response.
Not paying attention	Establish eye contact to hold his attention.	Lower your expectations (ask him to listen to a story for 3 minutes instead of 10; don't insist he sit through a full church service).
Refuses to pick up toys	Don't let him play until he does his job.	Show him how to do the task and help him with it; praise him when he finishes.

* Note: In all these situations, try to determine what influences might cause or prolong the behavior: Is the child in need of attention, tired, worried, fearful? What is your own mood or behavior? Remember, you always should praise your child for good or improved effort.

tion, or intensity by making sure your child does not get overtired, overly anxious, or unnecessarily frustrated. Your child's temper may become very short if she doesn't have enough "quiet time," particularly when she is sick or anxious, or has been unusually active. Even if she doesn't sleep, lying down for fifteen or twenty minutes can help restore her energy and reduce the likelihood of tantrums caused by exhaustion. Children who do not nap may be particularly prone to tantrums and often need such a quiet period on a daily, scheduled basis. If your child resists, you might lie down with her or read her a story, but do not allow her to play or talk excessively.

Children whose parents fail to set appropriate limits, are overly strict, or forget to reinforce good behaviors tend to have more frequent and severe tantrums than children whose parents take a moderate approach. As a rule, it's best to set very few limits but to be firm about those that are set. Expect your child to tell you "no" many times each day. She needs to assert herself this way and would not be normal if she never challenged you. You can allow her to have her way when the issue is minor—for example, if she wants to wander around slowly instead of walking quickly to the park, or if she refuses to get dressed before breakfast. But when she starts to run into the street, you must stop her and insist that she obey you, even if you have to hold her back physically. Be loving but firm, and respond the same way every time she violates the rule. She won't learn these important lessons immediately, so expect to repeat these interventions many times before her behavior changes. Also, make sure that every adult who cares for her observes the same rules and disciplines her in the same way.

How to Respond

When your child has a temper tantrum, it's important that you try to remain calm yourself. If you have loud, angry outbursts, your child naturally will imitate your behavior. If you shout at her to calm down, you probably will make the situation worse. Maintaining a peaceful atmosphere will reduce the general stress level and make both you and your child feel better and more in control. In fact, sometimes gentle restraint, holding, or distracting comments such as "Did you see what the kitty is doing?" or "I think I heard the doorbell" will interrupt behavior such as breath-holding before it reaches the point of fainting. (See also the box on page 539.)

Sometimes, if you feel yourself losing control, humor will save the day. Turn a dispute over taking a bath into a race to the bathroom. Soften your command to "eat your dinner" by making a funny face. Unless your child is extremely irritable or overtired, she is more likely to be distracted into obedi-ence if you temper discipline with a bit of fun or whimsy. Doing this also will make you feel better.

Some parents feel guilty every time they say "no" to their children. They try too hard to explain their rules, or apologize for them. Even at age two or three, children can detect uncertainty in a tone of voice, and they will try to take advantage of it. If the parent sometimes gives in, the child becomes even more outraged on those occasions when she doesn't get her way. There is no good reason to be apologetic about enforcing your rules. It only makes it more difficult for your child to understand which of them are firm and which can be questioned. This does not mean that you should be un-friendly or abusive when you say no, but state your position clearly. As your child gets older, you can offer brief, simple rea-sons for your rules, but do not go into long, confusing explanations.

When you ask your child to do something against her will, follow through on the order with her. If you've asked her to put away her toys, offer to help her. If you've told her not to throw her ball against the window, show her where she *can* throw it. If you've re-minded her not to touch the hot oven door, either remove her from the kitchen or stay there with her to make sure that she minds you. (Never issue a safety order to a two- or three-year-old and then leave the room.)

When to Call the Pediatrician

Although occasional temper tantrums dur-ing the preschool years are normal, they should become less frequent and less in-tense by the middle of the fourth year. Be-tween tantrums, the child should seem normal and healthy. At no time should the behavior cause the child to harm herself or others or destroy property. When the outbursts are very severe, frequent, or prolonged, they may be an early sign of emotional disturbance.

Consult your pediatrician if your child shows any of the following warning signs.

- Tantrums persist or intensify after age four.

- Your child injures herself or others, or destroys property during tantrums.

- Tantrums are accompanied by frequent nightmares, extreme disobedience, reversal of toilet training, development of headaches or stomachaches, refusal to eat or go to bed, extreme anxiety, constant grumpiness, or clinging to parents.

- Your child holds her breath and faints during tantrums.

If your child holds her breath and faints, you probably should call the pediatrician. The doctor may want to examine her and possibly check for other causes of "fainting," such as seizures (see page 660). The pediatrician also can offer suggestions for disciplining the child and suggest parent education groups that might provide additional support and guidance. If the doctor feels the tantrums indicate a severe emotional disturbance, she will refer you to a child psychiatrist, psychologist, or mental health clinic.

Thumb and Finger Sucking

Do not be upset if your baby begins sucking his thumb or fingers. This habit is very common and has a soothing and calming effect. Some experts feel that nine out of every ten children engage in this activity at some time in their early life. It is largely the result of the normal rooting and sucking reflexes present in all infants. There is evidence that some infants suck their thumbs and fingers even before delivery, and some, particularly finger suckers, will show that behavior immediately after being born.

Because sucking is a normal reflex, thumb and finger sucking can be considered a normal habit. The only time it might cause you concern is if it continues too long or affects the shape of your child's mouth or the alignment of his teeth. Over half of thumb or finger suckers stop by age six or seven months. Sometimes young children, especially when they are feeling most vulnerable, even until age eight or so, still will suck their thumb occasionally. Thumb sucking beyond the fifth birthday may cause changes in the roof of the mouth (palate) or in the way the teeth are lining up. At that time, you and the child's dentist might become concerned. This also is the time when your child might begin to be affected by the negative comments of his playmates, siblings, and relatives. If these factors become worrisome, consult your pediatrician about treatment.

Treatment

Severe emotional or stress-related problems that might cause this habit to be prolonged should be ruled out before any treatment program is begun. Also, your child should want to stop the habit and should be directly involved with the treatment chosen. Treatment usually is limited to children who persist in thumb sucking beyond their fifth birthday.

The techniques used usually begin with gentle reminders, particularly during the daytime hours. Friends or relatives might suggest that you use a pacifier, but there is no evidence that this is effective. It only substitutes one sucking habit for another.

If these measures are ineffective and your child is still interested in breaking the habit, your pediatrician might recommend trying some type of "aversive" (unpleasant) treatment. These treatments are designed to serve as a reminder when your child begins to suck. They include coating the finger or thumb with a bitter substance, covering it with a bandage or "thumb guard" (an adjustable plastic cylinder that can be taped to the thumb), or using an elbow restraint to prevent the elbow from bending and thus keeping the fingers and thumb from being brought up close to the mouth. Before you use any of these methods, you should explain them to your child. Discontinue their use if they cause undue anxiety or tension. In rare cases where there is severe tooth misalignment and the techniques just described have all failed, some dentists will install a device in the mouth that prevents the fingers or thumb from putting pressure on the palate or teeth. In fact, this apparatus usually makes placement of the thumb or finger into the mouth unpleasant enough that your child will withdraw it.

It is important to remember that your child may be one of the very few who for one reason or another cannot seem to stop thumb and finger sucking. Be assured that all of these children stop daytime sucking habits before they progress very far along in school due to the peer pressure that is exerted. These same children might still use sucking as a way of going to sleep or calming themselves when they are particularly upset. They usually do this away from the observation of strangers and it causes no harm, either emotionally or physically. Exerting excessive pressure on your child to stop this type of behavior probably would cause more harm than good, and even these children eventually stop the habit on their own.

Tics

Children who have tics experience involuntary movements or muscle spasms, most often of the face and neck. Their eyes may blink, their shoulders may shrug, their face may grimace, or they may stretch their neck.

Healthy newborns frequently have rhyth-mic tremors, most often of the chin or leg. They may appear to be a spasm, but they are quite normal. Most noticeable while the baby is crying, such tremors usually disappear after the second week of life. By contrast, true tics tend to develop later in childhood, sometimes as early as two to three years of age, but more often between ages seven and nine. These tics may start suddenly, typically in the aftermath of a physical or social stress. They can worsen when a child is anxious or tense, and become less frequent when he is able to relax.

The most serious tic disorder is called *Tourette's syndrome.* Children with this condition usually have a number of motor tics, starting in the face but before long affecting other parts of the body. These youngsters may have vocal tics, as well, such as uttering obscene words or phrases, coughs, hiccups, sniffs and snorts. The specific sounds and movements may change over time. Tourette's syndrome often is associated with other disorders, including hyperactivity, ADHD (attention deficit hyperactivity disorder), and obsessive thoughts. It usually has its onset toward the middle of the first decade of life.

Management

You may find tics in your child annoying, and although you might be tempted to ask him to "stop doing that," they are beyond his control. In fact, when you call attention to them, they are more likely to persist or worsen.

If your pediatrician believes that there is a psychological component to your child's tics, these underlying emotional difficulties should be treated. Make an effort to reduce the stress, worries, or conflicts in your youngster's life, which may help relieve the severity of his tics. For Tourette's syndrome, your doctor may prescribe medications to control the condition.

18

CHEST AND LUNGS

Asthma

Asthma is a lung disorder affecting the bronchial tubes. In the last twenty years, there has been a major increase in the number of people with asthma, especially young children and those living in urban areas. In fact, asthma is now one of the most common chronic diseases of childhood, affecting about 5 million children. The cause of the recent increase in prevalence is not completely understood, but probably air pollution, exposure to allergens, and respiratory illnesses are the main reasons.

Asthma is the most common condition that causes wheezing in children. Wheezing is the high-pitched sound that occurs when the airways in the lungs are narrowed, typically due to inflammation. In asthma, wheezing occurs on expiration (breathing out), most often at night or in the early morning. Even though wheezing is the hallmark symptom of asthma, not everyone who wheezes has asthma. Although no specific test can make the diagnosis of asthma, children with this disorder usually experience three or more episodes of wheezing; between these episodes, the wheezing often goes away.

Many things can trigger an attack of asthma, but in children under five, an attack most commonly occurs after a viral respiratory infection inflames the lining of the bronchial tubes and stimulates the muscles surrounding them.

Other common triggers of asthma attacks include:

- Air pollutants such as cigarette smoke or paint fumes

- Allergens such as dust, dust mites, cockroaches, animal dander, grasses, pollens and molds

- Exercise, in some children

- Inhaling cold air

- Certain medications

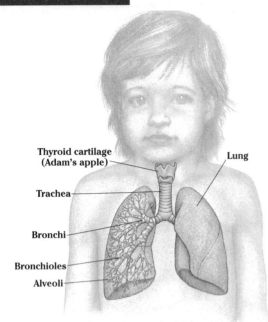

Thyroid cartilage
(Adam's apple)

Lung

Trachea

Bronchi

Bronchioles

Alveoli

Chest and Lungs

Some less common triggers are:

- Stress and emotional upset

- Sinus infections

- Allergic reactions to certain foods

- Previous injury to the airways (e.g., in children who have had an endotracheal tube or inhaled cigarette smoke)

Signs and Symptoms

When your child has an asthma attack, the major symptom will be a cough that gets worse at night, with physical activity, or after contact with an irritant (i.e., cigarette smoke) or an allergen (i.e., animal hair, dander, dust mites, or cockroaches). She will make a wheezing sound as she breathes out. As the attack progresses the wheezing actually may decrease, as less air is able to move in and out. She also may experience shortness of breath during an asthma episode.

Most children with asthma have chronic symptoms, such as daily (or nightly) cough, cough whenever they exercise, or cough with certain daily exposures such as pets, dust, and plants. In some children, the physician may hear wheezes (especially when the child blows out hard) even in the absence of symptoms. In the older child, abnormalities may be detected by pulmonary function testing.

When to Call the Pediatrician

If your child has asthma, you should know the situations that require immediate medical attention. As a rule, call your pediatrician immediately or consider going to the emergency room if:

- Your child has *severe* trouble breathing and seems to be getting worse, especially if she is breathing rapidly and there is pulling in of the chest wall when she inhales and forceful grunting when she exhales.

- Your child's mouth or fingertips appear blue, or she acts agitated, unusually sleepy, or confused.

- She has chest, throat, or neck pain.

You also should call your pediatrician without delay if:

- Your child has a fever and persistent coughing or wheezing that is not responding to treatment.

- She is vomiting, and cannot take oral medication.

- She has difficulty speaking or sleeping because of wheezing, coughing, or troubled breathing.

Treatment

Asthma always should be treated under your pediatrician's supervision. The goals of treatment are to:

1. Decrease the frequency and severity of attacks, reducing or preventing the chronic symptoms of coughing and difficulty breathing.

2. Gain control of the wheezing and return lung function to normal.

3. With your pediatrician, develop a sensible "plan of response" for any serious asthma attack to reduce the need for emergency medical treatment.

4. Allow your child to grow and develop normally, and take part in normal childhood activities as fully as possible.

5. Control your youngster's symptoms with the least amount of medication to decrease the risk of drug side effects.

6. Ensure regular school attendance.

7. Decrease the use of emergency room care.

With these goals in mind, your pediatrician will prescribe medication and may refer you to a specialist who can evaluate your child's lungs. Your doctor also will help you plan your child's specific home treatment program. This probably will include learning how to use the medicines and treatments that are prescribed and developing a plan to avoid the irritants and allergens that may be causing your child to wheeze.

If your child's asthma seems to be triggered by severe allergies, your pediatrician may refer you to a pediatric allergist or pulmonologist (lung specialist) for comprehensive evaluation, including pulmonary functions and skin testing. The allergist also may recommend giving your child vaccines to lessen her sensitivity to the allergens that are triggering her attacks. This procedure involves regular injections of a dilute form of the allergenic materials, which commonly include dust, molds, mites, and pollens. In addition, significant focus on education about causes will diminish future exposures and attacks, it is hoped.

The medication prescribed for your child will depend on the nature of the asthma. There are two types of asthma drugs. One type opens up the breathing tubes and relaxes the muscles causing the obstruction. These quick-relief or rescue medicines are called bronchodilators. The second type is the controller or maintenance medications, which are used to treat the airway inflammation.

If your child's symptoms occur on an intermittent basis, the pediatrician might prescribe a bronchodilator only when there is an episode of coughing or wheezing. If the asthma is chronic or persistent, he usually will prescribe medications for regular daily use. These medicines may take some time (weeks) to provide their full effect. Anti-inflammatory medications are recommended for all asthmatic children who have persistent symptoms. Inhaled corticosteroids are the most commonly used of these medications. They are very effective and safe, and are given in a metered dose inhaler (MDI, or puffer) or by "nebulization." With an MDI, the medication is sprayed into a "spacer" or holding chamber, and then your child breathes in the medication from the spacer. (You and your youngster must be taught how to use the spacer correctly to ensure that the medication gets to the lungs.) After taking the inhaled steroid, it is important for your child to clear her mouth by drinking something or brushing her teeth.

"Nebulizers," or pulmonary nebulizer machines, are particularly useful for children under two years of age who frequently have problems using metered dose inhalers and spacers.

Anti-inflammatory medications must be taken regularly to be effective. Often they fail because they are not taken consistently. Because they do not have an immediate effect, it is tempting to stop them. Doing so, however, leaves the airways unprotected, and an asthma attack may occur.

A new class of medications called leukotriene modifiers, which are taken in pill form, have become available recently. They also act as anti-inflammatory medicines and should be taken every day.

During severe attacks, the use of the rescue medicine should be increased. Your doctor may prescribe additional medication.

Give medications according to your pediatrician's directions. *Do not stop medicines too soon,* give them less often than recommended, or switch to other drugs or treatments without first discussing the change with the doctor. If you do not understand why a particular treatment has been recommended, ask for an explanation.

Prevention

To keep your child from having asthma attacks, you need to reduce the asthma triggers in your home by:

- Covering your youngster's bed mattress and pillow with airtight covers (usually plastic)

- Using pillows or comforters filled with polyester instead of feathers and cotton, or acrylic blankets that can be machine-washed

- Washing sheets, blankets, pillows, throw rugs, and stuffed animals often; use hot water to kill dust mites

- Limiting stuffed animals

- Keeping pets (especially cats and dogs) out of your child's room (or out of the house, if possible)

- Encouraging your child to stay off carpets, which collect dust and allergens

- Carefully watching your child's diet at home and school to avoid allergy-causing foods

- Keeping your child out of rooms while you're vacuuming

- Investing in a special air filter to keep your child's room clean

- Maintaining the humidity in your house below 50 percent when possible; dust mites and mold grow best in damp areas

- Keeping your child away from cigarette, cigar, or pipe smoke.

Bronchiolitis

Bronchiolitis is an infection of the small breathing tubes (bronchioles) of the lungs. It occurs most often in infants. (Note: The term *bronchiolitis* sometimes is confused with bronchitis, which is an infection of the larger, more central airways.)

Bronchiolitis is almost always caused by a virus, most commonly the respiratory syncytial virus (RSV). Other viruses that can cause this condition are parainfluenza, influenza, measles, and adenovirus. The infection causes inflammation and swelling of the bronchioles, which in turn causes blockage of air flow through the lungs.

Most adults and many children who are infected by RSV get only a cold. In children under two years of age, however, the infec-

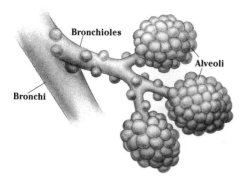

Bronchioles

Alveoli

Bronchi

tion is more likely to lead to bronchiolitis. It also may cause episodes of apnea (a temporary pause in breathing). Many infants who develop RSV bronchiolitis go on to develop asthma later in life. We do not know why these youngsters are more susceptible, but it is likely that the RSV infection is the first trigger for the airway reaction.

RSV infection is the most likely cause of bronchiolitis from October through March. During the other months, bronchiolitis usually is caused by other viruses.

The RSV is highly contagious and is spread by contact with secretions from an infected person. It often spreads through families, child care centers, and hospital wards. Careful handwashing can help prevent this.

Signs and Symptoms

If your infant has bronchiolitis, it will start with signs of an upper respiratory infection (a cold): runny nose, mild cough, and sometimes fever. After a day or two the cough becomes more pronounced, and the child begins to breathe more rapidly and with more difficulty.

If your baby shows any of the following signs of breathing difficulty, or if his fever lasts more than three days (or if it is present at all in an infant under three months), call your pediatrician immediately.

- He makes a high-pitched whistling sound, called a wheeze, each time he breathes out or exhales.

- He may be unable to drink fluids well because he is working so hard to breathe that he has difficulty sucking and swallowing.

- He may develop a bluish tint around his lips and fingertips. This indicates that his airways are so blocked that not enough oxygen is getting into the blood.

Also call the pediatrician if your child develops any of the following signs or symptoms of dehydration, which also can be present with bronchiolitis.

- Dry mouth

- Taking less than his normal amount of fluids

- Shedding no tears when he cries

- Urinating less often than normal

If your child has any of the following conditions, notify your pediatrician as soon as you suspect that he has bronchiolitis.

- Cystic fibrosis

- Congenital heart disease

- Bronchopulmonary dysplasia (seen in some infants who were on a respirator as newborns)

- Low immunity

- Organ transplant

- A cancer for which he is receiving chemotherapy

Home Treatment

There are no medications you can use to treat RSV infections at home. All you can do during the early phase of the illness is ease your child's cold symptoms. You can relieve some of the nasal stuffiness with a humidifier, nasal aspirator, and perhaps some mild salt-solution nasal drops.

Also, to avoid dehydration, make sure your baby drinks lots of fluid during this time. (See *Diarrhea,* page 505.) He may prefer clear liquids rather than milk or formula. Because of his breathing difficulty, he also may feed more slowly and may not tolerate solid foods very well.

Professional Treatment

If your baby is having mild to moderate breathing difficulty, your pediatrician may try using a bronchodilating drug (one that opens up the breathing tubes) before considering hospitalization. These drugs seem to help a small number of patients.

Unfortunately, some children with bronchiolitis need to be hospitalized, either for breathing distress or for dehydration. The breathing difficulty is treated with oxygen and bronchodilating drugs, which are inhaled periodically.

Very rarely, an infant will not respond to these treatments and might have to be assisted by a breathing machine (respirator). This treatment usually is only a temporary measure to help him until his body is able to overcome the infection.

Babies who are born very prematurely and those who have chronic lung disease may be candidates for receiving an injection of a special antibody that reduces the severity of RSV infections. Ask your pediatrician if your child should receive this medication.

Prevention

The best way to protect your baby from bronchiolitis is to keep him away from the viruses that cause it. When possible, especially while he's an infant, avoid close contact with children or adults who are in the early (contagious) stages of respiratory infections. If he is in a child care center where other children might have the virus, make sure that those who care for him wash their hands thoroughly and frequently.

Cough

Coughing is almost always an indication of an irritation in your child's air passages. When the nerve endings in the throat, windpipe, or lungs sense the irritation, a reflex causes air to be ejected forcefully through the passageways.

Coughs usually are associated with respiratory illnesses, such as colds/upper respiratory infection (see page 577), bronchiolitis (see page 546), croup (see page 550), flu (see page 551), or pneumonia (see page 553). If your child's cough is accompanied by fever, irritability, or difficulty breathing, he probably has such an infection.

When a child has a cold, the cough may sound wet (productive or congested), or dry and irritating; the cough may last longer than the accompanying runny nose. If he has a cough, a fever, and difficulty breathing, pneumonia may be present. A baby or a child who has pneumonia often breathes rapidly. If this happens, see your doctor.

To a large extent, the location of the problem determines the sound of the cough: An irritation in the larynx (voice box), such as croup, causes a cough that sounds like the bark of a dog or seal. Irritation of the larger airways, such as the trachea (windpipe) or bronchi, is characterized by a deeper, raspy cough that gets worse in the morning.

Allergies and sinus infections can cause a chronic cough because mucus drips down the back of the throat producing a dry, hard-to-stop cough, particularly at night. A child who coughs only at night may have asthma (see page 543).

Here are some other cough-related issues in the lives of children.

- Anything more than an occasional cough in an infant has to be taken seriously. The most common causes are colds and bronchiolitis, which usually get better in a few days. It is important to watch for signs of breathing difficulties and seek medical help if needed. These signs include not only rapid breathing, especially while asleep, but also drawing in of the ribs and breastbone (sternum).

- Sometimes children cough so hard that they throw up. Usually they vomit liquid and food from the stomach, but there may be a lot of mucus, as well, especially during a cold or an asthma attack.

- Wheezing is a high-pitched sound during breathing that occurs when there is an obstruction of the airway inside the chest. It is one of the symptoms of asthma, but also can occur if your child has bronchiolitis, pneumonia, or certain other disorders.

- Children with asthma often cough and wheeze together. This may happen when they are active or playing, or at night. Sometimes their cough can be heard, but the wheezing may be evident only to your doctor when she listens with a stethoscope. The cough and the wheeze usually get better after using asthma medications.

- A cough is commonly worse at night. When your child coughs at night, it may be caused by irritation in the throat or a sinus infection. Asthma is another major reason for a nighttime cough.

- A sudden cough can develop in children and may start with a choking episode. It could mean that some food or liquid has "gone down the wrong way" and ended up in the lungs. The coughing helps clear the airway. However, if coughing continues for more than a few minutes, or if your child is having difficulty breathing, seek medical help right away. Don't put your fingers in your youngster's mouth to clear the throat because you may push the food or other cause of the obstruction down farther. (See *Choking,* page 481.)

When to Call the Pediatrician

An infant under two months of age who develops a cough should be seen by the doctor. For older infants and children, consult your physician if:

- The coughing makes it difficult for your child to breathe.

- The coughing is painful, persistent, and accompanied by whooping, vomiting, or turning blue.

- The cough lasts longer than one week.

- The cough appears suddenly and is associated with fever.

- The coughing begins after your child chokes on food or any other object. (See *Choking,* page 481.)

Your pediatrician will try to determine the cause of your child's cough. When the cough is caused by a medical problem other than a cold or the flu, such as a bacterial infection or asthma, it will be necessary to treat that condition before the cough will clear. Occasionally when the cause of a chronic cough is not apparent, further tests such as chest X rays or tuberculosis skin tests may be necessary.

Treatment

The treatment for a cough depends on its cause. But whatever the cause, it is always a good idea to give extra fluids. Adding moisture to the air with a humidifier or vaporizer also may make your child more comfortable, especially at night.

A cold-water humidifier is just as effective as a hot-water vaporizer and is considerably safer if accidentally knocked over. However, be sure to clean the device thoroughly with detergent and water each morning, so it doesn't become a breeding ground for harmful bacteria or fungi.

Nighttime coughs, particularly those associated with allergies or asthma, can be especially annoying, because they occur when everyone is trying to sleep. In some cases it may help to elevate the head of the child's bed. If the night cough is due to asthma, bronchodilators should be used.

Although cough medicines can be purchased without a prescription, their ingredients vary widely, so ask your pediatrician to recommend a brand and specify the appropriate dosage and frequency for your child. These medicines should be given only with your doctor's approval.

Croup

Croup is an inflammation of the voice box (larynx) and windpipe (trachea). It causes a barking cough and a high-pitched sound when inhaling. Although croup is sometimes associated with allergies, it usually is caused by a virus, most commonly the parainfluenza

virus. The illness most often is "caught" from someone who is infected, sometimes from air droplets or from your child's own hand, which he uses to transfer the virus into his nose or eyes.

Croup tends to occur in the fall and winter when your youngster is between three months and three years old. Initially he may develop nasal stuffiness resembling a cold, and he may have a fever. After a day or two, the sound of the cough will turn into something resembling barking. The cough tends to become worse at night.

The greatest danger with croup is that your child's airway will continue to swell, further narrowing his windpipe and making it difficult, at times almost impossible, to breathe. As your child tires from the effort of breathing, he may stop eating and drinking. He also may become too fatigued to cough. Some youngsters, by the way, are particularly prone to getting croup and seem to develop the infection whenever they have a respiratory illness.

Treatment

If your child awakens in the middle of the night with croup, take her into the bathroom and steam it up by turning on the shower with the hottest available water. Close the door and sit in the steamy bathroom with your child. Inhaling the warm, humidified air should ease her breathing within fifteen to twenty minutes. For the rest of that night and the next few nights, use a cold-water vaporizer or humidifier in your child's room.

Do *not* try to open your child's airway with your finger. Her breathing is being obstructed by swollen tissue beyond your reach, so you can't clear it away. She may throw up because of the coughing, but don't try to make her vomit. Pay close attention to your child's breathing. Take her to the nearest emergency room *immediately* if:

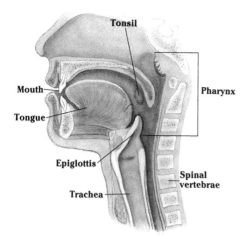

- She makes a whistling sound that gets louder with each breath.

- She can't speak because of a lack of breath.

- She seems to be struggling to get a breath.

- She turns blue when she coughs.

Your pediatrician may prescribe steroid medications to help treat croup. These drugs may reduce swelling in the throat, and they'll usually shorten the illness. Antibiotics are not helpful for croup because the problem is caused by a virus or an allergy. Cough syrups usually do not help, either.

In the most serious cases, which are quite rare, your child will have a lot of difficulty breathing, and your pediatrician may admit her to the hospital for a few days until the swelling in the airway gets better. Sometimes a tube will be inserted through the nose or mouth into the windpipe to help your child breathe.

Flu/Influenza

Flu is the short term for influenza. It is an illness caused by a respiratory virus. There are three influenza viruses, types A, B, and C; the usual epidemics of the flu are caused by either A or B. Each of these viruses also has different subgroups, or strains, so that each year, the flu virus that causes most flu cases is slightly different. That's why individuals at high risk for serious or complicated influenza infection should receive a flu shot every year.

Influenza epidemics often occur in the winter months, although the flu season extends from the beginning of October through March. The infection can spread rapidly through communities as the virus is passed from person to person. When someone with the flu coughs or sneezes, the influenza virus gets into the air, and people nearby, including children, can inhale it. The virus also can be spread when your child touches a hard surface, such as a door handle, and then places his hand or fingers in his mouth or nose.

When there is an outbreak or epidemic, usually during the winter months, the spread tends to be most pronounced in preschool or school-age children. Adult caregivers are easily exposed and can contract the disease. The virus usually is transmitted in the first several days of the illness.

You can suspect that your child has the flu if you observe the following signs or symptoms.

- Sudden onset of fever (usually above 101 degrees Fahrenheit, or 38.3 degrees Celsius)

- Chills and shakes accompanying the fever

- Extreme tiredness or fatigue

- Muscle aches and pains

- Dry, hacking cough

After the first few days of these symptoms, a sore throat, stuffy nose, and continuing cough become most evident. The flu can last a week or even longer. A child with a common cold (see *Colds/Upper Respiratory Infection,* page 577) usually has a lower degree of fever, a runny nose, and only a small amount of coughing. Children with the flu—or adults, for that matter—usually feel much more sick, achy, and miserable.

Healthy people, especially children, get over the flu in a few days, or perhaps a week or two, without any lingering problems. However, you might suspect a complication if your child says that his ear hurts or that he feels congested in his face and head or if his cough and fever persist.

Very rarely, there is a risk of developing Reye syndrome (see page 520), although the incidence of this disorder seems to have diminished significantly with the awareness that it may be associated with aspirin use during viral illnesses and the consequent decrease in the use of aspirin to treat symptoms of the flu or chickenpox.

Children who appear to be at greatest risk for complications from the flu are those with an underlying chronic medical condition, such as heart or lung disease, an immune problem, some blood diseases, or malignancy. As these children may have more severe disease or complications, they should, when possible, be kept away from children with the flu, and additional precautions should be taken for them.

(Children with certain flulike symptoms—such as a fever and a severe sore throat—as well as drooling or difficulty breathing could have a rare illness called epiglottitis, which is a serious condition that may require hospitalization. For more information about epiglottitis, see page 585).

Treatment

For all children with the flu who don't feel well, lots of tender loving care is in order. Children can benefit from extra bed rest, extra fluids, and light, easy-to-digest meals. A cold-water vaporizer in the room may add additional moisture to the air and make breathing through inflamed mucous membranes of the nose a little easier.

If your child is uncomfortable because of a fever, acetaminophen or ibuprofen in doses recommended by your pediatrician for his age and weight will help him feel better. (See Chapter 23, "Fever.") Ibuprofen is approved for use in children six months of age and older; however, it should never be given to children who are dehydrated or who are vomiting continuously. *It is extremely important not to give aspirin to a child who has the flu or is suspected of having the flu. Aspirin use during bouts of influenza is associated with an increased risk of developing Reye syndrome.*

Prevention

Since the flu virus is transmitted from person to person, a first step you can take to decrease the chances of family members getting the flu is to practice and teach good hygiene. If, for example, you have a child with the flu, do the following to prevent its spread.

- Avoid kissing your infected child on or around the mouth, although he will need plenty of hugs during the illness.

- Teach your child not to cough or sneeze without covering his nose and mouth with a tissue, and make sure the tissue is disposed of properly.

- Make sure you and other caregivers wash hands both before and after caring for your child.

- Wash your child's utensils in hot, soapy water or in the dishwasher.

- Don't allow others to share drinking glasses or utensils, and never share toothbrushes.

- Use disposable paper cups in the bathroom and kitchen.

There is a vaccine to protect against the flu. The current vaccine is considered safe, effective, and associated with minimal side effects. Those children, six months or older, for whom yearly influenza vaccination is recommended include those with the following conditions:

- Asthma

- Cystic fibrosis

- Chronic lung disease

- Congenital heart disease

- Sickle cell anemia

- HIV (human immunodeficiency virus) infection

- Diabetes and other metabolic diseases

- Chronic kidney disease

- A condition that requires your child to take medications that suppress his immune system

The American Academy of Pediatrics recommends that the influenza vaccination be given to *all* healthy children ages six months through twenty-three months because children in this age group have a high likelihood of being hospitalized because of flu. Children and adults who live in the same household as someone who has a high risk for flu complications also may be candidates for vaccination. However, the flu vaccine is *not* approved for use in infants younger than six months old.

Even though few side effects appear to be associated with the vaccine, production of the vaccine involves the use of eggs. If a child or an adult has had a serious allergic reaction to eggs or egg products, he should be skin-tested before receiving the vaccine. If skin testing confirms hypersensitivity, the influenza vaccine should not be given.

Antiviral medications to treat an influenza infection are now available. Such treatments must be initiated within forty-eight hours of the beginning of illness. Also, for chronically ill children, prevention of influenza is important. If the child has not been immunized, use of antiviral medication before the exposed child gets the disease can make the flu less severe.

Pneumonia

The word *pneumonia* means "infection of the lung." While such infections were extremely dangerous in past generations, today most children can recover from them easily if they receive proper medical attention.

Most cases of pneumonia follow a viral upper respiratory tract infection. Typically, the viruses that cause these infections (respiratory syncytial virus [RSV], influenza, parainfluenza, adenovirus) spread to the chest and produce pneumonia there. Other viruses—such as those related to measles, chickenpox, herpes, infectious mononucleosis, and rubella—might travel from various parts of the body to the lungs, where they also can cause pneumonia.

Pneumonia also can be caused by bacterial infections. Some of these are spread from person to person by coughing or by direct contact with the infected person's saliva or mucus. Also, if a viral infection has weakened a child's immune system, bacteria that ordinarily are harmless may begin to grow in the lung, adding a second infection to the original one.

Children whose immune defenses or lungs are weakened by other illnesses, such as cystic fibrosis, asthma, or cancer (as well as by the chemotherapy used to treat cancer), are more likely to develop pneumonia. Children whose airways or lungs are abnormal in any other way also have a higher risk.

Because most forms of pneumonia are linked to viral or bacterial infections that spread from person to person, they're most common during the fall, winter, and early spring, when children spend more time indoors in close contact with others. The likelihood that a child will develop pneumonia is *not* affected by how she is dressed, by the temperature of the air she is in, or by whether she is exposed to fresh air when ill.

Signs and Symptoms

Like many infections, pneumonia usually produces a fever, which in turn may cause sweating, chills, flushed skin, and general discomfort. The child also may lose her appetite and seem less energetic than normal. If she's a baby or toddler, she may seem pale and limp, and cry more than usual.

Because pneumonia can cause breathing difficulties, you may notice these other, more specific symptoms, too:

- Cough (see page 548)

- Fast, labored breathing

- Increased activity of the breathing muscles below and between the ribs and above the collarbone

- Flaring (widening) of the nostrils

- Wheezing

- Bluish tint to the lips or nails, caused by decreased oxygen in the bloodstream

Although the diagnosis of pneumonia usually can be made on the basis of the signs and symptoms, a chest X ray sometimes is necessary to make certain and to determine the extent of lung involvement.

Treatment

When pneumonia is caused by a virus, there is no specific treatment other than rest and the usual measures for fever (see Chapter 23). Cough suppressants containing codeine or dextromethorphan should not be used, because coughing is necessary to clear the excessive secretions caused by the infection. Viral pneumonia usually disappears after a few days, although the cough may linger up to several weeks. Ordinarily, no medication is necessary.

Because it is often difficult to tell whether the pneumonia is caused by a virus or by bacteria, your pediatrician may prescribe an antibiotic. All antibiotics should be taken for the full prescribed course and at the specific dosage recommended. You may be tempted to discontinue them early, since your child will feel better after just a few days, but if you do this, some bacteria may remain and the infection might return.

Your child should be checked by the pediatrician as soon as you suspect pneumonia. Check back with the doctor if your youngster shows any of the following warning signs that the infection is worsening or spreading.

- Fever lasting more than a few days despite the use of antibiotics

- Breathing difficulties

- Evidence of an infection elsewhere in the body: red, swollen joints, bone pain, neck stiffness, vomiting, or other new symptoms or signs

Prevention

Your child can be vaccinated against pneumococcal infections, a bacterial cause of pneumonia. The American Academy of Pediatrics recommends that all children younger than two years old receive this immunization (called the heptavalent pneumococcal conjugate vaccine, or PCV7). A series of doses needs to be given at two, four, six, and twelve to fifteen months of age, at the same time that youngsters receive other childhood vaccines.

The vaccine also is recommended for older children (twenty-four to fifty-nine months of age) who are considered to have a high risk of developing an invasive pneumococcal infection. These youngsters include those with sickle cell anemia and HIV (human immunodeficiency virus) infection, and other children with a weakened immune system.

(See also: *Asthma,* page 543, *Colds/Upper Respiratory Infection,* page 577; Chapter 23, "Fever.")

Tuberculosis

Tuberculosis (TB) is an airborne infection that primarily affects the lungs. For decades, the incidence of TB had been on the decline. However, it increased in the late 1980s and early 1990s. Since 1992 the trend has reversed again, and the rate has begun to decrease.

Some groups of children have a higher risk of developing tuberculosis, including:

- Children living in a household with an adult who has active tuberculosis or has a high risk of contracting TB

- Children infected with HIV or another condition in which the immune system is weakened

- Children born in a country that has a high prevalence of TB

- Children from communities that generally receive inadequate medical care

Tuberculosis usually is spread when an infected adult coughs the bacteria into the air. These germs are inhaled by the child, who then becomes infected. (Children with TB of the lungs rarely infect other people, because they tend to have very few bacteria in their mucus secretions and also have a relatively ineffective cough.)

Fortunately, most children exposed to tuberculosis don't become ill. When the bacteria reach their lungs, the body's immune system attacks them and prevents further spread. These children have developed a symptom-free infection indicated only by a positive skin test. (See page 556 for a description of this test.) However, the symptom-free child still must be treated, as noted below, to prevent an active disease from ever occurring. Occasionally, in a small number of children, the infection does progress, causing fever, fatigue, irritability, a persistent cough, weakness, heavy and fast breathing, night sweats, swollen glands, weight loss, and poor growth.

In a very small number of children (mostly those less than four years old), the tuberculosis infection can spread through the bloodstream, affecting virtually any organ in the body. This illness requires much more complicated treatment, and the earlier it is started, the better the outcome. These youngsters have a much greater risk of developing tuberculosis meningitis, a dangerous form of the disease that affects the brain and central nervous system.

The signs and symptoms of childhood TB

can be difficult to detect. Often the only way you can tell for sure that a child has been exposed to this infection is by performing a skin test. Your pediatrician will perform this so-called PPD (purified protein derivative of tuberculin) test, which is done by injecting a purified, inactive piece of TB germ into the skin. If there has been an infection, your child's skin will swell and redden in the area of the injection. You'll be asked to check for this area two days after the test is administered, since the reaction takes about forty-eight hours to appear. Your pediatrician should examine any reaction. This skin test will reveal past exposure to the bacteria, even if the child has had no symptoms and even if his body has fought the disease successfully.

If your child's skin test for TB turns positive, a chest X ray will be ordered to determine if there is evidence of active or past infection in the lungs. If the X ray does indicate the possibility of active infection, the pediatrician also will search for the TB bacteria in your child's cough secretions or in his stomach contents (obtained with a tube inserted into the nose down to the stomach). This is done in order to determine the type of treatment to be given.

Treatment

If your child's skin test turns positive, but he does not have symptoms or signs of active tuberculosis infection (typically in an X-ray finding or the detection of TB bacteria in his saliva or stomach contents), he still is infected. In order to prevent the infection from becoming active, your pediatrician will prescribe a medication called isoniazid (INH). This medication must be taken by mouth once a day for a minimum of nine months.

For an *active* tuberculosis infection, your pediatrician may prescribe three or four medications. You'll have to give these to your child for six to twelve months. Your youngster may have to be hospitalized initially for the treatment to be started, although most of it can be carried out at home.

Prevention

If your child has been infected with TB, regardless of whether he develops symptoms, it's *very* important to attempt to identify the person from whom he caught the disease. Usually this is done by looking for symptoms of TB in everyone who came in close contact with him, and having TB skin tests performed on all family members, babysitters, and housekeepers. Anyone who has a positive skin test should receive a physical examination and a chest X ray.

When an actively infected adult is found, he'll be isolated as much as possible—especially from young children—until treatment is under way. All family members who have been in contact with that person usually are also treated with INH, regardless of the results of their own skin tests. Anyone who becomes ill or develops an abnormality on a chest X ray should be treated as an active case of tuberculosis.

Tuberculosis is much more common in underprivileged populations, which are more susceptible to disease due to crowded living conditions, poor nutrition, and the probability of inadequate medical care. AIDS patients, too, are at a greater risk of getting TB, because of their lowered resistance. If untreated, tuberculosis can lie dormant for many years, only to surface during adolescence, pregnancy, or later adulthood. At that time, not only can the individual become quite ill, but he also can spread the infection to those around him. Thus, it's very important to have your child tested for TB if he comes in close contact with any adult who has the disease and to get prompt and adequate treatment for him if he tests positive.

Whooping Cough (Pertussis)

Pertussis, or whooping cough, is uncommon now, as the pertussis vaccine has made most children immune. Before this vaccine was developed, however, there were several hundred thousand cases of whooping cough each year in the United States. Now there are approximately 4,000.

This illness is called pertussis because it is caused by the pertussis bacterium, which attacks the lining of the breathing passages (bronchi and bronchioles), producing severe inflammation and narrowing of the airways. Severe coughing is a prominent symptom. If not recognized properly, the bacteria may spread to those in close contact with the infected person, through her respiratory secretions.

Infants under one year of age are at greatest risk of developing severe breathing problems and life-threatening illness from whooping cough. Because the child is short of breath, she inhales deeply and quickly between coughs. These breaths (particularly in older infants) frequently make a "whooping" sound—which is how this illness got its common name. The intense coughing scatters the pertussis bacteria into the air, spreading the disease to other susceptible persons.

Pertussis often acts like a common cold for a week or two. Then the cough gets worse, and the older child may start to have the characteristic "whoops." During this phase (which can last two weeks or more), the child often is short of breath and can look bluish around the mouth. She also may tear, drool, and vomit. Infants with pertussis become exhausted and develop complications such as susceptibility to other infections, pneumonia, and seizures. Pertussis can be fatal in some infants, but the usual course is for recovery to begin after two to four more weeks. The cough may not disappear for months, and may return with subsequent respiratory infections.

When to Call the Pediatrician

Pertussis infection starts out acting like a cold. You should consider the possibility of whooping cough if the following conditions are present.

- The child is a very young infant who has not been fully immunized and/or has had exposure to someone with a chronic cough or the disease.

- The child's cough becomes more severe and frequent, or her lips and fingertips become dark or blue.

- She becomes exhausted after coughing episodes, eats poorly, vomits after coughing, and/or looks "sick."

Treatment

The majority of infants with whooping cough who are less than six months old, and slightly less than one-half of older babies with the disease, initially are treated in the hospital. This more intensive care can decrease the chances of complications. These complications can include pneumonia, which occurs in slightly less than one-fourth of children under one year old who have whooping cough. (If your child is older, she is more likely to be treated only at home.)

While in the hospital, your child may need to have the thick respiratory secretions suctioned. His breathing will be monitored, and he may need to have oxygen administered. For several days, your youngster will be isolated from other patients to keep the infection from spreading to others.

Whooping cough is treated with antibiotics, usually for two weeks. These medications are most effective when they are given in the first stage of the illness before coughing spells begin. Although antibiotics can stop the spread of the whooping cough infection, they cannot prevent or treat the cough itself. Because cough medicines do not relieve the coughing spells, your pediatrician probably will recommend other forms of home treatment to help manage the cough. Let your child rest in bed and use a cool-mist vaporizer to help soothe his irritated lungs and breathing passages. A vaporizer also will help loosen secretions in the respiratory tract. Ask your pediatrician for instructions on the best position for your child to help drain those secretions and improve breathing. Also ask your doctor whether antibiotics or vaccine boosters need to be given to others in your household to prevent them from developing the disease.

Prevention

The best way to protect your child against pertussis is with DTaP (immunizations at two months, four months, and six months of age, and booster shots at twelve to eighteen months and before entering school). The DTaP vaccine, known as the "acellular" type, protects your child against diphtheria (D), tetanus (T), and pertussis (aP). It has fewer side effects than earlier versions of the vaccine, causing less fever, irritability, and probably less risk of brain injury. The risk to your child from pertussis disease is greater than risking serious reactions from DTaP.

Therefore, the *American Academy of Pediatrics urges parents to continue immunizing their infants against pertussis but to be aware of the following reactions that can occur, and the conditions under which the vaccine should not be used.*

Severe reactions to the DTaP vaccine that should alert you and your pediatrician not to give another pertussis immunization include:

- An allergic reaction (hives or rash within minutes of the injection, or shock)

- An acute, severe central nervous system disorder, which is otherwise unexplained, within seven days of receiving injection

In addition, certain adverse reactions that occur in relation to DTaP vaccines are considered warnings against giving further administration of these vaccines. Because these events have not been proven to cause permanent injury, you and your pediatrician must weigh carefully the benefits of future vaccinations against risks. Adverse reactions in this category are:

- Fever of 105 degrees Fahrenheit (40.6 degrees Celsius) or greater

- Prolonged, continuous crying

- An episode of limpness or paleness

- Unusual high-pitched cry

- Convulsions

In addition to the above, certain children probably should never get the "P" part of the injection in the first place: any child with a progressive neurological disorder or a neurological (nervous system) condition that increases the likelihood of developing a seizure.

Fortunately, the number of children to whom these rules apply is very small. Do not make the mistake of refusing to immunize your child if she is normal and healthy. The benefits of the vaccine far outweigh the risks.

19

DEVELOPMENTAL DISABILITIES

It's natural to compare your child with others his age. When the neighbor's baby walks at ten months, for example, you may worry if yours does not crawl until thirteen months. And if your toddler is using words at an earlier age than his playmates, probably you'll be very proud. Usually, however, such differences are not significant. Each child has his own unique rate of development, so some learn certain skills faster than others.

Only when a baby or preschooler lags far behind, or fails altogether to reach the developmental milestones outlined in Chapters 6 through 12 of this book, or loses a previously acquired skill, is there reason to suspect a mental or physical problem serious enough to be considered a developmental disability. Developmental disabilities that can be identified during childhood include mental retardation, language and learning disorders, cerebral palsy, autism, and sensory impairments such as vision and hearing loss. (Some pediatricians include seizure disorders in this category, but a large percentage of children who have seizures develop normally.)

Each of these developmental disabilities can vary greatly in severity. For example, one child with mild cerebral palsy may have no obvious handicap other than a slight lack of coordination, while another with a severe form may be unable to walk or feed himself. Also, some children have more than one disability, each requiring different care.

If your child does not seem to be developing normally, he should have a complete medical and developmental evaluation, perhaps including a consultation with a developmental pediatrician who is a specialist in this field. Doing this will give your pediatrician the information needed to determine whether a true disability exists and, if so, how it should be managed. Depending on the results of the evaluation, the doctor may recommend physical, speech and language, or occupational therapy. Educational intervention or psychological counseling also might be necessary. Your pediatrician should be able to help you arrange these

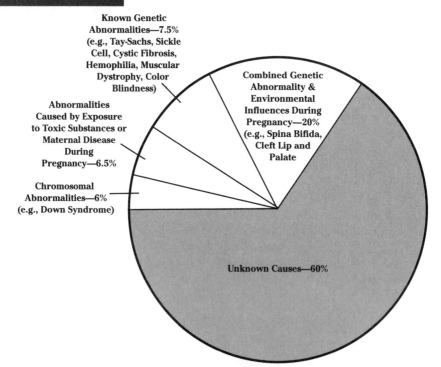

Known Genetic Abnormalities—7.5% (e.g., Tay-Sachs, Sickle Cell, Cystic Fibrosis, Hemophilia, Muscular Dystrophy, Color Blindness)

Combined Genetic Abnormality & Environmental Influences During Pregnancy—20% (e.g., Spina Bifida, Cleft Lip and Palate

Abnormalities Caused by Exposure to Toxic Substances or Maternal Disease During Pregnancy—6.5%

Chromosomal Abnormalities—6% (e.g., Down Syndrome)

Unknown Causes—60%

consultations. In some states and cities these evaluations are offered free of charge or are partially paid for by local government. Your local board of education can tell you if this is the case in your area.

Today every child over the age of three years who has a developmental disability is entitled by federal law to special education in a preschool or school program. Most states also offer special programs for infants and toddlers who have developmental delays or disabilities or who are at risk for these difficulties.

The families of children with disabilities also need special support and education. It's not so easy to accept the fact that a child has a developmental problem. To understand what the child is facing and how he can be helped to realize his full potential, each member of the family should be educated about the specific problem and counseled about how to deal with it.

Cerebral Palsy

Children with cerebral palsy have an impairment in the area of the brain that controls movement and muscle tone. Many of these youngsters have normal intelligence, even though they have difficulty with motor control and movement. The condition causes different types of motor disability, which can vary from quite mild and barely noticeable to very profound. Depending on the severity of the problem, a child with cerebral palsy may simply be a little clumsy or awkward, or he may be unable to walk. Some children have weakness and poor motor control of one arm and one leg on the same side of the body (called hemiparesis). Many have problems with paralysis of both upper or lower extremeties; this is called diplegia. In some children the muscle tone generally is increased (called spasticity or hypertonia), while others are abnormally limp (called hypotonia). Speech may be affected, as well.

Cerebral palsy frequently is caused by malformation or damage to the brain during pregnancy, delivery, or immediately after birth. Premature birth is associated with an increased risk of cerebral palsy. A baby also can get cerebral palsy from very severe jaundice after birth, or later on in infancy from an injury or illness affecting the brain. In most cases the cause is unknown. However, a recent report issued by the American Academy of Pediatrics and the American College of Obstetricians and Gynecologists did conclude that the majority of cerebral palsy cases are not the result of events during labor and delivery, such as an insufficient supply of oxygen (hypoxia).

Signs and Symptoms

The signs and symptoms of cerebral palsy vary tremendously because there are many different types and degrees of disability. The main clue that your child might have cerebral palsy is a delay in achieving the motor milestones listed in Chapters 5 through 12 of this book. Here are some specific warning signs.

In a Baby over Two Months

- Head lags when you pick him up while he's lying on his back.

- He feels stiff.

- He feels floppy.

- When held cradled in your arms, he seems to overextend his back and neck—constantly acts as if he is pushing away from you.

- When you pick him up, his legs get stiff and they cross or "scissor."

In a Baby over Six Months

- He continues to have the asymmetrical tonic neck reflex (see page 146).

- He reaches out with only one hand while keeping the other fisted.

In a Baby over Ten Months

- He crawls in a lopsided manner, pushing off with one hand and leg while dragging the opposite hand and leg.

- He scoots around on buttocks or hops on knees, but does not crawl on all fours.

If you have any concerns about your child's development, talk to your pediatrician at your routine visit. Because children's rates of development do vary so widely, it is sometimes difficult to make a definite diagnosis of mild cerebral palsy in the first year or two of life. Often a consultation from a developmental pediatrician or pediatric neurologist will assist in the diagnosis. A CAT/CT (computed tomography) or MRI (magnetic resonance imagery) of the head may be recommended to determine whether a brain abnormality exists. Even when a firm diagnosis is made during these early years, it often is difficult to predict how severe the disability will be in the future. However, usually by three to four years of age there is enough information to predict accurately how a child will function in years to come.

Treatment

If your pediatrician suspects that your child has cerebral palsy, you will be referred to an early intervention program. These programs are staffed by early childhood educators; physical, occupational, and speech and language therapists; nurses; social workers; and medical consultants. In such a program you'll learn how to become your child's own teacher and therapist. You will be taught what exercises to do with your infant, what positions are most comfortable and beneficial to him, and how to help with specific problems such as feeding difficulties. You'll be introduced to some of the newer treatment options, such as baclofen therapy, that may be able to manage the spasticity associated with cerebral palsy, and botulinum toxin type A (Botox), which is a muscle-relaxing drug that can help relieve the toe-walking that is related to muscle tightening. You'll receive information about so-called adaptive equipment that can help your child participate in everyday activities despite the physical problems he may have; this equipment includes special utensils to make eating easier, pencils that can be held more easily, wheelchairs, and walkers. Through these programs you also can meet parents of other children with similar disabilities and share experiences, concerns, and solutions.

The most important thing you can do for your child is to help him develop competence and grow up feeling good about himself. When he is old enough to ask or understand, explain to him that he has a disability and reassure him that he'll be able to make adjustments in order to succeed in life. Encourage him to perform the tasks he is ready for, but do not push him to do things at which you know he will fail. The professionals at early intervention centers can help you evaluate your child's abilities and teach you how to reach appropriate goals.

Do not make the mistake of searching for magical cures or undertaking controversial treatments. They will waste your time, energy, and money. Instead, ask your pediatrician, or contact the United Cerebral Palsy Association at www.ucpa.org, for information about resources and programs available in your area.

Associated Problems

Mental Retardation

It has been estimated that more than half of children with cerebral palsy have problems with intellectual functioning (thinking, problem solving). Many are classified as mentally retarded, while others have average abilities with some learning disorders. Some have perfectly normal intelligence. (See also page 572.)

Seizures

One out of every three people with cerebral palsy has or will develop seizures. (Some start having them years after the brain is damaged.) Fortunately, these seizures usually can be controlled with anticonvulsant medications. (See also page 660.)

Vision Difficulties

Because the injury to the brain often affects eye muscle coordination, more than three out of four children with cerebral palsy have strabismus, a problem with one eye turning in or out, with or without nearsightedness. If this problem is not corrected early, the vision in the affected eye will get worse and eventually will be lost permanently. Thus it is extremely important to have your child's eyes checked regularly by your pediatrician. (See also *Strabismus*, page 602.)

Limb Shortening and Scoliosis

Of those children with cerebral palsy affecting only one side of the body, over half will develop a shortening of the involved leg and arm. The difference between the legs is rarely more than two inches (5 cm), but an orthopedic surgeon should be consulted if shortening is noticed. Depending on the degree of difference between the legs, a heel or sole lift may be prescribed to fit into the shoe on the shorter side. This is done to prevent a tilt of the pelvis, which can lead to curvature of the spine (scoliosis) when standing or walking. Sometimes surgery is required to correct a serious degree of scoliosis. Scoliosis also can develop in the other forms of cerebral palsy involving both sides of the body.

Dental Problems

Many children with cerebral palsy have more than the average number of cavities. One reason may be that it is difficult for them to brush their teeth. However, they also have enamel defects more frequently than normal children, which make their teeth more susceptible to decay.

Hearing Loss

Some children with cerebral palsy have a complete or partial hearing loss. This happens most often when the cerebral palsy is a result of severe jaundice at birth. If you find that your baby does not blink at loud noises by one month, is not turning his head toward a sound by three to four months, or is not saying words by twelve months, discuss it with your pediatrician. (See also page 569.)

Joint Problems

In children with spastic forms of cerebral palsy, it is often difficult to prevent "contracture," an extreme stiffening of the joints caused by the unequal pull of one muscle over the other. A physical therapist, developmental pediatrician, or physiatrist (doctor of physical medicine) can teach you how to stretch the muscles to try to prevent the onset of contracture. Sometimes braces, casting, or medication may be used to improve joint mobility and stability.

Problems with Spatial Awareness

Over half the children with cerebral palsy affecting one side of the body cannot sense the position of their arm, leg, or hand on the affected side. (For example, when his hands are relaxed, the child cannot tell whether his fingers are pointing up or down without looking at them.) When this problem is present, the child rarely will attempt to use the involved hand, even if the motor disability is minimal. He acts as if it is not there. Physical or occupational therapy can help him learn to use the affected parts of his body, despite this disability.

Congenital Abnormalities

Thanks to improved medical care during pregnancy and to progress in early detection of chromosomal and other genetic abnormalities through amniocentesis, chorionic villus sampling, and other newer diagnostic tests, there are fewer and fewer newborns with congenital problems. About three of every hundred babies born in the United States have congenital abnormalities that will affect the way they look, develop, or function—in some cases for the rest of their lives.

Congenital abnormalities are caused by problems in the development of the infant before birth. There are five categories, grouped according to the cause of the abnormality.

Chromosome Abnormalities

Chromosomes are the structures that carry the genetic material inherited from one generation to the next. Normally, twenty-three chromosomes come from the father and twenty-three from the mother, and all are found in the center of every cell in the body except the red blood cells. The genes carried on the chromosomes determine how the baby will grow, what she will look like, and to a certain extent how she will function.

When a child does not have the normal forty-six chromosomes, or when pieces of the chromosomes are missing or duplicated, she may look and behave differently from others her age, and she may develop serious health problems, as well. Down syndrome is an example of a condition that can occur when a child is born with an extra chromosome.

Single-Gene Abnormalities

Sometimes the chromosomes are normal in number, but one or more of the genes on them are abnormal. Some of these genetic abnormalities can be passed on to the child if one of the parents is affected with the same abnormality. This is known as autosomal dominant inheritance.

Other genetic problems can be passed to the child only if both parents carry the same defective gene. (Cystic fibrosis, Tay-Sachs disease, and sickle-cell anemia are all examples of this type of abnormality.) In these cases both parents are normal, but one in four of their children would be expected to be affected. This is known as autosomal recessive inheritance.

A third type of genetic abnormality is called sex-linked, and generally is passed on to boys only. Girls may carry the abnormal gene that causes these disorders but not show the actual disease herself. (Examples of this problem include hemophilia, color blindness, and the common forms of muscular dystrophy.)

Damaging Conditions During Pregnancy

Certain illnesses during pregnancy, particularly during the first nine weeks, can cause serious congenital abnormalities—German measles and diabetes, for example. Excess alcohol consumption and the use of certain drugs during pregnancy significantly increase the risk that a baby will be born with abnormalities. Certain medications, if taken during pregnancy, also can cause permanent damage to the fetus, as can certain chemicals that can pollute air, water, and food. Before using any medication during pregnancy, women should check with their doctors.

Combination of Genetic and Environmental Problems

Spina bifida and cleft lip and palate are types of congenital abnormalities that may occur when there is a genetic tendency for the condition combined with exposure to certain environmental influences within the womb during critical stages of the pregnancy.

Unknown Causes

The vast majority of congenital abnormalities have no known cause. This situation is particularly troubling for parents who plan to have more children, because there is no way to predict if the problem will recur. If you and your family have experienced such a genetic-related birth abnormality, ask your pediatrician for a referral to a genetic counseling service. These services have expertise with a variety of genetic abnormalities and may be able to advise you as to the proper course of action.

Learning to Live with the Problem

If your newborn has a congenital abnormality, the first hours and days of her life will be very difficult for you. At the same time that you are learning about your child as she is, you probably will be mourning the perfect baby you'd imagined she would be. Meanwhile, all your relatives and friends are calling to hear the "good news." One way to relieve the social pressure you're bound to feel is to appoint one family member and one friend to inform other friends and relatives about your newborn's condition.

If you have other children, you'll need to explain the situation to them as soon as possible. It is difficult to predict how siblings will react to such news; but, whether they show it or not, many feel guilty. They may have felt jealous and resentful about the baby during the pregnancy—perhaps even wished secretly that the baby would never come. If so, when they learn that their new brother or sister has a problem, they may feel that their wishes were responsible. Encourage them to ask questions, answer them in terms that they can understand, and be sure to explain that the problem is no one's fault.

Try not to blame yourself for what's happened, either. Except in cases where the congenital abnormality is caused by the mother's use of drugs or alcohol during pregnancy, there is nothing that could have been done to prevent an abnormality of this kind. Don't allow yourself to feel guilty or responsible. Guilt will only get in the way of the love and affection that are especially vital in these special circumstances.

As overwhelmed as you may be by the problems facing your family and your newborn, this child needs to receive all the nurturing and affection you would give any baby. It's easy to forget this during the first days of her life, when you are confronting many difficult decisions and feeling anxious, fearful, and disappointed. Yet this is precisely the time when touching, holding, and comforting are especially critical to the child and to you.

Coping with the Medical Necessities

Congenital abnormalities are so diverse, and require such different types of treatment, that it would be impossible to discuss them all in this section. Instead, we will look only at the medical management of the two most common problems, Down syndrome and spina bifida.

Down Syndrome

Approximately one out of every eight hundred babies is born with Down syndrome. Fortunately, with the use of amniocentesis, Down syndrome can be detected prenatally. This problem—which is caused by the presence of an extra chromosome—results in a number of physical abnormalities, including up-slanted eyes with extra folds of skin at the inner corners, flattening of the bridge of the nose, a relatively large tongue, and a decrease in the muscle and ligament tone of the body.

A major serious effect of Down syndrome is mental retardation. All but a very small number of these children develop more slowly than average, although the extent of the delay can vary widely from one youngster to the next. Some seem to border on normal development, while others are severely retarded. However, even though children with Down syndrome may be retarded in development as children and young adults, most eventually are able to feed and dress themselves and to be toilet-trained. Many, with special education, can learn basic job skills.

Early detection of Down syndrome is very

important, since many babies with the disorder require early treatment for related abnormalities of the heart, intestinal tract, and/or blood. Early detection also allows parents to adjust to the situation and gather support and information. Once suspected, the condition is confirmed by a blood test. (It takes a few days to produce results.) Since newborns with Down syndrome usually have no medical problems that require immediate treatment, most can leave the hospital after the normal newborn stay.

If you have a newborn with Down syndrome, your pediatrician may recommend a special early-intervention program for you and your baby. If so, you should begin it as soon as possible. These programs employ specially designed services to help your child make the most of her developmental and physical capabilities.

You probably will hear about other types of "therapy" that are *not* proven or recommended, such as multivitamin ("orthomolecular") treatments and a system known as "patterning," which focuses on the child's behavior. These approaches receive a lot of media attention because they claim to have great success, but no long-term benefits have ever been proven for them, and large doses of some vitamins may be harmful. These programs also may delay effective methods of treatment and be very expensive. If you hear of any treatments that you think may help your child, always discuss them first with your pediatrician to see if they are valid before spending your money or trying them.

In addition to developmental delay, Down syndrome can result in physical problems as your child gets older. Her growth should be closely watched, since extremely slow growth in height and/or excessive weight gain may indicate a lack of thyroid hormone, a problem that affects many youngsters with Down syndrome. Even without thyroid problems, chances are that she'll be shorter and weigh less than average for her age as an infant. When they're older, children with Down syndrome tend to be overweight. One-half of children with Down syndrome also have heart problems that may require medication or surgery. Over one-half have vision and hearing defects.

Another problem, which affects fifteen of every hundred children with Down syndrome, is an abnormality in the ligaments of the neck that can cause serious spinal injury if the neck is extended (bent backward) during exercise. For this reason, consult your pediatrician for advice regarding the need for your child's neck to be X-rayed before she's allowed to participate in vigorous athletic activities (especially tumbling and gymnastics). If X rays show this abnormality, her physical activities should be limited to movements that cannot cause injury. Currently there is some controversy over the value of these X rays.

For all its difficulties, raising a child with Down syndrome can be deeply rewarding. Children with this condition are usually loving and openly affectionate, and will thrive if nurtured and loved in return. As with all children, each achievement they make can be a triumph shared by everyone in the family.

Spina Bifida

Spina bifida occurs when the spinal bones fail to close properly during early formation. Spina bifida occurs less often than Down syndrome, or in about one in one thousand births. It is, however, the most common of the physically disabling congenital abnormalities. A parent who has one child with spina bifida has a greater chance (one out of a hundred) of having another. This increased frequency appears to be due to some combined effect of heredity and environment. There are now tests available to screen for spina bifida early in pregnancy.

A newborn with spina bifida appears at first glance to be normal, except for a small sac protruding from the spine. However, the sac contains spinal fluid and damaged nerves that lead to the lower body. Within the first few days, surgery must be performed to remove the sac and close the opening in the spine. Unfortunately, little can be done to repair the damaged nerves.

Most babies with spina bifida develop further problems later on, including the following.

Hydrocephalus. Up to nine out of ten children with spina bifida eventually develop hydrocephalus, caused by an excessive increase in the fluid that normally cushions the brain from injury. The increase occurs because the spina bifida abnormality blocks the path through which the fluid ordinarily flows. This condition is serious and, if not treated, may lead to death.

The pediatrician should suspect hydrocephalus if the baby's head is growing more rapidly than expected. The condition is confirmed by a computerized X ray of the head, called a CT (computed tomography) scan or magnetic resonance imagery (MRI). If hydrocephalus is present, surgery will be necessary to relieve the fluid buildup.

Latex allergies. People with spina bifida have an increased risk of developing an allergy to latex. Preventing the child from being exposed to latex will reduce the likelihood that he will acquire the sensitivity. Many products used by infants contain latex (bottle nipples, pacifiers, teething toys, changing pads, mattress covers, and some diapers) and should be avoided.

WHERE WE STAND

In an effort to reduce the prevalence of spina bifida, the American Academy of Pediatrics endorses the recommendation of the U.S. Public Health Service that all women capable of becoming pregnant consume 400 micrograms per day of folic acid (a B vitamin). Folic acid has been shown to help prevent neural tube defects (NTD), which include spina bifida. Although some foods are fortified with folic acid, it is not possible for women to meet the 400 microgram goal through a typical diet. Thus, a recent policy statement of the Academy recommends the use of a daily multivitamin tablet that contains folic acid in the recommended dose. Studies show that if all women of childbearing age met these dietary requirements, 50 percent or more of NTDs could be prevented.

We advise women who are considered at high risk for having an NTD-affected pregnancy (e.g., because of a previous NTD-affected pregnancy, the presence of diabetes mellitus, or the need to take antiseizure medications) to discuss their risk with their doctor, including the possibility of treatment with very high doses of folic acid (4,000 micrograms per day), beginning one month before becoming pregnant and continuing throughout the first trimester. As the doctor will explain, however, women should not attempt to achieve this very high dose of folic acid by taking multivitamin supplements, but rather only under the care of a physician.

Muscle weakness or paralysis. Because the nerves leading to the lower part of the body are damaged, the muscles in the legs may be very weak or even paralyzed in children with spina bifida. Their joints also tend to be very stiff, and many babies with this disorder are born with abnormalities of the hips, knees, and feet. Surgery can be performed to correct some of these problems, and the muscle weakness can be treated with physical therapy and special equipment, such as braces and walkers. Many children with spina bifida eventually can stand and some do walk, though the learning process is often long and extremely frustrating.

Bowel and bladder problems. Often the nerves that control bowel and bladder function are damaged in children with spina bifida. As a result, these children are more likely to develop urinary tract infections and damage to the kidneys due to abnormal urine flow. Special techniques are available to develop urinary control and minimize infections. Your pediatrician will advise you.

Bowel control also is a problem, but usually can be achieved by children with this disorder. It may, however, take a great deal of time, patience, careful dietary management (to keep the stools soft), and the occasional use of suppositories or other bowel stimulants, or special enemas.

Infection. Parents of children who have spina bifida and hydrocephalus or urinary tract problems must be ever alert for signs of infection. Fortunately, the types of infections that occur in these cases usually can be treated effectively with antibiotics.

Educational and social problems. Seven out of ten children with spina bifida have developmental and learning disabilities requiring some sort of special education. Many also need psychological counseling and tremendous emotional support in order to deal with their medical, educational, and social problems.

Parents of a child with spina bifida need more than one physician to manage their child's medical care. In addition to the basic care your pediatrician delivers, this disorder requires a team approach that involves neurosurgeons, orthopedic surgeons, urologists, rehabilitation experts, physical therapists, psychologists, and social workers. Many medical centers run special spina bifida clinics, which offer the services of all these health professionals in one location. Having all members of the team together makes it easier for everyone to communicate and usually provides better access to information and assistance when parents need it.

Resources

Information and support for parents are available from various organizations.

The National Down Syndrome Congress
1370 Center Drive
Suite 102
Atlanta, GA 30338
1–800–232–NDSC
www.ndsccenter.org

The Spina Bifida Association of America
4590 MacArthur Boulevard, NW
Suite 250
Washington, DC 20007–4226
1–800–621–3141

United Cerebral Palsy Association
1660 L Street, NW
Suite 700
Washington, DC 20036
1–800–872–5827
www.ucpa.org

For information about congenital abnormalities, write:

The March of Dimes Resource Center
1275 Mamaroneck Avenue
White Plains, NY 10605

Hearing Loss

Most children experience mild hearing loss when fluid accumulates in the middle ear in response to allergies or colds. This hearing loss is temporary. In many children, perhaps one in ten, fluid stays in the middle ear because of ear infection (see page 580). They don't hear as well as they should during the infections, and sometimes have delays in talking. Much less common is the permanent kind of hearing loss that always endangers normal speech and language development. This difficulty varies from mild or partial to complete or total.

Although they can occur at any age, the most serious effects come from hearing losses that are present from birth or develop during infancy and the toddler years. Hearing loss during this time demands immediate attention, because it directly affects the child's ability to understand and produce spoken language. Even a temporary severe hearing loss during infancy or early in the preschool years can make it very difficult for the child to learn proper oral language.

There are two main kinds of hearing loss:

Conductive hearing loss. When a child has a conductive hearing loss, there may be an abnormality in the structure of the outer ear canal or middle ear, or there may be fluid in the middle ear that interferes with the conduction of sound.

Sensorineural hearing loss (also called nerve deafness). This type of hearing impairment is caused by an abnormality of the inner ear or the nerves that carry sound messages from the inner ear to the brain. The loss can be present at birth or occur shortly thereafter. If there is a family history of deafness, the cause is likely to be inherited (genetic). If the mother had rubella (German measles), cytomegalovirus (CMV), or another infectious illness that affects hearing during pregnancy, the fetus could have been infected and may lose hearing as a result. The problem also may be due to a malformation of the inner ear. Most often the cause of severe sensorineural hearing loss is unknown. In such cases, the probability that the hearing loss is genetic is high, even when no other family members are affected. Future brothers and sisters of the child have a greatly increased risk of being hearing impaired themselves.

Hearing loss must be diagnosed as soon as possible, so that the child isn't delayed in learning language—a process that begins the day she is born. The American Academy of Pediatrics recommends that before a newborn infant goes home from the hospital, she needs to undergo a hearing screening. Most states, in fact, now have Early Hearing Detection Intervention (EHDI) programs, which attempt to ensure that all newborns are screened for hearing loss.

At any time during your child's life, if you and/or your pediatrician suspect that she has a hearing loss, insist that a formal hearing evaluation be performed promptly. (See "Hearing Loss: What to Look For" on page 571.) Although some family doctors, pediatricians, and well-baby clinics can test for fluid in the middle ear—a common cause of hearing loss—they cannot measure hearing precisely. Your child should go to an audiologist, who can perform this service. She may also be seen by an ear, nose, and throat doctor (ENT; an otolaryngologist).

If your child is under age two, or is uncooperative during her hearing examination, she may be given one of two available screening tests, which are the same tests used for newborn screening. They are painless, take just five to ten minutes, and can be performed while your child is sleeping or lying still. They are:

- The auditory brainstem response test, which measures how the brain responds to sound. Clicks or tones are played into the baby's ears through soft earphones, and electrodes placed on the baby's head measure the brain's response. This allows the doctor to test your child's hearing without having to rely on her cooperation.

- The otoacoustic emissions test, which measures sound waves produced in the inner ear. A tiny probe is placed just inside the baby's ear canal, which then measures the response when clicks or tones are played into the baby's ear.

These tests may not be available in your immediate area, but the consequences of undiagnosed hearing loss are so serious that your doctor may advise you to travel to where one of them can be done. Certainly, if these tests indicate that your baby may have a hearing problem, your doctor should recommend a more thorough hearing evaluation as soon as possible to confirm whether your child's hearing is impaired.

Treatment

The treatment of a hearing loss will depend on its cause. If it is a mild conductive hearing loss due to fluid in the middle ear, the doctor may simply recommend that your child be retested in a few weeks to see whether the fluid has cleared by itself. Use of antihistamines or decongestants is an ineffective treatment for fluid in the middle ear. Antibiotics are of limited value, but a trial for one to two weeks is usually worth it. (See *Middle Ear Infections,* page 580.)

If there is no improvement in hearing over a three-month period, and there is still fluid behind the eardrum, the doctor may recommend referral to an ear, nose, and throat (ENT) specialist and drainage of the fluid through ventilating tubes, which are surgi-

cally inserted through the eardrum. This is a minor operation and takes only a few minutes, but the child must receive a general anesthetic for it to be done properly, so he usually will spend part of the day in a hospital's "one-day surgery center."

Even with the tubes in place, future infections can occur, but the tubes help reduce the amount of fluid and decrease your child's risk of repeated infection. They also improve the hearing. Your pediatrician also might place the child on a low-dose antibiotic regimen to decrease the possibility of infection.

If a conductive hearing loss is due to a malformation of the outer or middle ear, a hearing aid may restore hearing to normal or near-normal levels. However, a hearing aid will work only when it's being worn. You must make sure it is on and functioning at all times, particularly in the very young child. Reconstructive surgery may be considered when the child is much older.

Hearing aids will not restore hearing completely to those with significant sensorineural hearing loss, but they may help.

Implantation of an electronic replacement for the inner ear in children and adults with hearing impairments has attracted a lot of publicity recently, but this procedure still is considered experimental. At best, these "cochlear implants" help a person to become aware of sounds. They do not restore hearing nearly well enough for the child to learn spoken language without additional help, including hearing aids to amplify sounds, as well as special education and parent counseling. Recently there have been a number of cases of serious infections complicating cochlear implants even months after surgery. Many are being removed. Because of this, if your child has a cochlear implant, contact your ENT surgeon or pediatrician immediately for the best next step.

Parents of children with sensorineural hearing loss usually are most concerned

When to Call the Pediatrician

Hearing Loss:
What to Look For

Here are the signs and symptoms that should make you suspect that your child has a hearing loss and alert you to call your pediatrician.

- Your child doesn't startle at loud noises by one month or turn to the source of a sound by three to four months of age.

- He doesn't notice you until he sees you.

- He concentrates on gargles and other vibrating noises that he can feel, rather than experimenting with a wide variety of vowel sounds and consonants. (See *Language Development* in Chapters 8 and 9.)

- Speech is delayed or hard to understand, or he doesn't say single words such as *dada* or *mama* by one year of age.

- He doesn't always respond when called. (This is usually mistaken for inattention or resistance, but could be the result of a partial hearing loss.)

- He seems to hear some sounds but not others. (Some hearing loss affects only high-pitched sounds; some children have hearing loss in only one ear.)

- He seems not only to hear poorly but also has trouble holding his head steady, or is slow to sit or walk unsupported. (In some children with sensorineural hearing loss, the part of the inner ear that provides information about balance and movement of the head is also damaged.)

---

about whether their child will learn to talk. The answer is that all children with a hearing impairment can be taught to speak, but not all will learn to speak clearly. Some children learn to lip-read well, while others never fully master the skill. But speech is only one form of language. Most children learn a combination of spoken and sign language. Written language also is very important because it is the key to educational and vocational success. Learning excellent oral language is highly desirable, but not all people who are born deaf can master this. Sign language is the primary way deaf people communicate with one another and the way many express themselves best.

If your child is learning sign language, you and your immediate family also must learn it. How else can you share life with your child? You must be able to teach her, discipline her, praise her, comfort her, and laugh with her. You should encourage friends and relatives to learn signing, too. It is a lot of work, but it is also fun.

Although some advocates in the deaf community prefer separate schools for deaf children, there is no reason for children with severe hearing impairment to be isolated from other people because of their hearing loss. With proper treatment, education, and support, these children will grow to be full participants in the world around them.

Mental Retardation

The term *mental retardation* is used when a child's intelligence and abilities to adjust to his surroundings are significantly below average and affect the way he learns and develops new skills. The more severe the retardation, the more immature a child's behavior will be for his age.

Intelligence in children over age two years generally is measured in terms of IQ (intelligence quotient). To determine IQ, the child is given tasks in a variety of areas to assess his problem-solving skills and other specific abilities. An average IQ score is 100, which is achieved when the child's mental age score is identical to the average score for his age group.

In some cases, standard IQ tests are not accurate or reliable, because cultural differences or language problems or a physical handicap affect a child's understanding of the questions or his ability to respond appropriately. In such cases, special tests that measure the child's ability to function and reason, despite these problems, should be used.

Signs and Symptoms

Generally, the more severe the degree of mental retardation, the earlier the signs are noticeable. However, even though such signs may be present, it still may be difficult to predict in young children the ultimate degree of retardation that will be present as the child grows. Children born with Down syndrome, for example (see page 565), can vary greatly in their ultimate level of mental retardation, from mild to severe.

When a baby is late in developing basic motor skills (i.e., holding his head up by himself by three to four months or sitting unsupported by seven to eight months), there also may be some associated mental disability. However, this is by no means always the case. Nor does normal motor development guarantee normal intelligence. Some children with mild to moderate degrees of mental retardation appear to have normal physical development during the first few years of life. In such cases, the first sign of mental retardation may be a delay in language development or in learning simple imitation skills, such as waving bye-bye or playing pat-a-cake.

In many cases of mild retardation, except for delays in speech, the young child otherwise may appear to be developing normally. Later, when he begins preschool or school, he may have difficulty performing academic skills at his grade level. He might have trouble completing puzzles, recognizing colors, or counting when his classmates already have mastered these tasks. Remember, however, children do develop at very different rates, and problems in school certainly are not always a sign of retardation. Developmental delays also can be caused by disorders such as hearing loss, vision problems, learning disabilities, or emotional difficulties.

When to Call the Pediatrician

If you are concerned about a delay in your child's development (see the sections on development in Chapters 6 through 12), call your pediatrician, who will review your child's overall development and determine whether it is appropriate for his age. If the pediatrician is concerned, she will probably refer you to a pediatric developmental specialist, a pediatric neurologist, or a multidisciplinary team of professionals for further assessment. With older children, referral for formal psychological testing may be helpful. However, your pediatrician may suggest waiting awhile, to see if your child's rate of development improves or speeds up. This is more likely to happen if the child has been seriously ill, or if his pattern of development does not seem significantly delayed. If you remain worried despite your pediatrician's reassurances, ask for a referral to an appropriate specialist.

If you take your child to a developmental pediatrician or a pediatric neurologist, a variety of tests will be performed to determine the nature and cause of the problem. In addition to identifying what is wrong, these tests should help you discover some of your child's physical and intellectual strengths. Once the testing is completed, you should be given a full explanation of the problem, what (if anything) is known about its cause, what can be done to help your child, and generally what to expect in the future. Remember, especially when there are related physical disabilities, such as those caused by cerebral palsy, making accurate predictions about how a young child with delayed development will function later in life can be very difficult.

Treatment

The main treatment for children with mental retardation is education and training. Most individuals with *mild* retardation can be educated to a fourth- or fifth-grade level and can learn to read and write, be relatively independent in daily activities, learn to travel, and hold a job. Adults with *moderate* retardation may read or write on a first- or second-grade level and can be trained to perform the activities of daily living, but need special transportation and supported employment. Although people with *severe* or *profound* retardation do not read or write, except in rare cases, and often require supervision, they may be trained to dress, feed, and toilet themselves, with assistance. They also may be trained to participate in specialized vocational settings.

One of the most common questions parents ask is "Will my child be able to function independently when he is older?" The answer to that question varies, depending on the level of mental retardation and whether the child has any additional problems.

Today many adults with mental retardation live at home or in small, supervised group homes. The number of these group homes has increased markedly in the past decade, and they are an accepted presence in communities all over the United States. The residents of these facilities go out to programs, workshops, or jobs by day, attend community recreation facilities on weekends or evenings, and visit their families on holidays and at other times.

Prevention

Only a few causes of mental retardation can be treated medically and early enough to prevent significant disability. Among the more common ones are metabolic disorders such as phenylketonuria (PKU) and hypothyroidism. If these conditions are detected soon after birth through the standard screening tests performed in the hospital nursery, they can be treated, and mental retardation will be prevented. Another condition that can cause mental retardation if not detected early in life is hydrocephalus (excess fluid causing increased pressure in the brain; see page 567). This condition usually is treated by draining the fluid to another part of the body to release the pressure and thereby prevent damage to the brain. The possibility of a genetic cause for a child's mental retardation should be evaluated, since this may help with projecting the child's future needs and allow the family to receive genetic counseling for future pregnancies.

In many cases of mental retardation, there is no clearly identifiable cause, and in the vast majority of cases, little, if anything, could have been done to prevent it. Despite claims you may hear, there are no complete cures for most children with mental retardation, and a great deal of money or emotional energy can be wasted looking for one. It is much more important to invest your energy in coming to terms with your child's disability and helping him to develop his abilities to the maximum. Consult your pediatrician, local advocacy organizations such as the Association for Retarded Citizens (ARC) at www.thearc.org, and other reputable professionals to find out what programs (i.e., the Special Olympics) are available in your community. Professional assistance can be extremely helpful. In the long run, however, you are your child's most important advocate.

Overprotecting your child can result in more harm than good. A child with a disability, like any youngster, needs to be challenged in order to develop to his full potential. If you overprotect your child, you will prevent him from trying new things and you will limit his opportunities to expand his abilities. Help him make the most of the strengths he does possess. Set realistic objectives for him, and encourage him to reach them. Assist him if necessary, but let him do as much as possible on his own. You and your child will feel most rewarded when he reaches a goal by himself.

20

Ears, Nose, and Throat

Allergic Rhinitis

If your child's nose starts to run and his eyes become itchy, red, and swollen, but there are no other symptoms of a cold or an infection, he may be having an attack of allergic rhinitis, an allergic reaction to "allergens" in the environment. The most common allergens that trigger allergic rhinitis are dust, mold, and animal dander.

Like other allergies, allergic rhinitis often is inherited, so if you or your spouse has it, your child is more likely to develop it. The symptoms may not appear immediately, however. Respiratory allergies are quite uncommon in children under age three.

It is sometimes difficult to tell the difference between a common cold and allergic rhinitis, because many of the symptoms are the same. Here are some of the signs of allergic rhinitis.

- Sneezing, sniffling, stuffiness; itchy and runny nose (usually clear discharge)

- Tearing; itchy, red, or swollen eyes

- Coughing

- A crease on the top of the nose from frequent wiping

- Nosebleeds or sores around the outside of the nose (see *Nosebleeds,* page 587)

- Dark rings (or "allergic shiners") under the eyes

- Constant red throat

- Snoring at night and breathing through the mouth because of stuffiness

- Fatigue (mostly from not sleeping well at night)

- Frequent throat clearing

- Cough at night resulting from a postnasal drip

- Headache without fever

If your child has nasal allergies, it might open the door to other problems, as well.

Common Household Allergens

Source	What to Do
Pets (dogs, cats, guinea pigs, and hamsters): There's no such thing as a "nonallergic" dog or cat, although some people are less sensitive to certain breeds. For dogs and cats, it's the *dander* (or skin sheddings) that trigger allergies, while for rodents, their urine is the major allergen.	If your child is allergic to an animal, don't allow that animal in the house. When choosing your next pet, think in terms of snakes, lizards, fish, and frogs.
Mold (small pieces of plants that contain spores or seeds): Mold grows outdoors in cool, damp, dark places, such as in soil, grass, and dead leaves. Indoors, it's found in damp cellars, closets, attics, old mattresses, and pillows and blankets that haven't been aired out in a long time.	The key to controlling mold is to limit humidity. Avoid using vaporizers, humidifiers, and swamp coolers. A dehumidifier in a damp basement can be helpful. Throughout the house, replace any carpet that's been saturated by a big water spill, or dry it completely. You can destroy mold with several types of disinfectants, but be careful to store them in a safe place, away from curious toddlers.

For example, he may get more sinus and ear infections (see *Middle Ear Infections,* page 580, and *Sinusitis,* page 661), or if the allergy causes eye irritation, he may be more susceptible to eye infections (see page 604). Since chronic allergies also can interfere with sleep, your child often may be tired and cranky, which in turn can lead to behavior problems.

Treatment

Call your pediatrician when your child's allergy starts to interfere with sleeping or with school, social, or other activities. To prevent or treat mild allergy symptoms, the doctor probably will recommend an antihistamine, sometimes combined with a decongestant. The most common side effects of these medications are drowsiness, dry mouth, constipation, decreased appetite, and, occasionally, change in behavior. Sometimes an antihistamine will have a stimulating effect, causing unusual activity and/or nervousness in the child; several of the newer prescription antihistamines, however, do not cause either hyperactivity or drowsiness. For more severe or persistent allergy symptoms, your physician may recommend a prescription nose spray.

You may be tempted to use decongestant nose drops or sprays that you can buy over the counter, but do so for no more than three days. After a few days' use, these medications actually may cause more nasal congestion rather than less. Ironically, this increased congestion can be even more uncomfortable and difficult to treat than the original allergy. If your youngster's eyes are swollen, itchy, and red, the physician may

Source	What to Do
House Dust Mites: Many people are allergic to house dust mites, which are found in bedding (pillows, blankets, sheets, mattresses), upholstery, furniture, and carpet. These mites, which are too small to be seen without a magnifying glass or microscope, thrive in humid environments (humidity greater than 50 percent).	The most important measures for reducing exposure to house dust mites are focused on the bedroom. Put mite-proof covers on mattresses and pillows, and wash sheets and blankets in hot water every one to two weeks to remove allergens and and kill the mites. Remove stuffed animals from the bed, or wash them every two weeks along with the bedding. It's also helpful to keep the humidity in the home at less than 50 percent to prevent the growth of mites. Using specially designed "double bags" in the vacuum cleaner may help limit the amount of airborne allergens during cleaning. Air cleaners are of no value in controlling exposure to dust mites. If you're remodeling the bedroom, consider removing carpets from the room.

prescribe eyedrops in addition to oral antihistamines.

Perhaps the best thing you can do for your allergic child is to remove the sources of allergens from your home. Refer to the chart on page 576 and above for the most common culprits—and how to avoid them.

Colds/Upper Respiratory Infection

Your child probably will have more colds, or upper respiratory infections, than any other illness. In the first two years of life alone, most youngsters have eight to ten colds. And if your child is in child care, or if there are older school-age children in your house, she may have even more, since colds spread easily among children who are in close contact with one another. That's the bad news, but there is some good news, too: Most colds go away by themselves and do not lead to anything worse.

Colds are caused by viruses, which are extremely small infectious organisms (much smaller than bacteria). A sneeze or a cough may directly transfer a virus from one person to another. The virus also may be spread indirectly, in the following manner.

1. A child or adult infected with the virus will, in coughing, sneezing, or touching her nose, transfer some of the virus particles onto her hand.

2. She then touches the hand of a healthy person.

3. This healthy person touches her newly contaminated hand to her own nose, thus

How Allergies Develop

If your child has a tendency to develop allergies, he probably has inherited it from you and your spouse. When an allergic-prone youngster is exposed to an allergen, his immune system produces an antibody (called IgE) in a process called allergic sensitization.

Then the IgE sticks to so-called mast cells in the skin and the linings of the airways, stomach, and intestines. The next time he comes in contact with allergens, these cells release chemicals (i.e., histamine and leukotrienes) that cause allergic symptoms.

---

introducing the infectious agent to a place where it can multiply and grow—the nose or throat. Symptoms of a cold soon develop.

4. The cycle then repeats itself, with the virus being transferred from this newly infected child or adult to the next susceptible one, and so on.

Once the virus is present and multiplying, your child will develop the familiar symptoms and signs:

- Runny nose (first, a clear discharge; later, a thicker, often colored one)

- Sneezing

- Mild fever (101–102 degrees Fahrenheit [38.3–38.9 degrees Celsius]), particularly in the evening

- Decreased appetite

- Sore throat and, perhaps, difficulty swallowing

- Cough

- On-and-off irritability

- Slightly swollen glands

- *Pus on the tonsils, especially in children three years and older, may indicate a strep infection* (see page 589).

If your child has a typical cold without complications, the symptoms should disappear gradually after seven to ten days.

Treatment

An older child with a cold usually doesn't need to see a doctor unless the condition becomes more serious. If she is three months or younger, however, call the pediatrician at the first sign of illness. With a young baby, symptoms can be misleading, and colds can quickly develop into more serious ailments, such as bronchiolitis (see page 546), croup (see page 550), or pneumonia (see page 553). For a child older than three months, call the pediatrician if:

- The noisy breathing of a cold is accompanied by the nostrils' widening with each breath, or difficulty with moving breath in and out.

- The lips or nails turn blue.

- Nasal mucus persists for longer than ten to fourteen days.

- The cough just won't go away (it lasts more than one week).

- She has pain in her ear (see *Middle Ear Infections,* page 580).

- Her temperature is over 102 degrees Fahrenheit (38.9 degrees Celsius).

- She is excessively sleepy or cranky.

Your pediatrician may want to see your child, or he may ask you to watch her closely and report back if she doesn't improve each day and is not completely recovered within one week from the start of her illness.

Unfortunately, there's no cure for the common cold. Antibiotics may be used to combat *bacterial* infections, but they have no effect on viruses, so the best you can do is to make your child comfortable. Make sure she gets extra rest and drinks increased amounts of fluids. If she has a fever and is very uncomfortable, give her acetaminophen or ibuprofen. Ibuprofen is approved for use in children six months of age and older; however, it should never be given to children who are dehydrated or who are vomiting continuously. (Be sure to follow the recommended dosage for your child's age.) Never give her any other kind of cold remedy without first checking with your pediatrician. Over-the-counter treatments often dry the respiratory passages or make the nasal secretions even thicker. In addition, they tend to cause side effects, such as drowsiness.

If your infant is having trouble nursing because of nasal congestion, clear her nose with a rubber suction bulb before each feeding. When doing so, remember to *squeeze the bulb part of the syringe first, gently stick the rubber tip into one nostril, then slowly release the bulb.* This slight amount of suction will draw the clogged mucus out of the nose

and should allow her to breathe and suck at the same time once again. You'll find that this technique works best when your baby is under six months of age. As she gets older, she'll fight the bulb, making it difficult to suction the mucus.

If the secretions in your baby's nose are particularly thick, your pediatrician may recommend that you liquefy them with salt-water (saline) nose drops, which are available without a prescription. Using a dropper that has been cleaned with soap and water and well rinsed with plain water, place two drops in each nostril fifteen to twenty minutes before feeding, and then immediately suction with the bulb. *Never use nose drops that contain any medication, since excessive amounts can be absorbed. Only use normal saline nose drops.*

Placing a cool-mist humidifier (vaporizer) in your child's room also will help keep nasal secretions more liquid and make her more comfortable. Set it close to her so that she gets the full benefit of the additional moisture. Be sure to clean and dry the humidifier thoroughly each day to prevent bacterial or mold contamination. *Hot-water vaporizers are not recommended since they can cause serious scalds or burns.*

One final note about medications: *Never use cough medicines or cough/cold preparations in a child under three years of age unless prescribed by your pediatrician.* Coughing is a protective mechanism that clears mucus from the lower part of the respiratory tract, and ordinarily there's no reason to suppress it.

Prevention

If your baby is under three months old, the best prevention against colds is to keep her away from people who have them. This is especially true during the winter, when many of the viruses that cause colds are circulating in larger numbers. A virus that causes a mild illness in an older child or an adult can cause a more serious one in an infant.

If your child is in child care and has a cold, instruct her to cough and sneeze away from others, and to use a tissue to cough into and wipe her nose. Doing this may prevent her from spreading the cold to the others. Similarly, if your child would be in contact with children who have colds and it is convenient for you to keep her away from them, by all means do so. Also teach her to wash her hands regularly during the day; this will cut down on the spread of viruses.

By the way, the use of a tissue or a handkerchief is preferable to having your child cover her mouth with her hand when sneezing and coughing. If the virus lands on her hand, it can be transmitted to whatever she touches—a sibling, a friend, or a toy.

Middle Ear Infections

During your child's first few years of life, there's a significant chance that he'll get a middle ear infection. At least 70 percent of the time, middle ear infections are preceded by virus colds that impair the local defenses which, in the healthy state, prevent bacteria from entering the middle ear. Doctors refer to this middle ear infection as acute otitis media.

Middle ear infections are the most prevalent treatable childhood illness, occurring most often in youngsters between six months and three years of age. Two-thirds of all children have at least one ear infection by their second birthday. It's a particularly common problem among young children because they are more susceptible to viral upper respiratory infections and because of the length and shape of their tiny eustachian tubes, which normally ventilate the middle ear.

Children under one year of age who spend time in group child care settings tend to get more middle ear infections than those cared for at home, primarily because they are exposed to more viruses. Also, infants who self-feed when lying on their backs are susceptible to ear infections since this may allow small amounts of formula to enter the eustachian tube. Children in certain ethnic groups, notably Native Americans and Inuits, seem to have more ear infections, too. This may be due to the configuration of the eustachian tube in these groups. Two things may explain the fact that, as your child enters school, his likelihood of getting a middle ear infection will decrease: The growth of his middle ear structures reduces the likelihood of fluid blockage, and the body's defenses against infection improve with age.

Other characteristics may place children at a higher risk of middle ear infections:

Sex. Although researchers are not sure why, boys have more middle ear infections than girls.

Heredity. Ear infections can run in families. Children are more likely to have repeated middle ear infections if a parent or a sibling also had numerous ear infections.

Tobacco smoke. Children who breathe in nearby tobacco smoke have a markedly increased risk of developing health problems, including ear infections.

Signs and Symptoms

Middle ear infections are usually, but not always, painful. A child old enough to talk will tell you that his ear hurts; a younger child may pull at his ear and cry. Babies with ear infections may cry even more during feedings, because sucking and swallowing cause painful pressure changes in the middle ear. A baby with an ear infection may have trouble sleeping. Fever is another warning signal; ear infections sometimes (one out of three) are accompanied by elevated temper-

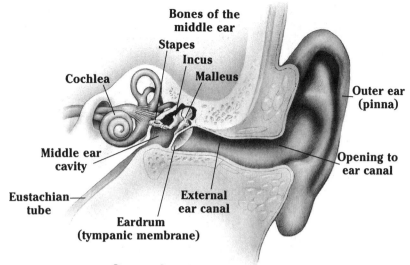

Bones of the
middle ear
Stapes
Incus
Malleus
Cochlea
Outer ear
(pinna)
Middle ear
cavity
Opening to
ear canal
Eustachian
tube
External
ear canal
Eardrum
(tympanic membrane)

Cross Section of Ear

atures ranging from 100.4 to 104 degrees Fahrenheit (38–40 degrees Celsius).

You might see blood-tinged yellow fluid or pus draining from the infected ear. This kind of discharge means that the eardrum has developed a small hole (called a perforation). This hole usually heals by itself without complications, but you will want to describe the discharge to your pediatrician.

You also may notice that your child may not hear well. This occurs because the fluid behind the eardrum interferes with sound transmission. But the hearing loss is usually temporary; normal hearing will be restored once the middle ear is free of fluid. Occasionally, when ear infections recur, fluid may remain behind the eardrum for many weeks and continue to interfere with hearing. If you feel your child's hearing is not as good as it was before his ear became infected, consult your pediatrician. If you remain concerned, request a consultation with an ear, nose, and throat doctor (ENT; otolaryngologist). After several months of watchful waiting, your pediatrician may recommend a hearing test if your child has had more than four ear infections in a year, hearing loss for twelve weeks

or longer, and middle ear fluid that remains in both middle ears for more than three months.

Ear infections are most common during the cold and flu season of winter and early spring. When your child complains of moderate or severe pain in his ear during the summer, particularly after a day at the pool or the beach, he could be suffering from an infection of the *outer* ear canal, called swimmer's ear. This poses no danger to hearing, although it can be very painful and should be treated. (See *Swimmer's Ear,* page 590.)

Treatment

Whenever you suspect an ear infection, call your pediatrician. In the meantime, follow these steps to make your child more comfortable.

- If he has a high fever, cool him using the procedures described in Chapter 23.

- Give acetaminophen or ibuprofen in the dose appropriate for his age. (Don't give aspirin to your child; it has been associated with Reye syndrome, a disease that affects the liver and brain.)

- Your pediatrician might suggest placing warm (not hot) compresses or a heating pad on your child's ear to help relieve pain. (This is not recommended for young babies.) Instillation of a pain-relieving drop (prescribed by your pediatrician) into the ear canal may help reduce pain, but never do this if the ear is draining.

- An extra pillow at night also may help. (Never use pillows in a crib.)

- Do not use eardrops unless your pediatrician authorizes them after seeing your child.

The pediatrician will look into your child's ears with a lighted magnifying instrument called an otoscope. To determine whether there is fluid in the middle ear space behind the eardrum, the doctor may attach a piece of rubber tubing to the otoscope and press on a rubber bulb or blow gently into the ear to check for sensitivity and eardrum movement. Objective tests can help determine whether there is fluid in the middle ear. One test uses an instrument that produces a printed report called a tympanogram; another test is called Ear Check.

If a fever is present, the doctor will perform an examination to determine whether your youngster has any other problem in addition to an ear infection. To treat infections of the middle ear, the doctor will recommend steps to ease pain and may prescribe an antibiotic. Antibiotics are available as flavored liquids, tablets, capsules, and sometimes in chewable form. Eardrops sometimes are used to relieve pain. Unless your child's ear infections are associated with allergies, antihistamines and decongestants probably won't help.

An antibiotic is one of the treatment options for ear infections. Your doctor will specify the schedule for giving it to your child; it may be two or three times a day. Follow the schedule precisely. As the infection begins to clear, some children experience a sense of fullness or popping in the ears; these are normal signs of recovery. There should be clear signs of improvement and disappearance of ear pain and fever within three days.

When your child starts feeling better, you may be tempted to discontinue the medication—but don't. Some of the bacteria that caused the infection still may be present. Stopping the treatment too soon may allow them to multiply again and permit the infection to return with full force. The usual course of antibiotic treatment is ten days for children less than two years and seven days to ten days for older children.

Your pediatrician may want to see your child after the medication is finished, to check if any fluid still is present behind the eardrum, which can occur even if the infection has been controlled. This condition (fluid in middle ear), known as otitis media with effusion, is extremely common: five out of every ten children still have some fluid three weeks after an ear infection is treated. In nine out of ten cases, the fluid will disappear within three months without additional treatment.

Occasionally an ear infection won't respond to the first antibiotic prescribed. If your child continues to complain of significant ear pain and still has a high fever for more than two days after starting an antibiotic, call the pediatrician. To determine if the antibiotic is working, your doctor or a consulting ENT specialist may take a sample of the fluid from the ear by inserting a needle through the eardrum. If the analysis of this sample reveals that the infection is caused by bacteria resistant to the antibiotic your child has been taking, your pediatrician will prescribe a different one. In very rare instances, an ear infection may linger even though other drugs are used. In these cases, a child may be hospitalized so that antibiotics can be given intravenously and the ear can be drained surgically.

Should a child with an ear infection be kept home? It won't be necessary if he's feeling well, as long as someone at child care or school can administer his medication properly. Talk with the staff nurse or your child's caregiver, and review the dosage and the times when it should be given. You also should check to be sure that storage facilities are available if the medication must be refrigerated. Medicine that doesn't require refrigeration should be kept in a locked cabinet separate from other items, and its container should be clearly identified with your child's name and the proper dosage. Most antibiotics can be given once or twice daily.

If your child's eardrum is perforated, he'll be able to engage in most activities, although he may not be permitted to swim. Ordinarily, there's no reason to prevent him from flying in an airplane.

Prevention

Occasional ear infections cannot be prevented. In some children, ear infections may be related to seasonal allergies, which also

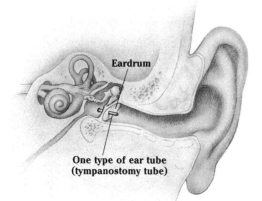

Eardrum

One type of ear tube (tympanostomy tube)

can cause congestion and block the natural drainage of fluid from the ear to the throat. If your child seems to get ear infections more frequently when his allergies flare up, mention this to your pediatrician, who may suggest additional testing or prescribe antihistamines.

If your baby is being bottle-fed, hold his head above the stomach level during feedings. Doing this keeps the eustachian tubes from becoming blocked. You and others also should not smoke cigarettes around your baby.

And what about children who recover from one ear infection only to get another shortly thereafter? If your youngster has had at least three separate middle ear infections during the season, your pediatrician may suggest preventive antibiotics to reduce the chances of still another infection. These drugs usually are prescribed at a low dosage that is taken once or twice a day. Although ear infections may recur while this medicine is being taken, they usually happen less often. Some specialists do not approve of this approach because of the possibility of contributing to antibiotic resistance (see page 584).

If your child continues to have ear infections, he probably will be referred to an ear specialist, who may recommend that tiny ventilation tubes be inserted in the eardrum. These tubes also may be prescribed if fluid remains behind the eardrum more than three months after an ear infection and hearing is impaired, as indicated by a hearing test. While the tubes are in place, they usually restore hearing to normal and also prevent fluid and harmful bacteria from becoming trapped in the middle ear, where they can cause another ear infection.

The long-term benefit of these tubes is still unproven. Also, general anesthesia usually is required to place the tubes in the eardrum. Use of tubes has become standard care for the following specific indications:

Risks of Antibiotic Overuse

Antibiotics are a very important treatment in the management of ear infections. But in recent years many pediatricians have been prescribing antibiotics with much more care to minimize the growing problem of "antibiotic resistance." If antibiotics are used when they are not needed—or if patients do not take a complete course of the drug—new strains of bacteria may develop. When that happens, antibiotics eventually may stop working and the infections they're designed to treat will no longer be curable by the use of these medications, because the bacteria have become "resistant" to them.

Here are some important points to keep in mind to reduce the risk of antibiotic resistance.

- Antibiotics work only against bacterial illnesses, not those caused by viruses. Thus, while they may be appropriate for treating ear infections, you should not ask your pediatrician for a prescription for antibiotics to treat your child's colds and flu (as well as many sore throats and coughs), which are viral infections.

- When your pediatrician recommends antibiotics for an ear infection or other bacterial infection, make sure that your child takes them exactly as your doctor instructs. That means taking all of the medicine that was prescribed, even if your child seems well before he has finished the entire course.

- Don't give your child antibiotics that have been prescribed for another family member or for another illness.

persistent fluid in both middle ears for more than three months with hearing loss or persistent fluid in one middle ear longer than six months.

In an older child, the procedure might be postponed in favor of close monitoring of his hearing to see if it improves with time. If the placement of ventilation tubes is proposed for your child, discuss his specific problem with your child's pediatrician so you fully understand the advantages and disadvantages.

If your child is given ventilation tubes, he should avoid getting water in his ears. Bathing rarely causes a problem, and swimming on the surface of the water is all right, although the doctor may want him to use custom-made earplugs. Even with earplugs, however, don't allow him to dive or swim underwater.

Repeated ear infections can be very trying for you and your child. However, rest assured that it is only a temporary problem that almost always improves as he gets older. Keep in mind that although ear infections are bothersome and uncomfortable, they are usually minor and clear up without causing any lasting problems. Most children stop getting ear infections by the time they are four to six years old.

Epiglottitis

The epiglottis is a tonguelike flap of tissue at the back of the throat. Ordinarily it prevents inhalation of food and liquid into the windpipe when one swallows. In epiglottitis, a rare but serious condition, this structure becomes infected, usually by bacteria called *Haemophilus influenzae* type B. This condition is life-threatening, because when the epiglottis is swollen, it can block the trachea (windpipe) and interfere with normal breathing. Children between two and six years old are most susceptible to this problem. Fortunately, this condition is now very uncommon thanks to the Hib vaccine, which prevents infections due to *Haemophilus influenzae* type B.

The infection begins with a sore throat and a fever that usually is greater than 101 degrees Fahrenheit (38.3 degrees Celsius) and quickly makes your child feel very sick. Her throat will become extremely sore. With each breath, she may make a harsh or raspy noise, called stridor. She may have such difficulty swallowing that she begins to drool. She probably will refuse to lie down and will be most comfortable sitting and leaning forward.

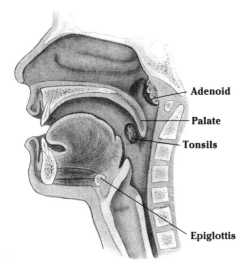

Adenoid

Palate

Tonsils

Epiglottis

Treatment

If your child has an unusually sore throat and is drooling and/or breathing with difficulty, call your physician immediately. Because epiglottitis progresses so rapidly and has such serious consequences, do not attempt to treat it at home. After contacting your pediatrician, try to keep your child calm. Don't try to examine her throat or insist that she lie down. Also, avoid offering food or water, because that might cause vomiting, which often makes breathing even more difficult.

If you take your child to the pediatrician during the early stages of epiglottitis, the doctor may not be able to diagnose the disease. Don't hesitate to call back if the sore throat becomes much worse or drooling or hoarse breathing begins after you return home.

If your pediatrician suspects epiglottitis, you will be asked to take your child directly to the hospital emergency room. With the help of an anesthesiologist and an otolaryngologist (an ear, nose, and throat specialist; ENT), the doctor will examine your child's epiglottis. If it is severely inflamed, an anesthetic will be given and a tube will be inserted through the nose and into the trachea, bypassing the swelling and allowing your child to breathe comfortably again. In very severe cases, a tracheostomy (a breathing tube placed into the trachea through a small incision in the neck) may be necessary, but this is done much less often now than in the past. Your child also will be given antibiotics.

All these decisions are likely to be made very quickly, and you may feel shocked that your child needs such extreme treatment for what looks like a simple though severe sore throat. It's important to remember that epiglottitis progresses very rapidly and can become life-threatening if it goes untreated.

Prevention

The Hib vaccine is available to combat the bacteria that cause epiglottitis. Your child should receive the Hib vaccine at two, four, and six months, and a booster at twelve to fifteen months. However, even if she has had the vaccine, consult your doctor if you know there has been an exposure to another child who has the infection. Your physician might want to take added precautions.

Herpes Simplex

Oral herpes is one of the most common viral diseases of childhood. This condition produces sores ("cold sores"), blisters ("fever blisters"), and swelling of the inside of the mouth and lips. (When most people hear the word *herpes,* they associate it with genital herpes, the sexually transmitted disease; however, a different strain of this virus usually causes cold sores in children.) Oral herpes is highly contagious, and is spread by direct contact, frequently by kissing. Most infants are protected by their mothers' antibodies up to about age six months, but they become susceptible after that.

When the virus is transmitted to a child for the first time, she is said to have primary herpes. This may cause pain, swelling and reddening of the gums, and an increase in saliva, followed a day or two later by blisters inside the mouth. When the blisters break, they leave sore areas that take several days to heal. The child also may develop a fever and headache, act irritably, lose her appetite, and have swollen lymph glands for a week or so. Many children, however, have such mild symptoms that no one realizes they have the virus.

Unfortunately, once a child has had primary herpes, she becomes a carrier of the virus. This means that the virus, usually in an inactive state, remains within her system.

However, during episodes of stress (including other infections), injury to the mouth, sunburn, allergies, and fatigue, the virus can become reactivated, producing what's called secondary herpes. This is a condition similar to but generally milder than the primary infection, and usually doesn't occur until later in childhood or adulthood. Cold sores and fever blisters are the usual symptoms of secondary herpes.

Treatment

If your child complains of symptoms resembling those of herpes, consult your pediatrician. Primary herpes is not a serious illness, but it can make your child uncomfortable. The treatment, which should be aimed at reducing this discomfort, includes:

- Bed rest and sleep.

- Plenty of cold fluids, including nonacidic drinks like apple or apricot juice.

- Acetaminophen, if fever or excessive discomfort is present.

- Mouth rinse or gargles prescribed by your pediatrician. These medications may contain a painkiller that will numb the areas affected by the mouth sores. Carefully follow the directions for use of these preparations.

- A soft, bland but nutritious diet.

- Antiviral medications that may be prescribed by your pediatrician. They will stop the virus from mutiplying, but will not prevent reactivation after the medications are stopped.

Occasionally a child infected with primary herpes must be hospitalized because of dehydration.

Never use any creams or ointments containing steroids (cortisone) if there is the slightest suspicion that the mouth sores are due to herpes. These preparations can make the viral infection spread.

Prevention

Direct contact is required to spread the herpes virus, so you should not let anyone with herpes blisters or sores kiss your child. People with oral herpes often shed the virus even when they have no sores, and these sores are contagious. In general, discourage individuals from kissing your baby or child directly on the lips.

Also, try to discourage your child from sharing eating utensils with other children. (This is more easily said than done.) If your child has primary herpes, keep her home to prevent other children from getting this infection from her.

Nosebleeds

Your child is almost certain to have at least one nosebleed—and probably many—during these early years. Some preschoolers have several a week. This is neither abnormal nor dangerous, but it can be very frightening. If blood flows down from the back of the nose into the mouth and throat, your child may swallow a great deal of it, which in turn may cause vomiting.

There are many causes of nosebleeds, most of which aren't serious. Beginning with the most common, they include:

- Colds and allergies: A cold or allergy causes swelling and irritation inside the nose and may lead to spontaneous bleeding.

- Trauma: A child can get a nosebleed from picking his nose, or putting something into it, or just blowing it too hard. A nosebleed also can occur if he is hit in the nose by a ball or other object or falls and hits his nose.

- Low humidity or irritating fumes: If your house is very dry, or if you live in a dry climate, the lining of your child's nose may dry out, making it more likely to bleed. If he is frequently exposed to toxic fumes (fortunately, an unusual occurrence), they may cause nosebleeds, too.

- Anatomical problems: Any abnormal structure inside the nose can lead to crusting and bleeding.

- Abnormal growths: Any abnormal tissue growing in the nose may cause bleeding. Although most of these growths (usually polyps) are benign (not cancerous), they still should be treated promptly.

- Abnormal blood clotting: Anything that interferes with blood clotting can lead to nosebleeds. Medications, even common ones like aspirin, can alter the blood-clotting mechanism just enough to cause bleeding. Blood diseases, such as hemophilia, also can provoke nosebleeds.

- Chronic illness: Any child with a long-term illness, or who may require extra oxygen or other medication that can dry out or affect the lining of the nose, is likely to have nosebleeds.

Treatment

There are many misconceptions and folktales about how to treat nosebleeds. Here's a list of dos and don'ts.

Do...

1. Remain calm. A nosebleed can be frightening, but is rarely serious.

2. Keep your child in a sitting or standing position. Tilt his head slightly forward. Have him gently blow his nose if he is old enough.

3. Pinch the lower half of your child's nose (the soft part) between your thumb and finger and hold it firmly for a full ten minutes. If your child is old enough, he can do this himself. *Don't release the nose during this time to see if it is still bleeding.*

Release the pressure after ten minutes and wait, keeping your child quiet. If the bleeding hasn't stopped, repeat this step. If after ten more minutes of pressure the bleeding hasn't stopped, call your pediatrician or go to the nearest emergency room.

Don't...

1. Panic. You'll just scare your child.

2. Have him lie down or tilt back his head.

3. Stuff tissues, gauze, or any other material into your child's nose to stop the bleeding.

Also call your pediatrician if:

- You think your child may have lost too much blood. (But keep in mind that the blood coming from the nose always looks like a lot.)

- The bleeding is coming only from your child's mouth, or he's coughing or vomiting blood or brown material that looks like coffee grounds.

- Your child is unusually pale or sweaty, or is not responsive. *Call your pediatrician*

immediately in this case, and arrange to take your child to the emergency room.

- He has a lot of nosebleeds, along with a chronically stuffy nose. This may mean he has a small, easily broken blood vessel in the nose or on the surface of the lining of the nose, or a growth in the nasal passages.

If your pediatrician sees your child during a nosebleed, she probably will repeat the nose-holding routine described in Step 3. (If the nose is full of blood clots, it may be suctioned clean first.) The doctor also may use nose drops that constrict the blood vessels, or put cotton soaked with medication inside the child's nose. The doctor may decide to examine your child's nose with a special light to find the origin of the bleeding. If a blood vessel is found to be causing the problem, the doctor will touch that point with a chemical substance (silver nitrate) to stop the bleeding.

If the bleeding still cannot be controlled, the nose may have to be packed with gauze. Your child won't like this—it is uncomfortable—but it may be necessary. The packing is generally left in for at least twenty-four hours.

If your doctor thinks it's necessary to explore the cause of the bleeding further or to make sure your child didn't lose too much blood, a blood test will be ordered. It's extremely rare that a child will need a blood transfusion to replace lost blood.

Prevention

If your child gets a lot of nosebleeds, ask your pediatrician about using salt-water (saline) nose drops every day. Doing so may be particularly helpful if you live in a very dry climate, or when the furnace is on. In addition, a humidifier or vaporizer will help maintain your home's humidity at a level high enough to prevent nasal drying. Also tell your child not to pick his nose. If he picks it at night or in his sleep, put him to bed wearing thin cotton gloves or socks over his hands and pinned to his pajama sleeve.

Sore Throat (Strep Throat, Tonsillitis)

The terms *sore throat, strep throat,* and *tonsillitis* often are used interchangeably, but they don't mean the same thing. Tonsillitis refers to tonsils that are inflamed. (See *Tonsils and Adenoid,* page 595.) When your child has a strep throat, the tonsils are usually very inflamed, and the inflammation may affect the surrounding part of the throat, as well. Other causes of sore throats are viruses and may only cause inflammation of the throat around the tonsils and not the tonsils themselves.

In infants, toddlers, and preschoolers, the most frequent cause of sore throats is a viral infection. No specific medicine is required when a virus is responsible, and the child should get better over a seven- to ten-day period. Often children who have sore throats due to viruses also have a cold at the same time. They may develop a mild fever, too, but they generally aren't very sick.

One particular virus (called Coxsackie), seen most often during the summer and fall, may cause the child to have a somewhat higher fever, more difficulty swallowing, and a sicker overall feeling. If your child has a Coxsackie infection, she also may have one or more blisters in her throat and on her hands and feet. Infectious mononucleosis can produce a sore throat, often with marked tonsillitis; however, most young children who are infected with the mononucleosis virus have few or no symptoms.

Strep throat is caused by a bacterium called *Streptococcus pyogenes.* To some extent, the symptoms of strep throat depend on the child's age. Infants with strep infections may have only a low fever and a thickened or bloody nasal discharge. Toddlers (ages one to three) also may have a thickened or bloody nasal discharge with a fever. Such children are usually quite cranky, have no appetite, and often have swollen glands in the neck. Children over three years of age with strep are often more ill; they may have an extremely painful throat, fever over 102 degrees Fahrenheit (38.9 degrees Celsius), swollen glands in the neck, and pus on the tonsils. It's important to be able to distinguish a strep throat from a viral sore throat, because strep infections are treated with antibiotics.

Diagnosis-Treatment

If your child has a sore throat that persists (not one that goes away after her first drink of juice in the morning), whether or not it is accompanied by fever, headache, stomachache, or extreme fatigue, you should call your pediatrician. That call should be made even more urgently if your child seems extremely ill, or if she has difficulty breathing or extreme trouble swallowing (causing her to drool). This may indicate a more serious infection (see *Epiglottitis,* page 585).

The doctor will examine your child and may perform a throat culture to determine the nature of the infection. To do this, he will touch the back of the throat and tonsils with a cotton-tipped applicator and then smear the tip onto a special culture dish that allows strep bacteria to grow if they are present. The culture dish usually is examined twenty-four hours later for the presence of the bacteria.

Some pediatric offices perform quick-result strep tests that provide findings within minutes. However, when these tests are negative, their results still need to be confirmed with a twenty-four-hour culture. If the result of the culture is still negative, the infection usually is presumed to be due to a virus. In that case, antibiotics (which are antibacterial) will not help and need not be prescribed.

If the test shows that your child does have strep throat, your pediatrician will prescribe an antibiotic to be taken by mouth or by injection. If your child is given the oral medication, it's very important that she take it for the full course, as prescribed, even if the symptoms get better or go away.

If a child's strep throat is not treated with antibiotics, or if she doesn't complete the treatment, the infection may worsen or spread to other parts of his body, causing more serious problems, such as ear and sinus infections (see *Middle Ear Infections,* page 580, and *Sinusitis,* page 661). If left untreated, a strep infection also can lead to rheumatic fever, a disease that affects the joints and the heart. However, rheumatic fever is rare in the United States and in children under five years old.

Prevention

Most types of throat infections are contagious, being passed primarily through the air on droplets of moisture or on the hands of infected children or adults. For that reason, it makes sense to keep your child away from people who have symptoms of this condition. However, most people are contagious before their first symptoms appear, so often there's really no practical way to prevent your youngster from contracting the disease.

In the past when a child had frequent sore throats, her tonsils might have been removed in an attempt to prevent further infections. But this operation, called a tonsillectomy, is recommended much less often today. (See *Tonsils and Adenoid,* page 595.) Even in difficult cases, where there is repeated strep throat, treatment with antibiotics is usually the best solution.

(See also *Swollen Glands,* page 592.)

Swimmer's Ear (External Otitis)

Swimmer's ear is an infection of the skin of the ear canal (or outer ear) that occurs most often after swimming or other activities that admit water into the ears. Swimmer's ear develops because moisture in the ear canal encourages the growth of certain bacteria and, at the same time, causes the skin that lines the ear canal to soften (like the white, swollen area that forms under a wet bandage). The bacteria then invade the softened skin and multiply there.

Children who play for long periods in warm water are most likely to get this infection. However, for reasons that are not clear, some children are more prone to it than others: Infants, for instance, rarely get swimmer's ear; preschool and school-age children develop it most often, usually in the summertime. At any age, injury to the canal (cotton swab abuse), and conditions such as eczema (see page 693) and seborrhea (see page 692), can increase the likelihood of getting swimmer's ear.

With the mildest form of swimmer's ear, your child will complain only of itchiness or a plugged feeling in the ear, or—if he's too young to tell you what's bothering him—you might notice him sticking his finger in his ear or rubbing it with his hand. These symptoms often progress to dull pain, beginning anytime from six hours to five days after being in the water. By this time the opening of his ear canal may become swollen and slightly red, and if you push on the opening or pull up on his ear, it will hurt him.

In more severe cases of swimmer's ear,

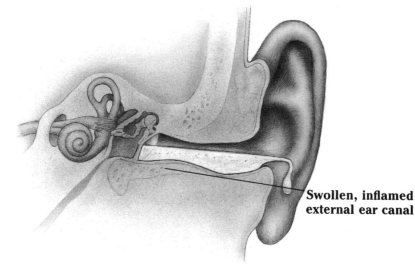

**Swollen, inflamed
external ear canal**

the pain will be constant and intense, and your child may cry and hold his hand over his ear. The slightest motion, even chewing, will hurt a lot. The ear canal opening actually may be swollen shut, with a few drops of pus or cheesy material oozing out, and there may be a low-grade fever (rarely more than one or two degrees above normal). In the most serious infections, the redness and swelling may spread beyond the ear canal to the entire outer ear.

Since swimmer's ear doesn't involve the middle ear or the hearing apparatus, any loss of hearing due to blockage of the canal is temporary. The infection rarely spreads beyond the canal into deeper tissues. If it does, however, this can be very serious, and more intensive treatment is required.

Treatment

If your child has pain in his ear, or if you suspect swimmer's ear, call your pediatrician. Although the condition usually isn't serious, it still needs to be examined and treated by a doctor. Unfortunately, sometimes it's impossible for a parent to tell whether a young

child suffers from swimmer's ear, a middle ear infection, or some unrelated condition, so you should not attempt to treat it by yourself.

Until you see your pediatrician, you can help relieve your child's pain with acetaminophen, along with a heating pad (on low setting) or a hot-water bottle placed around the ear. For more severe pain in an older child, you might also be able to use a codeine preparation, but you should check with your pediatrician before giving your child this or any medication other than acetaminophen.

Do *not* insert a cotton swab or anything else into the ear in an attempt to relieve itching or promote drainage; doing so will only cause further skin damage and provide additional sites for bacteria to grow. As a matter of fact, using cotton swabs to clean out a child's ears can, by itself, lead to infection of the ear canal. Using the swab can irritate the skin and remove the thin layer of earwax that's there to coat and protect the canal against moisture and bacteria.

At the pediatrician's office, the doctor first will examine the affected ear and then, perhaps, carefully clean out pus and debris from the canal. In mild cases this may be the only treatment your child needs, although most doctors also prescribe eardrops for five to seven days. The eardrops combat infection and thereby decrease swelling, which helps to relieve the pain. In order to be effective, however, eardrops have to be used properly. Here's how to administer them:

1. Lay your child on his side with his affected ear up.

2. Put the drops in so that they run along the side of the ear canal, permitting air to escape as the medicine flows in. You can gently move the ear to help the drops along.

3. Keep your child lying on his side for two or three minutes to make sure that the drops reach the deepest recess.

4. Use these drops as directed for the length of time prescribed. Occasionally oral antibiotics are prescribed also.

If the ear canal is too swollen for drops to enter, your pediatrician may insert a "wick"—a small piece of cotton or spongy material that soaks up the medicine and holds it in the canal. In this case, you'll need to resaturate the wick with the drops three or four times per day.

Rarely, a swimmer's ear infection is so severe that the child has to be hospitalized to receive intravenous antibiotic therapy and pain medication.

When your child is being treated for swimmer's ear, he should stay out of the water for about a week. However, he can take brief showers or baths daily and have his hair washed, as long as you dry the ear canal afterward with the corner of a towel or a blow-dryer (on a very low setting, held away from the ear). Once that's done, put in more eardrops. Incidentally, swimmer's ear is not contagious, so you don't have to keep your child home from school or camp, as long as someone there can put in his drops properly.

Prevention

There's no need to try to prevent swimmer's ear unless your child has had this infection frequently or very recently. Under these circumstances, limit his stays in the water, usually to less than an hour. Then, when he comes out, remove the excess water from his ear with the corner of a towel, or have him shake his head. His ears should dry out for at least twenty minutes before he enters the water again.

As a preventive measure, many pediatricians recommend acetic acid eardrops. They are available in various preparations, some of which require a prescription. These are preferred over those that are "home-made." They usually are used in the morning, at the end of each swim, and at bedtime. Earplugs or a bathing cap sometimes helps keep the ears dry and prevent this problem from occurring.

There's still another sound way to prevent swimmer's ear—by following the advice your grandmother gave you: "The only thing you should stick in your ear is your elbow." That goes for your child's ears, too. Resist the temptation to clean out your child's ears with cotton swabs, your finger, or any other object. Your doctor can show you how to remove the wax from the ear with an ear bulb syringe or an earwax softener.

Swollen Glands

Lymph glands (or lymph nodes) are an important part of the body's defense system against infection and illness. These glands normally contain groups of cells, called lym-

Common Causes of Swollen Glands

- Swollen glands in the front or sides of the neck usually are caused by an inflamed or sore throat, most often caused by a virus, but sometimes due to strep bacteria. (See *Sore Throat,* page 589.) At times, swollen glands in the back of a child's neck may mean that there is (or has been) an infection of the scalp. Occasionally a swollen gland in the neck area is mistaken for mumps (see page 658.) However, this disease usually causes swelling of the parotid gland, which is located on the jaw in front of the ear and does not extend down the neck.

- Swollen glands under the jawbone may be caused by infection in the cheek or gum or a tooth.

- Although slight swelling of the glands at the lower back of the head is often normal, it also could indicate, particularly if the glands are large and tender, that the child has a viral illness or infection.

- Swollen glands occurring only in the groin usually are a sign of an infection in the leg.

- Swollen glands in the underarm typically indicate an infection on the arm or hand on the same side as the swelling.

- Swollen glands all over the body usually are related to a general illness, such as a viral infection.

- Scratches from cats may result in swollen glands near the site of the break in the skin or even farther away, depending on the location of the glands normally draining that body area.

- Swollen glands at the base of the neck and just above the collarbone may be evidence of an infection or even a tumor within the chest, and should be examined by a physician as soon as possible.

---

phocytes, which act as barriers to infection. The lymphocytes produce substances called antibodies that destroy or immobilize infecting cells or poisons. When lymph glands become enlarged or swollen, it usually means that the lymphocytes have increased in number due to an infection or other illness and that they are being called into action to produce extra antibodies. Rarely, swollen glands, particularly if long lasting and without other signs of inflamma-

tion, such as redness or tenderness, may indicate a tumor.

If your child has swollen glands, you'll be able to feel them or actually see the swelling. They also may be tender to the touch. Often, if you look near the gland, you can find the infection or injury that has caused it to swell. For example, a sore throat often will cause glands in the neck to swell, or an infection on the arm will produce swollen glands under the arm. Sometimes the illness may be a generalized one, such as those caused by a virus, in which case many glands might be slightly swollen. In general, because children have more viral infections than adults, lymph nodes, particularly in the neck, are more likely to be enlarged.

Treatment

In the vast majority of cases, swollen glands are not serious. Lymph node swelling usually disappears after the illness that caused it is gone. The glands gradually return to normal over a period of weeks. You should call the pediatrician if your child shows any of the following:

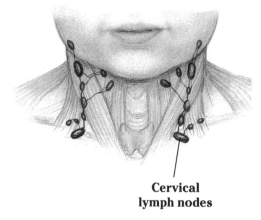

**Cervical
lymph nodes**

- Lymph glands swollen and tender for more than five days

- Fever higher than 101 degrees Fahrenheit (38.3 degrees Celsius)

- Glands that appear to be swollen throughout the body

- Tiredness, lethargy, or loss of appetite

- Glands that enlarge rapidly, or the skin overlying them turning red or purple

As with any infection, if your child has a fever or is in pain, you can give her acet-

aminophen in the appropriate dosage for her weight and age until you can see the pediatrician. When you call, your doctor probably will ask you some questions to try to determine the cause of the swelling, so it will help if you do a little investigating beforehand. For instance, if the swollen glands are in the jaw or neck area, check if your child's teeth are tender or her gums are inflamed, and ask her if there is any soreness in her mouth or throat. Mention to your doctor any exposure your child has had to animals (especially cats) or wooded areas. Also check for any recent animal scratches, tick bites, or insect bites or stings that may have become infected.

The treatment for swollen glands will depend on the cause. If there's a specific bacterial infection in nearby skin or tissue, antibiotics will clear it, allowing the glands gradually to return to their normal size. If the gland itself has an infection, it may require not only antibiotics but also warm compresses to localize the infection, then surgical drainage. If this is done, the material obtained from the wound will be cultured to determine the exact cause of the infection. Doing this will help the doctor choose the most appropriate antibiotic.

If your pediatrician cannot find the cause of the swelling, or if the swollen glands don't improve after antibiotic treatment, further tests will be needed. For example, infectious mononucleosis might be the problem if your child has a fever and a bad sore throat (but not strep), is very weak, and has swollen (but not red, hot, or tender) glands, although mononucleosis occurs more often in older children. Special tests can confirm this diagnosis. In cases where the cause of a swollen gland is unclear, the pediatrician also may want to do a tuberculosis skin test.

If the cause of prolonged swelling of lymph nodes cannot be found in any other way, it may be necessary to perform a biopsy (remove a piece of tissue from the gland) and examine it under a microscope. In rare cases this may reveal a tumor or fungus infection, which would require special treatment.

Prevention

The only swollen glands that are preventable are those that are caused by bacterial infections in the surrounding tissue. Proper cleansing of all wounds (see *Cuts and Scrapes,* page 485) and early antibiotic treatment in cases of suspected infection are the keys to avoiding involvement of the lymph nodes.

Tonsils and Adenoid

If you look into your child's throat, you will see a pink, oval-shape mass on each side. These are the tonsils. The tonsils are small in infants and increase in size over the first five years of life. They produce antibodies during periods when the body is fighting infection.

Like the tonsils, the adenoid is part of your child's defense against infections. Although it is often referred to as adenoids, this is incorrect because the adenoid is actually a single mass of tissue. The adenoid is located in the very upper part of the throat, above the uvula and behind the nose. This area is called the nasopharynx. The adenoid can be seen only with special mirrors or instruments passed through the nose.

The most common illness associated with the tonsils is tonsillitis. This is an inflammation of the tonsils usually due to an infection. There are several signs of tonsillitis, including:

- Red and swollen tonsils

- White or yellow coating over the tonsils

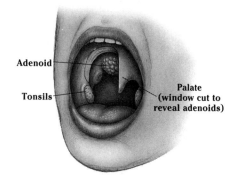

- A "throaty" voice

- Sore throat

- Uncomfortable or painful swallowing

- Swollen lymph nodes ("glands") in the neck

- Fever

It is not always easy to tell when your child's adenoid is enlarged. Some children are born with a larger adenoid. Others may have temporary enlargement of their adenoid due to colds or other infections; this is especially common among young children. Constant swelling or enlargement can cause other health problems, such as ear and sinus infections. Some signs of adenoid enlargement are:

- Breathing through the mouth instead of the nose most of the time

- Nose sounds "blocked" when the child talks

- Noisy breathing during the day

- Snoring at night

Both the tonsils and the adenoid may be enlarged if your child has the above symptoms along with any of the following:

- Breathing stops for a short period of time at night during snoring or loud breathing (called sleep apnea)

- Choking or gasping during sleep

- Difficulty swallowing, especially solid foods

- A constant "throaty voice," even when there is no tonsillitis

In extreme cases, your child may have such difficulty breathing that it interferes with the normal exchange of oxygen and carbon dioxide in his lungs. This is very rare, but important to recognize. If your child has severe breathing difficulties, seems drowsy during waking hours, and lacks energy despite what should have been adequate amounts of sleep, consult your pediatrician.

Treatment

If your child shows the signs and symptoms of enlarged tonsils or adenoid, and doesn't seem to be getting better over a period of weeks, mention it to your pediatrician. If the doctor decides that there is significant tonsil or adenoid enlargement, she will recommend one of several courses of treatment.

Watching and Waiting

If you have only just noticed the symptoms, the doctor may delay further action until she is sure there's an ongoing problem. Most enlarged tonsils or adenoid simply get smaller by themselves.

Treatment with Antibiotics

Your pediatrician may decide to give your child antibiotics in an attempt to eliminate any infection that might be causing the swelling.

Surgery to Remove Tonsils and/or Adenoid (Tonsillectomy and Adenoidectomy)

Although these two operations (often combined and called T & A) were done almost routinely in the past and remain the most common major operations performed on children, not until recently has their long-term effectiveness been adequately tested. In light of current studies, today's physicians are much more conservative in recommending these procedures, even though some children still need to have their tonsils and/or adenoid taken out.

According to the guidelines of the American Academy of Pediatrics, your pediatrician may recommend surgery in the following circumstances:

- Tonsil or adenoid swelling makes normal breathing difficult. (This may or may not include sleep apnea.)

- Tonsils are so swollen that your child has a problem swallowing.

- An enlarged adenoid makes breathing uncomfortable, severely alters speech, and possibly affects normal growth of the face. In this case, surgery to remove only the adenoid may be recommended.

- The child has an excessive number of severe sore throats each year.

- Lymph nodes beneath the lower jaw are swollen or tender for at least six months, even with antibiotic treatment.

If your child needs surgery, make sure he knows what will happen before, during, and after surgery. Don't keep the surgery a secret from your child. An operation can be scary, but it's better to be honest than to leave your child with fears and unanswered questions.

The hospital may have a special program to help you and your child get familiar with the hospital and the surgery. If the hospital allows, try to stay with your child during the entire hospital visit. Let your child know that you'll be nearby during the entire operation. Your pediatrician also can help you and your child understand the operation and make it less frightening. A little ice cream afterward won't hurt, either.

21

Eyes

Your child relies on the visual information he gathers to help him develop throughout infancy and childhood. If he has difficulty seeing properly, he may have problems in learning and relating to the world around him. For this reason it is important to detect eye deficiencies as early as possible. Many vision problems can be corrected if treated early but become much more difficult to care for later on.

Your infant should have his first eye examination by a pediatrician at birth to check for problems that may be present then. Routine vision checks then should be part of every visit to the pediatrician's office. If your family has a history of serious eye diseases or abnormalities, your pediatrician may refer your baby to an ophthalmologist (an eye specialist with a medical degree) for an early examination and follow-up visits if necessary.

If a child is born prematurely, he will be checked for a vision-threatening condition called retinopathy of prematurity, especially if he required oxygen over a prolonged period of time during his early days of life. The risk is greater in the more premature, lower–birth weight infant. This condition may not be prevented even with ideal neonatal care, but in many cases, if detected early, it can be treated successfully. All neonatologists are aware of the threat of retinopathy and will advise parents of the necessity for ophthalmological evaluations. Parents also should be advised that all premature children are at greater risk for developing astigmatism, myopia, and strabismus and that they therefore should be screened periodically throughout childhood.

How much does a newborn baby see? Until fairly recently, it was thought that the newborn infant could see very little; however, the information now available indicates that even during the early weeks of life, an infant can see light and shapes and can detect movement. Far vision remains quite blurry, with the optimal focal length being 8 to 15 inches (20 to 38 cm), roughly the distance from his eyes to yours as you are nursing or feeding your baby.

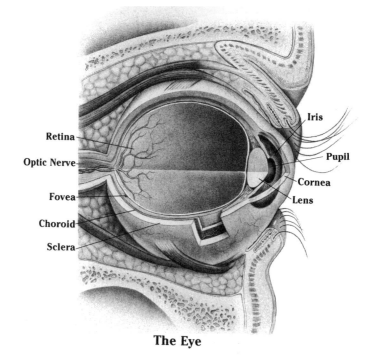

Retina

Optic Nerve

Fovea

Choroid

Sclera

Iris

Pupil

Cornea

Lens

The Eye

Until your baby learns to use both eyes together, they may "wander," or move randomly. This random movement should be decreasing by two to three months of age. Around three months of age, your baby probably will focus on faces and close objects and follow a moving object with his eyes. By four months of age, the baby should be using his vision to detect various objects close to him, which he probably will reach for and grasp. By six months of age, the baby should be able to visually identify and distinguish between objects.

Between one and two years of age, your child's ability to see develops rapidly, so that the average two-year-old can see at approximately the 20/60 level. (He sees at 20 feet what the normal mature eye sees at 60 feet.) Between the ages of two and three years, the child's vision gradually reaches an acuity level of 20/25, and by ages three to four, the child with normal vision will reach the adult visual acuity level of 20/20.

By the time a child is ten, his motor sys-

tems are fully developed. At this point, many eye and vision problems can no longer be reversed or corrected. This is why early detection and treatment of eye problems in children is so important and why your pediatrician will examine your baby's eyes at every routine physical examination.

If regular eye checks during pediatric visits indicate that your baby's eyes are developing normally, he should not need more formal testing until three to four years of age. By that age, most children can follow directions and describe what they see, so testing is much more reliable. Your pediatrician may use the E-game vision screen or similar testing, which enables him to estimate your child's visual acuity in reportable terms. As visual acuity should have reached the 20/40 level, any child with less than 20/40 vision should be referred to an ophthalmologist to determine the cause of the visual deficiency.

Your pediatrician's screening also will check for any evidence of eye disease and will evaluate the alignment of your child's eyes to make sure both eyes are working together.

Vision Screening Recommendations

Vision screening is a very important factor in identifying vision-threatening conditions. The American Academy of Pediatrics recommends that children be screened in four stages:

1. In the newborn nursery: Pediatricians should examine all infants prior to their discharge from the nursery to check for infections and structural defects, cataracts, or glaucoma. If a problem is suspected, a pediatric ophthalmologist should see the newborn. All children with multiple medical problems or with a history of prematurity and/or oxygen exposure should be examined by an ophthalmologist.

2. By the age of six months: Pediatricians should screen infants at the time of their well-baby visits to check for alignment (eyes working together) and the presence of any eye disease.

3. At the age of three to four years: All children should be examined by a pediatrician. At this age, the visual acuity is checked and the eyes are examined for any other abnormality that may cause a problem with the child's educational development. Any abnormality requires referral to an ophthalmologist.

4. At the age of five years and older: Pediatricians should screen children annually, if such screenings are not provided by school personnel or volunteer organizations. These tests measure visual acuity and evaluate other ocular functions.

When to Call the Pediatrician

Routine eye checks can detect hidden eye problems, but occasionally you may notice obvious signs that your child is having trouble seeing or that his eyes are not normal. Notify the pediatrician if your child shows any of the following warning signs.

- Persistent (lasting more than twenty-four hours) redness, swelling, crusting, or discharge in his eyes or eyelids

- Excessive tearing

- Sensitivity to light, especially a change in the child's sensitivity to light

- Eyes that look crooked or crossed, or that don't move together

- Head held in an abnormal or tilted position

- Frequent squinting

- Drooping eyelids

- Pupils of unequal size

- Continuous eye-rubbing

- Eyes that "bounce" or "dance"

- Inability to see objects unless he holds them close

- Eye injury (see page 607)

- Cloudy cornea

You also should take your child to the pediatrician if he complains of any of the following:

- Seeing double

- Frequent headaches

- Dizziness

- Nausea after doing close-up eye work (reading, television)

- Inability to see clearly

- Itching, scratching, or burning eyes

- Difficulty with color vision

Depending on the symptoms your child displays, the pediatrician probably will check for vision difficulties and/or some of the other problems discussed in the remainder of this chapter.

Vision Difficulties Requiring Corrective Lenses

Nearsightedness

The inability to see distant objects clearly is the most common visual problem in young children. This inherited trait occasionally is found in newborns, especially premature infants, but it's more often detected after two years of age.

Contrary to popular belief, reading too much, reading in dim light, or poor nutrition cannot cause or affect nearsightedness. It's usually the result of an eyeball that's longer than its focusing ability. Less frequently, it's due to a change in the shape of the cornea or lens.

The treatment for nearsightedness is corrective lenses—either eyeglasses or contact lenses. Keep in mind that when your child grows rapidly, so do his eyes, so he may need new lenses as often as every six months or less. Nearsightedness usually changes very rapidly for several years and then stabilizes before or during adolescence.

Farsightedness

This is a condition in which the eyeball is shorter than its focusing ability. Most children are actually born farsighted, but as they grow, their eyeballs get longer and the farsightedness diminishes. Glasses or contact lenses rarely are needed unless the condition is excessive. If your child has eye discomfort or frequent mild headaches related to prolonged reading, she may be suffering from a severe degree of farsightedness and should be examined by your pediatrician or pediatric ophthalmologist.

Astigmatism

Astigmatism is an uneven curvature of the surface of the cornea and/or lens. If your child has an astigmatism, vision both near and far may be blurred. Astigmatism can be corrected with either glasses or contact lenses.

Strabismus

Strabismus is a misalignment of the eyes caused by an imbalance in the muscles controlling the eye.

A newborn baby's eyes commonly and normally wander. However, within a few weeks, he learns to move his eyes together, and the wandering should disappear within a few months. If this intermittent wandering continues, or if your baby's eyes don't turn in the same direction (if one turns in, out, up, or down), he needs to be evaluated by a pediatric ophthalmologist. This condition, called strabismus, makes it impossible for the eyes to focus on the same point at the same time.

If your child is born with strabismus, it's important for his eyes to be realigned early in life so he can focus them together on a single object. Eye exercises alone cannot ac-

**Left eye
turning inward**

complish this, so the treatment usually involves eyeglasses, eyedrops, or surgery.

If your child needs an operation, it is frequently done between six and eighteen months of age. The surgery is usually safe and effective, although it's not uncommon for a child to need more than one procedure. Even after surgery, your youngster still may need glasses.

Some children look as if they have strabismus because of the way their faces are structured, but in fact their eyes are perfectly aligned. These children may have a flat nasal bridge and broad skin folds alongside the nose, termed *epicanthus,* which can distort the appearance of the eyes, making these youngsters appear cross-eyed when they really aren't. This condition is called pseudostrabismus (meaning false eyeturn). The child's vision is not affected, and, in most cases, as the child grows and the nasal bridge becomes more prominent, the child loses the pseudostrabismic appearance.

Because of the importance of early diagnosis and treatment of the true eyeturn (or true strabismus), if you have any suspicion

that your baby's eyes may not be perfectly aligned and working together, you should bring it to the attention of your pediatrician, who can best determine whether your baby has an actual problem.

Strabismus occurs in about 4 of 100 children. It may be present at birth (infantile strabismus), or it may develop later in childhood (acquired strabismus). Strabismus may develop if your child has another visual impairment, sustains an eye injury, or develops cataracts. Always report the sudden onset of strabismus to your pediatrician immediately. Although very rare, it may indicate the development of a tumor or other serious nervous system problem. In all cases, it is important to diagnose and treat strabismus as early in your child's life as possible. If a turned eye is not treated early, the child may never develop the ability to use both eyes together (binocular vision); and if both eyes are not used together, it is common for one to become "lazy," or amblyopic.

Amblyopia

Amblyopia is a fairly common eye problem (affecting about 2 of 100 children) that develops when a child has one eye that doesn't see well or is injured, and begins to use the other eye almost exclusively. The idle eye then relaxes and becomes even weaker. In general, the problem must be detected by the age of three in order to treat and restore normal vision in the affected eye by age six. If this situation persists for too long (past the age of seven or nine years), vision may be lost permanently in the unused eye.

Once an ophthalmologist corrects the problems in the unused eye, your child may need to wear a patch over the "good" eye for periods of time. This forces her to use and strengthen the eye that has become "lazy." Patching therapy will be continued for as long as necessary to bring the weaker eye up to its full potential. This could take weeks, months, or even up to age ten or older. As an alternative to the patch, the ophthalmologist might prescribe eyedrops or ointment to blur the vision in the good eye, thereby forcing your child to use the amblyopic eye.

Eye Infections

If the white of your child's eye and the inside of his lower lid become red, he probably has a condition called conjunctivitis. Also known as pinkeye, this inflammation, which can be painful and itchy, usually signals an infection, but may be due to other causes, such as an irritation, an allergic reaction, or (rarely) a more serious condition. It's often accompanied by tearing and discharge, which is the body's way of trying to heal or remedy the situation.

If your child has a red eye, he needs to see the pediatrician as soon as possible. The doctor will make the diagnosis and prescribe necessary medication if it is indicated. *Never put previously opened medication or someone else's eye medication into your child's eye. It could cause serious damage.*

In a newborn baby, serious eye infections may result from exposure to bacteria during passage through the birth canal—which is why all infants are treated with antibiotic eye ointment or drops in the delivery room. Such infections must be treated early to prevent serious complications. Eye infections that occur after the newborn period may be unsightly, because of the redness of the eye and the yellow discharge that usually accompanies them, and they may make your child uncomfortable, but they are rarely serious. Several different viruses, or occasionally bacteria, may cause them. If your pediatrician feels the problem is caused by bacteria, antibiotic eyedrops are the usual

treatment. Conjunctivitis caused by viruses should not be treated with antibiotics.

Eye infections typically last up to ten days and may be contagious. Except to administer drops or ointment, you should avoid direct contact with your child's eyes or drainage from them until the medication has been used for several days and there is evidence of clearing of the redness. Carefully wash your hands before and after touching the area around the infected eye. If your child is in a child care or nursery school program, you should keep him home until the pinkeye is no longer contagious. Your pediatrician will tell you when you can safely send her back to child care or nursery school.

Eyelid Problems

Droopy eyelid (ptosis) may appear as an enlarged or heavy upper lid; or, if it is very slight, it may be noticed only because the affected eye appears somewhat smaller than the other eye. Ptosis usually involves only one eyelid, but both may be affected. Your baby may be born with a ptosis, or it may develop later. The ptosis may be partial, causing your baby's eyes to appear slightly asymmetrical; or it may be total, causing the affected lid to cover the eye completely. If the ptotic eyelid covers the entire pupillary opening of your child's eye, or if the weight of the lid causes the cornea to assume an irregular shape (astigmatism), it will threaten normal vision development and must be corrected as early as possible. If vision is not threatened, surgical intervention, if necessary, is usually delayed until the child is four or five years of age or older, when the eyelid and surrounding tissue are more fully developed and a better cosmetic result can be obtained.

Most **birthmarks** and growths involving the eyelids of the newborn or young child are benign; however, because they may increase in size during the first year of life, they sometimes cause parents to become concerned. Most of these birthmarks and growths are not serious and will not affect your child's vision. Many decrease in size after the first year of life and eventually disappear entirely without treatment. However, any irregularity should be brought to the attention of your child's pediatrician so that it can be evaluated and monitored.

Some children are born with or develop **tumors** that can impair eyesight. In particular, a flat, purple-colored skin tumor (hemangioma), if it involves the child's upper eyelid, may put the child at risk for glaucoma (a condition where pressure increases inside the eyeball) or amblyopia. Any child having such a mark should be examined periodically by an ophthalmologist.

Small dark moles, called **nevi,** on the eyelids or on the white part of the eye itself rarely cause any problems or need to be removed. Once they have been evaluated by your pediatrician, these marks should cause concern only if they change in size, shape, or color.

Small, firm, flesh-colored bulges on your child's eyelids or underneath the eyebrows are usually **dermoid cysts.** These are noncancerous tumors that usually are present from birth. Dermoids will not become cancerous if not removed; however, because they tend to increase in size during puberty, their removal during preschool years is preferred in most cases.

Two other eyelid problems—**chalazia** and **hordeola** or **sties**—are common, but not serious. A chalazion is a cyst resulting from a blockage of an oil gland. A sty, or hordeolum, is a bacterial infection of the cells surrounding the sweat glands or hair follicles on the *edge* of the lid. Call your pediatrician regarding treatment of these conditions. He probably will tell you to apply warm compresses directly to the eyelid for twenty or thirty minutes three or four times a day until the chalazion or sty clears. The doctor may want to examine your child before prescribing additional treatment, such as an antibiotic ointment or drops.

Once your child has had a sty or chalazion, she may be more likely to get them again. When chalazia occur repeatedly, it's sometimes necessary to perform lid scrubs to reduce the bacterial colonization of the eyelids and open the oil gland pores.

Impetigo is a very contagious bacterial infection that may occur on the eyelid. Your pediatrician will advise you on how to remove the crust from the lid and then prescribe an eye ointment and oral antibiotics.

Tear (or Lacrimal) Production Problems

Tears play an important role in maintaining good eyesight by keeping the eyes wet and free of particles, dust, and other substances that might cause injury or interfere with normal vision. The so-called lacrimal system maintains the continuous production and circulation of tears, and depends on regular blinking to propel tears across the surface of the eye, finally draining into the nose.

This lacrimal system develops gradually over the first three or four years of life. Thus, while a newborn will produce enough tears

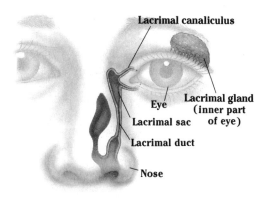

Lacrimal canaliculus

Eye

Lacrimal gland (inner part of eye)

Lacrimal sac

Lacrimal duct

Nose

to coat the surface of the eyes, it probably will be about seven to eight months after birth before he "cries real tears."

Blocked tear ducts, which are very common among newborns and young babies, can cause the appearance of excessive tearing in one or both eyes, because the tears run down the cheek instead of draining through the duct and into the nose and throat. In newborns, blocked tear ducts usually occur when the membrane covering them at birth fails to disappear. Your pediatrician will demonstrate how to massage the tear duct. She'll also show you how to clean the eye with moist compresses to remove all secretions. Until the tear duct finally opens, the purulent infectious discharge may not go away. Since this is not a true infection or pinkeye, antibiotics should not be used.

Sometimes a membrane or small cyst can cause blocked or inflamed tear ducts. When this occurs and the methods described above are unsuccessful, the ophthalmologist may decide to open the blocked tear duct surgically. Rarely, this procedure must be repeated more than once.

Cataracts

Although we usually think of cataracts as affecting elderly people, they also may be found in infants and young children, and are sometimes present at birth. A cataract is a clouding of the lens (the transparent tissue inside the eye that helps bring light rays to focus on the retina). While rare, congenital cataracts are nonetheless a leading cause of visual loss and blindness in children.

Cataracts in children need to be detected and treated early so their vision can develop normally. A cataract usually shows up as a white reflection in the center of the child's pupil. If a baby is born with a cataract that blocks most of the light entering the eye, the affected lens has to be removed surgically to permit the baby's vision to develop. Most pediatric ophthalmologists recommend that this procedure be performed during the first month of life. After the clouded lens is removed, the baby must be fitted with a contact lens or with an eyeglass correction. At the age of about one year, the placement of a lens within the eye is recommended. In addition, visual rehabilitation of the affected eye will almost always involve use of a patch until the child's eyes are fully mature (at age nine or older).

Occasionally a child will be born with a small cataract that will not initially impede visual development. These cataracts often do not require treatment; however, they need to be monitored carefully to ensure that they do not become large enough to interfere with normal vision. In addition, even if too small to pose a direct threat to visual development, cataracts may cause secondary amblyopia (loss of vision), which will need to be treated by your ophthalmologist.

In most cases the cause of cataracts in infants cannot be determined. Cataracts may be attributed to a tendency inherited from parents; they may result from trauma to the eye; or they may occur as a result of viral infections such as German measles and chickenpox or infection from other microorganisms, such as those that cause toxoplasmosis. To protect the unborn child from cataracts and from other serious disorders, pregnant women should take care to avoid unnecessary exposure to infectious diseases. In addition, as a precaution against toxoplasmosis, pregnant women should avoid handling cat litter or eating raw meat, both of which may contain the organism that causes this disease.

Glaucoma

Glaucoma is a serious eye disorder caused by increased pressure within the eye. It may be due to either overproduction of or inadequate drainage of the fluid within the eye. If this increased pressure persists too long, it can damage the optic nerve, resulting in loss of vision.

Although a child can be born with glaucoma, this is quite rare. More often it develops later in life. The earlier it is detected and treated, the better the chance of preventing permanent loss of vision. If any of the following warning signs occur, call your pediatrician promptly.

- Excessive tearing

- Extreme sensitivity to light (The child will turn her head into the mattress or blankets to avoid light.)

- Blinking tightly

- Hazy or overly prominent-appearing eyes

- Increased irritability

- Eyelid spasms

- Persistent pain

Glaucoma must be treated surgically to create an alternate route for fluid to leave the eye. Any youngster who has this disease must be watched very carefully throughout her life so that the pressure is kept under control and the optic nerve and cornea are not harmed.

Eye Injuries

When dust or other small particles get in your child's eyes, the cleansing action of tears usually will wash them out. If that fails to occur, or if a serious accident affecting the eye takes place, call your pediatrician or take your child to the nearest emergency room after heeding the following emergency guidelines.

Chemicals in the Eye

Flush the eye with water for fifteen minutes, making sure you get the water into the eye itself. Then take the child to the emergency room.

Large Particle in the Eye

If the particle won't come out with tears or by flushing with water, or if your child is still complaining of pain after an hour, call your pediatrician. The doctor will remove the object or, if necessary, refer you to an ophthalmologist. Sometimes such particles cause scratches on the cornea (corneal abrasions), which are quite painful but heal rapidly with eye ointment and patching. Corneal injuries also can be caused by blows or other injuries to the eye.

Cut Eyelid

Minor cuts usually heal quickly and easily, but a deep cut requires emergency medical attention and probably will need stitches. (See *Cuts and Scrapes,* p. 485.) Even if the cut is minor, check to make sure it isn't on the border of the eyelid or near the tear duct. If it is, call your pediatrician right away for advice on how to handle the situation.

Black Eye

To reduce swelling, apply a cold pack or towel to the area for ten to twenty minutes. Then consult the doctor to make sure there is no internal damage to the eye or the bones surrounding the eye.

Preventing Eye Injuries

Nine out of ten eye injuries are preventable, and almost half occur around the home. To minimize the risk of such accidents in your family, follow these safety guidelines.

- Keep all chemicals out of reach. That includes detergents, ammonia, spray cans, Super Glue, and all other cleaning fluids.

- Choose your child's toys carefully. Watch out for sharp or pointed parts, especially if your child is too young to understand their danger.

- Keep your child away from darts and pellet and BB guns.

- Teach your preschooler how to handle scissors and pencils properly. If she's too young to learn, don't allow her to use them.

- Keep your child away from power lawn mowers, which can hurl stones or other objects.

- Don't let your child near you when you're lighting fires or using tools. If you want her to watch you hammer nails, make her wear protective goggles.

- If your child begins participating in youth sports, have him wear eye protectors appropriate for his sport. Baseball is the leading cause of sports-related eye injuries in children, with many such injuries resulting from being struck by a pitched ball. Eye protectors (made of polycarbonate) should be seriously considered for use as part of his batting helmet. Protective sports eye equipment (again using polycarbonate lenses) also should be worn during soccer practice and competition.

- Tell your youngster not to look directly into the sun, even with sunglasses. Doing so can cause permanent and severe eye damage.

- Never allow your child near fireworks of any kind. The American Academy of Pediatrics encourages children and their families to enjoy fireworks at public fireworks displays rather than purchasing fireworks for home use. In fact, the Academy would like to see a ban on public sales of all fireworks.

- Never allow a child to look directly at an eclipse of the sun.

22

FAMILY ISSUES

Adoption

If you are about to adopt or have just adopted a child, you are likely to be experiencing conflicting emotions: Along with the excitement and delight, you understandably will feel some anxiety and apprehension. It's no different with couples who bear a child themselves, except that nature gives them nine months of preparation.

Having an understanding and supportive pediatrician will be very helpful as you begin your new job as a parent. Even before the child actually comes to your home, the doctor can help you understand your feelings. If you are adopting a child from overseas, the pediatrician will be able to alert you to special medical issues that may arise.

Once your child is home with you, schedule a visit to the pediatrician as soon as possible to make sure there are no existing medical problems. Schedule future examinations as required by the child's age and medical needs, but you should schedule several special counseling sessions during the first year to help you deal with the concerns that may arise as you and your child start to develop a relationship. Adoptive parents must face several issues and questions that natural parents do not encounter. They include the following:

■ How and when should I tell my child she is adopted?

Your child should learn the truth as early as she is able to understand, which probably will be between ages two and four. It's important to adjust the information to her maturity level, so that she can make sense of it. For example, "Your parents loved you very much, but they knew they could not take care of you. So they looked for someone who also loved little children, but could not have them on their own." As she gets older and asks more specific questions, give her honest answers, but do not press information on her if she seems uncomfortable or fearful about it.

■ **Are there special problems to watch for?**

Adopted children have no more or different problems from any other child of the same age and background. However, if you adopt an older child, you will need to learn as much as possible about her background, so you can provide the special support and understanding she requires.

■ **Should I tell others that my child is adopted?**

If you are asked, answer the question honestly and straightforwardly. Do not belabor the point or go into extensive detail if your child is nearby, however, as that may make her uncomfortable.

■ **What if she wants to find her "real parents"?**

Allow your child to discuss her feelings and desires, and tell her that you will help her locate them if she still wishes to do so when she is older. Don't push her into searching for them, and don't discourage her from doing so if it's important to her. As she gets older, explain any special circumstances, such as state guidelines or specific requests by the biological parents to not be identified, so she'll know how difficult it may be to trace them.

Your pediatrician may be able to help you with more detailed answers to these and other questions that arise in adoptive families.

Child Abuse and Neglect

Child abuse is common. The news is so full of reports about child mistreatment that you can't help but wonder how safe your child really is. Although it's a mistake to become overprotective and make your child fearful, it is important to recognize the actual risks and familiarize yourself with the signs of abuse. More than 2.5 million cases of child abuse and neglect are reported each year. Of these, thirty-five of one hundred involve physical abuse, fifteen of one hundred involve sexual abuse, and fifty of one hundred involve neglect. Studies show that one in four girls and one in eight boys will be sexually abused before they are eighteen years

---

WHERE WE STAND

Adoptions by gay or lesbian parents have become more common in recent years and have become political issues in some states. Amid this debate, a number of small studies have shown that a parent's sexual orientation has no measurable effect on the quality of parent-child relationships, or on the children's mental health or social adjustment, even though some of the experiences are unique. Parents' sexual orientation is much less important than the presence of loving and nurturing parents.

The American Academy of Pediatrics recognizes the diversity of lifestyles. We believe that children who are born to, or adopted by, one member of a gay or lesbian couple deserve the security of two legally recognized parents. Therefore, we support legal and legislative efforts that provide for the possibility of adoption of those children by the second parent or co-parent in same-sex relationships.

old. About one in twenty children are physically abused each year.

Most child abuse occurs within the family, often by parents or relatives who themselves were abused as children. Neglect and mistreatment of children is also more common in families living in poverty and among parents who are teenagers or are drug or alcohol abusers. Although there has been a recent increase in child abuse outside the home, it is still true that most often children are abused by a caregiver or someone they know, not a stranger.

Sexual abuse is any sexual activity that a child cannot comprehend or consent to. It includes acts such as fondling, oral-genital contact, and genital and anal intercourse, as well as exhibitionism, voyeurism, and exposure to pornography. Physical abuse involves injuring a child's body. This could include bruising, burns, bone injury, head injury, and injury to an internal organ. Because a bruise indicates that body tissue has been damaged and blood vessels have broken, any discipline method that leaves bruises is by definition physical abuse.

Child neglect can include physical neglect (withholding food, clothing, shelter, or other physical necessities), emotional neglect (withholding love, comfort, or affection), or medical neglect (withholding needed medical care). Psychological abuse results from all of the above, but also can be associated with verbal abuse.

Signs and Symptoms

It's not always easy to recognize when a child has been abused. Children who have been mistreated are often afraid to tell anyone, because they think they will be blamed or that no one will believe them, or because the person who abused them is someone they love very much. Parents also tend to overlook symptoms, because they don't want to face the truth. This is a serious mis-

take. A child who has been abused needs special support and treatment as early as possible. The longer he continues to be abused or is left to deal with the situation on his own, the less likely he is to make a full recovery.

The best way to check for signs of abuse is to be alert to any unexplainable changes in your child's body or behavior. Don't conduct a formal "examination" unless you have reason for suspicion, as this may make the child fearful, but do look further if you notice any of the following:

Physical Abuse

- Any injury (bruise, burn, fracture, abdominal or head injury) that cannot be explained

Sexual Abuse

- Fearful behavior (nightmares, depression, unusual fears)

- Abdominal pain, bedwetting (especially if the child had already been toilet trained), genital pain or bleeding, sexually transmitted disease

- Attempts to run away

- Extreme sexual behavior that seems inappropriate for the child's age

Psychological Maltreatment

- Sudden change in self-confidence

- Headaches or stomachaches with no medical cause

- Abnormal fears, increased nightmares

- Attempts to run away

- School failure

Part-time Care and Child Abuse

The media sometimes publicize frightening stories about child abuse in child care settings. As a result, many parents are reluctant to leave their child in the hands of anyone outside their families. The truth is that child abuse in child care settings is extremely rare. More often, child care homes and centers are places where children who are abused elsewhere can get help.

Still, for your own peace of mind, you can minimize any chance of abuse by inspecting the center program fully before enrolling him and making unannounced visits after he starts going there. (If parental visits are restricted, don't enroll your child.) However, because parental visits can be disruptive and distracting, stay in the background as much as possible. If you yourself are unable to visit, you might ask other adults (relatives, close friends) to drop in and observe from time to time. Also get to know other parents with children in the program, and share your observations and concerns.

How will you know if your child is being physically abused, in child care or elsewhere? You might be alerted by changes in his behavior or appearance. Pay special attention to the following:

- Any injury that does not have a reasonable explanation.

- Repeated injuries, even if apparently accidental.

- Changing accounts from the caregiver about injuries to a child.

- Hand-shape bruises; burns in patterns that don't look accidental;

Emotional Neglect

- Failure to gain weight (especially in infants)

- Desperately affectionate behavior

- Voracious appetite and stealing of food

Long-term Consequences

In most cases, children who are abused or neglected suffer greater emotional than physical damage. A child who is severely mistreated may become depressed or develop suicidal, withdrawn, or violent behavior. As he gets older, he may use drugs or alcohol, try to run away, refuse discipline, or abuse others. As an adult, he may develop marital and sexual difficulties, depression, or suicidal behavior.

Not all abuse victims have severe reactions. Usually the younger the child, the longer the abuse continues, and the closer the child's relationship with the abuser, the more serious the emotional damage will be. A close relationship with a very supportive adult can reduce some of the impact.

marks in the shape of a cord, belt, or other object.

- Bruises, infections, and bleeding around the genital or anal area.

- A child who has been toilet trained for a long time who suddenly starts having accidents without any other logical explanation.

- Open, inappropriate sexual behavior by the child. (Be careful not to confuse normal experimentation and curiosity with something more sinister; three- to four-year-olds, for example, normally masturbate and develop a heightened interest in sexuality; see page 367.)

As a general guideline, if your child has been comfortable in his child care program for a while but then suddenly starts to protest, look for explanations—but don't automatically assume the worst. This shift of attitude simply may reflect a developmental change. Between seven and nine months, for example, most babies suddenly become afraid of "strangers," which could include anyone other than Mom and Dad. Between thirteen and eighteen months, most toddlers go through separation anxiety, clinging to parents whenever they leave. If you can't reasonably explain your child's change in behavior, consult your pediatrician for advice before launching an investigation of the child care program.

Finally, pay attention to the way your child plays and talks. The stories he makes up, the pictures he draws, and the fantasies he acts out all reflect his recent experiences, interests, and fears. If something unpleasant has happened to him, it may come through in his play, even if he can't tell you any other way. Learn to read this special language.

Getting Help

If you suspect your child has been abused, get help immediately through your pediatrician or a local child protective agency. Physicians are legally obligated to report all suspected cases of abuse or neglect to state authorities. Your pediatrician also will detect and treat any medical injuries or ailments, recommend a therapist, and provide necessary information to investigators. The doctor also may testify in court if necessary to obtain legal protection for the child or criminal prosecution of a sexual abuse suspect. Criminal prosecution is rarely sought in mild physical abuse cases but will occur in cases involving sexual abuse.

If he has been abused, your child will benefit from the services of a qualified mental health professional. You and other members of the family may be advised to seek counseling so that you'll be able to provide the support and comfort your child needs. If someone in your family is responsible for the abuse, a mental health professional may be able to treat that person successfully, as well.

If your child has been abused, you may be the only person who can help him. There is *no* good reason to delay reporting your suspicions of abuse. Denying the problem will only make the situation worse, allowing the abuse to continue unchecked and decreasing your child's chance for a full recovery.

In any case of child abuse, the safety of the abused youngster is of primary concern. He or she needs to be in a safe environment free of the potential for continuing abuse.

Preventing Abuse

The major reasons for physical and psychological mistreatment of children within the family often are parental feelings of isolation, stress, and frustration. Parents need support and as much information as possible in order to raise their children responsibly. They need to be taught how to cope with their own feelings of frustration and anger without venting them on children. They also need the companionship of other adults who will listen and help during times of crisis. Support groups through local community organizations often are helpful first steps to diminish some of the isolation or frustration parents may be feeling.

Personal supervision of and involvement in your child's activities are the best ways to prevent physical and sexual abuse outside the home. Any school or child care program you select for your child should allow unrestricted and unannounced parental visits without prearrangement. Parents should be allowed to help in the classroom on a volunteer basis and be informed about the selection or changes of staff members. Parents should pay careful attention to their child's reports about and reactions to his experiences at school. Always investigate if your child tells you he's been mistreated or if he undergoes a sudden unexplained change in behavior.

Although you don't want to frighten your child, you can teach him some basic rules of safety in a nonthreatening manner. Teach him to keep his distance from strangers, not to wander away from you in unfamiliar territory, to say "no" when someone asks him to do something against his will, and always to tell you if someone hurts him or makes him feel bad. Emphasize that he will not get in trouble if he tells you about abuse. Emphasize that you need to know this to be able to keep him safe and that he will be OK if he tells you. Instead of teaching him that he's surrounded by danger, teach him that he is strong, capable, and can count on you to keep him safe. Teach him that it is not OK for adults to touch his body if he does not consent or understand what is occurring.

Divorce

Every year over 1 million children in the United States are involved in a divorce. Even those youngsters who had lived with parental conflict and unhappiness for a long time may find the changes that follow divorce more difficult than anything they'd experienced before. At the very least, the child must adjust to living apart from one parent (usually the father) or, if in shared custody, to dividing her life between two homes. Because of financial changes, she also may have to move to a smaller home and a different neighborhood. A mother who stayed at home before now may have to go to work. Even if she doesn't, the stress and depression that accompany divorce may make her less attentive and loving with her child.

No one can predict specifically how divorce will affect your child. Her response will depend on her own sensitivity, the quality of her relationships with each parent, and the parents' ability to work together to meet her emotional needs during this time. It also will depend to some extent on her age. In a very general way, you can anticipate how your child will react to divorce based on her age at the time it occurs.

Children under two often revert to more infantile behavior. They may become unusually clinging, dependent, or frustrated. They may refuse to go to sleep and may suddenly start waking up during the night.

Children between three and five also may act more babylike, but they may feel that they are responsible for their parents' breakup. At this age, children do not fully understand that their parents' lives are separate from their own. They believe that they are the center of their family's universe and therefore blame themselves when it falls apart. Boys often become more aggressive and defiant toward the mother. Girls may become insecure and mistrustful of males. The less contact the child has with the noncustodial parent, or the more tense the postdivorce relationship, the more serious these reactions are likely to be.

Your child's response to the divorce probably will be most intense during and immediately following the breakup. As she grows older, she may continue to think about the past and struggle to understand why her parents separated. For years she may have some sense of loss, which might become especially painful during holidays and on special occasions like birthdays and family reunions.

Most children of divorce wish desperately for their parents to get back together. However, it is much more difficult for them if the parents repeatedly attempt to reconcile and then part again than if the initial separation is final. When the parents act indecisively, the child is likely to become suspicious, confused, and insecure.

In some cases, a child's behavior and self-esteem actually improve after the parents' divorce. Sometimes this is because the parents are relieved of the tension and sadness of an unhappy marriage and now can give the child more affection and attention. Sometimes it is because the divorce ends an emotionally or physically abusive situation.

Often, however, even children who have been abused by a parent still yearn for that parent's love and for the restoration of the family.

How Parents Can Help the Child

Children integrate and mirror their parents' emotions. If her parents are angry, depressed, or violent during the separation process, a child is likely to absorb these disturbing feelings and may turn them against herself. If the parents argue about her, or if she hears her name during their disputes, she may believe even more strongly that she is to blame. Secrecy and silence probably won't make her feel much better, however, and actually may intensify the unhappiness and tension she feels around her. The best approach is to be honest about your feelings but make a special effort to be loving and reassuring with your child. She will have to accept that her parents no longer love each other—and you shouldn't try to pretend otherwise—but make sure she understands and feels that both parents love her just as much as ever.

If your child is younger than two years, you can't get this message across very well with words. You will have to convey it through your actions. When you are with your child, try to put your own pain and worries aside and concentrate on her needs. Keep the daily routine as consistent as possible, and do not expect her to make any other major changes (i.e., toilet training, moving from a crib to a bed, or, if avoidable, adjusting to a new babysitter or home arrangement) during this transitional period. In the beginning, try to be understanding and patient if your child's behavior regresses, but if this regression continues even after the divorce is completed and your life has settled back into a regular routine, ask your pediatrician for advice.

If your child is older, she needs to feel that both of her parents care about her and that they are willing to put their differences aside when it comes to her welfare. This means that you both must maintain an active involvement in her life. In the past, most fathers gradually withdrew from their children following divorce. Today courts and psychologists are trying to correct this pattern, in part by making a distinction between physical and legal custody. In this way, one parent can be granted physical custody, so that the child can have a home base, while legal custody can be awarded jointly, so that both parents remain involved in decisions about the child's education, medical care, and other basic needs. The child can visit regularly with the parent who does not have physical custody.

It is also possible to have both joint physical custody and joint legal custody. This arrangement has the advantage of keeping both parents fully involved with the child. However, it also may have serious drawbacks. Especially if they are under ten, the children may feel split between two homes, two sets of friends, and two routines. Many parents who have joint physical custody find it difficult to manage all the day-to-day decisions about scheduling, birthday parties, lessons, and schoolwork. Unless both parents are fully committed to making this arrangement work, it can lead to more conflict, confusion, and stress for the youngster. Any custody arrangement selected should give a high priority to the children's emotional and developmental needs.

Whatever your custody arrangement, both of you, as your child's parents, will continue to play key roles in her life. Try to support each other in these roles. As much as possible, avoid criticizing each other. Your child needs reassurance that it's still OK for her to love both of you. She needs you to help her feel that she's safe with either of you and that there's no need for secrets or guilt.

If you and her other parent can't actively cooperate, at least be tolerant of each other's routines, rules, and plans, even if you have minor reservations. Under the circumstances, arguments over how much television your child watches or what foods she eats can cause her far more damage than will the TV or the snacks. If necessary, discuss your concerns when your child is not present. If a child hears you trying to undermine each other's authority, she may come to feel that she can't trust either of you or that she can't talk about her feelings openly. An atmosphere of hostility may make it hard for her to enjoy herself with either parent.

As your child reaches age four or five, her life will broaden to include school and neighborhood activities, and she will develop much more complex feelings about her place in the world. You and your former spouse should discuss how she behaves and what she talks about when she is with each of you. Even though you are divorced, you still share responsibility for your child, and you need to work together to resolve any emotional or behavioral problems she may develop. Be especially alert for any signs of low self-esteem, unusual moodiness or depression, or excessive apologizing or self-criticism. These signs may indicate that she is blaming herself for the divorce. If this is the case, and you cannot convince her that she is blameless, talk to your pediatrician. She may advise you to consult a child psychiatrist or psychologist or other mental health professional.

If you feel very depressed or disturbed after your divorce and cannot seem to regain control of your life, you cannot give your child the nurturing and support she needs and that you wish to provide. For everyone's sake, consult a professional for psychological counseling as soon as you realize you are having difficulty.

Although there are always difficult moments in any divorce, you and your spouse can help your child adjust by making an effort to keep the divorce as nonconfrontational as possible. Consider using a "collaborative law" approach, where couples reach a settlement outside of the court system. Although each partner often hires his or her own lawyer, both sides have the same goal—namely, to reach an agreement that's acceptable to everyone, with the intent to cooperate and avoid antagonism—for their own sake and the sake of their children. A growing number of divorce lawyers now specialize in this collaborative law; your attorney is an advocate on your behalf, but is trained to minimize problems and reach a harmonious resolution that everyone finds acceptable.

If your divorce is full of tension and anger, you may worry that the battles will never end and that your child will never recover. Although it's true that some of the emotional effects of divorce may remain with your youngster permanently, she will have every chance to grow up healthy and happy if she receives the love, affection, and support she needs from her parents and other caregivers.

(See also *Single-Parent Families,* page 623; *Stepfamilies,* page 625.)

Grief Reactions

Losing a parent is one of the most traumatic events that can happen to any child, and grief is the natural response. Your child may experience grief not only if a parent dies but also if one becomes chronically or seriously ill, or if there is a divorce. (Even if he remains in touch with both parents following divorce, he may mourn the loss of the family

unit as he's known it.) Children also may grieve for siblings, grandparents, a beloved caregiver, or a pet.

When a Child Loses a Parent

For a young child, the loss of a parent is an overwhelming crisis, impossible to understand. Children under five cannot grasp the permanence of death. Because of this, the first stage of grief is often a period of protest and hope that the lost parent will return. Many children will try to use fantasy to make this happen, imagining the missing parent in familiar situations or places.

Once the child begins to realize that his parent is truly gone forever, despair sets in. Infants, with their limited communication skills, generally express their distress by crying, feeding poorly, and being difficult to console. Toddlers will cry and be easily excitable and uncooperative, and may regress to infantile behavior. Older children may become withdrawn. A preschooler might have a faraway look on his face, be less creative and less enthusiastic about play during this period. The more anguished or emotionally distant the other members of the family are, the more intense a young child's despair is likely to be.

Eventually he will emerge from this mood of despair and begin to shift his love and trust to others. This does not mean that he's forgotten the missing parent or that the hurt has gone away. Throughout his life there will be times when he will experience conscious and unconscious feelings of loss, especially on birthdays and holidays, during special occasions such as a graduation, and when he's ill. At these times the child may voice his sadness and ask about his missing parent.

If the deceased parent was the same sex as the child, these questions probably will come up frequently between ages four and seven, when he is struggling to understand his own gender identity. In the best of outcomes, these remembrances will be brief and positive and will not create serious distress. If they are prolonged or if they noticeably disturb the child, you should discuss them with the pediatrician.

When a Child Loses a Sibling

Losing a sibling also is a devastating experience. Although it might not strike as deeply as the loss of a parent, it may be more complicated because many children, even those old enough to understand how their sibling died, may feel that in some way they are to blame. These feelings may be intensified if parents, deep in their own despair, become withdrawn or angry and unwittingly shut themselves off from the child.

The surviving sibling must watch helplessly as his parents go through the same agony of grief that he would experience if he'd lost them. First he will see the shock and emotional numbness, then denial, then anger that such a cruel thing could possibly happen. Through it all, he is likely to hear guilt in his parents' words and voices. He may interpret this guilt to mean that they were devoting time or attention to him that should have been given to his lost sibling.

His mother may feel driven to talk about her lost child, how the death occurred, and what she could have done to prevent it. The child may struggle to comfort her even as he's trying himself to comprehend what has happened. The realization that he cannot make her happy, no matter what he does, may seriously damage his feelings of security and self-esteem. If his father unwittingly reacts, as many men do, by becoming restrained, short-tempered, and preoccupied with distractions outside the family, the surviving sibling may feel frightened and rejected by him.

In a household where the mother intensively feels the need to talk and the father avoids talking, the essential mutual support and understanding they each need is difficult to achieve. As a result, the marriage may suffer. The surviving child, feeling this stress as keenly as his grief for the sibling he's lost, may assume that he's responsible for his parents' disputes as well as for his sibling's death. The entire family may benefit from professional counseling after a child dies. Your pediatrician can recommend a qualified family therapist, psychologist, or child psychiatrist to help you all cope with your grief and bring your family back together.

Helping Your Grieving Child

When you are grieving for your spouse or your child, it is easy to overlook your surviving child's needs. The following suggestions can help you provide the love, comfort, and trust your child needs during and after the grieving process.

1. Maintain your child's familiar day-to-day routine as much as possible. Ask the people he loves and trusts—family members, familiar babysitters, or preschool teachers—to be there for him when you are unavailable.

2. Offer frequent, calm explanations, keeping in mind your child's level of understanding and possible feelings of guilt. Keep the explanations as simple as possible, but be truthful. Do not construct fairy tales that will leave him more confused or hopeful that the death can be reversed. If your child is older than three, reassure him that nothing he did or thought caused the death and that no one is angry with him. To help ensure that he understands, it may help to ask him to repeat what you've said.

3. Get help from loved ones. It is difficult to give your grieving child all the attention and support he needs when you are grief-stricken yourself. Close friends and family members may be able to give you some relief, while at the same time providing a comforting sense of family and community when he may feel alone and lost. If you have lost a child, it is especially important for the family's sake that you and your spouse try to be mutually supportive during this time.

4. Be open to discussions about the loss over the ensuing weeks, months, and years. Even if your child appears to recover from grief faster than you do, his grieving process will go on below the surface for many years—possibly, in a quiet way, for a lifetime. He will need your continuing support and understanding as he tries to come to terms with his loss. As he grows older, he will ask more sophisticated questions about the circumstances and reasons for the death. As painful as it may be for you to recall these events, try to answer him honestly and directly. The more he understands what happened, the easier it will be for him to make his peace with it.

Should Your Preschooler Attend the Funeral?

Whether a young child attends a funeral for a loved one depends on the child's individual level of understanding, emotional maturity, and desire to participate in this ritual. If he seems very fearful and anxious, and can't understand the purpose of the ceremony, then he probably should not attend. On the other hand, if he seems able to control his responses and wishes to be present to say good-bye one last time, attending may be consoling and actually help him deal with his grief.

If you decide to have him present, prepare him for what will happen. Also, make arrangements ahead of time for a close family member or caregiver to take the child if he needs to leave, so you can remain at the funeral. Having this extra help also will free you to meet your own emotional needs during the ceremony.

If you decide not to have your child at the funeral, you might arrange a private, less formal visit later to the gravesite. Although this, too, will be stressful, it may make it easier for him to understand what has happened.

When to Get Professional Help

You may want to consult your pediatrician for advice soon after the death has occurred. With the experience and knowledge to help you guide your child through the grieving process, the physician can help you decide how and what to tell your child, and can discuss how your child may be feeling and behaving in the months to come.

It is not possible to say how long your child will continue to grieve. Ordinarily, a grieving child will show signs of gradual recovery, with, at first, hours, then days, and eventually weeks when he acts pretty much as he did before the death. If he does not start to have these periods of normalcy within four to six weeks, or if you feel that his initial despair is too intense or is lasting too long, talk to your pediatrician.

Although it is normal for a child to miss a deceased parent or sibling at times, it is not normal for the preoccupation to overshadow the child's entire life for years to come. If your child seems to be thinking constantly about the death, so that his grief dominates every family occasion and interferes with his social and psychological development, he needs psychological counseling. Your pediatrician can refer you to a qualified mental health professional.

Your child also needs you to return gradually to normal functioning. After you've lost a child or your spouse, it may take many months before you are able to return to your usual daily routine and much longer before your feelings of anguish begin to subside. If a year has passed since the death and you still don't feel that you can resume your former activities, or if your grieving is replaced by ongoing depression, it's good to seek psychological help, not only for your benefit but for your child's, as well.

One- and Two-Child Families

Most newly married couples today plan to have only one or two children, compared with three or more back in the early 1960s. The reasons for this shift include a trend toward later marriage, more emphasis on careers for women, more effective methods of contraception, and the rising cost of rearing and educating children.

There are some very clear benefits to having a small family.

- Each child receives more parental attention and educational advantages, which generally raise her self-esteem.

- Children in small families, especially first and only children, tend to have higher school and personal achievement levels than do children of larger families.

- The financial costs of maintaining a household are lower.

- It is easier for both parents to combine careers with family life.

- The general stress level is lower because there often are fewer conflicts and less rivalry.

There are also some trade-offs, especially in one-child families. When all the expectations, hopes, and fears are focused on just one child, parents easily can become overprotective and indulgent without even realizing it. The child may have fewer opportunities to meet other children or to develop a sense of independence. She may be pushed to overachieve, and she may receive so much doting attention that she becomes self-centered and undisciplined.

If you have just one or two children, you may become overprotective and overly attentive. This may make your child reluctant to be separated from you, hindering the development of new relationships with peers. In fact, you may have that same difficulty. Here are tips to help you keep these feelings in the proper perspective as your child matures.

- Make sure your expectations of your child are realistic for her age. Get to know other families with children the same age, and watch how these parents raise their children: when they're protective and when they let go; how they discipline the children; how much responsibility they expect of them.

- Maintain your own adult social life as a couple (or as an individual, if you are a single parent). Taking a few hours off from each other will help both you and your child develop your individual identities. The earlier you start this pattern of personal time (at least once a week, even during infancy), the easier it will be for you both to accept the increasing definition of personality that needs to occur as she grows older.

- Let your child get to know other trusted grown-ups by having them babysit and by including the child in group activities with other families.

- Give her plenty of opportunities to play with other children her age through playgroups, nursery schools, or other children's groups.

- If you are worried about your child's health or development, get advice from your pediatrician as soon as possible. Don't let your anxieties build, and don't limit your child with unnecessary concern.

Sibling Rivalry

If you have more than one child, you almost certainly will have to deal with some amount of sibling rivalry. Competition between youngsters in a family is natural. All children want parental affection and attention, and each child believes he rightly should receive all of yours. Your child does not want to share you with his brother or sister, and when he realizes he has no choice in the matter, he may become jealous, possibly even violent, toward his sibling.

Sibling rivalry between younger children tends to be most troublesome when the age difference is from one and a half to three years. This is because the preschool child is still very dependent on his parents and has not yet established many secure relationships with friends or other adults. However, even when the spread is as many as nine years or more, the older child still needs parental attention and affection. If he feels that he is being left out or rejected, he likely will blame the baby. In general, the older the child, the less jealousy he will feel toward his younger sibling. The jealousy is often most intense for preschoolers when the sibling is a newborn.

There may be days when you're convinced your children really do hate each other, but these emotional outbursts are only temporary. Despite their feelings of resentment, siblings usually have true affection for one another. You may have difficulty

seeing this, however, since they may reserve their worst behavior for moments when you are present, and they are competing directly for your attention. When you're absent, they may be fine companions. As they get older and their need for your complete and undivided attention decreases, their feelings of affection probably will overcome their jealousy of each other. Intense sibling rivalry that lasts into adulthood is rare.

What to Expect

You may notice the first signs of sibling rivalry even before your younger child is born. As the older one watches you preparing the nursery or buying baby equipment, he may demand gifts for himself. He may want to wear diapers again or drink from a bottle "like the baby will." If he senses that you're preoccupied with the baby, he may misbehave or act out in order to get your attention.

This unusual or regressive behavior may continue after the baby is home. Your older child may cry more frequently, become more clinging and demanding, or simply withdraw. He may imitate the baby by asking for his old baby blanket, sucking on a pacifier, or even demanding to nurse. School-age children often appear very interested and affectionate toward the baby, but are aggressive or misbehave in other ways to get attention. Among all siblings, the demand for attention is usually greatest when the parents are actively and intimately involved with the baby—for example, during breastfeedings or bath time.

As your younger child gets older and becomes more mobile, quarrels will erupt over the older child's toys and other possessions. The toddler will go straight for what he wants, without caring who owns it, while your preschooler will guard his own territory jealously. When the toddler intrudes on this space, the older child usually reacts strongly.

Sometimes, particularly when the children are several years apart, the older one is accepting and protective of the younger sibling. However, as the younger one grows and begins to develop more mature skills and talents (in schoolwork, athletics, talking, singing, or acting, e.g.), the older child may feel threatened or embarrassed by "being shown up." He may then become more aggressive or irritating, or start to compete with the younger sibling. The younger child, too, may experience jealousy about the privileges, talents, accomplishments, or advantages that his older sibling accumulates as he gets older. Often it is almost impossible to tell which child is contributing more to the rivalry.

How Should Parents React?

It's important not to overreact to jealousy between your children, especially if the older child is a preschooler. Feelings of resentment and frustration are understandable—no child wants to give up the spotlight of parental affection. It takes time for a youngster to discover that his parents don't love him any less because they have a second child.

If your older child starts imitating the baby, don't ridicule or punish him. You can indulge his fantasies briefly by allowing him to drink from a bottle or climb into the crib or playpen, but only once or twice at the most, and don't reward this behavior by giving him extra attention. Make it absolutely clear that he does not have to behave like a baby to gain your approval, love, or affection. Praise him when he acts "grown-up," and give him plenty of opportunities to be a "big brother" (or, in the case of a girl, a "big sister"). It shouldn't take long for him to re-

alize that he benefits more by acting maturely than by behaving like a baby.

If your older child is between three and five years old, try to minimize conflicts over space by guaranteeing some secure, protected area. Separating his private possessions from shared ones will help reduce quarreling.

It's natural for parents to compare their children, but don't do this in front of them. Each child is special, and should be treated as such. Comparisons inevitably make one child feel inferior to the other. A statement such as "Your sister is always so much neater than you," for example, will make a child resent both you and his sister, and actually may encourage him to be messy.

When your children get into an argument, usually the best strategy is to stay out of it. Left alone, they probably will settle it peacefully. If you get involved, you may be tempted to take sides, making one child feel triumphant and the other betrayed. Even if they bring their fight to you, try to be impartial and tell them to settle it peacefully on their own. Instead of blaming either one, explain that they're both responsible for creating the dispute and for ending it.

Obviously, you must intervene if the situation becomes violent, especially if the older child might harm the younger one. In this case you must first protect the baby. Make sure the older youngster understands that you will not tolerate such abusive behavior. If the age difference is large or if there is any reason to suspect that violence may erupt, supervise them closely when they are together. Preventing aggressive behavior is always better than punishment, which all too often increases rather than decreases the older child's feelings of rivalry.

It is important to spend time separately with each child. Finding the right balance of attention is not always easy, but if your older child's acting out is becoming extreme, it could be a signal that he needs more of your time.

If the older sibling remains extremely aggressive, or if you feel that you don't know how to handle the situation, consult your pediatrician, who can determine whether this is normal sibling rivalry or a problem that requires special attention. The pediatrician also can suggest ways to ease the tensions. If necessary, she will refer you to a qualified mental health professional.

(See also *Preparing Your Other Children for the Baby's Arrival,* page 23.)

Single-Parent Families

Single-parent families are becoming more common. Most children of divorce spend at least some years in single-parent households. Another increasingly large group of children live with single parents who were never married or involved in a long-term relationship. A smaller number of children have widowed parents.

From a parent's viewpoint, there are some benefits to being single. You can raise the child according to your own beliefs, principles, and rules, with no need for conflict or resolving differences. Single parents often develop closer bonds with their children. When the father is the single parent, he may become more nurturing and more active in his child's daily life than most fathers in two-parent households. Children in single-parent households may become more independent and mature because they have more responsibility within the family.

Single parenthood is not easy, though, for parents or children. It generally means less income and a lower standard of living. If you can't arrange or afford child care, getting and holding a job may be difficult. (See Chapter 13, "Part-time Care for Your Child.") Without another person to share the day-in, day-out job of raising the child and maintaining the household, you may find yourself socially isolated. When you are under stress, the child may sense and share this stress. You can easily become too tired and distracted to be as emotionally supportive or consistent about rules and discipline as you would like to be. This can lead to distress and behavior problems for the child. Some single parents worry that the lack of a same-sex parent may deprive their son or daughter of a potential role model.

Here are some suggestions that may help you meet your own emotional needs while providing your child with the guidance she needs.

- Take advantage of all available resources in finding help in caring for your child. Use the guide to part-time care in Chapter 13.

- Maintain your sense of humor as much as possible. Try to see the positive or humorous side of everyday surprises and challenges.

- For your family's sake as well as your own, take care of yourself. See your doctor regularly, eat properly, and get enough rest, exercise, and sleep.

- Set a regular time when you can take a break without your child. Relax with friends. Go to a movie. Pursue hobbies. Join groups. Do things that interest you. Pursue a social life of your own.

- Don't feel guilty because your child has only one parent. There are plenty of families in the same situation. You didn't "do it to her," and you don't need to penalize yourself or spoil her to make amends. Feeling and acting guilty won't help anyone.

Parenting in Military Families

A parent in the military can present unique challenges, particularly in times of deployment or military conflict, when the stresses of being away from a child can be difficult for the entire family. Young children may demonstrate a number of behaviors in response to being separated from a parent, such as clinginess to the other parent and/or a caregiver; regressive behaviors (e.g., bedwetting after having being toilet-trained), anxiety over new people or circumstances, and being quiet and pulling away from others.

If you're the parent remaining at home with your child, try to keep things as normal as possible, including maintaining usual daily routines. Answer questions as honestly as possible (keeping in mind his level of understanding), and reassure him that the deployed parent is fine and doing well. Try to maintain as much communication as possible with the absent parent, letting your child communicate by phone, letter, or e-mail. If your child seems to be in particular distress, talk with your pediatrician, who might make a referral to a mental health professional.

- Don't look for problems where none exist. Many children grow up very well in single-parent homes, while others have a great many problems in two-parent homes. Being a single parent doesn't necessarily mean you'll have more problems or have more trouble resolving them.

- Set firm but reasonable limits for your children, and don't hesitate to enforce them. Children feel more secure and develop responsible behavior better when limits are clear and consistent. Expand these limits as the child demonstrates the ability to accept increased responsibility.

- Find some time each day with your child—playing, talking, reading, helping with homework, or watching television.

- Praise your child often, showing genuine affection and unconditional, positive support.

- Create as large a support network for yourself as possible. Keep active lists of relatives, friends, and community services that can help with child care. Establish friendships with other families who will let you know of community opportunities (soccer, cultural events, etc.) and are willing to exchange babysitting.

- Talk to trusted relatives, friends, and professionals such as your pediatrician about your child's behavior, development, and relationships within the family.

Smaller Extended Families

Until the last few generations, most American families were two-parent ones; living nearby, perhaps even in the same house, were grandparents, aunts, uncles, and cousins. The women were primarily responsible for caring for the children and running the household while the men worked outside the home. In many ways, this formula worked well: There were plenty of adults to look after the children. There was a built-in support system and roles were clearly defined. The children benefited the most because they had so many close social contacts and received love from so many different directions.

The extended family is not as common in American society today. Due to career obligations, opportunities, and the desire to go to new places, fewer and fewer newly married couples choose to or can live near their parents or close relatives.

Without regular contact with these relatives, parents and children need to create alternative support systems. A close friendship with another family, participation in a surrogate or foster grandparent program or in Big Brothers or Sisters, can help replace the missing ties. For many families, religious congregational activities are a source of support and close friendships. Many other community programs, such as youth and neighborhood activity centers, also can fulfill these needs.

Even if your relatives are scattered, try to strengthen your child's sense of family by keeping in touch by phone, letters, and e-mail. Encourage your child to draw pictures for relatives and to send his own letters when he learns to write. Exchange photographs, and make them into a photo album that grows with your child. If you have a tape recorder or video camera, make tapes of your family as "audiovideo letters" to bring you closer together.

The overall intent is to balance the intimate connections of a small nuclear family with continued meaningful contacts with loved ones outside the immediate family. The values fostered and nurtured through these family relationships will be important ones for the child to model and incorporate into his way of living when he grows up.

Your family's modeling of these values reinforces their importance for the growing child.

Stepfamilies

A single parent's remarriage can be a blessing for the parent and child alike—restoring the structure, stability, closeness, and security that were lost through divorce, separation, or death. A stepfamily arrangement is often financially beneficial. Moreover, the stepparent becomes an appropriate role model of the same sex as the former spouse.

But creating a stepfamily also requires many adjustments and can be very stressful for everyone involved. If the stepparent is presented to the child as a substitute for her absent parent, the child may feel torn by her loyalty to her biological parent and may reject the stepparent immediately. There's often a great deal of jealousy between stepparents and stepchildren, as well as competition for the love and attention of the parent who has brought them together. If a child feels that her new stepparent is coming between her and her parent, she may reject the stepparent and act out in order to regain her parent's attention. The situation becomes even more complex and stressful when there are children on both sides who are suddenly expected to accept each other's parents and get along as siblings. With time, most blended families do manage to sort through these conflicts, but it requires a great amount of patience and commitment on the part of the adults, as well as the willingness to get professional help if serious problems should develop.

As difficult as the transition may seem at first, try to keep in mind that relationships between stepparents and stepchildren tend to develop gradually, over a period of one to several years, rather than over weeks or months.

Suggestions for Stepfamilies

Making a smooth transition from a single-parent family to a successful stepfamily requires special sensitivity and effort from the biological parent and stepparent. Here are some suggestions that may help.

- Inform your former spouse of your marriage plans, and try to work together to make the transition as easy as possible for your child. Make sure everyone understands that the marriage will not change your former spouse's role in your child's life.

- Give your child time to get to know the stepparent (and stepsiblings, if any) before you begin living together. Doing this will make the adjustment easier for everyone and will eliminate a lot of your child's anxiety about the new arrangement.

- Watch for signs of conflict, and work together to correct them as early as possible.

- Parent and stepparent should decide together what will be expected of the child, where and how limits will be set, and what forms of discipline are acceptable.

- Parent and stepparent need to share the responsibilities of parent-

hood. This means that *both* will give affection and attention and that *both* will have authority in the household. Deciding together how the child should be disciplined, and supporting each other's decisions and actions, will make it easier for the stepparent to assume a role of authority without fear of disapproval or resentment.

- If a noncustodial parent visits the child, these visitations should be arranged and accepted so that they don't become an issue of contention within the stepfamily.

- Try to involve both biological parents and stepparent(s) in all major decisions affecting a child. If possible, arrange for all the adults to meet together to share insights and concerns; doing this will let the child know that the grown-ups are willing to overcome their differences for his benefit.

- Be sensitive to your child's wishes and concerns about his role within the stepfamily. Respect his level of maturity and understanding when, for example, you help him decide what to call the stepparent or introduce him to the stepparent's relatives.

An important factor in the development of the steprelationship may be support from the other biological parent. The child may resent a relationship with a biological parent that precludes closeness to the stepparent and may feel guilty whenever she is emotionally drawn to the stepparent. Harmonious communication among all three (or four) parents can minimize this guilt, as well as reduce the confusion that a child could feel when she tries to accommodate the values and expectations of several adults. For this reason, when a child is spending time in two households, occasional meetings including all of the parents, if possible, may be very helpful. Sharing perspectives on rules, values, and scheduling communicates to the child that all her parents can talk with one another, are mutually respectful, and have her development as a central priority.

In an atmosphere of mutual respect between biological and stepparents, the child can derive the benefits of stepfamilies mentioned earlier. The child again has the opportunity of living in a household with two parents. The remarried parent often is happier and thus better able to meet the child's needs. As the child gets older, her relationship to the stepparent may give her support, skills, and perspectives. These benefits, together with the economic advantages of the stepfamily situation, may give the child a broader range of opportunities.

Twins

Having twins means much more than simply having two babies at once, and this challenge goes beyond having twice the work or pleasure. Twins quite frequently are born early and therefore tend to be smaller than the average newborn, so you may need to consult your pediatrician even more frequently than you would with a single baby. Feeding twins, whether by breast or bottle, also requires some special strategies, and the doctor can provide advice and support. (See Chapter 4.)

Raising Twins

From the very beginning, it's important that you recognize your twin babies as two separate individuals. If they are identical, it's easy to treat them as a "package," providing them with the same clothing, toys, and quality of attention. But as similar as they may appear physically, emotionally they are different, and in order to grow up happy and secure as individuals, they need you to support their differences. As one twin explained, "We're not twins. We're just brothers who have the same birthday!"

Both identical and fraternal twins may become either competitive or interdependent as they grow. Sometimes one twin acts as the leader and the other as the follower. Whatever the specific quality of their interaction, however, most twins develop very intense relationships early in life simply because they spend so much time with each other.

If you also have other children, your twin newborns may prompt more than the usual sibling rivalry. They will require a large amount of your time and energy, and will attract a great deal of extra attention from friends, relatives, and strangers on the street. You can help your other children accept, and perhaps even take advantage of, this unusual situation by offering them "double rewards" for helping with the new babies and encouraging even more involvement in the daily baby care chores. It also becomes even more essential that you spend some special time each day alone with the other children doing their favorite activities.

As your twins get a little older, particularly if they are identical, they may choose to play only with each other, making their other siblings feel left out. To discourage the twins from forming such exclusive bonds, urge them to play individually (not as a unit) with other children. Also, you or their babysitter might play with just one twin while the other plays with a sibling or friend.

Twins: Fraternal vs. Identical

Identical twins come from the same egg, are always the same sex, and look very much alike. However, they have their individual personalities, styles, and temperament. We expect them to act alike and develop in similar ways as they grow up. Because of their many similarities, they may develop extremely close emotional bonds, possibly excluding even other family members to some extent.

Fraternal twins come from two separate eggs, which are fertilized at the same time. They may or may not be the same sex, and they will not be identical in appearance, temperament, or behavior. Because of these differences, they do not form the extremely close relationship found between identical twins.

Characteristic	Identical	Fraternal
Sex	Same	Same or different
Appearance	Identical	Many similarities, but not identical
Placenta	1	2
Chorion bag*	1 or 2	2
Amniotic sac†	1 or 2	2
Blood types	Identical	May be identical

* The cellular, outermost extraembryonic membrane
† Membrane around the fetus

You may find that your twins do not develop in the same pattern as do other children their age. Some twins seem to "split the work," with one concentrating on motor skills while the other perfects social or communication abilities. Because they spend so much time together, many twins communicate better with each other than with other family members or friends. They learn how to "read" each other's gestures and facial expressions, and occasionally they even have their own verbal language that no one else can understand. (This is particularly true of identical twins.) Because they can entertain each other, they may not be very motivated to learn about the world beyond them. This unique developmental pattern does not represent a problem, but it does make it all the more important to separate your twins occasionally and expose them individually to other playmates and learning situations.

Twins are not always happy about being apart, especially if they've established strong play habits and preferences for each other's company. For this reason, it's important to begin separating them occasionally as early as possible. If they resist strongly, try a gradual approach using very familiar children or adults to play with them individually but in the same room or play area. Being able to separate will become increasingly important as the twins approach school age. In nursery school most twins can stay together in the same room, but many elementary schools prefer twins to be in separate classes.

As much as you appreciate the individual differences between your twins, you no doubt will have certain feelings for them as a unit. There is nothing wrong with this, since they do share many similarities and are themselves bound to develop a dual identity—as individuals and as twins. Helping them understand and accept the balance between these two identities is one of the most challenging tasks facing you as the parent of twins. Your pediatrician can advise you on how to cope with the special parenting problems involved with twins. He also can suggest helpful reading material or refer you to organizations involved with helping parents who have multiple births.

Working Mothers

In the United States today, more than half of mothers with young children work, compared to about one third in the 1970s. Working mothers are now the rule rather than the exception. Women have been moving into the workforce not only for career satisfaction but also because they and their families need the income. Many married working women have husbands who earn less than $30,000 a year. More than one-fourth of all children live in single-parent homes, with their mothers providing most of their support. For the children in many of these families being raised by one or two parents, the alternative to a working mother is poverty.

In many families today, mothers continue to work because they have careers that they have spent years developing. Some women return to work soon after giving birth because they know that most employers in this country are not sympathetic to working mothers who wish to take time off to be with their young children. If these women stop working, even for several months, they may give up some of the advantages they have earned or risk losing certain career opportunities.

As a greater number of women enter the workforce and stay there, more and more children are cared for by adults other than their parents. Relatives sometimes take on child care duties, or children are cared for in a variety of child care settings. Not surprisingly, working mothers are more likely to have their infants and toddlers in an out-of-the-home child care center than nonemployed mothers. However, most three- to five-year-olds are in center-based or preschool programs regardless of whether their mother works outside the home. Parents all want their children to have the best possible start in school, so they are likely to enroll their three- and four-year-olds in a program.

Some people still think that a "good mother" is one who gives up work to stay home with her children. However, no scientific evidence says children are harmed when their mothers work. A child's development is influenced more by the emotional health of the family, how the family feels about the mother's working, and the quality of child care. A child who is emotionally well adjusted, well loved, and well cared for will thrive regardless of whether the mother works outside the home.

A mother who successfully manages both an outside job and parenthood provides a role model for her child. In most families with working mothers, each person plays a more active role in the household. The children tend to look after one another and help in other ways. The father is more likely to help with household chores and child rearing as well as breadwinning. These positive outcomes are most likely when the working mother feels valued and supported by family, friends, and coworkers.

Problems can arise if a woman does not want to work or if her husband does not want her to work. If a woman works because she needs the money, she may have to take a job that she does not like. In that case, she needs to be careful not to bring her frustration and unhappiness home, where it will spill over into family relationships. The message the children may receive in this situation is that work is unpleasant and damages instead of builds self-esteem.

Family relationships may suffer if both parents want to work but only one has a job. Problems also can occur if there is competition or resentment because one parent is earning more money than the other. Such conflicts can strain the marriage and may make the children feel threatened and insecure. With both parents working, the need for mutual support and communication is even more important.

Even when there are no problems, however, a two-career family has to deal with issues that do not come up in other families. Parents may feel so divided between family and career that they have little time for a social life or each other. Both parents need to share household and child care responsibilities so that one will not end up doing most of the work and feeling resentful. Parents will lose an average of about ten work days per year due to the need to tend to a sick child, to care for their child when child care arrangements have broken down, or to take their child to necessary appointments.

A woman's decision to return to work must take into account her own needs as well as those of her family. If you are considering returning to work, try to delay your return until three or four months after your child is born. Doing this will allow you to get to know your child and let her get to know you. Take the time to prepare yourself and your family, so that the adjustment is as easy as possible for everyone. Time your return to work so that stress is minimal. If at all possible, avoid having your return coincide with other major family changes, such as moving or changing schools, or personal crises, such as illness or death in the family; arrange trustworthy child care as far in advance as possible.

As a working parent, you are bound to be concerned about the loss of time with your child, especially if he is very young. You may worry that you will miss some of your child's important milestones, such as his first step or word. You may even feel jealous of the time your child spends with the caregiver. These are all normal feelings. Be aware of them and work to separate your own needs from concerns about your child's welfare.

The first few years of life are very important in shaping a child's future personality, but this does not mean that the mother is the only one able to do the shaping. In fact, child care seems to have some important benefits for young children. Youngsters who are routinely cared for by individuals other than their parents may be slightly more independent than other children. A high-quality, stimulating, and nurturing child care program also prepares children for school, both socially and intellectually.

Parents all wish for the best start for their child. Unfortunately, quality child care can be expensive and often hard to find. Many parents end up spending a large share of their paychecks for child care and still are not happy with the quality of the care their children receive. Lower-income families are much less likely to have their child in a quality center, and are more likely to have multiple changes in their child care arrangements, than middle- to higher-income families.

Finding quality child care is very important. Standards for child care settings may vary depending on the type of child care. Parents can, however, improve their children's child care programs by becoming actively involved. You can visit the program regularly and talk with the caregiver often and extensively. You also can get involved in fund raising and donating supplies, can volunteer to help, or can work with the staff to create developmentally appropriate activities for the children. It also helps to bring the child's activities home for family interaction, and on weekends, to try to maintain the child's weekday schedule.

Taking an active role in your child's care not only helps ensure a child's well-being, but also may reduce any guilt or misgivings you may feel about working. Having quality child care and a good relationship with the caregiver also can ease some of the worry. Parents need to be especially attentive when they are with their children. The more involved parents are in all aspects of their children's life—even when they are not physically with their children—the closer they will feel and the more effective they will be as parents.

Good child care helps children grow in every way and promotes their physical, social, and mental development. It offers support to working parents. Your pediatrician wants your child to grow and develop with enjoyment in a setting that supports you as a parent. For more information on choosing a child care arrangement for your family, ask your pediatrician about the brochure "Choosing Child Care: What's Best for Your Family" by the American Academy of Pediatrics (also see Chapter 13).

Stay-at-Home Fathers

Many of today's fathers spend much more time with their children than their own fathers did. But for a growing number of fathers, the caretaking of their youngsters has become their full-time job. Often their wives are in the workplace, and they have assumed the primary role of raising their children. They prepare baby bottles, do the bathing, and put the kids down for naps. They drive carpools and take their kids to the park. They participate in playgroups with their youngsters and become involved in their child's preschool.

Becoming a stay-at-home father is a major decision for many fathers, typically one that is made in collaboration with their spouse. More couples are deciding that it is best for their children for Dad to remain home, perhaps because his wife has greater earning power, because of their respective career goals, or because they've decided that it's simply best for their child. According to a recent U.S. Census estimate, slightly fewer than 2 million fathers in the United States remain at home with their children while their wife works outside the home.

Even so, many people still see this trend as a role reversal, and often a stigma goes with it. Some stay-at-home fathers say that they battle stereotypes and struggle for respect, often encountering comments from friends who wonder why they've chosen a job that, in most cultures, traditionally has been assumed by women. When taking their children to parks, they may be asked, "Why aren't you at work today? Did you lose your job?" At the same time, just like their female counterparts, these full-time fathers often feel isolated and deprived of contact with other adults. Even so, many feel it's the best and the most important and rewarding decision they've ever made.

Without a doubt, most fathers can fulfill the primary role of child raising as well as mothers can. If the roles in your family are different from what they were in the family you grew up in, it doesn't mean that they're wrong. It's a personal choice that couples should make together. As times change, and with so many more women in the workforce, each family should determine what works best for them and follow that path.

23

FEVER

Your child's normal temperature will vary with his age, activity, and the time of day. Infants tend to have higher temperatures than older children, and everyone's temperature is highest between late afternoon and early evening and lowest between midnight and early morning. Ordinarily, a rectal reading of 100 degrees Fahrenheit (37.8 degrees Celsius) or less, or an oral reading of 99 degrees Fahrenheit (37.2 degrees Celsius) or less, is considered normal, while higher readings indicate fever.

By itself, fever is *not* an illness. In fact, usually it is a positive sign that the body is fighting infection. Fever stimulates certain defenses, such as the white blood cells, which attack and destroy invading bacteria. However, fever can make your child uncomfortable. It increases his need for fluids and makes his heart rate and breathing faster.

Fever most commonly accompanies respiratory illnesses such as croup or pneumonia, ear infections, influenza (flu), severe colds, and sore throats. It also may occur with infections of the bowel or urinary tract and with a wide variety of viral illnesses.

In children between six months and five years, fever can trigger seizures, called febrile convulsions. These convulsions tend to run in families, and usually happen during the first few hours of a febrile illness. The child may look "peculiar" for a few moments, then stiffen, twitch, and roll his eyes. He will be unresponsive for a short time, and his skin may appear to be a little darker than usual during the episode. The entire convulsion usually lasts less than one minute but, although uncommonly, can last for up to fifteen minutes, and may be over in a few seconds, but it can seem like a lifetime to a frightened parent. It is reassuring to know that febrile convulsions almost always are harmless—they do not cause brain damage, nervous system problems, paralysis, mental retardation, or death—although they should be reported promptly to your pediatrician.

Children younger than one year at the time of their first simple febrile seizure have approximately a 50 percent chance of having another such seizure, while children over one year of age when they have their first seizure have about a 30 percent chance of

Upper Limits of Normal Temperatures

Method	Time	3 years and Under	Over 3 Years
Rectal temperature (digital thermometer)	1 minute	100.4°F (38° C)	99.6°F (37.5 Celsius)
Oral temperature (digital thermometer)	1 minute	99.2°F (37.3° C)	98.6°F (37 Celsius)

having a second one. Nevertheless, febrile seizures rarely happen more than once within a twenty-four-hour (1 day) period. Although many parents worry that a febrile seizure will lead to epilepsy, keep in mind that epileptic seizures are not caused by a fever, and children with a history of fever-related seizures have only a slightly higher likelihood of developing epilepsy by age seven.

A rare but serious problem that is easily confused with fever is *heat-related illness,* or *heat stroke.* This is caused not by infection or internal conditions, but by surrounding heat. It can occur when a child is in a very hot place—for example, a hot beach in mid-summer or an overheated closed car on a summer day. Leaving children unattended in closed cars is the cause of many deaths a year; *never* leave an infant or child unattended in a closed car, even for a few minutes. Heat stroke also can occur if a baby is overdressed in hot, humid weather. Under these circumstances, the body temperature can rise to dangerous levels (above 105 degrees Fahrenheit [40.5 degrees Celsius]), which must be reduced quickly by cool-water sponging, fanning, and removal to a cool place. After the child has been cooled, he should be taken immediately to a pediatrician or emergency room. Heat stroke is an emergency condition.

Whenever you think your child has a fever, take his temperature with a thermometer. (See *Which Thermometer Is Best?* on page 637.) Feeling the skin (or using temperature-sensitive tape) is not accurate, especially when the child is experiencing a chill.

What type of thermometer should you select? The American Academy of Pediatrics no longer recommends the use of mercury thermometers because these glass thermometers often break and, as their mercury vaporizes, it can be inhaled at toxic levels. Digital electronic thermometers and ear (tympanic) thermometers are better choices (see page 637).

- Digital devices can measure temperatures in your child's mouth, rectum, and under the arm. As with any device, some digital thermometers are more accurate than others. Follow the manufacturer's instructions carefully, and be sure the thermometer is calibrated.

- Ear thermometers are another acceptable choice. The accuracy of their readings depends on the ability of the beam emitted by the devices to reach the eardrum. Thus, some of these devices may not be reliable. For that reason, most pediatricians prefer that parents use digital electronic thermometers.

When to Call the Pediatrician

If your child is *two months or younger* and has a rectal temperature of 100.4 degrees Fahrenheit (38 degrees Celsius) or higher, call your pediatrician immediately. *This is an absolute necessity.* The doctor will need to examine the baby to rule out any serious infection or disease.

You also may need to notify the doctor if your child is between three and six months and has a fever of 101 degrees Fahrenheit (38.3 degrees Celsius) or greater, or is older than six months and has a temperature of 103 degrees Fahrenheit (39.4 degrees Celsius) or higher. Such a high temperature may indicate a significant infection or dehydration, which may require treatment. However, in most cases, your decision to call the pediatrician should depend on the presence of associated symptoms, such as a severe sore throat, a severe earache, a cough, an unexplained rash, or repeated vomiting or diarrhea. Also, if your child is very fussy or sleeping more than usual, call your doctor. In fact, your youngster's activity level tends to be a more important indicator than the height of the fever.

If your child is over one year of age, is eating and sleeping well, and has playful moments, there usually is no need to call the doctor immediately. If a high fever persists for more than twenty-four hours, however, it is best to call even if there are no other complaints or findings.

If your child becomes delirious (acts frightened, "sees" objects that are not there, talks strangely) while he has a high fever, call your pediatrician, particularly if this has not occurred before. These unusual symptoms probably will disappear when the temperature returns to normal, but the doctor may want to examine your child to make sure they are a response to the fever and not something more serious, such as an inflammation of the brain (encephalitis).

Other circumstances should prompt an immediate call to your pediatrician. For example, contact your doctor if your child is feverish and has been in an extremely hot place, such as an overheated car. Also, talk to your pediatrician if your youngster has a fever and has a condition that suppresses immune responses, such as sickle cell disease or cancer, or if he is taking steroids.

If your child has a febrile convulsion, he should be examined by your pediatrician as soon as possible, particularly if this is the first time it has occurred, or if it is more severe or prolonged than others he has had. You need to be sure that the seizure is due to fever and not to a more serious condition such as meningitis (see page 655).

Home Treatment

Fevers generally do not need to be treated unless your child is uncomfortable or has a history of febrile convulsions. Even higher temperatures are not in themselves dangerous or significant unless your child has a history of convulsions or a chronic disease. It is more important to watch how your child is behaving. If he is eating and sleeping well and has periods of playfulness, he probably doesn't need any treatment.

When your child has a fever and seems to be quite bothered by it, you can treat it with the following approaches.

Medication

Several medications can reduce body temperature by blocking the mechanisms that cause a fever. These so-called antipyretic agents include acetaminophen, ibuprofen, and aspirin. All three of these over-the-counter drugs appear to be equally effective at reducing fever. *However, since aspirin may cause or be associated with Reye syndrome (see page 520), the American Academy of Pediatrics does not recommend using it to treat a*

Acetaminophen Dosage Chart

Dosages may be repeated every four hours, but should not be given more than five times in twenty-four hours. (*Note:* Milliliter is abbreviated as ml; 5 ml equals 1 teaspoon [tsp]. Don't use household teaspoons, which can vary in size.)

Age	Weight	Drops 80 mg/0.8 ml	Elixir 160 mg/5 ml	Chewable Tablets 80 mg tabs
0–3 mos	6–11 lbs (2.7–5 kg)	0.4 ml	—	—
4–11 mos	12–17 lbs (5.5–7.7 kg)	0.8 ml	½ tsp	1 tab
1–2 yrs	18–23 lbs (8.2–10.5 kg)	1.2 ml	¾ tsp	1½ tabs
2–3 yrs	24–35 lbs (10.9–15.9 kg)	1.6 ml	1 tsp	2 tabs
4–5 yrs	36–47 lbs (16.3–21.4 kg)	2.4 ml	1½ tsp	3 tabs

We do not recommend using aspirin ever to treat a simple fever.

simple fever in children. Ibuprofen use is approved for children six months of age and older, although it should never be given to children who are dehydrated or vomiting continuously.

Ideally, the dose of acetaminophen should be based on a child's weight, not his age. The dose of ibuprofen also should be based on weight, not age. (See the dosage charts above and on page 638.) However, the dosages listed on the labels of acetaminophen bottles (which are usually calculated by age) are generally safe and effective unless your child is unusually light or heavy for his age. Keep in mind that at too-high doses of acetaminophen, a toxic response can develop, although it happens only rarely. When a toxic reaction does occur, the symptoms may include nausea, vomiting, and abdominal discomfort.

As a general guideline, read and follow the instructions on the manufacturer's label when using *any* medication. Following the instructions is important to ensure that your child receives the proper dosages. Also, other over-the-counter medications, such as cold and cough preparations, may contain acetaminophen. The simultaneous use of more than one acetaminophen-containing product may be dangerous, so read all medication labels to ensure that your child is not receiving multiple doses of the same medicine. Also, as a general rule, do not give a baby under two years old either acetaminophen or any other medication without the advice of your pediatrician.

Which Thermometer Is Best?

DIGITAL THERMOMETERS

How to Use: Wipe with soapy water or rubbing alcohol, then rinse with cool water. Turn on the switch, and place the sensor under the tongue, toward the back of the mouth. Hold the thermometer in place until you hear an electronic beep. You also can use a digital thermometer rectally, with a nonpetroleum lubricant, or in your child's armpit.

Pros:
- Easy to read
- Beeps when ready
- Cost: $10–$15

Cons:
- Needs batteries
- Fussy children may not sit still for this type of reading.

TYMPANIC (EAR) THERMOMETERS

How to Use: Position the end of the thermometer gently in the ear canal. Press the start button. You will get a digital reading of your child's temperature within seconds.

Pros:
- Very quick reading
- Easy to use on fussy or uncomfortable children

Cons:
- Needs to be placed correctly in the ear canal for an accurate reading
- Needs batteries
- Too much earwax can cause incorrect readings
- Cost: about $30–$40

Sponging

In most cases, using oral acetaminophen or ibuprofen is the most convenient way to make your feverish child more comfortable. However, sometimes you may want to combine this with tepid sponging, or just use sponging alone.

Sponging is preferred over acetaminophen or ibuprofen if:

- Your child is known to be allergic to, or is unable to tolerate, antipyretic (antifever) drugs (a rare case).

It is advisable to *combine* sponging with acetaminophen or ibuprofen if:

- Fever is making your child extremely uncomfortable.

Ibuprofen Dosage Chart

Dosages may be repeated every six to eight hours, but should not be given more than four times in twenty-four hours. (Note: Milliliter is abbreviated as ml; 5 ml equals 1 teaspoon [tsp]. Don't use household teaspoons, which can vary in size.)

Age*	Weight†	Drops 40 mg/1.5 ml	Elixir 100 mg/5 ml	Chewable Tablets 50 mg tabs
6–11 mos.	12–17 lbs. (5.5–7.7 kg)	1 dropper	—	—
1–2 yrs.	18–23 lbs. (8.2–10.5 kg)	1½ droppers	—	—
2–3 yrs.	24–35 lbs. (10.9–15.9 kg)	2 droppers	1 tsp	—
4–5 yrs.	36–47 lbs. (16.3–21.4 kg)	—	1½ tsp	3 tabs

* Note: Age is provided as a convenience only. Dosing for fever should be based on baseline weight.
† Weight given is representative of the age range.

We do not recommend using aspirin to treat a simple fever.

- He is vomiting and may not be able to retain the medication.

To sponge your child, place him in his regular bath (tub, bathinette, or baby bath), but put only 1 to 2 inches of tepid water (85–90 degrees Fahrenheit, or 29.4–32.2 degrees Celsius) in the basin. If you do not have a bath thermometer, test the water with the back of your hand or wrist. It should feel just slightly warm. Do not use cold water, since that will be uncomfortable and may cause shivering, which can raise his temperature. Seat your child in the water—it is more comfortable than lying down. Then, using a clean washcloth or sponge, spread a film of water over his trunk, arms, and legs. The water will evaporate and cool the body. Keep the room at about 75 degrees Fahrenheit (23.9 degrees Celsius), and continue sponging him until his temperature has reached an acceptable level. *Never put alcohol in the water; it can be absorbed into the skin or inhaled, which can cause serious problems, such as coma.*

Usually sponging will bring down the fever in thirty to forty-five minutes. However, if your child is resisting actively, stop and let him just sit and play in the water. If being in the tub makes him more upset and uncomfortable, it is best to take him out even if his fever is unchanged. Remember, a fever less than 105 degrees Fahrenheit (40.5 degrees Celsius) is in itself not harmful.

Other Suggestions for Mild Fever

- Keep your child's room comfortably cool, and dress him lightly.

- Encourage him to drink extra fluid (water, diluted fruit juices, commercially prepared oral electrolyte solutions).

- If the room is warm or stuffy, place a fan nearby to keep cool air moving.

- Your child does not have to stay in his room or in bed when he has fever. He can be up and about the house, but he should not run around and overexert himself.

- If the fever is a symptom of a highly contagious disease (e.g., chickenpox or the flu), keep your child away from other youngsters and elderly people.

Treating a Febrile Convulsion

If your child has a febrile convulsion, take the following steps immediately to prevent injury:

- Place him on the floor or bed away from any hard or sharp objects.

- Turn his head to the side so that any saliva or vomit can drain from his mouth.

- Do not put anything into his mouth; he will not swallow his tongue.

- Call your pediatrician.

24

Genitourinary Tract

Blood in the Urine (Hematuria)

If your child's urine has a red, orange, or brown color, it may contain blood. The medical term for this is *hematuria*. Many things, including a physical injury or inflammation or infection in the urinary tract, can cause it. Hematuria also is associated with some general medical problems, such as defects of blood clotting, exposure to toxic materials, hereditary conditions, or abnormalities of the immune system.

Sometimes there may be such small amounts of blood in the urine that you cannot see any color change, although it may be detected by a chemical test performed by the pediatrician. In some cases the reddish color may be due simply to something your child has eaten or swallowed. Beets, blackberries, red food coloring, phenolphthalein (a chemical sometimes used in laxatives), Pyridium (a medicine used to relieve bladder pain), and the medicine rifampin may cause the urine to turn red or orange if your child ingests them. Anytime you are not sure that one of these has caused the color change, or if the color change persists for more than twenty-four hours without explanation, call your pediatrician.

Treatment

The pediatrician will ask you about any possible injury or foods that might have caused the change in urine color. He will perform a physical examination, checking particularly for any increase in blood pressure, tenderness in the kidney area, or swelling (particularly of the hands or feet or around the eyes) that might indicate kidney problems. The doctor also will perform tests on a sample of urine and may order blood tests, X rays, or other examinations to check the functioning of your child's kidneys, bladder, and immune system. If none of these reveals the cause of the hematuria, and it continues to occur, your pediatrician may refer you to a children's kidney specialist, who will per-

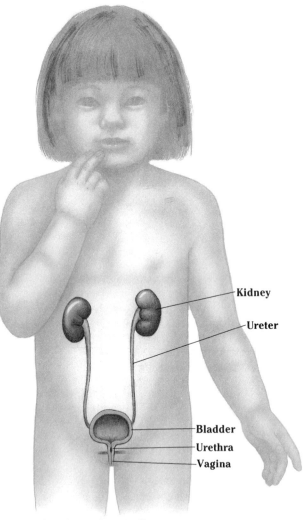

Kidney

Ureter

Bladder

Urethra

Vagina

Genitourinary System

form additional tests. (Sometimes these tests include an examination of a tiny piece of kidney tissue under the microscope. This tissue may be obtained by surgically operating or by performing what's called a needle biopsy.)

Once your pediatrician knows more about what is causing the hematuria, a decision can be made whether treatment is necessary and, if so, how it should be administered. Often no treatment is required. Occasionally

medication is used to suppress the immune system temporarily. Whatever the treatment, your child will need to return to the doctor regularly for repeat urine and blood tests and blood pressure checks. This is necessary to make sure that she isn't developing chronic kidney disease, which can lead to kidney failure. Occasionally hematuria is caused by kidney stones, or rarely by an abnormality that will require surgery. If this is the case, your pediatrician will refer you to a pediatric urologist who can perform such procedures.

Proteinuria

A child's urine sometimes can contain abnormally high amounts of protein. Although the body needs proteins to perform essential functions, such as guarding against infections and helping the blood to clot, protein detected in the urine may mean that the kidneys are not working properly and are allowing proteins (which are large molecules) to leak out into the urine. At times, the kidneys may be inflamed, and that inflammation may damage the kidneys' filtering mechanism, allowing leakage of protein.

Diagnosis

Proteinuria often causes no symptoms. But when high levels of protein appear in the urine, blood protein levels may drop and your child could develop symptoms such as swelling in the legs, ankles, or eyelids. Blood pressure may be elevated in some of these same situations. If your pediatrician suspects proteinuria, she can use a simple test in which a chemically treated paper strip is dipped into the urine, and will change colors if protein is present. She may recommend that you collect urine samples from your child just after awakening in the morning. She may recommend that a urine specimen be examined in the laboratory or that your child have some blood tests. Occasionally small amounts of protein are found in the urine and is of no consequence and disappears on its own.

At times, your pediatrician may decide to have your child seen by a kidney specialist (nephrologist), who might recommend performing a kidney biopsy to help evaluate what may be causing the problem. During a kidney biopsy, a needle is used to remove a small amount of kidney tissue for examination in the laboratory. Your child will usually be sedated for this procedure.

Treatment

Medication can be given to treat some underlying kidney problems associated with proteinuria. Your pediatrician might recommend that your child consume less salt to curtail the swelling associated with proteinuria. Children who have had an episode of proteinuria, even if it appears to be one of the harmless varieties, probably will be monitored over time with regular urine tests.

Hypospadias

In boys, the opening through which urine passes (the meatus) is located at the tip of the penis. A condition known as hypospadias is a birth defect that leaves the opening on the underside of the penis. There also may be an abnormal bending of the penis called chordee, which may cause sexual problems in adulthood. The meatus may direct the urinary stream downward, and in very rare cases there may be some blockage during urination. One of the important reasons to correct severe hypospadias, however, is to prevent the psychological complications that can arise quite early in childhood when peers may notice the abnormal appearance of the boy's penis.

Treatment

After detecting hypospadias in your newborn, the pediatrician probably will advise against circumcision until after consultation with a pediatric urologist or surgeon. This is because circumcision makes future surgical repair more difficult.

Mild hypospadias may require no treatment, but moderate or severe forms require surgical repair. This operation may be done as early as six months but usually is recommended just before toilet training. This surgery usually is performed on an outpatient basis. In severe cases, more than one operation may be needed to repair the defect completely. After surgery your child will have normal urinary and sexual function and a nearly normal-appearing penis.

Undescended Testicles (Cryptorchidism)

During a woman's pregnancy, the testes of the male fetus develop in his abdomen. As he nears birth, they descend through a tube (the inguinal canal) into the scrotum. In a small number of boys, especially those who are premature, one or both testicles fail to descend by the time of birth. In many of these boys, descent will occur during the

first nine months of life. In some, however, this does not happen.

All boys will have a normal retraction of the testes under certain situations, such as while sitting in cold water (i.e., the testes "disappear" temporarily up into the inguinal canal). However, in general, when the boy is warm, testes should be low in the scrotum. The cause of most cases of undescended testicles is unknown. However, in some boys, the following factors may play a role.

- There may not have been enough of certain hormones from the mother or the developing testicles to stimulate the testes' normal maturation, and descent.

- The testes themselves may respond abnormally to these hormones.

- A physical blockage may prevent descent.

- In some cases there may be a link with hormonal preparations taken by the mother during pregnancy (which is one reason why pregnant women are advised to avoid such medications).

If your child has undescended testicles, his scrotum may be small and appear underdeveloped. If only one testicle is undescended, the scrotum may look asymmetrical (full on one side, empty on the other). If the testicles sometimes are present in the scrotum and at other times (i.e., when he is cold or excited) are absent, and located above the scrotum, they are said to be retractile. This condition usually is self-correcting as the boy becomes more mature.

The undescended testicle may be twisted, and in the process, its blood supply may be stopped, causing pain in the inguinal (groin) or scrotal area. If this situation is not corrected, the testicle can be damaged severely

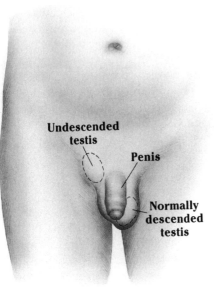

Undescended testis

Penis

Normally descended testis

and permanently. If your son has an undescended testicle and complains of pain in the groin or scrotal area, call your pediatrician immediately.

Undescended testicles should be reevaluated at each regular checkup. If they do not descend into the scrotum by age one to two, treatment should be started.

Treatment

Undescended testicles may be treated with hormone injections and/or surgery. The lower the testes, the more likely that hormone injections will be successful. Usually, but not always, treatment with hormones is tried first; if that is unsuccessful, the surgical approach is taken. Sometimes a hernia (see page 515) is also present and can be repaired at the same time.

If your son's undescended testicle is allowed to remain in that position for over two years, he has a higher than average risk of being unable to father children (infertility). He also has a slightly increased risk of developing testicular tumors in adult life, particularly if the testicle is left in its abnormal position. Fortunately, with early and proper treatment, all of these complications usually can be avoided.

Urethral Valves

Urine leaves the bladder through a tube called the urethra, which in boys passes through the penis. During early fetal development, tiny "valves" at the beginning of the urethra block the passage of urine. These normally disappear well before birth so that urine can flow freely out the end of the penis, although they can remain during the latter part of the pregnancy, continuing to block the urine flow. In some boys, however, these valves—called posterior urethral valves—

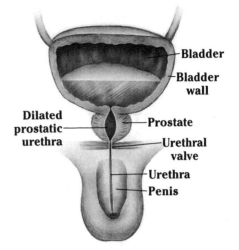

may be present after birth, causing serious problems by interfering with the flow of urine.

Often these valves are detected during pregnancy. They may be suspected if there appears to be a decrease in the amount of amniotic fluid. A consultation with a pediatric urology specialist is sometimes advisable before the baby is born.

Many times the posterior urethral valves are not discovered until the newborn period, when the pediatrician finds that the baby's bladder is distended and enlarged. Other warning signals include a continual dribbling of urine and a weak stream during urination. If you notice these symptoms, notify your pediatrician at once.

Posterior urethral valves require immediate medical attention to prevent serious urinary tract infections or damage to the kidneys. If the blockage is severe, the urine can back up through the ureters (the tubes between the bladder and the kidneys), creating pressure that can damage the kidneys.

Treatment

If a child has posterior urethral valves, the pediatrician may pass a small tube into the bladder to relieve the obstruction temporarily. Then X rays of the bladder and kidneys will be ordered to confirm the diagnosis and to see if any damage has occurred to the upper urinary tract. If the blockage is severe, it will have been present since early in pregnancy. In these cases, there may be damage to the kidneys and the bladder. Your pediatrician will consult with a pediatric nephrologist or urologist, who may perform surgery to remove the obstructing valves.

Labial Adhesions

Ordinarily the lips of skin (labia) surrounding the entrance to the vagina are separated. In rare cases, they grow together to block the opening, partially or completely. This condition, called labial adhesions (sticking together of labia), may occur in the early months of life or, less frequently, later on if there is constant irritation and inflammation in this area. In these latter cases, the problem is usually traceable to diaper irritation,

contact with harsh detergents, or panties made with synthetic fabric. Usually labial adhesions do not cause symptoms, but they can lead to difficulty with urination and increase a girl's susceptibility to urinary tract infection. If the vaginal opening is completely blocked, urine and/or vaginal secretions build up behind the obstruction.

Treatment

If the opening of your daughter's vagina appears to have closed or looks partially blocked, notify your pediatrician. He will examine your child and advise if any treatment is necessary.

At first, the doctor will attempt to spread the labia gently. If the connecting tissue is weak, this mild pressure may expose the opening.

If the connecting tissue is too strong, the doctor may prescribe a cream that contains the female hormone estrogen for you to apply to the area as you very gently and gradu-

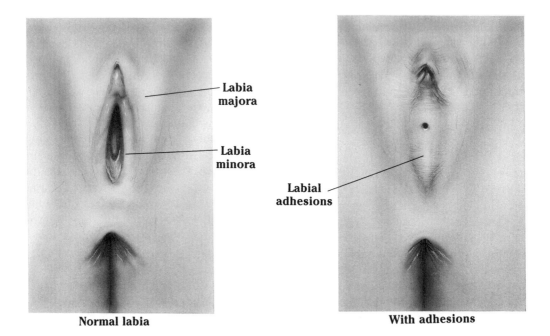

Labia majora

Labia minora

Labial adhesions

Normal labia   **With adhesions**

ally spread the labia apart over a period of time. Once the labia are separated, you will need to apply the cream for a short while (three to five days) until the skin on both sides heals completely.

Occasionally some adhesions return once the cream is discontinued. However, they usually disappear permanently at puberty. In rare cases, the adhesions (scarlike tissue that grows between the labia and holds them together) are so thick that they block the flow of urine. In this situation, they will need to be separated by a physician.

Meatal Stenosis

The meatus is the opening through which urine passes. Sometimes, particularly in circumcised boys, irritation of the tip of the penis causes scar tissue to form around the meatus, making it smaller. This narrowing, called meatal stenosis, may develop at any time during childhood, but is most commonly found between ages three and seven. Meatal stenosis is relatively rare.

Boys with meatal stenosis have a narrowed and abnormally directed urinary stream. Urination may take longer, and they have difficulty emptying the bladder completely. Although rare, recurrent urinary tract infections can result from this condition. Meatal stenosis in girls is very rare.

Treatment

If you notice that your son's urinary stream is very small or narrow, or if he strains to urinate or dribbles or sprays urine, discuss it with your pediatrician. Meatal stenosis is not a serious condition, but it should be evaluated to see if it needs to be corrected surgically. The operation is very minor and usually requires only local anesthesia. There will be some minor discomfort after the pro-

cedure, but this should disappear after a very short period of time.

Prevention

Decreasing the irritation caused by diapers, harsh detergents, and wet, rough underclothing may help prevent the condition.

Urinary Tract Infections

Urinary tract infections are common among young children, particularly girls. They generally are caused by bacteria that enter through the urethra, although they also can be caused by bacteria carried through the bloodstream to the kidneys from another part of the body. As the bacteria move through the urinary tract, they may cause infection in different locations. *Urinary tract infection* is a general term used for all the following specific infections.

- *Cystitis:* infection of the bladder

- *Pyelonephritis:* infection of the renal pelvis (the urine-collecting part of the kidney) and the kidney

- *Urethritis:* infection of the urethra

The bladder is the area most commonly infected. Usually cystitis is caused by bacteria that get into the urinary tract through the urethra. The urethra is very short in girls, so bacteria can get into the bladder easily. Fortunately, these bacteria normally wash out with voiding.

Cystitis can cause lower abdominal pain, tenderness, pain during urination, frequent urination, blood in the urine, and fever. Infection of the upper urinary tract (the kidneys) will cause a more general abdominal pain and higher fever, but is less likely to cause frequent and painful urination. In general, urinary tract infections in infants and young children (two months to two years of age) may have few recognizable signs or symptoms other than a fever; they also have a greater potential for causing kidney damage than those occurring in older children.

Urinary tract infections must be treated with antibiotics as quickly as possible, so you should notify your pediatrician promptly if you suspect your child has developed one. A urinalysis also should be performed if your child suffers vague symptoms that cannot be explained, since these can be caused by a chronic urinary tract infection. Even if your child has no symptoms, routine urinalyses should be performed according to the recommended schedule of the American Academy of Pediatrics (see pages 68–69), and blood pressure checks should be done when possible at each office visit for preschool age children.

Diagnosis/Treatment

The pediatrician will measure your child's blood pressure and examine her for lower abdominal tenderness that might indicate a urinary tract infection. The doctor will want to know what your child has been eating and drinking, because certain foods can irritate the urinary tract, causing symptoms similar to those of an infection. (Drinks containing citrus juice, carbonation, and caffeine may have this effect.)

Your child also will be asked to provide a urine sample for analysis. This must be collected by the "clean catch" method, so you will need to help. First, you'll use soap and water to cleanse the urethral opening (with an uncircumcised boy, hold the foreskin back). Then allow your child to start to urinate, but wait just a moment before you start to collect the sample in the container provided by the doctor. In this way, any bacteria around the outside of the urethral opening will be washed away by the first urine voided and won't contaminate the specimen. (Infants should be cleansed in the same manner but will have special urine collectors taped over the penis or vaginal opening until voiding occurs.) Infants who are very sick or have a fever may need to have their urine collected through a small tube called a catheter or by draining the urine out of the bladder with a needle inserted through the skin of the lower abdomen.

The urine will be examined under the microscope for any sign of blood cells or bacteria, and special tests (cultures) will be done to identify the bacteria. An antibiotic will be started if an infection is suspected, although it may need to be changed after the final results of the culture are obtained (up to forty-eight hours later).

Antibiotics may be prescribed for as long as a ten-day to two-week period. Prompt treatment is important in order to eliminate the infection and prevent its spread, and also to reduce the chances of kidney damage.

Make sure your child takes the full course of medication prescribed, even if the discomfort goes away after just a few days. Otherwise, the bacteria may grow again, causing further infection and more serious damage to the urinary tract. After treatment is complete, another urine sample will be taken to make sure that the infection is completely gone and no bacteria remain.

Most specialists now feel that further tests (ultrasound, X rays, or renal scans) should be done after your child's first serious urinary tract infection. Your pediatrician also may conduct other tests to check kidney function. If any of these examinations indicate a structural abnormality that should be corrected, your doctor will recommend that your child see a pediatric urologist or pediatric surgeon.

Wetting Problems or Enuresis

After toilet training is completed (usually between ages two and four), it is not uncommon for children to wet the bed at night. This may happen as often as two to three times per week early in this period and gradually become less and less until it is completely gone at around age five.

The best way to deal with incontinence (wetting) is to treat it as something natural and unimportant and not scold or punish. This wetting usually occurs because the child's bladder is not yet large enough to hold a full night's output of urine, or because he has not yet developed the ability to awaken in response to the urge of a full bladder.

Some children continue to wet at night past the age of five. When wetting occurs only during sleep, it is called nocturnal (nighttime) enuresis, or bed-wetting. It affects one out of every ten children over the age of five. Boys make up two-thirds of this group, and often there is a family history of bed-wetting (usually in the father). The reasons for bed-wetting are not fully understood, but may be related to the time it takes different children to develop control over the nervous, muscular, and nighttime full-bladder alarm systems. Bed-wetting generally is *not* associated with other physical or emotional problems.

A much smaller number of children over age five have daytime wetting problems, and an even smaller group is unable to hold their urine both day and night. When incontinence does occur both day and night, it may signal a more complicated problem with the bladder or the kidneys.

If your child wets at night, consider the following possible causes.

- Slow development of the ability to awaken when the bladder is full

- Urinary tract infections or urethral irritation from bubble bath or detergents in bathwater or, rarely, sensitivity to certain foods

- Constipation, which can cause extra pressure on the bladder from the rectum

- An early sign of diabetes mellitus (see page 719), urinary tract infection (see page 647), or emotional distress caused by an upsetting event or unusual stress—particularly if wetting began suddenly after a dry period.

Signs of a Problem

When your child is starting toilet training, he is sure to have "accidents." Therefore, there is no reason to be concerned about wetting until at least six months to a year after the training is successful. Even then, it is still normal for him to have some accidents, but they should decrease, so that by age six he should have only occasional accidents during the day, with perhaps a few more at night. If your child continues to wet frequently, or if you notice any of the following signals, consult your pediatrician.

- Wet underpants, nightclothes, and bed linens, even when the child regularly uses the toilet

- Unusual straining during urination, a very small or narrow stream of urine, or dribbling after urination

- Cloudy or pink urine, or bloodstains on underpants or nightclothes

- Redness or rash in the genital area

- Hiding of underwear to conceal wetting

- Daytime as well as nighttime wetting

Treatment

Occasional nighttime wetting or daytime accidents when a child is laughing, or engaged in physical activity, or just too busy playing, are perfectly normal up to the age of five or so and should be no cause for concern. Although annoying to you and perhaps embarrassing for your child, it should stop on its own. There probably is no need for a medical investigation. However, your pediatrician will want to know the answers to the following questions.

- Is there a family history of wetting?

- How often does your child urinate, and at what times of the day?

- When do the accidents occur?

- Do accidents occur when your child is very active or upset, or when he's under unusual stress?

- Does your child tend to have accidents after drinking caffeinated drinks, lots of water, or a lot of salty foods?

- Is there anything unusual about your child's urination or the appearance of his urine?

If your pediatrician suspects a problem, he may check a urine sample for signs of urinary tract infection (see page 647). If there is an infection, the doctor will treat it with antibiotics, and this may cure the wetting problems. Usually, however, infection is not the cause.

If there are other indications that wetting is due to more than just slow development of the full-bladder response, and the wetting persists beyond age five, your pediatrician may request additional tests, such as X rays of the bladder or kidneys. If an abnormality is found, the doctor may recommend that you consult a pediatric urologist.

If no physical cause can be found for wetting in a child who is over five years of age, and the wetting is causing significant family disruption, the pediatrician may recommend a home treatment program. The program will vary, depending on whether your child wets during the day or the night.

Home Treatment for Daytime Wetting after Toilet Training

1. Eliminate skin irritation in the genital area by avoiding the use of harsh detergents or underclothing and bubble-making products in the bathwater. Also, use mild soaps for bathing, and apply petroleum jelly to protect the affected areas from further irritation from the water and urine.

2. Eliminate dietary sources of excess urine output and irritation:

- Excessive water

- Drinks that contain caffeine

3. Prevent constipation or treat it if it occurs (see page 503).

4. Try using a timed voiding program, reminding your child to empty his bladder every two hours or so rather than waiting until he "has to go"—which by then may be too late.

Home Treatment for Nocturnal Bedwetting over the Age of Five

The following plan usually is helpful, but you should discuss it with your pediatrician before beginning.

1. Explain the problem to your child, emphasizing that you understand and know it's not his fault.

2. Discourage drinking large amounts of fluids right before bedtime.

3. Have your child use the toilet immediately before bedtime.

4. Awaken your child to use the toilet again right before *you* go to bed if he's been asleep for an hour or more. (This may be difficult if he's a very sound sleeper.)

5. Reward dry nights, but don't punish wet ones. This is very important, since this is an emotional issue for both of you.

If your child is still wetting after one to three months on this plan, your pediatrician may recommend using a bed-wetting alarm device. This alarm will awaken your child automatically as soon as he begins to wet, so he can get up and complete his urination in the toilet. When used consistently and according to your pediatrician's guidelines, this conditioning method is successful for one-half to three-fourths of children who try it.

If the bed-wetting alarm hasn't solved the problem after three or four months, your pediatrician may prescribe oral medication, but this should be a last resort. Although medication can be helpful, it also can pro-duce side effects, such as rapid heart rate, restlessness, and changes in blood pressure.

If None of the Treatments Works

A small number of children with bed-wetting simply do not respond to any treatment. Almost all will outgrow the problem by adolescence, however. Only one in a hundred adults is troubled by persistent bed-wetting. Until your child does outgrow his wetting problem, he will need a large amount of emotional support from the family, and he may benefit from counseling with his pediatrician or a child mental health professional. He should recognize that there still are things he can do to help his problem, however, and he should be encouraged to continue trying to increase his bladder capacity (holding for several minutes when he feels the urgency to urinate), and to avoid drinking large quantities of beverages that stimulate urination. Because bed-wetting is such a common problem, many mail-order treatment programs and devices are advertised. You should be wary of them, however, as many false claims and promises are made. Your pediatrician is still your most reliable source for advice, and you should ask for it before enrolling in or paying for any treatment program.

25

HEAD, NECK, AND NERVOUS SYSTEM

Autism

Autism is a serious and lifelong emotional, behavioral, and social disorder that traditionally has been thought of as relatively rare, although the number of reported cases has increased in recent years. Children with autism (or autistic spectrum) may develop a variety of behaviors, including abnormal or delayed communication skills and unusual use of language. Symptoms and their severity may vary, ranging from mild peculiarities to severe disabilities.

Genetics appears to play a role in autism, although there are probably other causes, as well. Although some parents have been concerned about a possible link between autism and certain childhood immunizations (in particular, the measles/mumps/rubella [MMR] vaccine), no scientific evidence supports such an association.

Autism occurs about four times as often in boys as in girls and affects about one in one thousand children. It usually becomes ap-

parent in the first three years of life. It is one of several *pervasive developmental disorders* (PDD), which include Asperger syndrome, another category of children with these problems. The term *autistic spectrum disorder (ASD)* also is used to describe autism and its related conditions; it has come into fashion to describe people with a wide range of functional disabilities, including autism, Asperger syndrome, and high-functioning autism. Most doctors now believe that autism is not a distinct disease, but instead is a collection of disorders of brain development.

Here are some characteristics typically seen in children with autism, although the signs and symptoms can differ from one child to another.

- Some children never develop the ability to speak, or their language skills may be delayed or poorly developed. They may use words without attaching the usual meanings to them or simply repeat what they hear others saying (known as echolalia).

- They may not be able to understand what people say to them, or interpret or respond appropriately to cues such as others' facial expressions and body language.

- These children may be socially withdrawn and have trouble relating to people and making eye contact. They may appear to be unaware of their surroundings.

- Their behavior and body movements are sometimes self-stimulating and repetitive (rocking, flapping their arms, hair twirling). They also may engage in self-injurious activity (head banging, biting), as well as demonstrating aggressiveness and having tantrums.

- They may become upset when there are changes in everyday routines (i.e., mealtimes).

- They may have a limited range of interests and activities. Their play may not be creative or imaginative in the usual sense of "play," in that it often includes repetitive behavior.

- They may play with toys in ways in which they are not designed to be used.

- In many cases, these children are mentally retarded.

Children with Asperger syndrome (AS) are considered to be at the high-functioning end of the ASD spectrum. But even though these youngsters have good language skills, they typically have impaired social skills and have difficulty understanding how they should interact with others. They may be preoccupied with their "own little world" and exhibit only limited facial expressions.

Other ASD syndromes include Rett syndrome (in which children develop skills such as talking and walking but then gradually lose those abilities), as well as childhood disintegrative disorder (severe impairment of mental and social functioning), and PDD not otherwise specified (PDD-NOS).

Diagnosis

If you are concerned about your child's language and social development, or any of the other signs just described, talk to your pediatrician. There is no laboratory test to diagnose autism, nor does a single set of symptoms always characterize it. The diagnosis is made based on the presence (or absence) of a collection of symptoms. A doctor or a team of health care specialists with expertise in autism should make the diagnosis. These specialists usually can be found in major medical centers; ask your pediatrician for a referral.

Treatment

There is no known cure for autism and other pervasive developmental disorders. A child with autism will need specialized services aimed at the management of his disorder. Early diagnosis and treatment is important, and may improve the ability of the youngster with autism to function more effectively in life.

Some children with autism do much better in specialized schools, particularly when they receive one-on-one attention or participate in small classes. They may benefit from special-education programs to help them develop language and improve their social skills. At times, medications are prescribed to manage the behavioral difficulties that can occur with autism and related disorders.

Keep in mind, however, that children with

autism and other types of ASD can vary considerably in their ability to function in the world, as well as in their behavior and intelligence. Youngsters with Asperger syndrome, for example, often are able to live on their own as adults and lead more independent lives than those with other forms of ASD.

Your pediatrician can help you find community agencies that provide services for your child, as well as family support networks, counseling, and advocacy groups. On the Internet, seek out reliable sources of information and education, such as the Autism Society of America (www.autismsociety.org; 1–800–328–8476).

If one of your youngsters is diagnosed with autism, there is an increased risk (of about 3 to 7 percent) that the same disorder will occur in subsequent children. Speak to your pediatrician about receiving counseling services to discuss this increased risk.

Meningitis

Meningitis is an inflammation of the tissues that cover the brain and spinal cord. The inflammation sometimes affects the brain itself. With early diagnosis and proper treatment, a child with meningitis has a good chance of getting well without any complications.

Today most cases of meningitis are caused by viruses. The *viral* form usually is not very serious, except in infants less than three months of age. Once meningitis is diagnosed as being caused by a virus, there is no need for antibiotics and recovery should be complete. *Bacterial* meningitis (several types of bacteria are involved) is a very serious disease. It occurs very rarely, but when it does, children under the age of two are at greatest risk.

The bacteria that cause meningitis often can be found in the mouths and throats of healthy children. But this does not necessarily mean that these children will get the disease. That doesn't happen unless the bacteria get into the bloodstream.

We still don't understand exactly why some children get meningitis and others don't, but we do know that certain groups of children are more likely to get the illness. These include the following:

- Babies, especially those under two months of age (Because their immune systems are not well developed, the bacteria can get into the bloodstream more easily.)

- Children with recurrent sinus infections

- Children with recent serious head injuries and skull fractures

- Children who have just had brain surgery

Before antibiotics (drugs that combat bacteria) were developed, nine out of ten children with bacterial meningitis died. Of those who survived, most were left mentally retarded or deaf, or had convulsions. Now the outlook is much brighter. With prompt diagnosis and treatment, seven out of ten children who get bacterial meningitis recover without any complications. Even most of those with complications usually have only minor ones that last just a short time. Hearing loss, however, remains a common, important, and long-lasting problem. Meningitis must be detected early and treated aggressively. This is why it's so important for you to notify your pediatrician immediately if your child displays any of the following warning signs.

If your child is less than two months old: The presence of fever, decreased appetite, listlessness, or increased crying or irritability warrants a call to your doctor. At this age,

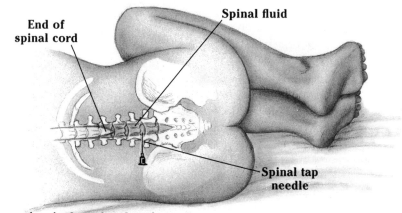

End of spinal cord

Spinal fluid

Spinal tap needle

A spinal tap is taken from the space below the spinal cord so that the needle will not touch the spinal cord.

the signs of meningitis can be very subtle and difficult to detect. It's better to call early and be wrong than to call too late.

If your child is two months to two years old: This is the most common age for meningitis. Look for symptoms such as fever, vomiting, decreased appetite, excessive crankiness, or excessive sleepiness. (His cranky periods might be extreme and his sleepy periods might make it impossible to arouse him.) Seizures along with a fever may be the first signs of meningitis, although most brief, generalized (so-called tonic-clonic) convulsions turn out to be simple febrile seizures, not meningitis. (See *Convulsions,* page 660.)

If your child is two to five years old: In addition to the above symptoms, a child of this age with meningitis may complain of a headache, pain in his back, or a stiff neck. He also may object to looking at bright lights.

Treatment

If, after an examination, your pediatrician is concerned that your child may have meningitis, she will conduct a blood test to check for a bacterial infection and also will obtain some spinal fluid by performing a spinal tap, or lumbar puncture (LP). This procedure in-volves inserting a special needle into your child's lower back to draw out the fluid. Any signs of infection in this fluid will confirm that your child has bacterial meningitis. In that case he'll need to be admitted to the hospital for intravenous antibiotics and fluids and for careful observation for complications. During the first days of treatment, your child may not be able to eat or drink, so intravenous fluids will provide the medicine and nutrition he needs. For certain types of meningitis, this may be necessary for seven to twenty-one days, depending on the age of the child and the bacteria identified.

Prevention

Some types of bacterial meningitis can be prevented with vaccines or antibiotics. Ask your pediatrician about the following.

Hib (*Haemophilus influenzae* type b) Vaccine

This vaccine will decrease the chance of children becoming infected with *Haemophilus influenzae* type b (Hib) bacteria, which was the leading cause of bacterial meningitis among young children before this immunization became available. The vaccine is given by injection to children at two months, four months, and six months, and then again between twelve and fifteen months of age. (Some combined vaccines may allow your doctor to omit the last injection.)

Pneumococcal Vaccine

This vaccine is effective in preventing many serious infections caused by the *pneumococcus* bacteria, including meningitis as well as bacteremia (an infection of the bloodstream) and pneumonia. Called Prevnar or PCV7 (or the heptavalent pneumococcal conjugate vaccine), it is recommended starting at two months of age, with additional doses at four, six, and between twelve and fifteen months of age. Some children who have an increased susceptibility to serious infections (these high-risk youngsters include those with abnormally functioning immune systems, sickle cell disease, certain kidney problems, and other chronic conditions) may receive an additional pneumococcal vaccine between ages two and five years. Your doctor can choose between two types of vaccine for this immunization.

Rifampin

If your child has been exposed either at home or at child care to a child with meningitis caused by *Haemophilus influenzae* or the *meningococcus* bacteria, he should be placed on an antibiotic called rifampin to prevent him from becoming infected. In some cases adults who are exposed (by means of close intimate contact) to someone with bacterial meningitis also should be placed on medication for a period of time. Your pediatrician will tell you how often and how long to use it. If your child shows any of the signs of meningitis, even though he is on the medication, call your pediatrician immediately.

Motion Sickness

Motion sickness occurs when the brain receives conflicting signals from the motion-sensing parts of the body: the inner ears, the eyes, and nerves in the extremities. Under usual circumstances, all three areas respond to any motion. When the signals they receive and send are inconsistent—for example, if you watch rapid motion on a movie screen, your eyes sense the motion, but your inner ear and joints do not—the brain receives conflicting signals and activates a response that can make you sick. The same thing can happen when a child is sitting so low in the backseat of a car that she cannot see outside. Her inner ear senses the motion, but her eyes and joints do not.

Motion sickness usually starts with a vague feeling of stomach upset (queasiness), a cold sweat, fatigue, and loss of appetite. This usually progresses to vomiting. A young child may not be able to describe queasiness, but will demonstrate it by becoming pale and restless, yawning, and crying. Later she will lose interest in food (even her favorite ones), and finally she will vomit.

We do not know why motion sickness happens more often in some children than others, but it is most likely due to an increased sensitivity to the brain's response to motion. This response can be affected by previous car trips that made them sick, but it usually improves over time.

Motion sickness occurs most often on a first boat or plane ride, or when the motion is very intense, such as that caused by rough water or turbulent air. Stress and excitement also can start this problem or make it worse.

Not infrequently, children with a history of motion sickness go on to develop migraine headaches.

What You Can Do

If your child starts to develop the symptoms of motion sickness, the best approach is to stop the activity that is causing the problem. If it occurs in the car, stop as soon as safely possible and let her get out and walk around. If you are on a long car trip, you may have to make frequent short stops, but it will be worth it. If this condition develops on a swing or merry-go-round, stop the motion promptly and get your child off the equipment.

She probably will be upset and scared, so try to help her relax. Otherwise, what should be a happy time will become a dreaded experience. Most important, do not get angry with your child, because she cannot help what is happening. Be as supportive of her as you can, or she may refuse to travel or have a temper tantrum the next time you ask her to get into the car or board a plane or boat.

Since "car sickness" is the most common form of motion sickness in children, many preventive measures have been developed. In addition to frequent stops, try the following.

- Place your young child in an approved car safety seat, facing forward if over 20 pounds (9 kg) *and* over one year old. Do not let her move around in the car. (You should not let her do this for safety reasons, anyway.)

- If she has not eaten for three hours, give your child a *light* snack before the trip—which also helps on a boat or plane. This relieves hunger pangs, which seem to add to the symptoms.

- Try to focus her attention away from the queasy feeling. Listen to the radio, sing, or talk.

- Have her look at things outside the car, not at books or games.

If none of the above works, stop the car and have her lie on her back for a few minutes (still in her lap belt) with her eyes closed. A cool cloth on the forehead also tends to lessen the symptoms.

If you are going on a trip and your child has had motion sickness before, you might want to give her medication ahead of time to prevent problems. Some of these medications are available without a prescription, but ask your pediatrician before using them. Although they can help, they often produce side effects, such as drowsiness (which means that when you get to your destination your child might be too tired to enjoy it), dry mouth and nose, or blurred vision. Less common reactions include skin rashes, blood pressure changes, nausea, and vomiting. Some children actually become agitated from these medicines rather than drowsy. Never use the skin patch–type motion sickness medications on young children.

Although it does not happen often, dehydration (see page 506) can occur from the vomiting and poor fluid intake that may accompany motion sickness. If you feel that your child is becoming dehydrated, take her to the nearest physician's office or to an emergency room.

If your child has symptoms of motion sickness at times when she is not involved with a movement activity—particularly if she also has a headache; difficulty hearing, seeing, walking, or talking; or if she stares off into space—tell your pediatrician about it. These may be symptoms of problems other than motion sickness.

Mumps

Mumps is a viral infection that usually causes swelling of the salivary glands (the glands that produce the digestive juices in the mouth). Thanks to the MMR (measles, mumps, and rubella) vaccine given at twelve to fifteen months and a booster at age four to six years, most of today's children will never get this disease. If your child has not been immunized, however, you should know how to identify mumps and distinguish it from similar ailments.

The parotid gland, located in front of the ear at and above the angle of the jaw, is the one most often affected by mumps. However, other salivary glands in and around the face may be involved. Although not all children with mumps appear swollen (milder case), anyone who has the virus in his system will become immune to it.

The mumps virus is transmitted when an infected individual coughs droplets containing the virus into the air or onto hands. A nearby child can inhale these particles, and the virus can pass through his respiratory system into his bloodstream, finally settling in his salivary glands. At this point, the virus usually causes swelling of the glands along the side of one or both cheeks. The child also may have a fever for three to five days, and will complain of pain when touching the swollen area, when opening his mouth, and while eating food—especially foods that stimulate the release of salivary juices. He also may experience nausea, occasional vomiting, headache, a general feeling of weakness, and loss of appetite.

In addition to the swelling of the salivary glands, there also can be swelling and pain in the joints and, in boys, swelling of the testes. In extremely rare cases, the virus can cause swelling of the brain in boys or girls, or swelling of the ovaries in girls.

Several days before the glands become noticeably swollen, the child with mumps will become infectious to others. He'll remain infectious until the swelling is gone—that is, for at least ten days after the first sign of inflammation.

It's important to note that salivary gland swelling can be caused by infections other than mumps. This explains why some par-ents are convinced that their children have had the disease more than once. If your child has been immunized or already has had mumps and his cheeks become swollen, consult your pediatrician to determine the cause.

Treatment

There is no specific treatment for mumps, aside from making the child as comfortable as possible with rest, lots of fluids, and acetaminophen for fever. Although a child with the disease won't be too eager to take fluids, you should keep a glass of water or noncitrus juice nearby, and encourage him to take frequent sips. Sometimes a warm compress over the swollen gland will give some short-term relief.

Eating solid, hard-to-digest foods may cause your child increased pain because they require extra saliva from the swollen glands. Instead, feed him soft, noncitrus foods that are easy to chew and swallow and that place minimal demands on the inflamed glands.

If your child's condition worsens, or if he

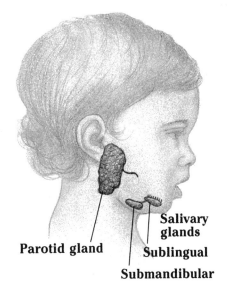

Parotid gland **Salivary glands** **Sublingual** **Submandibular**

develops complications such as painful testes, severe abdominal pain, or extreme listlessness, contact your pediatrician right away. The doctor will want to examine your child to see if he needs more extensive medical treatment. However, such complications from mumps are extremely rare.

Seizures, Convulsions, and Epilepsy

Seizures are sudden temporary changes in physical movement or behavior caused by abnormal electrical impulses in the brain. Depending on how many muscles are affected by the electrical impulses, a seizure may cause sudden stiffening of the body or complete relaxation of the muscles, which can make a person appear to be paralyzed temporarily. Sometimes these seizures are referred to as "fits" or "spells." The terms *convulsion* and *seizure* can be used interchangeably.

A convulsion (sometimes called a grand mal seizure) that involves the whole body (is "generalized") is the most dramatic type of seizure, causing rapid, violent movements and sometimes loss of consciousness. These sometimes can start with focal movements (those involving one specific part of the body) and progress to generalized movements. Convulsions occur in about five out of every hundred people at some time during childhood. By contrast, petit mal seizures (also called absence attacks) are momentary episodes associated with a vacant stare or a brief (one or two seconds) lapse of attention. These occur mainly in young children and may be so subtle that they aren't noticed until they begin affecting schoolwork.

Febrile convulsions (seizures caused by high fever) occur in three or four out of every hundred children between infancy and age five. They rarely occur after five years of age, however, and half of all children who have one febrile convulsion never have another. A febrile convulsion can cause reactions as mild as a rolling of the eyes or stiffening of the limbs, or as startling as a generalized convulsion with twitching and jerking movements that involve the whole body. Febrile convulsions usually last less than five minutes, and ordinarily the child's behavior quickly returns to normal. The risk of developing epilepsy later in life is extremely low.

The term *epilepsy* is used to describe seizures that recur over a long period of time. Sometimes the cause of the recurring seizures is known (symptomatic epilepsy), and sometimes it is not (idiopathic epilepsy). Chemical imbalances in the blood, brain damage due to infection or injury, and lead poisoning (see page 730) are some of the conditions that can lead to epilepsy.

Some children experience sudden episodes that include breath holding, fainting, facial or body twitching, and unusual sleep disorders. They may occur just once or may recur over a limited time period. Although these episodes may resemble epilepsy or true seizures, they are not, and they require quite different treatment.

Treatment

Most seizures will stop on their own and do not require immediate medical treatment. If your child is having a convulsion, protect her from injuring herself by moving her to a semisitting position or laying her on her side with her hips higher than her head, so she will not choke if she vomits.

If the convulsion does not stop within two or three minutes, is unusually severe (difficulty breathing, choking, blueness of the skin, having several in a row), call for emergency medical help. Do not leave the child unattended, however. After the seizure stops, call the pediatrician immediately and arrange to meet in the doctor's office or the nearest emergency room. Also call your doctor if your child is on an anticonvulsant medication, since this may mean that the dosage must be adjusted.

If your child has a fever, the pediatrician will check to see if there is an infection. If there is no fever and this was your child's first convulsion, the doctor will try to determine other possible causes by asking if there is any family history of seizures or if your child has had any recent head injury. He will examine the child and also may order blood tests, X rays, or an electroencephalogram (EEG), which measures the electrical activity of the brain. Sometimes a spinal tap will be performed to obtain a specimen of spinal fluid that can be examined for some causes of convulsions such as meningitis, an infection of the lining of the brain (see page 655). If no explanation or cause can be found for the seizures, the doctor may consult a pediatric neurologist, a pediatrician who specializes in disorders of the nervous system.

If your child has had a febrile convulsion, the doctor may advise you to control the fever using acetaminophen and sponging. However, if a bacterial infection is present, an antibiotic probably will be prescribed. If a serious infection such as meningitis is responsible for the seizure, your child will have to be hospitalized for further treatment. When seizures are caused by abnormal amounts of sugar, calcium, or magnesium in the blood, hospitalization may be required so that the cause can be found and the imbalances corrected.

If epilepsy is diagnosed, your child usually will be placed on an anticonvulsant medication. When the proper dosage is maintained, the seizures can almost always be completely controlled. Your child may need to have her blood checked periodically after starting this medication to make certain there is an adequate amount present. She also may need periodic EEGs. Medication usually is continued until there have been no seizures for a year or two.

As frightening as seizures can be, it's encouraging to know that the likelihood that your child will have another one drops greatly as she gets older. (Only one in a hundred adults ever has a seizure.) Unfortunately, a great deal of misunderstanding and confusion about seizures still exists, so it is important that your child's friends and teachers understand her condition. If you need additional support or information, consult with your pediatrician or contact your local or state branch of the Epilepsy Foundation.

Sinusitis

Sinusitis is an inflammation of one or more of the sinuses (bony cavities) around the nose. It usually occurs as a complication of a viral upper respiratory infection or allergic inflammation in children over two years of age. These conditions cause swelling of the lining of the nose and sinuses. This swelling blocks the openings that normally allow the sinuses to drain into the back of the nose, so the sinuses fill with fluid. Although nose blowing and sniffing may be natural responses to this blockage, they can make the situation worse by pushing bacteria from the back of the nose into the sinuses. Since the sinuses can't drain properly, the bacteria will multiply there, causing an infection.

Several signs of sinusitis should alert you to call your pediatrician:

■ The persistence of symptoms of a cold or upper respiratory infection, including cough and nasal discharge lasting for more than ten days, without any improvement. The nasal discharge may be thick and yellow, or clear, or whitish, and the cough usually will continue during the day as well as at night. In some cases a child with sinusitis will have swelling around the eyes when he wakes up in the morning. Also, a preschooler with sinusitis sometimes may have persistent bad breath along with cold symptoms. (However, this also could mean that he has put something into his nose or has a sore throat, or that he isn't brushing his teeth.)

- Your child's cold is severe and is accompanied by high fever and thick yellow nasal discharge. His eyes might be swollen in the early morning, and he might have a severe headache that he describes (if he's old enough) as behind or above the eyes.

In very rare cases, a sinus infection may spread to either the eye or the central nervous system (the brain). If this occurs, you'll see swelling around the eye not just in the morning but all through the day, and you should call your pediatrician immediately. If your child has a very severe headache, becomes sensitive to light, or is increasingly irritable, the infection may have spread into the central nervous system. This is serious and requires immediate medical attention.

Treatment

If your pediatrician thinks your child has sinusitis, she may prescribe an antibiotic, usually for a fourteen- to twenty-one-day period. Once your child is on the medication, his symptoms should start to go away very quickly. In most cases the nasal discharge will clear and the cough will improve over a week or two. *But even though he may seem better, he must continue to take the antibiotics for the prescribed length of time.*

If there's no improvement after two to

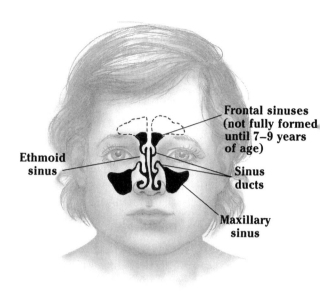

Frontal sinuses (not fully formed until 7–9 years of age)

Ethmoid sinus

Sinus ducts

Maxillary sinus

four days, your pediatrician might want to conduct some further tests, after which a different medication may be prescribed or an additional one added for a longer period of time.

Wryneck (Torticollis)

Wryneck is a condition that causes a child to hold her head or neck in a twisted or otherwise abnormal position. She may lean her head toward one shoulder and, when lying on her stomach, always turn the same side of her face toward the mattress. This can cause her head to flatten on one side and her face to appear uneven or out of line. If not treated, wryneck may lead to permanent facial deformity or unevenness and to restricted head movement.

There are several different causes of wryneck.

Congenital Muscular Torticollis

By far the most common cause of wryneck among children under age five, this condition is the result of injury to the muscle that connects the breastbone, head, and neck (the sternocleidomastoid muscle). The injury may occur during birth (particularly breech and difficult first-time deliveries), but it also can occur while the baby is still in the womb. Whatever the cause, this condition usually is detected in the first six to eight weeks of life, when the pediatrician notices a small lump on the side of the baby's neck in the area of the damaged muscle. Later the muscle contracts and causes the head to tilt to one side and look toward the opposite side.

Klippel-Feil Syndrome

In this condition, which is present at birth, the tilt of the neck is caused by a fusion or bony connection between two or more bones in the neck. Children with Klippel-Feil syndrome may have a short, broad neck, low hairline, and very restricted neck movement.

Torticollis Due to Injury or Inflammation

This is more likely to occur in older children, up to the age of nine or ten. This type of torticollis results from an inflammation of the throat caused by an upper respiratory infection, a sore throat, an injury, or some unknown factor. The swelling, for reasons still not known, causes the tissue surrounding the upper spine to loosen, allowing the vertebral bones to move out of normal position. When this happens, the neck muscles go into spasm, causing the head to tilt to one side.

Treatment

Each type of wryneck requires a slightly different treatment. It is very important to seek such treatment early, so that the problem is corrected before it causes permanent deformity.

Your pediatrician will examine your child's neck and may order X rays of the area in order to identify the cause of the problem. X rays of the hip also may be ordered, as some children with congenital muscular torticollis also have an abnormality known as developmental dysplasia of the hip. If the doctor decides that the problem is muscular torticollis due to a birth-related injury to the sternocleidomastoid muscle, you will be instructed on the use of an exercise program to stretch the neck muscles. The doctor will show you how to gently move your child's head in the opposite direction from the tilt. You'll need to do this several times a day, very gradually extending the movement as the muscle stretches.

When your child sleeps, it is best to place her on her back or side, with her head positioned opposite to the direction of the tilt. She can be placed on her stomach if she allows you to turn her face away from the side of the muscle injury, and if she then keeps her head in this position while sleeping. When she is awake, position her so that things she wants to look at (windows, mo-

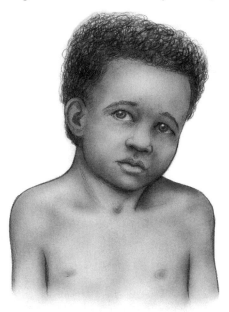

biles, pictures, activity) are on the side away from the injury. In that way, she'll stretch the shortened muscle while trying to see these objects. These simple strategies cure this type of wryneck in the vast majority of cases, preventing the need for later surgery.

If the problem is not corrected by exercise or position change, your pediatrician will refer you to a pediatric orthopedist. In some cases it may be necessary to lengthen the involved tendon surgically. If your child's wryneck is caused by something other than congenital muscular torticollis, and the X rays show no spinal abnormality, other treatment involving rest, a special collar, traction, application of heat to the area, medication, or rarely surgery may be necessary.

26

HEART

Arrhythmias

The regular rhythm or beat of the heart is maintained by a small electrical circuit that runs through nerves in the walls of the heart. When the circuit is working properly, the heartbeat is quite regular, but when there's a problem in the circuit, an irregular heartbeat, or arrhythmia, can occur. Some children are born with abnormalities in this heart circuitry, but arrhythmias also can be caused by infections or chemical imbalances in the blood.

Your child's heart rate normally will vary to some degree. Fever, exercise, crying, or other vigorous activity makes any heart beat faster. (That's why a person's base heart rate usually is measured when the body is at rest.) And the younger your child, the faster her resting heart rate will be. As she gets older, her rate will naturally slow down. For example, a resting heart rate of 130 beats per minute is normal for a newborn infant, but it's too fast for a six-year-old

child at rest. A resting heart rate of 50 or 60 beats per minute may be normal for an athletic teenager, but it is abnormally slow for a baby.

Even in healthy children, there can be other variations in the rhythm of the heartbeat, including changes that occur just as a result of breathing. Such a normal fluctuation is called sinus arrhythmia, and requires no special evaluation or treatment. It is not a sign of heart trouble.

So-called premature heartbeats are another form of irregular rhythm that requires no treatment at all. If these occur in your child, she might say that her heart "skipped a beat" or did a "flip-flop." Your pediatrician may check to see if the irregular beats disappear with exercise; if they do, they are not an indication of heart disease.

If your pediatrician says that your child has a true arrhythmia, it could mean that her heart beats faster than normal (tachycardia), very fast (flutter), fast and with no regularity (fibrillation), or slower than normal (bradycardia), or that it has isolated

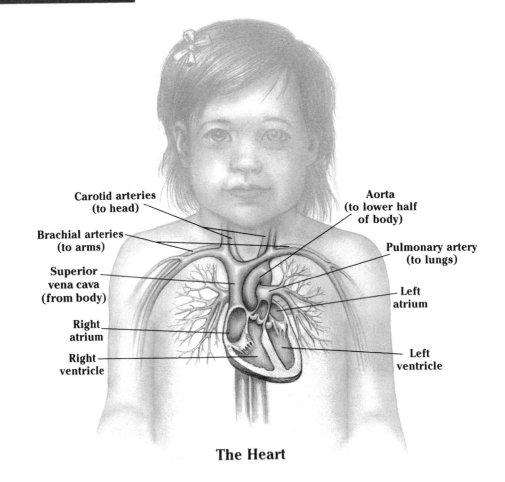

Carotid arteries
(to head)

Brachial arteries
(to arms)

Superior
vena cava
(from body)

Right
atrium

Right
ventricle

Aorta
(to lower half
of body)

Pulmonary artery
(to lungs)

Left
atrium

Left
ventricle

The Heart

early beats (premature beats). While true arrhythmias are not very common, when they occur they can be serious, causing fainting or even heart failure. Fortunately, they can be treated successfully with medication or a special kind of heart catheterization called ablation, so it's important to detect them as early as possible.

Signs and Symptoms

If your child has a true arrhythmia, your pediatrician probably will discover it during a routine visit. But should you notice any of the following warning signs between pediatric visits, notify the physician immediately.

- Your infant suddenly becomes pale and listless; her body feels limp.

- Your child complains of her "heart beating fast," even when she's not exercising.

- She tells you she feels uncomfortable, weak, or dizzy.

- She blacks out or faints.

It's *unlikely* that your child will ever experience any of these symptoms, but if she does, your pediatrician will perform additional tests and perhaps consult with a pediatric cardiologist. In the process the doctors may do an electrocardiogram (ECG), so as to better distinguish a harmless sinus arrhythmia from a true arrhythmia. An ECG is really just a tape recording of the electrical impulses that make the heart beat, and it will allow the doctor to observe any irregularities more closely.

Sometimes your child's unusual heartbeats may occur at unpredictable times, often not when the ECG is being taken. In that case the cardiologist may suggest that your child carry a small portable tape recorder that continuously records her heartbeat over a one- to two-day period. During this time you'll be asked to keep a log of your child's activities and symptoms. Correlating the ECG with your observations will permit a diagnosis to be made. For example, if your child feels her heart "flutter" and becomes dizzy at 2:15 P.M. and the ECG shows her heart suddenly beating faster at the same time, the diagnosis of tachycardia will probably be established.

Occasionally irregular heartbeats will occur only during exercise. If that's the case with your child, the cardiologist may have your youngster ride a stationary bicycle or run on a treadmill while her heartbeat is being recorded. When your child is old enough to participate in sports, ask your pediatrician if any special tests or restrictions are necessary.

Heart Murmur

Technically, a heart murmur is simply a noise heard between the beats of the heart. When a doctor listens to the heart, she hears a sound something like *lub-dub, lub-dub, lub-dub.* Most often, the period between the *lub* and the *dub* and between the *dub* and the *lub* is silent. If there is any sound during this period, it is called a murmur. Although the word is unsettling, murmurs are *extremely* common, and usually normal, occurrences.

In preschool and school-age children, heart murmurs almost always turn out to be harmless; the children require no special care, and the sound eventually disappears. These children have "normal" or so-called functional or innocent heart murmurs, caused simply by the way the blood is flowing through their hearts.

If your child has such a murmur, it probably will be discovered between the ages of one and five during a routine examination. The doctor then will listen carefully to determine if this is a "normal" heart murmur or one that might indicate a problem. Usually, just by listening to its sound and noting its location on the chest or back, the pediatrician will be able to tell into which group it falls. If necessary, she will consult a pediatric cardiologist to be certain, but additional tests are usually not necessary.

On rare occasions, a pediatrician will hear a murmur that sounds abnormal enough to indicate something more than just a noisy flow of blood through the heart. If the doctor suspects this, your child will be referred to a pediatric cardiologist for special tests that will enable a precise diagnosis to be made.

Heart murmurs that can be heard during the first six months of life usually are *not* functional or innocent, and most likely they will require the attention of a pediatric cardiologist. Your infant will be observed for changes in skin color (turning blue), as well as breathing or feeding difficulties. He also may undergo additional tests, such as a chest X ray, electrocardiogram (ECG), and an echocardiogram. The echocardiogram creates a picture of the inside of the heart by using sound waves. If all of these tests prove normal, then it is safe to conclude that the baby probably has an innocent murmur, but the cardiologist and pediatrician probably will want to see him again to be absolutely certain.

Treatment

Innocent heart murmurs require no treatment, nor should your child be excluded from sports or other physical activities because of one. The only people who need to know about such a heart murmur are the parents, the child, and the doctor who examines him. (This includes any physician who treats him in an emergency room or elsewhere.) You don't need to tell school officials. They might misinterpret the information, thinking your child has a heart problem, and they could try to keep him from being physically active. For the same reason, when you complete health forms for school or camp, you should write "normal" in the heart section if your child's murmur is innocent. If there's a specific question about a heart murmur, write "normal" in the space provided.

Innocent heart murmurs, incidentally, generally disappear by midadolescence. Cardiologists don't know why they go away, any more than we know why they appear in the first place. In the meantime, don't be discouraged if the murmur is softer on one visit to the pediatrician and loud again on the next. This may simply mean that your child's heart is beating at a slightly different rate each time. Most likely the murmur will go away eventually.

Hypertension/High Blood Pressure

We usually think of high blood pressure, or hypertension, as a problem that affects adults. But, in fact, this condition can be present at any age, even in infancy. About five of every hundred children have higher than normal blood pressure, although fewer than one in a hundred has medically significant hypertension.

The term *blood pressure* actually refers to two separate measurements: *systolic* blood pressure is the highest pressure reached in the arteries as the heart pumps blood out for circulation through the body; *diastolic* blood pressure is the much lower pressure that occurs in the arteries when the heart relaxes to take blood in between beats. If either or both of these measurements are above the range found in healthy individuals of similar age and sex, it's called hypertension.

Hypertension is more common among individuals of color than whites. It also seems to be more prevalent in some parts of the world; for example, it's very rare among Alaskan Inuit, but affects as many as forty of every hundred adults in northern Japan. In many cases hypertension seems to develop with age. As a result, your child may show no signs of high blood pressure as an infant, but may develop the condition as she grows. Youngsters who are overweight are also more prone to have hypertension (and other chronic diseases). Thus good eating habits (without overeating and without emphasizing high-fat foods) and plenty of physical activity are important throughout the early years of childhood (and for the rest of her life).

In most instances of high blood pressure, no known cause can be identified. However, when hypertension becomes *severe* in children, it's usually a symptom of another serious problem, such as kidney disease or abnormalities of the heart or of the nervous or endocrine (gland) system.

Fortunately, high blood pressure alone rarely causes serious problems in children, and can be controlled through dietary changes, medication, or a combination of

High-Sodium (Salt) Foods
(more than 400 milligrams/serving)

Seasonings: Bouillon, salted meat tenderizers, salted spices (i.e., garlic salt, onion salt, seasoned salt), soy sauce, teriyaki sauce

Snack foods: Salted pretzels, crackers, chips, and popcorn

Commercially prepared foods: Most frozen dinners and commercially prepared entrees; dry and canned soups

Vegetables: Any vegetables prepared in brine (i.e., olives, pickles, sauerkraut); vegetable juices (i.e., tomato juice)

Cheeses: Processed cheese foods, some types of cheeses including American cheese, blue cheese, cottage cheese, and Parmesan

Meat: Any smoked, cured, pickled, or processed products (i.e., corned beef, bacon, dried meat and fish, ham, luncheon meats, sausages, and frankfurters)

Low- and Moderate-Sodium (Salt) Foods
(less than 400 milligrams/serving)

Seasonings: Spices without added salt (i.e., garlic powder, onion powder); "plain" spices (oregano, thyme, dill, cinnamon, etc.); condiments (mayonnaise, mustard, hot pepper sauce, steak sauce, catsup)

Vegetables: All fresh, frozen, and canned, particularly those canned with no added salt

Fruits and fruit juices: Fruit juices; all fresh, canned, frozen, and dried fruits

Grain products: Pasta, bread, rice, cooked cereals, most ready-to-eat cereals, pancakes, pastries, cakes, cookies

Dairy products: Milk, yogurt, custard, pudding, ice cream

Meat and other protein foods: Fresh meat, fish, and eggs; unsalted nuts; dried beans and peas

the two. However, if hypertension is allowed to continue or become worse over many years, the prolonged extra pressure can lead to heart failure. In addition, the stress on blood vessels in the brain can cause them to burst, producing a stroke. Also, long-term hypertension causes changes in blood vessel walls that may result in damage to the kidneys, eyes, and other organs. For these reasons it's important for children found to have hypertension to have their blood pressure checked regularly by their pediatrician, and for you to follow the doctor's advice carefully.

Treatment

In most routine physical examinations, your child's blood pressure will be measured. This is how hypertension is usually discovered. Most often this condition causes no noticeable discomfort, but any of the following may indicate high blood pressure:

- Headache

- Dizziness

- Shortness of breath

- Visual disturbances

- Fatigue

If your child is found to have high blood pressure, your pediatrician will order tests to see if there is an underlying medical problem causing it. These tests include studies of the urine and blood. Sometimes special X rays are used to examine the blood supply to the kidneys. If, as in most cases, no causative medical problem can be found, the diagnosis of essential hypertension will be made. (In medical terms, the word *essential* refers only to the fact that no cause could be found.)

What will the doctor tell you to do? The first step toward reducing your child's blood pressure is to limit the salt in her diet. Giving up the use of table salt and restricting salty foods can reverse mild hypertension and will help lower more serious blood pressure elevations. You'll also have to be cautious when shopping for packaged foods; most canned and processed foods contain a great deal of salt, so check labels carefully to make sure the items have little or no salt added.

The pediatrician also may suggest that your child get more exercise. Physical activity seems to help regulate blood pressure and thus can reduce mild hypertension. Weight reduction in the obese individual also may serve to lower blood pressure; in addition, the avoidance of excessive weight provides other health benefits.

Once the pediatrician knows your child has high blood pressure, he'll want to check it frequently to make sure the hypertension is not becoming more severe. Depending on how high the blood pressure is, the pediatrician may refer the child to a child hypertension specialist, usually a kidney expert. If it does become worse, it may be treated with medication as well as diet and exercise. Many types of medications are available, which work through different parts of the body. At first the pediatrician may prescribe a diuretic, a medicine that increases urine output of salt (sodium), before trying stronger drugs. Alternatively, or if this doesn't return your child's blood pressure to normal, an antihypertensive drug will be prescribed. Initially the doctor will prescribe a single drug, adding others only if the blood pressure is difficult to control.

When your child's blood pressure is brought under control with diet or medication, you may be tempted to let her increase her salt intake or stop taking her medicine because the problem seems to be gone. However, doing this will only bring back the hypertension, so be sure to follow your pediatrician's instructions exactly.

Prevention

It's very important to detect hypertension early. It is now recommended that all children have their blood pressure checked beginning at age three, sooner for those at high risk (infants that were preterm, had a low birth weight, and who had a difficult or prolonged hospital stay, as well as in children who have congenital heart disease, who are receiving medications that might increase blood pressure, or who have any other condition that might lead to high blood pressure).

Because overweight children are more likely to develop hypertension (as well as other health problems), watch your child's caloric intake and make sure she gets plenty of exercise.

It's also wise to keep excess salt out of your child's diet, even if she doesn't have high blood pressure. There's no clear evidence that salt causes this problem, but your child doesn't need extra salt, and once she develops a taste for it, she'll have more difficulty decreasing salt intake if she develops blood pressure problems later in life.

Kawasaki Disease

Kawasaki disease is a serious and perplexing disease, the cause of which is unknown. Some researchers believe, however, that it is caused by a virus or bacteria. Signs of this disease include fever, usually quite high, that lasts for at least five days and doesn't respond to antibiotics. Fever should be present to consider the disease in the acutely ill child.

In addition, four of the six following signs are present in the typical case:

1. Rash over some or all of the body, often more severe in the diaper area, especially in infants under six months of age.

2. Redness and swelling of the palms and soles and/or cracking of the skin around the base of the nails.

3. Red, swollen, and cracked lips and/or a strawberry tongue.

4. Red, inflamed eyes, especially the sclerae (white part).

5. A swollen gland, particularly on one side of the neck.

6. Irritability or listlessness. Children with Kawasaki disease are usually crankier or more lethargic than usual. They also may complain of abdominal pain, headache, and/or joint pain.

Kawasaki disease causes inflammation of the blood vessels; in some cases this includes the arteries of the heart (the coronary arteries). This inflammation weakens the walls of the blood vessels. In most cases the blood vessels return to normal after several months, but in some cases they remain weakened and may even balloon out, causing aneurysms (blood-filled swellings of the blood vessels).

Kawasaki disease occurs most frequently in Japan and Korea and in individuals of Japanese and Korean ancestry, but it can be found among all racial groups and on every continent. In the United States alone, more than three thousand cases are reported each year, typically among older infants and preschoolers.

Kawasaki disease does not appear to be contagious. It is extremely uncommon for two children in the same household to get the disease. Likewise, it does not spread among children in child care centers, where there is daily close contact. Although Kawasaki disease can occur in community outbreaks, particularly in the winter and early spring, no one knows the cause. The peak age of occurrence in the United States is between six months and five years. Evidence suggests that Kawasaki disease may be linked to a yet-to-be identified infectious agent, such as a virus or bacteria. However, despite intense research, no bacteria, virus, or toxin has been identified as a cause of the disease. No specific test makes the diagnosis. The diagnosis is established by fulfilling the signs of illness mentioned above and by excluding other possible diseases.

Treatment

Because the cause of Kawasaki disease is unknown, it can be treated but not prevented. If it is diagnosed early enough, intravenous gamma globulin (a mixture of human antibodies) can minimize the risk of a child developing aneurysms. In addition to gamma globulin, the child should receive aspirin, initially in high doses, then, after the fever is gone, in lower doses. Aspirin can decrease the tendency of blood to clot in damaged blood vessels. Although it's appropriate to use aspirin to treat Kawasaki disease, treating children with minor illnesses (i.e., a cold or influenza) with aspirin has been linked with a serious disease called Reye syndrome. Always consult your pediatrician before giving aspirin to your child.

27

IMMUNIZATIONS

Routine immunizations are available to protect your child against eleven major childhood diseases: polio, measles (page 702), mumps (page 658), rubella (German measles, page 706), chickenpox (page 691), pertussis (whooping cough, page 557), diphtheria, tetanus, haemophilus infections (meningitis, page 655; epiglottitis, page 585), pneumococcal infections (meningitis, page 655), and hepatitis B (page 512). Any of these diseases can disable or kill, so your child should be immunized against all of them. Immunizations also are available against influenza and rabies for special circumstances.

Certain children may need protection against influenza virus (flu vaccine) or rabies virus (rabies vaccine). For example, the flu vaccine is recommended each year for children six months of age and older who have certain high-risk characteristics, such as asthma, diabetes, HIV infections, heart disease, and sickle cell anemia. This vaccine also is recommended for all healthy children ages six to twenty-three months. In areas of the country where the hepatitis A virus is most common, the vaccine protecting against it is recommended for all children; your pediatrician will tell you if it is necessary in your state or region. *All* of the immunizations are injections.

When your child is given a vaccine, he actually receives that part of the "weakened" or killed infectious organism that is able to stimulate his body to produce antibodies against it. These antibodies then protect

The American Academy of Pediatrics recommends the schedule of immunizations appearing on page 73. Please refer to the chart on that page for complete details of the immunizations your child needs and when they should be administered. Chapter 3 provides additional information about the immunizations themselves.

him against the disease, should he ever come in contact with it.

Side Effects

Each of the vaccines has some potential reactions or side effects, but they are usually mild. Severe reactions are very rare. Symptoms of a more serious reaction include:

- Very high fever

- Generalized rash

- A large amount of swelling at the point of injection.

Many studies have shown that vaccines used for routine childhood immunizations can be given together safely. Side effects when multiple vaccines are administered at the same time are no greater than when each vaccine is administered on separate occasions. Talk to your pediatrician if you are concerned about the number of vaccines your child is scheduled to receive.

The side effects associated with various vaccines are listed below.

Diphtheria, Tetanus, and Pertussis

Protection against these three diseases is provided in a single vaccine, abbreviated DTaP (the "a" stands for acellular). The side effects for the diphtheria and tetanus portions of the vaccine are similar: pain and swelling at the site of the injection and, on rare occasions, skin rash within twenty-four hours. The pertussis portion of the vaccine may cause heat, redness, and tenderness at the injection site in about half the children who receive it. It also may cause fever and irritability. Inflammation of the brain also has been known to occur following vaccination, although it is so rare (1 in 110,000 im-

munizations) that it is not definitely known whether it is caused by the vaccine or by some other substance or infection.

These side effects and complications must be weighed against the fact that the disease itself causes far more complications than the vaccine.

No scientific evidence links DTaP vaccines with the sudden infant death syndrome (SIDS). However, the myth of such an association continues because the first dose is given at two months of age, when the risk of SIDS is greatest. Nevertheless, these events are not connected.

Polio

IPV, or inactivated polio vaccine, has not been shown to cause any major problems except mild soreness at the site of the injection.

Since the year 2000, the oral polio vaccine has not been recommended for use in the United States because of a very small risk of vaccine-associated paralytic polio (VAPP), which occurred in 1 in 1 million children receiving this live oral vaccine. VAPP is *not* associated with the injectable polio vaccine.

Measles, Mumps, and Rubella

These vaccines usually are given together in one injection. The measles part of the vaccine sometimes causes a mild rash and fever beginning five to ten days after it is given. Very rarely, children will have slight swelling over the jaw, as if they had mild mumps from the mumps vaccine. The rubella part of the vaccine sometimes causes joint pains and swelling or, very rarely, an inflammation of the nerves of the arms or legs.

Haemophilus influenza Type B (Hib) Vaccine

Your child might be sore, red, or swollen around the site of the injection. This reaction occurs in 2 of every 100 children. Mild fever may develop.

Pneumococcal Vaccine

A small number of children may experience local reactions such as redness, tenderness, and swelling at the site where the injection is given. Some youngsters also may develop a fever of short duration.

Hepatitis B Vaccine

No serious reactions are associated with this vaccine, although minor side effects may include soreness, redness or swelling at the site of the injection, as well as fussiness.

Chickenpox (Varicella) Vaccine

Adverse reactions from the chickenpox vaccine generally are mild and occur only in a small number of children. These reactions include redness, stiffness, soreness, and swelling where the shot was given; tiredness; fussiness; fever; and nausea. Also, a rash of a few small bumps or pimples may develop at the spot where the shot was given or, infrequently, on other parts of the body. This rash can occur up to one month after immunization and can last for several days.

Influenza

The newer vaccines have few side effects except for one or two days of soreness at the injection site; febrile (fever) reactions are infrequent.

Rabies

The current rabies vaccines have few side effects in children; they require five injections in a series.

Treatment for Side Effects

Before immunizing your child, your pediatrician should review with you what reactions you can expect and how to treat them. Generally, fever is managed with acetaminophen. For local reactions, your pediatrician may recommend that you apply cool compresses for symptomatic relief. If your child has any reaction that makes him uncomfortable for more than four hours, notify your pediatrician, who will want to note it in your child's records and prescribe appropriate treatment. Together, you also can decide whether your child should receive another dose of the same vaccine, depending on the severity of the reaction.

Children Who Should Not Receive Certain Vaccines

These vaccines do not cause serious reactions in most children. However, in some cases they should not be given.

Diphtheria and Tetanus

If your child has had a serious reaction (petechial rash [pinpoint rash]), hives (swelling), or anaphylaxis (loss of consciousness) to a previous dose of these vaccines, he should not receive another one.

Pertussis

If your child has had a seizure *before* getting the pertussis vaccine, your pediatrician may delay giving the aP part of the DTaP until the cause of the seizure is known, and at least six months have gone by without the occurrence of another seizure. The pertussis vaccine also may be postponed, or not given at all, if your child is suspected of having a progressive disease of the nervous system.

If your child had a serious reaction to a previous dose of the pertussis vaccine, care-

Personal Immunization Chart

Keep a record of your child's immunization by filling in this chart. Fill in the date each time your child is immunized. If you need more of these records, contact the American Academy of Pediatrics, 141 Northwest Point Boulevard, P.O. Box 927, Elk Grove Village, IL 60009–0927.

	DTaP	Polio	MMR	Hepatitis B	Hib	Pneumococcal	Chicken-pox
Birth	:	:	:	:	:		:
1–2 months	:	:	:	:	:		:
2 months	:	:	:	:	:		:
4 months	:	:	:	:	:		:
6 months	:	:	:	:	:		:
6–12 months	:	:	:	:	:		:
12–15 months	:	:	:	:	:		:
15 months	:	:	:	:	:		:
15–18 months	:	:	:	:	:		:
4–6 years	:	:	:	:	:		:
11–12 years	:	:	:	:	:		:
14–16 years	:	:	:	:	:		:

ful consideration to future doses of the aP part may be given, and Pediatric DT (without pertussis protection) will be substituted. Serious reactions include high fever (105 degrees Fahrenheit [40.5 degrees Celsius] or greater), seizures, prolonged high-pitched and peculiar crying or screaming, or collapse. Severe reactions (contraindications) that should alert you and your pediatrician not to give any more doses of DTaP and substitute Pediatric DT are allergic reactions and/or otherwise unexplained inflammation of the brain (called encephalopathy) within seven days of the injection.

Chickenpox (Varicella)

Although the chickenpox vaccine is approved for use in otherwise healthy children, certain groups of people, such as children with a weakened immune system or pregnant women, should not receive it. Talk to your pediatrician about whether your child falls into any of the high-risk categories and should not be vaccinated against chickenpox.

Measles, Mumps, Rubella

Because these vaccines contain live viruses, children with weakened immune systems (as well as pregnant women) should not receive them.

Rabies

As a general rule, because of the life-threatening nature of rabies, the vaccine is indicated. Often consultation with a specialist in rabies is needed.

Influenza

Flu vaccines are prepared from egg protein, so children who are severely allergic to eggs should not receive them.

Hepatitis B

Although severe allergies to yeast are rare in children, they are an indication that the hepatitis B vaccine should not be given.

Haemophilus influenzae Type b (Hib), Pneumococcal, and Polio Vaccines

There are no reasons for withholding these vaccines from your child unless he has a sensitivity to one or more of its ingredients. Your pediatrician will help you determine this.

Live Virus Vaccines (Measles, Mumps, Rubella, and Varicella)

No live virus vaccine should be given to a child with a weakened immune system. Because measles is more dangerous to a child infected with HIV (the virus that causes AIDS) than is the measles vaccine, children with HIV may receive the MMR vaccine.

28

MUSCULOSKELETAL PROBLEMS

Arthritis

Arthritis is an inflammation of the joints that produces swelling, redness, heat, and pain. Although we usually think of it as a disease of the elderly, some children also have this condition. There are four main types of childhood arthritis.

Toxic Synovitis of the Hip

This is the most common form of arthritis in children. It develops suddenly in youngsters between two and ten years old and then disappears after a short time, with no serious aftereffects. A virus is the probable cause.

Bacterial Infection

When a joint becomes infected with bacteria, a child may limp or refuse to walk (if the hip, knee, or ankle is infected), run a fever, and feel pain on moving the affected joint. See your pediatrician immediately if these signs or symptoms appear. If this is a bacte-

rial infection of the hip, it can be a serious condition and needs to be properly diagnosed and treated as an emergency.

Lyme Disease

An infection transmitted by the deer tick can cause a form of arthritis (known as Lyme

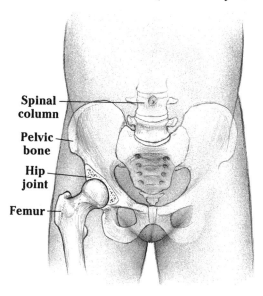

Spinal column

Pelvic bone

Hip joint

Femur

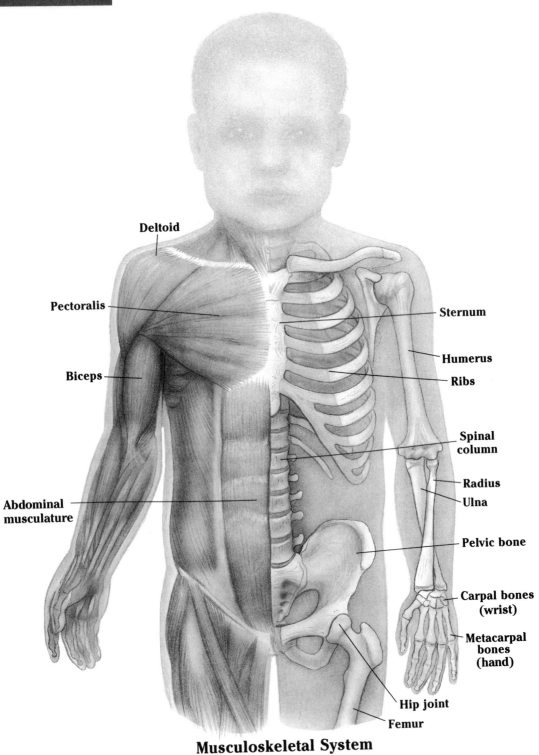

Deltoid

Pectoralis

Biceps

Abdominal
musculature

Sternum

Humerus

Ribs

Spinal
column

Radius

Ulna

Pelvic bone

Carpal bones
(wrist)

Metacarpal
bones
(hand)

Hip joint

Femur

Musculoskeletal System

How to Remove a Tick

1. Gently cleanse the area with an alcohol-soaked sponge or cotton ball.

2. Using forceps, tweezers, or fingers (protected by a tissue or cloth), grasp the tick as near to the mouth parts and as close to the skin as possible.

3. Using gentle but steady tension, pull the entire tick up and out. Be sure the tick is dead before disposing of it. (Alternatively, save the tick if your local health department wants it for surveillance purposes.)

4. After the tick is out, cleanse the bitten area thoroughly with alcohol or other cleansing (soap) agent.

---

arthritis because it was first diagnosed in a child of Old Lyme, Connecticut). The disease starts with a rash surrounded by a light ring or halo, which is where your child was bitten. Additional rashes may then appear on other body areas. Later, there are flulike symptoms such as headaches, fever, chills, swollen glands, fatigue, and muscular aches and pains. Weeks to months later, the child often develops an arthritis.

Although this Lyme infection (caused by bacteria called spirochetes) can be disabling, it tends to last for just a limited time. Since its original discovery, it has been found in many other parts of the world. Antibiotics are helpful if the diagnosis is made within one month of the tick bite. Sometimes a high dose of antibiotics is useful in those children with chronic, relapsing Lyme disease. However, the American Academy of Pediatrics does not recommend that antibiotics be taken routinely by someone who has received a tick bite in an effort to prevent the illness (due to the medication's cost, possible side effects, and the risk of infections associated with antibiotic-resistant bacteria). We also don't recommend blood tests for Lyme disease immediately after a youngster has received a tick bite, since your child probably won't yet have detectable antibodies associated with the bite.

Although a vaccine for Lyme disease is available, it is not approved for children under fifteen years old. You should try to keep your child away from tick-infested areas, which may include wooded regions, high grasses, and marshes. Or she should wear protective clothing (i.e., long-sleeved shirts, and pants tucked into socks) and insect repellent (containing a substance called DEET) when in these areas. See page 702 for more information on DEET.

Juvenile Rheumatoid Arthritis

Commonly referred to as JRA, this is the most common chronic (long-term) form of joint inflammation in children. Unfortunately, it also sometimes can lead to permanent damage. JRA is a puzzling disease that is often difficult for the pediatrician to diagnose and for parents to understand.

If your child has any of the symptoms described below—particularly unexplained fever, persistent joint stiffness, pain, or swelling of the joints—call your pediatrician. These all could signal the presence of arthritis.

Juvenile rheumatoid arthritis occurs most often in children between the ages of three and six or around the time of puberty. It's unusual for JRA to begin under one year of age or after age sixteen. Although this disease can be disabling, with proper treatment most children recover fully, and the condition usually disappears after puberty.

Although the exact cause of JRA is unknown, a combination of factors probably comes into play. Researchers believe that JRA may be triggered by or perhaps is related to a viral infection in children who have an abnormality in their immune (disease-resistance) system. In nonsusceptible children, the viruses probably would cause only a mild illness with no lasting effect. But the immune system of some children overreacts to the viruses, particularly in the joint areas. It is this overreaction that causes the inflammation, swelling, pain, and joint damage.

The signs, symptoms, and long-term effects can vary depending on the type of JRA present. A form of JRA known as systemic JRA, for instance, causes not only fever and painful joints, but also may damage internal organs. When systemic JRA strikes the internal organs, the child can develop inflammation of the outside covering of the heart (pericarditis) or of the heart muscle (myocarditis), or of the lining of the lungs (pleuritis) or the lung tissue itself (pneumonitis). Much less commonly, inflammation occurs in the brain and its lining (meningoencephalitis).

There are two other types of JRA—pauciarticular (affecting one or two joints) and polyarticular (affecting many joints). Pauciarticular JRA can be associated with inflammation of the eye, which in turn can cause glaucoma or cataracts. Pauciarticular JRA is the most common form, and most often it affects young girls. It also has the best prognosis in terms of disability and ultimate outcome.

Treatment

Great strides are being made in the treatment of JRA and other forms of arthritis, and often the disease can be controlled completely. Treatment varies depending on the type of arthritis your child has. It may include medications, exercise, physical therapy, or the use of splints. Whatever treatments are prescribed, it is essential that every step be carried out exactly as recommended.

For JRA, therapy is aimed at reducing inflammation. Aspirin may be used initially (this is one of the very few indications for using aspirin in children) because it's a safe and inexpensive anti-inflammatory drug. It does have some undesirable side effects, such as stomach irritation. Also, because of its link to Reye syndrome (see page 520), aspirin must be discontinued if your child has chickenpox or flulike illnesses. If aspirin doesn't work or produces unacceptable side effects, your pediatrician may decide to use one of the newer nonsteroidal anti-inflammatory drugs (sometimes referred to as NSAIDs). Like aspirin, these are rapid-acting drugs, but less likely to cause side effects. They are also much more expensive.

If JRA is severe and is still getting worse, your pediatrician might prescribe a "slow-acting" drug containing gold. Given by injection, it is effective in six out of ten cases. (A pill form of this medication is available for adult use, but it hasn't been approved for children.)

Although there is no way to prevent JRA, it is possible to slow the progression of the disease. At times it will require a parent to do some difficult things, such as forcing a child to exercise when any movement hurts. It's necessary, however, because if a child with JRA is inactive, her pain and deformities will increase. Remember, with JRA and other types of arthritis, it is important to carry through on treatment recommendations, even when your child is in pain, in order to prevent deformities and disability later on.

JRA requires a great deal of adjustment, not only for the ill child but also for her parents and other family members. By working as a team you'll markedly decrease your child's chances of suffering permanent damage. If you need more support, your pediatrician can refer you to arthritis organizations that can assist you.

What about treatments for other types of arthritis? If *infectious arthritis* is diagnosed, the child may be placed on antibiotics for a time. A *bacterial infection* of the hip must be treated immediately with a needle aspiration of the hip joint, surgical drainage, and intravenous (IV) use of antibiotics.

When *toxic synovitis* is diagnosed, only bed rest may be prescribed, or in some cases traction (gentle stretching of the joint with a system of weights and pulleys). *Lyme disease,* if diagnosed early (within one month of the tick bite), is treated with antibiotics. If the arthritis is severe, other medications usually will be prescribed to control the inflammation and pain until the condition gradually disappears on its own.

Bowlegs and Knock-Knees

If your toddler's legs seem to curve outward at the knees, there's probably no reason for concern. Look around, and you'll see that few young children have truly straight legs. In fact, many children between the ages of one and two appear quite bowlegged, and it's common for children from three to six to look knock-kneed. Their legs may not look straight until the age of nine or ten.

Bowlegs and knock-knees usually are just variations of normal, and they require no treatment. Ordinarily the legs straighten out and look perfectly normal by adolescence. Bracing, corrective shoes, and exercise are not helpful, and may hinder a child's physical development and cause emotional difficulty.

Rarely, bowlegs or knock-knees are the result of a disease. Arthritis, injury to the growth plate around the knee (see *Fractures,* page 490), infection, tumor, and rickets all can cause changes in the curvature of the legs. Here are some signs that suggest a child's bowlegs or knock-knees may be caused by a serious problem:

- The curvature is extreme.

- Only one side is affected.

- The bowlegs get worse after age two.

- The knock-knees persist after age seven.

- Your child also is unusually short for his age.

If your child's condition fits any of these descriptions, you should talk to your pediatrician, who can determine the exact cause and prescribe the necessary treatment. In some cases the pediatrician will refer you to a pediatric orthopedist for consultation and possible corrective surgery.

Elbow Injuries

A pulled elbow (also known as nursemaid's elbow) is a common, painful injury among children under four years old. It occurs when nearby soft tissue slips into the elbow joint and is trapped there. This can happen because your child's elbow joint is loose enough to separate slightly when her arm is pulled to full length (when she's being lifted, yanked, or swung by the hand or wrist, or if she falls on her outstretched arm). The nearby tissue slides into the space created by the stretching and is trapped there when the joint returns to its normal position.

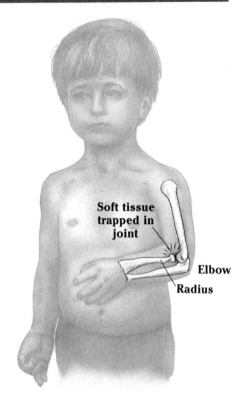

Soft tissue trapped in joint

Elbow

Radius

Nursemaid's elbow usually doesn't cause swelling, but your child will complain that it hurts. She probably will hold her arm close to her side, with her elbow slightly bent and her palm turned toward her body. If you try to straighten the elbow or turn her palm upward, she will resist because of the pain.

Treatment

Don't try to treat this injury yourself, because elbow pain also might be caused by a fracture. Instead, your pediatrician should examine the injury as soon as possible. To make your child more comfortable until she sees the doctor, support the arm in a sling made from a soft cloth, such as a dish towel. Don't give her food, water, or pain medication unless your physician advises you to do so.

The doctor will check the injured area for swelling and tenderness and any limitation of motion. If an injury other than nursemaid's elbow is suspected, X rays may be taken. If no fracture is noted, the doctor will manipulate the joint gently to release the trapped tissue. Although this procedure causes some pain as it's being done, your child should feel relief almost immediately afterward. Infrequently, the doctor may recommend the use of a sling for comfort for two or three days, particularly if several hours have passed before the injury is treated successfully.

Prevention

Nursemaid's elbow usually can be prevented by lifting your young child properly. Grasp her under the arms or around her body. *Do not pull or lift her by holding her hands or wrists, and never swing her by the arms.*

Flat Feet/Fallen Arches

At some point during your baby's first year or two, you'll probably notice that he seems to have very little arch to his feet. This flat-footedness, which may persist well into later childhood, occurs because children's bones and joints are very flexible, causing their feet to flatten when they stand. Also, young babies have a fat pad on the inner border of their feet that hides the arches. You still can see the arch if you lift your baby up on his toes, but it disappears when he comes down on his heels. Often the foot also turns out, increasing the weight on the inner side and making it appear even more flat.

This natural flat-footedness usually disappears by age six as the feet become less flexible and the arches develop. Only about one or two out of every ten children will continue to have this kind of flat-footedness into

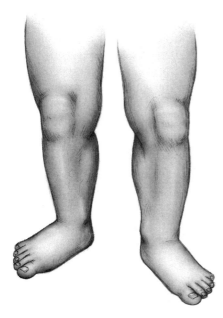

evaluated promptly. If your child has any foot pain, sores or pressure spots on the inner side of the foot, or if the foot is stiff, with limited side-to-side or up-and-down ankle motion, see your pediatrician. If rigid flat-footedness is diagnosed, you'll probably be referred to a pediatric orthopedist for further treatment.

Limp

Limping in a child can be caused by something as simple as a stone in the shoe, a blister on the foot, or a pulled muscle. But a limp also can be a sign of more serious trouble, such as a broken bone or an infection, so it should be investigated early to make sure no serious problems are present.

Some children limp when they first learn how to walk. Among the causes of early limping are neurological damage (e.g., cerebral palsy; see page 560). Any limp at this age needs to be investigated as soon as possible, since the longer it goes untreated, the more difficult it may be to correct.

Once walking is well established, significant sudden limping usually indicates one of several conditions:

- A "toddler" fracture

- Hip injury or inflammation (synovitis)

- Previously undiagnosed developmental dysplasia (abnormal development) of the hip (DDH)

- Infection in the bone or joint

A toddler fracture is a so-called spiral fracture of the tibia (the leg bone extending from the knee to the ankle; see page 490) that can occur with minor accidents such as a slip on a newly waxed floor or a jump from a porch step or swing. The bone fracture itself oc-

adulthood. Even for these youngsters, however, as long as the feet remain flexible, there's no cause for concern and no need for treatment. In fact, all the special shoes, inserts, and exercises that are promoted and sold may cause more problems than the flat feet themselves, and will *not* develop an arch in your child's foot.

Other forms of flat-footedness may need to be treated differently. For instance, a child may have tightness of the heel cord (Achilles tendon) that limits the motion of his foot. This tightness can result in a flat foot, but it usually can be treated with special stretching exercises to lengthen the heel cord.

Rarely, a child will have truly rigid flat feet, a condition that definitely can cause problems. Such youngsters have difficulty moving the foot up and down or side to side at the ankle. The rigid foot can cause pain—although it usually does not occur until the teenage years—and, if left untreated, can lead to arthritis. This rigid type of flat foot is seldom seen in an infant or very young child, but when it does develop, it should be

curs in a spiral or twisted pattern. Sometimes the child can explain how the injury occurred, but youngsters do so many things in one day that they may have difficulty recalling exactly what happened. Sometimes an older sibling or babysitter can solve the mystery.

Hip problems that cause a limp at this age usually are due to a viral joint infection and need to be brought to the attention of your pediatrician. When a child has an infection in the bone or joint, there usually is fever, swelling of the joint, and redness. If the infection is in the hip joint, the child will hold her leg flexed or bent at the hip and be extremely irritable and unwilling to move the hip and leg in any direction.

Sometimes a child is born with a dislocated hip (DDH) that, in rare cases, goes undetected until she starts to walk. As one leg is shorter than the other, the child will walk with an obvious limp, which will be persistent.

Treatment

If you know that your child's limp is due to a minor injury, such as a blister, cut, splinter in the foot, or mild sprain, you can apply simple first-aid treatment at home. However, most other causes need to be examined and treated by a physician.

If your child has just started walking and is limping, the pediatrician should see her as soon as possible. Calls about limping in an older child may be delayed for twenty-four hours, since many of these problems disappear overnight.

X rays of the hip or the entire leg may be necessary to make the diagnosis. This is most certainly true if there is a suspicion of developmental dysplasia of the hip. If an infection is present, antibiotics will be started immediately. The IV antibiotics get a much higher dose to the infection. (Hospitalization is required if the infection is in the joint or bone.) If a bone is broken or dislocated, it will be placed in a splint or cast, probably after consultation with a pediatric orthopedic specialist. If a congenital dislocated hip is diagnosed, you will be referred immediately to a pediatric orthopedist, as proper treatment, including special casting and/or bracing, should not be delayed.

Pigeon Toes (Intoeing)

If your child's feet turn inward, he is said to be pigeon-toed, or have intoeing. It's a very common condition that may involve one or both feet, and occurs for a variety of reasons.

Intoeing During Infancy

This intoeing usually is due to a turning in of the front part of the foot (the forefoot), and is called metatarsus adductus (see figure on page 687). It may be due to the baby's position in the uterus or to other causes.

You can be suspicious if:

- When you look at the foot from the bottom while the child is resting, you see that the front portion turns inward.

- The outer side of your child's foot (opposite his big toe) is curved like a half-moon.

Usually this condition is mild and will resolve before the child's first birthday. Sometimes it is more severe, or is accompanied by other foot deformities that result in a problem called clubfoot. This condition requires a consultation with a pediatric orthopedist and early casting or splinting.

Intoeing in Later Childhood

If you notice that your child is toeing in during his second year, it is most likely due to inward twisting of the shinbone (tibia). This condition is called internal tibial torsion (see figure below). If your child is between ages three and ten and has intoeing, it is probably due to an inward turning of the thighbone (femur), a condition called media femoral torsion. Both of these conditions tend to run in families.

If the condition seems severe enough to affect your child's walking or running, ask the pediatrician to examine your child's feet.

Treatment

Some experts feel no treatment is necessary for intoeing in an infant under six months of age. For severe metatarsus adductus in infancy, brief, early casting is appropriate. In cases where there are different opinions, it is best to follow the advice of your own pediatrician. It does appear that the majority of infants who have intoeing in early infancy will outgrow it with no treatment.

If your baby's intoeing persists after six months, or if it is rigid and difficult to straighten out, your doctor may recommend a series of casts applied over a period of three to six weeks. The pediatrician also will refer you to a pediatric orthopedist. The main goal is to correct the condition before your child starts walking.

Intoeing in early childhood usually clears on its own, but if your child has trouble walking because of turning of the tibia, further discussion with your pediatrician and orthopedic consultant is required. A night brace (special shoes with connecting bars) used in the past for this problem, has not been shown to be an effective treatment.

If your child's intoeing remains severe when he is nine or ten years old, he may require surgery to correct it.

Because intoeing so often corrects itself over time, it is very important not to use nonprescribed "treatments" such as corrective shoes, twister cables, daytime bracing, exercises, shoe inserts, and back manipulations. These do not correct the problem and may be harmful because they interfere with normal play or walking. Furthermore, a child wearing these braces faces unnecessary emotional strain caused by his playmates' ridicule.

Sprains

Sprains are injuries to the ligaments that connect bones to one another. A sprain occurs when a ligament is stretched excessively or torn. Sprains are very uncommon in young children, because their ligaments are usually stronger than the growing bones and cartilage to which they are attached. Therefore, the growing part of the bone might separate or tear away before the ligament is injured.

In young children, the ankle is far and away the most commonly sprained joint, followed by the knee and wrist. In a mild sprain

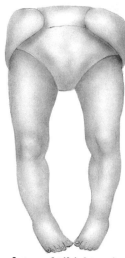

Appearance of foot in metatarsus adductus

Internal tibial torsion

(grade 1), the ligament simply is over-stretched. More severe sprains can involve partial tearing of the ligament (grade 2) or complete tearing (grade 3). The signs and symptoms of sprains in young children can be quite similar to those for fracture: pain, swelling around the joint, and inability to walk, bear weight, or use the joint.

Call your child's pediatrician if there is any evidence that a joint injury has occurred. Often the doctor will want to examine the child. If the pain and swelling are excessive or if there is concern about a fracture, your pediatrician may recommend a consultation with an orthopedic surgeon. The orthopedist may need to perform special X rays to distinguish between an injury to a ligament or a bone.

When a sprain is diagnosed, the joint is usually immobilized with an elastic bandage or a splint. Crutches may be necessary in the case of a leg sprain, to prevent continued stress on the injured ligament. A cast may be necessary if the injury has been severe.

Most grade 1 sprains will heal within two weeks without subsequent complications. In certain grade 3 injuries, especially around the knee, an operation may be necessary to repair the damage. Your child's physician should be called any time a joint injury fails to heal or swelling recurs. Ignoring these signs could result in more severe damage to the joint and long-term disability.

29

SKIN

Birthmarks and Hemangiomas

Dark-Pigmented Birthmarks (Nevi or Moles)

Nevi, or moles, are either congenital (present at birth) or acquired. Composed of so-called nevus cells, these spots are often dark brown or black.

Congenital Nevi

Small nevi present at birth are relatively common, occurring in one of every hundred Caucasian children. They tend to grow with the child and usually don't cause any problems. Rarely, however, these moles may develop into a type of serious skin cancer (melanoma) at some later time. Therefore, while you don't have to worry about them right away, it's a good idea to watch them carefully and have them checked by your pediatrician at regular intervals or if there is any change in appearance (color, size, or shape). She may refer you to a pediatric dermatologist who will advise you on removal and any follow-up care.

A much more serious type of nevus is a large congenital one that varies in size from a half-dollar to as large as this book. It might be flat or raised, may have hair growing from it (although small, insignificant nevi sometimes also have hair), and can be so large that it covers an arm or a leg. Fortunately, these nevi are very rare (occurring in one of every twenty thousand births). However, they are much more likely than the smaller ones to develop into a melanoma, so early consultation with a pediatric dermatologist is advisable.

Acquired Nevi, or Moles

Most Caucasian people develop ten to thirty pigmented nevi, or moles, throughout the course of their lives. They usually occur after the age of five, but sometimes develop earlier. These acquired moles are seldom a cause for worry. However, if your child develops one that's irregularly shaped (asymmetrical), has multiple colors within its structure, and is larger than a pencil eraser, your pediatrician should examine it.

One final note: Probably the most common acquired dark spots on the skin are freckles. They can appear as early as ages two to four years, are found more often on parts of the body exposed to the sun, and tend to run in families. They often become darker or larger during the summer and are less prominent in the winter. They represent no danger and should not cause concern.

Blood Vessel Birthmarks on the Skin (Hemangiomas)

Your young infant has a red raised bump growing rapidly on his forehead and a flat dark-red patch on one arm. They're quite unsightly, but are they harmful?

These birthmarks occur when a certain area of the skin develops an abnormal blood supply during early childhood. This, in turn, causes the tissue to enlarge over the course of several weeks or months and become reddish blue. When the condition involves only the capillaries (the smallest blood vessels), the birthmark is called a strawberry hemangioma. When the blood vessels are larger, they may be of a different type and have a different appearance.

Flat Angiomata (Stork Bites)

These most common blemishes on the skin usually appear on the eyelids or back of the neck. They usually disappear over the first months to years of life and are not serious.

Hemangiomas

Hemangiomas (sometimes called strawberry patches), a common form of this condition, are found in at least two of every hundred babies born. Although frequently they are not noticeable at birth, they appear within the first month of life as a red raised dot. They can occur on any area of the body, but are seen most commonly on the head, neck, and trunk. Usually a child has just a single strawberry hemangioma, but occasionally these marks will be scattered over several parts of the body.

If your infant develops a strawberry hemangioma, have your pediatrician examine it so he can follow its course from the start. During the first six months of life, strawberry hemangiomas usually grow very rapidly, which can be quite alarming. But they soon stop enlarging and almost always disappear by the time the child is nine years old.

Quite often, the large reddish-purplish appearance of these birthmarks so upsets parents that they want to have them removed immediately. However, since the vast majority will gradually reduce in size over the second to third year of life, it's generally best to leave them alone. Studies have shown that when this type of hemangioma is left untreated, few complications or cosmetic problems result. By contrast, those that are treated either with medication or surgery have a greater chance of complications or unwanted changes in appearance.

At times, hemangiomas may need to be treated or removed—namely, when they occur close to vital structures, such as the eye, throat, or mouth; when they seem to be growing much faster than usual; or when they are likely to bleed profusely or become infected. Such uncommon conditions will require careful evaluation and management by your pediatrician and pediatric dermatologist.

Very rarely, hemangiomas are found in large numbers on the face and upper trunk. On such occasions, hemangiomas also may be present on organs inside the body. If this is suspected, your pediatrician may need to conduct further tests.

Port Wine Stains

Port wine stains are flat malformations of small blood vessels, usually present at birth. They are dark red and often found on the face or limbs (usually only on one side of the body), although they may occur anywhere. Unlike hemangiomas, port wine stains don't go away, although they sometimes fade. Even so, they rarely cause any problems. On occasion, however, if they are found on the upper eyelid and/or forehead, there is a chance of a related problem in the underlying brain structures (Sturge-Weber syndrome). If the birthmark is located immediately around the eye, there is a possibility that glaucoma (see page 606) may develop in that eye.

Port wine stains should be examined from time to time to evaluate their size, location, and appearance. If your child is very unhappy with this birthmark, a special covering makeup can be used. Laser treatment has been successful in many cases, but other types of surgery are rarely recommended. (See also *How Your Newborn Looks,* page 122.)

Chickenpox

Chickenpox is one of the most common childhood illnesses. This highly contagious infection causes an itchy, blisterlike rash that can cover most of the body. Children often get a mild fever along with the rash.

After your child is exposed to the virus that causes chickenpox, it can take ten to twenty-one days for the rash to appear. Small blisters, which may have a red area around them, will begin to appear on the body and scalp, then spread to the face, arms, and legs. Normally the blisters will crust over and then heal, but tiny sores and possibly small scars may develop if your child scratches them and they become in-fected. The skin around some of the blisters may become darker or lighter, but this change in coloring will disappear gradually after the rash is gone.

Treatment

From your own childhood, you may remember just how itchy chickenpox can be. You should discourage your child from scratching, because that can cause additional infection. Acetaminophen (in the appropriate dose for your child's age and weight) may decrease the discomfort and also reduce any fever she has (although keep in mind that fever helps her body fight the virus). Trimming her fingernails and bathing her daily with soap and water also can help prevent secondary bacterial infection. Oatmeal baths, available without prescription from your pharmacy, will ease the itch. Antihistamines can be used to decrease the itch. (Be sure to follow the dosing instructions carefully.) A prescription medicine (acyclovir) also can decrease the severity of the symptoms if started within twenty-four hours of the onset of the disease. This medicine, while not needed by everyone, is especially valuable for children with eczema (a skin disorder), children with asthma, or adolescents.

Do not give your child aspirin or any medication that contains aspirin or salicylates when she has chickenpox. These products increase the risk of Reye syndrome (see page 520), a serious illness that involves the liver and brain. You also should avoid steroids and any medicines that interfere with the immune system. If you are not sure about what medications you can safely use at this time, ask your pediatrician for advice.

Incidentally, the doctor probably won't need to see your child unless she develops a complication such as a skin infection, trouble breathing, or if her temperature rises above 102 degrees Fahrenheit (38.9 degrees Celsius) or lasts longer than four days. Let the pediatrician know if areas of the rash become very red, warm, or tender; this may indicate a bacterial infection. Be sure to call your pediatrician *immediately* if your youngster develops any signs of Reye syndrome or encephalitis: vomiting, nervousness, confusion, convulsions, lack of responsiveness, increasing sleepiness, or poor balance.

Your child may be contagious one to two days before the rash starts and for twenty-four hours after the last new blister appears (usually five to seven days). Only individuals who have never had chickenpox (or the chickenpox vaccine) are susceptible. Keep her away from youngsters who have not been vaccinated, have never had the disease, or who aren't sure that they've had it. After she's recovered from the chickenpox, your child will be immune to it for the rest of her life.

Prevention

A vaccine to protect against chickenpox is recommended for all healthy children between twelve and eighteen months of age who have never had the disease. Until your child has received this vaccine, the only sure way to protect her is to avoid exposure. Protection from exposure is important for newborn infants, especially premature babies, in whom the disease can be more severe.

Most infants whose mothers have had chickenpox are immune to the disease for the first few months of life. Susceptible children who have diseases affecting the immune system (i.e., cancer) or who are using certain drugs (i.e., cortisone) also must avoid being exposed to chickenpox. If these children or normal adults are exposed, they may be given a special medication to provide immunity to the disease for a limited period. It's important to remember that since varicella vaccine is a live virus vaccine, children who have a weakened immune system may not have a normal response to it and should not be vaccinated.

Cradle Cap and Seborrheic Dermatitis

Your beautiful one-month-old baby has developed scaliness and redness on his scalp. You're concerned and think maybe you shouldn't shampoo as usual. You also notice some redness in the creases of his neck and armpits and behind his ears. What is it and what should you do?

When this rash occurs on the scalp alone, it's known as cradle cap. But although it may start as scaling and redness of the scalp, it also can be found later in the other areas just mentioned. It can extend to the face and diaper area, too, and when it does, pediatricians call it seborrheic dermatitis (because it occurs where there are the greatest number of oil-producing sebaceous glands). Seborrheic dermatitis is a noninfectious skin condition that's very common in infants, usually beginning in the first weeks of life and slowly disappearing over a period of weeks or months. Unlike atopic or contact eczema (see page 693), it's rarely uncomfortable or itchy.

No one knows for sure the exact cause of this rash. Some doctors have speculated that it may be influenced by the mother's hormonal changes during pregnancy, which stimulate the infant's oil glands. This overproduction of oil may have some relationship to the scales and redness of the skin.

Treatment

If your baby's seborrheic dermatitis is confined to his scalp (and is, therefore, just cradle cap), you can treat it yourself. Don't be afraid to shampoo the hair; in fact, you should wash it (with a mild baby shampoo) more frequently than before. This, along with soft brushing, will help remove the scales.

Baby oil is not very helpful or necessary. Many parents tend to use the unperfumed baby oil or mineral oil and do nothing else. But doing this allows scales to build up on the scalp, particularly over the rear soft spot, or fontanelle. If you decide to use oil, use only a little, rub it into the scales, and then shampoo and brush it out.

Stronger medicated shampoos (antiseborrhea shampoos containing sulfur and 2 percent salicylic acid) may loosen the scales more quickly, but since they also can be irritating, use them only after consulting your pediatrician. The doctor may prescribe some additional medication to treat the scales and redness.

If frequent shampooing doesn't improve cradle cap, or if the rash spreads to your baby's face, neck, and crease areas, call your pediatrician, who may suggest a stronger, scale-dissolving shampoo and also might prescribe a cortisone cream or lotion. One percent hydrocortisone cream is a commonly used preparation.

Once the condition has improved, you can prevent it from recurring, in most cases, by frequent hair washing with a mild baby shampoo. Occasionally you may need a stronger medicated shampoo, but let your pediatrician decide.

Sometimes yeast infections become superimposed on the affected skin, most likely in the crease areas rather than on the scalp. If this occurs, the area will become extremely reddened and quite itchy. In this case, your pediatrician might prescribe some specific antiyeast cream containing the medicine nystatin. If this is necessary, apply a small amount to the area three or four times a day, and rub it in well.

Rest assured that seborrheic dermatitis is not a serious infection. Nor is it an allergy to something you're using, or due to poor hygiene. It will go away without any scars, and your baby will be beautiful again.

Eczema (Atopic Dermatitis and Contact Dermatitis)

Eczema is a general term used to describe a number of different skin conditions. It usually appears as reddened skin that becomes moist and oozing, occasionally resulting in small, fluid-filled bumps. When eczema becomes chronic (persists for a long time), the skin tends to thicken, dry out, and become scaly with coarse lines.

There are two main types of eczema: atopic dermatitis and contact dermatitis.

Atopic Dermatitis

Atopic dermatitis often occurs in infants and children who have allergies or a family history of allergy or eczema, although the problem is not necessarily caused by an allergy. Atopic dermatitis usually develops in three different phases. The first occurs between two and six months of age, with itching, redness, and the appearance of small bumps on the cheeks, forehead, or scalp. This rash then may spread to the arms or trunk. Although atopic dermatitis often is confused with other types of dermatitis, especially seborrheic dermatitis, severe itching and the absence of previous allergy are clues that this is the problem. In many cases the rash disappears or improves by two or three years of age.

The second phase of this skin problem occurs most often between the ages of four and ten years, and is characterized by circular, slightly raised, itchy and scaly eruptions on the face or trunk. These are less oozy and more scaly than the first phase of atopic dermatitis, and the skin tends to appear somewhat thickened. The most frequent locations for this rash are in the bends of the elbows, behind the knees, and on the backs of the wrists and ankles. All types are very itchy, and the skin generally tends to be very dry.

The third phase, characterized by areas of itching skin and a dry, scaly appearance, begins at about age twelve and occasionally continues on into early adulthood.

Contact Dermatitis

Contact dermatitis can occur when the skin comes in contact with an irritating substance. One form of this problem results from repeated contact with irritating substances such as citrus juices, bubble baths, strong soaps, certain foods and medicines, and woolen or rough-weave fabrics. In addition, one of the most common irritants is the child's own saliva. Contact dermatitis doesn't itch as much as atopic dermatitis and usually will clear when the irritant is no longer present and improves when babies no longer salivate over their skin.

Another form of contact dermatitis develops after skin contact with substances to which the child is allergic. The most common of these are:

- Certain flavorings or additives to toothpastes and mouthwashes (These cause a rash around or in the mouth.)

- Glues and dyes used in the manufacture (or in the leather) of shoes (They produce a reaction on the tops of the toes and feet.)

- Dyes used in clothing (These cause rashes in areas where the clothing rubs or where there is increased perspiration.)

- Nickel jewelry or snaps on jeans or pants

- Plants, especially poison ivy, poison oak, and poison sumac (see page 704)

- Medications such as neomycin ointment

This rash usually appears within several hours after contact (one to three days with poison ivy). It is often itchy, and may have small blisters.

Treatment

If your child has a rash that looks like eczema, your pediatrician will need to examine it to make the correct diagnosis and prescribe the proper treatment. In some cases she may arrange for a pediatric dermatologist to examine it.

Although there is no cure for atopic dermatitis, it generally can be controlled and often will go away after several months or years. The most effective treatment is to prevent the skin from becoming dry and itchy and to avoid substances that cause the condition to flare. To do this:

- Avoid frequent long, hot baths, which tend to dry the skin.

- Use skin moisturizers (e.g., creams or ointments) regularly and frequently to decrease the dryness and itchiness.

- Avoid harsh or irritating clothing (wool or coarse-weave material).

- If there is oozing or exceptional itching, use tepid (lukewarm) compresses on the area, followed by the application of prescribed medications.

Your pediatrician usually will suggest a medicated cream or ointment to control inflammation and itching. These preparations often contain a form of cortisone, and should be used only under the direction of your doctor. In addition, other lotions or bath oils might be prescribed. It's important to continue to apply the medications for as long as your pediatrician directs. Stopping too soon will cause the condition to recur.

In addition to the skin preparations, your child also may need to take an antihistamine by mouth to control the itching and antibiotics if the skin becomes infected.

The treatment of allergic contact dermatitis is similar, although your pediatric dermatologist or allergist also will want to find the cause of the rash by taking a careful history or by conducting a series of patch tests. These tests are done by placing small patches of common irritants (or allergens) against your child's skin. If the skin reacts with redness and itching, that substance should be avoided.

Alert your pediatrician if any of the following occurs:

- Your child's rash is severe and is not responding to home treatment.

- There is any evidence of fever or infection (i.e., blisters, redness, yellow crusts, pain, or oozing of fluid).

- The rash spreads or another rash develops.

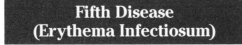

Fifth Disease (Erythema Infectiosum)

Rosy cheeks usually are a sign of good health, but if your child suddenly develops bright-red patches on her cheeks that are also raised and warm, she may have a viral illness known as fifth disease. Like so many other childhood illnesses, this one is spread from person to person. The virus causing this disease is called a parvovirus. Once the virus is in your child's body, it may take from four to fourteen days for symptoms to appear.

This is a mild disease, and most children feel well even when the rash is present. However, there can be mild coldlike symptoms: sore throat, headache, pinkeye, fatigue, a mild fever, or itching. In rare cases there may be aches in the knees or wrists. The disease process may be more severe in children with abnormalities of their hemoglobin or red blood cells, such as sickle cell anemia, and in children with cancer.

The rash usually begins on the cheeks, causing them to look as if they've been slapped. During the next few days, the arms and then the trunk, thighs, and buttocks will develop a pink, slightly raised rash that has a lacelike pattern. Fever is usually absent or mild. After five to ten days the rash will fade, with the face clearing first, followed by the arms, and then the trunk and legs. Interestingly, the rash may reappear briefly weeks or months later, particularly if your child becomes hot from bathing, exercise, or sunlight, or spends time in the sun.

Treatment

While fifth disease is not serious in most children, it may be confused with a rash that is. It also may mimic certain drug-related rashes, so it's important to inform your pediatrician about any medications your child may be taking. When you describe the symptoms over the phone, the doctor may suspect fifth disease, but he still may want to examine your child to be certain.

There is no specific medicine for fifth disease; treatment is geared to symptomatic relief. For instance, if there's a fever or aches and pains, you can use acetaminophen. When cold symptoms are interfering with sleeping or eating, check with your pediatrician about using a decongestant. Itching can be relieved by using an antihistamine. Also, if your child exhibits new symptoms, feels sicker, or develops a high fever, call your pediatrician.

The child is contagious when she is suffering the coldlike symptoms that precede the rash. By the time your child has a rash, she is no longer contagious. Nevertheless, as a rule, whenever your child has a rash or a fever, you should keep her away from other children until the illness is identified by your doctor. As a precaution, wait until she no longer has a fever and is feeling normal before allowing her to play with other children. Also keep your youngster away from pregnant women (particularly in their first trimester), since the virus that causes this disease may have a damaging effect on the fetus if the mother becomes infected.

Hair Loss (Alopecia)

Almost all newborns lose some or all of their hair. This is normal and to be expected. The baby hair falls out before the mature hair comes in. Thus hair loss occurring during the first six months is not a cause for concern.

Very commonly, a baby loses her hair where she rubs her scalp against the mattress or as a result of a head-banging habit. As she starts to move more and sit up or outgrow this head-banging behavior, this type of hair loss will correct itself.

In very rare cases, babies may be born with alopecia (hair loss), which can occur by itself or in association with certain abnormalities of the nails and the teeth. Later in childhood, hair loss may be due to medications, a scalp injury, or a medical or nutritional problem.

An older child may also lose her hair if it's braided too tightly or pulled too hard when combing or brushing. Some youngsters (under age three or four) twirl their hair as a comforting habit and innocently may pull it out. Other children (usually older ones) may pull their hair out on purpose but deny doing it; this often is a signal of emotional stress, which you should discuss with your pediatrician.

Alopecia areata, a condition common in children and teenagers, seems to be an "allergic" reaction to one's own hair. In this disorder, children lose hair in a circular area, causing a bald spot. In general, when it's limited to a few patches, the outlook for complete recovery is good. But when the condition persists or worsens, steroid creams and even steroid injections and other forms of therapy at the site of the hair loss often are used. Unfortunately, if the hair loss is extensive, it may be difficult to renew its growth.

Because alopecia and other types of hair loss can be a sign of other medical or nutritional problems, bring these conditions to your pediatrician's attention whenever they occur after the first six months of age. The doctor will look at your child's scalp, determine the cause, and prescribe treatment. Sometimes referral to a pediatric dermatologist is necessary.

Head Lice

Head lice commonly occur in young children who play together, share clothing or hats, or are generally in close contact. Although often misunderstood and embarrassing to parents, head lice are neither a painful nor a serious medical problem. Head lice do not transmit diseases or cause permanent problems. Many parents with children in school or child care have received a note informing them of a case of head lice in their child's classroom. This problem used to be confined to school-age children, but now that more children are in preschool, there are more cases at earlier ages. Head lice occurs in all socioeconomic groups and is most common in children ages three to twelve.

Usually you first become aware of the presence of head lice by noticing that the child has an extremely itchy scalp. On close inspection, you may see little white dots in the hair or on the neck at the hairline. Sometimes you may confuse this with dandruff or seborrhea. Dandruff generates larger flakes, however, while lice infestation results in more discrete dots that usually are stuck onto the shaft of the hair. On close examination, you may see them move on the hair shaft. Also, the itchiness of the scalp is usually far more uncomfortable with lice than with seborrhea or dandruff.

These symptoms may indicate the presence of the head louse, *Pediculus humanus capitis,* and its eggs or nits. Try not to overreact when you first realize this or when your child's school phones or sends home a note. It is a very common condition that does not reflect negatively on your level of personal hygiene. It is merely the result of having your child in contact with other children infected with head lice. Because youngsters in the same family spend so much time together in such close proximity, it is not unusual for lice to be spread from one sibling to another.

A child with head lice probably contracted them through direct contact with the head of another infected person, such as a classmate or a sibling. Lice also can spread by sharing brushes, combs, and hats or other articles of clothing, but this means of transmission is much less common.

Treatment

Once you recognize that your child has head lice, there are several treatments available.

The following agents are most widely used in treating head lice.

- Permethrin 1% (brand name NIX) is the treatment currently recommended by the American Academy of Pediatrics. It has advantages over the other treatments, such as low toxicity, and it does not cause allergic reactions in individuals with plant allergies. Apply the permethrin 1%, a cream rinse, to the hair after the hair has been shampooed with a nonconditioning shampoo and towel-dried. Leave the permethrin on for ten minutes before rinsing. You may need to apply it again in seven to ten days if you still see live lice.

- Lindane (brand names Kwell, Scabene) is used as a shampoo for no more than ten minutes. This preparation can be toxic if it is not used according to directions.

- Pyrethrins plus piperonyl butoxide (brand names A200, RID, R&C, among others) are applied as shampoos, then left on for ten minutes before rinsing. Often you will have to apply a second treatment seven to ten days later. Do not use pyrethrins in children allergic to chrysanthemums.

Medications to kill lice are potentially dangerous insecticides. Use only according to package instructions and your pediatrician's recommendations.

Whichever treatment you use, you do not have to remove nits manually after using the medication to prevent the spread of head lice, although doing so may be prudent for aesthetic reasons. Careful combing of the hair with a fine-tooth comb can remove the dead egg cases and any nits or eggs that have survived treatment. This nit removal is tedious and often requires more than one sitting, depending on the number of nits.

To prevent reinfection, you also must wash all bedclothes and clothing (hats are a big culprit) that have been in contact with the child for the forty-eight hours immediately preceding your noticing the head lice. Use the hot cycles to wash the clothes, or have them dry-cleaned if you prefer. Wash combs and brushes in a shampoo specific against lice, or soaked in hot water. Temperatures exceeding 128.3 degrees Fahrenheit (53.5 degrees Celsius) for five minutes are lethal to lice and eggs.

In addition, if your child has lice, it's important to inform the child care center or school. However, the American Academy of Pediatrics believes that no healthy child should be excluded from or allowed to miss school because of head lice. The Academy also discourages "no nit" policies that require the absence of lice in order for a child to return to school. A youngster with an active head lice infestation likely has had this outbreak for a month or more by the time it is discovered. Thus because he poses little risk to others, he should remain in class while trying to avoid direct head contact with other children. Also, to prevent your child from contracting head lice infestations, teach him not to share personal items such as hats, combs, and brushes. If your active, engaging three-year-old has head lice, someone else in the group probably does, too. Because head lice are very contagious, *other family members also may need to be examined and treated* and have their clothing and bedding laundered.

Hives

If your child has an itchy rash that consists of raised red bumpy areas, perhaps with pale centers and no flaking skin over the lesions, he probably has hives (welts). This rash may occur all over the body or just in one region, such as the face. The location may change, with the hives disappearing in one area of the body and appearing in another, often in a matter of hours.

Among the most common causes of hives are:

- Foods (berries, cheese, nuts, eggs, milk, sesame oils, shellfish)

- Drugs, either over-the-counter or prescribed (Penicillin and aspirin are two frequent culprits.)

- Pollen from trees, grass, ferns

- Plants

- Response to infection

- Cold water

- Bites or stings from bees or other insects

In at least half of the cases, it is not possible to identify the cause.

Treatment

An oral antihistamine will relieve the itching of hives. Many can be obtained without a prescription, but you should ask your doctor to recommend one. You may need to use this type of medication for several days and give it as often as every four to six hours. Applying cool compresses to the area of itching and swelling also may help.

Other treatments may be necessary if internal parts of the body are involved in the allergic reaction. If your child is wheezing or having trouble swallowing, seek emergency treatment. The doctor usually will prescribe a more effective antihistamine and may even give an injection of epinephrine to stop the allergic response. If the allergy causing the hives also results in severe breathing difficulties, your pediatrician will help you obtain a special emergency-care kit for possible use with such reactions in the future.

Prevention

In order to prevent subsequent outbreaks of hives, your doctor will try to determine what is causing the allergic reaction. If the rash is confined to a small area of skin, it probably was caused by something your child touched. (Plants and soaps are frequent culprits.) But if it spreads all over her body, something she ingested or inhaled, or possibly an infection, is most likely to blame.

Often the pattern to the appearance of the hives provides a clue to the allergy. For example, does it usually happen after meals? Does it seem to occur more during certain seasons, or when traveling to particular places? If you discover a specific pattern, alter your routine to see if your child improves. You will need to consider every food your child eats, even those that she has eaten without difficulty in the past. Sometimes hives will occur if your child eats an unusually large amount of a food to which she is only mildly allergic.

Once you've discovered the cause of the problem, try keeping your child away from it as much as possible. If you know in advance that she will or may be exposed, send or bring along an antihistamine. If her allergy is to insects, keep a bee sting kit available. (See *Insect Bites and Stings,* p. 700.)

Impetigo

Impetigo is a contagious bacterial skin infection that often appears around the nose, mouth, and ears. It is caused by either streptococcus bacteria, which also are responsible for "strep" throat and scarlet fever, or staphylococcus, or "staph," bacteria.

If staph bacteria are to blame, the infection may cause blisters filled with clear fluid. These can break easily, leaving a raw, glistening area that soon forms a scab with a honey-colored crust. By contrast, the strep bacteria usually are not associated with blisters, but they do cause crusts over larger sores and ulcers.

Treatment

Until your child can see the doctor, cleanse the rash well with soap and water. You can use a mild medicated soap. Impetigo needs to be treated with antibiotics, but your pediatrician may wish first to determine which bacteria are causing the rash in order to know what specific medication to prescribe. Make sure your child takes the medication for the full prescribed course, or the impetigo could return.

One other important point to keep in mind: Impetigo is contagious until the rash clears, or until at least two days of antibiotics have been given and there is evidence of improvement. Your child should avoid close contact with other children during this period, and you should avoid touching the rash. If you or other family members do come in contact with it, wash your hands and the exposed site thoroughly with soap and water. Also, keep the infected child's washcloths and towels separate from those of other family members.

Prevention

The bacteria that cause impetigo thrive in breaks in the skin. The best ways to prevent this rash are to keep your child's fingernails clipped and clean and to teach him not to scratch minor skin irritations. When he does have a scrape, cleanse it with soap and water, and apply an antibiotic cream or ointment. Be careful not to use washcloths or towels that have been used by someone else who has an active skin infection.

When impetigo is caused by certain types of strep bacteria, a rare but serious complication called glomerulonephritis can develop. This disease injures the kidney and may cause passage of blood in the urine and high blood pressure.

Insect Bites and Stings

Your child's reaction to a bite or sting will depend on her sensitivity to the particular insect's venom. While most children have only mild reactions, those who are allergic to certain insect venoms can have severe symptoms that require emergency treatment.

Treatment

Although insect bites can be irritating, they usually begin to disappear by the next day and do not require a doctor's treatment. To relieve the itchiness that accompanies bites by mosquitoes, flies, fleas, and bedbugs, apply a cool compress and/or calamine lotion freely on any part of your child's body *except* the areas around her eyes and genitals. If your child is stung by a wasp or bee, soak a cloth in cold water and press it over the area of the sting to reduce pain and swelling. Call your pediatrician before using any other treatment, including creams or lotions containing antihistamines or home remedies. If the itching is severe, the doctor may prescribe oral antihistamines.

If your child disturbs a bee nest, get him away from the nest as quickly as possible. The base of a honeybee's sting emits an alarm pheromone (hormone) that makes other bees more likely to sting, as well.

It is very important to remove a bee stinger quickly and completely from the skin. The quick removal of a bee stinger will prevent a large amount of venom from being pumped into the skin. If the stinger is visible, remove it by gently scraping it off horizontally with a credit card or your fingernail. Avoid squeezing the stinger with a pair of tweezers; doing this may release more venom into the skin. Bee stings and mosquito bites may be more swollen on the second or third day after the incident.

Keep your child's fingernails short and clean to minimize the risk of infection from scratching. If infection does occur anyway, the bite will become redder, larger, and more swollen. In some cases you may notice red streaks or yellowish fluid near the bite. Have your pediatrician examine any infected bite, because it may need to be treated with antibiotics.

Call for medical help immediately if your child has any of these other symptoms after being bitten or stung:

- Sudden difficulty in breathing

- Weakness, collapse, or unconsciousness

- Hives or itching all over the body

- Extreme swelling near the eye, lips, or penis that makes it difficult for the child to see, eat, or urinate

Prevention

Some children with no other known allergies may have severe reactions to insect bites and stings. If you suspect that your child is allergy-prone, discuss the situation with

Insect/ Environment	Characteristics of Bite or Sting	Special Notes
Mosquitoes Water (pools, lakes, birdbaths)	Stinging sensation followed by small, red, itchy mound with tiny puncture mark at center.	Mosquitoes are attracted by bright colors, sweat, and sweet odors, such as perfumes, scented soaps, and shampoos.
Flies Food, garbage, animal waste	Painful, itchy bumps. May turn into small blisters.	Bites often disappear in a day but may last longer.
Fleas Cracks in floor, rugs, pet fur	Small bump that looks like a hive. Often in groups where clothes fit tightly (waist, buttocks).	Fleas are most likely to be a problem in homes with pets.
Bedbugs Cracks of walls, floors, crevices of furniture, bedding	Itchy red bumps surrounded by a blister. Usually two or three in a row.	Bedbugs are most likely to bite at night and are less active in cold weather.
Fire ants Mounds in pastures, meadows, lawns, and parks	Immediate pain and burning. Swelling up to ½ inch (1.3 cm). Cloudy fluid in area of bite.	Fire ants usually attack intruders. Some children have reactions such as difficulty in breathing, fever, and stomach upset.
Bees and wasps Flowers, shrubs, picnic areas, beaches	Immediate pain and rapid swelling.	A few children have severe reactions, such as difficulty in breathing and swelling all over the body.
Ticks Wooded areas	May not be noticeable. Hidden in hair or on skin.	Don't remove ticks with matches, lighted cigarettes, or nail polish remover. Grasp the tick firmly with tweezers near the head. Gently pull the tick straight out; don't leave any parts embedded in the skin.

your doctor. He may recommend a series of hyposensitization injections. In addition, he will prescribe a special kit for you to keep on hand for use if your child is stung.

It is impossible to prevent all insect bites, but you can minimize the number your child receives by following these guidelines.

- Avoid areas where insects nest or congregate, such as garbage cans, stagnant pools of water, uncovered foods and sweets, and orchards and gardens where flowers are in bloom.

- When you know your child will be exposed to insects, dress her in long pants and a lightweight long-sleeved shirt.

- Avoid dressing your child in clothing with bright colors or flowery prints, because they seem to attract insects.

- Don't use scented soaps, perfumes, or hair sprays on your child, because they also are inviting to insects.

Insect repellents are generally available without a prescription, but they should be used sparingly on infants and young children. In fact, the most effective insecticides include DEET (N,N-diethyl-m-toluamide), which is a chemical *not* recommended for use in children under two months of age. Do not apply DEET-containing repellents more than once a day on older children.

The concentrations of DEET vary significantly from product to product—ranging from less than 10 percent to over 30 percent—so read the label of any product you purchase. The higher the concentration of DEET, the longer the duration of action and the greater the effectiveness of the product. Efficacy plateaus at a concentration of 30 percent, which is also the maximum concentration currently recommended for children. The safety of DEET does not appear to be related to its level of concentration; therefore, a prudent approach is to select the lowest effective concentration for the amount of time your child spends outdoors. Check the label for percent but it will usually be 10–30%.

Repellents are effective in preventing bites by mosquitoes, ticks, fleas, chiggers, and biting flies, but have virtually no effect on stinging insects such as bees, hornets, and wasps. Contrary to popular belief, giving antihistamines continuously throughout the insect season does not appear to prevent reactions to bites.

The table on page 701 summarizes information about common stinging or biting insects.

Measles

Thanks to vaccinations, cases of measles are very uncommon in America today. In 2000, fewer than one hundred cases were reported in the United States. However, people still get the measles. If your child has never been immunized or had the measles, he can get them if he is exposed. The measles virus is passed through the air droplets transmitted by an infected person. Anyone who breathes the droplets and is not immune to the disease can become infected.

Signs and Symptoms

For the first eight to twelve days after being exposed to the measles virus, your child probably will have no symptoms; this is called the incubation period. Then he may develop an illness that seems like a common cold, with a cough, runny nose, and pinkeye (conjunctivitis; see page 604). The cough may be severe at times and will last for about a week, and your child probably will feel miserable.

During the first one to three days of the illness, the coldlike symptoms will become worse, and he'll develop a fever that may run as high as 103 to 105 degrees Fahrenheit (39.4–40.5 degrees Celsius). The fever will last until two to three days after the rash first appears.

After two to four days of illness, the rash will develop. It usually begins on the face and neck, and spreads down the trunk and out to the arms and legs. It starts as very fine red bumps, which may join together to form larger splotches. If you notice tiny white spots, like grains of sand, inside his mouth next to his molars, you'll know the rash will follow soon. The rash will last five to eight days. As it fades, the skin may peel a little.

Treatment

Although there is no treatment for the disease, it is important that the pediatrician examine your child to determine that measles is, in fact, the cause of the illness. Many other conditions can start in the same way, and measles has its own complications (i.e., pneumonia) that the doctor will want to watch for. When you call, describe the fever and rash, so that the doctor knows that you suspect measles. When you visit the office, the pediatrician will want to separate your child from other patients, so that the virus is not transmitted to them.

Your child is contagious from several days before the rash breaks out until the fever and rash are gone. During this period he should be kept at home (except for the visit to the doctor) and away from anyone who is not immune to the illness.

At home, make sure your child drinks plenty of fluids and give acetaminophen in the proper dose if your child is uncomfort-

able due to the fever. The conjunctivitis that accompanies measles can make it painful for the child to be in bright light or sunshine, so you may want to darken his room to a comfortable level for the first few days.

Sometimes bacterial infections develop as a complication of the measles. These most often include pneumonia (see page 553), middle ear infection (see page 580), and strep throat (see page 589). In these cases, your child must be seen by the pediatrician, who may prescribe antibiotic treatment.

Prevention

Almost all children who receive two doses of the MMR (measles, mumps, rubella) vaccine after their first birthday are protected against measles for life. Because up to 5 percent of children may not respond to the initial vaccination, a second (booster) dose is recommended later in childhood. Your pediatrician will tell you what is best for your child. (See Chapter 27, "Immunizations.")

If your unimmunized child has been exposed to someone who has the measles, or if someone in your household has the virus, notify your pediatrician at once. The following steps can help keep your child from getting sick.

1. If he is under one year old or has a weakened immune system, he can be given immune globulin (gamma globulin) up to six days following exposure. This may temporarily protect him from becoming infected, but will not provide extended immunity.

2. An infant six to eleven months of age may receive the measles vaccine alone if he is exposed to the disease or if he is residing in a community where exposure is highly likely or in an epidemic situation. If doses are given during these months, your child still may need additional doses to be fully immunized.

3. If your child is otherwise healthy and over one year old, he can be vaccinated. The vaccine may be effective if given within seventy-two hours of his exposure to an infected person, and *will* provide extended immunity. If your child has received one dose of the measles vaccine and at least one month has elapsed since that dose, he may be given a second dose after exposure.

Poison Ivy, Poison Oak, Poison Sumac

Contact with poison ivy, poison oak, or poison sumac is a common cause of skin rashes in children during the spring, summer, and fall seasons. An allergic reaction to the oil in these plants produces the rash. The rash occurs from several hours to three days after contact with the plant and begins in the form of blisters, which are accompanied by severe itching.

Contrary to popular belief, it is not the fluid in the blisters that causes the rash to spread. That occurs when small amounts of oil remain under the child's fingernails, on her clothing, or on a pet animal's hair that then comes in contact with other parts of her body. The rash will not be spread to another person unless the oil that remains also comes in contact with that person's skin.

Poison ivy grows as a three-leafed green weed with a red stem at the center. It grows in vinelike form in all parts of the country except the Southwest. Poison sumac is a shrub, not a vine, and has seven to thirteen leaves arranged in pairs along a central stem. Not nearly as abundant as poison ivy, it grows primarily in the swampy areas of the Mississippi River region. Poison oak grows as a shrub, and it is seen primarily on the West Coast. All three plants produce similar skin reactions. These skin reactions are forms of contact dermatitis. (See Eczema, page 693.)

Treatment

Treating reactions to poison ivy—the most frequent of these forms of contact dermatitis—is a straightforward matter.

- Prevention is the best approach. Know what the plant looks like and teach your children to avoid it.

- If there is contact, wash all clothes and shoes in soap and water. Also, wash the area of the skin that was exposed with soap and water for at least ten minutes after the plant or the oil has been touched.

- If the eruption is mild, apply calamine lotion three or four times a day to cut down on the itching. Avoid those preparations containing anesthetics or antihistamines, as often they can cause allergic eruptions themselves.

- Apply topical 1 percent hydrocortisone cream to decrease the inflammation.

- If the rash is severe, on the face, or on extensive parts of the body, the pediatrician may need to place the child on oral steroids. These will need to be given for about ten days, with the dose tapering in a specific schedule determined by your pediatrician. This treatment should be reserved for the most severe cases.

Call the pediatrician if you notice any of the following:

- Severe eruption not responsive to the previously described home methods

- Any evidence of infection, such as blisters, redness, or oozing

- Any new eruption or rash

- Severe poison ivy on the face

- Fever

Ringworm

If your child has a scaly round patch on the side of his scalp or elsewhere on his skin, and he seems to be losing hair in the same area of the scalp, the problem may be a contagious infection known as ringworm or tinea.

This disorder is caused not by worms but by a fungus. It's called ringworm because the infections tend to form round or oval spots that, as they grow, become smooth in the center but keep an active red scaly border.

Scalp ringworm often is spread from person to person, sometimes when sharing infected hats, combs, brushes, and barrettes. If ringworm appears elsewhere on your child's body, he may have the type spread by infected dogs or cats.

The first signs of infection on the body are red scaly patches. They may not look like rings until they've grown to half an inch in diameter, and they generally stop growing at about one inch. Your child may have just one patch or several. These lesions may be mildly itchy and uncomfortable.

Scalp ringworm starts the same way the body variety does, but as the rings grow, your child may lose some hair in the infected area. Certain types of scalp ringworm produce less obvious rings and are easily confused with dandruff or cradle cap. Cradle cap, however, occurs only during infancy. If your child's scalp is continually scaly and he's over a year old, you should suspect ringworm and notify your pediatrician.

Treatment

A single ringworm patch on the body can be treated with an over-the-counter cream recommended by your pediatrician. The most frequently used ones are tolnaftate, miconazole, and clotrimazole. A small amount is applied two or three times a day for at least a week, during which time some clearing should begin. If there are any patches on the scalp or more than one on the body, or if the rash is getting worse while being treated, check with your pediatrician again. She will prescribe a stronger medication and, in the case of scalp ringworm, will use an oral antifungal preparation. Your child will have to take medicine for several weeks to clear the infection.

You also may need to wash your child's scalp with a special shampoo when he has scalp ringworm. If there's any possibility that others in the family have caught the infection, they also should use this shampoo and be examined for possible signs of infection. Do not allow your youngster to share combs, brushes, hair clips, barrettes, or hats.

Prevention

You can help prevent ringworm by identifying and treating any pets with the problem. Look for scaling, itchy, hairless areas on your dogs and cats, and have them treated right away. Any family members, playmates, or schoolmates who show symptoms also should be treated.

Roseola Infantum

Your ten-month-old doesn't look or act very ill, but she suddenly develops a fever between 102 degrees Fahrenheit (38.9 degrees Celsius) and 105 degrees Fahrenheit (40.5

degrees Celsius). The fever lasts for three to seven days, during which time your child has less appetite, mild diarrhea, slight cough, and runny nose, and seems mildly irritable and a little sleepier than usual. Her upper eyelids appear slightly swollen or droopy. Finally, *after her temperature returns to normal,* she gets a slightly raised, spotty, pink rash on her trunk, which spreads only to her upper arms and neck and fades after just twenty-four hours. What's the diagnosis? Most likely it's a disease called roseola—a contagious viral illness that's most common in children under age two. Its incubation period is seven to fourteen days. The key to this diagnosis is that the rash appears *after* the fever is gone.

Treatment

Whenever your infant or young child has a fever of 102 degrees Fahrenheit (38.9 degrees Celsius) or higher for twenty-four hours, call your pediatrician, even if there are no other symptoms. If the doctor suspects the fever is caused by roseola, he may suggest ways to control the temperature and advise you to call again if your child becomes worse or the fever lasts for more than three or four days. For a child who has other symptoms or appears more seriously ill, the doctor may order a blood count, urinalysis, or other tests.

Since illnesses that cause fever can be contagious, it's wise to keep your youngster away from other children, at least until you've conferred with your pediatrician. Once she is diagnosed as having roseola, don't let her play with other children until the rash clears.

While your youngster has a fever, dress her in lightweight clothing. If she is very uncomfortable because of the fever, you can give her acetaminophen in the appropriate dose for her age and weight. (See Chapter 23, "Fever.") Don't worry if her appetite is decreased, and encourage her to drink extra fluids. As soon as her rash is gone, she may return to all normal activities, including contact with other children.

Although this disease rarely is serious, be aware that early in the illness, when fever climbs very quickly, there's a chance of convulsions (see *Seizures, Convulsions,* and *Epilepsy,* page 660). There may be a seizure regardless of how well you treat the fever, so it's important to know how to manage convulsions even though they're usually quite mild and occur only briefly, if at all, with roseola.

Rubella (German Measles)

Although some of today's parents had rubella, or German measles, during their childhood, it is a rare illness now, thanks to the availability of an effective vaccine. Even when it was quite prevalent, however, rubella was usually a mild disease.

Rubella is characterized by a mild fever (100–102 degrees Fahrenheit [37.8–38.9 degrees Celsius]), swollen glands (typically on the back of the neck and base of the skull), and a rash. The rash, which varies from pinhead size to an irregular redness, is raised and usually begins on the face. Within two to three days it spreads to the neck, chest, and the rest of the body as it fades from the face.

Once exposed to rubella, a child usually will develop the disease in fourteen to twenty-one days. The contagious period for rubella begins several days before the rash appears and continues for five to seven days after it develops. Because the disease can be so mild, it goes unrecognized in about half the children who contract it.

Before the rubella vaccine was developed, this illness tended to occur in epidemics every six to nine years. Since the vaccine was introduced in 1968, there have been no significant epidemics. Even so, the disease still occurs. Each year unvaccinated and susceptible teenagers, often in college campus settings, develop the illness. Fortunately, except for causing fever, discomfort, and occasional pain in the joints, these small epidemics are of little consequence.

The situation is quite different when rubella infects an unvaccinated, susceptible woman in the first three months of her pregnancy. In this case it can cause severe, irreversible damage to the unborn fetus. Babies born with this form of rubella (congenital rubella) may have eye disorders (cataracts, glaucoma, small eyes), heart problems, deafness, severe mental retardation, and other evidence of central nervous system damage.

What You Can Do

If your pediatrician diagnoses rubella in your child, you may be able to make him more comfortable by giving him extra fluids, bed rest (if he's fatigued), and acetaminophen if he has a fever. Keep him away from other children or adults unless you are sure that they're immunized. As a general rule, children with rubella should not be in child care or any other group setting for seven days after the rash first appears. In particular, make a special effort not to expose pregnant women to a child with rubella.

If your child is diagnosed as having the congenital form of rubella, your pediatrician can advise you on the best way to manage his complex and difficult problems. Infants born with congenital rubella are often infectious for a year after birth and therefore should be kept out of any group child care setting, where they could expose other susceptible children or adults to the infection.

When to Call the Pediatrician

If your child has a fever and a rash and appears uncomfortable, discuss the problem with your pediatrician. If rubella is diagnosed, follow the guidelines suggested earlier for treatment and isolation.

Prevention

Prevention of German measles through immunization is the best approach. The vaccine usually is administered as part of a three-in-one shot called MMR (measles, mumps, rubella), given when the child is twelve to fifteen months old. Booster doses need to be given. (See Chapter 27, "Immunizations.")

There are relatively few adverse reactions to the rubella vaccine. Occasionally children will get a rash, a slight fever, and some joint pain in the first one to three weeks after the vaccine is given. (Joint pain is much less common with the newest version of the vaccine.) *A child can be immunized even if his mother is pregnant at the time.* However, a susceptible pregnant woman should *never* be immunized herself. She also should be extremely careful to avoid contact with any child or adult who may be infected with the virus. After delivery, she should be immunized immediately.

Scabies

Scabies is caused by a microscopic mite that burrows under the top layers of skin and deposits its eggs. The rash that results from scabies is actually a reaction to the mite's body, eggs, and excretions. Once the mite gets into the skin, it takes two to four weeks for the rash to appear.

In an older child, this rash appears as numerous itchy, fluid-filled bumps that may be located under the skin next to a reddish burrow track. In an infant, the bumps may be more scattered and isolated and often are found on the palms and soles. Because of scratch marks, crusting, or a secondary infection, this annoying rash often is difficult to identify.

According to legend, when Napoleon's troops had scabies, one could hear the sound of scratching at night from over a mile away. A bit of exaggeration perhaps, but it illustrates two key points to remember if you think your child has scabies: It's very itchy and contagious. Scabies is spread only by person-to-person contact, and this happens extremely easily. If one person in your family has the rash, the others may get it, too.

Scabies can be located almost anywhere on the body, including the area between the fingers. Older children and adults usually don't get the rash on their palms, soles, scalp, or face, but babies may. Adult women often develop scabies sores around their breasts, and adults of both sexes often get them on their genitals, armpits, arms, wrists, midriff, and lower buttocks.

Treatment

If you notice that your child (and possibly others in the family) is scratching constantly, suspect scabies and call the pediatrician, who will examine the rash. The doctor may gently scrape a skin sample from the affected area, and look under the microscope for evidence of the mite or its eggs. If scabies turns out to be the diagnosis, the doctor will prescribe one of several anti-scabies medications. Most are lotions that are applied over the entire body—from the scalp to the soles of the feet—and are washed off after several hours. You may need to repeat the application one week later.

Some experts feel the whole family must be treated—even those members who don't have a rash. Others feel that although the entire family should be examined, only those with a rash should be treated with antiscabies medications. Any live-in help, sleep-over visitors, or frequent babysitters also should receive care.

To prevent infection caused by scratching, cut your child's fingernails. If the itching is very severe, your pediatrician may prescribe an antihistamine or other anti-itch medication. If your child shows signs of bacterial infection in the scratched scabies, notify the pediatrician. She may want to prescribe an antibiotic or other form of treatment.

Following treatment, the itching could continue for two to four weeks, because this is an allergic rash. If it persists past four weeks, call your doctor, because the scabies may have returned and need retreatment.

Incidentally, there is some controversy over the possible spread of scabies from clothing or linen. Evidence indicates that this occurs very rarely. Thus, there's no need for extensive washing or decontamination of the child's room or the rest of the house, since the mite usually lives only in people's skin.

Scarlet Fever

When your child has a strep throat (see page 589), there's a chance that he'll get a rash known as scarlet fever or scarlatina. The symptoms of scarlet fever begin with a sore throat, a fever of 101 to 104 degrees Fahrenheit (38.2–40 degrees Celsius), and headache. This is followed within twenty-four hours by a red and sometimes itchy rash covering the trunk, arms, and legs. The rash is slightly raised, which makes the skin feel like fine sandpaper. Your child's face will turn red, too, with a pale area around his mouth. This redness will disappear in three to five days, leaving peeling skin in the areas where the rash was most intense (neck, underarms, groin, fingers, and toes). He may also have a white-coated, then reddened, tongue and mild abdominal pain.

Treatment

Call your pediatrician whenever your child complains of a sore throat, especially when a rash or fever also is present. The doctor will examine him and check for the presence of strep bacteria. If strep throat is found, an antibiotic (usually penicillin) will be given either by injection or by mouth. If your child takes the antibiotic by mouth, it's extremely important to complete the entire course because shorter treatment sometimes results in a return of the disease.

Most children with strep infections respond very quickly to antibiotics. The fever, sore throat, and headache usually are gone within twenty-four hours. The rash, however, will remain for about three to five days.

If your child's condition does not seem to improve with treatment, notify your pediatrician. If other family members develop fever or sore throat at this time—with or without a rash—they, too, should be examined and tested for strep throat.

If not treated, scarlet fever (like strep throat) can lead to ear and sinus infections, swollen neck glands, and pus around the tonsils. The most serious complication of untreated strep throat is rheumatic fever, which results in joint pain and swelling and sometimes heart damage. Very rarely, the strep bacteria in the throat can lead to glomerulonephritis, or inflammation of the kidneys, causing blood to appear in the urine and sometimes high blood pressure.

Sunburn

While those with darker skin coloring tend to be less sensitive to the sun, everyone is at risk for sunburn and its associated disorders. Children especially need to be protected from the sun's burning rays, since most sun damage occurs in childhood. Like other burns, sunburn will leave the skin red, warm, and painful. In severe cases it may cause blistering, fever, chills, headache, and a general feeling of illness.

Your child doesn't actually have to be burned, however, in order to be harmed by the sun. The effects of exposure build over the years, so that even moderate exposure during childhood can contribute to wrinkling, toughening, freckling, and perhaps cancer of the skin in later life. Also, some medications can cause a skin reaction to sunlight, and some medical conditions may make people more sensitive to the effects of the sun.

Treatment

The signs of sunburn usually appear six to twelve hours after exposure, with the greatest discomfort during the first twenty-four hours. If your child's burn is just red, warm, and painful, you can treat it yourself. Apply cool compresses to the burned areas or bathe the child in cool water. You also can give acetaminophen to help relieve the pain. (Check the package for appropriate dosage for her age and weight.)

If the sunburn causes blisters, fever, chills, headache, or a general feeling of illness, call your pediatrician. Severe sunburn must be treated like any other serious burn, and if it's very extensive, hospitalization sometimes is required. In addition, the blisters can become infected, requiring treatment with antibiotics. Sometimes extensive or severe sunburn also can lead to dehydration (see *Diarrhea,* page 506, for signs of dehydration) and in some cases fainting (heatstroke). Such cases need to be examined by your pediatrician or the nearest emergency facility.

Prevention

Many parents incorrectly assume that the sun is dangerous only when it's shining brightly. In fact, it's not the visible light rays but rather the invisible ultraviolet rays that are harmful. Your child actually may be exposed to more ultraviolet rays on foggy or hazy days because she'll feel cooler and therefore stay outside for a longer time. Exposure is also greater at higher altitudes. Even a big hat or an umbrella is not absolute protection because ultraviolet rays reflect off sand, water, snow, and many other surfaces.

Try to keep your child out of the sun when the peak ultraviolet rays occur (between 10 A.M. and 4 P.M.). In addition, follow these guidelines.

- Always use a sunscreen to block the damaging ultraviolet rays. Choose a sunscreen made for children with a sun protection factor (SPF) of at least 15. (Check the label.) Apply the protection half an hour before going out. Many sunscreens are waterproof, but even these may need to be reapplied every two to three hours if your child spends a lot of time in the water. Consult the instructions on the bottle.

- Dress your child in lightweight cotton clothing with long sleeves and long pants.

- Use a beach umbrella or similar object to keep her in the shade as much as possible.

- Have her wear a hat with a wide brim.

- Babies under six months of age should be kept out of direct sunlight. If adequate clothing and shade are not available, sunscreen may be used on small areas of the body, such as the face and the backs of the hands.

(See also *Burns,* page 476.)

Warts

Warts are caused by a virus—the human papilloma virus. These firm bumps (although they also can be flat) are yellow, tan, grayish, black, or brown. They usually appear on the hands, toes, around the knees, and on the face, but can occur anywhere on the body. When they're on the soles of the feet, doctors call them plantar warts. Although warts can be contagious, they appear infrequently in children under the age of two.

Treatment

Your pediatrician can give you advice on the treatment of warts. Sometimes he will recommend an over-the-counter medication that contains salicylic acid. If any of the following are present, he may refer you to a dermatologist.

- Multiple, recurring warts

- A wart on the face or genital area

- Large, deep, or painful plantar warts (warts on the soles of the feet)

- Warts that are particularly bothersome to your child

Some warts will just go away themselves. Others can be removed using prescription preparations. However, surgical removal by scraping, cauterizing, or freezing is sometimes necessary with multiple warts, those that continue to recur, or deep plantar warts. Although surgery usually has a good success rate, it can be painful and results in scarring. Laser treatment may help. The earlier the warts are treated, the better the chance of permanent cure, although there is always the possibility that they will recur even after treatment that is initially successful.

If a wart comes back, simply treat it again the way you did the first time, or as directed by your pediatrician. Don't wait until it becomes large, painful, or starts to spread.

West Nile Virus

The West Nile virus has received plenty of attention in recent years. It is spread to humans through the bite of an infected mosquito. The first outbreak occurred in the United States in 1999. Although some children have become ill when infected with the virus, in most cases the symptoms are mild.

Mosquitoes become carriers of the virus by feeding on infected birds. Although other animals have been infected with the virus—including horses, bats, squirrels, and domestic animals—birds are the most common reservoir. Once the virus has been transmitted to a human through a bite, it can multiply in an individual's bloodstream and in some cases cause illness. However, even if your child is bitten, she'll probably have only mild symptoms or none at all. Among people who have been bitten and contracted the infection, about one of five develop mild flulike symptoms (i.e., a fever, headaches, and body aches) and at times a skin rash. These symptoms tend to last only a few days. In less than one of one hundred of infections, a severe ill-ness can occur (so-called West Nile encephalitis or meningitis), with symptoms such as a high fever, a stiff neck, tremors, muscle weakness, convulsions, paralysis, and loss of consciousness.

Mosquitoes infected with the West Nile virus have been found only in certain (but a growing number of) regions of the United States. Even in those areas, however, only a small number of mosquitoes carry the virus.

Prevention

Like all people, your own child's risk of West Nile virus comes from mosquito bites. She cannot catch the disease from an infected playmate or from touching or kissing a person with the infection (or even by touching a bird infected with the virus).

There is no vaccine to protect your child from the West Nile virus. But you can reduce her likelihood of developing the disease by taking steps to reduce the chance that she'll be bitten by a mosquito infected with the virus. Here are some strategies to keep in mind. (Some of them appear in the previous section, as well).

- Apply insect repellent to your child, using just enough to protect her exposed skin.

- Choose a repellent containing the chemical DEET (N,N-diethyl-m-toluamide). The more DEET in the formulation, the longer your child will be protected.

- Do not use DEET preparations on infants under two months of age. In older children, apply it sparingly around the ears, and don't use it on the mouth or the eyes. Don't put it over cuts.

- Once your child comes indoors, wash off the repellent.

- Whenever possible, dress your youngster in long sleeves and long pants while she's outside. Use mosquito netting over a baby's infant carrier.

- Keep your youngster away from locations where mosquitoes are likely to congregate or lay their eggs, such as standing water (e.g., in birdbaths and pet water dishes).

- Because mosquitoes are more likely to bite humans at certain times of day—most commonly at dawn, dusk, and in the early evening—consider limiting the amount of time your child is outdoors during those hours.

- Repair any holes in your screens.

30

CHRONIC CONDITIONS AND DISEASES

Coping with Chronic (Long-Term) Health Problems

We tend to think of childhood as a carefree and healthy time of life, but some youngsters face chronic health problems during these early years. (By *chronic,* we mean conditions that last for at least three months, or require at least a month of hospitalization.) While most long-term health problems in children are relatively mild, any type of lengthy illness or disability is stressful for both them and their families.

The specific medical treatment of many chronic conditions is discussed elsewhere, under the names of those conditions. (See index.) The information that follows is aimed at helping parents deal with the emotional and practical challenges of living with any child who has a long-term illness or disability.

Getting Help

If your child is born with a serious medical problem or develops a chronic medical condition during her first years, you may face some of the following stresses and decisions.

- The realization that your child is not perfectly healthy often leads to feelings of disappointment and guilt, and fear for her future. In trying to deal with these feelings, you may find yourself struggling with unexplained emotional swings ranging from hopefulness to despair and depression.

- You will need to select and work with a team of medical professionals who can help your child.

- You may face decisions about treatment or surgery.

- You may have to accept responsibility for giving your child certain medications, guiding her in the use of special equipment, or helping her perform special therapies.

- You will be called on to provide the time, energy, money, and emotional commitment necessary for your child to receive the best possible treatment.

- You will need to learn how to access appropriate services and information to help your child.

- In adapting your life to meet your child's needs without neglecting other family members, you will face many difficult choices, some of which may require compromise solutions.

To avoid becoming overwhelmed, it is helpful to select one medical person as the overall coordinator of your child's medical care. This person may be your pediatrician or another health professional who is most closely involved with your child's treatment. It should be someone who knows your family well, makes you feel comfortable, and is willing to spend time answering your questions and working with other doctors and therapists involved in your child's care.

Not all of your child's special needs will be medical, of course. She may require special schooling, counseling, or other therapy. Your family may need outside financial or governmental assistance. The person who coordinates your child's medical care also should provide some guidance in obtaining this extra help, but the best way to make sure you and your child get the services and support you need is to learn about the resources and regulations that apply to special services for children with chronic illnesses or disabilities. You also should find out what you can do if the services your family receives do not meet your child's needs.

Balancing the Needs of Family and Child

For a while, the child with special needs may take all your attention, leaving little for other family members and outside relationships. Although this is normal, everyone will suffer unless you find some way to restore a sense of balance and routine to your activities. Neither your sick child nor the rest of the family will benefit if the health problem becomes the central and overwhelming issue in your family's life. Eventually your child's medical care must become a part of your daily routine rather than its focus.

If your child must be hospitalized, returning her to normal family and community life is vital, not only for the family but also for her health and well-being. The longer she is treated like a "patient" instead of a growing child, the more problems she may have socially and emotionally later on. Although it's natural to want to protect a sick child, overprotection may make it more difficult for her to develop the self-discipline she needs as she matures. Also, if you have other children, you can't expect them to observe rules that you allow the child who is sick or disabled to ignore.

Your child needs your encouragement far more than your protection. Rather than concentrating on what she cannot do, try to focus instead on what she *can* do. If given a chance to participate in normal activities with children her age, she probably will do things that surprise everyone. Establishing this sense of normalcy is difficult if your child's condition is uncertain. You may find yourself withdrawing from your friends because you're so worried about your child, and you may hesitate to plan social activities if you're not sure she'll be well enough to attend. If you give in to these feelings all the time, resentment is bound to build up, so try not to let this happen. Even if there is a chance that your child's condition may worsen unexpectedly, take the risk and plan special outings, invite friends to your home, and get a babysitter from time to time so you can go out for an evening. Both you and your child will be better off in the long run if you take this approach.

Special Tips

The following suggestions may help you cope more effectively with your child's condition.

- Whenever possible, include both parents in discussions and decisions about your child's treatment. Too often, mothers go alone to medical appointments and then must explain what was said to the father. This may prevent the father from getting some of his own questions answered or learning enough about the choices.

- Keep an open line of communication with your pediatrician. Express your concerns and ask questions.

- Don't be offended if your child's doctors ask personal questions about your family life. The more they know about your family, the better they can help you manage your child's care. For example, if your child has diabetes, she may need a special schedule of meals, so the pediatrician may want to suggest ways to work this diet into your family's normal meal plan. Or if your child needs a wheelchair, the doctor may ask about your home in order to suggest the best places for wheelchair ramps. If you have concerns about the doctor's suggestions, discuss them with him so you can reach an acceptable plan of action together.

- Remember that although you and your doctor want to be optimistic about your child's condition, you must be honest about it. If things are not going well, say so. Your child depends on you to speak up at these times and to work with the doctor to adjust the treatment or find a solution that will make the situation as good as possible.

- Discuss your child's condition frankly with her and the other members of your family. If you do not tell your child the truth, she may sense that you are lying; this can lead to feelings of isolation and rejection. Furthermore, she will imagine all the things that could be wrong—most of which may be worse than her real problem. So talk to her openly, and listen to responses to make sure she understands. Answer her questions in clear, simple language.

- Call on friends and family members for support. You cannot expect to handle the strain created by your child's chronic condition all by yourself. Asking close friends to help you meet your own emotional needs will in turn help you to meet your child's.

- Remember that your child needs to be loved and valued as an individual. If you let the medical problems overshadow your feelings for her as a person, they may interfere with the bond of trust and affection between you. Don't let yourself become so worried that you cannot relax and enjoy your child.

Anemia

Blood contains several different types of cells. The most numerous are the red blood cells, which absorb oxygen in the lungs and distribute it throughout the body. These cells contain hemoglobin, a red pigment that carries oxygen to the tissues and carries away carbon dioxide (the waste material). *Anemia* is the name for the condition in which a decreased amount of hemoglobin is available in the red blood cells, making the blood less able to carry the amount of oxygen necessary for all the cells in the body to function and grow.

Anemia may occur for any of the following reasons.

1. The production of red blood cells slows down.

2. Too many red blood cells are destroyed.

3. There is not enough hemoglobin within the red blood cells.

4. Blood cells are lost from the body.

Young children most commonly become anemic when they fail to get enough iron in their diet. Iron is necessary for the production of hemoglobin. This iron deficiency causes a decrease in the amount of hemoglobin in the red blood cells. A young infant may get iron-deficiency anemia if he starts drinking cow's milk too early, particularly if he is not given an iron supplement or food with iron. The deficiency occurs because cow's milk contains very little iron and the small amount present is poorly absorbed through the intestines into the body. In addition, cow's milk given to an infant under six months of age can cause irritation of the bowel and small amounts of blood loss. This results in a decrease in the number of red blood cells, which can cause anemia.

Other nutritional deficiencies, such as a lack of folic acid, also can cause anemia, but this is very rare. It is probably seen most often in children fed goat's milk, which contains very little folic acid.

Anemia at any age can result from exces-sive blood loss. In rare cases, the blood loss may occur because the blood does not clot properly. A newborn infant with difficulty clotting may bleed heavily from his circumcision or a minor injury and become anemic. Because vitamin K promotes blood clotting and is often lacking in newborns, an injection of this vitamin generally is given right after birth.

Sometimes the red cells are prone to being easily destroyed. This condition, called hemolytic anemia, can result from disturbances on the surface of the red cells or other abnormalities in or outside the cells.

A severe condition that involves an abnormal structure of hemoglobin, seen most often in children of African heritage, is called sickle cell anemia. This disorder can be very severe and is associated with frequent "crises," often requiring repeated hospitalizations.

Finally, certain enzyme deficiencies also can alter the function of the red blood cells, increasing their susceptibility to destruction.

Signs and Symptoms

Anemia frequently causes a mild paleness of the skin, usually most apparent as a decreased pinkness of the lips, the lining of the eyelids (conjunctiva), and the nail beds (pink part of the nails). Anemic children also may be irritable, mildly weak, or tire easily. Those with severe anemia may have shortness of breath, rapid heart rate, and swelling of the hands and feet. If the anemia continues, it may interfere with normal growth. A newborn with hemolytic anemia may become jaundiced (turn yellow), although many newborns are mildly jaundiced and don't become anemic.

If your child shows any of these symptoms or signs, or if you suspect he is not getting enough iron in his diet, consult your pediatrician. A simple blood count can diagnose anemia in most cases.

Some children are not anemic but still are deficient in iron. These youngsters may have a decreased appetite and be irritable, fussy, and inattentive, which may result in delays in their development or poor school performance. These problems will reverse when the children are given iron. Other signs of iron deficiency that may be unrelated to anemia include a tendency to eat unusual things, such as ice, dirt, clay, and cornstarch. This behavior, called pica, is not harmful unless the material eaten is toxic (i.e., lead). Usually the behavior improves after the anemia is treated and as the child becomes older, although it may persist longer in children who are developmentally delayed.

Children with sickle cell anemia may have unexplained fever or swelling of the hands and feet as infants, and they are extremely susceptible to infection. If there is a history of sickle cell anemia or sickle cell trait in your family, make sure your child is tested for it at birth.

Treatment

Since there are so many different types of anemia, it is very important to identify the cause before any treatment is begun. Do not attempt to treat your child with vitamins, iron, or other nutrients or over-the-counter medications unless it is at your physician's direction. This is important, because such treatment may mask the real reason for the problem and thus delay the diagnosis.

If the anemia is due to a lack of iron, your child will be given an iron-containing medication. This comes in a drop form for infants and a liquid or tablet form for older children. Your pediatrician will determine how long your child should take the iron by checking his blood at regular intervals. Do not stop giving the medication until the physician tells you it is no longer needed.

Following are a few tips concerning iron medication.

- It is best not to give iron with milk because milk blocks iron absorption.

- Vitamin C increases iron absorption, so you might want to follow the dose of iron with a glass of orange juice.

- Since liquid iron tends to turn the teeth a grayish black color, have your child swallow it rapidly and then rinse his mouth with water. You also may want to brush your child's teeth after every dose of iron. Although tooth-staining by iron is unattractive, it is not permanent.

- Iron medications cause the stools to become a dark black color. Don't be worried by this change.

Safety precautions: Iron medications are extremely poisonous if taken in excessive amounts. (Iron is one of the most common causes of poisoning in children under five.) *Keep this and all medication out of reach of small children.*

Prevention

Iron-deficiency anemia and other nutritional anemias can be prevented easily by making sure your child is eating a well-balanced diet and by following these precautions.

- Do not give your infant cow's milk until he is over one year old.

- If your child is breastfed, give him iron-fortified foods such as cereal when solid foods are introduced. Before then, he will absorb enough iron from the breastmilk. If you choose to breastfeed solely beyond four months, an iron supplement is recommended. However, the introduction of iron-poor solid foods will decrease the amount of iron he absorbs from the breastmilk.

- If your baby is formula-fed or partially breastfed, the current recommendation is to give him formula with added iron (containing from 4.0 to 12 milligrams per liter of iron), beginning at birth and continuing through age twelve months.

- Make sure your older child has a well-balanced diet and eats foods that contain iron. Many grains and cereals are iron-fortified. (Check labels to be sure.) Other good sources of iron include egg yolks, green and yellow vegetables, yellow fruits, red meat, potatoes, tomatoes, molasses, and raisins. Also, to increase the iron content of your entire family's diet, use the fruit pulp in juices, and cook potatoes with the skins on.

Cystic Fibrosis

Cystic fibrosis (CF) is a disease that changes the secretions of certain glands in the body. It is inherited from parents who carry the gene that causes CF. Although the sweat glands and the glandular cells of the lungs and pancreas are affected most often, the sinuses, liver, intestines, and reproductive organs also can be involved.

Great progress has been made in treating this disease and its symptoms, but there is still no cure. However, children with CF are living longer, thanks to the scientific progress that has occurred.

For a child to get cystic fibrosis, both parents must be carriers of the gene that causes it. In the United States, CF is most common in the Caucasian population, where 1 out of every 20 people is a carrier, and 1 of every 2,000 to 3,000 Caucasian babies have CF. The disease is much less common in African Americans (1 in 17,000 live births) and Hispanics (1 in 11,500 live births), and even rarer among Asians. About 60,000 children and adults worldwide have been diagnosed with CF; approximately half of them (30,000) are in North America.

In 1989 researchers discovered the gene that causes CF. Couples planning to have children can undergo genetic testing and counseling to find out if they are carrying the CF gene.

Signs and Symptoms

The majority of CF cases are diagnosed within the first two years of life; in many states, newborn screenings now include mandatory testing for CF. (In some cases, CF is diagnosed even before the baby is born, either with genetic testing or because of an abnormality found on an ultrasound in the later stages of pregnancy). Your pediatrician may suspect CF if your child is failing to gain weight, which often accompanies this disease. Other signs and symptoms vary with the degree of the involvement of organs like the lungs.

More than half of the cases of CF are diagnosed because of repeated lung infections. These infections tend to recur because mucus in the airways is thicker than normal and more difficult to cough out. A child with CF is likely to have a persistent cough that gets worse with colds. Since the secretions of the lungs remain in the airways longer than normal, the airways are more likely to become infected, increasing the chances of pneumonia or bronchitis. Over time, these lung infections cause damage to the lungs, and are the major cause of death in CF.

Most children with CF are deficient in digestive enzymes, making it difficult for them to digest fats and proteins as well as they should. As a result, these children have large, bulky, foul-smelling stools. Loose stools may result from an inability to digest formula or food, and are one of the causes of the child's failure to gain weight.

To confirm the diagnosis, your pediatrician will order a sweat test to measure the amount of salt your child loses as he perspires. Children with cystic fibrosis have much more salt in their sweat than do children who do not have CF. Two or more of these tests may be required to ensure an accurate diagnosis, since the results are not always clearly positive or negative. If your child is diagnosed as having the disease, your pediatrician will help you get the additional specialized medical help that is necessary.

Treatment

Treatment of CF's lung infections is the most important aspect of your child's care. The goal is to help clear the thick secretions from your youngster's lungs, which may involve various techniques that help him cough out the sputum more easily. The lung infections themselves are treated with antibiotics. Periods in which the lung infections worsen are called exacerbations, which are associated with more coughing and sputum production, and may require treatment with the use of intravenous antibiotics.

To treat the lack of digestive enzymes in CF, your child will be prescribed capsules containing enzymes to be taken with every meal and every snack. The amount of enzymes is based on the level of fat in the diet and the weight of your child. Once the correct amount of enzymes is taken, your youngster's stool pattern will become more normal and he'll begin gaining more weight.

He also will need to take supplemental vitamins.

Emotional Burden of Cystic Fibrosis

Because CF is a hereditary disease, many parents feel guilty about their child's illness. However, CF is a genetic disease that is no one's fault, so there's no reason to blame anyone. Instead, you should channel your emotional energies into your child's treatment.

It is important to raise your child as you would if he did not have this disease. There is no reason to limit his educational or career goals. The majority of children with CF can expect to grow up and lead productive adult lives. Your child needs both love and discipline, and should be encouraged to develop and test his limits.

Balancing the physical and emotional demands created by this disease is hard on both the CF patient and his family, so it is very important that you get as much support as possible. Ask your pediatrician to put you in touch with the nearest CF center and CF support groups. The Cystic Fibrosis Foundation also can be of help. Write to: Cystic Fibrosis Foundation, 6931 Arlington Road, Bethesda, MD 20814, or visit the foundation's website (www.cff.org).

Diabetes Mellitus

Diabetes mellitus occurs when specialized cells of the pancreas (a gland located behind the stomach) do not produce adequate amounts of the hormone insulin. Insulin permits the body to process proteins, fat, and sugars in food to make body tissues, produce energy, and store energy. In people without diabetes, insulin is produced as needed to process food. But people with diabetes have a reduced supply of insulin or none at all. Therefore, the nutrients cannot be used by the cells but remain in the blood. Without a source of energy, the cells think they are starving. In an attempt to nourish the starving cells, the liver makes sugar from the body stores of protein and fat. This leads to weight loss and weakness, because muscle is being broken down and is not getting the energy it needs. The body tries to flush out the excess sugar circulating in the blood by making more urine. This is why people who have diabetes urinate more frequently and can become very thirsty as they try to replace the fluid loss. Without insulin, fat breaks down to form certain kinds of acids known as ketones, which are also excreted in the urine.

At the present time, there is no way to prevent the development of diabetes. Although there is a genetic predisposition to develop this disease, most children with type 1 diabetes (previously known as insulin-dependent diabetes) don't have any close relatives with the disease. The destruction of the cells that make insulin results from a process in which the body views these cells as foreign invaders and mounts an immune response against them. This autoimmune process starts years before the first symptoms of diabetes show up. The trigger for this process may be viruses or other agents in the environment.

Type 1 diabetes is very different from type 2 diabetes, which is much more common and occurs in nine out of ten adults with diabetes. In type 2 diabetes, the body does not respond properly to insulin. Type 2 diabetes usually is associated with obesity, and is increasing in frequency as the rates of obesity grow. (Among children diagnosed with type 2 diabetes, eighty-five out of one hundred are obese.) Youngsters who are inactive, overeat, and have a family history of diabetes have the greatest risk of developing type 2 diabetes. Children in minority groups also have a higher incidence of type 2 diabetes. In recent years, many more school-age and teenage children are being diagnosed with type 2 diabetes.

Diabetes can appear at any time, even in the first year of life. The diagnosis often is delayed in infants and toddlers until the child is very sick, because the symptoms at this age are not very specific. It is important to notify your pediatrician immediately if your child displays any of the following warning signs and symptoms of diabetes:

- Increased thirst.

- Increased urination. A toilet-trained child may start wetting, or a baby in diapers will need more frequent changes.

- Weight loss with either increased appetite and food intake or loss of appetite (more common in the younger child).

- Dehydration (see page 506 for signs).

- Severe diaper rash that does not respond to the usual treatment.

- Vomiting that is persistent, particularly if it is accompanied by weakness or drowsiness.

If your child goes to the doctor with any suspicious symptoms, be sure that a urine or blood test is done to determine whether his sugar levels are too high. This simple test will provide a clue to diabetes and prevent further deterioration, which can be dangerous.

Treatment

When blood tests confirm the diagnosis of diabetes, treatment is begun immediately with injections of insulin. When the child does not require intravenous fluids to correct dehydration and vomiting, most specialists do not hospitalize patients with diabetes. A diabetes education team will teach the entire family how to deal with diabetes. You'll learn how to test blood glucose levels from a drop of blood from a finger stick and how to give insulin injections, usually twice a day at the beginning. Your acceptance and ability to carry out these basic tasks will help your child adjust to the treatment with the least anxiety and fear. By the time your child reaches age seven or eight, he will be playing a part in the management of his diabetes, and by age eleven most children are giving themselves their own insulin injections and doing their own blood tests, under adult supervision.

Children with diabetes do not need to be on a special diet, but particular attention should be paid to good nutrition and regular eating schedules. These youngsters have the same nutritional needs for growth and development as other children, but they can't miss meals and shouldn't delay them. Main meals should be similar in size and content to each other, with about the same amount of carbohydrates and the same amount of protein. Because the insulin is being absorbed constantly, these children need to eat more often, with between-meal snacks and a bedtime snack. The use of the insulin pump or the long-acting insulin glargine allows for more flexibility in the timing of meals and snacks and in the amounts of food eaten. Also, children with diabetes need to increase their food intake or decrease their insulin dose if they are more physically active than usual, since this activity increases the effect of insulin and lowers blood glucose levels.

A good diet for children with diabetes at all ages is the same as that recommended for everyone. This includes: plenty of complex carbohydrates, such as whole-grain breads, pastas, potatoes, beans, and peas; unprocessed foods, such as bran cereals, oatmeal, and fresh fruits and vegetables; and no more than 30 of every 100 calories from fat. The fat should be mostly unsaturated, such as liquid oils. Special diabetic and dietetic foods are a waste of money, and some, such as those that replace sugar with extra fat, actually can be harmful.

Snacks are important to maintain a supply of food for the insulin to work on and thus prevent hypoglycemia (low blood sugar). Good snack choices include fresh fruit, dried fruit, cheese crackers, peanut butter crackers, yogurt, trail mix, vanilla wafers, grain crackers, or granola bars, if strenuous exercise is planned. These snacks also are used for treating mild symptoms of hypoglycemia (low blood sugar) after initial treatment with juice to raise blood glucose quickly. Desserts that are good for all members of the family include fresh fruit, low-fat yogurt or pudding, and fruit pies made with sugar substitute.

Child care and school personnel need to know about the youngster's diabetes and snack needs and how to recognize and treat hypoglycemia.

Having children participate as much as possible in their care gives them some measure of control. Children under age three can choose which finger to stick for blood sugar tests or which place to use for the insulin injection. Parents should handle treatment with a matter-of-fact yet affectionate attitude, and the American Academy of Pediatrics suggests that all adults in the family share responsibility for shots and blood tests. Children four to seven years old can help with monitoring blood sugar and with injections. Children in this age group are likely to think that diabetes is a punishment for something they have done. They need regular reassurance from you that the diabetes is not their fault and they are not being punished.

Emotional support for the entire family is

very important. You can get this—and learn more about the disease—from the Juvenile Diabetes Research Foundation (120 Wall Street Avenue South, New York, NY 10005; www.jdf.org) and the American Diabetes Association (1701 North Beauregard Street, Alexandria, VA 22311; www.diabetes.org).

The more you understand about diabetes and deal with it matter-of-factly, the better the chance that your child will do well. The tools available for managing diabetes today make it possible to control diabetes to a degree that will reduce the risk of later complications and permit children to grow up and lead productive, fulfilling lives.

Failure to Thrive

If you plot your child's weight and measurements, you should see a continuous upward trend, although there will be times when she gains very slowly and perhaps some weeks when she actually loses a little weight due to illness. It is not normal for her to stop growing or to decrease in weight except for the small amount she loses during the first few days of life. If she does lose weight, it's a clear sign either that she's not getting enough to eat or that she's ill. The medical term for this condition is *failure to thrive*. Although it can occur in older children who are seriously ill or undernourished, it is most common and most dangerous during the active growth period of the first three years.

If allowed to continue for a prolonged period, this condition can become serious. Steady weight gain is especially important for infants and toddlers because it indicates that they are receiving adequate nutrition and care for normal physical, mental, and emotional development.

Usually when a child stops growing, it's due to a feeding problem that prevents her from getting as many calories as she needs.

As a newborn, she may be too fussy to eat as much as she needs, or, if breastfed, she may not be getting enough milk while nursing. Some children may require more food than their parents are able to provide. These problems must be detected and treated early in order to avoid long-term or permanent damage.

Sometimes failure to thrive signals a medical problem. The newborn may have an infection passed on from her mother during pregnancy, or she may have a hormonal difficulty, allergy, or digestive problem that prevents nutrients from being absorbed into the body properly. Diseases such as cystic fibrosis (page 718), diabetes (page 719), or heart disease also can interfere with normal growth. If one of these is present, the child may need a special diet as well as medical treatment.

When to Get Help

Regular charting of your child's growth and comparison of her general development with others her age is the best way to make sure she is thriving. If she does not gain weight, grow in length, or otherwise develop normally, consult your pediatrician, who will measure and examine your child, ask about her diet and eating patterns, and review her medical history for signs of illness that may be contributing to her failure to thrive. The physician will try to establish exactly when the growth or weight gain stopped, and ask about any incidents or events that may have contributed to this. The pediatrician also may watch the youngster eating or nursing to see how much she consumes and how she responds to food. Sometimes a short period of in-hospital observation may be necessary.

If the doctor discovers a physical cause for the decrease in growth rate, the appropriate treatment will be recommended. If there is no physical reason, however, the pediatrician will look for emotional or social problems, particularly within the family. Such disturbances can decrease a child's appetite or alter her normal food intake and digestion. Once discovered, these difficulties can be treated with individual or family counseling.

HIV Infection and AIDS

No one who has read newspapers or watched television newscasts in recent years could have avoided learning something about HIV infection (which frequently leads to AIDS, or acquired immune deficiency syndrome). This infection is caused by the human immunodeficiency virus (HIV).

Half of all new HIV infections in the United States occur among adolescents and young adults, usually via sexual activity. Heterosexually acquired infections have increased in the United States, and now heterosexual activity is the identified risk behavior responsible for the majority of HIV infections in women. Intravenous drug use has become a proportionately less frequent cause of HIV infection, and currently only an exceedingly rare instance of blood-related or blood product–related transmission occurs in the United States, because testing of these materials is done routinely.

Children, on the other hand, acquire the infection primarily from their HIV-infected mothers, either in utero (as the virus passes across the placenta), during delivery (when the newborn is exposed to the mother's blood and body fluids), or by ingestion of infected breastmilk. An HIV infection will develop in thirteen to thirty-nine of one hundred infants born to HIV-infected mothers who are untreated. Zidovudine (or AZT) treatment of the mother and newborn diminishes the risk of transmission of the HIV

infection from mothers to babies to about eight of one hundred, and more powerful combinations of drugs can reduce this figure to two of one hundred or less.

Once a person is infected with HIV, the virus will be present in his body for life. People with the HIV infection may be free of symptoms for years. AIDS occurs only after the progressive erosion of the immune defense system by HIV, a process that may take many months or years. Without treatment, children usually develop signs of HIV infection by the age of two, but the average time to develop AIDS is about five years.

Infants with the HIV infection initially may appear well, but problems gradually develop. For example, their weight and height fail to increase appropriately within the first six months to one year. They have frequent episodes of diarrhea or minor skin infections. The lymph nodes (glands) anywhere in the body may enlarge, and there is a persistent fungus infection of the mouth (thrush). The liver and spleen may enlarge.

All the above symptoms are suggestive of HIV infection. Eventually, if the HIV infection progresses as the body's immune system further deteriorates, AIDS-related infections and cancers may occur. The most common of these, *Pneumocystis jiroveci* pneumonia, is accompanied by fever and breathing difficulties. This common infection occurs predominantly in infants between three months and one year of age. It is possible to prevent this infection with antibiotics, and it is now recommended that all babies born to HIV-infected women be placed on preventive antibiotics as early as six weeks of age. Before deciding to stop therapy, the doctors must determine if the baby is HIV infected.

Care of the Child with HIV Infection

It is clear from overwhelming and consistent evidence that children who are HIV positive should be played with, interacted with, and loved just like all other children. HIV infections cannot be transmitted by just holding a child who is HIV positive. These children need all we can give them, whether it is in a child care center, on a one-to-one basis, or in any group, large or small. Caregiving adults should take every opportunity to make them feel no different from any other child. Often, in fact, their circumstances have placed them in a situation or an environment that is less conducive to optimum growth and development. We must all do everything we can to counteract those negative factors and contribute to their positive outlook on life.

Parents of children with HIV infection sometimes hide the diagnosis from relatives, feeling the youngster will be shunned by them. However, most families are very supportive; indeed, often they have taken over the responsibility for care during periods when the parents need assistance. Common infections can cause serious complications in children with HIV infection. Children with HIV infection should attend child care and school when they are able. They may be accidentally exposed to communicable illnesses like chickenpox, and parents should be informed of these exposures and report them to their child's doctor. Call the doctor immediately if your child with HIV develops a fever, breathing difficulties, diarrhea, swallowing problems, or skin irritation, or if he's been exposed to a communicable disease. In fact, any change in the child's health status should prompt you to seek medical attention, since the child with HIV may have few reserves to combat even minor illnesses.

Whenever seeking any medical attention for your youngster, be sure to inform the physician of the HIV infection so that she can assess and care for the illness appropriately and give correct immunizations.

Currently a number of approved and licensed anti-HIV or antiretroviral drugs are available for use in children. Others are in the process of being tested and approved. These agents suppress virus replication (reproduction) and have been demonstrated to improve growth and neurologic development and delay disease progression. It is essential that your doctor knows about the baby's HIV infection as early in life as possible and that you administer antiretroviral therapy as the doctor advises. With more treatments now available, complete suppression of the virus now is possible in many cases. There are specific guidelines for the treatment of HIV-infected children that your pediatrician will provide.

Immunizing the Child Born to the HIV-Infected Mother

Your pediatrician has up-to-date guidelines on which vaccines should and shouldn't be given to a child with the HIV infection. Below is a summary of the current recommendations.

Children with HIV infection should receive the following vaccines at the usual recommended age:

- DTaP (diphtheria, tetanus, pertussis vaccine).

- IPV (inactivated poliovirus vaccine).

- Hepatitis B vaccine.

- Hib (*Haemophilus influenzae* type b vaccine).

WHERE WE STAND

The American Academy of Pediatrics supports legislation and public policy directed toward eliminating any form of discrimination based on whether a child is infected with HIV (the virus that causes AIDS).

- **AIDS in the schools:** All children infected with HIV should have the same right as those without the infection to attend school and child care. Infected children should be provided with access to special education and other related services (including home instruction) if their disease progresses. The confidentiality of a child's HIV infection status should be respected, with disclosure given only with the consent of the parent(s) or legal guardian(s).

- **AIDS legislation:** As the number of HIV-infected children, adolescents, and young women continues to grow, the Academy supports federal funding for AIDS research and health care services for HIV-infected individuals and their families.

- **AIDS testing:** The Academy recommends documented routine HIV education and routine testing with consent for all pregnant women in the United States. Routine education about HIV infection needs to be part of a comprehensive program of health care for women. All pregnant women, with their consent, should be tested for their HIV status. The Academy also recommends HIV testing with consent for *newborns* whose mothers' HIV status (whether the virus is present in her blood) is not determined.

- The live measles, mumps, rubella vaccine (MMR) and varicella vaccine *unless* the child is severely immunocompromised. Your doctor will know how to determine if the vaccine should be administered.

- The pneumococcal and influenza vaccines.

HIV-infected children may experience especially severe illness due to chickenpox or measles. Following exposures to these infections, the physician should be notified and HIV-infected children should receive special immune globulin by injection.

If You're Pregnant

All pregnant women should be counseled about HIV and offered HIV testing. It is important for the appropriate care of the mother and because treatment (with drugs such as zidovudine [AZT]) can reduce transmission of the virus from the mother to her infant. Once the baby is born, women who are HIV infected should not breastfeed their infant because of the risk of transmitting the virus via breastfeeding; safe alternative sources of infant nutrition are available, such as infant formulas.

In the Classroom

There is no risk of HIV transmission in routine classroom activities. The virus is not spread through casual contact. It is not transmitted through the air, by touching, or via toilet seats. Almost all school-age children with HIV infection can attend a regular school.

Although transmission of HIV has not occurred in schools and child care centers, transmission of other infectious agents requires that all these settings adopt routine precautionary procedures for handling blood, stool, and bodily secretions. The standard precaution is to wash exposed skin immediately with soap and water after any contact with blood or body fluids. Soiled surfaces should be cleaned with disinfectants such as bleach (a 1-to-10 dilution of bleach to water). Disposable towels or tissues should be used whenever possible. Gloves are recommended when contact with blood or blood-containing body fluids may occur, and therefore gloves should be available in schools and child care centers. It is important to wash one's hands thoroughly after changing diapers, whether gloves are used or not. Schools should ensure that children wash their hands before eating; staff should wash their hands before food preparation or feeding children. Though many parents worry about biting, there has not been transmission of HIV in the preschool setting; therefore this fear appears to be theoretical only.

Also, it is critically important that schools incorporate education about HIV infections into their curriculum. All children should be educated about the risks of HIV transmission through sexual activity and intravenous drug use. They should be taught how to avoid exposure to blood and body fluids that might contain HIV. They should also learn that HIV is *not* spread through casual contact.

31

THE ENVIRONMENT AND YOUR CHILD

Although we live in an environmentally conscious society, there are still plenty of potential environmental health risks to which your child might be exposed. As your youngster grows, he breathes more air, consumes more food, and drinks more water pound for pound than an adult. This could put him at greater risk for health problems if the world in which he lives is environmentally tainted.

Of course, you can't protect your child from every environmental hazard that exists, but you can lower his exposure by taking the steps described in this chapter.

Asbestos

Asbestos is a natural fiber that was widely used as a spray-on material for fireproofing, insulation, and soundproofing in schools, homes, and public buildings from the 1940s through the 1970s. It does not pose health risks unless it deteriorates and becomes crumbly, when it can release microscopic asbestos fibers into the air. When asbestos fibers are inhaled, they can cause chronic health problems involving the lungs, throat, and gastrointestinal tract, including a rare type of lung cancer (called mesothelioma) that can occur as long as five decades after exposure to asbestos.

Today schools are mandated by law to either remove asbestos or otherwise ensure that children are not exposed to it. However, it is still present in some older homes, especially as insulation around pipes, stoves, and furnaces, as well as in walls and ceilings.

Prevention

Follow these guidelines to keep your child safe from asbestos.

- If you think there may be asbestos in your home, have a professional inspector check for it. Local health departments and regional offices of the Environmental Protection Agency can provide the names of individuals and labs certified to inspect homes for asbestos.

- Do not let your youngster play near any exposed or deteriorating materials that could contain asbestos.

- If asbestos is found in your home, it may be acceptable to leave it there if it is in good condition. But if it is deteriorating, or if it might be disturbed by any renovations you're planning, have a properly accredited and certified contractor remove the asbestos, which must be taken off in a safe manner. Again, ask the local health department or the EPA for information on finding a certified contractor in your community.

Carbon Monoxide

Carbon monoxide is a toxic gas that is a possible by-product of appliances, heaters, and automobiles that burn gasoline, natural gas, wood, oil, kerosene, or propane. It has no color, no taste, and no odor. It can become trapped inside your home if appliances are malfunctioning, if a furnace or stove has a clogged vent or chimney, or if a charcoal grill is used in an enclosed area. Carbon monoxide also might enter your home when an automobile is left idling in an attached garage.

When your child breathes carbon monoxide, it impairs the ability of his blood to transport oxygen. Although everyone is at risk for carbon monoxide poisoning, it is particularly dangerous for children because of their higher metabolic rate. Symptoms may include headaches, nausea, shortness of breath, fatigue, confusion, and fainting. Persistent exposure to carbon monoxide can lead to personality changes, memory loss, severe lung injury, brain damage, and death.

Prevention

You can reduce your child's risk of carbon monoxide poisoning by:

- Buying and installing carbon monoxide detectors in your home, particularly near the bedrooms

- Never leaving your car idling in an attached garage (even if the garage door is open)

- Never using a charcoal grill, hibachi, or portable camping stove indoors or in an enclosed area

- Scheduling an annual inspection and servicing of oil and gas furnaces, woodstoves, gas ovens and ranges, gas water heaters, gas clothes dryers, and fireplaces

- Never using your nonelectric oven to heat your kitchen or your house

Drinking Water

Children drink much more water for their size than adults. Most of this water comes from the tap, and the quality of this water is regulated by standards instituted by Congress, included in the Safe Drinking Water Act of 1974. Subsequent laws have implemented drinking water standards for chemicals that were known to be present in some water supplies.

Today the drinking water in the United States is among the safest in the world, although problems can occur from time to time. Violations in water safety standards are most likely to occur in small systems that serve less than a thousand people. Also, keep in mind that private wells are not federally regulated.

Contaminants that can cause illness when present in the drinking water include: germs, nitrates, manmade chemicals, heavy metals, radioactive particles, and by-products of the disinfecting process.

Although bottled water can be purchased in markets, many brands are just tap water that has been bottled for sale. Bottled water is generally much more expensive than tap water, and unless there are known contamination problems in your community's water supply, it may not be necessary.

Prevention

To ensure that your child is consuming safe drinking water, you can check the water quality by contacting the county health department, the state environment agency, or the Environmental Protection Agency's Safe Drinking Water Hotline (1–800–426–4791). Your local water company is mandated to tell you what is in the water if you request this information. Water that is not regulated—such as well water—should be tested yearly.

Other guidelines include:

- Use cold water for cooking and drinking. Contaminants can accumulate in hot water heaters.

- If you are concerned about the quality of your plumbing, run the faucet for two minutes each morning prior to using the water for cooking or drinking. This will flush the pipes and lower the likelihood that contaminants will end up in the water you consume.

- Have well water tested for nitrates before giving it to infants under one year of age.

- Prepare water supplies that may be contaminated with germs for drinking by boiling the water and then allowing it to cool before drinking. Boil for no more than one minute.

Pesticides

Pesticides are used in a variety of settings, including on farms and in home gardens. While they may kill insects, rodents, and weeds, some are toxic to people when consumed in food and water.

More research is needed to determine

with precision the short- and long-term effects of pesticides. Although some studies have found associations between some childhood cancers and an exposure to pesticides, other studies have not reached the same conclusions.

Prevention

Try to limit your child's unnecessary exposure to pesticides. To reduce such exposure:

- If possible, avoid foods in which chemical pesticides were used by farmers.

- Wash all fruits and vegetables with water before your child consumes them.

- Produce that is in season is less likely to have been heavily sprayed with pesticides than out-of-season produce.

- For your own lawn and garden, use non-chemical pest control methods whenever possible. If you keep bottles of pesticides in your home or garage, make sure they're out of the reach of children to avoid any accidental poisoning.

Lead Poisoning

During the first two to three years of life, your child is bound to go through a phase of putting things other than food into his mouth. He'll chew on his toys, taste the sand in the playground, and sample the cat's food if given the opportunity. As annoying as this behavior can be for you, few of these things will cause him any serious harm, as long as you keep poisons and sharp objects out of his reach. Lead is one dangerous substance, however, that your child can consume without your knowledge.

Contrary to popular belief, lead poisoning is not caused by chewing on a pencil or being stabbed with its point. The so-called lead in a pencil actually is harmless graphite, and there is no lead in the paint coating the outside. Lead poisoning is caused most often by eating lead contained in dust, bits of old paint or dirt, by breathing lead in the air, or by drinking water from pipes lined or soldered with lead. There also may be lead in hobby materials such as stained glass, paints, solders, and fishing weights. It might be present in miniblinds manufactured outside the United States prior to July 1997. If you buy new miniblinds, look for those that have a label that says "new formulation" or "nonleaded formula." Lead also might be present in food cooked or stored in some imported ceramic dishes. Do not serve acidic (e.g. orange juice) substances in these dishes, since the acids can leach lead from the dishes into the food.

Lead was an allowable ingredient in house paint before 1978 and therefore may be present on the walls, doorjambs, and window frames on many older homes. As the paint ages, it chips, peels and comes off in the form of dust. Toddlers may be tempted by such bite-size pieces and will taste or eat them out of curiosity. Even if they don't intentionally eat the material, the dust can get on their hands and into their food. Sometimes the lead-containing finish has been covered with other layers of newer, safer paints. This can give you a false sense of reassurance, however, since the underlying paint still may chip or peel off with the newer layers and fall into the hands of toddlers.

Although there has been a decline in high lead levels detected in the blood of youngsters, somewhere between one-half to one million children in the United States still have unacceptably high levels. Living in a city, being poor, and being African American or Hispanic are all risk factors that increase the chances of having an elevated blood-

WHERE WE STAND

Lead causes serious damage to children's brains at relatively low levels of exposure—the effects of which are largely irreversible. The American Academy of Pediatrics supports widespread lead screening of children, as well as the funding of programs to remove lead hazards from the environment.

lead level. But even children living in rural areas or who are in well-to-do families still can be at risk.

As the child continues consuming lead, it accumulates in the body. Although it may not be noticeable for some time, ultimately it can affect many areas of the body, including the brain. Lead poisoning can cause learning disabilities and behavioral problems. Very high levels will likely cause the most severe problems, but the extent of damage due to lead for any individual child cannot be predicted. Lead also can cause stomach and intestinal problems, loss of appetite, anemia, headaches, constipation, hearing loss, and even short stature. (See *Abdominal Pain,* page 497.)

Prevention

You can make certain that your child doesn't eat or inhale lead by removing any sources of leaded paint. If your home was built after 1977, when federal regulations restricted the amount of lead permitted in paint, the risk for having dangerous amounts of lead in the dust, paint, or soil of your residence is low. However, if your home is older, the likelihood of having dangerous amounts of lead there can be very high, especially for the oldest homes (those built before 1960). Older homes in the Northeast or Midwestern areas of the United States are particularly likely to have lead. If you think your home may contain lead, your first

course of action is to look for areas of peeling or chipping paint and to clean them up using water. Adding a detergent to the water helps bind the lead into the water. Keeping surfaces (floors, window areas, porches, etc.) clean may lower your child's chance of being exposed to lead-containing dust. Older windows are of particular concern as paint on wood frames frequently is damaged and the action of opening and closing windows can produce lead-containing dust. In older homes, lead-containing dust can also contaminate carpets and it is not removed by vacuuming. A next step is to positively identify surfaces in your home with lead-contaminated paint, or areas with dangerous amounts of lead in the dust or dirt. A home inspection is necessary to do this and you can get help from your local or state health department in identifying a lead inspector in your area. Sometimes the health departments will provide the inspection, but most often you will have to pay for it. If you live in an older home that needs repairs, you should assume that the repair process could potentially generate dangerous amounts of lead dust. So, unless you know positively that any paint that will be disturbed does not contain lead you need to seek expert advice before starting repairs. Renovation projects that disturb lead paint need to be done by individuals with special training in lead-safe work practices. Sanding and scraping of paint can generate large amounts of dust. Exposure to dust during or following renovation is a common way for children to get lead poisoned. The safest thing to do is for the family to move out while the renovation is ongoing and until the final cleaning has been completed. Contact your state or local health department for more detailed information.

In a rented home, the landlord is responsible for all maintenance, and this includes necessary repainting and repairs. If you suspect unhealthy levels of lead in the building, and your landlord is unresponsive or is not using lead-safe work practices when doing repairs, ask your community's department of health for help. Sometimes legal actions can compel the landlord to make safe repairs.

All children need a well-balanced diet. Having adequate stores of iron in the body in particular helps reduce the amount of lead absorbed and retained from the intestine. Adequate intake of calcium may also play a role, but this is less clear. Although food cans with soldered seams could add lead to the food inside them, these cans generally have been replaced by seamless aluminum containers in the United States. It's also a good idea to have your child wash his hands often, particularly before he eats.

Call your local health department, checking to see if lead in the water is a problem in your community. Or contact the Environmental Protection Agency's Safe Drinking Water Hotline (1–800–426–4791) to find out whether your local water supply presents a risk of lead exposure.

Treatment

Children who have lead poisoning rarely show any physical symptoms. However, the learning and behavior problems due to lead may be seen in the preschool child or may not be seen until the child reaches school age. At that point they need to learn more complicated tasks like reading or arithmetic and may have trouble keeping up with classwork. Some may even seem overly active, due to the effects of the lead. For this reason, the only sure way to know if your child has been exposed to excessive lead is to have him tested. A blood test for lead at ages 1 and 2 years is recommended for children at high risk for exposure to lead. In communities where the risk of elevated blood lead is low, questions to evaluate the child's risk for exposure are used to determine whether a blood test is necessary. Local and state health departments have developed guidelines based on the risks for their areas.

The most common screening test for lead poisoning uses a drop of blood from a finger prick. If this test indicates that a child has been exposed to excessive lead, a second test will be done using a larger sample of blood obtained from a vein in the arm. This test is more accurate and can measure the precise amount of lead in the blood.

Children who have lead poisoning may require treatment with a drug that binds the lead in the blood and greatly increases the body's ability to eliminate it. The treatment may involve hospitalization and a series of injections. Today the more common treatment consists of new oral medicines used on an outpatient basis.

Some children with lead poisoning require more than one course of treatment, and all require months of close follow-up. Unfortunately, standard treatments of lead-poisoned children produce only a short-term or marginal lowering of the child's body lead burden so have not been shown to lower the child's chance of behavioral or learning problems due to lead. Children who have experienced lead poisoning will need to have their behavior and academic performance monitored for many years and should receive special schooling and therapy to help them overcome their problems.

Outdoor Air Pollution

The outdoor air contains several substances that could be harmful to children. One of the most worrisome is ozone, which is a colorless gas that can cause harm when it is present near the ground. Ozone is formed by the action of sunlight on certain chemicals (nitrogen oxides, reactive hydrocarbons) emitted by automobiles and industry. Concentrations of ozone are likely to be greatest in the summer on warm, sunny days, peaking in the mid- to late afternoon.

Because children spend time playing outdoors, they are particularly susceptible to ozone's effects, with breathing difficulties most likely to occur in youngsters with asthma. Children also breathe more rapidly than adults and inhale more pollutants per pound of body weight.

Prevention

To protect your child from air pollution, limit his playtime outdoors when local agencies have issued health advisories or smog alerts. Newspapers and TV news programs often provide information about the air quality in the community.

To reduce the air pollution caused by automobiles on smoggy days, keep your car in the garage and use public transportation or carpools instead.

Radon

Radon is a gas that is a product of the breakdown of uranium in soil and rock. It also may be present in water, natural gas, and building materials.

High levels of radon are found in homes in many regions of the United States. It makes its way into homes through cracks or openings in the foundation, walls and floors, or occasionally in well water. It does not cause health problems immediately upon inhalation. Over time, however, it can increase the risk of lung cancer. In fact, next to cigarette smoking, radon is thought to be the most common cause of lung cancer in the United States.

Prevention

To reduce your child's risk of exposure to radon:

- Ask your pediatrician or the local health department whether radon levels are high in your community.

- Have your home tested for radon, using an inexpensive radon detector. (Hardware stores sell these detectors.) A certified laboratory should analyze the results of this test.

- If the levels are too high in your home, call the Radon Hotline (operated by the National Safety Council in conjunction with the Environmental Protection Agency) at 1–800–767–7236; this is also a good resource for information on reducing the radon risk in your home.

- You may need to make home repairs (i.e., sealing cracks in the foundation) to eliminate the presence of radon.

Second-Hand Smoke

Nearly half of the homes in the United States have at least one smoker residing in them. If you or someone else in your home uses cigarettes, pipes, or cigars, your child is being exposed to their smoke. This smoke contains thousands of chemicals, some of which have been shown to cause cancer and other illnesses, including respiratory infections, bronchitis, and pneumonia. Children exposed to cigarette smoke also have a greater likelihood of developing ear infections and asthma, and they may have a more difficult time getting over colds. They are more susceptible to headaches, sore throats, hoarseness, irritated eyes, dizziness, nausea, lack of energy, and fussiness. In fact, children who are exposed to as few as ten cigarettes per day have an increased chance of getting asthma, even if they've never had any symptoms.

If a parent smokes around her newborn, the baby has a greater risk of dying from sudden infant death syndrome (SIDS). In addition, nicotine and other dangerous chemicals from cigarettes are present in the breastmilk of nursing mothers, who thus expose their babies.

When children are exposed to tobacco smoke, they might develop life-threatening illnesses later in life, including lung cancer and heart disease. They also may be more likely to have cataracts as adults.

When you smoke in your home, you create a risk of fires and burns to your child and others. Children can suffer burns if they find and play with a lit cigarette or with matches or a lighter.

As your child grows, keep in mind that you are a role model. If your child sees you smoking, she may want to try it, as well, and you could be laying the foundation for a lifetime of smoking.

Prevention

Here are some steps you can take to reduce your child's exposure to environmental tobacco smoke.

- If you or other family members smoke, stop! If you've been unable to quit, talk to your doctor, who can refer you to low-cost stop-smoking programs available in your community. Or contact the American Lung Association, 61 Broadway, 6th floor, New York, NY 10006, www.lungusa.org; the American Cancer Society, 1599 Clifton Road, Atlanta, GA 30329, www.cancer.org; and the American Heart Association, 7272 Greenville Avenue, Dallas, TX 75231, www.americanheart.org, and inquire about their stop-smoking classes.

- Don't allow anyone to smoke in your home or your car, particularly when children are present. Don't place ashtrays around your house that can encourage people to light up. Your home and car should always remain smoke-free.

- Store matches and lighters out of reach of children.

- When selecting a babysitter or child care provider, make it clear that no one is permitted to smoke around your youngster.

- When you're in public places with your child, ask others not to smoke around you and your youngster. Choose restaurants that don't allow smoking.

Index

Page numbers of illustrations and charts appear in italics